Thou awakest us to delight in praise; for thou hast made us for thyself, and our heart is restless until it rests in thee.

— Augustine
The Confessions

As to the situation of this town [of Mansoul], it lies just between the two worlds; and the first founder and builder of it, so far as by the best and most authentic records I can gather, was one SHADDAI; and he built it for his own delight.

— Bunyan
The Holy War

Who We Are:
Our Dignity as Human

A NEO-EVANGELICAL THEOLOGY

Paul K. Jewett

edited, completed, and with sermons by
Marguerite Shuster

WILLIAM B. EERDMANS PUBLISHING COMPANY

GRAND RAPIDS, MICHIGAN / CAMBRIDGE, U.K.

© 1996 Wm. B. Eerdmans Publishing Co.

255 Jefferson Ave. S.E., Grand Rapids, Michigan 49503 /

P.O. Box 163, Cambridge CB3 9PU U.K.

Printed in the United States of America

01 00 99 98 97 96   7 6 5 4 3 2 1

Library of Congress Cataloging-in-Publication Data

Jewett, Paul King.

Who we are: our dignity as human: a neo-evangelical theology /
Paul K. Jewett; edited, completed, and with sermons by Marguerite Shuster.

p.   cm.

Includes bibliographical references.

ISBN 0-8028-4075-2 (pbk.: alk. paper)

1. Man (Christian theology)   2. Sociology, Christian.

3. Sex — Religious aspects — Christianity.

4. Presbyterian Church — Sermons.   5. Sermons, American.

I. Shuster, Marguerite.   II. Title.

BT701.2.J48   1996

233′.5 — dc20   96-5064

CIP

To Grandson
Eric Edward Jewett

Contents

Editor's Preface

When Paul Jewett died late in 1991, this volume was about two-thirds complete. As he rather wistfully surveyed his unfinished work, too weak to write any more, he said, "You know, in a way it doesn't matter if it ever gets published because doing it was such fun." That is the way he felt about theology: he loved it with a purity that did not stop to worry about what measure of recognition would accrue to him on account of his labors. So, too, he gave his work the passionate care that refused to bow to pressures, including those of the calendar. Time ran out on him.

Not that he was entirely surprised at that. Initially, he had planned a single-volume systematics; but partway through the first volume, he confessed it would run to two. By the time *God, Creation, and Revelation* was finished, he had resigned himself to three volumes. And when he was well into this present volume, which covers only part of a single locus in theology, he was sheepishly admitting he might need Karl Barth's little wheelbarrow before he was done, were he to proceed at this rate. Even though he felt well until only three months before his death, he knew years if not illness would overtake him before such a project could be brought to a close.

When it became clear that he would get far less close to his goal than he had presumed, we discussed what might become of the work; and I — having been his student and teaching assistant before becoming his pastor and friend — agreed to try my hand at completing it. (He thought that I would enjoy the work, too; and I must admit that he was right about that, as about so many other things.) He had collected for the remainder of this volume piles of materials and references not to be counted in pages but to be measured in feet. He also had some transcribed classroom lecture material, much of which I have incorporated, though generally not in quite its original form. I added materials that I had gathered and sermons to supplement those he had already selected, as well as edited the earlier pages and updated some notes. Here is a case where Jewett's longtime penchant for the editorial "we" can be seen as indicating a genuinely plural subject and may thus perhaps escape Mark Twain's acerbic remark that such usage should be reserved for editors, royalty, and people with tapeworm. Obviously, then, deficiencies in any part of this volume must be attributed to me and not to him. Lest the reader become confused, however, even in the later pages anecdotes in the first person refer to Jewett's experience and are taken directly from his notes.

My deep thanks go to Dr. Jewett for giving me the pleasure and doing me the honor of entrusting me with this work. Thanks are also due, as always, to the faithful and patient people in the Fuller word-processing department, most particularly David Sielaff and Jone Bosch, who turned Dr. Jewett's barely legible pencil and my floppy disks, supplemented by oceans of red ink, into a presentable manuscript.

Marguerite Shuster
Pasadena, California
Advent, 1993

WHO WE ARE:
OUR DIGNITY AS HUMAN

I. Introduction

A. HUMANKIND IN SPACE AND TIME

The doctrine of creation, we have argued, teaches us that the world was made by God.[1] It cannot be understood, therefore, in terms of itself but only in terms of its origin in the will and word of the Creator. Since we are part of this world, the same is true of us. We can understand who we are only as we acknowledge that it is he who has made us and not we ourselves (Ps. 100:3). The human story, like the story of creation as a whole, begins with a divine word: "Let us make humankind in our image, according to our likeness" (Gn. 1:26 NRSV). Indeed, with this word God consummates his work as Creator. He summoned the light into being; gathered the waters into seas; clothed the land with verdure; placed the sun, moon, and stars in the heavens; and filled the earth with living creatures in order that the world might be a fit abode for the man and woman. Having called them into being and having endowed them with his image, he entrusts to them the world he has made and all that is in it (Gn. 1:28).[2]

To many in our day, such an understanding of humankind seems hopelessly naive, since it reflects the view that we humans are not only the lords of earth but the heirs of heaven as well. How, it is asked, can one possibly suppose, this side of Copernicus and Galileo, that God in his heaven — if there is such — could be concerned with earthlings like ourselves? Earth not only revolves around a very average sun, but our sun is

---

1. See the extended discussion in our *God, Creation, and Revelation* (Grand Rapids: Eerdmans, 1991).

2. To this effect see John Calvin, *Institutes of the Christian Religion* (hereafter *Inst.*), trans. John Allen (Philadelphia: Presbyterian Board of Christian Education, 1936), 1.14.22.

one of a rotating congregation of millions of suns in a galaxy we call the Milky Way; the Milky Way, in turn, is a member of a "local group" of some twenty clustered galaxies; this "local group" is a member of a galactic supercluster that is all but lost in a universe made up of many galactic superclusters observable in every direction and all moving away from each other as they push out the horizons of the universe to a diameter of perhaps 28 billion light years.[3]

When we look out toward the edge of a universe of such magnitude, we are looking, of course, back in time — billions of years in time. Were one to compress the history of the universe into a year, planet Earth would appear during the last month of the year, and the first humans would strut onto life's stage on the last day of the last month of the year at about 10:30 in the evening.[4] To contemplate the span of an individual life measured on the yardstick of such unimaginable time only adds to the vague sense of unease felt by many in our day.[5]

Awareness of who and where we are in the universe has naturally spawned all sorts of speculation about extraterrestrial life. Although Martians and their canals have ceased to exist even in the astronomers' imagination, now that our Mariner spaceships have given us a good look at the red planet, UFO enthusiasts still believe Martian-like creatures have visited us in their mysterious, antigravity machines. (See Ted Peters, *UFOs: God's Chariots?* [Atlanta: John Knox, 1977], for an interesting survey of the lore and lure of flying saucers.) Meanwhile, many scientists, convinced that there can be no singularities in the universe, and noting that the same chemical building blocks exist everywhere, assume that there must be millions of suns and orbiting planets, on some of which, at least, there are intelligent beings like ourselves. Listening devices have even been set up to monitor any messages coming from "out there," but so far the phone has not rung in any SETI (Search for Extra-Terrestrial Intelligence) office. Nor will it ever, we suspect. To have life, as we know it, on other planets, there must be the right kind of sun — not just any old sun will do; the right kind of planet; and the right kind of atmosphere on that planet to set the stage for "life" as science defines it. Should all these conditions be present, even then no one knows how life could get started and, if it did, what turn it would take as it began to develop. Here on planet Earth, the differing histories of organisms do not repeat themselves.

3. One hundred and seventy-four sextillion miles and increasing at the rate of nearly 10 million miles a minute!

4. See the *Los Angeles Times,* Dec. 31, 1975, pt. II, p. 3. Also Karl Heim, *Christian Faith and Natural Science* (New York: Harper and Brothers, 1953), pp. 11-12, for Paul Dorn's original calculations postulating a somewhat different age for the universe.

5. One is reminded of Pascal's comment, "When I consider the short duration of my life, swallowed up in the eternity before and after, the little space which I fill and even can see, engulfed in the infinite immensity of spaces of which I am ignorant and which know me not, I am frightened and am astonished at being here rather than there; for there is no reason why here rather than there, why now rather than then" (*Pensées,* no. 205).

No species has ever evolved twice. Dinosaurs are gone forever. Nothing quite like them occurred before the Mesozoic and nothing like them will ever emerge again. For evolution to follow the same path on another planet [as on ours] would require at every moment all over that planet an exact duplication of every environmental change that took place on the earth as well as the same selection of alternatives from randomly changing genetic pools as was made here. (Wm. G. Pollard, *Science and Faith: Twin Mysteries* [New York: Nelson, 1970], p. 76)

Pollard goes on to note that here on earth, while all the continental land masses started at the same time with the same primate stock, only in Africa did humans appear, whence they spread over the earth, not by evolution but by migration. The Americas never got any further than the new world monkeys.

Over and beyond all the mysteries and improbabilities surrounding the origin and development of living creatures like ourselves on other planets, there is the sheer size of the space that separates us from "possible others" when it comes to tuning in on them. Had we celestial neighbors on the nearest star (which is sans planets), we would hear the response to our "hello" nine years later — if we were still alive to listen for it. The first radio signals emitted from planet Earth have little more than left the solar system; and the same is true of Pioneer 10, with its information about what humans are like and where they live. Out there is the void, a symbol of the eternal silence that envelops planet Earth. It is an awesome silence, indeed, for what technology can ever overcome it? Even the Space Telescope, which lifts the veil of earth's atmosphere, will never detect planets. Hence we are not excited about the prospects for "exotheology."

For those whose ultimate trust is in science and the knowledge it affords, the Christian understanding of the meaning and uniqueness of human life has little appeal, for it is — if we might so speak — on a different wavelength. Yet even apart from the Christian faith there are hints, which none can deny, that we humans are remarkably different, somehow, from the rest of the created order. Of course, the universe as a whole is remarkable. But what is more remarkable: that the universe in which we live is as it is, or that *we* should have discovered that it is as it is? Is it not a wonder of the first order that on a speck of cosmic dust called planet Earth there lives a creature whose mind has penetrated with incredible acumen the equally incredible disguises of her environment?[6] While it is

6. Although we seem to stand on terra firma, we know that we are actually whirling on a bullet, spinning and gyrating through space. Our earth that is "established; it shall never be moved" (Ps. 96:10) is actually rotating on its axis at 1000 miles per hour and revolving around the sun at almost 20 miles per second. The sun, meanwhile, moves in a local star system at 13 miles per second, while the local star system moves in our galaxy at 200 miles per second. Our galaxy, in turn, moves in relation to the others in its cluster at 100 miles per second. See Lincoln Barnett, *The Universe and Dr. Einstein* (New York: Wm. Sloane, 1959), p. 32.

humbling to know how small we are, at the same time it is a tribute to our
powers of self-transcendence that the empire of our thought is coterminous
with the universe itself. As Kant observed, while we have decreased as
objects, we have increased as subjects.[7]

But since we are subjects, why should we estimate our significance in
terms of our size as objects? Or again, why should we consider the life of
a star more significant than our own because of its vastly greater duration
in cosmic time? Even the Scriptures, which know nothing of an expanding
universe, give us little reason to preen ourselves on our significance as
creatures in time and space. Our life in this world is compared to a dream
and a vapor. Like grass we flourish in the morning and wither away in the
evening (Ps. 90:6-7; Jas. 4:14; 1 Pt. 1:24). Whole nations are likened to a
drop in the bucket and dust in the balance (Is. 40:15).

> Speaking of nations, it is easy, especially for Americans, to forget this biblical
> perspective and to equate significance with size. Ours is the biggest army,
> biggest navy, biggest gross national product — biggest everything. But God's
> people Israel suffered no such illusions. While they worshiped a great God,
> Creator of heaven and earth, they knew that this God did not choose them
> because of their numbers, for they were the fewest of all people (Dt. 7:7).
> They lived out their history surrounded by mighty powers who further re-
> duced their modest numbers to a pitiful remnant. Hence they took their hope
> and encouragement in God only and in the promise of his covenant; it was
> his word that gave their lives meaning and significance. So it is with Chris-
> tians, who are the heirs of Israel's faith. They know (though as Americans
> they sometimes forget) that significance in God's sight has no more to do
> with size than the significance of words has to do with the size of the letters
> with which they are printed. True, newspapers use headlines to convey sig-
> nificant messages. But consider the messages on billboards, the biggest of
> all — "Come to Marlboro Country," etc.

The Christian doctrine that human life is significant because God
has made us in his image is not, then, altogether unreasonable. And if it
is true, as Christians believe it is, then the meaning of our lives is to be
found not in our size but in our unique relationship to God, who, as
Augustine said, has made us for himself. Contemporary men and women
feel lonely and lost in the vast universe, Christians would say, because
they are not in fellowship with God. "Separated from Christ," they are
"alienated from the commonwealth of Israel, and strangers to the
covenants of promise, having no hope and without God in the world"
(Eph. 2:12). Their cosmic loneliness is a projection of their personal

---

7. Einstein's wife is said to have remarked that her husband could compute the size of
the universe on the back of an envelope — no mean boast!

loneliness. By contrast, the awesome universe that is opened to us by science is not threatening to the Christian; it evokes, rather, the worship of him who created heaven and earth. As the psalmist says, "The heavens declare the glory of God; and the firmament showeth his handiwork" (Ps. 19:1 KJV).[8]

B. HUMANITY AND MECHANISTIC REDUCTIONISM

As the synthetic sweep of astrophysics has seemed to reduce the human subject to the vanishing point, so the analytic study of the material world has seemed to reduce her in an even more drastic way. Each individual becomes a subsystem to be understood solely in terms of those objective laws according to which all the parts of the system function. The Christian view that each man and woman is a unique creation of God is dismissed as a religious judgment of a purely subjective nature. Religion is simply psychology, which is simply biology, which is simply the chemistry of the large molecule. And since the large molecule is made up of atoms that function according to the laws of physics, physics ultimately accounts for everything. The human brain, to be sure, is a very complex instance of physics and a highly efficient physical mechanism with its 100 billion nerve cells (neurons) and ten times as many glia cells. Just to keep the body's metabolism going, it energizes thousands of enzymes in over two million reactions per second. When it comes to conscious acts like lifting a spoon to our mouths, tens of thousands of neurons are involved in a series of chemical reactions that are mind-boggling. Nonetheless, the brain is not qualitatively different from the other mechanisms of nature. While it may be true that the brain is presently as little understood as the remote reaches of space, our ever increasing knowledge confirms that this inner universe functions according to the same laws that govern the outer universe — "thoughts are related to the brain in much the same way as gall to the liver and urine to the kidneys."[9]

8. One's size in relation to one's environment is admittedly an interesting subject, as is entertainingly demonstrated in Swift's account of *Gulliver's Travels*. See especially part I, "A Voyage to Lilliput," and part II, "A Voyage to Brobdingnag."

9. Karl Vogt, *Köhlerglaube und Wissenschaft*, as quoted by Barth, *Die Kirchliche Dogmatik* (hereafter *KD*) (Zurich: Evangelischer Verlag, 1959), III/2, p. 461 (cf. *Church Dogmatics* [hereafter *CD*], trans. G. W. Bromiley, et al., ed. Bromiley and T. F. Torrance [Edinburgh: T. & T. Clark, 1960], III/2, pp. 384-85). Barth goes on to remind the reader of Feuerbach's well-known quip, *"Der Mensch ist was er isst"* ("One is what one eats"). Put

Viewing the human person as simply a complex machine has created a large discussion about computers, robots, and an assortment of cybernetic contraptions. The first robots were Vulcan's "golden handmaids, who also worked with him, and were like real young women, with sense and reason, voice also and strength" (*The Iliad of Homer,* Great Books [Chicago: Britannica, 1952], 18.410). Today science fiction regales the reader with stories of robots, especially bad robots that even outdo Mary Shelley's monster, usually called by the name of its fictional creator, Frankenstein. Meanwhile, some theologian types have darkly observed that as God created us in his image, so cyberneticists are creating computers in our image. In the same vein, we are solemnly assured in science museum exhibits that computers can think, choose, create, and do whatever else sounds impressive. However, bionic humans, once predicted for the 1980s, have not made their debut, and one need not be apprehensive over the prospect that they will.

There can be little doubt that the presence of computers has made our lives quite different, as have the telephone, the automobile, and many other marvelous devices. But it is absurd to suppose that computers are capable of thought and will one day outthink us. Computers do not think; even human brains do not think. *We* think *with* our brains. The thing that makes computers helpful, as we do our thinking, is their capability for storing vast amounts of information that we can recall almost instantly when needed. A computer can, for example, give space scientists a trajectory in a few seconds. But this happens only after a half-dozen people have worked for several months to store in the computer the right information. This programming process is never reversed. Computers do not want to know about trajectories, *people* do. In fact, a computer does not "know" what a trajectory is because it does not "know" anything. "I am appalled," says Eccles, "at the naïveté of the statements and arguments that are made by the proponents of the computer simulation of man" (*Facing Reality* [New York: Longman, 1970], p. 171). Between 1964 and 1966 Joseph Weizenbaum composed a computer program in which one could "converse" in English with a computer named "Eliza," a psychiatrist. In his *Computer Power and Human Reason* (New York: W. H. Freeman, 1976), Weizenbaum writes of the shock he felt at the response of learned people to his program, a response that simply assumed there was no difference between human and machine intelligence. "What I had not realized is that extremely short exposures to a relatively simple computer program could induce powerful delusional thinking in quite normal people" (ibid., p. 7).

Such mechanistic reductionism represents a totally different view of humankind from the one that will determine the ensuing discussion. Christian doctrine understands the human self from above (created in God's likeness) rather than from below (a complex congeries of particles and electromagnetic forces). Yet the mechanistic view, though it espouses a

---

a bit more genteelly and in the sophisticated lingo of modern neurological research: "When we call a fellow human 'brilliant,' we are not far off the mark: his or her brain can generate impressive electromagnetic waves. A dull person just isn't sparking" (Philip Dunne in "Guess Who Isn't Coming to Dinner," *Harvard Magazine,* March-April 1985, p. 50).

gross falsehood, is not wholly without truth. The same brain that was indispensable to Shakespeare's metabolism was also indispensable to his writing *Romeo and Juliet;* and it functioned according to the same physical laws in both instances. Not mechanism, then, but mechanistic reductionism is the view that Christian thought rejects. Christian faith postulates a qualitative difference between a machine and a person. True, we are given our personal being in a bodily form; hence our being as persons has a mechanistic aspect; but this mechanistic aspect of our being as persons is secondary, not primary, to our understanding of who we are. To be materially *conditioned* as conscious selves is not to be materially *constituted* as such.

The Christian view that human beings are creatures made in the Creator's image is, of course, a faith judgment. But it is not a judgment that is contrary to the "assured results of science." The evidence that humans are persons is that they alone are self-reflecting, conscious of themselves as selves. Science gives one no hard data that warrants the relegating of this self-consciousness to the meaningless category of an epiphenomenon.[10] There is something transcendent about self-consciousness. Each self, conscious of itself through memory, links all of life together in a continuity of inner experience. Thus the self comes to recognize its existence as a self, that is, a person who is an "I."

To be sure, an indefeasible relationship exists between ongoing brain states and self-consciousness or mind.[11] But the brain does not function by channeling all the incoming sensory data into a single, centralized, pontifical cell that integrates such data into a meaningful whole. Brain functions are rather like a democracy involving millions of cells that weave a pattern in the cerebral cortex that has been likened to the operation of an "enchanted loom."[12] What happens as this pattern is woven defies all mechanistic analysis. Conscious thought takes over, integrating the patterns of neural activity in a mysterious way that gives them meaning.[13]

10. In the ensuing comments on the brain-mind problem we reflect the position taken by J. C. Eccles in his *Facing Reality* (New York: Springer, 1970). See also his *Neurophysiological Basis of Mind* (New York: Oxford University Press, 1960); and Marilyn Ferguson, *The Brain Revolution* (New York: Taplinger, 1973).

11. "Mind," as here used, does not refer exclusively to "reason" or "understanding," but to all that is indicated by self-consciousness; hence, it overlaps in meaning with what has been traditionally called "soul" or "spirit" in theology.

12. Sherrington, *Man on His Nature,* as quoted by Eccles, *Facing Reality,* p. 54.

13. This integration takes place even when patterns are being woven on different parts of the loom simultaneously. One hears a book being read and follows the reading with the eyes, or with the fingers in the case of the blind; but these auditory, visual, and tactile stimuli, though channeled to different parts of the brain, all yield one and the same result, namely, one's understanding of what the author is saying.

Equally mysterious is the way in which thought brings about a shifting of the patterns of neural activity so that the loom weaves a new pattern that translates into acts in the external world. Thus a transcendent, spiritual reality (the mind) interpenetrates the material world, though we know not how.[14] Such acts in the external world are the acts of a conscious self. They differ in a qualitative way both from the involuntary acts caused by the stimulation of the motor cortex and the activity of the autonomic nervous system in that they reflect decision, choice, will. To dismiss them as a mere illusion is folly. They rather evidence a brain-mind liaison that is basic to all we shall have to say here about the Christian view of the human self as a responsible subject made in the image of the Creator.[15]

14. "Those who take seriously the existence of Mind are often taunted with being worried by 'a ghost in the machine'; I suggest it is high time we refuse to let our critical faculties be paralyzed any longer by this pert gibe" (Beloff, *The Existence of Mind,* as quoted by Eccles, *Facing Reality,* p. 64).

15. While we know that there are specific areas of the brain concerned with one's ability to feel, hear, speak, and see, interestingly, no such area has been located for the will. No one has been able to stimulate the cerebral cortex so as to make one choose to do something. See Huston Smith, *Forgotten Truth* (New York: Harper & Row, 1976), pp. 64-65.

Who Are We?

A Sermon Preached by Marguerite Shuster
at Knox Presbyterian Church, Pasadena, California,
Lord's Day, March 4, 1990.

O Lord, our Lord, how majestic is thy name in all the earth! Thou whose glory above the heavens is chanted by the mouth of babes and infants, thou hast founded a bulwark because of thy foes, to still the enemy and the avenger. When I look at thy heavens, the work of thy fingers, the moon and the stars which thou hast established; what is man that thou art mindful of him, and the son of man that thou dost care for him? Yet thou hast made him little less than God, and dost crown him with glory and honor. Thou hast given him dominion over the works of thy hands; thou hast put all things under his feet, all sheep and oxen, and also the beasts of the field, the birds of the air, and the fish of the sea, whatever passes along the paths of the sea. O Lord, our Lord, how majestic is thy name in all the earth!

Psalm 8

A book I recently purchased has on its cover a very striking picture. One sees first the image of a man ascending a ladder stretching up into the sky until it disappears into the clouds. That part is common enough and could be seen as one more example of the relentless human pride that has, ever since the Tower of Babel, sought to scale the heavens. But as one looks again, one sees that the ladder no longer rests on the earth. Indeed, the earth does not even appear in the drawing. Furthermore, each rung of the ladder breaks and falls away as soon as the man steps on it. He cannot go

11

back; he must go forward, though he knows not where, for there is nothing under his feet.[a]

In another volume, Loren Eiseley writes,

> In the more obscure scientific circles which I frequent there is a legend circulating about a late distinguished scientist who, in his declining years, persisted in wearing enormous padded boots much too large for him. He had developed, it seems, what to his fellows was a wholly irrational fear of falling through the interstices of that largely empty molecular space which common men in their folly speak of as the world. A stroll across his living-room floor had become, for him, something as dizzily horrendous as the activities of a window washer on the Empire State Building. Indeed, with equal reason, he could have passed a ghostly hand through his own ribs.
>
> The quivering network of his nerves, the awe-inspiring movement of his thought had become a vague cloud of electrons interspersed with the light-year distances that obtain between us and the farther galaxies. This was the natural world which he had helped to create, and in which, at last, he had found himself a lonely and imprisoned occupant.[b]

Again, there was nothing, he feared, under his feet. The world, as we have learned more about it, has become increasingly strange and vast and, paradoxically, unknown.

Once upon a time, a long time ago, there was a nice, tidy, three-story universe. The earth stood on pillars above the underworld, and the heavens were a vault stretched overhead, serving safely to enclose the earth and to provide a place to spread the stars. Everything pretty much stayed put — a very satisfactory arrangement. Once upon a somewhat later time, some more sophisticated astronomers got rid of the pillars and the vault, but in all their calculations simply assumed the earth as the central and stable point in the universe. Everything turned around it. And then came Copernicus and Galileo. The earth is not central and, what is more, it moves. In response to this new understanding John Donne penned the famous lines, the

> new Philosophy calls all in doubt,
> The Element of fire is quite put out;
> The Sun is lost, and th' earth, and no man's wit

a. Cover illustration by R. Dunnick, for J. D. Meindl, ed., *Brief Lessons in High Technology* (Stanford: Stanford Alumni Association, 1989).

b. *The Firmament of Time* (New York: Atheneum, 1984), p. 153.

Can well direct him where to look for it.

. . . .

'Tis all in pieces, all coherence gone.[c]

What, indeed, would Donne have written had he known that the sun is but a no-account star in a perfectly average galaxy — one among who knows how many galaxies spread out over distances so great that the numbers used to express the miles between them are, humanly speaking, simply meaningless, miles beyond our traversing even in a lifetime and thus beyond our truly conceiving. What would he have written had he known that the subatomic universe within is as vast and mysterious as the astronomer's universe without? Would he not have added exclamation points to the psalmist's query as he meditated on the night sky, "When I look at thy heavens, the work of thy fingers, the moon and the stars which thou hast established; what is man that thou art mindful of him, and the son of man that thou dost care for him?" Have we any particular significance, really? Why do we not just, so to speak, fall through the cracks? What is there under our feet?

The psalmist's question is clearly based on a keen sense of humankind's frailness, impotence, and mortality, compared to the power and expanse of the creation. To emphasize this point, he employs an unusual word for humankind, a word used especially in the book of Job, because it carries overtones of human littleness and weakness. This question of human significance is heightened in our day by our every discovery of the size and complexity of the universe, until we feel lost and lonely and rather dizzy in the midst of the great cosmic dance. However, the basic import of the psalmist's question remains the same today as it always was. After all, we have always been small and frail and short-lived compared to mountains or redwood trees, not to mention galaxies. Elephants are stronger than we. Dogs have better noses. Fish swim better. Birds have more sensitive navigation systems. Flowers are more lovely and colorful. So what's so special about us?

It matters, profoundly, how we answer that question; because if, in false humility, we say, "nothing," we will do terrible evil. If we say that, obviously enough, we are simply animals and not very impressive animals at that, we will surely act like animals.[d] Similarly but more chillingly, Abraham Heschel suggests that there may be a connection between believ-

c. Quoted in Alexandre Koyré, *From the Closed World to the Infinite Universe* (Baltimore: Johns Hopkins University Press, 1957), p. 29 (spelling modernized).

d. See Emil Brunner, *Our Faith,* trans. John W. Rilling (New York: Scribner's, 1954).

ing that one is simply made up of enough "fat to make seven cakes of soap, enough iron to make a medium sized nail," and so on; and "what the Nazis actually did in the extermination camps: make soap of human flesh."[e] Rob human beings of their unique dignity, and we will treat them as beasts or objects. Again, then, it matters that we take a proper view of ourselves, and therefore of other human selves, because what we believe makes a difference in how we behave.

But what constitutes a proper view of a person, as opposed to a proper view of a star or a tree or a dog? Heschel, again, remarks that if a person wakes up one day and insists that he is a rooster, we do not know what he means, and we put him in an insane asylum. But it is also true that when a person wakes up one day and insists he is a human being, we do not know what he means.[f] We are mysterious to ourselves. Not fundamentally mysterious as *objects:* we explore and seek to manipulate the way our own bodies and brains work, from their chemical constituents to their genetic code to the assaults made on them by disease, the same way we explore and seek to manipulate the rest of the world. We make the same sort of progress in these endeavors, meet the same sorts of obstacles, and find the same sorts of unexpected new vistas continuing to open up that we do in the other sciences. The mysteries of the human object we approach as problems to be solved, problems that, we are confident, one day will be solved. But the real mystery of humankind is the mystery not of the human object but of the human *subject:* How is it that one creature, and one creature only, asks the question about its own significance and then proceeds to seek to understand the whole created order? How is it that one creature alone has the power not just to *look* at the heavens and see them, as any animal can, but to *consider* them, as the King James Version puts it?

Perhaps you are familiar with Rodin's sculpture of a man pensively reflecting upon the human skull he holds in his hand — reflecting, one assumes, on the mystery of reflection. A couple of my friends — theologians both — have in their offices parodies of this statue: the form of a large ape, in exactly the same position as the man in the sculpture, looking down, pensively, at a human skull. But whatever the ape is supposedly thinking, his thoughts are not like our thoughts. No ape ever sculpted a statue, much less a parody of a statue. That is why the parody is both funny and provocative.

No ape ever sculpted a statue. No elephant ever exulted in its own strength. No flower ever rejoiced in its own beauty or mourned the brevity of its life. No star ever admired its brilliance or the brilliance of its neighbors or marveled

e. *Who Is Man?* (Stanford: Stanford University Press, 1965), p. 24.
f. Ibid., pp. 51-52.

that its light would be seen years after it burnt itself out. No galaxy ever thought of making its size a ground for ruling other galaxies, or making its ancient age a reason that it should be venerated. No mountain, however high it rears its peak toward heaven, and no quark or gluon, however nearly it enters into the inner secret of things at the physical level, ever asked who made it or bowed down to worship or wrote a psalm in praise of the wonders of creation. Human beings alone among all God's creatures do these things. Human beings alone can consider, can reflect upon, themselves and the world. They alone respond with awe to beauty. They alone have a longing for the ultimate, for God, and seek to worship him. A mystery and a marvel indeed.

But to take a proper view of ourselves, we must not only consider the incredible difference between us and the rest of the creation, which gives us a peculiar dignity and might despite our physical insignificance and weakness; we must also consider the meaning of this difference. If it has no meaning — if it is nothing but some sort of evolutionary fluke — then, without doubt, the higher we climb in our quest for knowledge and power, the more surely we will find that there is nothing under our feet, and the more surely we will feel befuddled and baffled by the powers of thought and self-transcendence that leave us increasingly aware of being alone in a universe that, no matter how loudly we call, has no ability to utter so much as a rational whisper in reply.

The psalmist, however, makes clear that we are not alone. Throughout this psalm we see the possessive pronoun. The heavens are the Lord's heavens, declaring his glory; the earth is his workmanship. As Augustine put it in describing his contemplation of the world:

> And what is this God? I asked the earth, and it answered: "I am not he," and all things that are on the earth confessed the same. I asked the sea and the deeps and the creeping things with living souls. . . . I asked the blowing breezes . . . the heaven, the sun, the moon, the stars. . . . Tell me something about my God. And they cried out in a loud voice: "He made us": My question was in my contemplation of them, and their answer was in their beauty.[g]

The whole creation testifies not to itself, but to God. And, if we consider rightly, so do we. For the Lord who made the heavens not only made us, but made us what we are. And what is that? What are human beings? Creatures, says the psalmist, a little less than God, creatures whom, despite their weakness, despite their impotence, despite their utter insignificance in terms of size and strength, God has chosen in his abundant goodness to

g. *Confessions*, 10.6.

crown with glory and honor, attributes of royalty bestowed upon the chosen rulers of his creation. All of our human uniqueness is simply God's gift to us, and finally a revelation of his unfathomable majesty rather than a manifestation of our own achievement.

But it also follows that, precisely because the Lord has expressly given us authority over the works of his hand, our exercise of power in and over nature is not, or at least is not necessarily, a manifestation of rebellion against God. The very possibility of exercising such authority is both gift and commission from him. Thus we see the psalmist referring not only to tame animals like sheep and oxen, which we might see as proper objects of domestication, but also wild animals, the beasts of the field, and birds and fish and "whatever passes along the paths of the sea." Our rightful dominion extends not only to what we have currently brought under our control, but also to those realms where it is hard for us to conceive ever having control. Perhaps, then, the whole impulse of learning and science and technology and the exploration and use of the created world may find here a sort of incipient sanction. Although they may be and certainly have been seriously abused, these are basically good things, not bad ones, activities fitting the creature who is a little less than God and, in their own way, activities that, in revealing more and more about the wonders of God's world, may thereby increase our impulse to worship him.

What, then, shall we say now about our place in the universe? Have we something under our feet after all? Have we a firm place to stand while traveling on a world comprised more of empty space than of solid matter and whirling through inconceivable reaches of space at hundreds of miles per second? The answer depends on our ability to say, as the psalmist says at both the beginning and ending of this psalm, "O LORD, our Lord, how majestic is thy name in all the earth!" If and only if we know the Lord of heaven and earth as our Lord will we know that we are not a fluke, or a mistake, or alone in the universe. We will know that the whole universe, including us, bears witness to his glory. And we will also know that our security is in the Lord who has crowned us with glory and honor in that he has put all things under our feet.

C. HUMANITY VIEWED AS FELLOWSHIP WITH GOD AND NEIGHBOR

Knowledge of the outer world of the universe where we live and the inner world of the mind by which we perceive where we live — knowledge of the "phenomena of humanity," as Barth calls it — gives us genuine knowledge about ourselves. Such knowledge, however, will never disclose the ultimate mystery of our humanity; it will never tell us what it means to say "I."[16] Am I, the individual, naught but "a tribute to the subtlety of matter" (Sagan)? Is it true that "I" first exist, turn up, appear on the scene, and then define *myself* (Sartre)?[17] The admonition "Know yourself" (γνῶθι σ'αὐτόν), carved over the entrance of the temple at Delphi, is easier to hear than to heed. Indeed, self-knowledge has proved to be the hardest of all to acquire. Some would say it is because we are so near to ourselves. It is as when one tries to read a page held too close to the eyes; we lack the distance to be objective. Yet we cannot help but seek such self-knowledge, for it is simply impossible to lose ourselves in the immediacy of our experience as do the animals. We not only exist but we know we exist, and such self-awareness compels us, inevitably, to pursue the knowledge of ourselves that we may understand who we are and the meaning of our existence.

The problem, as Christians see it, is not that we seek to understand ourselves, but that we seek such understanding in terms of ourselves alone.[18] Such a procedure is doomed to failure because only God, who made us, truly knows who we are and can disclose to us the mystery of our existence. Were we to follow Pope's advice,

> Know then thyself, presume not God to scan,
> The proper study of mankind is man,

we could only conclude with him that indeed we are "the glory, jest, and riddle of the world."[19] But since God has made us, and not we ourselves

16. In limiting our previous comments to the "hard" sciences of cosmology and physiology, especially neurophysiology, we do not mean to ignore the insights gained about the human condition through philosophy, psychology, and sociology. These disciplines, however, yield such a plethora of opinion about what it means to be human that we found it difficult to summarize the discussion without losing the thread of our argument in the maze of material. We thought it best, therefore, simply to comment on the thought of a Plato or an Aristotle, a Freud or a Jung, a Marx or an Engels, as may be indicated, in the course of our ongoing effort to frame a Christian anthropology. For a good summary of the Marxian and Freudian conceptions of humankind, see David Cairns, *The Image of God in Man* (New York: Philosophical Library, 1953), chaps. 15 and 16.

17. For comment on Sagan, see J. R. Nelson, *Human Life* (Philadelphia: Fortress, 1984), pp. 56-57; concerning Sartre's insistence that "existence precedes essence," see A. C. Cochrane, *The Existentialists and God* (Philadelphia: Westminster, 1954), pp. 65-66.

18. Here one is reminded of the opening sentence in the Creed of St. Euthanasia (commonly called the Athenaeum Creed): "I believe in Man, Maker of himself and inventor of all science; and in Myself, his Manifestation, and Captain of my Psyche; and that I should not suffer anything painful or unpleasant" (Dorothy Sayers, *Christian Letters to a Post-Christian World* [Grand Rapids: Eerdmans, 1969], p. 10).

19. Alexander Pope, "An Essay on Man," in Louis Untermeyer, ed., *A Treasury of Great Poems* (New York: Simon and Schuster, 1955), p. 532.

(Ps. 100:3), he can tell us who we are; his word resolves the riddle of our existence. The same divine word that gives us a knowledge of God also gives us knowledge of ourselves. Hence an adequate self-understanding is indissolubly bound up with our knowledge of God. "True and substantial wisdom," Calvin reminds us, "principally consists in two parts, the knowledge of God and the knowledge of ourselves." These two branches of knowledge are intimately related, he argues, because we live and move and have our being in God. Indeed, "it is evident that the talents which we possess are not from ourselves, and that our very existence is nothing but a subsistence in God alone."[20]

Christians believe that this interlocking of the knowledge of God and the self is because human existence is by definition an existence in relation to God. The being that is human has no existence in itself, but only in its unique relationship to the Creator. In disclosing himself as the God-who-has-made-us-for-himself, the Creator discloses to us that we are the creature-uniquely-related-to-him.[21] While all creation is grounded in the word of the Creator (Ps. 33:6), to be human is to be grounded in that word in a unique way. The Creator is both the God in whom we live, move, and have our being (Acts 17:28), and the God with whom we have to do (Heb. 4:13). To say that God is the God "with whom we have to do" is just to say that we have our being in a way that makes us responsible to him.[22] Even sinful humanity is uniquely related to God and, therefore, responsible to him though not in fellowship with him. As the Creator, he is the true "Thou" of every human "I." To be human is to live one's life *coram Deo.*[23]

20. *Inst.,* 1.1.1.

21. See Otto Weber, *Foundations of Dogmatics,* trans. D. L. Guder, 2 vols. (Grand Rapids: Eerdmans, 1981-83), 1.529-33. To be sure, we are brought to confess that our being is a being-in-relation-to-God, our Creator, only through our knowledge that God is our Redeemer. It is in Christ that we clearly perceive that God is the God-who-has-made-us-for-himself and therefore freely acknowledge that we are the creature-who-is-uniquely-related-to-him. But we should not confuse the noetic and the ontological. It is not our experience of salvation, but God's act of creation, that is the basis of a Christian understanding of humanity.

22. "Only if we understand responsibility literally as the necessity of giving an account to the Judge who judges impartially and knows everything — only then do we understand ourselves as really responsible. The idealistic philosophy has attempted to circumvent this 'theological' interpretation of responsibility by making man responsible to a moral law. This is the monological . . . interpretation of responsibility" (Emil Brunner, *Dogmatics,* vol. 3: *The Christian Doctrine of the Church, Faith, and the Consummation,* trans. David Cairns in collaboration with T. H. L. Parker [Philadelphia: Westminster, 1962], p. 419).

23. See G. C. Berkouwer, *Man: The Image of God,* trans. Dirk W. Jellema (Grand Rapids: Eerdmans, 1962), p. 35. The Bible does not teach us to say, "I think, therefore I am" (Descartes), but, "The Creator thought of me before all time. Therefore I am." And, "He thinks of me still. Therefore, at all times, I am responsible to him."

This fundamental affirmation of Christian anthropology that the human I can never understand itself in isolation because it is not autonomous, not the measure of all things, but rather created in and for fellowship with God, is an offense to.the modern mind that seeks to understand humanity apart from all metaphysical or religious considerations. This secular self-understanding, whether oriented in terms of wealth (Marx), power (Nietzsche), sex (Freud), or whatever, is ultimately a monologue, a talking to the self about the self. Even in the Idealistic tradition, the transcendental Self is talking to the empirical self. Theological anthropology that is Christian enters the field not simply to add one more voice to this multifarious soliloquy, but to proclaim that it has something to say that is new and decisive for humankind, whoever they may be and whatever their self-understanding.

Admittedly such a claim is astounding. What do Cro-Magnons have in common with the citizens of Pericles' Athens; the Indians of the Amazon rain forest with the astronauts whose footprints are on the moon? The theologian best answers this question not by appeal to common, human qualities, supposedly evident to all through reasoned analysis of empirical data, but by appeal to the implications of biblical revelation. According to Scripture, humanity has its origin in the word of God in a way that no other creature has. As humans we are not simply summoned into existence by divine fiat — "let the dust bring forth humankind." Rather, we are given our existence as a gift of love in order that in love we may respond to the Creator's love with gratitude and obedience. According to the biblical narrative, our first parents knew the divine love through the Creator's blessing and provision. They also knew how they were to respond to that love, that is, they knew their *responsibility,* for they were addressed by their Maker as those who could distinguish between "thou shalt" and "thou shalt not." Thus they were summoned (and we with them) to a life of responsible love toward God and one another (Gn. 2:16; 3:2-3; 1:28-29). Such love toward God and neighbor is not simply a desirable attribute of our existence as human; it is rather the very essence of that existence. *Our being-in-responsibility is fulfilled in our being-with-and-for-others-in-love, first the divine Other who is our Maker, and also the human other who is our neighbor.*[24]

---

24. As we have noted, this "dynamic" understanding — as it has been called — of the *imago,* describes our humanity even as fallen and sinful. Original sin, which is the radical perversion of the love to which we are summoned in creation, will concern us in another volume. For now we simply wish to note that while the sin of the creature turns the love of God and neighbor into a selfish love that rebels against God and exploits the neighbor, it cannot utterly destroy the responsible relationship to God and neighbor given us in and by creation.

Christians, it is true, believe that the Creator's love by which we were created is revealed supremely in the love through which we are redeemed. This is the love of a Father for a sinful world — from aborigine to astronaut (Jn. 3:16); a love shown in the death of his Son (Rom. 5:8) and shed abroad in our hearts by the Spirit whom he has given us (Rom. 5:5). This love of the Redeemer reveals the love of the Creator because Creator and Redeemer are one and the same triune God. Likewise, the purpose of the love that redeems is to fulfill the love that creates by restoring the creature to fellowship with the Creator. For the Christian, then, God's final revelation in Christ illumines his original revelation in creation.[25]

While such a Christian understanding of humankind rests on revelation rather than on a rational analysis of empirical data, it surely does not contradict the data. All must agree that the ineluctable encounter with the human other, the neighbor, entails responsible behavior toward the other. In this respect humans are essentially different from animals, whatever one may say about a common biological ancestry and the evidence of primitive intelligence in animal behavior. The basic human act is to affirm, "I am." And to posit the self as an "I" in this way is to posit the other who is a "thou." I am "I" not in isolation but in encounter with others. "No man is an island" (Donne).[26]

Our being as a being-in-encounter is evidenced particularly by the fact of human speech. Speech is not the making of sounds like a talking parrot, or the stringing of arbitrary symbols in a linear way like a computer; but the disclosing of the self to others and placing oneself at the disposal of others. Such fellowship, flawed though it is by sinful self-interest, is of the essence of humanity. In a remarkable passage in the preface to his *Das Wort und die geistigen Realitaten: Pneumatologische Fragmenta,* Ferdinand Ebner observes,

> It does not appear entirely superfluous to me, here in the foreword, to reduce the fundamental thought in the *Fragments* to as brief a formula as possible. This fundamental thought is: presupposed that human existence in its kernel has a spiritual significance, viz., a significance that is not exhausted in its natural manifestation in the

25. See our remarks on the meaning of the Sabbath rest of creation in *God, Creation, and Revelation,* pp. 483, 492.

26. It is noteworthy that prisoners look on solitary confinement as the worst form of punishment. Vietnam War prisoners viewed it as the "ultimate ordeal." "The isolation and monotony of the prison," they said, "surpasses in psychological horror and human degradation all the beatings and rats and diarrhea and morning emptyings of the honeybucket. 'If you think only in terms of physical torture, you miss the subtlety of what we mean by inhumane treatment' " (*Los Angeles Times,* Dec. 5, 1970, pt. I, p. 10).

course of a world event; presupposed that one may speak of something spiritual in humankind otherwise than in the sense of a fiction of a poetic or metaphoric nature, or of a fiction demanded on "social" grounds: then this spiritual entity is essentially defined thereby, that it is fundamentally connected with something *outside* it, *through* which and in which it exists. An evidence, and indeed, an "objectively" tangible evidence, of dependence on a relation of such a sort and one that is therefore accessible to objective knowledge, is to be found in the fact that humans are speaking beings, that they have the "word." They do not, however, have the word on a natural or social basis. Society in the human sense is not the presupposition of speech, but rather itself has as the presupposition of its existence that the word is lodged in humans.

If, then, in order to have an expression for it, we call this spiritual entity in humans "I," and that which is *outside* them, in relationship to which the "I" exists, "thou," we must remember that this I and this thou are given to us precisely *through* the word and *in* it, in its "inwardness"; not as an empty word in which dwells no relationship to reality . . . but rather as a word that "duplicates" its content and real form in the concreteness and actuality of its being pronounced, that is, in and through the situation created by speech. That, in brief, is the fundamental thought.[27]

If Ebner is correct, and we believe that he is, the uniqueness of the human situation, illumined by the fact of speech, gives plausibility to the Christian view that I-thou relationships at the human level reflect the relationship between the human I and the divine Thou that is fundamental to the right understanding of our humanity. Ebner himself draws this conclusion. He seeks to escape what he calls (following Johann Georg Hamann) the misunderstanding of the self with the self, which leads to the absolute Self of the metaphysician and the transcendental Self of the ethicist. Such an autonomous self knows no authority outside itself and will not allow itself to be *spoken to*. This is the self that refuses to hear the voice of God, who is the true Thou of the human I, the God who created humankind in and for fellowship with himself.

> What life have you if you have not
> life together?
> There is no life that is not in

27. Ebner, *Das Wort und die geistigen Realitaten, Pneumatologische Fragmenta* (Innsbruck: Brenner, 1921), p. 12. Italics his.

community.

And no community not lived in praise of God.[28]

Only the one addressed by God is human, concludes Ebner; only the one who responds affirmatively to that address escapes the death of the human spirit.[29]

According to Ebner, it was Johann Georg Hamann, "that marvelously profound philologist," and Wilhelm von Humboldt who saw the significance of speech in its spiritual roots as of divine origin, "something absolutely transcendent" (*Das Wort,* p. 16). John Cullberg cites a similar observation of Martin Buber to the effect that the great contribution of Israel was not monotheism but the teaching that we may address God as "Thou" precisely because he so addresses us (*Das Du und die Wirklichkeit* [Uppsala: Lundequistska, 1933], p. 42, citing Buber's *Die chassidischen Bucher,* XI). To affirm the transcendent character of speech is to deny that apes do not speak simply because they never evolved the right-shaped larynx. "Why do animals not speak?" asks Goez. "Because they have nothing to say!" (*Naturwissenschaft und Evangelium* [Heidelberg: Quelle & Meyer, 1954], p. 77). To affirm this transcendent character of speech is also to deny that the multimillion-dollar effort to achieve machine translation will ever succeed. If animals cannot speak, how much less machines.

To see human speech as rooted in transcendence, however, is not to affirm that Adam and Eve, on the first day they met, had the vocabulary Milton gives them in *Paradise Lost.* In the matter of speech, no doubt, the experience of the human species as a whole may be likened to the experience of the self as an individual. Although our speech has a transcendent basis, each of us in our immanence must learn to speak by speaking — which takes time. A little child "begins by babbling, learns by stammering, but one day announces its 'I' with all clarity" (Goez, *Naturwissenschaft,* p. 101). Even Shakespeare needed a little time to learn to "speak that we might see him." (One of the most fascinating stories in this regard is that of Helen Keller, who one day suddenly perceived that the sign made on her palm by Anne Sullivan was the word for what she felt running over her hand at the pump. See her *The World I Live In* [New York: Century, 1908]. Also Roger Shattuck, *The Forbidden Experiment: The Story of the Wild Boy of Aveyron* [New York: Farrar Straus Giroux, 1980]. For an interesting account of the shift away from behaviorism on the part of psychologists and the positing of some sort of innate knowledge to account for a child's learning of language — "the jewel in the crown of cognition" — see John de Cuevas, "No, she holded them loosely," *Harvard*

---

28. T. S. Eliot, *The Complete Poems and Plays, 1909-1950* (New York: Harcourt Brace and World, 1962), p. 101.

29. See Ebner, *Das Wort,* pp. 17, 21, 26. According to the Christian, this affirmative response that gives life to the human spirit and so restores fellowship with the Creator is faith in Jesus Christ, who is God's final Word (Heb. 1:2). It is such faith that enables the Christian to sing,

Be Thou my true wisdom and Thou my true Word;
I ever with thee and thou with me Lord.

(Ancient Irish)

Magazine, Sept.-Oct. 1990, p. 61. De Cuevas reviews the work of Harvard psychologist Roger Brown.)

D. HUMANITY VIEWED AS INDIVIDUAL SELVES

The truth that we have our being as human only in a fellowship of an I and a thou in no way impugns the distinction between them. True, I cannot rightly understand myself apart from God who gave me my existence and my neighbor with whom I share that existence. But the boundary between the self and the other is an ineluctable one. Hence Christian theology rejects all pantheistic, mystical merging of the creature with the Creator and recognizes, at the human level, the uniqueness and worth of the personal self over against all other selves.[30] To say "*I* am" is to say I am given my existence as an individual. While I am summoned to an existence of responsible love by my Creator, it is I, an individual self, who am summoned to such an existence. While I never exist apart from my neighbor, I am, in my existence, ever distinct from my neighbor. I am not you, even as you are not I.[31] Only I know myself as a subject, as only you know yourself as a subject. To recognize this "opacity of the self-knowing self" (Simone de Beauvoir) is to recognize that each has her being as an individual. Having reflected on the I in relation to the thou, we must now reflect on the I as distinct from the thou, the I as an individual self.

According to Christian teaching, the individual is the locus of that

---

30. "According to mysticism, even when interpreted in Meister Eckhardt's semi-Christian sense, virtue can be achieved only by the annihilation of the individual's will. . . . Mysticism, in other words, insists on the full dimension of height in the human spirit, but identifies unique individuality with a creatureliness which must be overcome" (Reinhold Niebuhr, *The Nature and Destiny of Man,* 2 vols. [London: Nisbet, 1941-43], 1.61).

31. Even in the "one flesh" of the marriage bond, the most intimate of all I-thou relationships at the human level, the thou remains the ever mysterious other:

> Why, having won her, do I woo?
>   Because her spirit's vestal grace
> Provokes me always to pursue,
>   But spirit-like, eludes embrace . . .
>
> Because, tho' free of the "outer court"
>   I am, this Temple keeps its shrine
> Sacred to Heaven; because, in short,
>   She's not and never can be mine.
>
>   (From Coventry Patmore's "The Married Lover,"
>   in Untermeyer, ed., *Treasury of Great Poems,* pp. 927-28)

value, dignity, and worth which belong to all who are human. This is because each individual is endowed at creation with the image and likeness of God. Furthermore, it is the individual who is the object of God's gracious call in the *new* creation. True, the individual is saved in and for fellowship (the church), but it is only as an individual that each becomes a member of the body of Christ. Admittedly, the inexhaustible inventiveness of the Creator in bringing myriads of individual selves into being overwhelms our powers of comprehension. Yet we know that God creates humanity not in a general but in an individual way. He creates us as unique persons, giving each a name and a face. He clothes our being, as it were, with the garment of individuality and thus gives each self a basic identity forever. Hence our individual existence is as significant as it is mysterious.[32]

It was Kierkegaard's burden as a philosopher to rescue the individual from being swallowed up Jonah-like in the belly of Hegel's system. The thinker should never forget that *she* exists. It is the individual that is important. In particular, I am important to me — and to God.[33] The fact that God, who is one, has given us our being in the oneness of the individual self, so that each is aware of herself as an "I," opens up before us many issues that we cannot here pursue in detail. Our main concern is to understand this I, who is I and not another, in the light of biblical revelation. What does the Bible say about this "I" surrounded by countless other

32. According to the Bible, the human story begins with the creation not of a group but of Adam and Eve (Gn. 2), and concludes with the promise that in the new creation each one who overcomes will receive a white stone with a new name written on it that no one knows but the one who receives it (Rv. 2:17). We are given a parable of this profound truth in the uniqueness of our bodily existence. There are no two people living on the planet who are physically identical. Nor, statistically speaking, has there been sufficient time in the entire history of the race, given the number of genetic variables, to produce a single clone. In our reckoning, the thought that biologists will one day confer immortality on the individual by reproducing her replica from a piece of her skin, treated with appropriate potions, is a piece of science fiction. On the possibility of replicating Einstein, see the *Los Angeles Times,* Jan. 7, 1967, pt. II, p. 7.

33. Kierkegaard's break with Hegel is powerfully formulated in his *Concluding Unscientific Postscript,* in *Kierkegaard's Writings,* 12.1, ed. and trans. H V. Hong and E. H. Hong (Princeton: Princeton University Press, 1992). In his *Attack on Christendom* (trans. Walter Lowrie [Princeton: Princeton University Press, 1949], passim), Kierkegaard presses the same point, as a Christian believer, against the Lutheran Church of Denmark. Everyone in Denmark is reckoned a Christian by virtue of her baptism and confirmation. Such mass Christianity is faceless, mediocre, with no passion, no existence. There is no individual choice for or against Christ as demanded by the New Testament. This is what is really rotten in Denmark. Kierkegaard's insistence that the individual becomes truly an individual in the choice for or against Christ shows that he is not thinking of the individual as an I in isolation but as confronted by the divine Thou. Hence Ebner pays him the high tribute: "Kierkegaard was perhaps the only genius who made the proper use of that genius" (*Das Wort,* p. 40).

selves, yet consciously identifying itself with none other than itself? This is the question we must now seek to answer.

The Christian acknowledges that every atom, snowflake, plant, and animal has its own particularity. But such individuation is different from that of a self-conscious self. This fact explains why our ecological efforts are directed toward threatened species of plants and animals; the individual condor, whooping crane, or blue whale is valuable as a carrier of a threatened population. But in the human realm the value of the individual is of the same order as that of the human family as a whole. In other words, the Christian does not accept the thought that at the human level the individual is of less worth than the species. If we think of ourselves Christianly, we cannot suppose that universal, ideal being is our essential being, while our individual, historical being is accidental, non-essential being. Such an ontology is rejected by Christians because of the belief that the Creator has endowed each self with his own likeness. Therefore human individuality is unique; each individual has value as a personal self in the image of God. When the good vicar of Wakefield seeks to commend his plan for reforming prisoners to the members of his family, he concludes: "Perhaps I may catch up even one from the gulf, and that will be a great gain; for is there upon earth a gem so precious as the human soul?" (Oliver Goldsmith, *The Vicar of Wakefield* [New York: Macmillan, 1924], p. 138).

By the same token, one who embraces the Christian doctrine of humankind must deplore any social, political, or economic order that reduces the individual to the anonymity of the masses, whether they be the slaves that built the pyramids of Egypt and propelled the galleys of the Roman navy or the men and women of today who work on the assembly lines and sew in the sweatshops.

> O men, with sisters dear!
> O men, with mothers and wives!
> It is not linen you're wearing out,
>> But human creatures' lives.
>>> Stitch-stitch-stitch
>> In poverty and dirt, —
> Sewing at once, with a double thread,
>> A shroud as well as a shirt!
>>>>> (Thomas Hood, "The Song of the Shirt")

II. On Being Human:
A Christian Perspective

A. INTRODUCTION

To the question, How should one understand the human self in the light of biblical revelation, we are given the answer: the "I" is an "I" in relation to the "other," the divine Thou of the Creator and the human thou of the neighbor. This relationship is one of responsible love. At the same time, we have argued, this relationship is a relationship of distinct selves; we are given our humanity as individual persons. A human "I" is always aware of itself not only in relation to the "other" but also as distinct from and over against the "other." Assuming this general approach to human "ontology," we must now ask what, specifically, the Scripture teaches about the nature of the individual self. What has the Creator given each of us as individuals? What are the endowments that make each one's relationship to God and neighbor unique? Some have argued that we should not ask such questions, since the *being* of a person that makes her relationship to God unique *is* the relationship. Only as we perceive this, it is alleged, can we overcome the traditional, static understanding of personhood with a dynamic understanding.[1]

---

1. Brunner, for one, sometimes goes to this extreme. The being *(Wesen)* of humanity *is* relationship to God. "Personhood is a total act." The verb in this sentence is sui generis. The "act which constitutes a person relates itself to the individual 'acts' of the person" as the constitution of the state which, as a governmental act, is related to the ongoing "acts" of government *(Dogmatik,* 2.71; cf. *Dogmatics,* vol. 2: *The Christian Doctrine of Creation and Redemption,* trans. Olive Wyon [Philadelphia: Westminster, 1952], p. 60). Also *Man in Revolt,* trans. Olive Wyon (London: Lutterworth, 1939), pp. 150-52.

For us, such an approach has insuperable problems. As Cairns has noted,

> If personal being is reduced to decision or act or relation, the objection is perfectly justified that one cannot think of a decision which is not the decision of a subject, and that relations are meaningless without related terms. This does not mean that the terms can [always] exist outside of the relations. It will be remembered that our contention is that in the God-man relation, man cannot exist as man outside of his relation of confrontation with God. In response to God's creative act, he exists. But were our life nothing but decisions following one upon another, there would be no personal continuity. Our being would be like a pearl necklace without a thread.[2]

While the human self is actualized in its relationship to God and neighbor, it is not itself this relationship *simpliciter*. Indeed, had the Creator not endowed the individual with unique faculties and powers in the act of creation, the self could never actualize itself as a personal subject in relationship to other personal subjects. One must ask, then: What *is* a human being? Obviously, Christians are not the only ones who have asked this question; nor is the Christian answer — with which we shall be concerned — the only answer that has been given. However, the many answers to our question are all variations of two basic types: either (1) individual humans are viewed as highly evolved animals ("naked apes"); or (2) individual humans are viewed as unique; they differ from the animals not only in degree but in kind. There are many varieties of this latter view — some stressing the powers of reason, some the freedom of the will; all seek to understand the self-conscious self in terms of a dimension beyond the purely empirical.[3]

For Christians, the answer to the question of our humanity is found in a story that begins with its own "once upon a time." Once upon a time God said, "Let us make humankind" (Gn. 1:26 NRSV). So God took the dust of the ground and made a man, breathing into his nostrils the breath of life. Thus the man became a "living being" from whose side God made a woman and brought her to the man (2:7, 22). This man and this woman

---

2. Cairns, *Image,* pp. 190-91. In many respects Cairns follows Brunner's approach, as do we, but here his criticism is well taken.

3. "Consciousness is a capacity for surveying the world and determining action from a governing centre [will]. Self-consciousness represents a further degree of transcendence in which the self makes itself its own object in such a way that the ego is finally always subject and not object. . . . The self knows the world, insofar as it knows the world, because it stands outside both itself and the world, which means that it cannot understand itself except as it is understood from beyond itself and the world" (Niebuhr, *Nature and Destiny,* 1.13-14).

in their reciprocity and complementarity are the humankind to whom he gives dominion over all the earth, the male and female made in his image and likeness (1:26-27). Obviously, then, the Christian answer to what it means to be human is an instance of the second option mentioned above. Though sharing a bodily existence with the animals, we humans are unique; we differ from the animals in that we are like God.

In the above summary of the biblical account of human origins, we are assuming the essential oneness, theologically, of the two narratives with which the Bible begins. While these narratives paint different pictures, this visual difference does not alter their functional unity. The first narrative begins with chaos (1:2), the second with a barren desert (2:5); the first associates humankind with the animals, both being created on the sixth day (1:24-25); the second speaks of the man's being formed from the dust of the ground (2:7), the same ground that brought forth the animals; the first speaks of dominion over the creatures of the earth (1:26-27), the second of naming the animals (2:19). (See Thorleif Boman, *Hebrew Thought Compared with Greek,* trans. J. L. Moreau [reprint, New York: Norton, 1970], p. 181.) We shall presently speak more at length about the biological origins that we share with the animals. Our present concern is with our uniqueness as human, our dominion over and naming of the animals.

The biblical story of human beginnings, both in its later (1:1-23) and earlier (2:4-24) form, underscores some truths that have had, through the centuries, a commanding place in the faith of the church. These truths may be summarized as follows:

1. Although one among many creatures, humans are somehow different. When God made the human species, he began by taking counsel with himself — "let us make humankind."[4] As a diamond cutter contemplating a priceless gem pauses before the initial stroke, so the Creator paused, as one especially engaged in what he was about to do (1:26). Furthermore, he did not simply command the dust to bring forth but stooped to gather it in his hands that he might form the man (2:7). Then, taking a rib from his side, God made the woman as man's counterpart, the "helper fit for him" (2:18-22). By such studied deliberation and intimate involvement, the Creator commends to us the dignity of our nature as human.

2. Although one among many creatures, humans alone reflect a divine prototype. God, we are told, made the man and the woman in his image (צֶלֶם), after his likeness (דְּמוּת) (1:26). While all living creatures have their breath from God, in the case of the human creature God imparted his breath directly; human life, in distinction to life generally, is given by an imme-

---

4. On the plural usage in Gn. 1:26, "And the Elohim [אֱלֹהִים, i.e., the *gods*], said, 'Let *us* make (נַעֲשֶׂה),'" see *God, Creation, and Revelation,* p. 269.

diate impartation (sufflation) from the Creator's own mouth (2:7). Thus we are taught to think of ourselves not only as like other creatures but also as like the Creator. Although we are creatures, such direct endowment implies that we have uncommon worth in God's sight.[5]

3. Although one among many creatures, God made special provision for the man and woman. Not only did he give them food to eat (1:29-30), but he planted a garden in Eden where he put the man and the woman to till it and keep it (2:8, 15, 22). While they shared the garden with other creatures, they were given dominion over them (1:28). Thus we are taught that ours is a privileged place in the created order, a place that brings with it extraordinary responsibility. We are the stewards of creation, vested with authority as the vicegerents of the Creator. This dignity, worth, and responsibility with which the biblical story of creation invests the human creature comes to its sharpest focus, for theologians, in the concept of the image of God (the *imago Dei*). It is the gift of the image that grounds the I-thou relationship we have with God and with one another. For the Christian, then, the study of the doctrine of the image awakens thoughts of wonder at the majesty and mystery of our being and of God's purpose in so making us that we may enjoy a privileged fellowship with him.

As we have noted, however, the oldest form of the human story begins not with the divine image but with animated dust (Gn. 2:7). Thus we are reminded that though we may understand ourselves in terms of the God who made us rather than the dust of which he made us, we must not forget that we are the progeny of "the first man who is of the earth, earthy" (χοϊκός, "made of dust," 1 Cor. 15:47). We begin our theological elaboration of the biblical view of human nature, therefore, not with the concept of the *imago* but with a comment on the obvious fact that, with all other creatures in this time-space world, we humans have our existence in a bodily form.

On Persons and Personalities

Before we discuss the question of human nature on its material side, a brief word is in order concerning human nature in the secondary sense of "character." While theology is primarily concerned with the question of nature (personhood), it should not leave

---

5. "It is true that the life of all other beings is also ascribed to this divine breath of life, and that even the animals are classified with Man as *nepeš ḥayyā* [living creatures]. However, it was clearly the narrator's intention to mark Man out from the other creatures, since only in his case does he relate a direct transfer of the divine breath. . . . Man receives his life by a special act of God, and is thus treated as an independent spiritual I, and accorded a closer association with God than the animals" (Walther Eichrodt, *Theology of the Old Testament,* trans. J. A. Baker, 2 vols. [Philadelphia: Westminster, 1961-67], 2.121).

the study of character (personality) to psychology altogether. Of course the theologian can be no expert on "dominant" and "submissive," "extroverted" and "introverted" personality types. But she does have something to say about character. Character is our personal nature as it is shaped and matured through the experience of living our lives in response to God and neighbor. It is the self, not simply as given by the Creator but as formed by the creature. A newborn child is a self on the way to becoming a particular kind of self. Our character — the particular kind of self we become — may be viewed as unified decision, decision made up of all our particular decisions as they are taken up into the ongoing unity of the personal self. Classically, theologians have called this unified decision the *habitus* of the soul. It is the "primal" decision that lies beneath the particular decisions of each day. (For an unparalleled depiction in words of some fifty different types of human character — egocentric, hedonistic, heroic, dominant, submissive — see Browning's series of poems under the title *Men and Women*.)

Who we are (nature, personhood), therefore, and what we are like (character, personality) are inseparable. As a result, though our character is determined by God's decision to make us as persons in his image, it is also determined by our own decisions day by day as we live our lives in the world in which we find ourselves. When we speak of our character as "determined," we do not mean to say that it is *causally* determined, for character is the actualization of a nature that is essentially free. Although we are not free as God is free, we are free within the limits of our creaturehood. (See Niebuhr's comments on the invalidity of every effort to do psychology as a purely empirical science because of the freedom of transcendence with which we are endowed as persons, even in our sinful alienation from God [*Nature and Destiny,* 1.76-79].) The locus where "character" most concerns the theologian is not anthropology but soteriology. We are thinking, specifically, of the doctrine of sanctification, which has to do with the holy life, i.e., the life of those who are born of the Spirit and progressively conformed to the image of Christ as they seek, day by day, to die to sin and live to righteousness. We shall reserve further comment on "character," therefore, until we have occasion to ruminate on the nature of the Christian life when dealing with the doctrine of salvation.

B. HUMAN NATURE ON ITS MATERIAL SIDE: OUR EXISTENCE IN THE BODY[6]

Since God is without bodily parts, theologians have never said that our bodily existence *is* the image of God, but rather that we who are creatures

---

6. "Body" (σῶμα) describes our nature on its material side; it is the physical organism viewed as the sum total of its related members. "Flesh" (σάρξ) describes the matter or material of which the σῶμα (body) is made. As such, it carries overtones of the finitude and transitory nature of human existence. In many passages in the New Testament, "body" and "flesh" are used more or less interchangeably. In a theological anthropology, therefore, they

in his image have a bodily existence. Yet they have generally concurred in the thought that our bodily existence affords intimations of that image.

The decision to discuss the material aspect of our being before discussing the immaterial is not to suggest the body/soul antithesis of Greek dualism, much less an anthropology done from below. Humans are not simply cerebrating animals. Nonetheless, we do have something in common with the animals in that we are taken from the same dust, as the second creation narrative reminds us. Indeed, though the first narrative emphasizes the image of God, it also teaches us that we are given this image in the differentiation of male and femaleness, which surely has something to do with the bodily form of existence we share with the animals.

With regard to our bodily existence as an existence shared with the animals, it helps us not to think of ourselves more highly than we ought to think when we remember that animals, in some ways, are better endowed physically than we. The keen eye of the eagle, the reflexes of the mountain goat, the respiratory powers of the cheetah, the olfactory feats of the bloodhound — all are a constant reminder not only of our finitude in general, but of our limitations in particular. (To equal the metabolic achievement of the migrating blackpolls we would have to run a four-minute mile for eighty hours nonstop!) Yet we really have no grounds for begrudging the Creator's bounty toward the marvelous creatures that share the planet with us. For the body with which we are endowed, culminating in the brain, is no ordinary chunk of clay. Made up of seven octillion atoms organized into ten trillion cells, it is, beyond all doubt, the most highly organized piece of matter in the universe. Given such an endowment, along with our relative freedom from instinct and specialization, we can with instruments sharpen our ears to hear the universe being born and our eyes to track the furtive path of atomic particles.

While the writers of Scripture were unaware of these achievements of modern science, they knew that we humans are "fearfully and wonderfully made" (Ps. 139:14 NRSV). Paul's familiar parable (1 Cor. 12:14-16) of the one body with many members — the eye, the ear, the hand, the foot — all arranged by God to serve the needs of the whole person, reflects a similar reverence for the Creator's work and wisdom. What present-day science has brought to light only enhances this sense of awe on the part of the believer.

To speak of the reverence reflected in Scripture for the body is not to endorse the Greek — and modern — cult of the body. Though living in the midst of Greek culture, the authors of the New Testament were well aware that Praxiteles' models, bowed down with age, had long since died, and that "dust had closed Helen's eyes." Women were admonished, therefore, to adorn themselves with good deeds, not with braided hair and costly attire (1 Tm. 2:9-10). And Timothy (1 Tm. 4:8) was reminded that bodily exercise profits only a little. (Back in 1961 Americans spent $121,680,000 on lipstick alone, and another $127,600,000 on facial creams [*The Body,* Life Science Library (New York:

---

do not warrant separate treatment. The use of the term "flesh" in the New Testament to describe human nature in its sinful opposition to the Spirit of God ("the desires of the *flesh* are against the Spirit," Gal. 5:17) is a matter of soteriology, not anthropology. The same is true of passages like 1 Pt. 2:11, which admonishes: "abstain from the passions of the flesh that wage war against your soul."

Time, 1964), p. 35]. By 1991 these figures combined for a total of four billion [*Los Angeles Times,* Feb. 8, 1991, p. E1].) Nonetheless, Paul readily drew analogies from Greek athletic games to illustrate spiritual truths, admonishing his converts to run the race of the Christian life so as to win the prize (1 Cor. 9:24-25) and likening his own life as a Christian to that of a Greek runner (Phil. 3:13-14).

As for intimations of transcendence in the bodily form of our existence, it has been frequently observed that humans do not creep and crawl on the ground but walk upright with head held high. The face and eyes, particularly, have been cited as revealing a spirit that transcends the noblest creatures in the animal kingdom. When Cain was angry with his brother, his countenance fell (Gn. 4:5); again, Jacob's relation to Laban changed radically when he perceived that Laban's countenance had changed toward him (Gn. 31:2). Jesus said nothing when Peter denied him; he simply looked at him. But when Peter's eyes met the Master's, he was reduced to tears (Lk. 22:61-62). Such encounters at the bodily level are true I-thou encounters, for the I always meets the thou in the mutuality of a concrete, bodily existence.[7]

Poets have sung of the "sweet, silent rhetoric of loving eyes," and Milton tells us that the visage of those who drink the pleasing poison of the Sorcerer is transformed so that

> the inglorious likeness of a beast
> Fixes instead, unmoulding reason's mintage
> Character'd in the face.

Comus, 528-29

Among painters, Rembrandt, especially, saw the face as the mirror of the soul. "He painted his own image not because he was enamored of its ill-proportioned and coarsening features but because it was a face in which he could ponder the question of man's nature" (John Canaday, *Metropolitan Seminars in Art* [New York: Metropolitan Museum of Art, 1959], Portfolio F, p. 24).

The body, then, is not a mere, physical instrument at the discretionary disposal of the essential self; it is rather the visible form of the self in its specific individual existence.[8] In fact, since the body localizes one in space,

---

7. Anyone who has ever made eye contact with apes and monkeys in the zoo will sense the difference: such encounters are obviously not I-thou encounters.

8. This holistic view of our humanity is reflected in the way the Old Testament genealogies begin. As God, in the beginning, created humankind in his image and likeness, Adam is said to have become the father of a son in his image and likeness (Gn. 5:3). It would be difficult to suppose this text is in no way concerned with the body. See also Gn. 9:6, where shedding the blood of another, an affront to the body, is said to be an affront to God. Likewise in our everyday speech, the body becomes the synonym for the self. "She embraced me," one says, not "she embraced my body."

it is the most obvious symbol, at the objective level, that God has given us our humanity as distinct individuals.[9] Although theologians have had little to say about the body when framing their doctrine of anthropology, what they have said has important implications for several other areas of Christian doctrine yet to be discussed.[10] Because we are concerned in this study with theology in its systematic form, we shall conclude our remarks on the material aspect of our humanity with brief comments on the implications of our bodily existence for other doctrines, specifically the doctrines of sin, incarnation, salvation, and hope.

As for *sin,* since the body is integral to our humanity as originally given us by the Creator, our sinfulness cannot be explained as due to our bodily existence. We do, indeed, manifest our sinful nature in bodily acts, but our sin is not because of the contamination of the soul by a material body that is evil. The body is not evil; it is rather the good gift of the Creator and should be celebrated as such.

As for the *Incarnation,* a central doctrine of the Christian faith, since our humanity is given us as a bodily existence, the Son of God, in identifying with us, assumed our bodily existence. He was "born of a woman" (Gal. 4:4 NRSV) with a true, real, and substantial body, as are we. "The Word became flesh" (Jn. 1:14). John's remark that only the spirit which "confesses that Jesus Christ has come in the flesh is of God" (1 Jn. 4:2) is probably a repudiation of early, inchoate Docetism that the church eventually rejected as heresy.

> All depends upon the fact that the Word did become flesh, and this means that the Eternal has entered into the sphere of external historical fact. To be "made flesh" means among other things an actual state of presence, sensible, external, non-spiritualized. Incarnation means entering into the realm of visible fact, being the object of police reports, a subject of the photographers, for the commonplace journalist, and other things of that kind. It is a state in which any individual can be touched, handled, or photographed; it is an isolated fact within time and space, the filling of a certain point within time and space which apart from this fact would have remained empty,

9. This truth is dramatically illustrated in the individuality of the fingerprint. Of the hundreds of millions on file, no two are sufficiently alike to give the expert pause.

10. Polanus was an exception, devoting three chapters of his exposition of Christian theology (1609) to the human body. But he indulges in "astonishing allegories" (Barth). We have two ears and one mouth because we should listen more and talk less, etc. (*KD,* III/2, p. 457 [cf. *CD,* III/2, p. 381]).

and which can be filled in by this fact alone: all that belongs to the activity of the Incarnation of the Word.[11]

As for *salvation,* since our bodies are the gift of the Creator, salvation can never be a matter of an ascetic denial of the body. The theology we have espoused has no place for the ideals of Romuald of Camaldoli and the Camaldolensian monks who mercilessly beat their bodies to overcome the temptations of the devil. Not ascetic denial but the temperate expression of bodily appetite is the way of that "holiness without which no one will see the Lord" (Heb. 12:14). While we cannot but admire the zeal of the ascetic in this day when so many indulge every fleshly appetite, we must not forget that our calling as Christians is to overcome the *sins* of the flesh, not to overcome the flesh as such. Rather than depreciating the body, we should recall the apostle's word that our bodies are the temple of the Holy Spirit (1 Cor. 6:19); we should heed his admonition to present our bodies as a living sacrifice to God, which is our spiritual worship (Rom. 12:1); and, God helping us, we should emulate his resolve that Christ shall be honored in our bodies, whether by life or by death (Phil. 1:20). We should remember, too, that if our gospel teaches it is an act of worship to present our bodies a living sacrifice to God, then we can never close our eyes to the so-called social implications of that gospel. We only discredit our witness to the gospel if we say to "a brother or sister who is ill-clad and in lack of daily food . . . 'Go in peace, be warmed and filled,' without giving them the things needed for the body" (Jas. 2:16). In other words, the gospel is concerned with the salvation of the whole person.

As for the Christian *hope,* it is nothing less than the resurrection of the body, the overcoming of the sting of death and the victory of the grave (1 Cor. 15:55). Christians do not scoff at the idea of a resurrection, as did the Athenians (Acts 17:32). Believing, rather, that God as Creator has given us our being in a bodily existence, they also believe that as the Redeemer he will consummate our salvation with the resurrection of the body, even as he raised Christ Jesus from the dead (Rom. 8:11).

In due course we shall have more to say about all these matters. Here we only pause to speak of the implications of one doctrine for our understanding of several others — a little exercise in *systematic* theology.

---

11. Emil Brunner, *The Mediator,* trans. Olive Wyon (London: Lutterworth, 1934), pp. 153-54.

C. HUMAN NATURE ON ITS IMMATERIAL SIDE: OUR TRANSCENDENCE OF THE BODY

1. INTRODUCTION

When the Christian speaks of human nature as body and soul, she is not speaking, as did Socrates, of a soul that is "enshrined in the living tomb which we carry about, now that we are imprisoned in the body, like an oyster in his shell."[12] The church as a whole (despite the deliverances of certain of its members) has never taught that body and soul are related in terms of struggle and conflict.[13] The biblical witness to the essential unity and wholeness of the personal self is antithetical to a dualism that posits an evil body and a good soul. This is not to deny, however, that there is a distinction between the outer and the inner, the visible and the invisible, the physical and the spiritual, aspects of our humanity.[14] Beginning with "dust" and "breath" as distinguished in the creation narrative of Genesis, a two-sided view of human nature pervades the whole Bible. In death "the dust returns to the earth as it was, and the spirit returns to God who gave it" (Eccl. 12:7). For this reason one easily understands the telling remark of Jesus to his disciples, "The spirit indeed is willing, but the flesh is weak" (Mt. 26:41).

The twofold view of human nature reflected in biblical usage also dominates that of Christian piety. To the question, "What is your only comfort in life and in death?" the Heidelberg Catechism teaches us to answer: "That I — *body and soul,* in life and in death — belong not to myself but to my faithful Savior, Jesus Christ." And through the years thousands have stood by a graveside and joined in some such prayer as, "Receive then our souls unto yourself, and suffer our bodies, when they have rested in their graves, to rise . . . to everlasting life." It is in such moments as these, when we renew our hope in the presence of death, that we best articulate the Christian understanding of our humanity.

In contemporary theological anthropology, "dualism" is not a popular word. Zealous to exorcise Greek philosophy from Christian theology, and influenced by the monism

---

12. Dialogues of Plato, *Phaedrus,* Great Books, p. 126, §250.

13. Anchises tells Anaeus of the "fiery vigor" and "heavenly sense" of souls: "Save as impaired by flesh corruptible, / Dulled with frames earthly, and limbs prone to death" (Virgil, *Aeneid,* 6.732-33).

14. We use the term "aspects" here much as Barth uses *Momente* when he affirms that soul and body are two *Momente* of the one human nature constituted as a soul that enlivens and a body that is enlivened (*KD,* III/2, p. 471 [cf. *CD,* III/2, pp. 394-95]).

of modern thought, present-day theologians have emphasized the unity of the personal self over the duality of body and soul. Such an emphasis is not altogether unwarranted, since theologians have traditionally inclined to the opposite extreme of treating body and soul as independent, distinct "substances." For example, Thomas Aquinas begins his "Treatise on Humankind" (*Summa Theologica,* pt. 1, q. 75) by referring to humans as "composed of a spiritual and a corporeal *substance.*" This two-substance view is found in Protestant thought as well. "We also affirm that humankind consists of two different substances in one person: an immortal soul . . . and a mortal body" (Second Helvetic Confession, chap. VII). Such an approach has led theologians into fruitless speculation about the "nature" of the soul in contrast to the body — whether it is composed of matter and form; whether, unlike animal souls, it is subsistent; whether it is incorruptible, like angels, etc.

While the two-substance doctrine is inadequate, nonetheless, those who would frame a Christian and biblical anthropology must speak of the human subject not only in terms of a unity of the personal self but also in terms of a distinction between soul and body. Although the personal self is not apart from the body (Idealism), yet it cannot be equated with the body (Materialism). Hence our Lord's admonition that we should not fear those who may kill the body but cannot kill the soul (Mt. 10:28). To be a person is to be a soul in and with a body. In this regard it is noteworthy that the Vatican's well-known *Pastoral Constitution on the Church in the Modern World (Gaudium et Spes),* for all the new ground that it breaks, still speaks in a traditional way of humankind as "made of body and soul" (*The Documents of Vatican II,* ed. W. M. Abbott and J. Gallagher [Piscataway, N.J.: New Century, 1966], p. 212). Likewise, contemporary Protestant thinkers continue to speak of the "diversity-in-unity" that marks our humanity, of its "center and periphery," its "inevitable twoness" (e.g., Berkouwer, who, though he opposes "dualism," yet acknowledges "diversity.") In the ensuing discussion, therefore, though we assume the personal unity of each individual as an embodied self, we also seek to do justice to the diversity-in-unity reflected in the way Scripture speaks of this self both in its material and in its immaterial aspects.

2. SOUL AND SPIRIT

The body, we have argued, is not simply an instrument, something incidental and indifferent to our essential humanity. It is rather the God-given medium in which we live our lives as personal selves in the objective world of time and space. We are, then, part of the world of things; specifically, we are mammals with large brains, subject to the same laws of physics and chemistry that govern all of God's creatures in this world. If we slip when climbing, gravity will pull us down the mountain like a stone; if we inhale the gaseous oxides of nitrogen, our lungs will become fatally inflamed.

Yet, we have also argued, we humans are not simply cerebrating animals. Rather, we are so created that while we are in the world as objects, we transcend the world as subjects.[15] But how can this be? How is our nature constituted that we should be aware of ourselves as personal subjects? To answer this question we must speak of "soul" and "spirit." What is "soul"? What is "spirit"? And how are they related to each other and the body? Before we consider these difficult questions in depth, we pause to summarize the relevant biblical data.

The language of "body," "soul," and "spirit," familiar in theology, rests, of course, on biblical usage. Because that usage is rather complex, we offer the following overview, in which we have been helped by Walther Eichrodt, "The Place of Man in the Creation," §16 in *Theology of the Old Testament*, trans. J. A. Baker (Philadelphia: Westminster, 1967), 2.118-50; and by various articles on ψυχή and πνεῦμα, especially in *TDNT*. Franz Delitzsch's *System of Biblical Psychology* (trans. Robert E. Wallis, 2nd ed. [Edinburgh: T. & T. Clark, 1875]) should also be mentioned.

In the Old Testament, נֶפֶשׁ, often translated "soul," describes the breath proceeding out of the throat that distinguishes the living from the dead. Hence it comes to mean just "life" in the physical sense, whether it be animal or human life. Such life is always bound up with a body; and when it departs, the body becomes a corpse. Thus נֶפֶשׁ comes to mean the living individual creature or just the creature that is described as living. When God breathed into man's nostrils the breath of life, he became a "living being" (נֶפֶשׁ חַיָּה, Gn. 2:7). As the vitality of the individual self, the נֶפֶשׁ is the seat of psychical impulses and emotions. Because these emotions are often of a spiritual sort, the meaning of נֶפֶשׁ in some passages comes close to that of "spirit" (רוּחַ). For example, Hannah tells Eli (1 Sam. 1:15) that she has poured out her soul (נֶפֶשׁ) to the LORD because she is a woman of a troubled spirit (רוּחַ). The obvious parallelism makes it impossible to find, in such a passage, any significant theological distinction between נֶפֶשׁ and רוּחַ, the Hebrew words for "soul" and "spirit," respectively.

In the New Testament, the broad equivalent of נֶפֶשׁ is ψυχή, also generally translated "soul." All that has been said of נֶפֶשׁ may be said of ψυχή, though the use of the latter term in the New Testament is generally limited to humans in distinction to animals. (Rv. 8:9, however, refers to the death of sea creatures having "life," literally, having "souls," ψυχάς; and in the judgment scene of Rv. 16:3 it would seem that ψυχή is used in a way that includes even plant life.) Paul reassures all concerned that Eutychus's life (ψυχή) is in him (Acts 27:22) and encourages his fellow travelers in the storm at sea with the assurance that there shall be no loss of life (ψυχή) among them (Acts 20:10). When so used, ψυχή connotes life not only in the biological but also in the spiritual sense, as when Jesus asks what it would profit one to gain the whole world and lose one's life (i.e., one's soul, ψυχή, Mk. 8:36). Given this spiritual meaning, we can understand how ψυχή can be used to describe those who survive the death of

---

15. This fact is obvious in everyday life. A physician, for example, can know a great deal about a comatose patient as object — age, race, sex, blood pressure, pulse; yet because the patient transcends the cause-effect world as subject, the physician can know her as a person only as she opens her eyes and discloses herself to him, tells him her *name* in an I-thou encounter. See *God, Creation, and Revelation*, pp. 177, 207-18.

the body. When, for example, the fifth seal of the Apocalypse is opened, under the altar the seer sees the souls (ψυχάς) of the martyrs who cry out for justice (Rv. 6:9-10). Although ψυχή, like נֶפֶשׁ in the Old Testament, tends to be used of embodied life, it can be used, as in this vision of the seer, of those in an interim state who await the resurrection of the body and the final judgment.

As for the word "spirit," also frequently used in the Bible to describe human nature on its spiritual (immaterial) side, the biblical data is even more complex than it is in the case of "soul." In the Old Testament, "spirit" usually translates רוּחַ, a word that also refers to the wind that blows over the surface of the earth, or to the breath that proceeds from one's mouth or nostrils. It is a word used both of the "Spirit" of the LORD, that is, the energizing breath of God that gives life to all, and also of the "spirit" of the human creature who receives life from God.

Of course, God and the creature are sharply distinguished in the thought of Israel. Yet the use of the same word to describe the "Spirit" of God and the "spirit" of the creature who is in his image reflects Israel's awareness that the organ of psychic life in humankind is, in a special way, related to and derived from the divine, transcendent source of all life. It is true that as the organ of psychic phenomena the רוּחַ (spirit), like the נֶפֶשׁ (soul), may be viewed as the seat of the all too human emotions and passions to which the creature is prone as a sinner alienated from God. Ahab's petulant display when Naboth refuses to sell his vineyard is said to be a manifestation of his willful and rebellious spirit (רוּחַ). Basically, however, the human "spirit" designates that aspect of our nature most immediately related to God. (Animals are virtually never said to have רוּחַ, i.e., "spirit.") Accordingly, the meaning of "spirit" (רוּחַ) has a somewhat different nuance than that of "soul" (נֶפֶשׁ) when used to describe humankind in relation to God. To one who has a sense for this difference, the usage of the penitent in his prayer for forgiveness is natural:

> Create in me a clean heart, O God,
>   and put a new and right spirit (רוּחַ) within me.
> Cast me not away from thy presence,
>   and take not thy holy Spirit (רוּחַ) from me.
>
> Psalm 51:10-11

The psalmist assumes that his own spirit can be a right spirit only when the divine Spirit is present in his life. In the messianic age of salvation, this Spirit of Yahweh will indwell his people; and they themselves will have a new "spirit," resulting in an altered inward disposition that will incline them to love and obey God. Thus by the work of the Redeemer the original work of the Creator will be restored and the purpose of creation fulfilled.

In the New Testament, the equivalent of רוּחַ is πνεῦμα, which also means "wind" (Jn. 3:8). Ordinarily translated "spirit," πνεῦμα, like רוּחַ in the Old Testament, is used of both God and humankind. When used of the human creature, "spirit" refers to that vital principle which animates the body and enables one to feel, think, will, and desire. As such, it is the seat of psychic experience and has essentially the same meaning as "soul" (ψυχή). Being the seat of psychic experience, the human spirit is especially engaged as one relates to God. "God is spirit (πνεῦμα), and they who worship him must worship him in spirit (πνεῦμα) and truth" (Jn. 4:24). As the righteous who have departed this life may be described as "souls" (ψυχάς) under the altar (Rv. 6:9-10), so they may also be described as the "spirits" (πνεύματα) of the just made perfect in the presence of God (Heb. 12:23). Again, as in the age of messianic promise God will give his people a new "spirit" (Ezk. 11:19), so in the fulfillment of that promise, the "Spirit" of Christ bears witness with our "spirits" that we are the children of God (Rom. 8:16). Thus we are renewed in the likeness of him who created us for fellowship with himself, a fellowship expressed in the prayer that we utter in the Spirit/spirit: "Abba! Father!" (Rom. 8:15-16).

While "soul" and "spirit" are the traditional terms used in theology to designate the inner life of the personal self, the body, one must remember, is more than the incidental instrument of that self; indeed, it is the self in its objective manifestation in the time-space world. This truth is underscored by the way the biblical authors describe the psychic experiences that manifest the life of the soul and spirit in terms of the physical organs of the body. The kidneys or "reins" (KJV) (כְּלָיוֹת, Ps. 7:9 [MT 10]; νεφρούς, Rv. 2:23), deep within the body, are the seat of distress and the source of understanding. The bowels (מֵעִים, Lam. 1:20; σπλάγχνα, Col. 3:12) may be convulsed with seething emotions in affliction and moved with tender compassion in the presence of suffering. Even the flesh cries out for the living God and the bones are troubled in the hour of distress.

But of all the physical organs associated with the inner life of the human subject, none has the preeminence in Scripture that is given to the "heart" (לֵב, לֵבָב; καρδία). As the organ that circulates the blood, which is the life, and quickens the pulse in a time of inner stress and crisis, the heart has a central place in biblical anthropology. Every psychic experience of the individual self — feeling, thought, memory, will — and every spiritual experience as well — aspiration after God and fellowship with him — are associated with the heart. On the heart of all who are human the law is written by the Creator (Rom. 2:15); and to love God with all the heart (Mk. 12:30) is to keep the law and so fulfill the counsel of perfection. Hence the "heart," though literally an organ of the outer (material) self, has all the meaning of "soul" and "spirit" as descriptive of the inner (immaterial) self.

Such usage is a striking testimony to the Bible's holistic understanding of human nature. At the same time, such usage also shows us how interlocking and complex are the terms whereby Scripture tells us what it means to be human and to live humanly in this world where the Creator has placed us. As we have noted, theologians, in reflecting on these terms, have given special attention to the concepts of "soul" and "spirit" as they relate to the body and to one another. We must now consider the conclusions to which they have come as they have pondered these difficult matters.

Taking up the question of how our nature is constituted that we should be aware of ourselves as subjects, the church has answered: God has created us embodied souls endowed with his image. The church has never reversed this usage by saying that we are "besouled bodies."[16] The reason is ob-

---

16. "Soul" and "spirit" are often interchangeable terms in Scripture, and the former has tended to be the operative word in theological discourse, covering for both. However, this

vious. While we are given our humanity in the body, our body is not the center and focal point of that humanity.[17] This is evident in the way the writers of the New Testament speak. For example, Paul calls the body his "outer nature" that is wasting away in contrast to his "inner nature" that is daily renewed (2 Cor. 4:16); it is an earthly "tent" (σκηνή) in which we sigh with anxiety (2 Cor. 5:4).[18] Peter uses the same figure: "I think it right, as long as I am in this body [lit. 'tent,' — 'tabernacle' (KJV), 'tent of this body' (NIV)] — to arouse you by way of reminder, since I know that the putting off of my body [lit. 'tent'] will be soon" (2 Pt. 1:13-14). When Paul was "caught up to the third heaven" and heard what no mortal may utter, it did not concern him whether he was "in or out of the body" (2 Cor. 12:1-4). Peter calls Christ the Shepherd and Guardian of our *souls* (ψυχαί), not our bodies (1 Pt. 2:25); though obviously the well-being of our bodies is also the concern of our Savior. The writer of Hebrews admonishes his/her readers to submit to the leaders in the church, who shall give account for the watch they have kept over the souls of their people (Heb. 13:17). This is not to say that their leaders were concerned only with their souls; but it is a way of speaking that implies that the essential self is not a body but an embodied *soul*. The soul, then, is the seat of those endowments given by the Creator that make one human. As Calvin observes, referring to our creation in the divine image, "For though the glory of God is displayed in our external form, yet there is no doubt that the proper seat of the image is the soul."[19]

The traditional Christian emphasis on the soul over the body is one that needs to be made in this day of the cult of the body. Not that the Christian faith contemns the body,

---

traditional usage does reflect the unfortunate way in which the language of philosophical anthropology has dominated the discourse of theological anthropology. As our previous review of the scriptural data has shown, we need to speak not only of the "soul" but also and especially of the "spirit" if we would speak biblically of human nature on its immaterial side.

17. The penultimate place of the body in the Christian understanding of our humanity is indicated by the empirical fact that the individual is aware throughout life of continuity as a personal self even though the body undergoes several complete changes at the atomic level in the course of that life.

18. Such texts as these would seem to be what Calvin had in mind when he speaks of the "soul's liberation from the prison of the body" (*Inst.*, 1.15.2), for he surely was not thinking Platonically.

19. *Inst.*, 1.15.3. In a similar vein is Luther's moving prayer at Worms, ending with the words: "And though the world may be filled with devils; though my body, which is still the work of your hands, should be slain, be stretched upon the pavement, be cut in pieces, be reduced to ashes — my *soul* is yours! Yes, I have the assurance of your word. My soul belongs to you! It shall abide forever with you. Amen. O God! Help me! Amen" (Clyde L. Manschreck, *A History of Christianity* [Englewood Cliffs, N.J.: Prentice-Hall, 1964], p. 53).

but our dignity and worth as human does not center in the body. It is better, Jesus said, to go through life maimed than so to use the body as to endanger the soul (Mk. 9:43-48).

One should also note that since the soul, not the body, is the essential self, the Christian faith is denied whenever the physically handicapped are treated as persons of lesser worth and dignity. True, in the Levitical law the mutilated, injured, and deformed are denied the priestly privilege (Lev. 21:16-21). But such ceremonialisms are concerned with the perfection of God and his law (Dt. 32:4; Ps. 19:7), not the worth of the creature; hence even a physically handicapped person "may eat the bread of his God, both of the most holy and of the holy things" (Lev. 21:22). Indeed, when Christ comes, to whom belongs the substance of these shadows (Col. 2:17), all such ceremonialisms are done away. Hence Jesus admonishes his disciples not to invite to their feasts their friends and wealthy neighbors but the poor, the maimed, the lame, and the blind (Lk. 14:12-14). And when such were brought to him, he received them gladly and healed them (Mt. 15:30; Heb. 12:12-13). The gospel is good news for the handicapped in the body as well as in the soul. (See the comments on "physical integrity" in Albert Vanhoye, "Perfection" [trans. John J. Kilgallen], in Xavier Léon-Dufour, ed., *Dictionary of Biblical Theology,* 2nd ed. [New York: Seabury, 1973], p. 422.)

Philosophers have generally admitted that the knowledge of the soul rests on inferences drawn from the facts of experience rather than on demonstration.[20] Plato thought of the soul as an individualized instance of the rational essence of the universe. As such, it was antithetical to the body, which is a part of the material world of flux and change. Aristotle begins his treatise on the soul *(De Anima)* by acknowledging that to obtain knowledge of the soul is among the most difficult things in the world, though he did not doubt its existence. In fact, he believed it was the animating principle of all living things. Plants have a vegetative soul, animals a sensitive soul, and humans a rational soul, which is the specific agent of thought. Unlike Plato, Aristotle postulated an integral relationship between body and soul. The soul not only animates but also gives form to the body, as the die gives shape to the wax. The soul is the "essential whatness" of the body without which it would cease to be the body that it is. In this view of the soul and its relation to the body, Aristotle was followed by Thomas.[21]

Theologians, influenced by the philosophers, have traditionally spoken of the soul as a "substance," not, to be sure, a material substance like the body, but rather a substance of a spiritual sort existing along with and in the body. This "two substance" doctrine is not (Barth to the contrary

20. Kant, for example, postulates "soul" by appealing to the practical reason, giving up all attempts at theoretical proof.

21. *Summa Theologica,* pt. 1, q. 76, "Of the Union of Body and Soul," art. 1, "Whether the Intellectual Principle Is United to the Body as Its Form."

notwithstanding) altogether wrong, for the soul is not simply a concept of thought; it has objective reality, though not the reality of a material object.[22] But it is a doctrine that is less than adequate, in our judgment. For one thing, it tends to invite questions that the Scriptures do not ask — and the theologs cannot answer — such as, Where is the soul located and how is it related to the body?[23] It is better, therefore, to think of the soul in personal categories. While there is an ineluctable relationship between soul and body, the soul is not some spiritual substance "in" the body as a fetus is "in" the womb. Nor is it a spiritual substance diffused through the body as blood "through" the veins. Rather, the soul is just the personal self, the "I," animating the body and manifest in a bodily way. I am my soul, not my body; yet this soul that is "I" is the soul of my particular body and of no others.

As for the body-soul relationship, we find Thomas's treatment of the subject (*Summa Theologica,* pt. 1, q. 76) much more plausible than nineteenth-century theories of preestablished harmony, psychophysical parallelism, and the like. Furthermore, to view the soul, with Thomas, as the *form* of the body is surely nearer Christian thought than to view the soul as the *function* of the body (Materialism). But, as a theoretical question, it is best to leave the relationship of body and soul to philosophy; as a question of applied theory, to psychosomatic medicine. (The difficulty with Thomas's argument, as we see it, is that the Scriptures have little interest in his subject; hence they throw virtually no light on it.) Theologians can do no better than to settle for the commonsense view found by a tacit consent throughout Scripture. This commonsense view simply assumes that there is a constant interplay, a mutual influence, between body and soul. When the design of the wallpaper and the print on the page begin to assume a democratic likeness, the soul of the theology student preparing for an exam is being overcome with the fatigue of the body. When "comes the wanton blood up in the cheeks" of Juliet upon hearing of Romeo's nuptial plans, the body of Juliet is being overcome by the wounds Cupid's arrow has inflicted on her soul. But such experiences defy all theoretical explanation. We know not how the mind of Augustine moved his hand to write the *Confessions,* nor how the eye conveys to our mind the meaning of what he wrote. We only know that for all their disparity, our body and soul are meant for each other in the mysterious purpose of the Creator. As a result, each person experiences herself as a unitary self, an "I," in and through the changing life of the body.

As for "spirit," the other basic word used in Scripture to describe our nature on its immaterial side, the difficulty is to say how it does and yet does not differ in meaning from "soul." "Spirit" is obviously not different from "soul" as is "soul" from "body." The spirit is not manifest in the

---

22. On the meaning of οὐσία/*substantia* as used in the doctrine of God, see *God, Creation, and Revelation,* pp. 278-80, especially Sayers's comment.

23. For a humorous comment on Descartes's location of the soul in the pineal gland, see Laurence Sterne, *Tristram Shandy,* Great Books, pp. 270-71.

soul as is the soul in the body; rather, soul and spirit are both manifest in the body. Hence Scripture generally uses the terms interchangeably over against the body.[24] Yet this interchangeable use of "soul" and "spirit" in scriptural and theological usage cannot be made without qualification. As living creatures, we, like the animals, are said to have "soul" (נֶפֶשׁ/ψυχή). But, as we have noted, the Scriptures do not say that animals have "spirit" (רוּחַ/πνεῦμα).[25] This would seem to be because the term "spirit" not only describes our inner nature as persons but emphasizes the source of that nature in God, who is himself Spirit. Each of us, indeed, like the animals, is a living creature (נֶפֶשׁ חַיָּה), a sort of animated dust; but the direct impartation to the dust of the divine breath (נְשָׁמָה, Gn. 2:7) makes each one of us unique among living creatures. We are spirits because he who is the Creator Spirit has given us "spirit."

To describe our inner self as "spirit" is not to deny that we share the gift of life with the animal world. Our life, like theirs, is physical and psychical; it is the life of an embodied soul (ψυχή). But in our case this life of the soul is not simply an instance of animal life, for it is directly from God, who is Spirit. He "who created the heavens . . . , who spread forth the earth and what comes from it," is he "who gives breath to the people upon it and spirit to those who walk in it" (Is. 42:5). To speak, therefore, of the human self as "spirit" (רוּחַ/πνεῦμα) is to focus on the unique relationship we have with God, who is "the Father of spirits" (Heb. 12:9), and to confess that human life is not only physical and psychical but also spiritual in nature. We are created as spirits that we might enjoy God who is "Spirit" and worship him in "spirit" and in truth (Jn. 4:23-24). Of all God's creatures, only we are so endowed that our life finds its true meaning in fellowship with him.[26] The unique endowment of the human

---

24. This is why we have given a twofold rather than a threefold structure to our own discussion, speaking (a) of the material and (b) of the immaterial aspect of our nature as human. We will comment on the threefold, trichotomistic view presently.

25. The striking exception is Eccl. 3:21. In this passage the "Preacher" (Qohelet), commenting on the vanity of life and the certainty of death, asks: "Who knows whether the human spirit goes upward and the spirit of animals goes downward to the earth?" (NRSV). Such a rhetorical question reflects the pessimism of the author (see vv. 19-20) and does not characterize Scripture as a whole. The New Testament, by comparison, never attributes πνεῦμα (spirit) to the animals.

26. The particular nuance of meaning that the term "spirit" has as denoting the ground of our unique relationship to the Creator may bear on Paul's obvious preference for "spirit" over "soul" when speaking of the inner self. The message he proclaimed concerned primarily the creature's fellowship with the Creator through the saving work of Christ's *Spirit*. It is the *Spirit* who bears witness with our *spirit* that we are the children of God (Rom. 8:16). In any event, since Paul is the primary interpreter of the work of God the Redeemer, his preference explains why theological usage tends to shift from "soul" in anthropology to "spirit" in soteriology.

spirit that grounds our fellowship with God is, according to the theologians, the divine image. We must now give our attention to this doctrine of the image, which is central to the Christian understanding of humanity.

ADDENDUM: CONCERNING TRICHOTOMY

Having taken the position that our humanity has a material and an immaterial aspect, we pause to comment on a view that challenges such a dichotomistic approach by insisting that human nature is tripartite — body, soul, and spirit. In the ancient church, the effort to "explain" the relation between the divine and the human in the person of Christ led Apollinaris and others to assume a trichotomistic anthropology. When the eternal Son assumed our humanity, Apollinaris reasoned, he took upon him a human body and soul, but not a human spirit. Being himself the God who is Spirit, he had no need of a human spirit. When the church rejected this view of the Incarnation as heresy, insisting that the Son was fully human (vere homo), the tripartite anthropology that it presupposed also came under a cloud. From time to time, however, it has resurfaced in one form or another. Of course, the argument is no longer Christologically oriented, and even in anthropology it is often muted. The human "spirit" is said to be associated with our humanity in its higher aspirations, in contrast to the soul, which is the seat of animal appetites and passions. (American dispensationalists and various other fundamentalist groups often espouse some such trichotomistic anthropology.)

The most thoroughgoing exposition and defense of trichotomy with which we are familiar is J. B. Heard's *The Tripartite Nature of Man: Spirit, Soul, and Body.*[27] It is an erudite study reflecting a devout reverence for Scripture and full of theological curiosities. In the concluding summary of his argument, Heard affirms "that man is a τριμέρης ὑπόστασις, a union, not of two, but of three essential parts. These are, body or sense-consciousness; soul or self-consciousness; and spirit or God-consciousness."[28] This last category, "spirit," is the subject of an entire chapter (IX) in which the author argues that in contrast to the soul, the spirit is the unique chamber of God-consciousness. It is the spirit, as distinct from the soul, that distinguishes human beings from brutes. But if this is the case, one wonders about Jesus' statement of the first and greatest commandment. According to our Lord, we

27. Edinburgh: T. & T. Clark, 1882. By this date the work had gone through five editions.
28. Ibid., p. 338.

are to love God with all our heart and with all our soul, and with all our mind, and with all our strength (Mk. 12:30). How is it that Jesus makes no mention of the "spirit" if the spirit is the very component of our nature whereby we are uniquely related to God? Heard does not reflect on this question.

While Heard passes over the bulk of the biblical data on soul and spirit in silence, he finds a few passages "conclusively" in favor of the tripartite position. On these he dwells at some length. Among them is 1 Thessalonians 5:23: "May the God of peace himself sanctify you wholly; and may your spirit and soul and body be kept sound and blameless at the coming of our Lord Jesus Christ."[29] But if such a threefold description — spirit, soul, body — teaches us that human nature is tripartite, does not the counsel of perfection — that we should love God with all our heart, soul, mind, and strength — teach us that it is quadripartite? No one has ever argued for the latter position, however. It is commonly understood that the first and greatest commandment simply means that we should love God with our whole being. By the same token, may we not say that Paul's hope for the Thessalonians is that they may be sanctified in their whole being and thus blameless at the coming of Christ?

Along with 1 Thessalonians 5:23, Heard also finds Hebrews 4:12, which speaks of God's word as "piercing to the division of soul and spirit, of joints and marrow," to be "decisive testimony of the distinction between soul and spirit."[30] However, the text does not speak of a dividing of the soul *from* the spirit, but rather of the piercing power of God's word. It is a word that cleaves (splits open) both soul and spirit, both joints and marrow. The passage is best understood, then, not as a comment on the constituent elements of human nature (of which four are here mentioned, not three), but as an affirmation that the divine word is effectual, laying bare the inner self before God.

Not only does Heard defend a full-blown trichotomy on doubtful exegetical grounds, but he also finds the trichotomistic approach to be the "key" to resolving some intractable theological problems.[31] The subtitle of his work holds forth much promise in this respect. The doctrine of tripartite human nature is: *Applied to Illustrate and Explain the Doctrines of Original Sin, the New Birth, the Disembodied State, and the Spiritual Body.* Having laid out this ambitious program, the author proceeds, with the help of a tripartite anthropology, to cut several Gordian knots that most

29. For Heard's discussion, see ibid., pp. 97-98.
30. Ibid., p. 88.
31. This feature of his work reminds one of how trichotomy became prominent in the first place, as an effort to resolve the theological difficulty of the Incarnation.

theologians have found notably difficult. To give one example only, original sin is "explained" as the death of the human spirit. By the "death" of the spirit, Heard does not mean, as theologians generally affirm, that the spirit becomes enslaved by sin. In his thinking, the spirit is incapable of sin! A sinful human spirit is simply a contradiction in terms. To speak of the death of the spirit rather means that, as sinners, we are born without a spirit or, at least, without a functioning spirit. When the spirit is quickened to life by the new birth, then the sinner, who has lived as a soulish (ψυχικός) person, becomes a spiritual (πνευματικός) person — and so on.

In striking contrast to such a view, theologians have generally held that the human spirit is not only capable of sin but is the very place where our sin and rebellion originate. Original sin, therefore, is spiritual in nature. As for the thought that unbelievers are "soulish" people in that their lives are dominated by their souls, whereas believers are "spiritual" people in that their lives are dominated by their spirits, this seems to us a strange conceit. After all, the Corinthians, whom Paul admonished as carnal rather than spiritual (1 Cor. 3:1-3), were confessing Christians whom he addresses as such.[32] They may have come short of the Christian ideal, but they were not unbelievers. It seems best, therefore, to understand the apostle as speaking of those whose lives were dominated more by fleshly appetite and desire than by the Spirit, that is, the Holy Spirit.

As for trichotomy in general, the basic problem, as we see it, is the sharp distinction of an ontological sort that it posits between soul and spirit. In Scripture, by contrast, the terms are often used interchangeably. "And Mary said, 'My *soul* magnifies the Lord, and my *spirit* rejoices in God my Savior" (Lk. 1:46-47). In his last public discourse, Jesus declares: "Now is my *soul* troubled" (Jn. 12:27). Shortly thereafter, having spoken to his disciples whose feet he had washed, John tells us that "he was troubled in *spirit*" (13:21). In such instances it is difficult to suppose that soul and spirit are to be distinguished in an essential (ontological) way. Stephen, the first martyr, died with the prayer on his lips, "Lord Jesus, receive my *spirit*" (Acts 7:59). Surely this is the same prayer as that which Wesley has taught us all to sing,

> Hide me, O my Saviour, hide,
> Till the storm of life be passed;
> Safe into the haven guide,
> O receive my *soul* at last.

---

32. Here Paul uses σάρκινος and σαρκικός rather than ψυχικός, but with the same sense of not being under the control of the Spirit.

Well-being

A Sermon Preached by Marguerite Shuster
at Knox Presbyterian Church, Pasadena, California,
Lord's Day, March 25, 1990.

The elder to the beloved Gaius, whom I love in the truth. Beloved, I pray that all may go well with you and that you may be in health; I know that it is well with your soul. For I greatly rejoiced when some of the brethren arrived and testified to the truth of your life, as indeed you do follow the truth. No greater joy can I have than this, to hear that my children follow the truth.

3 John 1-4

If you want to know the basics about people, ask a child. In particular, all children sooner or later get around to inquiring about just how God creates people, and in their answers reveal something of what they think people are like. When two brothers were discussing the origin of a new baby, six-year-old Donald, a budding carpenter, proclaimed simply, "God made him all, without any glue or nails or anything." Another youngster saw it differently. She said of God's creative activity, "He draws us first, then cuts us out." Or take this response of a five-year-old to his four-year-old sister's query about where babies come from. He initially asserted, "Babies come from Heaven, of course." His sister was not satisfied. She said, "If babies come from Heaven, why did Mommy have to go to the hospital?" After a long pause her brother said, "To get the skins put on."[a]

---

a. Adapted from Dick Van Dyke, *Faith, Hope, and Hilarity,* ed. R. Parker (Garden City, . N.Y.: Doubleday, 1970), pp. 51-52.

In these responses, we can discern a progression from the truth that God does indeed make the whole of us, in all of our constituent parts, miraculously put together without glue or nails or anything; to the further truth that not only do people have an inside and an outside, so to speak, but also the inside is in some sense even more fundamental than the outside. The last little boy knew with some incipient understanding that persons are not to be fully identified with their skins. Not that skins are unimportant; people cannot live in this world without them. But skins are not everything. We are forced to acknowledge as much as soon as we acknowledge that something central about a person survives all the changes of skin, all the transformations of form, that an individual undergoes from babyhood to adulthood to old age.

Which leads me to my text, 3 John 2: "Beloved, I pray that all may go well with you and that you may be in health; [just as] I know that it is well with your soul." Note the clear distinction here between the physical and the spiritual life: the elder hopes that the physical circumstances of Gaius, to whom the letter is addressed, might be as satisfactory as his spiritual condition.

This is, of course, the beginning of a letter, and it follows some ancient letter-writing conventions. Today, we write, "Dear [Whoever]," to every-body; the "dear" implies no sentimental attachment. Similarly, in letters of John's day, the wish that one's correspondent might be in health was an opening formula that implied nothing in particular about his actual circum-stances. But still, the context of this conventional expression is distinctive, compared with other ancient letters, and is significant. For one thing, the health wish comes not first but second, after the wish that all might go well with Gaius. That first wish has a less secular flavor than the health wish because it carries implicitly, just beneath the surface, the thought of God, on whom all prosperity and health depend.[b] And for another thing, it is followed by the entirely nonsecular reference to the prosperity of his soul, an addition *not* part of a standard opening formula and one that refers to his life in relationship to God in Christ.

Thus from this single verse I think we can learn at least two important things. First, it is obviously desirable that one's physical and one's spiritual life be in harmony, that all might go well in both respects. We see here no assumption that affliction is to be desired as part of some program of self-improvement and spiritual growth. But, second, it is likewise clear that

b. Wilhelm Michaelis, "ὁδός, κτλ.," *Theological Dictionary of the New Testament* (hereafter *TDNT*), ed. G. Kittel and G. Friedrich, trans. and ed. G. Bromiley, 10 vols. (Grand Rapids: Eerdmans, 1964-76), 5.114.

there is no *necessary* or *inevitable* relationship between the two: the health of Gaius's soul does not guarantee the health of his body; nor, we may safely assume, would success and prosperity in the world lead certainly to the prosperity of his soul.

It is desirable that people prosper and be healthy. I said it two weeks ago, and I must say it again: in the Lord's initial intention, body and soul are not at war. Let us make this point as clearly as the elder makes it, who obviously did not consider the sentiment underlying his conventional greeting to be unworthy of a Christian. Or, better yet, let us make the point as clearly as Jesus makes it by his behavior as recorded in the Gospels. When an unnamed woman at the dinner in Simon the Pharisee's house bathed Jesus' feet with her tears and wiped them with the hair of her head, Jesus assured her with the words: "Your faith has saved you; go in peace" (Lk. 7:50). But the same words could equally mean: "Your faith has made you well," which is what he said to blind Bartimaeus (Mk. 10:52).ᶜ The granting of salvation does not make physical healing somehow irrelevant. Similarly, when Jesus blessed the poor, he was not so much suggesting that the degradations of poverty are somehow good for people as he was indicating that God knew and cared about them and their need. Illness and poverty do not necessarily make people better spiritually; as often as not, they make people embittered and helpless and despairing. Heaven is not a place where we are so spiritual that we sit glorying in the contribution sickness and misery make to our spiritual growth, but a place where affliction is given no room at all. It is not wrong for Christians to desire good health and a decent standard of living, provided that they extend their concern to others and not just to themselves.

To say that it is basically desirable that body and soul be in harmony, and that people prosper and be healthy, is not to deny that longings for wealth and for the indulgence of bodily urges can be directed so as to imperil the soul. Jesus obviously had a lot to say about this matter, too. He said that it was better that the body be maimed than that it be allowed to indulge in sin and lead the person to eternal destruction. He said that it constituted the ultimate foolishness to store up wealth in barns when at any moment one's soul might be required of one — that is, when one might at any time die. He told the rich young ruler to sell all that he had, discerning, evidently, that this man's wealth prevented him from following Jesus wholeheartedly. Yes, it is indeed desirable that body and soul be in harmony, but only when a rightly directed soul has the priority. The evident,

---

c. In the Gospels the same Greek verb is used in both instances.

if mysterious, interrelationship of body and soul is such that in any other case, the whole person is in jeopardy.

My second point, then, is that while it is desirable that body and soul be in harmony, there is no necessary and inevitable relationship between the relative prosperity of one and the relative prosperity of the other. Obviously they interact: undue fatigue of body may virtually prevent one from studying or praying; and worry over a besetting sin may give one an ulcer. Still, one's physical circumstances do not completely *determine* one's spiritual life, either for better or for worse; nor are bad physical circumstances necessarily a sign of spiritual ill health.

Consider improved physical circumstances: as I have said, they do not necessarily improve the state of one's soul. A Christian psychologist I once met told the story of a physician he had treated who, following a heart attack, seemed to be getting worse day by day, despite the fact that the finest heart specialists could find no reason for his continuing illness. It seems that this physician had had a miserable childhood and had had to earn his way through medical school by working nights in a flour mill. The strain and trauma of it all was such that he promised himself that when he finally became an M.D., he was going to ensure his security by making a million dollars. He delayed achievement of his goal by supporting his brother and sister while they were working toward their M.D.'s. But when they had all finished, they went into a joint practice and invested their money in the stock market. Every month for years he asked his accountant jokingly how much more money he needed before he would be a millionaire. Then one day, when he was fifty years old, his accountant told him that he had his million. Initially he felt very happy, but just a few days afterward, he had his heart attack.[d]

Now, the point the psychologist was making in telling this story was *not* that this doctor was suddenly, mysteriously, inexplicably, and unfairly struck down in the prime of life, and that we all need to be ready for the event that no amount of wealth can spare us. That is true enough, but it was not his point. His point was that this doctor, having met the one goal he had set for himself in life, had nothing left to live for. That was why he continued to get worse rather than improve. He had no future, nothing to which to give himself. The million dollars, the symbol that all was going well with him and that he would never suffer material want again, proved mightily destructive at the level of his inner person. And note that it was not deadly because he had obtained it illegally or was using it sinfully, but

d. K. V. Rajan, "Man and His Potential," address presented at annual meeting of Friendly Hills Fellowship, Hemet, California, March 8, 1963.

simply because no such outward well-being is in itself *enough* to make human life worthwhile.

What, then, shall we say to the 1983 survey of college freshmen that shows students to be "more materialistic and less altruistic" than freshmen of ten years before? It seems that 69.3% of these freshmen considered being well off very important, up from 50% ten years before; and only 44% thought it important to develop a meaningful philosophy of life, compared to 70% ten years before. (I suspect the figures would be still worse today.) An interpreter correlated the two statistics and remarked, "If your goal is to be rich, this obviates the need to develop a philosophy of life. Making money becomes a philosophy of life in itself."[e] The better these young people succeed, the more surely they will learn that outer prosperity does not in itself provide inner prosperity. Their attention to the material side of life will not bear the whole weight of their souls.

Likewise, the most desperate outer circumstances do not necessarily imperil the state of one's soul. The elder presumably did not know for sure what Gaius's circumstances might be. All he knew — or gathered from the reports he heard of Gaius's "walking in the truth," being faithful in both doctrine and life — was that it was well with his soul. And the testimony of faithful people across the centuries is indeed that the well-being of the inner person does not depend on favorable conditions of body or bank account.

Take the words of Samuel Coleridge, the nineteenth-century poet who certainly was not, during much of his life, an orthodox Christian, but who wrote a very Christian letter to his godson some twelve days before his death. After reflecting briefly on the very real blessings of health and learning and the pleasures of life, he notes that he had suffered many infirmities in his later life, had been essentially confined to bed for the preceding three or four years, and was hopeless of recovery. He continues,

> I, thus on the very brink of the grave, solemnly bear witness to you that the Almighty Redeemer, most gracious in His promises to them that truly seek Him, is faithful to perform what he hath promised, and has preserved under all my pains and infirmities, the inward peace that passeth all understanding, with the supporting assurance of a reconciled God, who will not withdraw His Spirit from me in the conflict, and in His own time will deliver me from the Evil One.[f]

e. A. W. Astin, *The American Freshman*, quoted in *Context* 16, no. 9 (May 1, 1984): 6.
f. Quoted in John Baillie, *A Diary of Readings* (Nashville: Abingdon, 1955), Day 2.

Or take the life of Christopher Smart, an eighteenth-century poet rejected in his time but today considered a genius. His religious devotion resulted in his being confined for years in an insane asylum, despite the fact that no less than the great Samuel Johnson himself thought he ought not to be locked up. Although he was eventually released from the insane asylum, his poetry sold badly, and he eventually died of starvation and fever in a debtors' prison. This man, whose whole adult life could hardly have been more miserable, wrote *Hymns for the Amusement of Children* with verses like this:

> Whate'er thy sacred will ordains,
> O give me strength to bear;
> And let me know my Father reigns,
> And trust his tender care.
>
> Whate'er thy providence denies
> I calmly would resign;
> For thou art just, and good, and wise,
> Lord, bend my will to thine.
>
> Be this the purpose of my soul,
> And my determin'd choice,
> To yield to thy supreme control,
> And in thy will rejoice.g

Or take the well-known story of Horatio Spafford, a story so crushing it hardly seems possible. A Presbyterian layman born in New York in 1828, he was always a faithful churchman and Bible student despite great financial success as a lawyer. Only a few months before the Chicago Fire of 1871, he had invested heavily in real estate on the shore of Lake Michigan. His holdings were destroyed by the fire. A short while earlier, his son had died. He then planned a European trip for the rest of his family, both to get some rest and to assist D. L. Moody in one of his campaigns in Great Britain. He was held up but sent his wife and four daughters on ahead. Their vessel was struck by another and sank in twelve short minutes. When the survivors landed in Wales, his wife cabled him two short words: "Saved alone." Soon thereafter Spafford himself left by ship to join her; and it is thought that he penned the words of his well-beloved hymn on the sea near the place where his four daughters drowned:

g. In David L. Jeffrey, ed., *A Burning and a Shining Light: English Spirituality in the Age of Wesley* (Grand Rapids: Eerdmans, 1987), p. 340.

When peace, like a river, attendeth my way,
When sorrows like sea-billows roll —
Whatever my lot, Thou hast taught me to say,
It is well, it is well, with my soul.
It is well with my soul, it is well, it is well with my soul.[h]

"Beloved, I pray that all may go well with you and that you may be in health; I know that it is well with your soul." If we can write thus to a friend or a dear one, if we can confess thus our own condition, we have nothing finally to fear.

D. HUMANKIND: THE IMAGE AND LIKENESS OF GOD

1. INTRODUCTION

Having pursued at some length the Christian effort to understand what it means to be human, we come now, at last, to the most distinctive feature of that understanding presaged in the Creator's resolve to make humankind "in our image, after our likeness" (Gn. 1:26).[33] Such a way of speaking is not characteristic of Scripture as a whole. Although theologians commonly describe the human subject as created in God's image and likeness, the writers of Scripture seem reticent to do so. This reticence, especially in the Old Testament, is due, at least in part, to an overriding sense of the divine transcendence, the otherness of God. The writers of the Old Testament knew that God is not to be confused with "the likeness of anything that is in heaven above, or that is in the earth beneath, or that is in the water under the earth" (Ex. 20:4). Since Israel was to give no divine qualities to the creature, it was a bold affirmation, indeed, to say that the Creator himself had done so in the case of the creature who is human.

While the intent of the author of Genesis 1:26 is not to suggest that the human creature is essentially divine, it is important to note that when he touches on the mystery of human nature, he is constrained, as it were, to use such a striking theologoumenon. This is because he understands the origin of the man and the woman in terms not of the mundane, but of the transcendent. Although their being is earthly, it is an earthly reflection of

h. See Kenneth W. Osbeck, *101 Hymn Stories* (Grand Rapids: Kregel, 1982), p. 127.
33. בְּצַלְמֵנוּ כִּדְמוּתֵנוּ; κατ' εἰκόνα ἡμετέραν καὶ καθ' ὁμοίωσιν (LXX). The use of different particles in the Hebrew text — בְּ ("in") and כְּ ("after") — is, in our judgment, of no theological significance.

the being of the God who gives it.[34] The reason why the concept of the
divine image has become so prominent in Christian anthropology is obvious: it confers on the human subject the highest possible distinction,
leaving the world of the animals far behind. Here is language used of no
other creature, language that teaches us to understand ourselves in terms
of God rather than in terms of the animals. While we share with them a
common mortality in the flesh, the Creator has endowed us with uncommon
gifts in the spirit. Our mammalian ancestry, whatever it may be, is therefore
a matter essentially indifferent so far as a Christian understanding of
humankind is concerned. In other words, Christian anthropology is done
from above, not from below.[35]

The term "image" (צֶלֶם, εἰχών, *imago*) may be given a very concrete meaning lexically.
It denotes a two-dimensional copy (a picture), or a three-dimensional one (a statue).
The text of Gn. 1:26 is saying, literally, that a human being is a copy of God. This
literal view is reflected in some Sumerian and Babylonian texts, even to the point of
physical appearance. (See Eichrodt, *Theology*, 2.122.) In the first creation narrative, it
is probably a desire to soften the implication of such a literal meaning that leads the
author to add the word "likeness" (דְּמוּת, ὁμοίωσις, *similitudo*) to his narrative. God
created humankind in his image, that is, in his likeness. Humankind is not an exact
replica of God but only a likeness or reflection of him. To be human is to be like God
somehow and somewhat; between the Creator and the creature who is human there is
a similarity; but it is a similarity only, an approximate correspondence. The plural, "let
us make humankind in *our* image," rather than "*my* image," looks in the same direction.
It distances God from the creature that is human by implying that this creature is not
alone the bearer of the divine image. This "plural of majesty" is echoed in Psalm 8,
where the psalmist says that humankind is made a little lower than the *elohim* (translated
"God" in the RSV, "angels" in the KJV, "heavenly creatures" in the NIV). Yet, granting
this reserve, the biblical text plainly makes the astonishing affirmation that the creature
who is human bears the stamp of Godlikeness. And this makes human life, for all its
affinity with the life of other creatures, somehow different and unique.

To the question, In what way is it unique? the creation narratives, naturally, do
not give an elaborate, theological answer. However, they do contain pointers to the
direction in which the answer lies. The God whose likeness the human creature bears
is a God who accomplishes his purpose in the act of freely creating the world. In this
act he shows himself to be a God who is personal, in that he speaks; he is the God who
summons the creation into being by his word. Since this is the God who is revealed in
the act of creation, the implication is that the creature in his image is also a personal

34. See G. von Rad, *TDNT,* 2.391-92.
35. When the psalmist ponders the Lord's mindfulness of humankind, he concludes:
"Yet you have made them a little lower than God. . . . You have put all things under their
feet, all sheep and oxen, and also the beasts of the field" (Ps. 8:5-7). "Here there is an echo
of Eden, even in the midst of sin and mortality; here there is a promise of what will yet be"
(Cairns, *Image,* pp. 27-28).

self. Such a conclusion is confirmed by the fact that in the biblical narrative God speaks to the man and the woman as self-conscious subjects in whom the word is lodged. To be in the divine image is to be the creature addressed by the Creator as one who is aware of oneself, one who freely determines oneself in conscious and responsible acts. To be in the divine image is to hear the divine command as the norm that determines what one ought and ought not to do. "Of the tree of the knowledge of good and evil you *shall not* eat" (Gn. 2:17). To be in the divine image is also to name the animals rather than to be named by them (2:19-20). For this reason the man can find no counterpart in the animal world, but only in the woman who is given him as "bone of his bone and flesh of his flesh" (2:18-23). Even the act of procreation, which the man and the woman share with the animals, carries with it, in their case, the obligation to act responsibly. They are to fill (not overfill) the earth (1:28).

Given these pointers in the biblical story of creation, together with other data found throughout Scripture, the teachers of the church began early on to frame a doctrine of humanity in which the concept of the *imago Dei* had a central place. To be in God's image, according to the theologians, is not something added to humanity but just humanity as such in its uniqueness and transcendence.

While Scripture plainly teaches that we should understand ourselves primarily in terms of our Godlikeness, the biblical data with which the theologians work in their efforts to frame a Christian anthropology have confronted them with an obvious problem from the start. This problem is due to the fact that the Bible uses the language of "image" and "likeness" to speak not only of our creation but also of our salvation.

On the one hand, we are told that even after our first parents fell into transgression, they and their offspring remain in God's image (Gn. 5:1-3).[36] This is why Abel's blood cried to the Lord from the ground (4:10). To take someone else's life is a capital offense — "whoever sheds the blood of a human, by a human shall that person's blood be shed" — because God made humankind in his own image (9:5-6 NRSV). In the same vein, James censures the unruly tongue with which "we bless the Lord and Father" and "curse those who are made in the likeness of God" (Jas. 3:9 NRSV). According to Scripture, then, even as sinners we remain creatures in the image of God. It is the divine image given in creation that makes us human and gives our lives, as human, a unique sacredness and dignity.

On the other hand, the apostle Paul says that *Christ* is the image of God (2 Cor. 4:4; Col. 1:15); and that those whom God has called, he "also predestined to be conformed to the *image* of his Son" (Rom. 8:29).

---

36. Actually, Gn. 5:1-3 says that Seth was in *Adam's* likeness and image. But since the passage begins by saying that God created Man (Adam) in *his* likeness, the meaning is clear. Seth, like his father who begot him, is in the image of God.

Obviously Paul does not simply mean that Christ is the ideal man, all that the first Adam was meant to be as the bearer of the divine image. In Philippians 2:6 he speaks of Christ as ἐν μορφῇ θεοῦ ("in the form of God"); and the writer of Hebrews (1:3) says that he is the χαρακτὴρ τῆς ὑποστάσεως αὐτοῦ, i.e., θεοῦ ("the express image of his [God's] person," KJV; "the very stamp of his nature," RSV). Christ, then, images God, not as the apogee of humanity but as incarnate Deity. (See Herman Ridderbos, *Paul,* trans. J. R. DeWitt [Grand Rapids: Eerdmans, 1975], pp. 70-72.) At the same time it is true that, as the incarnate Christ, he images God *in* our humanity. As Athanasius said, the Word himself came to earth and made visible the image we had lost "so that it might be copied afresh in the nature of humankind" (*De Incarnatione,* as quoted by Cairns, *Image,* p. 90).

This conformity of sinners to the image of God, manifested in his Son, is the blessing of the gospel. As we behold the glory of the Lord revealed in the gospel, we are being changed into his image (2 Cor. 3:18). Thus, "as we have borne the image of the man of earth, we shall bear the image of the man of heaven" (1 Cor. 15:49); for as Christians we have "put on the new nature which is being renewed in knowledge after the image of its Creator" (Col. 3:10).[37] It would seem, then, that God, in whose image we are made as humans, is also restoring us to that image as Christians. But how can this be? How can the gift of creation, which remains ours even as sinners, at the same time be restored to us in salvation? Can the sin of the creature so far undo the work of the Creator that what is unlosable is lost after all?

The first major theologian to address this question was Irenaeus. Writing some hundred and twenty years after the death of Paul, he sought to resolve the problem by postulating a fundamental difference between "image" and "likeness." This difference came to dominate the understanding of Genesis 1:26 in Western, scholastic theology. On the one hand, the *image* bestowed in creation, he argued, is unlosable. Even as sinners, all men and women are in God's image. On the other hand, the *likeness* to God with which our first parents were endowed is lost in the Fall. It can be restored only as we are sanctified by the Spirit of Christ.[38]

37. In all the above texts, εἰκών occurs. Although it does not occur in Eph. 4:24, the thought is implied. Hence the RSV translates: "put on the new nature, created after the likeness of God" (ἐνδύσασθαι τὸν καινὸν ἄνθρωπον τὸν κατὰ θεὸν κτισθέντα).

38. *Adv. Haer.,* 5.6.1; 4.4.3; 5.16.2; 5.8.1. For translation and comment, see Cairns, *Image,* pp. 73-74. Irenaeus's main agenda was the refutation of Gnosticism; hence his remarks on the image are often parenthetical. He and those who follow him in distinguishing "image" from "likeness" seem not to be bothered by the fact that both what is given in creation and what is restored in salvation are described in Scripture by the very same words, "image" (εἰκών) and "likeness" (ὁμοίωσις), a point that did not escape Luther, the first to challenge the tradition.

The distinction that the Scholastics, following Irenaeus, made between "image" *(imago)* and "likeness" *(similitudo)* led them to the view that humankind's original "likeness" to God was a gift over and beyond the image. The doctrine of a superadded gift *(donum superadditum)* became part of official Catholic doctrine. According to this doctrine, the gift of original righteousness *(justitia originalis),* with which our first parents were endowed by the Creator, and the state of integrity *(status integritatis)* in which they were so endowed are not the essential image *(imago essentialis).* If they were, the "image" could not have been lost in the Fall, since the "image" is endemic to our humanity. But our moral integrity, our "likeness" to God, *is* lost. This is the thrust of Thomas's argument when he reasons that the moral rectitude of the pristine state could not have been "from nature" or it would have remained after the Fall. He concludes, therefore, that it was not "a merely natural gift but a supernatural endowment of grace" *(Summa Theologica,* pt. 1, q. 95, art. 1). As an aside, we note that Emil Brunner would seem to have a point when he argues that since Thomas equated the essential image which is "from nature" with the human faculty of reason, this made reason inviolable. It was this supposed inviolability of reason that led Thomas to suppose that he could ground his natural theology rationally in Aristotelian metaphysics. (See Brunner, *Man in Revolt,* pp. 93-96.)

The Protestant Reformers rejected the scholastic distinction between "image" and "likeness," understanding Genesis 1:26 to be an instance of Hebrew parallelism, as we would say today. (See Calvin, *Commentary,* Gn. 1:26.) God created humankind in his image, that is, in his likeness. This means that the Reformers and their followers have had to take a quite different tack in their efforts to resolve the problem of the image. On the one hand, if one assumes the Protestant position, one obviously must work with the thought that our original likeness to God is not utterly lost in the Fall. All people remain in the image, that is, the likeness of God, no matter how depraved they may have become. On the other hand, as sinners we have lost something that is essential to our humanity, so essential, in fact, that apart from the restoring work of divine grace we ourselves are lost. The attempt to maintain a balanced theological position in one's approach to the question of the image as retained, yet lost and restored, has proved difficult to achieve. As with other paradoxes of the faith, theologians have sought to reduce this paradox, the paradox of the glory and the misery of our humanity, by speaking of humankind either too hopefully or too disparagingly. And of course there is Christian truth in both extremes, for no religious vision has ever esteemed humankind more highly than the Christian vision, nor judged it more severely. Hence the theologian who would frame a theological anthropology that is biblical must assert the genuine dignity of everyone who has a human face, while realistically avoiding the unbounded optimism of what might be called an anthropology-of-the-divine-spark. By the same token she must speak of the radical depravity of the human spirit while avoiding the pessimism of what might be called a miserable-sinner anthropology that can see no dignity or worth in anything human.

The Reliquiae (Relics, Remnants) of the Image

The problem of the unlosable image that is yet so far lost that only grace can restore it obviously compels theologians in the Protestant tradition to recognize that the term "image" is used in the Bible in two senses. A consensus has never been reached, however, on the best way to describe the twofold meaning of the term. Some speak of the "generic" and the "specific" image; some of the "formal" and the "material" image; others of the image in the "Old" and the "New Testament" sense; or of the image in the "broader" and "narrower" sense; or, again, of the "ontological" and the "moral" image. These theological distinctions are not, of course, found in the Scriptures in so many words. We do not read in Genesis that God said, "Let us make humankind in our broader image"; nor does Paul tell us that in Christ we are being restored to the "narrower image." But the use of "image" language to describe both our common humanity and our new humanity in Christ warrants some such distinction, however it may be qualified.

Luther was so opposed to the semi-Pelagianism in Roman Catholic thought that he often spoke of the sinner as having lost the image altogether; the image is something we now have in name only. (See Niebuhr's comment, *Nature and Destiny,* 1.171-72; also our remarks on the controversy between Barth and Brunner over the point of contact [*Anknüpfungspunkt*], in *God, Creation, and Revelation,* p. 75.) Yet even Luther had to acknowledge that some faint "relic" of the original image remained to the natural person. Luther's emphatic Augustinianism, as we might call it, is reflected in the creeds coming out of the Reformation. The sinner retains "a few remains" of the image (Belgic Confession, art. XIV); everyone shows some "glimmerings of natural light" that give a sufficient knowledge of God, of things natural and of good and evil, as to make possible "good order in society" (Canons of the Synod of Dort, III, art. IV), etc.

The position taken by Calvin, whose Augustinian doctrine of radical depravity cannot be doubted, is somewhat less extreme than one might suppose. He insists that it would be contrary to Scripture and common sense to deny the many admirable gifts of the Creator remaining to sinners.

> Whenever, therefore, we meet with heathen writers, let us learn from the light of truth which is admirably displayed in their works, that the human mind, fallen as it is, is yet invested and adorned by God with excellent talents. If we believe that the Spirit of God is the only fountain of truth, we shall neither reject nor despise the truth itself wherever it shall appear, unless we wish to insult the Spirit of God; for the gifts of the Spirit cannot be undervalued without offering contempt to the Spirit himself.

Calvin goes on to praise the ancient statesmen for their "just principles of civil order"; the philosophers for their "excellent contemplations"; the logicians who "have taught us to speak in a manner consistent with reason" and who, therefore, cannot be destitute of all understanding. Can we, he asks, accuse physicians, whose art is a benefit to many, of insanity, and esteem mathematics as "the delirious ravings of madmen" (*Inst.*, 2.2.15)? In such rhetorical questions, one hears the humanist in Calvin, who at the age of twenty-three (1532) published his *Commentary on Seneca*. However, Calvin held these gifts to be corrupted by sin even in matters terrestrial. And when it comes to celestial matters — the pure knowledge of God, the way of true righteousness, and the mysteries of the heavenly kingdom — Calvin affirms that the human mind is no longer capable of pursuing the right way of truth, but wanders in a morass of errors, groping and often stumbling in the darkness. In these matters, the understanding is "smothered by ignorance" and the will "fettered by inordinate desires" (*Inst.*, 2.2.12). For Calvin and his followers, then, the break between nature and grace is radical. It is only as the Spirit bears effectual witness through the Scripture to Jesus Christ, effacing the effects of sin and creating faith in our hearts, that the image is stamped anew upon us. Thus the image, which shone in our first parents at creation until vitiated by sin, is now being restored by the Spirit in believers.

In heaven, at last, this restored image will shine with an even greater glory than at the beginning (*Commentary*, 2 Cor. 3:18). Calvin's thought that the glory of the image restored will exceed that of the image lost is suggested by Paul's affirmation, "Just as we have borne the image of the man of dust, we shall also bear the image of the man of heaven" (1 Cor. 15:49). (Cairns observes that little really new on the subject of the image has been said since Calvin [*Image*, pp. 142-43].) Our present concern, as noted, is not with the image as restored by grace and confirmed in glory. It is rather with the broader image as given by the Creator when he made us in his likeness. What are those endowments of the human spirit that evidence this divine likeness, those endowments that make us not a little more than animals but a little less than God? To this question we must now give further attention.

2. THE MEANING OF THE IMAGE AS GIVEN IN CREATION: HUMAN SELF-TRANSCENDENCE

a. Introduction

In developing our doctrine of God, we spoke of the divine transcendence, but not of the divine *self*-transcendence. God is not a creature as we are; he has, therefore, neither need nor possibility of transcending himself. God is Subject in the absolute sense. By contrast, we are both object and subject, neither wholly other than the natural order nor wholly one with it.[39] Our

39. Cairns speaks, in this regard, of the "stereoscopic" effect of the concept of the image. While we experience ourselves in the body as objects in the world of nature, as subjects in the divine image we are aware of ourselves as lifted to a degree "out of the plane of nature" (*Image*, p. 19).

bodily existence, of course, puts us constantly in mind of the fact that we belong, with all the other creatures, to the natural order of this world. Nor can we escape the weakness, dependence, and finitude of this our creaturely existence in the body by ruminating on the fact that we are in the divine image. While it is true that we are in the image of *God,* we are only in the *image* of God, which is a long way from being God.[40]

Yet, as personal subjects, it is certainly true that we do not experience our creaturely finitude in the way the animals do. Although we are in the world with them, we are aware of this fact in a way that indicates our transcendence of the world.[41] The elaboration of the ways in which we evidence such transcendence of the world will enable us better to understand what it means to say that God has made us in his image. Clarity on this point is essential to prepare the way for our eventual discussion of sin and salvation. For how can the theologian say what is lost by the sinner and restored by the Redeemer if she cannot say what the Creator initially bestowed on humankind when he determined to make them?

Putting the question in this way anticipates our methodological approach. We shall seek to understand the doctrine of the image by working from creation to redemption. By contrast, contemporary theologians often argue that in framing a doctrine of the image we must begin not with the work of creation but with that of redemption. We can understand what the Bible means by "image of God" only in terms of the image as restored in Christ, who is himself the true image of God. Failure to observe this rule, it is alleged, led the church, generally, to follow the ancients and to develop the doctrine of the image in terms of a first human pair who were endowed at creation with original righteousness *(justitia originalis)* and lived in a state of moral integrity, the *status integritatis.* Compelled by the natural sciences to abandon the historicity of the creation and fall narratives, the church can no longer work with this traditional approach. But, it is often affirmed, such a circumstance has actually helped theologians to achieve a more biblical understanding of the doctrine of the image, one that is oriented in terms of the New Testament rather than the Old. It is not the First Adam but the Second Adam, Jesus Christ, who lives a righteous life with complete moral integrity. For this reason he is the full and final revelation of what it means to be the creature in God's image.

We would not dismiss this argument out of hand, for, as we have already affirmed, the revelation of the New Testament fulfills and consummates the Old. (See *God,*

---

40. Sin — to anticipate a later discussion — does not arise out of the finitude of our creaturely existence but out of our unwillingness to *accept* our finitude.

41. Niebuhr observes that this "essential homelessness of the human spirit is the ground of all religions; for the self that stands outside itself and the world cannot find the meaning of life in the world. It cannot identify meaning with causality in nature, for its freedom is obviously something different from the necessary causal links of nature" (*Nature and Destiny,* 1.14-15).

Creation, and Revelation, pp. 95-170.) The work of the Creator is fully revealed only in the work of the Redeemer. Therefore it is not in terms of our union with "the first man [who] was from the earth, a man of dust," that we know and define what we mean by the "image." It is rather in terms of our union with "the second man [who] is from heaven," the man by whom the lost image is restored (1 Cor. 15:47-49). Paul is not in travail for the Galatians until an unfallen Adam be formed in them, but until *Christ* be formed in them (Gal. 4:19).

Nonetheless, the structure of biblical revelation is obviously historical in nature. It is not just that sin is the logical *prius* of salvation, and creation in the image the logical *prius* of the Fall; but that Scripture always supposes these three — creation, fall, and salvation — to be related in terms of *temporal* succession. They are connected not only in an orderly way of thought, but also sequentially, as a series of events in time. Our approach, therefore, will reflect this temporal structure. (We will look at the question of "primal" history in more detail presently. See below, pp. 390-92.) To speak theologically, we will assume that salvation history *(Heilsgeschichte)* is imbedded in world history *(Weltgeschichte)*. Creation and fall, therefore, like salvation, involve events in time and space, not simply ideas that afford different perspectives on the human situation. (On the nature of the "event" of creation, see *God, Creation, and Revelation,* pp. 470-84.) Consequently, we will seek to answer the question of the meaning of the image in terms of events on a time line that begins, for the human race, with God's creative act recorded in Gn. 1:27: "So God created humankind in his image" (NRSV). Our answer, however, will be framed in the light of God's redemptive act in Christ, whereby we are conformed to the image of his Son. In other words, our understanding of what it means to be created in the divine image will prepare the way for our subsequent discussion of the loss of the image in the Fall and its restoration in Christ.

The answer we shall give to the question, What does it mean to say we are "created in the image of God"? presupposes all that we have said about the human self as a subject, an "I," who responds in freedom to the address of the divine "Thou." All creatures act in a way that is consonant with the being given them by the Creator. Objects roll downhill and animals react to stimuli. But neither objects nor animals *respond* to the word of the Creator; only the creature who is in the divine image does that. This response to the Creator's word, given by the creature that is human, is an act differing from all other creaturely acts. It is a free act of self-determination by the creature who is spirit.[42]

This freedom of the human spirit is the gift of the Creator. Being thus endowed, I, unlike other creatures that simply *reflect* God's glory, should also *give* him glory and thus "enjoy him forever."[43] Since this freedom is

---

42. On the meaning of "spirit," see above, pp. 36-44.

43. In this regard, see Barth's comment on Calvin's *Catechism* of 1542, *KD,* III/2, pp. 218-19 (cf. *CD,* III/2, pp. 182-84).

the gift of the Creator, I cannot boast of my freedom (self-transcendence) as though I were God; I can only use it as the creature having the ability to respond to God; use it, that is, in response-ability.[44] The univocal element in the analogy between God's being as the Creator and my being as the creature in his image is *my freedom to be who I am, the power of self-determination.* All other creatures come from God's hand complete; their natures are minted and stamped on them like the coinage of the realm. The human I, by contrast, determines itself in its response to the Creator's love. This response is either the obedient yes of reciprocated love or the disobedient no of a would-be autonomy. In either case, in this response I determine in a profound sense who I am as a human subject. This freedom to determine myself as a subject is the basis of my responsibility to myself, to my neighbor, and ultimately to my God.[45] Since I am not determined as a human self in the way a fox is determined as a fox, but rather determine myself, I must answer to God for the *way* I determine myself. Responsibility before my Maker is, in brief, essential to my humanity.[46]

Christian doctrine teaches that in our freedom as human subjects, we have answered God with a No! so profound that it can never be turned into a Yes! apart from grace. This sinful use of our freedom whereby we have perverted the image in which we were created will concern us when we speak of the Fall and original sin. For the present, we need only note that while we have lost the fellowship with God in and for which we were created, we are and remain responsible to him who has given us our being as human. No act of creaturely rebellion can utterly destroy the work of the Creator, who has made us in his image. We are sinners who "fall short of the glory of God" (Rom. 3:23) only because we are and remain creatures in the image and likeness of God.

How, then, do we understand the image of God that is ours as human even in our sinful revolt against the Creator? We answer: *the image is the human spirit (soul) imprinted by the Creator with those endowments that enable us to transcend the world of lesser creatures and live our lives in a unique I-thou relationship with God and neighbor.* Indeed, not only are

44. As the Germans would say, I have my being as *Gabe und Aufgabe* (gift *and* task).

45. As Bonhoeffer notes, the freedom that is the *tertium comparationis* between God and the creature in his image is not freedom in itself but freedom for him who wills to be free for the creature. The purpose of creation is that created freedom should worship Uncreated Freedom. See his *Creation and Fall,* trans. John C. Fletcher (New York: Macmillan, 1959), p. 36-38.

46. Brunner calls responsibility the formal definition of humanity, the irreducible ingredient of *humanitas.* Responsibility is not an attribute of humanity but its "substance" (*Man in Revolt,* pp. 50-51). For further comment, with sources, see our *Emil Brunner's Concept of Revelation* (London: James Clarke, 1954), pp. 80-81.

we *able* so to live, but we can live in no other way.[47] The time has now come to speak more at length of these endowments that theologians have viewed as evidence that the human spirit is the image of God, that is, stamped with his likeness. True, there is no formal listing of such endowments in Scripture, after the analogy of the lists of vices that mar the lives of sinners and virtues that adorn the lives of saints (Gal. 5:19-23). Yet terms like "mind" (νοῦς), "will" (θέλημα), "conscience" (συνείδησις), and others of a similar nature occur regularly in Scripture. One also finds in Scripture many references to feelings and emotions whose meaning is integrally related to these endowments.[48] Hence, in one way or another, a discussion of the image always involves comment on the nature of these endowments and the emotions associated with them, as these are seen to evidence the presence of the human spirit.

Memory

As we turn to a discussion of the unique endowments of the human spirit, a word is in order concerning "memory." As self-transcendent, we escape the present by recalling the past and contemplating the future. Along with reason, will, and conscience, therefore, Christian theology has had much to say about memory and its correlate, hope. Most of this comment is part of the Christian doctrine of soteriology, the doctrine concerned with the new past Christ has given us and the new future he has promised us. As for the new past, the divine mercy revealed in Christ relieves the anxiety evoked by the memory of our sins; thus we are freed for a new future that we contemplate in hope.

> No condemnation now I dread,
> Jesus, and all in him, is mine!
> Alive in him, my living Head,
> And clothed in righteousness divine,
> Bold I approach the eternal throne,
> And claim the crown through Christ my own.
>
> (Wesley)

But obviously, in the dogmatic order of things, soteriology presupposes anthropology. Hence we pause at this juncture to note that theologians, following Augustine, have

---

47. However, the *way* we live our lives, the so-called dynamic image, both expresses and presupposes the *nature* God has given us, the so-called ontic image. Having developed at length the "dynamic" view of the image in our discussion of human existence as an I-thou relationship, we now turn to the question of the "ontic" image which makes that relationship possible.

48. Emotions have traditionally been ignored in the discussion of the *imago* because God's unchanging character has been understood in terms of a strict impassibility. For our rejection of this view of the divine immutability, see *God, Creation, and Revelation*, pp. 396-412.

given considerable attention to memory viewed as an essential manifestation of the self-transcendence of the creature made in the divine image. Of course, not only our memory, by which we relate to the past, but also our creative imagination, by which we relate to the future, manifests our self-transcendence as human. But the discussion of this latter subject has become, for the theologian, part of the larger discussion of the "dominion" of humankind over nature that makes possible the "creation" of culture and technology. Through culture and technology, we both anticipate the future and shape it as well. (See below, pp. 357-76.)

As for memory, it is like a silken cord let down each morning from the sky. As we open our eyes, we reach up and grasp it, and in doing so are drawn into the light of a new day that has its meaning for us as memory recalls all our past days. Few may have the specialized memory of a Mozart, whose recall of pitch and all other things musical is legendary; but without memory in the ordinary sense, we could not so much as finish a sentence, let alone live out our days as human beings. It is memory that gives our lives continuity and the span of our years meaning. No doubt animals also have memory and therefore know something of what it means to transcend the present moment. But our memory, as human, is not simply the capacity to recall sights, sounds, and smells. Rather, we recall ideas in the abstract. As Augustine notes, our memory of numbers is not simply the recall of Greek or Latin sounds; nor is it the recollection of an image whereby we recognize a "4" or a "IV" or a "IIII" as it appears on a page. It is rather the recall of the thought itself, the concept of fourness. Such access to imageless, abstract concepts makes possible not only mathematics and metaphysics but theology also, a discipline in which we have to do with truths we can conceive but cannot picture in the mind. The implications of this remarkable capacity will have a tacit place throughout the ensuing discussion of the *imago*. (For Augustine's remarks on memory, see his *Confessions,* 10.7-20. Also Niebuhr's comments, *Nature and Destiny,* 1.167-68.)

b. Self-Transcendence and Reason[49]

From earliest times, Christian thinkers have affirmed that the universal image is manifested especially in humanity's powers of reason. Such a view, which dominated the tradition for a thousand years, is fully elaborated in Thomas's "Treatise on Humankind."[50] In his encyclical letter on the working classes, Pope Leo XIII simply assumes the Thomistic position as self-evident: "It is the mind, or reason, which is the predominant element in us who are human creatures; it is this which renders a human being human, and distinguishes one essentially and generically from the brute."[51]

49. The reader will recall that Bunyan tells us that reason's name was "Lord Understanding" and that he was the mayor, no less, of the famous town of Mansoul (*Holy War,* chap. 1).
50. See *Summa Theologica,* especially pt. 1, q. 79, in thirteen articles.
51. *Rerum Novarum,* May 15, 1891, in Manschreck, *History of Christianity,* p. 384.

This tendency to define the image in terms of rationality is reflected in the fact that theologians have traditionally spoken of the soul as the "rational" or "intellectual" soul to distinguish it from the animating principle (sensitive soul) of the lesser animal creatures. Thomas argued that this intellectual soul cannot be produced from the *semen* in procreation (he never bothered to ask if it could be produced from the *ovum*) because a material cause cannot produce an immaterial effect. That the soul is immaterial he deemed to be obvious, since he viewed thought as an operation of the soul "in which the body takes no part whatever" (*Summa Theologica,* pt. 1, q. 118, art. 2). This notion that "pure thought" is an operation of the soul apart from all bodily functions was embraced by Protestant theologians also, since they knew nothing of brain-wave activity. (Even now, with all we know about such activity, it is hard to believe the fact that participation in a world champion chess match consumes, on a given day, more *physical* energy than playing in the Super Bowl!)

In their doctrine of the *imago,* the Reformers followed the Thomistic tradition, emphasizing the preeminence of reason. Understanding the image to consist of that "excellence in which the nature of humankind surpasses all the other species of animals," Calvin speaks of Adam as created with a "right understanding when he had affections regulated by reason." Like Thomas, he argues that it is the office of the understanding to distinguish the good from the evil in order that the will may make the right choice. Thus "the understanding is, as it were, the guide and governor of the soul," whose authority the will respects.[52]

In present-day theologizing, dogmaticians tend to be much less inclined to give reason the prominent place it has traditionally enjoyed in defining the image. For some, such a view suggests the ancient Greek idea that the human soul is essentially a spark of the divine, a participation in the universal Logos. Others have argued that to equate the image with rationality is to imply that the phrase "image of God" is simply a religious figure of speech for what the philosophers have meant when they speak of a human being as a "rational animal" (Aristotle). Given such a philosophic view, the traditional emphasis on reason becomes a clandestine way of understanding ourselves in terms of ourselves; whereas the true intent of the doctrine of the image is that we should understand ourselves in terms of God and our relationship to him.[53]

In modern times, the study of animal psychology has humbled the traditional emphasis on reason as the key to understanding the image. The evidence is plain that the more

---

52. *Inst.,* 1.15.3-6.

53. A further problem is that the Greeks embraced a hierarchy of rational transcendence. The philosopher-king is maximally rational, concerned as he is with thinking; artisans and craftsmen sufficiently so; women and children partially so; slaves and animals not at all. Therefore the slave was a chattel without rights as a person.

highly developed animals are capable of mental acts. There can be no doubt, in the light of this evidence, that the theologians and philosophers have drawn the line between humans and animals rather too nicely in this regard. We shall have more to say on this matter presently when we take up the subject of evolution. (See below, pp. 385-88.)

Yet when all the caveats have been duly entered, one must conclude that our powers of reason have something to do with our likeness to God. Reason is the capacity to interpret the infinite flow of sensations so that we comprehend ("perceive," as psychologists would say) the world as intelligible. It gives us the ability not only to understand our experience, but also to draw inferences as we think; the ability, that is, to follow the path of implication. Reason, then, is not simply the movement of the mind from one affirmation to another; rather it is an "if — then" movement, a movement from premise to conclusion.[54] This capacity to comprehend the meaning of sense data, to draw logical inferences and reach valid conclusions, makes possible what has been called "technical intelligence," which, in its restless quest, its "unending reflection" (Kierkegaard), is the basis of human civilization and technology.[55] The creature who possesses such freedom to transcend the rule of instinct is destined to inherit the earth.

Reason (νοῦς) is that faculty of the spirit whereby we not only probe the secrets of nature but also hear and answer the call of God; it is the ground and substratum of our relationship to him who is the divine I of the human thou. To be sure, fallen reason, in its would-be autonomy, seeks to understand itself solely in terms of itself; the only religion it will embrace is a "religion within the limits of reason alone" (Kant). Faith, we grant, is opposed to such rationalism. But this does not mean that faith is opposed to reason as such, for reason is the reflection in the soul of the divine Logos. It is the light of the One who is the true light that enlightens everyone coming into the world (Jn. 1:9). Indeed, faith may be viewed, in a sense, as reason open to a word from beyond itself, a word that is not spoken *by* the creature but by the Creator *to* the creature.

---

54. Such logical movement of the mind finds its quintessential expression in the science of mathematics, which is a universal language bearing on just about everything human from philosophy and art to economics and parlor games. Space scientists assume that the laws of mathematics are understood wherever there is intelligent life in the universe, which would make the language of mathematics a truly universal language.

55. The traditional emblem of this intelligence is the flaming torch, an apt symbol since it implies the use of fire. The deathly fear of fire on the part of all animals makes it impossible for them to domesticate it.

First Addendum: The Retarded and the Gifted

To recognize our rational powers as evidence of the divine image compels one to say a word about the severely retarded, those who do not show "reason's mintage charactered in the face" (Milton). Are such unfortunate ones creatures in the divine image? Are they human? This question has always been given an affirmative answer by the church; that such persons are incapable of *manifesting* the image does not mean they are not *in* the image. With this conclusion we emphatically agree. We grant that there is virtually nothing in the Bible bearing directly on this matter one way or the other. But this is not to be wondered at, since Scripture is a word of God spoken *to* us rather than a theoretical word spoken *about* us. It is a word to those who can — and must — respond in a way the retarded cannot. What God's purpose for such disabled people might be, we cannot say. But this does not warrant the conclusion that they are without dignity and worth in his sight.

As we seek to make a Christian statement concerning our understanding of such people and our relationship to them, it is of help to recall the distinction already made between personhood and personality. As we see it (and we can do no more than give our own opinion), those who are retarded are *persons* in God's image who, in this life, are unable to respond to their environment in a way that would manifest and develop *personality.* In the technical language of theology, they cannot actualize the ontic image; therefore they live their lives apart from any manifestation of the image in the dynamic sense. That is, they possess the image as given by the Creator but not as actualized by the creature. One might illustrate the distinction we are making by observing that Paganini was a great violinist; yet he *became* one only as he took his violin in hand and played a concerto with its pizzicato, double stoppings, and gorgeous cadenza. And so it is, we would suggest, with those who are incapable of responding as an "I" in the presence of a "thou." They are like a musician without an instrument. Why God should have created Paganinis without violins is his secret. Here we see "through a glass darkly"; we can discern no meaning in the earthly life of such persons. But then, to name the name of Christ is to acknowledge that this life does not have its meaning in itself. We are all but pilgrims and strangers on our way to a better land and a better life. They whose eyes have shown no human awareness will in death, we believe, cross the narrow sea with us into the life beyond. Then we who have known the Lord's compassion will also know the gratitude of these hapless ones to whom we have shown compassion.

I was once escorted by a chaplain through a large mental institution. Greeting those who were on the lawn and in their porch chairs, we moved ever inward until at last a door was unlocked and a room filled with those incapable of any intelligent response opened before us. Backing instinctively away from their uncomprehending stares, I commented on the futility of a chaplain's ministry to such persons. I was surprised and rebuked to hear that they were dressed and taken to chapel every Lord's Day for prayers, Scripture reading, and the singing of hymns. Not long before, I was told, a woman from this room, as she lay dying, began to sing one of the hymns she had heard in the chapel, the first intelligent act of her life.

This incident occurred near the city of Bern a few years after World War II. One cannot but contrast such concern with the attitude of the Nazi in the land just to the north of Switzerland. Commenting on genocide as social policy in Hitler's Third Reich, George Kren notes: "It is a matter of record that beginning in September, 1939, with an implementation order from Hitler, several killing centers were organized to dispose of mentally deranged and retarded individuals." This inhuman program became "an indiscriminate method of cleaning out the back wards in various medical institutions" (*The Holocaust and the Crisis of Human Behavior* [New York: Holmes & Meier, 1980], p. 10.) Kren goes on to note that while a public outcry led to its termination, this program proved to be the first step toward the Holocaust.

The highly gifted, like the retarded, have evoked theological comment. But unlike the case of the retarded, it is easy to assume that such people are in God's image. This prejudice is reinforced by the Greek component in our cultural inheritance. Pericles' Athens, with its glorious Parthenon, was a city of not more than sixty to seventy thousand inhabitants. Yet in this city, as Gibbon reminds us, there was

> condensed, within the period of a single life, the genius of ages and millions. Our sense of the dignity of human nature is exalted by the simple recollection that Isocrates was the companion of Plato and Xenophon; . . . that his pupils Aeschines and Demosthenes contended for the crown of patriotism in the presence of Aristotle.[56]

But the ground beneath our feet is treacherous when we equate human worth with giftedness. One cannot deny that through the centuries a small handful of highly endowed people have vastly enlarged the horizons and influenced the destiny of the human race. Some geniuses, especially scientific ones, seem to be aware of reality in a way that enables them not only to see problems but also to discern the hidden paths leading to their solutions. Others, especially artists, have the capacity to create that which is so essentially new that it seems to ordinary mortals to have been brought forth almost ex nihilo. We all stand in awe of such genius — one may even

56. *Decline and Fall*, Great Books, 1.669.

wonder if Mozart had a human father and a human mother. Yet, though we easily recognize it, we do not know what genius is.[57] Nor can we cultivate it as we do the ordinary gifts of the Creator. In fact, it may leave one altogether or drive one to madness. And, if it is depraved, it will profane all it touches.

In any case, Jesus, whose life reveals what it means to be truly human, was no religious genius — liberals to the contrary notwithstanding. Nor does he tell us that the kingdom belongs to geniuses. Rather, he tells us that it belongs to little children and those who are like them (Mk. 10:14 and par.). And Paul reminds us that God has not called many who are wise by earthly standards; rather, he "chose what is foolish in the world to shame the wise" (1 Cor. 1:26-27). One may wonder what Paul thought when he visited the magnificent city of Athens and gazed on the art of Praxiteles; but whatever he thought, his soul was more vexed by the many idols the Athenians worshiped than moved by the genius that crafted them (Acts 17:16). In truth, he was not at home in Athens. The city for which he — and all Christians — look is not named Athens but Jerusalem (see Gal. 4:26; Heb. 11:10, 16; 12:22). Christians, then, are grateful for the gifts the Creator has granted the few; but they reverence their neighbor, not for her gifts but because she is the image and glory of God.

Second Addendum: Concerning Humor

We have argued that to be in the divine image is to be aware of our presence in the world in a way that transcends the world. Not only do we look back and ahead in a way the animals do not, but even the present we share with them has, for us, a quality of which the animals know nothing. A striking evidence of this is the fact that animals never laugh — only people do. Our sense of humor is the gift of the Creator that helps us cope with life as we perceive and reflect on its incongruities. In *Paradise Lost,* Milton is bold to put a jest on the lips of Deity. When Lucifer and the angels revolt against heaven, the sheer incongruity of it all elicits the Almighty's satirical response, .

> Nearly it now concerns us to be sure
> Of our Omnipotence.[58]

57. Emily Brontë in her poem, "God of Visions," calls her own genius that "ever present, phantom thing — / My slave, my comrade, and my king."

58. *Paradise Lost,* 5.718-19. Milton's lines were no doubt suggested by Ps. 2:1-6. That the kings of earth should conspire against the King of heaven evokes the divine laughter. See also Ps. 59:8.

Our sense of humor also relieves, though it does not resolve, the angst of our creaturely existence as sinners. Lincoln is said to have impressed some as more a jester than a sage; but those closest to him knew that his humor provided a necessary relief from the pressures that beset him in office and the anxieties they evoked. Black Americans have often used humor to cope with the ordeal of caste in a society that boasts of its democratic freedoms. Possibly the greatest baseball pitcher who ever lived, Leroy (Satchel) Page, had a sense of humor that turned his personal tragedy into triumph. The great Dizzy Dean once boasted, "If me and Satch was on the same team, we'd win sixty games between us." To which Page replied, "Maybe I'd win all sixty by myself."

To see the humor in a situation is a manifestation of rational transcendence, and the masterpieces of wit and humor in our literature are the creative achievements of pure intellect. Theologians, however, have paid little attention to humor; some have even been suspicious of it.[59] Our Puritan forebears, especially, are well known for their "stern mien" and somber approach to life. While they wrote voluminously, they seldom penned a light line. They took Jesus' warning about the "idle word" (Mt. 12:36 KJV), and Paul's proscription of "foolish talking" and "jesting, which are not convenient" (Eph. 5:4 KJV), very seriously. "Laughter," opines Edward Irving, "is a kind of bacchanalian state of mind, just as drunkenness is a bacchanalian state of the body."[60] Yet the Puritans knew how to smile. Matthew Henry's commentaries sparkle with genuine wit, and the original Psalter version of Psalm 100, which read "Him serve with *fear,*" was changed in the *Scottish Psalter* of 1650 to "Him serve with *mirth,* his praise forth tell."[61]

In fact, our laughing, more than our weeping, evidences our likeness to God. The seer tells us that in heaven God will wipe away our tears (Rv. 21:4) but not our smiles, for he is the God who has smiled on us in Christ. "Weeping may tarry for the night, but joy comes with the morning" (Ps. 30:5).[62] Thus, given their doctrine of the divine image, Christians, of all people, should enjoy following Don Quixote as he sallies forth to deliver the world; they should join Gulliver in his travels and meet the architect

59. We included Robert McAfee Brown's parody of the theistic proofs in *God, Creation, and Revelation* (pp. 57-58) to show that theologians can laugh — even at themselves.

60. As quoted by Charles Stanford, *The Wit and Humour of Life: Being Familiar Talks with Young Christians* (London: E. Stock, 1886), p. 64.

61. John Julian, *Dictionary of Hymnody* (London: John Murray, 1907), p. 44. If we can believe Longfellow's *Courtship of Miles Standish,* when John Alden brought a proposal of marriage to Priscilla Mullins from Standish, there must have been a smile on her face as she replied, in effect, "Speak for yourself, John."

62. Sarah's laughter at the birth of Isaac (Gn. 21:6) anticipates these eschatological smiles; hers was a kind of heavenly ecstasy. The absurd, the ridiculous, the unbelievable had actually happened to her.

at the Academy of Lagado "who had contrived a new method of building houses, by beginning at the roof, and working downward to the foundation." In so doing they may learn to take some of their own grand schemes and ideas a little less seriously.[63]

Wit has been commonly recognized as the highest form of humor. A poet named Waller presented a copy of congratulatory verses to King Charles upon his restoration after the fall of Cromwell's house. The monarch read them and observed: "Mr. Waller, these verses are very good, but not so fine as you made on the Protector." Whereupon Waller replied: "Your Majesty will please to recollect that we poets always write best upon fictions."[64] By contrast, the pun is at the lower end of humor's scale; yet Paul may have given it canonical status. In Philippians 4:2 he exhorts two women, one of whom is named Euodia, to a oneness of mind. Later, in the same chapter, he refers to the gift that the Philippians had sent him as "an odor of a sweet smell," literally, "an odor of *euodia*" (ὀσμὴν εὐωδίας, 4:18), a pleasant pun, it may be, on the name of the woman he knew to have been influential in preparing the gift for him.

Yet laughter is not the solution to all life's problems. There is, Scripture says, a time to weep as well as a time to laugh (Eccl. 3:4). To laugh at the wrong time is not an evidence of our creation in the divine image, but of our perversion of the image.[65] In our day we laugh about everything; we feed on flippancy; we pay professional comedians millions of dollars a year to keep us convulsed in one unending guffaw. But to use laughter as the final solution to life's fearsome unease is like beating drums in battle to drown out the groans of the dying. Those who name the name of Christ, who call themselves Christians, should remember that one's laughter is an index to one's soul. They must, therefore, exercise themselves in this regard not to "let the world around them squeeze them into its own mold but to let God remold their minds from within" (Rom. 12:2, Phillips).[66]

---

63. One might almost think, when looking at some of the animals, that the Creator must have laughed when he made them.

64. Corbyn Morris, *An Essay Toward Fixing the True Standards of Wit, Humour, Raillery, Satire, and Ridicule* (London: J. Roberts, 1744; reprint, New York: Garland, 1970), p. 7.

65. Consider, for example, Stephen Leacock's inclusion of Nathaniel Hawthorne's *The Celestial Railway* in *The Greatest Pages of American Humor* (New York: Sun Dial, 1936). Here one should read Screwtape's advice to his nephew, Wormwood. See C. S. Lewis, *The Screwtape Letters* (New York: Macmillan, 1960), Letter XI.

66. This is especially true for those who occupy the office of Christian ministry. Phillips Brooks, in his Yale *Lectures on Preaching,* admonishes the divinity students to whom he lectured not to become "clerical jesters" who turn doctrines that mean life or death into so much chaff (Manchester: James Robinson, 1899, pp. 55-56). How, for example, can one who jokes about hell claim to speak for him who told us the story of the rich man and Lazarus?

c. Self-Transcendence and Will[67]

To be in God's image, we have argued, is to have our being in such a way
that our presence in the world as subjects is, at the same time, a transcendence of the world. As subjects, we transcend ourselves as objects in the
world. Such self-transcendence is evidenced not only in our powers of
reason, whereby the world of experience becomes intelligible to us, but
also in our ability to act in the light of what we perceive and understand.
This ability to act we call "will." Will may be defined as the faculty (power)
whereby we translate thought into action through a conscious choice. The
acts of which we speak when we speak of "acts of will" are not to be
confused with such events as the beating of the heart or the inflation of
the lungs. There is a dimensional difference between such "acts" of the
autonomic nervous system and the acts of the conscious self. While it is
my heart that beats and *my* lungs that inflate, they do so involuntarily, not
by my will or choice. True, acts that result from the exercise of will or
choice depend on an awesome instrument called the central nervous system,
which functions by the same laws as the autonomic nervous system. Yet,
although the electrochemical impulses that underlie voluntary acts are the
same as those that produce involuntary acts, voluntary acts are qualitatively
different from involuntary ones. In the latter, the human I is passive as
object; in the former, active as subject.

To use the traditional language of theology, involuntary acts have to
do with the body, voluntary acts with the spirit. Will, then, is not a function
of the brain; the brain does not choose to do or not to do something — *I*
do. It is granted that my decisions are not apart from brain functions. But
they cannot be reduced to brain functions, for brain functions are a part of
the larger cause-effect nexus and therefore determined, whereas acts of will
are free, that is, transcendent.[68] All efforts to explain the relationship between the acts of personal will in which I make decisions and choices, and
the brain functions by which I make them as an embodied self, are futile.
When I decide to write this sentence, I can trace the movement of my hand
from the energized muscles in the arm to the stimulation of nerve impulses
originating in the brain; but here the path of causal explanation mysteriously

---

67. As we turn to the subject of the will, the reader will recognize Bunyan's "Lord
Willbewill, another of the gentry of the famous town of Mansoul. This Willbewill was as
high born as any man in Mansoul, and was much, if not more, a freeholder than many of
them were; besides, if I remember my tale aright, he had some privileges peculiar to himself
in the famous town of Mansoul. Now, together with these, he was a man of great strength,
resolution and courage" (*Holy War,* chap. 1).

68. See above, pp. 7-10, for our rejection of mechanistic reductionism.

ends. At this point one becomes aware of an invisible command center that cannot be understood through the study of physiology, yet cannot be doubted because the self knows itself as a subject who acts freely. I do not infer myself from my acts. Rather I am aware of myself in my acts with an undeniable immediacy.[69]

"When I will, I raise my hand. This is an experiment I can very simply carry out: it works. We can in such an instance analyze the bodily movement physically and chemically . . . but we have no possibility of building a bridge from the material to the spiritual. We simply have a certain inner experience: I will. It is an act of will. My hand obeys my spirit which wills that it should." (Goez, *Naturwissenschaft*, p. 143. See also Marguerite Shuster, "Against Reductionism: Problems of Conscious Experience," in *Power, Pathology, Paradox* [Grand Rapids: Zondervan, 1987], pp. 25-30.) It is true, of course, that such acts of will can be hindered by sickness or injury, especially by motor damage. But the very awareness of resistance, as one strives in physical therapy to overcome the hand's failure to grasp objects, is itself an act of self-transcendence. As for the resistance to the will experienced when one encounters the will of another, who is also a self, and the transcendence implied in this I-thou encounter, see *God, Creation, and Revelation*, pp. 211-12.

We have affirmed that an act of will is a free act of the self (spirit) — I decide to do or not to do something. Yet at the same time we have affirmed that such an act never takes place apart from the activity of the central nervous system culminating in the brain, which functions according to the laws of science. But if this instrument of the spirit, the brain, functions deterministically, must we not, then, say that a so-called free decision and choice only *seems* to be free, whereas in reality it is determined? We answer that while the brain functions according to fixed laws, this does not mean that the self is causally determined, *unless one assumes that the only reality that can have an impact on the brain from without is a reality belonging to the same cause-effect realm*. Rejecting such a view of reality, which reduces everything to a single ontological plane, we have argued that the human person is a self-transcending spirit. As the brain makes an impact on the spirit, so also the spirit on the brain. As the function of the brain has to do with the life of the spirit, so the life of the spirit has to do with the function of the brain.

To use a figure we have already employed, the spirit weaves a pattern of neural activity on the loom of the cerebral cortex. How it does so we cannot say. The relationship between the functions of the brain and the acts of the conscious self (spirit) is mysterious. The immediacy of the relation-

69. See Karl Heim, *The Transformation of the Scientific World View* (New York: Harper and Brothers, 1953), pp. 176-77.

ship between brain and spirit contributes, perhaps, to this sense of mystery. The movement of the hand in painting a picture is, by comparison, somewhat more distant from the center of the self in its awareness of itself, than is the brain activity that initiates such movement. A painter who loses the use of the hands may learn to paint with her toes. By contrast, the loss of brain function is just the loss of the self insofar as the self is aware of itself as embodied spirit in the time and space world. One is dead, in terms of this world, when all brain functions cease.

The question of the will, not only in theology but also in philosophy and science, has been overshadowed by the question of the *freedom* of the will. Leo XIII, in his encyclical letter *Rerum Novarum,* simply defines "will" in terms of freedom: "freedom of choice is the property of the will, rather, is identical with the will" (see Manschreck, *History of Christianity,* p. 384). In the present discussion we too have understood the will as free, a faculty of a self-determined spirit. In this discussion, however, we are simply setting the stage for further analysis down the theological road. We are affirming the freedom of the will internally, that is, in relation to the self. We leave until a later time the question of the freedom of the will externally, that is, in relation to the external world and to God who created the world. Our concern, for the present, is not whether the will is free to choose between options A and B, which are external to the choosing subject, the so-called *liberum arbitrium indifferentiae.* Did our first parents have a choice between eating and not eating the forbidden fruit? If we answer yes, does this mean that the creature has the freedom either (A) to fulfill or (B) to frustrate the purpose of God? These are important questions and must be answered in due course. But how we will answer them is not determined by the position we have taken here. Of course, when we do answer them, we will seek to do so in a way that is congruent with the position we here affirm, namely, that the choices we make are really free because the will, as a faculty of the spirit, transcends brain functions and therefore is not causally determined.

As we draw our discussion of the will to a close, we do well to remember that all the endowments of the human spirit that evidence the divine image are best understood not in terms of themselves but in terms of our relationship to God, who made us in his image that we might have fellowship with him. As reason is that endowment of the spirit whereby we hear the word of God, so will is that endowment whereby we respond to what we hear. It must be granted that, as sinners, we are not able, apart from grace, to respond to God's word with the Yes! of affirmation for which we were created. Yet even as sinners, we retain the ability to respond; otherwise we would not be sinners. Our No! to God is an act of self-determination; we are sinners by our own will and choice.

Although the will of sinners is "fettered by inordinate desire" (Calvin) so that they "who are in the flesh *cannot* (οὐ δύναται) please God" (Rom.

8:8), the will is by no means destroyed in its essential nature as the power of self-determination. When Saul the persecutor, consenting to Stephen's death (Acts 8:1), laid waste the church (Acts 8:3), his will was just as active as it was when he became Paul the apostle who proclaimed Christ in obedience to God's gracious call (Gal. 1:15) and so built up the church. Both Saul the persecutor and Paul the apostle did what "they" did freely; that is, without constraint or compulsion.[70] When, therefore, we speak of will as that faculty by which we transcend the givenness of our crea-tureliness and, under God, determine ourselves, we are speaking of that which is essential to our humanity. As Goez observes,

> the human *will* is a *conscious power;* here one is clearly and completely oneself. *"It* drives me" — but *"I* will." In this pregnant sense, the animals do not *will,* but simply *desire.* But human beings *will* — all reflections, conceptions, ethical goals, world views, reli-gious values, all feelings for the beautiful, all passions, all the powers of love and goodness, are taken up into this will; they are the *"mo-tives"* that move and direct it. Here, then, we have the central place in our inner lives, the will is the I.[71]

In a Christian anthropology, this will that is the I, the self, in its powers of self-determination, is given us by God. To be created in the image of God is to have the freedom to determine who we are and shall be. Since we are given this freedom by God, however, it is a freedom grounded in utter dependence on him. Our freedom, therefore, is not the freedom to do whatever we please with impunity. It is rather a freedom that makes us accountable to the One who has given us our freedom. Because our freedom is a freedom under God, all our decisions and choices are ultimately a response to him with whom we have to do. That human decisions and choices have this quality of responsibility gives us further insight into the nature of our being as creatures in the divine image. To describe the unique quality of such responsible decisions, theologians have used the terms "moral" and "immoral." Human choices are choices that have a moral quality; they have to do with what ought or ought not to be; they may be judged to be right or wrong, good or evil. To speak thus of the acts of the human spirit is to speak in a way that leaves the animals far behind. They

---

70. Some theologians have referred to Saul's freedom as "formal," that is, the freedom pertaining to the form of our humanity, as given by the Creator. His freedom as Paul the apostle to close in with the truth and say "yes" to the call of the risen Christ is, by contrast, spoken of as "material" freedom, that is, the freedom pertaining to the matter or essence of our humanity, namely, fellowship with God.

71. Goez, *Naturwissenschaften und Evangelium,* p. 100.

too live in dependence on the will of the Creator, but his will, quite apart from their own, determines how they shall live. They do not find their beatitude in submission to God's will nor the loss of it in revolting against his will. But we do, a fact whose implications will concern us in our next section, having to do with conscience.

Freedom or Mechanism? A Further Comment

Some researchers in our day have sought to arrive at a Christian view of the human will as the source of free and responsible choices without the dualism of body and soul with which theologians have traditionally worked. While they do not wish to foreclose the possibility that the traditional approach may turn out to be correct, and readily grant that the *onus probandi* is with the reductionists, they argue that the Christian view of freedom of choice does not entail such dualism. For example, Malcolm Jeeves proposes that we no longer think in terms of a mind/body dualism but rather in terms of a relationship between dual aspects of a unity ("Man as Mechanism," in *Christianity in a Mechanistic Universe and Other Essays,* ed. Donald MacKay [London: InterVarsity Press, 1965], pp. 51-52). He speaks of this relationship in terms of different levels of reality. There is the "level of the mechanical" appropriate to the outside observer who sees the choice made by the human agent, and the "level of the personal" appropriate to the acting agent who makes the choice (ibid., p. 67). Following what he calls MacKay's "dualism-of-aspect" approach, in contrast to the theologian's "dualism-of-stuff" approach, Jeeves argues that "freedom and determinism are concepts expressed in two different languages. There is the actor language used by the person who is freely choosing, and there is the spectator language used by the scientist observing the same set of events, namely the choice being made" (*The Scientific Enterprise and Christian Faith* [London: Tyndale, 1969], pp. 137-38). An analogy is seen in Niels Bohr's theory of complementarity in dealing with the wave/particle model of light.

We can only applaud such an effort to escape the "hard" determinism of a B. F. Skinner and others. (By "soft" determinism — implied in our use of the expression "hard" determinism — we have in mind the sort of determinism assumed in the actuarial calculations of insurance companies. As we see it, such determinism is of no concern in framing a Christian view of the freedom of the will.) But one cannot escape the suspicion that this sincere Christian effort to escape a thoroughgoing determinism without postulating the traditional dualism of the theologians is an argument that moves in a different thought world from that of the New Testament. One can sense that the argument rests on thin ice when one applies it to other, related areas of Christian doctrine. For example, MacKay attempts a similar "dualism-of-aspect" approach in order to explain what he calls "spiritual life," that is, the life that is given by grace to the sinner who is converted. "Could we perhaps agree," he asks, "that in the kind of way that we see psychological life 'embodied' in the physical brain, it is at least not implausible to see, in biblical terms, spiritual life as 'embodied' in the psychological mechanism of a man? . . . The suggestion would then be that this acquisition of life, in the New Testament sense, does not necessarily entail something which is inexplicable *psychologically*" ("Man as Mechanism," p. 67). In this way, MacKay continues, we can make our peace with the psychology of religious conversion, even as we have with the physiology of brain function. We grant that Christian conversion involves one's psychological life, even as one's act of will involves one's physiological life. But where does the New Testament speak in a way that suggests that the spiritual life of the Christian is "embodied in the human psychological mechanism"? Does not such a way of speaking show the influence of what we have called the "monism of modern thought"? If a dualism of body and spirit reflects Greek thought, do we better understand the New Testament (which was written in the Hellenistic world) when we use the monistic thought of the modern world?

Finally, while one may, with some plausibility, try to state a Christian anthropology sans dualism, how is one to manage such a monistic approach when it comes to Christian hope, namely, the doctrine of individual eschatology? How are we to understand our Lord's dying words, "Father, into thy hands I commit my spirit" (Lk. 23:46), if we think of spirit as one "aspect" of an indissoluble unity? If a similar prayer by the first martyr, "Lord Jesus, receive my spirit" (Acts 7:59), is in the "actor language" of the person praying it, what does it mean in the "spectator language" of the observer who hears it? Again, when the apostle Paul speaks of his desire to "depart and be with Christ," in contrast to "remaining in the flesh" (Phil. 1:23-24), how are we to understand him if we reject the dualism of flesh and spirit with which theologians have traditionally worked? We confess that such dualistic language is far from adequate. But is it not better to use inadequate language than language that threatens to lose altogether the meaning of what Scripture intends because it comes from a thought world that has no place for the otherness of the transcendent?

d. Self-Transcendence and Conscience[72]

1) Introduction

Josiah Royce describes a liar as "one who willfully misplaces his onto-logical predicates."[73] To speak of *placing* predicates implies the power of reason; to speak of *willfully* placing them implies the freedom of the will; to speak of willfully *misplacing* them implies the knowledge of right and wrong. Our primary concern at this time is not with the fact that all of us, like the Cretans, are liars (Ti. 1:12); but with the fact that we know we are liars because we are human and therefore can tell the difference between truth and falsehood, right and wrong. We have already determined the course our present discussion will take by what we have said about the knowledge God has given us of himself and the freedom of choice with which he has endowed us as creatures in his image. When God created us, he wrote the work of his law on our hearts (Rom. 2:15), with the result

---

72. The name Bunyan gives to conscience is "Mr. Recorder." He tells us that "before the town [of Mansoul] was taken, Mr. Recorder was a man well read in the laws of his King, and also a man of courage and faithfulness to speak truth at every occasion: and he had a tongue as bravely hung as he had a head filled with judgement" (*Holy War,* chap. 1).

73. "Truth," in *The Great Ideas: A Syntopicon,* Great Books, 2.915.

that we are aware of our freedom as a freedom-in-responsibility. We know that we ought to do God's will and that we must render an account to him when we do not. We are not, then, mere natural objects, but subjects who are responsible for our behavior. Our existence is not only an existence *by* God's word, but *in* it; we exist as human, in distinction from the animals, in that we hear his word as a word that approves our obedience and condemns our disobedience. Our existence is an existence-in-decision, a decision, that is, to do right or wrong, to conform or not to conform to the will of our Maker.

To the objection that such a view actually robs us of our freedom, and therefore of our responsibility, by binding us to a higher will, the Christian answers that to think of human freedom as autonomy is to deny rather than to affirm our responsibility. One cannot be responsible to abstract moral principles of one's own choosing or even to the higher (transcendental) self. Such responsibility to oneself is really not responsibility but irresponsibility. To be responsible is to be related to someone whose right it is to command our obedience and condemn our disobedience. For the Christian, this someone is the Creator, who said to our first parents when he made them in his image, "you shall," and "you shall not" (Gn. 2:16-17; 3:2-3).[74] The endowment of the human spirit whereby we perceive the difference between what God commands and what he condemns is called "conscience."

The meaning of the term "conscience" is admittedly difficult to render exactly. Helmut Thielicke is no doubt right in saying that lack of agreement as to what conscience is is due to the fact that the anthropological framework within which one works determines one's understanding of the term (*Theological Ethics,* trans. John W. Doberstein, ed. William H. Lazareth, 3 vols. [reprint, Grand Rapids: Eerdmans, 1979], 1.298). In our own discussion we have found helpful, among others, Martin Kähler's article, *"Gewissen"* (*Realencyclopädie für protestantische Theologie und Kirche* [Leipzig: J. C. Hinrichs'sche, 1899], 6.647ff.). This article is based on Kähler's great work, *Das Gewissen,* published by J. Fricke in Halle in 1878.

As Kähler notes, evangelical thought, following Calvin, has assumed that conscience presupposes an inner knowledge of God's law. "Conscience" is that added witness to this inner knowledge (*"con"-scientia*) which does not allow us to conceal our sins but pursues us till we are brought to conviction before the divine tribunal (*Inst.,* 3.19.15). In contrast to this evangelical view, Wolf, et al., understood conscience as a judgment of the understanding that depends solely on the training of the faculty of insight. According to Kähler, such an approach anticipates the subsequent development in Protestant Liberalism. In liberal thought, the term "conscience" is focused on moral feelings. Along with this emphasis on feeling there emerges an ever-increasing skepticism concerning the objective validity of the moral law. As a result,

74. See above, pp. 36-44.

the meaning of the term "conscience" becomes quite different from that understood by the Reformers, since it is cut off from any objective religious basis. For example, Rousseau defined conscience as the feeling for the moral and indestructible in human nature; thus he tried to eliminate such traditional terms as "guilt" and "duty" altogether. By contrast, Kähler himself argues that conscience is the point of contact in the soul for that aspect of divine revelation that concerns moral rectitude. As such, it constitutes the evidence that the basis of all morality is finally religious (theological) in nature.

As we seek to make our own theological statement on the meaning of the term "conscience," we shall follow the tradition that goes back to Augustine. In this tradition, conscience is that faculty of the soul which both witnesses to, and judges concerning, the moral quality of our thoughts and acts in God's sight. As Luther would say, conscience is the testimony that something is right; or, as he says at other times, it is the place where God "reckons with us through the law." In the former function, conscience makes us aware of what we ought and ought not to do; in the latter it acquits us when we do what we know we should and condemns us when we do not.

Luther's life affords dramatic illustrations of both these functions of conscience. On the one hand, in Luther's memorable appearance before the Diet of Worms, the emperor pressed him to give a direct answer to the question, Will you or will you not recant what you have written against the church? He replied that he could not and would not do so because "I am conquered by the holy Scriptures I have quoted, and my conscience is bound by the word of God: I cannot and I will not recant anything, since it is unsafe and dangerous to do anything against the conscience." (See Schaff, *History of the Christian Church*, 8 vols. [1910; Grand Rapids: Eerdmans, reprinted 1980-81], 7.305, n. 1, on variations in the original text.) Here we see conscience as Luther's awareness of duty *(Pflichtbewusstsein)*. When he became a party to the bigamy of the Landgrave, Philip of Hesse, on the other hand, we see Luther's conscience at work as the accuser. In fact, Melanchthon, who also had a part in the sordid affair, was so overcome by the accusations of conscience *(Gewissensanklage)* that he was physically ill until Luther prayed for him, urging him to lay hold of the doctrine of justification by faith alone.

2) The Biblical Data

The biblical data on which the doctrine of conscience is based call for comment on several scores. For one, it is somewhat surprising that the word, as such, is not found in the Old Testament. It is evident, however, that in the Old Testament the term "heart" sometimes has the function attributed to "conscience" in the New. When Nabal's churlish spirit provokes David, his wife Abigail placates David's wrath, reminding him that if he does not shed blood, he shall suffer no "offense of the heart"

(מִכְשׁוֹל לֵב). The RSV simply translates, "pangs of conscience" (1 Sam. 25:31).[75] "I bless the LORD who gives me counsel," says the psalmist, adding, "in the night also my heart instructs me" (Ps. 16:7). Not only does the heart instruct one in the right way of the Lord, but it rebukes the transgressor, which is also the function of conscience. After David had numbered the people of Israel, his "heart smote him"; and David said to the Lord, "I have sinned greatly in what I have done" (2 Sam. 24:10). This same usage is found in the New Testament. At Pentecost, those who heard Peter preach were "cut to the heart" (κατενύγησαν τὴν καρδίαν) and said, "Brethren, what shall we do?" (Acts 2:37). When they heeded the apostle's response and repented (2:38), their hearts that condemned them (the accusing conscience) became hearts that no longer condemned them (the acquitting conscience). As John says, "If our hearts do not condemn us, we have confidence before God" (1 Jn. 3:21).

In the New Testament, in contrast to the Old, the word "conscience" itself (συνείδησις) occurs from time to time, especially in the writings of Paul.[76] "I have lived before God," the apostle protests before the Sanhedrin, "in all good conscience up to this day" (Acts 23:1). He admonishes the Christians in Rome to be subject to the civil magistrate "for the sake of conscience" (Rom. 13:5). When Christians so live, they are able to say with the apostle that they have a "clear" conscience, that is, a conscience "void of offense" (ἀπρόσκοπον, Acts 24:16); theirs is a conscience that is "pure" (καθαρός, 1 Tm. 3:9), that is, "good" (ἀγαθός, 1 Tm. 1:5, 19); it testifies that they "have behaved in the world . . . with holiness and godly sincerity" (2 Cor. 1:12).

One of the striking things about the New Testament's appeal to conscience is that so little is said about the *accusing* conscience. The reason would seem to be that while the writers of the New Testament had a clear doctrine of original sin, they had an equally clear doctrine of redeeming grace. They speak as those who have been redeemed, whose consciences no longer accuse them. In the words of Hebrews, their consciences have been purified "from dead works to serve the living God" (Heb. 9:14).

75. See also Job 27:6, where Job protests, "I hold fast my righteousness, . . . my heart [conscience] does not reproach me." Concerning the use of "heart" in Scripture generally, as descriptive of all aspects of the inner life, see above, p. 39.

76. Paul's use of the term reflects that of Philo, whose doctrine of conscience combined Jewish and Hellenistic thought. (See Maurer, *TDNT,* 7.911.) The fact that Jesus never uses the term hardly seems to warrant a questioning of the Pauline usage. Granted the reading in Jn. 8:9 is not authentic, there is ample material reported elsewhere in the Gospels having to do with the function of conscience. Consider, for example, Jesus' account of the tax collector and his prayer (Lk. 18:10-14). "God, be merciful to me a sinner," the tax collector pleaded, as he "beat his breast," language obviously reflecting an accusing conscience.

Noting how little Paul has to say about the conscience that condemns, Christian Maurer observes that this fact

> is connected with the new thing which Paul has to tell with his Gospel of Jesus Christ. The accusing voice of conscience is overcome because the incomparably sharper accuser, the revealed Law by God which does not merely accuse but also slays (R. 7:7ff.), is done away and set aside by the pardoning voice of the God who makes new in Christ.[77]

We shall have more to say about this purifying of the conscience from dead works by the blood of Christ (Heb. 9:14) when we speak of salvation. Only the grace of God in Christ can close the insurmountable gap between "what is" and "what ought to be" *(Sein und Sollen)* in the life of the transgressor so as to give her peace with God. Our concern for the present, however, is our creation in God's image; and our thesis is that though the conscience may be "seared" by sin, it is not "dead as seared flesh" — Phillips's doubtful paraphrase of κεκαυστηριασμένων in 1 Timothy 4:2.[78] Though by no means always reliable, the conscience of the sinner is very much alive, for human sin can never utterly undo the work of the Creator. Just as we could not laugh at the gospel, as did the philosophers on Mars Hill (Acts 17:32), were we not rational; nor choose that wide gate that leads to destruction (Mt. 7:13) had we no powers of self-determination and will; so we could not say (with Milton's Satan), "Evil, be thou my good," did we not retain some awareness of the difference between them. Conscience, then, is essential to the understanding of our humanity. It is indeed the "place" where God reckons with us through his law and so reveals himself as the divine "Thou" in relation to whom each one of us becomes a responsible subject, an "I," that is truly human.

In view of his doctrine of grace, it is a misunderstanding of Paul (and the New Testament as a whole) to suppose that he thought of a "good" conscience in the Enlightenment sense of a last bastion of human rectitude. The conscience is not the unsullied habitus of the soul, the place where the still, small voice of the Divine is heard in a way that is beyond the reach of sin. It is not the moral self that needs only the cultivation afforded by education and social progress to achieve the ethical ideal. Rather, the "clear conscience" of which the New Testament speaks (Heb. 13:18) is the tranquility of mind that comes from the knowledge that our sins are forgiven and that we are reconciled to God in Christ. Paul can call his conscience to witness to the truth of his concern for Israel's salvation because it is a conscience that bears him witness "in the Holy Spirit" (Rom. 9:1).

77. Ibid., p. 917.
78. *The New Testament in Modern English.*

For all the difference between the Enlightenment and the New Testament view of conscience, we cannot, however, escape the impression that Brunner's reaction to the Enlightenment view is an overreaction. "Conscience," he reminds us, "is not the 'Voice of God,' as it used to be described in the theology of the Enlightenment." True. But then he goes on to say, "The sinister thing about conscience is precisely this, that it has nothing to do with God at all, that it attacks man like an alien, dark, hostile power" (*The Divine Imperative,* trans. Olive Wyon [Philadelphia: Westminster, 1947], p. 156). This, in our judgment, is to say too much. Yet we would agree with him that conscience is involved in that feeling, at the center of our sinful existence, that all is not well; that we are who we are, not by fate but by fault. Berkouwer is more cautious. While he expresses a concern that we should not suppose conscience has escaped the effects of sin so as to constitute the basis of an optimistic anthropology, yet there is that about conscience which is inviolable. Although the conscience can be "seared" (1 Tm. 4:2), leading people into all kinds of errors, at the same time it has an aura of holiness which makes us aware that it cannot be violated with impunity. Conscience, therefore, can be "identified with the voice of God in man. This means there is present in every man, even in his alienation from God, a truly transcendent element (*Man: The Image of God,* p. 171).

3) Conclusion

In keeping with our systematic approach, we conclude the discussion of human self-transcendence manifest in conscience with a comment on how an evangelical doctrine of conscience bears on other doctrines yet to be discussed, especially the doctrines of sin, salvation, and the church.

As for *sin,* while it is not the most popular doctrine, it is certainly an essential one so far as the Christian faith is concerned. The doctrine as such is an objective affirmation about the human condition. But our understanding and exposition of the doctrine will by no means be purely objective, for conscience will not let us simply reflect on sin without acknowledging our own sinfulness. It is conscience that makes God's commandment, which is holy, just, and good, the means by which sin works death in us. Thus sin is shown to be what it really is, sin that is sinful beyond measure (Rom. 7:7ff.). In other words, it is because of conscience that sin becomes that "damned spot" that "will not out," that disease which is "beyond the physician's practice."[79]

As for *salvation,* it begins, so far as the individual is concerned, with "repentance toward God and . . . faith in our Lord Jesus Christ" (Acts 20:21). Such repentance is a godly sorrow for sin joined with trust in God's mercy. It enables us to draw near to God with "hearts sprinkled clean from an evil [accusing] conscience and our bodies washed with pure water" (Heb. 10:22). In the same vein, Peter speaks of baptism as that which now

---

79. Shakespeare, *Macbeth,* act 5, scene 1.

saves us, "not the putting away of the filth of the flesh, but the answer of a good conscience toward God" (1 Pt. 3:21 KJV).[80] Thus the whole course of the Christian life may be summed up as serving God with a good conscience (2 Tm. 1:3).

Finally, as for the *church,* the doctrine of the "liberty of conscience" is the key to resolving the vexed question of church-state relationships. The Reformers' doctrine of the liberty of conscience was not concerned primarily with the political order. Rather, it was a protest against the exclusive right claimed by the Roman Catholic Church to determine how God is to be worshiped. Their response to this claim was that "God alone is Lord of the conscience, and has left it free from the doctrines and commandments of men which are in anything contrary to his word, or beside it, in matters of faith and worship."[81] But once the insight was gained that one cannot coerce the conscience in the worship of God, it was given a much broader interpretation by the so-called Radical Reformers — the Anabaptists, Mennonites, and Quakers. "Since God has assumed to himself the power and dominion of the conscience, . . . therefore it is not lawful for any whatsoever, by nature of any authority or principality they bear in the government of this world, to force the conscience of others."[82] This breaking away from the theocratic view of church and state was first achieved in America by Roger Williams, who founded Rhode Island in 1736 with a view to its becoming "a shelter for persons distressed for conscience." Our own ecclesiology will presuppose this "separation of church and state." Consonant with this view, we will defend the thesis that the church is a voluntary society whose right to worship God is an expres-

---

80. Assuming an evangelical approach, we do not understand this passage (1 Pt. 3:21) to refer to baptism as securing the salvation that it signifies, but as signifying, to the one baptized, the salvation that is secured through Christ's resurrection. The exact meaning of the passage is admittedly difficult. Baptism saves us, we are told, because it has to do, not with the cleansing of the flesh, ἀλλὰ συνειδήσεως ἀγαθῆς ἐπερώτημα εἰς θεόν, δι' ἀναστάσεως 'Ιησοῦ Χριστοῦ. This could mean that the efficacy of baptism is evidenced in the earnest appeal on the part of those baptized that God would grant them a good conscience. Or it could mean that the efficacy of baptism is evidenced in the earnest seeking after God, out of a good conscience, by those baptized. We incline to the latter view. Either way, the saving efficacy of baptism is grounded in the resurrection of Jesus Christ; for had our Lord not risen, our rising up out of the waters of baptism (in which we were buried to a sinful past) would signify nothing.

81. Westminster Confession, chap. 20, §2. This ringing affirmation is echoed in the well-known hymn: "Our fathers chained in prisons dark, / Were still in heart and *conscience* free" (Faber).

82. The Confession of the Society of Friends, "The Fourteenth Proposition," published in 1675, only twenty-eight years after the Westminster Confession.

sion of that liberty of conscience which should be guaranteed by the state to all its citizens in matters religious.[83]

Addendum: Conscience and the Moral Absolute

When he was a child, Paul tells us, he spoke as a child, thought as a child, and understood as a child, but when he became a man, he put away childish things (1 Cor. 13:11). Such growth and development is everyone's experience, the mark of our creaturely finitude. Not only the insights of reason and the resolutions of will, but also the perceptions of conscience reflect the history of the individual self. And what is true for the individual is true for the human race as a whole. "The history that gives us our will and thought," observes Adolf Schlatter,

> also influences our conscience. The appearances that are indicative of the development of the individual and of the human race remain, in this respect, parallel. The child has a conscience that is other than that of the adult, the profane person one that is other than that of a Christian. Likewise, in the sequence of human generations, morality moves through a history that rises and falls.[84]

A Christian theological statement about conscience, then, must reckon with the fact that conscience is conditioned by our finitude as creatures. Furthermore, such a statement must also reckon with the fact that conscience is compromised by our sin as rebellious creatures. But if our conscience is both historically conditioned and sinfully compromised, how is it that it confronts us with a moral absolute?

The answer to this question is implicit in what we have already said. So

---

83. The view that God only is Lord of the conscience has, of course, created an ongoing tension in the Christian community. On the one hand, the Christian acknowledges the state as a divine ordinance; the civil magistrate, therefore, is to be obeyed "for the sake of conscience" (Rom. 13:5). Yet Protestants have often revolted against civil magistrates in good conscience. History affords many instances of such conflicts of conscience, of which we shall speak in due course. For insightful comment on the tensions the United States presently faces in church-state relations, see M. W. McConnell, "Why 'Separation' Is Not the Key to Church-State Relations," *Christian Century* 106, no. 2 (Jan. 18, 1989): 43-44. It would be better, in our judgment, to say that separation is not the key to *all* church-state relations.

84. Adolf von Schlatter, *Das christliche Dogma* (Stuttgart: Calwer, 1923), p. 172. Speaking of the difference between the conscience of a Christian and a profane person, what shall we say to the disclosure that the elaborate estate of a Columbian drug lord includes a private chapel with a ten-pew sanctuary dedicated to St. Francis of Assisi? See *Los Angeles Times*, Saturday, Aug. 26, 1989, pt. I, p. 18. One is reminded of the adage that hypocrisy is the homage vice pays to virtue.

far as our creaturely finitude is concerned, it cannot be denied that our perception of right and wrong never rises above that knowledge of the Creator's will given through *general* revelation. Such knowledge varies markedly from age to age and culture to culture. Yet it is never completely relative. Although it is knowledge mediated in and through the relativities of the human situation, it is knowledge of the absolute — the divine will.[85] As for the sinfulness that "sears" our conscience, the resolution of this problem, insofar as a resolution is possible within the discipline of dogmatics, is implicit in what we have said about the remnants *(reliquiae)* of the image.[86] Though radically perverted by sin, the image, we have argued, is retained as the inviolable gift of the Creator that cannot be utterly destroyed by the creature's sin. While ignorance may darken our understanding, the powers of reason are still ours; while inordinate desires may fetter our ability to choose the good, the ability to make responsible choices is still ours. So it is with conscience. Though wounded by sin, conscience is among those remnants of a glory that is ours as human even in the midst of rebellion and alienation from our Maker. Even though we are sinners, conscience enables us to discern God's will, which is the moral absolute that determines for the creature what is right and what is wrong. Though by no means infallible, this discernment is sufficient to make us responsible to our Creator.

Although reason, will, and conscience are closely related, there is something unique about conscience that makes it necessary to qualify the relationship. In other words, the affinity of both reason and will to the conscience is an affinity-in-difference. As for reason, we would hold that it enables us to understand our behavior when we choose to act. Conscience is that added witness *(con-scientia)* which gives this self-understanding its moral quality. This difference between reason and conscience can be seen in the fact that conscience does not blame the thinker whose mind falls into logical error, but it does blame the thinker who ignores or conceals such fallacies once they are perceived. For example, Augustus De Morgan relates how the mathematician Joseph-Louis Lagrange once wrote a memoir on the theory of parallels. While presenting it to the members of the French Academy, he withdrew the manuscript in the middle of the reading with the remark, "I must reflect on it some more."[87] It was the light of reason that enabled Lagrange to perceive the petitio principii in his argument, but it was conscience that told him to stop reading when the light dawned. Such experiences, which are common enough, show

85. See our discussion of general revelation in *God, Creation, and Revelation*, pp. 68-73.

86. See above, pp. 58-59.

87. H. B. Smith, *A First Book of Logic* (New York: F. S. Crofts, 1938), p. 46.

that while conscience acts in conjunction with reason, it yet acts independently, on its own reconnaissance, as it were.

As for the will and conscience, the same is true. The will gives us the freedom of self-determination, but conscience makes us aware that our self-determination is not a freedom to do whatever we please. It is rather a freedom-in-responsibility. While acting in conjunction with the will, at the same time conscience stands over against the will, making its own independent judgments, as it approves or condemns the choices we make. Although each individual's conscience is her own, conscience is not something that arises out of the self in the same way as does the will. It has an objectivity about it that the will does not have, an objectivity grounded in the categorical nature of the divine will of which it makes us aware in the moment of ethical decision. The uniqueness of conscience among the human endowments that evidence the divine image does not mean, however, that conscience is autonomous, as though it were a divine spark transcending our finitude and sin. To press the uniqueness of conscience to such a degree would threaten the unity of the personal self, a unity without which all anthropology is flawed. Yet, when we affirm as Christians that God only is "Lord of the conscience," we do declare conscience to be under God's word and will in a most direct way. It is the faculty above all others that makes us aware of God's will as the moral absolute when we stand at those ethical crossroads encountered throughout life's journey.[88]

As Luther told the emperor at the Diet of Worms, "my conscience is bound by the word of God." He was conquered by the Scriptures he had quoted, he said, because his conscience heard those Scriptures as the voice of God himself. While conscience is not the voice of God in the soul so as to take precedence over Scripture, it is the "place" in the soul where the voice of God is heard as nowhere else. Hence Luther went on to say that he could not recant anything, "since it is unsafe and dangerous to do anything against conscience." In the same land where Luther made this decision to obey the voice of conscience, centuries later (July 20, 1944) Dietrich Bonhoeffer and seven others were executed for their attempt on the life of *der Führer,* Adolf Hitler. On the twentieth anniversary of their death, Martin Niemöller declared that the greatness of these martyrs lay in their obedience to the voice of conscience. "The liberating sacrifice of one's life for others *when conscience demands it* overcomes humanity's guilt."[89]

88. We shall have more to say about the character of moral decision when we seek to frame a doctrine of the Christian life (sanctification).

89. *Christian Century* 81, no. 36 (Sept. 2, 1964): 1092. Italics added.

It may be that this close proximity between the voice of God and the voice of conscience bears on the difficult question posed by Paul's treatment of the conscience of the "weaker" brother or sister in his first letter to Corinth. One like himself, whose conscience is enlightened, eats freely of meat offered to idols, knowing that there is only one true God and that idols are nothing. But, the apostle goes on to observe, not all have attained to this liberating knowledge. Their conscience is weak. Were such encouraged (οἰκοδομηθήσεται, "emboldened," KJV) by the example of the strong to eat when the act would be against their conscience, their conscience would be defiled and they themselves destroyed as moral agents. Were the strong to occasion in this way the fall of the weak, for whom Christ died, they would be sinning against Christ. Therefore, if one who is weak tells a brother or sister who is strong: "This has been offered in sacrifice," the latter, in deference to the conscience of the weak, should not eat. In this way the strong display their love rather than flaunt their knowledge, and so the body of Christ is edified (1 Cor. 8:7-13; 10:25-30).

In this matter Paul does not give himself to theological analysis; his concern, rather, is pastoral. However, what he says in a pastoral way has theological implications. That he should consider an act against conscience, even when it errs, to be a sin, shows that he regarded the claims of conscience as having something of a transcendent character. Conscience epitomizes, as it were, the self as a knowing, acting subject in its accountability to God. When, therefore, one violates one's own conscience by following the heteronomous authority of someone else's conscience, the ethical self is compromised.[90] This, it seems, is the reason Paul felt it better to obey a weak (erroneous) conscience, if it was one's own, than to act on the basis of someone else's enlightened conscience in violation of one's own. And so for him, it would appear, conscience is the place where the soul hears the word of God, even though imperfectly.[91]

90. How often one hears the excuse, "I only did what everyone else was doing," or "I was simply following orders" — excuses that condemn the one who makes them as morally bankrupt.

91. One could wish Paul had encountered some of the cases that occur in today's world. For example, what would he say of the decision of deeply religious parents who, for conscience's sake, reject medical care for their children? As for the resolution of conscientious scruples and doubtful cases, we regard such to be the task of moral rather than systematic theology. We would simply note, in passing, that while we accept the approach which posits the general principles of moral law rather than the approach of situational ethics, we believe the former must be combined with the concreteness of casuistry to prevent ethics from becoming an abstract science. See Schlatter, *Das christliche Dogma*, pp. 572-73, n. 5.

That conscience is somehow related to the moral absolute has been assumed by many literary lights in the past. Dante's vision of Bertrand de Born, carrying his own head by the hair like a lantern, was so appalling that he should not have dared to speak of it, he tells us,

> Did not blameless conscience stead me well —
> That trusty squire that harnesses a man
> In his own virtue like a coat of mail.
> *(Divine Comedy,* I: Hell, canto 28, lines 115-17)

It is especially as the accuser that conscience has been acknowledged to have a trustworthy, if unwelcome, word. As the two hired assassins in Shakespeare's *King Richard III* enter the tower of London to dispatch the duke of Clarence, the first asks the second what he will do if his conscience, now securely in the duke of Gloucester's purse, should fly out when he opens it to reward them. To which the second replies, "I'll not meddle with it: it is a dangerous thing: it makes a man a coward: a man cannot steal, but it accuses him; he cannot swear, but it checks him; he cannot lie with his neighbor's wife, but it detects him" (Shakespeare, *King Richard III,* act 1, scene 4, lines 137-40).

Nonetheless, many have turned the accusation back on the accuser, and rightly so. Conscience is not always a "trusty squire." For one thing, it can be intimidated. As the vicar of Wakefield observes: "Conscience is a coward; and those faults it has not strength enough to prevent, it seldom has justice enough to accuse" (Oliver Goldsmith, *The Vicar of Wakefield,* chap. 13). Not only is conscience cowardly, but it often succumbs to rationalization and indulges the art of sophistry. (See Mark Twain, *Huckleberry Finn* [reprint, Baltimore: Penguin, 1966], pp. 120-21, for the humorous account of Huck's placating his conscience for stealing watermelons and cantelopes with the decision not to steal any crabapples and persimmons. He was happy with the outcome of this decision "because crabapples ain't ever good, and the p'simmons wouldn't be ripe for two or three months yet.") Furthermore, the conscience, even of religious people — *especially* of religious people, it would seem — is given to tendentious scrupulosity. It is forever majoring in minors. At the trial of Jesus some leaders of the Jews, who knowingly accused him falsely, yet scrupled to enter the praetorium lest they be ceremonially defiled and so unable to eat the Passover (Jn. 18:28). And when Judas threw down the thirty pieces of silver, saying, "I have sinned in betraying innocent blood," those same religious leaders answered coldly, "What is that to us?" (Mt. 27:4). Yet their conscientious scruples moved them to deliberate over what they should do with the silver, since it was "blood money" (27:6). Thus we are confronted with the sad truth that original sin compromises the human spirit even in that "place" where we hear the voice of God. One recalls the warning Jesus gave his disciples: "A time is coming when anyone who kills you will think he is offering a service to God" (Jn. 16:2). Yet even in such cases the conscience is not destroyed utterly. Having encountered the risen Lord, the best-known persecutor of the church was conscience-stricken for his sin (Gal. 1:13-14; 1 Tm. 1:15).

As we conclude our discussion of conscience and the moral absolute, it remains only to observe that we must never forget that when we hypostatize conscience, we are speaking of real people, not of an abstract "faculty" from which we can distance ourselves. When we say, for example, that "conscience is a coward," we are, as a matter of fact, acknowledging that *we,* as responsible subjects, are lacking in moral courage. At Jesus' trial, Pilate washed his hands and declared his innocence (Mt. 27:26). This act was not the act of a weak conscience in the abstract but of a morally weak man who did what he did to salve his conscience.

Conscience

A Sermon Preached by Marguerite Shuster
at Knox Presbyterian Church, Pasadena, California,
Lord's Day, April 1, 1990.

As I urged you when I was going to Macedonia, remain at Ephesus that you may charge certain persons not to teach any different doctrine, nor to occupy themselves with myths and endless genealogies which promote speculations rather than the divine training that is in faith; whereas the aim of our charge is love that issues from a pure heart and a good conscience and sincere faith. Certain persons by swerving from these have wandered away into vain discussion, desiring to be teachers of the law, without understanding either what they are saying or the things about which they make assertions. . . .

This charge I commit to you, Timothy, my son, in accordance with the prophetic utterances which pointed to you, that inspired by them you may wage the good warfare, holding faith and a good conscience. By rejecting conscience, certain persons have made shipwreck of their faith, among them Hymenaeus and Alexander, whom I have delivered to Satan that they may learn not to blaspheme.

1 Timothy 1:3-7, 18-20

Conscience, said H. L. Mencken, "is a mother-in-law whose visit never ends."[a] Or, again, conscience is "the inner voice which warns us that

---

a. Quoted in *Parables* 8, no. 5 (July 1988): 5.

someone may be looking."[b] Conscience is described in such sayings as an irritant, something that nags and snoops and picks on us and is generally unreasonable, when all we want to do is live our lives and have a moderately good time, without undue interference. It comes across, in these epigrams, as the sort of nuisance one placates as best one can while trying not to let it hamper too much one's ordinary activities.

Contrast the view of conscience conveyed in ancient Greek mythology, where it is personified as the Furies, those avengers of sin that could not be banished from the earth as long as sin remained.[c] When Orestes killed his mother Clytemnestra to avenge her murdering his father, he came from the scene of the deed with his eyes fixed on something no one else could see. He stammered to his friends:

> "Did she do it or did she not? O you, my friends. I say I killed my mother — yet not without reason — she was vile and she killed my father and God hated her."
>
> His eyes were fixed always on that unseen horror. He screamed, "Look! Look! Women there. Black, all black, and long hair like snakes." They told him eagerly there were no women. "It is only your fancy. Oh, do not fear." "You do not see them?" he cried. "No fancy. I — I see them. My mother has sent them. They crowd around me and their eyes drip blood."[d]

Conscience, like women with long hair, like snakes and eyes weeping blood, pursued him wherever he went, year after year. It was no mere nuisance, no ungrounded fancy, but a terror, giving him no rest.

These pictures, both non-Christian, are certainly different, and one definitely gets the impression that Aeschylus, author of the Orestes plays, saw having a bad conscience as somehow more terrible, more consuming of the whole person, than Mencken did. The strictures of conscience may indeed be regarded differently in different ages, and conscience may be molded differently by different cultures. Nonetheless, conscience is a fundamental human endowment, recognized by ancient Greek playwright and modern American literary critic alike as being in some sense that faculty by which we distinguish right from wrong. People have consciences not because they are Christians but because they are people. Someone *is* looking, always; and the someone is, first of all, that part of ourselves that not only can recognize what we have done, but also passes moral judgment on

b. Mencken, ibid., p. 8.
c. Edith Hamilton, *Mythology* (New York: Mentor, 1942), p. 65.
d. Ibid., p. 246.

it. In English, as in Latin and Greek, the prefix of the term ("con" in English) implies not just *knowing* but knowing *with* — a reflective judgment on one's actions.

Christians, however, believe that this moral faculty is not just an interesting phenomenon but part of God's endowment of all humankind; and they further believe that conscience witnesses not only to the fact that part of oneself is looking, but also to the even more important fact that God is looking. Conscience, though malleable and marked by sin and open to corruption, is not wholly arbitrary, but is an instrument through which the Lord himself confronts us with his will. That is why we see in 1 Timothy the solemn warning that by rejecting conscience, certain persons have made shipwreck of their faith; and the emphasis on the importance of a good conscience (1:5, 19; 3:9).

"The aim of our charge is love that issues from a pure heart and a good conscience and sincere faith." "This charge I commit to you . . . that . . . you may wage the good warfare, holding faith and a good conscience." What does it mean to have a good conscience?

To begin with the negative side, let it be clear that a "good" conscience is not one that never makes a mistake, is never weak or misinformed. You have probably heard that radio ad in which a man responds to the voice that has been advising him on a course of behavior, "Why is it you're always right?" The voice replies, "Because I'm your conscience, friend." That whole sequence is misleading. Conscience is *not* always right (especially as personified in radio ads!). In fallen humankind, there is *no* faculty that is uncompromised by sin, no faculty that is always right — not our emotions, not our reason, not our conscience. A good conscience is not a perfect, infallible conscience.

Further, a good conscience is not one that finds no moral flaws in a person. Precisely because none of us is free from sin as long as we are in this world, the conscience that finds no fault with us must be a seriously deadened one. In his allegory *The Holy War,* in which a great battle is being fought for the town of Mansoul, John Bunyan personifies the conscience as Mr. Recorder. Diabolus, who was besieging the town, did all he could to corrupt Mr. Recorder by drawing him gradually into sin and wickedness, hardening him against any awareness of sin. Diabolus had considerable, but not complete, success: every once in a while Mr. Recorder would throw one of his fits and make the whole town of Mansoul shake.[e] Mr. Recorder was not being a good conscience when he was quiet or when he smoothly excused sin; he was far better when he was throwing a fit, despite his disruptive and possibly foolish appearance.

e. Chapter 1.

No; a good conscience is neither a perfect nor a self-satisfied, quiescent conscience. It is rather, first of all (like a pure heart, which means much the same thing), a conscience made free from an overwhelming burden of guilt by the work of Christ and the renewing power of the Holy Spirit. It is a conscience "cleansed from past sin and wholeheartedly directed to God."[f] And as such, it is a conscience that is not just empty or blameless, but a conscience rightly oriented with regard to both doctrine and life.

What we need to note in this text is both the strong ethical concern of the letter as a whole and the striking connection in these verses, twice over, of conscience and faith. "Faith" here has to do not only with trust in God, as it generally does in Paul's letters, but with orthodoxy, with faithfulness to tradition. And taking it a step further, orthodoxy, right doctrine, must clearly be oriented toward right behavior if it is not to degenerate into mere "speculation" and "vain discussion," such as that promoted by the teachers this letter condemns. As our own Presbyterian Book of Order puts it,

> Truth is in order to goodness; and the great touchstone of truth, its tendency to promote holiness. . . . We are persuaded that there is an inseparable connection between faith and practice, truth and duty. Otherwise, it would be of no consequence either to discover truth or to embrace it.[g]

Doctrine and behavior must not be torn apart. And conscience in some sense is the glue keeping them together. It stands between the two, so to speak, looking in both directions: a good conscience is informed by right doctrine, which it recognizes as carrying an "ought" by which behavior should be governed; and when one fails to act rightly, a good conscience not only delivers the "guilty" verdict, but also receives pardon through a truly held faith. "The aim of our charge is love that issues from a pure heart and a good conscience and sincere faith."

If having a good conscience is, then, terribly important, rejecting conscience is a sure recipe for disaster. It compromises the integrity of the person in a fundamental way. No doubt that is why our Book of Order, in the same context, also quotes the Westminster Confession to the effect that "God alone is Lord of the conscience."[h] No one but an individual and God himself knows what the Lord might be speaking in and through a person's conscience; and to act as if either one's own impulses or the convictions

---

f. Rudolf Meyer and Friedrich Hauck, *TDNT,* 3.425. See also Christian Maurer, *TDNT,* 7.899-919.

g. G-1.0304.

h. G-1.0301.

or demands of others should take precedence is to make a deadly error. Martin Luther had a keen sense of this in his famous appearance before the Diet of Worms. The emperor insisted that he give a direct answer to the question as to whether he would recant what he had written against the church. Luther replied, "I am conquered by the Holy Scriptures quoted by me, and my conscience is bound in the word of God: I cannot and will not recant any thing, since it is unsafe and dangerous to do any thing against the conscience."[i]

"It is unsafe and dangerous to do anything against the conscience," said Luther. "By rejecting conscience, certain persons have made ship-wreck of their faith," says my text. The word for "rejecting" is a strong one, suggesting deliberate spurning and not mere carelessness; so one need not feel as if all is lost if one stumbles in this regard. Nonetheless, it remains true on the negative as on the positive side that belief and practice are closely related: what we do rests on what we believe and, conversely, what we believe often follows what we do.

Take the possibility of rejecting the demands of conscience on the theoretical level, taking conscience as something less than that place where, however imperfectly and faintly, we hear the Lord's voice regarding right and wrong. Perhaps we label those twinges as mere neurotic guilt, to which we ought not to listen, and we go off and do as we please. Or perhaps, if we are materialists, we take conscience as a somewhat aberrant and out-moded function of the brain, having no transcendent purpose or meaning. In one of her mystery novels, Dorothy Sayers creates a character, a neurosurgeon, who believes that "the knowledge of good and evil is . . . attendant upon a certain condition of the brain-cells, which is removable."[j] Gentleman detective Lord Peter Wimsey looks further in one of the man's scholarly books and reads,

> "Conscience in man may, in fact, be compared to the sting of a hive-bee, which, so far from conducing to the welfare of its possessor, cannot function, even in a single instance, without occasioning its death. The survival-value in each case is thus purely social; and if humanity ever passes from its present phase of social development into that of a higher individualism, . . . we may suppose that this interesting mental phenomenon may gradually cease to appear; just as the nerves and muscles which once controlled the movement of our ears and scalps have, in all save a few backward individuals, become atrophied and of interest only to the physiologist."

i. Schaff, *History,* 7.304-5.
j. *Whose Body?* (New York: Harper & Row, 1923), p. 111.

"By Jove!" thought Lord Peter, idly, "that's an ideal doctrine for
the criminal. A man who believed that would never — "[k]

And at that the mystery was solved: a man who believed that would never
hesitate, on the account of those hiccups of brain material that we call
pangs of conscience, to do murder or anything else he took a notion to do.
Rejecting conscience, he indeed made shipwreck, the sort of shipwreck
that would utterly destroy any remnants of faith he might have had.

For most of us, though, the danger is greater that we will reject the
demands of conscience not on the theoretical but on the practical level —
that for a thousand little reasons, in response to a thousand little impulses,
in the company of a friend or two or three who see things differently than
we do, we will do something our own conscience plainly tells us is not
right. And, whatever we may have been told, nothing particularly out of
the ordinary happens. No lightning strikes. God does not reach down and
zap us. So we begin to wonder if it was so wrong after all. We do it again
in company; soon we do it alone; soon we can hardly remember why once
we thought it was wrong. If someone gives us a doctrinal reminder of why,
we will see cause to revise the doctrine to fit the behavior that has become
simply normal. We, too, will make shipwreck of our faith — if not with a
resonating crash against a mighty rock, then by losing board after board
to the termites that work no less surely for working in silence. Wrong
behavior compromises faith as surely as wrong faith undoes behavior.

Honor your conscience. It is not perfect. It is not infallible. Sometimes
it will nag you as seemingly unfairly as that stereotypical mother-in-law.
Sometimes it will pursue you relentlessly with the terrors of the Furies.
Nonetheless, do not simply reject it, lest you make shipwreck of your faith.
It will not become a good conscience, one with which you are truly at
peace, by being stifled. It will become a *good* conscience only as it is both
cleansed and renewed by Christ, and rightly directed with regard to both
doctrine and life. After all, God *is* watching, as we at least from time to
time suspect. So it is with the knowledge of our need for a good conscience
before him in mind that we may pray with Kierkegaard,

> Father in Heaven, when the thought of Thee wakes in our hearts,
> let it not awaken like a frightened bird that flies about in dismay,
> but like a child waking from its sleep with a heavenly smile.[1]

Amen.

k. Ibid.
l. Quoted in John Baillie, *Diary of Readings,* Day 21.

3. THE IMAGE AND THE SENSE OF THE BEAUTIFUL

To be human is to know that "a thing of beauty is a joy forever."[92] An awareness of pleasure in the presence of the beautiful comes to us with an immediacy and unmistakable power that is like our awareness of the right in contrast to the wrong. For the theologian, this awareness of the beautiful is further evidence of our self-transcendence as human. But the theologian cannot ground this awareness in the work and word of the Creator directly, as she does the awareness of right and wrong. Scripture says nothing of God's having written the law of the beautiful in our hearts, and it is difficult to establish the thesis that our sense of the beautiful confronts us with the either/or of a categorical imperative. Furthermore, our judgments about what is and what is not beautiful vary at least as much as our judgments about what is right and what is wrong. This fact has made it comparatively easy for relativists to restrict the beautiful to the eye of the beholder and to argue that something is beautiful only because we think that it is. Thus the world we experience as "rich with color and sound, redolent with fragrance, filled with gladness, love and beauty . . . , is crowded into minute corners of the brains of scattered organic beings."[93] The real world, which is the objective, quantitative world of physical reality, is cold, color- less, and silent.

This tendency to relativism in aesthetics is given a fillip not only by the various notions of beauty found in differing cultures, but also by the conflicting judgments made by the connoisseurs of art and literature even within western European culture. Time seems to be the only ultimate judge of true artistic achievement, and it has cruelly revised the early verdicts of many a critic. But our frequent lack of initial agreement on what is beautiful does not entail the conclusion that the distinction between the beautiful and the ugly is only a subjective one with no objective basis in the real world. That such a conclusion is untenable can be seen from the fact that there is a material agreement across cultures on what is beautiful, even though it often takes time and effort to reach this consensus. (With satisfaction in his voice, a black African student followed our class lecture one day with an account of how, in his country, "they" had finally gotten "our" organ out of the church. Such a struggle does, indeed, remind one of how varied, at particular times and in specific cases, our sense of the beautiful can be. But it does not mean that organ music is an ugly sound to African ears. It rather means that Western missionaries have often been slow to appreciate the beautiful found in the rhythm of the drum and the movement of the dance when black Africans gather for worship.)

---

92. Keats, *Endymion*, bk. 1, line 1.
93. E. A. Burtt, *The Metaphysical Foundations of Modern Physical Science*, p. 236, as cited by John Baillie, *The Sense of the Presence of God* (New York: Scribner's, 1962), p. 49, n. 1.

Not only is the relativist left with a cold and silent world, but it is a world without truth and goodness as well.

> Beginning in the sphere of beauty, subjectivism or relativism spreads first to judgments of good and evil, and then to statements about truth, never in the opposite direction. It becomes complete when, as so frequently happens in our own time, what is good or true is held to be just as much a matter of private taste or customary opinion as what is beautiful.[94]

The Christian rejection of relativism in general obviously entails its rejection in this instance also. For the Christian, beauty is not ultimately in the eye of the beholder, but in the mind of God. To the degree that it is in the beholder's eye, it is there because behind that eye there is a soul made in God's likeness. The Bible, therefore, assumes rather than argues that beauty is part of our lives as created in God's image. And by sanctified intuition Christians sing with Cecil Alexander her children's hymn,

> All things bright and beautiful,
> All creatures great and small,
> All things wise and wonderful,
> The Lord God made them all.[95]

Although we may be persuaded that we can never say what beauty is, that it is felt rather than explained (Santayana), there can be little doubt that it has something to do with reason. Michael Polanyi observes that "it is on account of its intellectual beauty . . . that the mathematician feels compelled to accept mathematics as true" (*Personal Knowledge* [New York: Harper & Row, 1962], p. 189). Nature, we are told, abhors a vacuum; by contrast, it seems to love shapes and relations that can be expressed mathematically and that the mind experiences as beautiful. The senses, as Thomas observes, plainly "delight in things duly proportioned." Spirals of pleasing symmetry occur in plants and animals. Hexagonal snow crystals group themselves into snowflakes so intricate that no geometrician can assign them names. (See the volume on *Mathematics* in the Life Science Library Series.) Art, in this respect, reflects nature. Pythagoras discovered the underlying mathematics of the musical scale centuries before Christ,

94. *The Great Ideas: A Syntopicon,* Great Books, 1.113.
95. See below, in our treatment of the dominion of humankind, pp. 457-61. Yet further discussion of the place of beauty in the Christian vision — the adorning of the temple and the priestly vestments in the Old Testament, the building of Christian cathedrals, the development of church music — must await our discussion of the doctrine of the church. Such varied manifestations of beauty give expression to the essential beauty of the church as the community of those who herald the gospel: "How beautiful upon the mountains are the feet of him who brings good tidings, who publishes peace, who brings good tidings of good, who publishes salvation" (Is. 52:7; Rom. 10:15).

and painters in fifteenth-century Florence worked as mathematicians to codify the laws of perspective by which they created solid reality on a flat canvas. (See the *Metropolitan Seminars in Art* [New York: Metropolitan Museum of Art, 1959], Portfolio C.) In architecture, the Golden Ratio is exemplified most notably in the Golden Rectangle, a visually satisfying geometric form that occurs so frequently it can hardly be a coincidence. (The Parthenon in Athens incorporates many geometric balances, including the Golden Rectangle, though its builders could not have been consciously aware of this fact.) The rhythms of poetry and prose are metrical in nature, like those of music, though they show such freedom and pliancy, especially in prose, as to defy all mathematical rules. "Each phrase of each sentence, like an air or a recitative in music, should be so artfully compounded out of long and short, out of accented and unaccented, as to gratify the sensual ear. And of this the ear is the sole judge. It is impossible to lay down laws" (Robert Louis Stevenson, as cited by John Franklin Genung, *The Working Principles of Rhetoric* [Boston: Ginn, 1900], p. 202).

Beauty is related not only to the truth that reason apprehends, but also to the good that conscience approves. This can be seen in the fact that subjectifying the beautiful relativizes the good, while objectifying it absolutizes the good. This is not to equate moral decision with aesthetic pleasure, a fatal mistake against which Kierkegaard warns us. (For a summary of Kierkegaard's views on aesthetics see Jolwet Regis, *Introduction à Kierkegaard* [Paris: Éditions de Fontenelle, 1946].) But it is to say that the God whose will is the norm of the creature's good is the God who "has made everything beautiful in its time; also he has put eternity into [our] mind" (Eccl. 3:11). Hence, as in doing the good, so also in perceiving the beautiful, we enjoy God, who has made us for himself.

To be sure, our *perception* of the beautiful does involve subjectivity, for it is never apart from our decision and choice as individual selves. Indeed, it is the subjectivity of the will, as arising within the self, that explains why all efforts to understand the beautiful in terms of personal taste and preference end up in a relativism in which the human subject becomes the measure of all things. In distinction from our *perception* (awareness) of beauty, however, beauty *itself* is that quality which the Creator has given to the world he has made. We do not make something beautiful by choosing it any more than we make something true by understanding it or something good by doing it. In other words, it is God's word and wisdom, not our decision and choice, that makes something beautiful.

In conclusion, one should note that the presence of God's grace in our life enables us to see not only the wisdom of God in that which appears foolish to the world, but also the beauty of God in that which appears unlovely to the world. In this experience of redeeming grace, we come to realize that there is a beauty in the mind of God that cannot be found in the city of Athens. We read of the Messiah that "he had no form or comeliness that we should look at him, and no beauty that we should desire him"; he is "as one from whom [people] hide their faces" (Is. 53:2-3). Yet, when God takes our hands from our faces and we look into the face of the Savior, no longer do we see him as the one who is to be despised and rejected; rather he becomes for us the

> Beautiful Saviour, King of Creation,
> Son of God and Son of Man!

(trans. Seiss)[96]

---

96. An old Welsh carol summons "all poor folk and humble / all lame ones who stumble" to haste to the "lowly poor manger" where Jesus was laid. The carol goes on to observe that though wise men "laid rich gifts around him,"

> Yet oxen they gave him their hay:
> And Jesus in beauty
> Accepted their duty;
> Contented in manger he lay.

Noting the surprising juxtaposition of beauty and oppression in this carol, Robert McAfee Brown observes, *"Beauty and the oppressed come together in the Jesus story"* (*Creative Dislocation: The Movement of Grace* [Nashville: Abingdon, 1980], pp. 140-41).

III. Human Dignity and Racial Prejudice

A. INTRODUCTION

We have propounded the thesis that to be human is to bear the stamp of Godlikeness. Such a view obviously implies that a unique dignity belongs to everyone with a human face. When in wonder the psalmist asks, "What are human beings that you are mindful of them?" he goes on to observe, "yet you have made them a little lower than God, and crowned them with glory and honor" (Ps. 8:4-5 NRSV). The psalmist's use of the term "honor" (כָּבוֹד), which, in the Old Testament view of things, belongs preeminently to God, points to the dignity of our humanity in a striking way.[1] There is a *grandeur* (Pascal) that God has bestowed on all who bear his likeness.[2]

In the Christian view of things, to be sure, human dignity does not entail moral goodness. Our eminence as human does not alter the fact that we "all have sinned and fall short of the glory of God" (Rom. 3:23). Yet our failure to attain the moral ideal is not the loss of our dignity as human. In reacting to the liberal teaching of the "infinite value of the human soul" (Harnack), some theologians have, unfortunately, defended the biblical doctrine of original sin in such a way that our unworthiness as sinners implies our worthlessness as creatures. Such confusion can have serious theological repercussions. If we are not careful, we end up speaking of the sinner, who is unworthy before God, in a way that is unworthy of the God who made us in his image in the first place. We need to remember what

---

1. Von Rad observes that the "honor" which is ours as human is the mysterious point where the identity between God and humankind becomes visible ("εἰκών," *TDNT*, 2.391).

2. *Grandeur,* that is, "eminence," "magnificence," "stateliness," "sublimity," "majesty," "augustness." Pascal was, perhaps, the first to speak of "la grandeur et misère de l'âme."

we are told in Genesis 9:6: if we shed our neighbor's blood, we are guilty because we have slain one who was made in the image of God. Commenting on this passage, Calvin observes that in it God declares

> that he is not thus solicitous respecting human life rashly, and for no purpose. Men are indeed unworthy of God's care, if respect be had only to themselves; but since they bear the image of God engraven on them, he deems himself violated in their person. Thus, although they have nothing of their own by which they obtain the favour of God, he looks upon his own gifts in them, and is thereby excited to love and to care for them. This doctrine is, however, to be carefully observed, that no one can be injurious to his brother without wounding God himself. Were this doctrine deeply fixed in our minds, we should be much more reluctant than we are to inflict injuries.[3]

Calvin goes on to say that should one object that the image has been obliterated by sin, the answer must be made that a remnant of it remains so that humankind, even as sinful, is possessed of "no small dignity." Such a statement obviously grounds the doctrine of human dignity not in our moral worthiness but in the gift of God, who gives us our worth by making us in his image. When, therefore, we impugn the dignity of our neighbor, we offer an affront to our Creator, whose work we call in question and threaten to destroy.

At this juncture the sinful, sordid history of "man's inhumanity to man" opens up before us and demands comment. Such comment would be less threatening were it made in response to abuses in remote and unfamiliar lands. We could mourn (self-righteously) the pathetic lives of India's outcasts, whose very touch defiles the Brahmans. Or, were we to use an illustration from Christian lands, we could deplore the wretched lot of the German peasants who were "stabbed, killed, and strangled" at Luther's behest by a nobility that lived in a less genteel age. Or again, were we to move closer to the present, we could accuse apartheid in South Africa, where the human dignity of millions of blacks was traduced daily by the systemic violence of an unjust social structure, a structure allegedly based on Scripture.[4] But when, in the name of a Christian anthropology,

---

3. Calvin, *Commentary on the First Book of Moses Called Genesis,* trans. John King (reprint, Grand Rapids: Eerdmans, 1948), 295-96.

4. South African racists are not the only ones who have appealed to the Bible. "My friends, I am going to bring you today one of the most important and timely messages I have ever brought. . . . Now, we folks at Bob Jones University believe that whatever the Bible says is so. . . . When the Bible speaks clearly about any subject, that settles it. . . . The Bible makes some things plain. . . . I am going to show you that the Bible is perfectly clear on

American theologians protest the inhumanity that violates a neighbor's dignity, they need not search for illustrations in faraway times and places. They live in a country that was violently taken from Native Americans; and they enjoy an affluence achieved not only by their own work, but also by the grueling labor of countless slaves brought in chains from black Africa. In the ensuing discussion, it is the legacy of this institution of chattel slavery, a legacy of bigotry and racial prejudice on the part of white Americans against African Americans, that we shall cite to show how the denial of one's dignity as human threatens to destroy one's humanity as the creature in God's image.

Our decision to do a little theology that comes from the United States rather than Germany, by making the racial prejudice of white Americans against black Americans the principal paradigm for the ensuing discussion, is dictated not only by our desire to bring theology down to earth and make it "relevant," but also by the enormity of the wrong done by white people against black people in this, "the land of the free and home of the brave." The story of the Indian peoples is mournful, indeed, and American students of theology would do well to read Dee Brown's *Bury My Heart at Wounded Knee* (New York: Holt, Rinehart & Winston, 1971); and especially Richard Drinnon's *Facing West: The Metaphysics of Indian Hating and Empire Building* (Minneapolis: University of Minnesota Press, 1980). But the story of how white Americans have related to black Americans is certainly a tragedy whose enormity is without parallel in the history of our nation.

Not that we would suggest that the heinousness of moral evil is determined quantitatively. But just to think — while captives waiting deportation, or while being brought across the Atlantic, millions of black Africans died even before they arrived in America. The number who were fed to the sharks exceeds by many times the estimated number of Native Americans (1,000,000 plus) living in the continental United States when the Europeans arrived. It even exceeds the number of the Jewish victims (6,000,000 plus) of the Holocaust. When the slavers promised the delivery of 400, they packed 800 into their ships like sardines in a can, knowing from experience that half would die before they were ever placed on the auction block. (Toni Morrison's novel *Beloved* [New York: Knopf, 1987] bears the dedication: "To Sixty Million and More," a figure that reflects an educated guess based on her research here and abroad concerning

---

races — just as clear as it can be. . . . If you are against segregation and against racial separation, then you are against God Almighty. . . . God is the author of segregation . . . racially, we have separation in the Bible. Let's get that clear. . . . Now, I am appealing to you colored people and to you white people. Let's use our heads. Let's be intelligent. Let's not try to kick the Bible off the center table where it belongs" (Bob Jones Sr., *Is Segregation Scriptural?* [1960], as quoted by John Zens, *Searching Together* 16, no. 2 (summer 1987): 1. For a more sophisticated form of the same argument, "domesticated by the Christian faith," see G. T. Gillespie, "A Christian View of Segregation," an address before the Mississippi Synod of the Presbyterian Church, Nov. 4, 1954. Hundreds of thousands of reprints have been distributed by the White Citizens Council, according to George D. Kelsey, *Racism and the Christian Understanding of Man* (New York: Scribner's, 1965), pp. 107-8.

those who did not survive the voyage into bondage.) For a poetic depiction of the horrors of the Atlantic crossing, see Robert Hayden's "Middle Passage," with its haunting line: "Jesus, Savior, Pilot Me," in Arnold Adoff, ed., *I Am the Darker Brother* (New York: Collier, 1970), pp. 34-35. For a literal depiction, see Gustavus Varra's account in Milton Meltzer, ed., *In Their Own Words: A History of the American Negro* (New York: Thomas Crowell, 1964), pp. 4-8. Born in Benin in 1745, Gustavus, at age eleven, was kidnapped and sold into slavery. Never having seen the ocean before, much less the slave dealers and their ships, he later describes from memory what the voyage was like. It is simply incredible.

Of those who survived the voyage, many died in slavery or lived a life worse than death under the whip of the overseer. Even when the conscience of the nation was stirred and the chains of slavery broken by the Civil War, black Americans escaped from the slaveholder's lash only to be threatened by the lyncher's rope and, in more recent times, the guns of the police. (For some grim, gruesome, and ghastly reading, see the NAACP study, *Thirty Years of Lynching in the United States* [Westport, Conn.: Greenwood, 1919].) And if at present the sheer barbarity of former times is ameliorated and the offense of Jim Crow segregation outlawed, nonetheless, white American society is still a society flawed by racist attitudes and practices that are more pronounced against blacks than any other group. What white Americans have achieved, black Americans have achieved, in spite of their handicaps. They have patented inventions, from the telegraph to the traffic light; received all the military decorations for valor ever pinned on a uniform; pioneered in science; won Nobel and Pulitzer prizes; and commanded the highest salaries in sports and entertainment. But, to use the words of the preamble of the United Nations' *Universal Declaration of Human Rights,* the "recognition of the inherent dignity and of the equal and inalienable rights of all members of the human family, [which] is the foundation of freedom, justice and peace in the world," has been systematically denied black citizens in American society from the days of slavery down to the present.

Racial prejudice, of course, is a many-headed hydra. Gunner Myrdal's *An American Dilemma* (New York: Pantheon, 1975) illumines its socioeconomic mien; and Gordon Allport's *The Nature of Prejudice* (Reading, Mass.: Addison-Wesley, 1954), its psychological mien. But the *soul* of racial prejudice is not social, economic, or psychological, but *theological* in nature. Hence it is from the standpoint of theological anthropology that we approach the subject and offer our strictures.

B. RACISM: ITS ESSENCE AND ITS EFFECTS

Our being as human, we have argued, is a being-in-encounter, encounter with the divine Thou who is our Maker and the human thou who is our neighbor. Given such a view of our humanity, it is not difficult to perceive the problem with racism. Racism is an encounter in which the human other is defamed and denigrated. Belonging to a different ethnic group, the racist treats the other not as a "thou" but as an "it," not as a person but as an object. Thus the encounter with one's neighbor leads to alienation rather than fellowship and so destroys the humanity it was meant to fulfill.

> Racism is human alienation purely and simply; it is the prototype of all human alienation. It is the one form of human conflict that divides human beings as human beings. That which the racist glorifies in himself is his being. And that which he scorns and rejects in members of out-races is precisely their human being. Although the racist line of demarcation and hostility inevitably finds expression through the institutions of society, it is not primarily a cultural, political, or economic boundary. Rather it is a boundary of estrangement in the order of human being as such.[5]

In the United States, to be specific, racism assumes the superiority of the self as a member of the white race over the neighbor who is a member of the black race. The estrangement that such an assumption creates is not always apparent to white people because it is manifest in subtle and insidious ways. The subtlety of racist alienation can be seen, for example, in the tendency of white people to relate to black people, not as individual selves but as an amorphous group — "blacks" — and to ask what "they" want.

Speaking of American democratic values as they bear on freedom, equality, and the dignity of the individual, Kelsey (*Racism,* pp. 140-41) observes that in racist thought such values undergo a transformation so far as blacks are concerned. This transformation takes the form of "the substitution of the mass for the individual. In the racist consciousness, no Negro is ever a distinct person; rather all Negroes are an instance of a homogenized mass. Thus all the individualistic conceptions of democracy — rights, property, self-realization, the pursuit of happiness — are applied to Negroes collectively." As a result, the principle of individualism proclaimed on the mountaintops and fanatically defended when applied to whites is smothered beneath endless debates about "Negro rights." In this way, the rights that belong to white citizens as individuals are taken from black citizens by assigning them to a collectivity.

Such a collective approach ignores the essential truth that we all have our humanity as *individuals* in community. The univocal element in the analogy between God's being and my being as human, we have argued, is just my power of self-determination, my freedom to be who I am as an individual self. When, therefore, white Americans deny to one who is black her right as an *individual* to be who she is, they are guilty of an affront to her humanity.

5. Kelsey, *Racism,* p. 23. We are indebted to Kelsey's penetrating analysis for our own understanding of the theological dimensions of racism as set forth in this section.

Driven to near madness on the farm of the "slave-breaker" Covey, Frederick Douglass would stand "in the deep silence of a summer Sabbath" (his only day of respite) on the shores of the Chesapeake Bay. Seeing the ships come and go, he would address to them this piteous apostrophe:

> You are loosed from your moorings and free. I am fast in my chains and am a slave! You move merrily before the gentle gale, and I sadly before the bloody whip. You are freedom's swift-winged angels that fly around the world; I am confined in bonds of iron. O, that I were free! . . . O, why was I born a man of whom to make a brute! The glad ship is gone — she hides in the dim distance — I am left in the hell of unending slavery. O, God, save me! God deliver me! Let me be free![6]

It is the power of self-transcendence, that is, the freedom to determine our lives in a responsible I-thou relationship with God and neighbor, which makes the individual self the focal point of that dignity and value belonging to all that is human. That is why a black person whose rights are denied experiences that denial as an unbearable indignity to the self. Anyone who has read what black Americans have written knows that the literature is full of moving and powerful protests against these personal indignities. The following incident is given by way of illustration.[7]

INCIDENT

From early childhood, Sammy Davis Jr. traveled with his father and uncle, Will Martin, in show business. He never spent a day in school. Sheltered from the realities of racial prejudice by their studied efforts, he joined the newly "integrated" army shortly after Pearl Harbor. The whistle blew and without looking back Sammy walked down the platform and boarded the troop train that took him to a military training center in Cheyenne, Wyoming. Reporting to the corporal outside the barracks to which he had been assigned, he and another black, Edward Robbins, were told to sit on the steps while the whites were checked off the list and sent inside. When the corporal himself went inside, an argument ensued that Davis could plainly hear. "It was impossible," he says,

6. Frederick Douglass, *Life and Times of Frederick Douglass* (reprint, New York: Macmillan, 1962), p. 125.

7. Although we ordinarily speak in generalities, we shall from time to time give specific illustrations of the evils of racism drawn from various sources. We call these illustrations "incidents," borrowing the title of Countee Cullen's poem, "Incident," which describes his ride in Baltimore one day when he was "eight and very small," but not too small to suffer.

to believe they were talking about me. "Yeah, but I still ain't sleepin' nexta no nigger." "What the hell's the army need 'em for? They'll steal ya blind while ya asleep and there ain't one of 'em has any guts. The're all yeller bellies. . . ." "Awright, knock it off. I don't want 'em any more than you do but we're stuck with 'em. That's orders. . . ." There was the sound of iron beds sliding across the wooden floor. The corporal beckoned from the doorway. "Okay, c'mon in and I'll assign you your bunks. Let's go," he snapped, "on the double." We picked up our gear and followed him through the door. I felt like a disease he was bringing in.

When Edward later accepted the task of shining the brand new boots of the white soldiers, Sammy was revolted with disgust until Edward looked up at him. "For a split second he opened up to me and I saw the humiliation he was enduring because his fear of trouble was stronger than his need for dignity." After several weeks had passed, having endured constant harassment, Davis was finally goaded into action when a bottle of warm urine was poured over him. He fought till knocked unconscious by his tormentor, Jennings. "Still," he said to himself after it was over,

as much as I hurt, as awful as it had been, the worst pain wasn't so bad that I wouldn't do it again for the *dignity* I got from hitting back.

Jennings had beaten me unconscious and hurt me more than I'd hurt him, but I had won. He was saying, "God made me better than you," but he lost the argument the minute he had to use his fists to prove it. All he'd proven is that he was physically stronger than me, but that's not what we were fighting over.

I'd never been so tired in my life, but I couldn't sleep. I hated myself for those weeks of sneaking around trying to avoid trouble. I'd been insane to imagine there was anything I could do to make a Jennings like me. I hadn't begun to understand the scope of their hatred. I was haunted by that voice yelling, "Y'can't hurt 'im 'cept below the forehead." My God, if they can believe that then they don't even know who I am. The difference they see is so much more than color. I'm a whole other brand of being to them. (Sammy Davis Jr. and Jane and Burt Boyar, *Yes, I Can: The Story of Sammy Davis, Jr.* [New York: Pocket Books, 1966], pp. 46-58.)

The irrationality of the white racist assumption that blacks are "a whole other brand of being" is reflected in the Red Cross practice of throwing away blood donated by blacks in Wilmington, Delaware, during World War II. The bigoted notion that "one drop of Negro blood makes a Negro" not only reflects a scurrilous view of black people, but also reminds one of a poignant tragedy. Charles Richard Drew was the black surgeon whose brilliant scientific research made blood transfusions possible. Reviewing his numerous honors and achievements when he was given an honorary degree by Amherst College, the president cited him with the words: "Your genius and your devotion have saved the lives of tens of thousands." On April 1, 1950, Drew was injured in an auto accident near Burlington, North Carolina. Although he was bleeding profusely, he was turned away from the nearest "white" hospital. By the time he was admitted to an accepting hospital, he had bled to death.

The social structure that most obviously secures and perpetuates those racial indignities that degrade the lives of its victims is segregation. Segregation, one should note, is not just separation, but *enforced* separation. Life affords many instances of *voluntary* separation. To learn, one goes to a school, while those who make shoes go to work in a factory. Those who wish to witness a sports event gather in a stadium, while those who would worship God assemble in a church. Such voluntary separation enables one to pursue a chosen activity; it is not enforced for the purpose of serving the social separation of persons as such. By contrast, segregation is a form of enforced separation that is

> born of hatred, fear, pride, and contempt. It knows nothing of love and does not aim at the general well-being; it is inspired by the spirit of pride and hostility, generated by the racist faith. Segregation is anticommunity. It is the structured will to despise and reduce the life of the other. The appointed place of the other is *below,* and the functions of the other are the servilities of society.[8]

Although de jure segregation has been struck down, de facto segregation is endemic to contemporary American society. Its purpose is to keep black people in what white people have defined as "their place." When one reads the sources with a little discernment, one perceives that the segregated "place" that whites assign to blacks is not so much a *space* as a *relation;* and that relation is one which rests on the assumption that whites are superior to blacks as human beings.

We do not mean to deny that the question of space in the most literal sense is a real part of the evil of racial segregation. In South Africa, enforced removal of whole communities of blacks and their relocation in the Bantustans was official policy from the 1950s until remaining apartheid laws were finally repealed in 1991. Exact figures are not available, but the numbers of those affected are certainly in the millions. Now that de jure segregation has been outlawed in America, the very least white people can do is support every effort black citizens make to overcome the forced segregation of their race by striving for a society in which there are integrated schools, open housing, and equal job opportunities. As these goals are realized, blacks will be able to share the same *space* with whites and thus enjoy at least some measure of that freedom and self-determination which belongs to them as human. At the same time, one must recognize that when a Rosa Parks is ordered to the back of the bus in Montgomery, Alabama, more is involved than her right to occupy the space that prejudice has reserved for whites. The order that she should move to a different space was simply the symbol of a deeper spiritual evil to which we must now give our attention.

8. Kelsey, *Racism,* p. 98.

When we say that racial segregation is not so much a matter of space as of relation, we have in mind the fact that in the South where spatial segregation (Jim Crow) has been traditionally enforced, white people have often had closer contacts with blacks than with other whites, except for members of their own families. As Kelsey has observed, black people have served whites as cooks, waiters, maids, practical nurses, barbers, chauffeurs, butlers, confidants, and even advisers, often living under the same roof. So long as they are functioning in a servant role to white people, they have been able to enter any segregated place as a matter of course.

Thus we see that "place" in the physical sense is not the issue; such literal segregation is only the symbol of a deeper issue. It is this deeper issue that racists unwittingly acknowledge when they insist that they have no problem with blacks "who know their place." What they mean is that they have no problem with blacks who accept the place of inferiority and submission whites have traditionally assigned them.

> The Negro is required by the white man to "keep his place." But the Negro's place is not really a place but rather a manner and a mood; his "place" is spiritual rather than spatial. If his mood and manner are right, if his mood and manner reveal in him a genuine spirit of subjection, subordination, and dependency, then his place is almost anywhere. In such settings the physical nearness of the Negro is not abhorrent to the white man; all doors are open to him if he "knows his place." What is intolerable to the white man is the slightest suggestion on the part of the Negro that the Negro questions the fundamental and underlying assumption of his inferiority.[9]

INCIDENT

Malcolm Little was one of the three highest scoring students in his school at Mason, near Lansing, Michigan. Although his family was destroyed in his childhood by Klan activity, he continued down life's road with considerable promise until something happened that was to become the first major turning point in his life.

> Somehow I happened to be alone in the classroom with Mr. Ostrowski, my English teacher. He was a tall, rather reddish white man and he had a thick mustache. I had gotten some of my best marks under him, and he had always

9. Kyle Haselden, *The Racial Problem in Christian Perspective,* as quoted by Kelsey, *Racism,* p. 103. There is an all too obvious similarity between the white sentiment that blacks should "know their place" and the male sentiment that women should remember their place is "in the home."

made me feel that he liked me. . . . I know that he probably meant well in what he happened to advise me that day. I doubt that he meant any harm. It was just in his nature as an American white man. I was one of his top students, one of the school's top students — but all he could see for me was the kind of future *"in your place"* that almost all white people see for black people.

He told me, "Malcolm, you ought to be thinking about a career. Have you been giving it thought?"

The truth is, I hadn't. I never have figured out why I told him, "Well, yes, sir, I've been thinking I'd like to be a lawyer." Lansing certainly had no Negro lawyers — or doctors either — in those days, to hold up an image I might have aspired to. All I really knew for certain was that a lawyer didn't wash dishes, as I was doing.

Mr. Ostrowski looked surprised, I remember, and leaned back in his chair and clasped his hands behind his head. He kind of half-smiled and said, "Malcolm, one of life's first needs is for us to be realistic. Don't misunderstand me now. We all here like you, you know that. But you've got to be realistic about being a nigger. A lawyer — that's no realistic goal for a nigger. You need to think about something you *can* be. You're good with your hands — making things. Everybody admires your carpentry shop work. Why don't you plan on carpentry? People like you as a person — you'd get all kinds of work."

It was a surprising thing that I had never thought of it that way before, but I realized that whatever I wasn't, I *was* smarter than nearly all of those white kids. But apparently I was still not intelligent enough, in their eyes, to become whatever *I* wanted to be.

It was then that I began to change — inside.

I drew away from white people. I came to class, and I answered when called upon. It became a physical strain simply to sit in Mr. Ostrowski's class. (Excerpts from "Mascot," *The Autobiography of Malcolm X,* written with the assistance of Alex Haley [New York: Grove, 1966], pp. 35-37. For a gripping account of a similar incident, see Richard Wright, *Uncle Tom's Children* [New York: Harper & Row, 1936], pp. 3-8.)

How is it white people take for granted that black people have a "place" and that they must learn to keep it? The answer is, they think black people are inferior to themselves. This is obvious from the fact that an all-white Congress drafted the Declaration of Independence, with its ringing affirmation, "We hold these truths to be self-evident, that all men are created equal," while standing on the backs of countless black slaves. And right down to the present day white people who cherish this Declaration continue to deny the inalienable rights of which it speaks to black people.[10] But why

10. The Declaration of Independence does not teach that God made everyone alike. To some he has given many gifts, to others few, and the authors of the Declaration recognized this obvious fact. What they meant was that each and every person has some inalienable

do white people think that black people are so inferior to themselves? The answer, absurd as it sounds, is — skin. Black people are lower on the scale of humanity because of the color of their skin.

Before the science of physical anthropology was developed, it was generally supposed that the present-day inhabitants of earth all descended from Shem, Ham, and Japheth, who survived the flood with their father, Noah, and their wives. Such a view naturally invited speculation about why there should be such differences among the races, in the light of their common ancestry. In particular, how is it that the supposed descendants of Japheth (Europeans) are white, while the supposed descendants of Ham (Africans) are black? Given the ungodly relationship that whites in antebellum America had to their black slaves, it is hardly to be wondered at that they found an ungodly answer to this question: The black skin of African people is a mark of opprobrium that has been placed on them by the Creator. Sometimes this mark was construed as the mark of Cain that allegedly separated his descendants from those of his brother Seth (Gen. 4:8-16). More often it was construed as the sign of the curse placed on Canaan, the son of Ham, who had injured his father's honor by looking on his nakedness (9:20-27). "Cursed be Canaan, a slave of slaves shall he be to his brothers" (9:24) became the text on which many white racists based their ugly thesis that blacks were intended to be separated and subjugated as inferior.

The use of Scripture to suggest that black skin is a divine judgment signifying inferiority is an ad hoc argument unworthy of rebuttal. Nothing in the text suggests that the mark of Cain had aught to do with skin pigmentation. And whatever it was, it was not a curse but an act of mercy to preserve his life (4:15). Intractable problems likewise plague the racist interpretation of the curse on Canaan. Canaan was the progenitor of the Canaanites who lived in Palestine when the Israelites occupied the land. They were no more black than the Israelites who conquered them. But such considerations do not faze the racist mind. It is not a mind that is prone to investigate facts or weigh the merits of an argument. It is not a mind that ponders the meaning of Scripture; it simply uses Scripture to support answers deduced from its own premises. Such incorrigible bias is found even in the cultured and educated mind. (See Henry Lee Moon, "Woodrow Wilson: Educated Racist," *The Crisis* 77, no. 8 [October 1970], pp. 290-91.)

Although the Bible says that God made of one [blood][11] every nation to live on the face of the earth, racists remind us that he has also determined their allotted times and the boundaries of their habitations (Acts 17:24-26). Of course, for Christians there cannot be "Greek and Jew, circumcised and uncircumcised, barbarian, Scythian, slave, free man, but Christ is all, and in all" (Col. 3:11). This verse is in the racist Christian's Bible. But racists construe this unity of which the apostle speaks as an exclusively

---

rights as a human being. The only explanation for their exclusion of blacks, therefore, from the exercise of these rights has to be that they did not consider them fully human. Later on the Supreme Court removed the ambiguity in the Declaration by declaring (*Dred Scott* case) that blacks were two-fifths human.

11. Textual evidence is sharply divided as to whether αἵματος should be included — that is, whether "of one" or "of one blood" is the better reading.

spiritual unity having to do with the privileges and benefits of soul salvation in the world to come. It does not have to do with racial differences as established by the Creator. In other words, spiritual equality before God does not imply social equality between men and women who are racially different. This ruinous dualism that separates the spiritual from the mundane is endemic to the racist mentality. Speaking of his experience with Covey, the Methodist slave breaker, Douglass scornfully comments:

> His religion hindered him from breaking the Sabbath, but not from breaking
> my skin on any other day than Sunday. He had more respect for the day than
> for the man for whom the day was mercifully given, for while he would cut
> and slash my body during the week, he would on Sunday teach me the value
> of my soul, and the way of life and salvation by Jesus Christ. (*Life and Times*,
> pp. 138-39)

The argument that our oneness in Christ is spiritual and hence does not remove the racial differences whereby whites are superior to blacks is a slippery slope. Since this "spiritual" salvation culminates in the life to come, are we supposed to think of heaven as segregated? Is the white lady of whom Countee Cullen speaks, right after all?

> She even thinks that up in heaven
> Her class lies late and snores,
> While poor black cherubs rise at seven
> And do celestial chores.

("For A Lady I Know")

The black bards who created the spirituals had a more biblical view of heaven. They first heard of heaven from their master's preacher and found it an attractive place. Naturally they hoped to go there, but this created a problem. How could they and their master share the same heaven? None of the slave songs ever reflects segregation as the answer to this riddle. Even though they had not had a course in theological anthropology, the Christian slaves knew that the slave section reserved for them in church on Sunday had no place in heaven. Therefore they sang,

> I've got a shoes, you've got a shoes,
> All God's children got a shoes;
> When I get to heaven gonna put on my shoes,
> Gonna walk *all over God's heaven.*

This happy prospect of freedom to go where they pleased led slaves to suggest that just possibly their segregationist masters might not make it after all. Since heaven is a free and open society under God, those who deny such freedom on earth have no claim to citizenship in heaven. Those who practice segregation on earth, therefore, had better be prepared for the possibility that God will practice it on them in the world to come. Hence they concluded a veiled protest song with the refrain,

> Heav'n, heav'n,
> Everybody talking 'bout heav'n ain't goin' there,
> Heav'n, heav'n,
> Gonna shout all over God's heav'n.

The idea that black skin marks a person as inferior is, of course, the reductio ad absurdum of white racism. It is also a despicable affront to the dignity of black people and a kind of lese majesty against God himself, whose image they bear. Yet, in their behavior, white Americans continue to inflict on black Americans the traumatic experience of what Martin Luther King has called "color shock." For black children especially, it is a major emotional crisis. If one is uneducated, she may strive for learning; if one is poor, she may at least hope for a better day. But if one is rejected because of her color, she is rejected for what she *is*. Such rejection can make one's spirit faint with despair.[12] The gate to life closes for many black children even before they have opportunity to enter upon its promise. Black children, in the inner city especially, are aware from early childhood that their color is a stigma. In the movies, television, and mass-circulation magazines, successful and beautiful people have a white skin. Even the English language undercuts the dignity of black people with a hundred tacit humiliations. It is the "black" sheep who strays from the fold, the "white" lie that is pardonable.[13]

In an effort to escape from the prison in which white prejudice has incarcerated them, some blacks who have an "integrated" complexion seek to pass as whites. But their life is a wretched existence, a kind of living lie. It evokes not only a constant fear of exposure but invites an abiding contempt for those with whom they are constrained to be identified.

"I would doubt," says Malcolm X, "if anyone in America has heard Negroes more bitter against the white man than some of those I have heard. But I will tell you that, without any question, the *most* bitter anti-white diatribes that I have ever heard have come from 'passing' Negroes, living as whites, among whites, exposed every day to what white people say among themselves regarding Negroes — things that a recognized Negro would never hear. Why, if there were a racial showdown, those Negroes 'passing' within white circles would become the black side's most valuable 'spy' and ally."[14]

12. See Martin Luther King, *Where Do We Go From Here: Chaos or Community?* (New York: Harper & Row, 1967), pp. 109-11. The despair that stifles ambition, suffuses the soul with emptiness, and kills the spirit is a recurrent theme in the literature. Although blacks are not guilty of Sisyphus's sin, they must roll the stone of human aspiration up the hill of racial bias time after time, only to have it come tumbling down again.

13. See Charles E. Silberman, *Crisis in Black and White* (New York: Random House, 1964), pp. 47-50.

14. Malcolm X, *Autobiography,* pp. 276-77. A white man, John Howard Griffin, did not change his features, his dress, his voice, his manner of speech, or his name, but only his skin — with the help of medical science — and walked into the world of the black American. He lasted just two weeks and couldn't take it any longer. He describes his experience with the observation, "I knew I was in hell. Hell could be no more lonely and hopeless, no more

INCIDENT

Martin Luther King tells how he would drive past an amusement park called Fun Town when on his way to the Atlanta airport. When she wasn't in school, his daughter always liked to ride with him.

> As we passed Fun Town so often in the car, she would look over at me and say, "Daddy, I want to go to Fun Town." Well, I could always evade the question when we were going in the automobile. . . . I could jump to another subject. I didn't want to have to tell my little daughter that she couldn't go to Fun Town because of the color of her skin. Then the other day we went home and, like most children, she likes to look at television. She was looking at television and they were advertising Fun Town. She ran down stairs and said, "Daddy, you know I've been telling you I want to go to Fun Town and they were just talking about Fun Town on the television and I want you to take me to Fun Town." I stood there speechless. How could I explain to a little six-year-old girl that she couldn't go to Fun Town because she was colored? I'd been speaking across the country about segregation and discrimination and I thought I could answer most of the questions that came up, but I was speechless for the moment. I didn't know how to explain it. I said to myself, I've got to face the problem once and for all. . . .
>
> My wife was sitting on the other side of the table and I took my little daughter and I told her to have a seat on my knee. She jumped up on my lap and I looked at her and I said, "Yolanda, we have a problem. You know some people don't do the right things and they are misguided. And so they have developed a system where white people go certain places and colored people go certain places. And," I said, "they have Fun Town like that so that they don't allow colored children to go to Fun Town." Then I looked at her at that point because I didn't want her to develop a sense of bitterness. I didn't want her to grow up with a sense of hatred and bitterness in her heart. So I had to push on and say, "Now all white people aren't like this. There are some white people right here in Atlanta who would like for you to go to Fun Town. And there are some all over the country who are right on this issue. Still, there are those who have been misguided." Then I looked down into her eyes and I said to her at this point — and I saw tears flowing from her eyes — I said, "Yoke, even though you can't go to Fun Town, I want you to know you are as good as anybody that goes to Fun Town. I want you to know, Yoke, that some of us are working hard every day to get Fun Town open and to get many other places open. And I say to you that in the not too distant future, Fun Town, and every other town, *will* be opened to all of God's children because we are going to work for it."[15]

agonizingly estranged from the world of order and harmony" (*Black Like Me* [Boston: Houghton Mifflin, 1960], pp. 61-63).

15. Transcribed from a personal tape of the speech, "Fun Town," by the late Martin Luther King Jr.

The affront offered by whites to the personal dignity of black people exacts an enormous toll on the black psyche.[16] To deny black people their freedom, their right of self-determination, not only hurts their feelings but threatens them as persons. Furthermore, it insults their Maker, who gave black people the same "place" he gave white people when he made them both in his likeness. And that "place" is the *human* place. When white racists want blacks to stay in the place they have assigned them, they are trying to play God — and doing a miserable job of it.

This being the case, why should black theologians — or any theologians who would be biblical — be satisfied with the kind of theoretical disquisitions on race relations that emanate from the halls of academia? Black theologians have feelings like anyone else, and their angry response to white racism is a perfectly human response. (Did not Jesus experience a little "righteous indignation" on occasion?) One may not embrace all that has been written in the name of black theology, but the fundamental thesis of such theology is eminently biblical. It is simply the affirmation of the essential worth of all black people. Black theology teaches that black people must be freed from self-hatred and moved with a spirit of dignity.

"When," observes James Cone, "Saint Paul speaks of being 'a new creature' in Christ, the redeemed black man takes that literally. He glorifies blackness, not as a means of glorifying self in the egotistical sense, but merely as the acceptance of the black self as a creature of God" (James H. Cone, *Black Theology and Black Power* [New York: Seabury, 1969], p. 53). In other words, "black is beautiful," the gift of the Creator. Not blackness but racial hatred makes the human face ugly, inhuman. (See below on the "hate stare," p. 117.) During the Montgomery bus boycott, an elderly black woman was offered a ride. When she declined, she was asked, "Aren't you tired?" To which she responded, "My feets is tired, but soul is rested." Black theology aims to do anthropology in a way that gives black people rest of soul and relief from the indignities of white racism.

16. This soul suffering is poignantly expressed in the blues.

> Sometimes I feel like nothin';
>   somethin' throwed away;
> Then I get my guitar
>   And play the Blues all day.

While inditing the sorrows of an unwanted people, the blues are not a pathological form of self-pity. Rather, they are an artistic creation to bring comfort and satisfaction to the singer and her companions in distress. Though melancholy in mood, the blues contain an affirmation of life. Theirs is a "lusty lyrical realism charged with taut sensibility" (Richard Wright). In 1902, "Ma" Rainey, famed interpreter of the melancholy folk songs of black people, when asked what kind of song it was she sang, replied, in a moment of inspiration, "It's the Blues."

When black people live in a white racist society, they can obtain a proper sense of their dignity only when they seize their right to self-determination. They must be what God their Maker intended them to be rather than what white Americans have permitted them to be. Therefore, black theology speaks of "black power," which is not to be dismissed as a mere slogan taken from the militant wing of the civil rights movement of the 1960s.

> Black power believes that blacks are not really human beings in white eyes, that they never have been and never will be, until blacks recognize the unsavory behavior of whites for what it is. Once this recognition takes place, they can make whites see them as humans. The man of Black Power will not rest until the oppressor recognizes him for what he is — a man. He further knows that in this campaign for human dignity, freedom is not a gift, but a right worth dying for.[17]

This black "declaration of independence," with its notice that blacks will determine themselves as subjects rather than be determined as objects, even if they must die in the attempt, has led whites to declaim on the evils of violence, the necessity of "law and order," and the ideal of Christian love. There is an irony in this white fear of violence, when it is blacks who have suffered the violence of racism ever since they were brought to America as slaves. John Perkins, a leading spokesman for evangelical blacks, ruminates on the way his evangelical audiences bring up the question, "But you don't agree with violence, do you?" To which he would respond:

> Violence? I don't believe that, over all, black folks believe in violence. . . . *Violence, in relation to civil rights activities, is simply not a production of black people. Violence is a reaction of whites to black people who want nothing more than their freedom.* . . . In the overall history, in the social structure of black-white relations, it's a different story. The worst violence is the violence against blacks. That is *the* violence — violence that is accepted so nicely within the white system that it gets no publicity at all.
>
> The fact is that there are many more whites who believe in violence, or who believe in ignoring it when whites do it. But the black is always the person who gets asked about violence.[18]

17. Cone, *Black Theology,* p. 12. As one of the first American statements by a professional theologian, Cone's work constitutes a landmark to which all theologians are indebted.
18. John Perkins, *Let Justice Roll Down* (Glendale: Regal, 1976), pp. 110-11. The physical violence of white racists against blacks beggars description. From the Simon Legrees of slavery to the Ku Klux Klansmen with their lynching rope and the police with their hoses, dogs, and guns, America has been stained with a trail of black blood that cries out like that of Abel. See Wm. B. Huie, *Three Lives for Mississippi* (New York: Wee Books, 1965).

Along with the charge that black theology incites violence, one hears the further complaint that black theology is "secular" because it is concerned with civil justice here and now, when it should be concerned with salvation in the life to come. This is another red herring. There is, to be sure, a danger of the loss of transcendence in the black struggle for liberation from the structures of violence in American society. But white evangelicals seem to think that life on the other side of Jordan should be so attractive to black Christians that they will overlook present pain in anticipation of future bliss in the world to come. "But," says, Cone, "black theology refuses to embrace an interpretation of eschatology which would turn our eyes from injustice here and now. It will not be deceived by images of pearly gates and golden streets, because too many earthly streets are covered with black blood."[19] Black Christians, like white Christians, can sing with Katharina von Schlegel,

> Be still my soul: the hour is hastening on
> When we shall be forever with the Lord,
> When disappointment, grief, and fear are gone,
> Sorrow forgot, love's purest joys restored.

But this serenity of soul that the Christian faith inspires does not mean passivity in the face of injustice. Were blacks to exemplify the "stillness of soul" that white racists expect of them, it would be not the stillness but the death of the soul.[20]

Now that we have noted what racism does to black people as victims, a word is in order about what it does to white people as perpetrators. If our humanity is given us in an I-thou fellowship, every encounter that threatens this fellowship is mutually destructive. The "I" that is white cannot diminish the "thou" that is black without diminishing itself. Indeed, we venture the opinion that racism may dehumanize the racist, in God's sight, even more than the victim, though the victim's loss appears more obvious to us. Since our humanity is fulfilled in a relationship of responsible love, when that love is turned to hate it destroys the one who hates more than the one who — like our Lord — is "hated without a cause" (Jn. 15:25). By treating their black neighbors as less than human, white racists become inhuman themselves.[21]

19. Cone, *Black Theology,* p. 127.

20. Speaking of the "death" of the soul, Jonathan Kozol published a study on the loss of incentive among black students in the Boston public schools when they became old enough to perceive what the future held for them. He entitled it, ominously, *Death at an Early Age* (New York: Penguin, 1986).

21. Every white American should read Frederick Douglass's account of how the "fatal poison of irresponsible power" could change a slaveholder from "a saint into a sinner, and

INCIDENT

Stepping into a Greyhound bus depot in New Orleans in November of 1959, John Howard Griffin, a white man whose skin had been temporarily darkened by medical science, had the following experience.

> I walked up to the ticket counter. When the lady ticket-seller saw me, her otherwise attractive face turned sour, violently so. This look was so unexpected and so unprovoked I was taken aback.
>
> "What do you want?" she snapped.
>
> Taking care to pitch my voice to politeness, I asked about the next bus to Hattiesburg.
>
> She answered rudely and glared at me with such loathing I knew I was receiving what the Negroes call "the hate stare." It was my first experience with it. It is far more than the look of disapproval one occasionally gets. This was so exaggeratedly hateful I would have been amused if I had not been so surprised.
>
> I framed the words in my mind: "Pardon me, but have I done something to offend you?" But I realized I had done nothing — my color offended her.
>
> "I'd like a one-way ticket to Hattiesburg, please," I said and placed a ten-dollar bill on the counter.
>
> "I can't change a big bill," she said abruptly and turned away, as though the matter were closed. I remained at the window, feeling strangely abandoned but not knowing what else to do. In a while she flew back at me, "I *told* you — I can't change that big a bill."
>
> "Surely," I said stiffly, "in the entire Greyhound system there must be some means of changing a ten-dollar bill. Perhaps the manager — "
>
> She jerked the bill furiously from my hand and stepped away from the window. In a moment she reappeared to hurl my change and the ticket on the counter with such force most of it fell on the floor at my feet. I was truly dumbfounded by this deep fury that possessed her whenever she looked at me. Her performance was so venomous, I felt sorry for her. It must have shown in my expression, for her face congested to high pink. She undoubtedly considered it a supreme insolence for a Negro to dare to feel sorry for her. (John Howard Griffin, *Black Like Me,* pp. 52-53)

As Henry Aaron approached Babe Ruth's career record of 714 home runs, his hate mail increased accordingly. The thought that the great, white "Sultan of Swat" should be dethroned by "Hammerin' Hank," a black man, did not sit well with many of the fans. When he was 30 homers back of Ruth, Aaron observed: "Last week I got 416 pieces of mail one day and 600-some-odd the next. I'd say the ratio is sixty-forty. Sixty percent

---

an angel into a demon." In his *Life and Times,* pp. 74-83, he tells in graphic prose and with penetrating insight how the natural goodness of his mistress, Mrs. Hugh Auld, was gradually metamorphosed into the angry despotism of a tyrant when she married a slave-owning husband.

of it is of a racist nature. If I were a white man, all America would be proud of me. But I'm black. You have to be black in America to know how sick some people are" (*Los Angeles Times,* May 17, 1973, pt. III, p. 1).

Many whites, even in the South, are dismayed at the behavior of the red-necked racist.[22] They eschew the vicious hate that would lead bigots to bomb a church and kill children in Sunday school. But they fail to realize how deep is the estrangement of their own hearts. Thus, even those who stand within the circle of Christian faith and reckon themselves to be part of that new humanity which is the church of Christ deceive themselves concerning their own social bias. "It seemed to me," observes John Perkins, "that some of the institutions, supposedly promoted for helping blacks, actually contributed to the cycle of dependency. A Bible school, founded and run by white Southerners to help train the 'po', pitiful black people for the Gospel,' was, of course, not interested in anything that would be a challenge to the *status quo*."[23] Such patronizing "good-will" toward blacks helps white people feel noble about the crumbs they throw to blacks when they should feel guilty about the way whites exploit blacks. This is why Christian people are so often surprised and perplexed at the resentment of blacks toward them. They have "acted with no ill feeling"; hence they cannot understand why their benevolence appears despicable to the very people they have sought to help. Fortified in their self-righteousness, they transmute their contemptuous pride into Christian virtue with verbal sophistries. They do not "look down" on blacks; they simply have "race preferences" when it comes to accepting a son- or daughter-in-law. And so they deceive their souls with the great lie that they really *are* superior and fail to realize that by their passive acceptance of evil, they help to perpetuate it.

It is this endemic mind-set of white people that provokes the protest, "We have marched, we have cried, we have prayed, we have voted, we have petitioned, we have been good little boys and girls. . . . We have done every possible thing to make the white man recognize us as *human beings. And he refuses*" (Ernie W. Chambers, an Omaha barber, testifying before the National Advisory Commission on Civil Disorders. See *Ebony Magazine,* April 1968, pp. 22ff., for his full testimony). When on occasion the scales

22. A shift in attitude in the segregated South can be plausibly traced to the shocked response evoked by the discovery — televised nationwide — of the bodies of three civil rights workers at the bottom of a twenty-foot crater near Meridian, Mississippi, in 1964. Many Southern segregationists had apparently persuaded themselves that the disappearance of the three young "revolutionaries" was a hoax and that they would resurface in some bar in the North.
23. Perkins, *Let Justice Roll Down,* p. 109.

do fall from the eyes of a white racist, it is a great encouragement to the student of theology, a bit of realized eschatology. An example of such enlightenment is provided by the story of Sarah Patton Boyle, a Virginian who graphically tells her struggle with a racist soul in *The Desegregated Heart* (New York: Wm. Morrow, 1962). An Episcopalian in good and regular standing, a typical liberal who believed in the essential goodness of humankind, her encounter with racism introduced her to the darker side of our humanity, the awful mystery of original sin. Fortunately, her pilgrimage did not end here. The knowledge of sin led to the understanding of grace and the realization that Jesus, whose life is a revelation of the meaning of love, is true man as well as true God *(vere homo, vere Deus)*. The dogma she had ignored came alive. Thus she became not only an Episcopalian but a Christian. While this change did not make her view of the world more rosy, it did give her a clearer understanding of the nature of the struggle required, in this sinful world, of all those who purpose to live their lives as human beings and as Christians, whether they be black or white.

C. A CONCLUDING WORD

While the Christian knows that this world is a fallen world, a world which is "in the power of the evil one" (1 Jn. 5:19), nonetheless, she also knows that one of the triumvirate of "theological" virtues is hope (1 Cor. 13:13). Hope is the anchor of the soul; hence, all theology that is Christian is a theology of hope, done in hope. This hope, Christianly speaking, is the restoration of that fellowship with God and neighbor in and for which we were created. True, this hope transcends the present life; it enters, in the words of Hebrews, "the inner shrine behind the curtain, where Jesus has gone . . . on our behalf" (Heb. 6:19-20).[24] But it is Christian doctrine that this hope is not only a future reality but also a present one. It has already entered the world in Christ, through whose resurrection we have been born anew into a living hope (1 Pt. 1:3). While this hope surely should manifest its power in the church, it has a larger implication for the whole human family. Since the God whom Christians worship as their Redeemer is the God whom they confess to be the Creator of all people, Christians must join with all who strive for the ideal of a human race that lives together as

---

24. It was this transcendent hope that enabled the slaves to create the spirituals. Surely no hope ever relieved a profounder misery; no Christians ever sang their *gloria in excelsis* more truly *de profundis!* One of these spirituals is engraved on the tomb of Martin Luther King:

> Free at last, free at last
> Thank God Almighty
> I'm free at last.

a community of persons. Such a community is one in which there is mutual respect based on the dignity and worth of one's neighbor. We know that such a community is found in this sinful world only very imperfectly. In the United States some progress has been made in desegregating our society. For this, Christians, black as well as white, can be grateful.[25] Desegregation, however, is not the realization of true community. It is simply a necessary first step, for without legal desegregation we cannot hope to move toward that community in the human family which, in its mutuality and reciprocity, is spiritual in nature.

The spiritual nature of true integration is reflected in the fact that while the law can forbid segregation, it cannot secure integration. When court-ordered desegregation began in Atlanta in the 1960s, the school system was 55 percent white, 45 percent black. Twenty years later, it was 90 percent black. White parents either moved to the suburbs or sent their children to a private school. (See *The Wall Street Journal,* Monday, Sept. 29, 1980, p. 1.) This does not mean that just laws are useless; but it does mean that the human problem cannot be solved by law alone, as Christians know, being the heirs of grace. We are aware, of course, that today many African Americans, as well as people of other racial and cultural groups, reject the idea of integration, not least on the grounds that it threatens to cost them cherished cultural distinctives and hence rob them of their particular identity. We have already argued that voluntary separation is not the same thing as enforced separation (whether the "force" be that of law or of entrenched convention and attitude); and it may well be that African Americans (and others) should affirm those separate gatherings that reinforce their identity and dignity as a people. Nonetheless, the eschatological vision of people coming from east and west, north and south, to sit at table in the kingdom of God (Lk. 13:29) suggests that we need not fewer but more settings where we, whatever our differences, meet as equals. Heaven will not be the state of perfect realization of the "separate but equal" theory.

To say that life as human is spiritual in nature is simply to recognize what we have already affirmed in framing our anthropology. The human spirit actualizes itself in an I-thou relationship with God and neighbor. Christians, above all others, are called to manifest this relationship in a community of love. Only as they are obedient to this vision can they commend the Christian doctrine of humankind.

Insofar as the church is really the church, it does manifest this community, it *is* the *communio sanctorum.* This is what makes segregation in the church such an egregious

25. Not only should blacks be grateful for progress that has been made and not "blame whitey" for everything; they should also come to grips with the problems they face in today's society that are, to a large degree, of their own making. See Pete Hamill, "Breaking the Silence," *Esquire,* March 1988, pp. 91-92. Our present discussion, however, concerns racial prejudice; and in America today that is a white problem, not a black problem.

scandal. In that very place where we should see the future manifest in the present, we too often see, so far as human relations are concerned, the same sinful alienation we see in the world. In the church white Christians sing, "Blest be the tie that binds our hearts in Christian love." But can white Christians really sing this hymn in a way that pleases God unless black Christians sing it with them? No! This does not mean that the black church should be assimilated into the white church. But it does mean white Christians must learn to live in a way that will move black Christians, in freedom, to sing with them. This will happen only when they, in turn, are moved to sing with black Christians. Thus both will adorn the doctrine they confess, namely, that as Christians they are "one in the Spirit" and "one in the Lord."

Learning to live as Christians is a lifetime job, even with the help of the Holy Spirit. With the thought that the Spirit speaks to us through the lives of others, we close our discussion with the account of what one man did as a Christian — and a black — to show us all the path we must follow as pilgrims on our journey to the celestial city.

INCIDENT

Roland Hayes was born in 1887 "in a community of shacks in Georgia too small to have a name; today it is called Curryville." As a teenager he heard recordings of Caruso and determined to devote his life to singing. Working his way through Fisk University, he trained in Boston and at age thirty risked financial ruin by renting Boston's Symphony Hall. (The management would not venture the staging of a black performer.) Seven hundred people were turned away for want of seats! Master of virtually every vocal tradition, Hayes went on from this first triumph to gain an international reputation as one of the world's leading tenors. "No German," admitted a Viennese critic, "could sing Schubert with more serious or unselfish surrender." At the height of his career, he returned to Curryville and purchased six hundred acres of the farm where his mother had been a slave. There, by coincidence, he met a Mr. Horace Mann, son of his mother's former owner. He talked to him, not as "the enemy," but as a friend. As the world's leading interpreter of the Spirituals, Hayes was gratified to learn from Mann, who was 105 years old at the time, that his great-grandfather had been an African tribal leader. Converted as a slave, he created Christian songs, one of which Mann recalled from childhood:

> Wasn't it a pity an' a shame,
> An' he never said a mumberlin' word.

Finding Mann and his wife in poor health and abject poverty, Hayes prepared for them a small house on his newly purchased farm and moved them into it. Later Mann hobbled two miles and sat in the front row when Hayes gave a benefit concert for poor black and white children in the area. At a gala concert in honor of his 75th birthday,

Virgil Thompson said to the diminutive, white-haired tenor, "You do the human race an honor to exist."[26]

ADDENDUM: CONCERNING CAPITAL PUNISHMENT

When speaking of the divine attributes, we affirmed that a justice which includes retribution is the foundation of the Lord's throne (Ps. 89:14).[27] Here, we have affirmed that our creation in the divine image entails the dignity of all life that is human. These affirmations concerning divine justice and human dignity, so essential to a Christian theology, confront us with a difficult question: Does justice require capital punishment for a capital offense?

Our decision to comment on capital punishment in an addendum to our discussion of racial prejudice may appear arbitrary. For us, the common element in both discussions is the factor of human dignity — which is the subject of this entire volume. It is the dignity of the victim as human, the creature in the divine image, that makes murder so heinous and justice so demanding. At the same time it is the dignity of the offender, who is also human, that makes the administration of justice so difficult. In this addendum, then, we are still concerned with the basic question of human dignity. The fact that when we move from the issue of racial prejudice to that of capital punishment, our language shifts and we speak not so much of the "dignity" as of the "sanctity" of human life does not appear to us to be significant. It is the *dignity* of human life, that is, its exalted and noble character as endowed by the Creator with his likeness, that gives such life its sacred inviolability, that is, the quality of *sanctity*.

When one takes from one's neighbor, who is made in God's image, the right to life, what does justice demand of the offender? Although we do not exact "an eye for an eye and a tooth for a tooth" literally, does justice require, in the case of murder, that the state shall exact a life for a life literally? The argument leading to such a conclusion is a plausible one and may be summarized as follows: All retributive justice curtails the offender's rights to some degree. A fine is the abridgment of one's right to material goods; imprisonment, the deprivation of one's right to freedom. The obligation of society thus to curtail one's rights rests on the assumption that the offender has forfeited those rights by the abuse of them. To be

26. The above account was drawn from James Traub, "Vita: Roland Hayes," *Harvard Magazine,* March-April 1983, p. 39; and Warren Marr II, "Roland Hayes," *The Crisis* 81, no. 6 (June/July 1974), p. 206.

27. *God, Creation, and Revelation,* pp. 336-433.

sure, even criminals have some rights that a just society will not deny. But when one willfully takes the life of another, one denies the victim's rights altogether. In such a case, it is argued, the offender forfeits all rights, in turn, even the right to go on living in this world as a member of the human family. Having denied the right to live to one's neighbor, one loses it for oneself. In other words, a capital offense places the offender under the judgment of death.

That such a judgment is just, we grant; that it is the only judgment that is just, we doubt; that it can be justly implemented in a sinful society, we deny. What follows is intended as a comment on these three affirmations.

In our discussion of the divine attribute of justice, we identified ourselves with those who reject a positivistic approach to justice in favor of the view that grounds justice in the transcendent will of God. (See *God, Creation, and Revelation,* pp. 383-85). Such justice, we have argued, is distributive, in that it treats all equitably. But, we have argued, it is also retributive. It seeks to restore the order established by the Creator and violated by the sinful creature. To that end it protects the God-given rights of all people and exacts payment from (imposes a penalty on) those who offend against these rights. (One is reminded of Heim's observation that punishment is not simply pedagogical but penal in its ultimate meaning. It removes guilt by rendering satisfaction, as Raskolnikow sought to do in Dostoyevsky's *Crime and Punishment.* "Capital punishment is the 'sacrament of the State' " [*Jesus the World's Perfecter,* trans. D. H. van Daalen (Edinburgh and London: Oliver and Boyd, 1959), pp. 110-11].) For this reason we cannot agree with those who deplore capital punishment as a barbarous medievalism unworthy of the Christian God. Having told the parable of the vineyard and the unworthy tenants (husbandmen) who killed the owner's son that they might inherit the vineyard, Jesus asks: "What will the owner of the vineyard do? He will come," he answers, "and destroy (ἀπολέσει, "kill," NIV) the tenants, and give the vineyard to others" (Mk. 12:1-9). We accept Jesus' word as God's word. We would not, therefore, have our Lord change the answer to his own question. We shall, of course, have more to say about these matters when we speak of the death of Christ and Paul's understanding of that death as an act of God to atone for our sins.

As for our first affirmation, namely, that the death penalty is just, here our thought rests on the assumption that since human life is life in the divine image, it is sacred. To take such life by a willful and premeditated act, therefore, is an act deserving of death. "Whoever sheds the blood of man, by man shall his blood be shed; *for in the image of God has God made man*" (Gn. 9:6 NIV). This is the thought world that is reflected in Paul's remark before Festus, "If . . . I am guilty of doing anything deserving death, I do not refuse to die" (Acts 25:11 NIV). Unlike the Positivist who thinks of crime as sickness, prisons as hospitals, and punishment as purely remedial, we do not doubt that Adolf Eichmann deserved the sentence of

death that the Israeli court pronounced against him. In his death justice
was done; the original order that belongs to the creation was affirmed and
the wrong made right insofar as is possible when crimes of such enormity
are perpetrated against humanity.[28] We, therefore, affirm that capital punishment is just.

It does not follow, however, that capital punishment is the *only* form
justice can take in dealing with such crimes as high treason or premeditated
murder. The doubt we have expressed in our second affirmation concerning
this later position is reinforced by a consideration of the fact that Scripture
itself looks in more than one direction when it comes to capital punishment.
In the Mosaic law, for example, many offenses were punishable by death
— kidnapping, cursing of parents, adultery, incest, homosexuality, bestiality, sorcery, Sabbath desecration, and others (Lv. 20). Such an approach
reflects a severity that few would espouse today who advocate the death
penalty in the name of justice.

A rigor even beyond that of the Mosaic law can be seen in the use of the death penalty
in the course of Christian history. For example, under Charlemagne the refusal of
baptism, or the pretense of having received it, as well as relapse into idolatry, and even
eating meat during Lent, were all punishable by death. Surely such rigor reflects more
the culture and times than the absolutes of divine justice. "At the beginning of the
nineteenth century," we are told, there were in England, "more than 200 offenses in
the State Book for which capital punishment might be inflicted. Property, even more
than person, was under the guardianship of the gallows" (John Lawrence, *A History of
Capital Punishment* [New York: Citadel, 1960], p. 13). As in times past people were
executed for the violation of property rights, so today executions for political reasons
are rampant. They occur in a Muslim fundamentalist theocracy like Iran, in a Communist
country like China, and in a white "Christian" country like South Africa. "Well over
1,000 people have been executed at Pretoria Central Prison since 1980, and over 100
in South Africa's 'independent' bantustans. But the new element in the disturbing
readiness of the South African regime to execute people is the increasing execution of
political offenders who are being sentenced to death" (*News Letter,* International
Defense and Aid Fund for South Africa, 1989. The Fund is in consultative status with
the United Nations).

In contrast to the severity of the Mosaic law, the treatment of the
offender in the biblical story of the first murder gives one a different
perspective on the possibilities of justice.[29] We read that after the Lord

28. As his crimes were reviewed, some present at the trial testified that they felt
physically nauseated. See Hannah Arendt, *Eichmann in Jerusalem* (New York: Viking, 1964).
29. Speaking of the different perspectives reflected in the biblical data, one should
remember that Moses himself slew an Egyptian who was oppressing a Hebrew slave. Was
his escape to Midian a miscarriage of justice? (Ex. 2:11-12).

had condemned Cain to a restless wandering in the earth, surprisingly he placed a protective mark on him, implying the continuing sanctity of his life even as a murderer (Gn. 4:8-16). If justice demands the death of a murderer, surely Cain should not have been spared — a man who planned the death of his own brother, Abel, and carried it out in a fit of jealous anger.

We are aware of the many disquisitions aimed at harmonizing the story of Cain and Abel with the thought that capital punishment alone can fulfill the demands of justice in the case of premeditated murder. As one who espouses such a view, John Murray offers a typical resolution. The treatment of Cain, he suggests, teaches us no more than that even the life of a murderer must not be taken away with ruthless violence, since such an act would replicate the murderer's own crime. Hence the protective mark given him. Yet Murray does find "the halo of sanctity which God places around the life of Cain" an "arresting" fact (*Principles of Conduct* [Grand Rapids: Eerdmans, 1957], p. 108).

We have further affirmed that though the sentence of death may be just, it is not, and cannot be, justly implemented in a sinful society. Not only are people executed for the wrong reasons, but too often the wrong people are executed. Since to err is human, is it not better to err on the side of leniency than severity? Some have argued for the necessity of the death penalty on the score that murder is an irremediable crime. Justice, therefore, demands the death of the offender. That an irremediable crime demands an irremediable penalty is a doubtful argument, in our judgment. Many other crimes besides murder are irremediable. We would argue, rather, that an absolutely irremediable penalty should *not* be imposed in a fallible and sinful society where errors of judgment are inevitable. Were one to argue that anything less than the death of a murderer comes short of perfect justice, yet surely one must admit that when the state takes the life of an innocent person, it is not a matter of *imperfect* justice but an intolerable *miscarriage* of justice. Why? Because it is an injustice that is without any remedy whatsoever. In this respect it differs from other acts of injustice.

Curiously, some people seem to think that such tragic mistakes were made only in the past, as, for example, when Europe was seized with the witch mania. They do not reckon with the fact that even in a society where torture is not used to obtain a confession and where, as a general rule, every effort is made to ascertain the truth, mistaken judgments are not only possible — they are inevitable. Colman McCarthy cites a *Stanford Law Review* article detailing three hundred and fifty proved cases of Americans who have been wrongfully condemned for murder, a disproportionate number of whom were black. Of these, twenty-three were executed. Such figures represent only part of the whole story, which will never be fully known.[30]

The response of those who favor capital punishment — "killing the killers" — is curious to say the least. They seek to reduce such obvious injustice to a mere bagatelle in the name of a larger justice. Their argument is that the number of wrongful executions is sufficiently low to be acceptable when one averages everything out. After all, most things we do, from driving cars to engaging in sports, result in the death of innocent people. But we do not give up such activities because in the pursuit of them we believe there is a net gain in life. So also with the institution of capital punishment; "a net gain in justice is being done."[31] How can one reply to such reasoning? When does a net gain in justice become a net loss? A mind that will correlate the risks associated with the good and necessary activities of life with the risk that innocent people will lose their lives in a miscarriage of public justice is a mind that cannot be enlightened.[32]

James Berry was public hangman in England from 1884 to 1892. A deeply religious man, he always prayed the night before an execution for the soul of the condemned. He was increasingly sickened by various experiences accompanying his work. Convinced that in one case, at least, he had clearly hanged an innocent man, he found no comfort in the thought that in his work he had contributed to "a net gain in justice." In fact, for a time he suffered a nervous breakdown. Eventually he resigned his post and, as a lay preacher, spoke out against capital punishment, expressing the hope that he might live to see it abolished in England.

In America today, an effort is made to relieve Berry's problem by laws that protect the executioner's identity. Sometimes the executioner is not only hidden from public view but joined by several others, all of whom respond when the order is given. Under such circumstances not even the executioners know whose hand inflicted death.

Many who advocate the death penalty reason that it acts as a restraint against murder. Granted that sometimes individuals are wrongfully executed,

---

30. See Colman McCarthy, "Falsely Convicted but Truly Dead," *Los Angeles Times,* Jan. 24, 1989, pt. II, p. 7. Not only are mistakes made, but sometimes, even in capital cases, prosecutors suppress evidence, prosecution witnesses perjure themselves, judges allow misleading circumstantial evidence to be heard, incompetent defense lawyers are hired, and convictions reflecting community outrage at the crime rather than the merit of the evidence against the accused are handed down by juries. And when such things happen, it is the poor with no resources who are most apt to suffer the injustice.

31. Ernest van den Haag, as quoted by McCarthy, ibid.

32. See "His Test Told Lies," the story of an innocent man convicted of murder on the basis of a polygraph, *Los Angeles Times,* Monday, Dec. 22, 1980, pt. I, p. 1. When the truth subsequently came to light, the judge commented that he was glad Ohio did not have the death penalty.

the impact on society as a whole is remedial and thus a larger justice is served in that innocent lives are saved. This argument has a distinguished pedigree and has been widely accepted. For example, noting that the laws of all lands agree in punishing murder with death, Calvin argues that if a country did not inflict an "exemplary vengeance" on those who commit murder, it would soon be ruined by murderers and robbers.[33] The difficulty with such reasoning is that there is no evidence to support it. Fewer murders do not occur in societies that practice capital punishment.

It is true, of course, that were people able to commit murder with impunity, no one's life would be secure. In the case of a heinous crime like murder, a severe penalty must be imposed both to satisfy justice and to shackle the feet that are "swift to shed blood." But why may we not suppose that life imprisonment without parole is an "exemplary vengeance" to inflict on those who are condemned for murder? If it is true, as we have argued, that there can be no I without a thou; if this I-thou relationship is of the essence of our humanity; and if life, as human, is life together, life in community; then to have this freedom-in-community forever taken away by incarceration is surely a heavy price to pay for one's offense. It is not a coincidence that many prisoners look upon solitary confinement, the most rigorous form of incarceration, as the worst punishment of all.[34] But though imprisonment without the possibility of parole is a grievous abridgment of one's humanity, it is not irremediable, as is death. If the imposition of such punishment should prove to be a miscarriage of justice because inflicted on an innocent party, there is the possibility of making at least some restitution, the possibility of restoring to such persons the dignity and freedom that are theirs as human beings. This is the consideration above all others that commends prison bars over the gallows to many who espouse a Christian anthropology.

We do not mean to imply that the vindication of the wrongly condemned can ever really compensate for the wrong done. See the story of Oscar Walden Jr., an African Methodist Episcopal Church pastor in Chicago who was arrested while a student at Moody Bible Institute. Walden spent fourteen years behind bars, plus thirteen more on parole, for a murder committed by a look-alike (see *Ebony Magazine,* Feb. 1979, pp. 95-96). Also the story of James Richardson, an itinerant black farmworker in Florida, who was wrongfully convicted of the murder of his seven children by an all-white jury. After he had been bathed and shaved for execution, his sentence was stayed at the eleventh hour

33. *Inst.,* 4.20.16. This reasoning lay behind the traditional practice of making executions public events, a practice largely abandoned in our day. When we go from public hangings in the town square to secret executions in a gas chamber, are we not, by such action, rejecting the argument that executions will awe people into goodness?

34. See above, p. 20, n. 26.

by a legal fluke. Twenty-one years later he was acquitted and released through the tireless efforts of a lawyer investigating his case wholly outside the judicial system. " 'I felt so alone," he said when the ordeal was over. "It was terrible to suffer for so long. But I found strength in the Lord. I knew that even if nobody else loves you, God loves you, and that kept me strong" (*Amnesty Action,* published by Amnesty International, May/June 1989, p. 6).

A further consideration that commends incarceration over execution in the case of murder has to do with the dispassionate exercise of power on the part of the civil magistrate. Christian thinkers have universally insisted that the power of the civil magistrate should be used to maintain justice, not to wreak vengeance. A vindictive spirit of retaliation should be banished from the civil judicatory. We know that in a sinful society such a noble sentiment is maintained only with difficulty. Yet to the extent that the ideal informs the reality, some measure of humaneness will be preserved in the state.[35] By contrast, capital punishment, under the guise of justice, easily evokes the baser, sadistic impulses in the human spirit.[36]

Any history of capital punishment makes for gruesome reading. While the law should inculcate respect for the sanctity of life, in many cases of capital punishment one feels revolted by the cheapening of life. People have been drowned, boiled, burned, crushed, hanged, and quartered; in short, they have been done in by every torture that the mind can conceive. Even death by lethal injection is more a display of modern technology than a tribute to human kindness. Richard Moran, a journalist, supposed that such a form of execution would leave a person drifting off into a peaceful sleep. But after he had witnessed it, he wrote: "The execution ceremony has changed much over the years. In a way it has become even less humane. A detached, private kindness has replaced unrestrained public brutality" ("Invitation to an Execution — Death by Needle Isn't Easy," *Los Angeles Times,* March 24, 1985, pt. IV, p. 1). There may be a painless death, Moran concludes, but there is no such thing as a humane execution. (To feel the force of this observation, one should read Tolstoy's description of an execution by a firing squad, *War and Peace,* bk. 12, chap. 11.)

35. Consider Lincoln's remarks in his Second Inaugural Address: "With malice toward none, with charity for all, with firmness in the right as God gives us to see the right, let us strive to finish the work we are in, to bind up the nation's wounds, . . . to do all which may achieve a just and lasting peace among ourselves and with all nations." Noble resolves for one who, as the chief magistrate, carried the sword of the victor in war.

36. "It is my belief that a great many of the most vociferous cries for the abolition of capital punishment emanate from those areas of our society which have been insulated against the horrors man can and does perpetrate against his fellow human beings" (J. Edgar Hoover, as quoted in the *Los Angeles Times,* June 2, 1960, pt. I, p. 6). Such a visceral defense of capital punishment is understandable in the light of the vicious murders that are perpetrated. But too often it is inimical to the exercise of evenhanded justice.

*   *   *   *   *

When the reign of terror began in France, the guillotine took center stage. "It became *La Sainte Guillotine,* and became the model of ornaments for women and toys for children. Miniature guillotines were not only sold in the streets, but the vendors supplied living sparrows to be decapitated by them" (Lawrence, *History of Capital Punishment,* p. 73). This was back in 1792; but the same grotesque, carnival-like activity occurs today. The Texas execution of Andy Barefoot, witnessed by Moran, was celebrated by people dressed in Halloween costumes. One was an executioner, a black hood pulled over his head as he pranced about with his cardboard axe.

Finally, we should say a word about the argument that to proscribe the death penalty is somehow to threaten the foundation of all civil authority and power. Some have argued that the sword of justice which secures the individual citizen against the attack of the murderer is the same sword that secures the state against the attack of a hostile neighbor. Therefore, to reason that the state should not execute murderers implies that it should not defend itself against invaders. The problem with this argument is just that one who has been apprehended and condemned for a capital offense is already divested by the state of the power to hurt its citizens. By contrast, the troops of an invading army constitute a very definite threat to the well-being of the citizenry. Capital punishment, therefore, is not killing in self-defense, as when a country defends itself against invasion; it is rather premeditated, judicial killing of one against whom no defense is needed. We can only conclude, therefore, that the judgment of death is best left in the hands of the Giver of life, that Judge of all the earth who will do right (Gn. 18:25).

In American society today, a movement known as Reconstructionism (Dominion Theology, Theonomy) teaches that future massive conversions to Christ will usher in a glorious age in which the Mosaic law will be reestablished as the basis of godly government. The movement began to attract adherents with the publication of Rousas John Rushdoony's *Institutes of Biblical Law* (Phillipsburg: Presbyterian & Reformed, 1973). It appeals to many who see present-day American society as threatened with moral chaos and lawlessness because it offers a blueprint for reconstituting a just society along Old Testament theocratic lines.

Since we have been concerned with capital punishment, we thought it appropriate to offer some citations from reconstructionist writers who tell us how justice will function in this coming millennium. "The divorce problem will be solved in a society under God's law because any spouse guilty of capital crimes (adultery, homosexuality, sabbath desecration, etc.) would be swiftly executed, thus freeing the other party to remarry" (Mark Rushdoony, *Chalcedon Report,* no. 252, 1986). Again: "In a Christian society, the death penalty 'is still appropriate for the crime of worshipping another god on the Lord's Day' " (James Jordon, *The Geneva Papers,* July 1982). Both of the above quotations are from "Moses in the Millennium," by Jon Zens, in the magazine *Searching Together* 17, nos. 2, 3, 4 (1988). As editor of *Searching Together,* Zens was among the first to challenge some theses of the Theonomists (Reconstructionists) as in conflict with the teaching of the New Testament. See also Anson Shupe, "The Reconstructionist Movement on the New Christian Right," *Christian Century* 106, no. 28 (Oct. 4, 1989): 880-81. Shupe reflects on the political aspects of the movement, including its influence on Pat Robertson and his decision to run for the presidency of the United States.

IV. The Image and Sexual Polarity: "Male and Female He Created Them"

A. INTRODUCTION

A theological statement on human sexuality must begin with the thesis, reiterated these many times, that to be created in the divine image is to be so endowed that one lives one's life in an ineluctable relationship with God and neighbor. In theological anthropology, the neighbor is that human "other," that "thou," in relation to whom I know myself as "I." The time has now come to say a further word about this "other" in fellowship with whom "I" have my humanity. This other is obviously one who, like myself, says "I" and relates to me as a "thou." Yet, interestingly enough, Scripture does not say, "So God created humankind in his image, in the image of God he created him, I and thou he created them." Rather, we read, "male and female he created them" (Gn. 1:27). This affirmation would be the first surprise in the Bible were we not so familiar with the creation story.[1] One could hardly have anticipated the close conjunction found in this text between our creation in God's image, on the one hand, and the sexual polarity in which we are given that image, on the other. Theologians have traditionally had little to say about the implications of this striking association. In fact, they have bestowed on the subject a vast amount of silence. They have, indeed, spoken about sexuality, but always in the context of marriage and procreation, simply taking it for granted that our maleness

---

1. "In the whole long history of man's understanding of himself, this statement has only been made *once* and at this point. . . . On account of this one statement alone, the Bible shines out among all other books in the world as the Word of God" (Brunner, *Man in Revolt*, p. 346).

and femaleness has nothing to do with our being in the image of God. Our sexuality is something we share with the animals, not with God, for God transcends all sexual distinctions.

A long-standing tendency in the Eastern theological tradition affirms not only that God transcends sexual distinctions but that, in a sense, we do too, in that the masculine and feminine principles are united in ideal humanity. We must think of ourselves, therefore, in terms of oneness rather than diversity, of unity rather than duality. Hence it would only confuse the quest for self-understanding were we to regard true humanity as manifest in our sexual polarity. Assuming that sin is basically sensuality, of which sexual lust is a prime example, theologians in this tradition have related our sexual polarity to our fallen condition rather than our original creation (see Niebuhr, *Nature and Destiny,* 1.228). Origen, the greatest of the early Eastern theologians, actually mutilated himself to avoid the passion. In modern times, the mystic Nicolas Berdyaev of the Russian Orthodox Church has argued that the androgynous union of the masculine and feminine principles constitutes the true ideal of humanity. The great anthropological myth that alone can be the basis of an anthropological metaphysic is that of the androgyne, first told in Plato's *Symposium* and later occupying a central place in the Gnosticism of Böhme. As a sexual, halved, divided being, humanity is doomed to disharmony, to passionate longing and dissatisfaction. According to Berdyaev, the Oedipus complex, to which Freud and the psychoanalysts attach universal meaning, may be interpreted symbolically and mystically from the perspective of this cosmic struggle between the sexes. Original sin is associated with the fall of the androgyne, that is, the division into two sexes. This formation of the "bad masculine" and "bad feminine" has incalculable consequence for our moral life. Christian asceticism has made heroic efforts and attained commendable achievements in overcoming the horror and curse of sex. The problem, however, has never been completely solved. The human creature, in the thinking of Berdyaev, remains a sick, wounded, and disharmonous creature because it is a *sexual* creature, a bisected being who has lost its wholeness and original integrity. (See Berdyaev, *Destiny of Man,* trans. Natalie Duddington, 4th ed. [London: Geoffrey Bles, 1954], pp. 61-67.)

This androgynous understanding of humankind has never been widely accepted in Christian theology because it obviously conflicts with the biblical story of human origins. According to Scripture, God did not create humankind male-female, but male *and* female, giving *them,* not *him,* dominion over the earth (Gn. 1:26, 27). To the same effect is the statement in Gn. 5:2: "Male *and* female he created *them,* and blessed *them* and named *them* Man when *they* were created." As Barth observes, there is no room in the Bible for the thought that it would be glorious for humankind in this whole sordid realm if the man and the woman could somehow transcend their sex in terms of a humanity embracing a higher unity. This would be to suppose we know better than the Creator, who has made his will simple and clear by making us human beings of a particular sex, not only male *and* female but male *or* female. All is in order so long as, and only so long as, we are fully conscious of our sex and thankful for it, living our lives before God as a man or a woman with a sober and good conscience (*KD,* III/4, pp. 173ff. [cf. *CD,* III/4, pp. 156ff.]).

Since theologians have traditionally seen no significance in the way Genesis 1:27 associates our sexuality with our being in God's image, with what, then, have they associated it? The answer, briefly put, is: the bond of marriage and the propagation of the race. It has simply been assumed that the woman was given to the man as a helper in the one and only work in which he really needed her help, namely, the work of procreation. Therefore, obviously, the fellowship of the sexes should be understood, not in terms of our creation in the divine image, as implied in Genesis 1:27, but in terms of our obligation to be fruitful and multiply, as enjoined in 1:28. Even those theologians who in more recent times have acknowledged the dynamic, relational quality of the image and emphasized that "it is not good that the man should be alone," have given little attention to the fact that the other human being who stands over against the man as his "thou" is not only *like* the man, in distinction from the animals, but also *different* from him in that *she* is a *woman.*[2]

Some, like Brunner, while admitting that sexuality, not marriage, is the definitive question in a Christian anthropology, yet speak of the distinction between male and female in a way that merges with the respective roles that the man and the woman assume in the marriage relationship. Unlike the image of God, which is essential to our humanity in an ultimate way, our maleness and femaleness is a penultimate matter. In this life it is an appropriate expression of our creaturely dependence on the Creator, for it is precisely in the creative task of bringing new life into the world that we experience a mutual dependence of a unique sort on one another. Thus the form of our humanity as male and female points to the true purpose of life as community with God and neighbor. Yet, Brunner concludes, the ultimate fulfillment of this purpose in the life to come is one in which sexual differentiation will pass away, according to the word of our Lord: "When the dead rise, they will neither marry nor be given in marriage; they will be like the angels in heaven" (Mk. 12:25 NIV).[3]

Since the theologians of the church have commonly subsumed sexuality under the rubric of marriage, they have frequently construed what Jesus said in Mk. 12:25 as Brunner does. But our Lord did not say that when the dead rise they will be neither

2. For example, G. C. Berkouwer, while he notes that the words "God created humankind in his own image" are immediately followed by "male and female he created them," yet concludes that this does not mean that the second phrase in any way interprets the first. The relationship between male and female has no particular implication for our understanding of the image. See his *Man: The Image of God,* p. 73.

3. In *Man in Revolt,* Brunner discusses the question of the origin of the *imago Dei* in chap. 5, reserving the subject of "Man and Woman" for chap. 15, many pages later. See also his *Christian Doctrine of Creation and Redemption,* pp. 64-65.

male nor female. To Augustine's credit, he perceived this. When he put the question of whether the bodies of women will retain their own sex in the resurrection, he answered in the affirmative. Of course, he never asked whether men would rise as men, since the answer to that question was as self-evident to the good bishop as the axioms of Euclid. We would not, however, make this observation with too great severity. Considering his views of fallen sexuality, one is more inclined to commend the great theologian's candor in answering the question as he did than condemn his prejudice in framing it. When the Sadducees, who denied the resurrection, asked Jesus which of seven brothers should have as wife the woman whom all had successively taken to raise up offspring, Augustine observes that it would have been a fit opportunity for Jesus to have said, "She, about whom you inquire, will herself be a man and not a woman in the resurrection." But he said no such thing. Nor did he say simply, "When the dead rise, they will not marry"; but rather, "When the dead rise, they will neither marry nor be given in marriage; they will be like the angels in heaven." Only males can "not marry" and only females can "not be given in marriage" (*De civitate Dei*, 22.17).

As for our Lord's remark about angels, our slight knowledge of angelic being would hardly warrant the conclusion that to be like them is to cease to be male and female. The question of the sex of angels and how they love is best left where Milton's Raphael puts it when he rebuffs Adam's overweening curiosity. Adam asks whether celestial spirits express their love by looks only or by touch.

> To whom the angel with a smile that glow'd
> Celestial rosie red, love's proper hue,
> Answered: "Let it suffice thee that thou know'st
> Us happy, and without love no happiness."
>
> (*Paradise Lost,* 8.615ff.)

The first theologian to associate human sexuality in a direct way with the doctrine of the image was Karl Barth. In doing so, he placed the male/female quality of human life at the very center of theological anthropology. Whether or not one finds his argument compelling in all its aspects, it does summon the church to develop a theology of humankind that is not only a theology of man but also of woman. If "it is not good that the man should be alone," then it is not good that one should frame an anthropology in terms of the man alone. If, by the Creator's decision and choice, humankind is male *and* female, and if the woman's creation is the completion of the man's creation, then a male-oriented anthropology is not one that is faithful to revelation, one that strives to think God's thoughts after him.

Surely one of the merits of Barth's approach is the way in which it makes clear that we should never speak of humankind without speaking of man *and* woman, man *or* woman. As human, we have our existence in a fellowship that is a fellowship in terms of this precise difference. Our lives, to be sure, reflect many differences: one may be gifted or not gifted;

one must be a child, one may be a parent; one must be young, one may be old; one must be of some time, place, or race; one may be of this or that time, place, or race. But in all of these necessary and not-so-necessary differences that mark the relationships of life, one is always and primarily a man or a woman. If one is a spouse, then either a husband or a wife; if a parent, then either a father or a mother; if a child, then either a son or a daughter. At the same time, this either/or in which we have our humanity is never ours in abstraction; there is no male as such or female as such, but only male in relation to female and female in relation to male. That is, the "or" in which we have our humanity — one is either a male or a female — is, in a theological anthropology that is Christian, taken up into the "and" of biblical revelation. We are created in God's image, male *and* female.

Should we, then, conclude that Barth supposes that our being male and female is what it means to be in the divine image? He does sometimes speak as though this were his thought — *simpliciter.* But in the fine print he makes some significant qualifications, for he knows well enough that God's being is not sexual in nature. To be in God's image is not to "replicate" the divine at the creaturely level. It is rather to be the creature that "reflects" God's being at the creaturely level, and that in a unique way. There is analogy, but only analogy, between the being of God and the being of the creature in his likeness. Barth sometimes speaks of this analogy as an analogy of relationship *(analogia relationis),* the univocal element in the analogy being that both God and the creature in his image have their being as being-in-relationship. What the divine "I" is to the divine "Thou" in the fellowship of the Trinity, the human "I" is to the human "thou" in the fellowship of humanity. God is the one God who is in himself not only "I," but "I" in relationship to himself who is also "Thou"; and not only "Thou," but "Thou" in relationship to himself who is also "I." That is, God's own being is a genuine, free, harmonious self-encounter, an open confrontation and reciprocity, a coexisting and cooperating. Humankind, as in the divine image, is a replication, a copy, a reflection of this form of the divine life in its confrontation and reciprocity.

For this reason, God sees, recognizes, and discovers himself in the creature whose being is also a being in an I-thou fellowship. This does not mean, however, that the fellowship in the Godhead is specifically a fellowship of male and female, as it is for the creature in his image. Analogy does not rest on exact correspondence but rather on a likeness that is a likeness in *un*likeness. While the I-thou fellowship at the human level is *like* the trinitarian fellowship of the Godhead, it is unlike it in that human fellowship is differentiated as male and female. This sexual quality of human fellowship belongs to the creature as human, not to the Creator as divine. It is the gift we share with other creatures.

It is also true for Barth, of course, that the fellowship in the Godhead is unlike that of the creature in his image in that the latter is a fellowship of discrete selves. Each human self is an individual. But Father, Son, and Spirit are not individual selves as are Peter, Paul, and Mary. Christians do not worship three Gods but one only; they are not tritheists but trinitarians. (See our exposition of the doctrine of the Trinity in *God, Creation, and Revelation,* pp. 261-331.)

To say that our sexuality is a gift shared with other creatures does not mean for Barth, however, that it should be viewed simply as a mechanism for procreation, something that God wills for us in this life only, a footnote to marriage and the family. Rather, our sexuality is a quality of being that penetrates the deepest ground of our humanity. As the creature in the divine image, we are given our humanity not only as shared humanity — humanity that is not shared is *in*humanity — but the primal form of this shared humanity is the fellowship of man and woman. This fellowship, therefore, is a fellowship that reminds us not only of our affinity with the animals but also and especially of our likeness to God, the God who made us in his image, male and female.[4]

B. THE MAN-WOMAN RELATIONSHIP

1. INTRODUCTION

Our fellowship as human, though it has many forms, is basically a fellowship of male and female. Even when an I-thou encounter is not between a man and a woman, it is always an encounter of a man or a woman. There are no personal encounters between persons as such, but only between persons who are male and persons who are female. While this male-female fellowship is preeminently exemplified in marriage, the fellowship of conjugal love, marriage is only one instance of a larger, complex, creative, dynamic, all-pervasive fellowship of men and women. This larger fellowship expresses itself in a variety of relationships beneficial to both the individual and society as a whole. This being so, the question of the

---

4. The above summary of Barth's position is taken from *KD,* III/1, §41, pts. 2 and 3; III/2, §45, pts. 2 and 3; and III/4, §54 (cf. *CD,* III/1, pp. 94-329; III/2, pp. 222-324; and III/4, pp. 116-323).

man-woman relationship in general is central in any anthropology done from a Christian point of view.

In framing a theological answer to the question, How ought men and women to be related? the church has traditionally argued that in the ordinance of creation the woman is subordinate to the man. Although the first creation narrative, with its affirmation that humankind is created in the divine image as male and female (Gn. 1:27), contains no hint of such a thought, the church has traditionally understood the second creation narrative (2:18-23) as plainly teaching a hierarchical relationship between the sexes. In this latter narrative, we are told that the woman was created *from* and *for* the man. What is the theological significance of this? Does the fact that the man was created first imply the headship of the male? And what shall we say of the woman's role in the subsequent story of the Fall? According to the biblical account, the woman was the first to be deceived by the Tempter, and she, in turn, seduced the man. Thus the whole human race came to ruin. Was her transgression the first instance of female insubordination? Should we conclude from this sad story of the woman's transgression that her proper place is one of quiet submission to the man? The theologians of the church have answered such questions in the affirmative. In doing so, they have simply taken over the rabbinic interpretation of the biblical accounts of the woman's creation and transgression, an interpretation obviously reinforced by the patriarchal society of Israel.

The woman's natural dependency on the man as provider (hunter) and protector (warrior) throughout the millennia of human history is reflected in the patriarchal society of the Old Testament. In such a society, the man is recognized as the head of the family or clan; he assumes the responsibility to provide and is invested with the authority to rule. Israel's unique relationship to Yahweh ameliorated the injustices against women to which such a social structure is prone. In ancient Israel women shared with men the blessings of God's grace as members of the covenant community; they participated in the cultic life of the people and, in exceptional cases, even assumed a prominent role of leadership. While the term "prophetess" may, at times, have been an honorary title given the wife of a prophet (Is. 8:3), at other times it clearly refers to women who exercised the prophetic gift: as Miriam in the days of Moses (Ex. 15:20), Deborah in the time of the Judges (Jgs. 4:4), and Huldah during the reign of Josiah (2 Kgs. 22:14). Women in Israel, especially in earlier times, associated freely with men, as did Rebekah and the young women who came to the well to draw water (Gn. 24:10-11); and Ruth, the Moabite, who gleaned with the women in the fields of Boaz (Ruth 2:2ff.). The law provided that a daughter should inherit the possessions of her father if he died without a male heir (Nm. 27:1-8), though such a woman had to marry in her own tribe in order to retain her inheritance (Nm. 36).

All in all, however, women lived in the shadows rather than in the light of life in Old Testament Israel. It was a man's world, a world in which men made the decisions and women obeyed them. A daughter remained under the authority of her father till she came under the authority of the man to whom she was given in marriage. Her father made the choice, though it was her body, indeed her very self, that was given. It was the custom for the groom to pay for the bride as for an object that could be bought. (This tendency was happily restrained in Israel and the bride might even receive gifts in her own right. See Gn. 24:53; 34:12. The Israelites also knew something of the mutuality and reciprocity with which genuine love informs marriage even in a patriarchal culture, as the erotic love poems in the Song of Songs evidence.)

Dominated by the male — first her father, then her husband — the woman was reduced to a second-class citizen in Israel. This fact was symbolically expressed in restricting the initiatory rite of circumcision, the sign of the covenant, to males. (See Gn. 12. Significantly, the corresponding New Testament rite of initiation reflects no such symbolic impediment. Women have always received baptism along with men.) As time went on, this symbolic exclusion of the woman from the full status of covenant privilege in Israel led to her physical exclusion in the worshiping congregation. In the temple built by Herod the Great, women were not permitted to enter the court of the men. Eventually even the synagogues were built so that men and women would not come into physical contact during worship. In fact, women were not even regarded as members of a congregation, properly speaking. For a congregation to be constituted there had to be ten men; nine men plus any number of women were not sufficient. Since the women were remanded to silence in worship, many authorities considered it undesirable to give girls serious religious instruction.

Concomitantly with this treating of women as inferior in their religious sensibilities, there emerged in Judaism an overt contempt of the female sex. Women were not to teach, nor were they allowed to bear witness. This latter proscription was based on Gn. 18:15, the passage in which Sarah denied her unbelieving laughter, which proved that women were liars by nature. (Although the Gospels speak of women as the first to encounter the risen Lord, Paul does not mention them when he lists the witnesses to the resurrection in 1 Cor. 15:5-8.) In brief, the Jewish conception of the man-woman relationship was one that obviously supposed that to the man belongs the preeminence as a person; to the woman, the place of submission as a lesser person. The man "is the image and glory of God; but woman is the glory of man" (1 Cor. 11:7). For further details, with sources concerning the place of women in the Old Testament and in Israel, see J. Leipoldt, *Die Frau in der Antiken Welt und im Urchristentum* (Gütersloh: Gütersloher Verlagshaus [Gerd Mohn], 1962); J. Jeremias, *Jerusalem in the Time of Jesus,* trans. F. H. and C. H. Cave (Philadelphia: Fortress, 1969); A. Oepke, "γυνή," *TDNT,* 1.781.

2. PAUL AND THE HIERARCHICAL VIEW OF THE MAN-WOMAN RELATIONSHIP

The hierarchical view of the man-woman relationship, in the Christian tradition, rests on the rabbinic understanding of the biblical story of the woman's creation and transgression. In affirming this hierarchical view, Christian thinkers have appealed especially to certain aspects of Pauline thought. A former rabbi who had become an apostle of Jesus Christ, Paul sometimes spoke of the headship of the man and the submission of the woman in clearly hierarchical terms. No effort to frame a Christian theology of the man-woman relationship, therefore, can ignore what Paul has to say on the subject. His most encompassing statement is found in the First Epistle to the Corinthians. Since Paul's letters deal with concrete, historical situations arising in the churches he had established, many scholars are of the opinion that the apostle must have been confronted in Corinth with what might be called the first "woman's emancipation movement." At least some of the women in the Corinthian congregation, it seems, were seeking to express the equality of the sexes, implied in the Christian message Paul had proclaimed, by laying aside their veils during worship. As members of the congregation, women were praying and prophesying without covering their heads, just as did the men. This behavior was their offense. "Now I want you to realize," says the apostle,

> that the head of every man is Christ, and the head of the woman is man, and the head of Christ is God. Every man who prays or prophesies with his head covered dishonors his head.[5] And every woman who prays or prophesies with her head uncovered dishonors her head — it is just as though her head were shaved. If a woman does not cover her head, she should have her hair cut off; and if it is a disgrace for a woman to have her hair cut or shaved off, she should cover her head. A man ought not to cover his head, since he is the image and glory of God; but the woman is the glory of man. For man did not come from woman, but woman from man; neither was man created for woman, but woman for man. For this reason, and because of the angels, the woman ought to have a sign of authority on her head.
>
> In the Lord, however, woman is not independent of man, nor is man independent of woman. For as woman came from man, so also man is born of woman. But everything comes from God. Judge for yourselves: Is it proper for a woman to pray to God with her head uncovered? Does not the very nature of things teach you that if a man has long hair, it is a disgrace to him, but if a woman has long hair, it is her glory? For long hair is given her as a covering. If anyone wants to be contentious about this, we have no other practice — nor do the churches of God.

(1 Cor. 11:3-16 NIV)

---

5. The custom whereby the Jewish man wears a head covering (the yarmulke) when he prays, as the mark of reverence and sorrow, did not begin until the fourth century and hence was unknown to the apostle.

The veil is that which screens, hides, protects, covers, masks, and disguises the one who wears it. It has been associated in Eastern cultures with the silence of anonymity and modesty belonging to the woman. In the Christian community, the nun, above all others, has personified this selfless surrender, so much so that the phrase "to take the veil" means to assume the cloistered life. For the apostle, therefore, the woman's covering of her head was not simply a cultural matter, as is so often affirmed today. It was rather the symbol of the woman's subordination to the man, a subordination that is part of a larger hierarchy that reaches up to God himself. As God is the head of Christ, so Christ is the head of the man, and the man the head of the woman (vv. 2, 3).[6] Hence it was very important to the apostles that one should accept one's place in this hierarchy and reflect this acceptance by conforming to the proper symbolism so far as one's literal head is concerned. For a man to violate this symbolism by covering the head while praying or prophesying in church, or for a woman to violate it by uncovering her head, is to deny one's place in a divinely constituted hierarchy of authority. Such a denial confuses the relationship that the Creator established between the sexes when he made the man the image and glory of God and the woman the glory of the man. The term "glory" (δόξα) refers to that which honors, magnifies, and brings praise to one. And how do we know that God created the woman to bring honor and praise to the man? From the account in Genesis 2 of the woman's creation: "For man did not come from woman," the apostle reminds us, "but woman from man; neither was man created for woman but woman for man." This is why the woman ought to have the sign of authority on her head.[7]

The same view of female subordination elaborated in 1 Corinthians 11 is found in Ephesians 5:22-33, a passage made familiar by its traditional use in the marriage ceremony of the church.

Wives, submit to your husbands as to the Lord. For the husband is the head (κεφαλή) of the wife as Christ is the head of the church,

6. The word "head" as used by Paul in 1 Cor. 11 denotes the one next above one in the order of authority established by the Creator. As the apostle uses it in this place, the Greek κεφαλή is probably synonymous, more or less, with ἀρχή, meaning "origin" or "first cause." In the apostle's thought, the male's superiority of place is grounded in his priority of creation. See D. S. Bailey, *Sexual Relation in Christian Thought* (New York: Harper and Brothers, 1959), pp. 295-96.

7. For a discussion of the detailed difficulties in the text of 1 Cor. 11:2-16, including the reference to angels (v. 10), see our *Man as Male and Female* (Grand Rapids: Eerdmans, 1975), pp. 51-57.

his body, of which he is the Savior. Now as the church submits to
Christ, so also wives should submit to their husbands in everything.
    Husbands, love your wives, just as Christ loved the church and
gave himself up for her.

(Eph. 5:22-25 NIV)

This analogy, the apostle goes on to say, between the relationship that unites
husband and wife in marriage and that which unites Christ and the church
in one body is a great mystery. This mystery, however, is no ground for
questioning the husband's authority. Hence the apostle concludes with the
admonition, "let every one of you in particular so love (ἀγαπάω) his wife
even as he himself; and the wife see that she reverence [φοβέω, literally
'fear'] her husband" (v. 33 KJV). This fear is not the cowering fear of a
slave but the reverential deference that should inform a woman's love for
her husband as the authoritative head of the family. As the love that
Christians have for the exalted Lord, the Head of the church, is mingled
with reverence, so, by analogy, is the love of a wife for her husband, who
is her head, her "lord," as Chaucer's immortal Greselda owned her husband
to be.[8]

    Obviously, then, the marriage relation is not a matter of mutuality as
between equal partners. While the apostle might well have said, "Wives,
love your husbands," he would never have said, "Husbands, reverence
your wives." Similar sentiments concerning wifely submission are found
in Colossians 3:18; also in Titus 2:5, which urges older women to teach
the younger women to be in subjection to their husbands, that the word of
God be not maligned. Peter, the apostle to the circumcision, speaks even
more emphatically, admonishing women to be submissive to their husbands
even if they are unbelievers, that their husbands may be won over by their
meek and quiet behavior. In so doing Christian women emulate the example
of holy women of old, like Sarah, who obeyed Abraham, calling him "lord"
(1 Pt. 3:1-2).

    In 1 Corinthians 14:33b-35 women are told to keep silent not only in
the church of Corinth but in "all the congregations of the saints" (NIV).
If they want to ask questions, they should ask them of their husbands at
home, for it is disgraceful or shameful (αἰσχρόν) for a woman to speak in
church. In 1 Timothy 2:11-15 women are reminded that they must not seek

---

8. The tendency today is to use the softest possible translation of φοβέω in Eph. 5:33,
rendering it as "respect": the wife should respect her husband. Of course the apostle also
believed that a husband should respect his wife. Thus a mutuality in marriage is achieved
by translation that is not present in the original text.

to teach or have authority over a man, "for Adam was formed first, then Eve. And Adam was not the one deceived; it was the woman who was deceived and became a sinner" (NIV). The author's thought seems to be that the Tempter was able to approach and seduce the woman because she did not have the critical acumen of the man. Obviously, then, she is not qualified to teach a man, but must "learn in quietness and full submission" (NIV). Yet women are assured that they "will be saved through childbearing — if they continue in faith, love, and holiness with propriety" (NIV).[9]

3. THE HIERARCHICAL VIEW OF THE MAN-WOMAN RELATIONSHIP ELABORATED AND DEFENDED

The woman's creation from the man (Gn. 2) and her seduction by the Tempter (Gn. 3) are the dominant themes in the "classical" defense of a hierarchical view of the man-woman relationship. In the *Summa Theologica,* pt. 1, q. 92, art. 1, Thomas puts the question: "Whether the Woman Should Have Been Made in the First Production [Creation] of Things?" While he answers in the affirmative, he raises no such question when speaking of the creation of the man. Obviously, *he* belongs to that first, pristine, unfallen creation, along with the stars, seas, plants, and animals that are pronounced good by the Creator. But one wonders about the woman; it takes a bit of theological analysis (four articles) to make sure she belongs in the first creation and did not come in with the serpent that crawls on its belly and the thorns that infest the ground. Thomas infers that the woman must have belonged to the original creation, since the Scripture says that "it is not good that the man should be alone." He notes, however, that she complements the man as his helper in the work of generation only, "since a man can be more efficiently helped by another *man* in other works." Thomas also engages in some nice distinctions when dealing with Aristotle's thesis that the woman is a "misbegotten male." He admits that the woman, as regards her particular nature (female), is indeed misbegotten, since the active force of the male seed (the female is a passive recipient and custodian in procreation) tends to the production of a perfect male likeness. But as to her universal nature (humanness), the female is not

---

9. The notion that women lack the critical perception to instruct men is sometimes fortified by listing all the female heretics from Priscilla and Maximilla to Mary Baker Eddy, a procedure that yields impressive results because of its selectivity. One shudders to think what the same approach to church history would do to the image of the male as a teacher of moral and religious truths!

misbegotten but included in the original intent of nature according to the will of the Creator, who made both the male and the female by his word.

As for the objection that the woman cannot have been created in the original production of things because she is subject to the man, Thomas distinguishes a twofold subjection. One is servile, in which the man uses the woman for his own benefit. This sort of subjection began with the Fall. The other is civil, as when a ruler rules over his subjects for their own good. This sort of subjection on the woman's part, entailed in her creation from the man, is for her own good. Such a subjection is also natural to the woman "because in man the discretion of reason predominates."[10]

As for the objection that the woman cannot belong to the original creation because she occasioned the sin of the man, Thomas grants the charge though he rejects the conclusion. True, as less endowed with reason, the woman was deceived by the Tempter; but she belongs to the original order of creation because she was taken from the man, who is the principle of the whole human race. Had only Eve sinned, Adam's children would not have inherited the taint of original sin. Had only Adam sinned, they would have. Following Thomas in this view of things, the Schoolmen laid the greater weight, therefore, on Adam's sin because of its consequences. However, they were more severe in condemning Eve's sin because of its motivation. Adam sinned by consenting to his wife out of conjugal love and fidelity, whereas Eve was moved by an ambitious desire to be like God (Gn. 3:5).[11]

While Protestants have not embraced the scholastic view of woman, they have traditionally agreed that the Tempter approached the woman as the "weaker vessel" (1 Pt. 3:7 KJV). This phrase, from the admonition of the apostle Peter to bestow honor, literally, "on the weaker vessel, the female one" (ἀσθενεστέρῳ σκεύει τῷ γυναικείῳ), has been traditionally understood to imply that the woman has lesser powers of perception and discernment. This traditional understanding of the text is probably closer to the author's thought than are the commentators' efforts in modern times to construe the passage as referring to the female's lesser muscular endowment. In any case, the supposedly intelligent and insightful male has been slow to discern that the stereotype

10. One may remember that Thomas believes the *imago* to be manifested especially in humanity's powers of reason. See above, p. 57. Therefore, in ascribing inferior powers of reason to the woman, he grounds her subordination in ontology: Woman, *per definitionem*, is subject to man. As for the distinction between the natural subjection of the woman in creation and the servile subjection she experiences after the Fall, Calvin reasons similarly in his *Commentary on 1 Timothy*. Thus he seeks to resolve the seeming contradiction in saying that the subjection of the woman is both the imposition of her creation and the punishment of her transgression.

11. This summary of Thomas's position is based on the *Summa Theologica*, pt. 1, q. 92, art. 1 (New York: Benziger Brothers, 1947).

of the female as the "weaker vessel" has been made plausible by the deprivations of her environment rather than the deficiencies of her nature. Furthermore, the male has not felt the absurdity in portraying the woman as both the dull-witted creature who was easily duped by the Devil and the one who accomplished the ruin of the man that the Tempter himself was not clever enough to pull off. This "paradox" of female stupidity and subtlety lingers on even to the present day, but it is nonsense. We have paradox when we do not fully understand; we have nonsense when we do not wish to understand. The asymmetry between the biblical data and the view that blames the woman for the fall of the man may be seen in the fact that in the Bible it is *fallen* Adam, seeking an *alibi,* who blamed the woman for his folly (Gn. 3:12). In this respect the theological tradition is little more than an elaboration of Adam's original attempt to expound the truth by obscuring it.

While the Reformers, Luther and Calvin, never spoke of the woman as in some sense misbegotten, they were, in the matter of male-female relations, largely children of their times. Luther, especially, retained unenlightened views of the woman's place: Her principal task was to bear children and to relieve the sexual appetite of the fallen male. He took an emphatic view of her subjection to the man in all things. A letter of advice to a friend begins, "Grace and peace in Christ and authority over your wife." The custom of nations, he admitted, sometimes allows for the rule of queens, as with the Ethiopian, Candace, mentioned in Acts 8:27. But in such cases a senate of prominent men actually administers the affairs of state, for women are not endowed to rule. "Everyone does best when he does that for which he was created. A woman handles a child better with her smallest finger than a man does with both hands. Therefore let everyone stick to that work to which God has called him and for which he was created."[12]

Calvin took somewhat higher ground, arguing that the woman's relation to the man was primarily social rather than procreative. She was not given to man simply as a "remedy" for his concupiscence, his comrade in the bedchamber, but to share life with him as his inseparable companion. Calvin also rejected the age-old propensity to blame the woman's dullness for the Fall. Commenting on 1 Timothy 2:14, he insisted that while the source of Adam's deception came from Eve, it was the same diabolical deception in his case as in hers. Nonetheless, though his views harbingered better things, Calvin, like Luther, held to the doctrine of female subordination, not only in the oversight of the church but in all of life. He saw no absurdity in a man's obeying in one relationship and commanding in

---

12. As translated by Elwald P. Plau, *What Luther Says* (Saint Louis: Concordia, 1959), p. 1458.

another. But this does not apply to women, "who by nature are born to obey. Hence wise men have always rejected the government of women as a natural monstrosity, a mingling of heaven and earth. Hence they are to be silent and abide within the limits of their sex according to the apostolic admonition." He made it plain that by the very order of creation, not simply as a result of the Fall, the woman is subject to the man. God did not create two "heads," but one. The woman was created later as "a kind of appendage," "a lesser helpmeet" to the man.[13]

Fuming in Dieppe, his return to Scotland impeded by Mary Tudor, John Knox spelled out the implications of his Calvinistic training about the woman's place with an explicitness that left nothing to be desired. His *First Blast of the Trumpet Against the Monstrous Regiment of Women* begins with the proposition, "To promote a woman to bear rule, superiority, dominion or empire above any nation, realm or city, is repugnant to nature, contumely to God, a thing most contrarious to his revealed will and approved ordinance; and finally it is a subversion of good order, of all equity and justice" (*The Works of John Knox*, ed. David Laing, 6 vols. [Edinburgh: John Thin, 1895], 4.365-66). This piece of polemical writing won the fiery Reformer the lasting resentment of Elizabeth.

Today no responsible theologian would say that the woman is a "kind of appendage" or "lesser helpmeet" to the man; yet the doctrine of sexual hierarchy is still defended in theory by some and assumed in practice by many.[14] Even Karl Barth, whose thinking points in the direction of the full equality of the man and the woman in the fellowship of life, still argues for female subordination. In framing his argument, Barth repudiates the traditional view that the woman is inferior and seeks to establish his case on the fact that she is different. Now it is an important point, all would agree, that men and women are different; and this difference is one that enriches the fellowship of human life at every level. No one ever stated this more eloquently than Barth. When we are dealing with the I-thou relationship in its most basic dimension, we are dealing with a relationship, he reminds us, that must be understood as coincident with the radical difference between male and female. Here it is not a question of the difference between parents and children, brothers and sisters, friends and relatives; between Europeans and Asiatics, Semites and Arians; between

13. See his Commentary on 1 Timothy, in *Calvin's New Testament Commentaries,* trans. T. A. Smail, ed. D. W. and T. F. Torrance (Grand Rapids: Eerdmans, 1964), pp. 217-18.

14. Consider, for example, the ongoing controversy over the ordination of women to the ministry of word and sacrament, and the refusal of the Roman Catholic Church so much as to discuss in any official way the possibility that women should be ordained to the priesthood.

rulers and subjects, teachers and students, rich and poor; or even between individual and individual. All such differences of whatever sort, and the relationships that these differences entail, are qualified by that ultimate difference-in-relationship whereby we are male and female. All aspects of our lives move around this center, by virtue of which each lives as man *or* woman coordinated with, belonging to, and turned toward each other as man *and* woman.[15] This closest of all relationships, which rests on this deepest of all differences, is never one of inequality. Though radical, it is a difference that is functional and only functional.

As he develops his thesis, it is evident that Barth wants to insist, on the one hand, that the woman is in no way inferior to the man; yet on the other, as different from him, she is subordinate to him. In his exposition of 1 Corinthians 11, Barth notes that the man-woman relationship is not one of reciprocity, since we are not told that the man is taken from the woman, but the woman from the man. The man does not belong primarily to her, but she to him. This supremacy of the man, however, must not be misunderstood; it is not a question of value, dignity, or honor, but of *order.* In fact, although the woman is the glory of the man, who is the image and glory of God, her glory is the greater glory because the man could not be the glory of God without her who is his glory as man. The woman's subordination, then, becomes not her humiliation but her exaltation! It is only because sin has disturbed the relationship of the man and the woman to God that their relationship to each other has been disturbed. It is sin that turns the creation ordinance of the man's preeminence without tyranny and the woman's submission without humiliation into one of blind dominion, on the one hand, and jealous zeal for emancipation, on the other.

As for the statement (1 Cor. 11:3b) that the man is "the head of the woman," Barth interprets it in the light of Ephesians 5:22-23: "The husband is the head of the wife as Christ is the head of the church." Whatever authority, therefore, is given to the man in relation to the woman, it is legitimate and effective only to the extent that the man merely attests and represents the authority that primarily and properly belongs to Christ as head of the church. Hence the order established in creation between the man and the woman and revealed in the church can imperil neither the man nor the woman in their self-fulfillment under God.

The verb ὑποτάσσεσθαι, meaning "to stand under" and translated "to submit to," "to be subject to," "to keep one's place," occurs no fewer than seven times in the New Testament when speaking of the woman's relation-

15. See *KD,* III/4, §54, p. 181 (cf. *CD,* III/4, p. 163), where Barth speaks of the *Zuordnung, Zugehörigkeit, Zuwendung* (order, relation, direction) of the man and the woman.

ship to the man (1 Cor. 14:34; Eph. 5:22, 24; Col. 3:18; 1 Tm. 2:11; Ti. 2:5; 1 Pt. 3:1). Noting this fact, Barth is careful to insist that we must never liken the man-woman relationship to that of owner and chattel, superior and subordinate, or even of prince and subject. The term does speak not only of sequence but of subordination, yet in such a way that the emphasis lies on a proper order in the relationship of the woman to the man. The authority to which the woman bows in her subordination to the man is not that of the man as such, but the τάξις (order) under which they both are placed. This order at the human level is only a token of the obedience that the church owes to Christ. Hence it is a mode of subordination that is sui generis; it is free, honorable, and meaningful, taking nothing from the woman and giving nothing to the man.

Yet there is a real subordination; one cannot avoid this fact in view of 1 Corinthians 11, Barth affirms. There is an express, irreversible order in the man-woman relationship. The divine command requires that we keep this order unchanged, though the circumstances in which the command is given vary greatly with time and place. We should not, then, regard the statements of the apostle about the woman's behavior as inflexible rules in their historical reference. A woman today may lay aside the veil, cut her hair, and break her silence in the assembly. While Paul spoke a specific word in a historical context, the important point is the eternal commandment he upheld, a commandment that directs the man and the woman to their proper place and forbids all attempts to violate the ordinance of creation that governs the relationship between them.

F. W. Grosheide, commenting on 1 Corinthians 11, observes that in this passage Paul postulates "a difference which puts the man *above* the woman, a difference we should never forget because it is an ordinance of creation." Yet, he continues, while the woman is given a place below the man, when the apostle acknowledges that the "man is not without the woman, in the Lord" (v. 11), he "fights on two fronts." On the one side it was necessary to "put the emancipated Corinthian ladies in their place; but on the other, Paul seeks to prevent the woman from being considered inferior."[16] However it may be with the apostle, one can hardly escape the impression that in defending his case for sexual hierarchy, Barth is "fighting on two fronts," to use Grosheide's phrase. As a result, his argument dies of a thousand qualifications. The woman is subordinate "in this respect," "from this standpoint," and "to this extent." But it is not always easy to determine in *what* respect, from *what* standpoint, and to *what* extent

---

16. F. W. Grosheide, *Commentary on the First Epistle to the Corinthians,* New International Commentary on the New Testament (Grand Rapids: Eerdmans, 1953), p. 258.

her subordination is to be understood. Reminding us of the fact that the man-woman relationship involves a definite order that must not be confused, reversed, or interchanged, but faithfully maintained, Barth appeals to the difference between the man and the woman. Over and over again he observes that the man and the woman are different: not an *A* and a second *A*, like two halves of an hourglass, but an *A* and a *B*. Such an affirmation can hardly be faulted, but so far as the question before us is concerned, it does not seem to advance anywhere; it does not move toward a resolution of the issue. The difference between the man and the woman is beyond dispute.[17] The issue is: Does this difference imply the subordination of the woman? Can Barth (or anyone else) establish the mooted point — woman's *subordination* to the man — by underscoring the obvious point — woman's *difference from* the man — without the help of the traditional point — woman's *inferiority* to the man? The answer, it appears to us, is no.

As we see it, the fundamental difficulty with Barth's argument for female subordination is just this: the theology of humankind as male and female that he himself has espoused is inimical to a doctrine of sexual hierarchy. In such a theology, the man and the woman are partners in life, so related to each other as to be a fellowship like God is in himself, the very image of him who is the Father, the Son, and the Holy Spirit. The plain implication of such a theology is obviously the equality of the man and the woman under God. Yet having gained this important insight, Barth nonetheless draws back from following its implications to the conclusion to which it leads. As a result, he seeks to maintain the traditional subordination of the woman to the man while repudiating the traditional theological grounds on which this subordination is based, namely, the superiority of the man as "the image and glory of God" in whom "the discretion of reason predominates." In this effort he has set himself a task that even his dialectical skills, extraordinary though they be, cannot accomplish.[18]

17. See the delightful book by Vivian Gussin Paley, *Boys and Girls: Superheroes in the Doll Corner* (Chicago: University of Chicago Press, 1984). Ms. Paley, a veteran kindergarten teacher, gathers vignettes from the classroom reflecting the striking difference between boys and girls at an early age.

18. We find Barth's argument in the defense of hierarchy both convoluted and protracted. Having stated his position for the first time in *KD*, III/1, he returns to the subject in III/2 and again in III/4. For a more detailed summary of the various facets of his argument, with sources, and an evaluation of greater length than we have attempted above, see our *Man as Male and Female*, pp. 69-86.

4. OTHER SCRIPTURES BEARING ON THE
MAN-WOMAN RELATIONSHIP

a. Introduction

Finding the theological argument for sexual hierarchy wanting both in its traditional and in its more contemporary forms, we shall now look at other data of Scripture bearing on the issue. In so doing, we hope to gain insight into the larger implications of biblical revelation for our understanding of the man-woman relationship. As we begin this task, one will recall that we have espoused the view that we are given our humanity as a shared humanity, an I-thou fellowship as male and female. "Male and female he created them" (Gn. 1:27b) is a direct comment on the affirmation, "in the image of God he created him" (1:27a).

It is our view that such an understanding of the first creation narrative implies that the man-woman relationship should be viewed as one of equality and complementarity in all of life. This understanding of the narrative was largely lost sight of in Israel, however, because the culture of God's ancient people was completely patriarchal. The Old Testament as a whole assumes that God's will for the ordering of human life is revealed in and through a patriarchal society that places the man over the woman. We would not dispute this assumption. But there is no more reason to absolutize patriarchy as found in the social order of the Old Testament than to absolutize monarchy as found in the political order of the Old Testament. Appeal to the divine right of the male over the female on the basis of Israel's patriarchy is like appealing to the divine right of kings over their subjects on the basis of Israel's monarchy. God, indeed, reveals some essential truths to his people concerning his relationship to them when he declares himself to be the true King of Israel in whose name the earthly king is to rule as his vicegerent. And the same may be said of the declaration, couched in patriarchal language, in which God speaks of himself as the Father of Israel, to whom obedience is to be rendered in all things. But surely there are other forms of government, consonant with the divine will, than that of monarchy in the political order; and the same is true of patriarchy in the social order. The latter, therefore, need not be understood as God's word for the ordering of the relationship between the man and the woman to perpetuity.

While patriarchy may be the best form of society under some circumstances, its obvious weakness is the occasion that the woman's dependency affords the man to suppress her rights as a person. Dependency, to be sure, does not necessarily imply subordination. A person who is ill may be *dependent* on a physician to regain her health; but she is not *subordinate* to the physician. Yet in a sinful world, it is unrealistic to suppose that half the human race could be made dependent on the other half without the latter abusing, the former suffering the abuse, that such a relationship allows. Indeed, it is only in terms of abuse and the amelioration of abuse that one can understand the revelatory character of many Old Testament laws and customs involving women who were victimized by the injustices of polygamy, made destitute by their husbands' repudiation of them, and reduced to slavery as the pawns of war. But such laws do not express the will of God for womankind in an absolute and final way; rather they secure a measure of justice for those of the oppressed and marginalized sex against their unrestrained exploitation by the male. If revelation is historical — as the church teaches — then it does not wholly transcend history and culture; rather, it redeems it. And such redemption is a process, sometimes a slow and gradual one.

Christians read the Old Testament as anticipatory, looking beyond itself. (That is why they call it the *"Old* Testament.") The end toward which it looks and for which it prepares is the coming of One who — as the Redeemer of all, male and female — fully lived out the implications of the original ordinance of creation. It is to the story of this One's life and ministry that we must now turn as we seek further insight into the biblical view of the male-female relationship.

b. Jesus and Women

That the submission of the woman to the man, exemplified in the Old Testament, is not the last word on the subject becomes indubitably clear when one turns to the account of our Lord's public ministry as recorded in the Gospels. Although Jesus was born and lived in a culture that assumed such submission, in his public ministry a new thing happened. This new reality is manifest not so much in what Jesus said as in how he related to women. In this relationship, his lifestyle was so remarkable that one can only call it astonishing. He treated women as fully human, equal to men in every respect; no word of depreciation about women as such is ever found on his lips. In this regard his ministry was truly revolutionary, in that it restored to the woman the full humanity that was given her when God made humankind in his image, male and female.[19]

How different Jesus' conception of the relationship between men and women was from that which prevailed in Israel can be seen in the way he attacked head-on the double standard of morality that condones in the male

19. Here see C. F. D. Moule, *The Phenomenon of the New Testament,* Studies in Biblical Theology 2/1 (Naperville: Allenson, 1967), "Jesus and the Women of the Gospels," pp. 63-64.

a behavior that is condemned in the female.[20] Having seized a woman taken in the act of adultery, the Pharisees dragged her before Jesus, reminding him of the law that she should be stoned.[21] To be sure, they were not concerned with Jesus' attitude toward women; they were simply using her case to impale him on the horns of a dilemma. Would he challenge the Roman rulers, who, it appears, may not at this time have allowed the Sanhedrin to impose the death penalty; or would he set aside the law of Moses? Yet they incidentally betrayed their prejudices in that they laid hold of the woman and not the man; *she* was the sinner who should be the test case. In his reply, Jesus not only sidestepped the snare that his critics had laid, but cut them down to size with his response: "Let him who is without sin among you be the first to throw a stone at her" (Jn. 8:3ff.). Of course our Lord did not condone this woman's act; "Go, and do not sin again" was his earnest admonition to her (8:11). But we should not so dwell on his admonition to female folly that we forget his devastating rebuke to male arrogance.

One cannot doubt that women in Jesus' presence sensed the difference somehow. Here was a man who violated no proprieties, yet broke through the barriers of tradition and custom in a way that put women completely at ease in his presence. This helps explain the significant fact that relatively early in his ministry (Galilean period), mention is made of a group of women disciples who accompanied him on his preaching missions along with the Twelve. Joachim Jeremias calls this

> an unprecedented happening in the history of that time. . . . Jesus knowingly overthrew custom when he allowed women to follow him. . . . Jesus was not content with bringing women up onto a higher plane than was the custom; but as Saviour of all, he brings them before God on an equal footing with men.[22]

Among their number, it would appear, were well-to-do women who helped support Jesus and his disciples out of their means (Lk. 8:1-3). These

---

20. Men have not only acted by a double standard but even justified it in theory. See Johnson's argument that the confusion of progeny means that "a woman who breaks her marriage vows is much more criminal than a man who does it" (Boswell's *Life of Johnson,* ed. G. B. Hill [New York: Harper, 1927], 1.372). All such arguments are miserable, indeed, and deserve the cutting observations made by Simone de Beauvoir, *The Second Sex,* trans. H. M. Parshley (New York: Knopf, 1953), p. 523.

21. Though omitted in the earliest manuscripts, the *pericope adulterae* (Jn. 7:53–8:11) is thought by some scholars to be an authentic account whose location has been lost. I personally incline to this view.

22. *Jerusalem in the Time of Jesus,* p. 376.

women, some married, some single, who left home and family to follow Jesus throughout the land, remained faithful even to the end. Of his male disciples, one betrayed him, another denied him, and most forsook him. But the women who followed him all the way from Galilee — Mary Magdalene, Mary the mother of James the Less, and many other women who came up with him to Jerusalem (Mk. 15:40-41) — were present at the scene of the crucifixion (Mt. 27:55-56).

Other women who did not follow him from place to place were also awakened to a new self-understanding through contact with Jesus. He took them seriously. When they were in his presence, the unheard-of happened: he spoke to them in a way that they could understand; he treated them as the real persons they were. Among such women were two sisters, Mary and Martha. Luke tells us (Lk. 10:38-42) that when Martha complained that her sister should be helping her prepare the meal rather than listening to him with his male disciples, Jesus reproved her gently for being so upset and told her, "Mary has chosen what is better, and it will not be taken away from her." "I think," observes Dorothy Sayers, tersely,

> that I have never heard a sermon preached on the story of Martha and Mary that did not attempt, somehow, to explain away the text. Mary's, of course, was the better part — the Lord said so, and we must not precisely contradict him. But we will be careful not to despise Martha. No doubt he approved of her too. We could not get on without her, and indeed (having paid lip service to God's opinion), we must admit that we greatly prefer her. For Martha was doing a really feminine job, whereas Mary was behaving just like any other disciple, male or female, and that is a hard pill to swallow.[23]

Early in Jesus' ministry, when he was still in Galilee, he was invited to dine at the home of a Pharisee named Simon (Lk. 7:36-50). While he reclined at dinner, an unnamed woman entered and, bending over his feet, began to weep.[24] As she wiped his feet with her hair, she anointed them with myrrh from a little flask and kissed them in sincere affection. Because of the cloak of anonymity with which the historian conceals her from an overweening curiosity, we can only surmise that she was a prostitute who had been redeemed through the ministry of Jesus, perhaps the first man

23. Dorothy Sayers, *Are Women Human?* (Grand Rapids: Eerdmans, 1971), p. 46. The observation that the term "disciple" (μαθητής) is never specifically used in the Gospels of Jesus' women followers is so much pedanticism. Since they possessed the qualifications by virtue of their relationship to Jesus, they are entitled to the name, as Sayers here assumes.

24. At such meals the guests first removed their sandals and reclined with their feet behind them. The subsequent intrusion of the uninvited was a common practice.

who had ever treated her as a person rather than a sex object. Her tears probably expressed not so much her repentance in suing for forgiveness as her gratitude in sensing that she had received it. Our Lord responded by acquitting her, publicly as it were, much to the displeasure of his fellow guests. Simon, his host, came off especially poorly. Having embraced a mean opinion of the woman, he censored Jesus for not acting according to his own supercilious standards, failing to perceive that the Lord was too noble to be bound by them. "Simon," Jesus asked, "do you see this woman?" The unspoken answer was, "No." Having dismissed her as a "sinner," he could not see her as a person.

Another celebrated instance of Jesus' speaking to a woman who was in the wrong social class altogether is recorded in John 4. In this instance, he converses with one who was not only a *woman,* not only a *sinful* woman, but a sinful *Samaritan* woman. While some Jews would not even travel through Samaria, Jesus' encounter with the woman at the well shows that he construed the commandment to love one's neighbor as knowing no boundaries of the sort that prejudice erects. Jesus once praised a poor widow for giving more than the rich (Mk. 12:41-44). He commended an importunate mother for her faith, and a Syrophoenician alien at that (Mt. 15:28). He was ever ready to heal women in need, such as Peter's mother-in-law, who was afflicted with fever (Mk. 1:30-31); the infirm woman bent over for eighteen years, whom he called a "daughter of Abraham" (Lk. 13:10-16); and the desperate woman with a flow of blood, who had endured many things at the hands of physicians (Mk. 5:25-34). This last case had a peculiar poignancy, since the woman had been ritually unclean for twelve years (see Lv. 15:19-20). When, however, she disclosed her secret, so far was Jesus from any concern that he had been touched by one who was unclean that he commended her for her faith and bade her depart in peace.[25]

The parables, so prominent in Jesus' teaching, differ from those of the rabbis in their use of materials drawn from the everyday world of a woman's cares and joys. In them Jesus refers to a woman putting leaven in her meal (Mt. 13:33); to maidens going forth to meet the bridegroom (Mt. 25:1); to an importunate widow who constrained a callous judge to render justice (Lk. 18:1ff.); and to a lowly housewife who swept her whole house till she found a lost coin (Lk. 15:8). In this last instance the woman stands for God himself, a matter that bears on the time-honored (but hardly honorable) argument that since God is masculine, only men may represent him in the office of Christian ministry.

25. On the subject of "female uncleanness," see our *Man as Male and Female,* pp. 103-5.

Little wonder, in the light of these things, that a multitude of women followed Jesus along the *via dolorosa,* lamenting and mourning him (Lk. 23:27). And in his response to them Jesus showed himself to be well aware of their place in his life. Even in this hour of his deepest distress, he had a pastoral word for them: "Daughters of Jerusalem, do not weep for me" (Lk. 23:28). Some of these faithful women who followed him to the cross — Mary Magdalene, Mary the mother of James, and Salome (Mk. 16:1) — were the first to whom the Lord appeared after he rose from the dead (Mt. 28:9, 10; cf. Mk. 16:9-11; Jn. 20:11-18). His male disciples first proclaimed the resurrection to the world; but his female disciples first received the revelation on which this proclamation was based.[26] Observing that women were the last at the cross and the first to the tomb, Dorothy Sayers gives the reason:

> They had never known a man like this Man — there never had been such another. A prophet and teacher who never nagged at them, never flattered or coaxed or patronized; who never made arch jokes about them, never treated them either as "The women, God help us!" or "The ladies, God bless them"; who rebuked without querulousness and praised without condescension; who took their questions and arguments seriously; who never mapped out their sphere for them, never urged them to be feminine or jeered at them for being female; who had no axe to grind and no uneasy male dignity to defend; who took them as he found them and was completely unselfconscious. There is no act, no sermon, no parable in the whole Gospel that borrows its pungency from female perversity; nobody could possibly guess from the words and deeds of Jesus that there was anything "funny" about woman's nature.[27]

c. The Pauline Argument Revisited

When one compares and contrasts the patriarchalism found in the Old Testament with the way in which Jesus related to women, one becomes aware of a dialectic in Scripture, a dialectic that is focused most sharply in Paul, the rabbi who became the apostle of Christian liberty. It was he, as we have seen, who spoke the clearest word concerning the woman's

---

26. In view of the central place witness to the resurrection had in the early kerygma of the apostles (Acts 2:22, 32), the appearance of the risen Lord first to women, with the command to tell his brethren (Mt. 28:9-10), is a fact too long overlooked in adjudicating the place of women in the Christian ministry.

27. Sayers, *Are Women Human?* p. 47.

subjection (1 Cor. 11:3-16). Yet it was he who also spoke the clearest word concerning her liberation (Gal. 3:28). We must, therefore, give further attention to Paul, whose teaching in this regard constitutes a *crux interpretum*.

In the Old Testament, as we have seen, the woman was dominated by the man and given an inferior status in the covenant community. Jesus, by contrast, never dominated women nor treated them as inferior. In his presence there were no "emancipated ladies" to be "put in their place." Rather, they were *truly* emancipated; *their place was the human place*. Hence in the church, the new Israel that Jesus is creating by his Spirit, there is no room for the thought that the male is superior to the female and therefore should rule over her.

The apostle Paul was the heir of this contrast between the old and the new. To understand his thought about the relation of the woman to the man, one must appreciate that he was both a Jew and a Christian. He was a rabbi of impeccable erudition who had become an ardent disciple of Jesus Christ. And his teaching about women — their place in life generally and in the church specifically — reflects both his Jewish antecedents and his Christian insight. The traditional teaching of Judaism and the revolutionary new approach implied in the life and teaching of Jesus contributed, each in its own way, to the apostle's thinking about the relationship of the sexes. So far as he thought in terms of his Jewish background, he thought of the woman as subordinate to the man, for whose sake she was created (1 Cor. 11:9). But so far as he thought in terms of the new insight he had gained through the revelation of God in Christ, he thought of the woman as equal to the man in all things, the two having been made one in Christ, in whom there is "no male and female" (Gal. 3:28).

Because these two perspectives — the Jewish and the Christian — are incompatible, there is no satisfying way to harmonize the Pauline argument for female subordination with the larger Christian version of which the great apostle to the Gentiles was himself the primary architect.[28] Something

---

28. This is not to deny that numerous efforts are continually being made to reconcile Paul with Paul in these matters. Especially when it comes to the apostle's instructing Christian women to keep silent in church and to cover their heads during worship, a great deal of novel exegesis is put forward. Its purpose is to show that this apostolic admonition in no way conflicts with the present-day recognition that such behavior is ethically indifferent. These labored efforts are elaborated especially by those who hold to the inerrancy of Scripture. Everything Scripture says about women is normative for the church today, according to the inerrantists — when, that is, the Scripture is *correctly interpreted.* These "correct" interpretations often prove to be more impressive for their erudite probing of Greek lexicography and grammar than for their theological substance.

of the tension can be felt as one evaluates the apostle's argument for male headship. Even when he states his case explicitly, it is evident that the apostle sensed the need to qualify the patriarchal view that he had inherited from Judaism as not altogether congruous with the gospel he preached. For example, although he will not say that the woman is "the image and glory of God," but only "the glory of man," he nonetheless affirms that as the woman is not without the man, so the man is not without the woman, in the Lord. For even as the woman is "out of" (ἐκ) the man, so the man is "through" (διά) the woman. And all things are of God (1 Cor. 11:7-12). He sees, in other words, a pointer in the direction of the equality of the sexes in that though the first woman was created from the man, all men, subsequently, are born of women. If the first woman owed her existence to the first man, from whose side she was taken, all other men owe their existence to those women who conceived them and brought them into the world. Thus the score is evened up somewhat.

Even as the apostle's reasoning, in his letter to Corinth, about the relation of the sexes looks in the direction both of sexual hierarchy and of sexual equality, so do his statements about female participation in public worship. On the one hand, he says that the woman is to keep silence in church as the law enjoins (1 Cor. 14:34-35). On the other, he plainly allows that the woman who covers her head may, like the man, lead the congregation in prayer and exhort its members with a word of prophecy (11:5).

In view of this difficulty, some scholars have suggested that the former passage is the interpolation of a later hand. In the best critical text, the editors, using a scale of A-D, give 1 Cor. 14:34-35 a B rating, as a text having "some degree of doubt." The doubt, however, is not sufficient to prevent most interpreters from attempting to relieve the seeming contradiction by other means. It is often suggested, for example, that the apostle did not mean that all women should keep silent (v. 34), but only the garrulous, who were disturbing the worshiping congregation by their unedifying and too-frequent questions. (So A. Oepke, "γυνή," *TDNT*, 1.788.) Not only does such a harmonizing effort lack historical evidence, but it implies that men, in contrast to women, did not offend in this respect, at least not so as to warrant an apostolic admonition. This is simply more female stereotyping, in our judgment.

It would seem, then, that while a feminine silence was rigorously observed in the Jewish synagogue, such was not the case in the Pauline churches. Although the woman's place was that of submissive silence, she could pray and prophesy in public worship if she covered her head (1 Cor. 11:5). Different churches in different ages have engaged in similar compromises. For example, women have been allowed to sing in virtually all churches, though in some they may not lead the singing.[29] In some churches they may not only sing but pray in the midweek prayer meeting (otherwise some prayer meetings would be sans prayers); yet they may not lead in the pastoral prayer on Sunday morning. In other churches — as in the congregation where I grew up — women may speak in most situations, but not preach the Sunday sermon. This is the way the New English Bible seeks to cut the Gordian knot of difficulty. "As in all congregations of God's people, women should not *address the meeting*. . . . It is a shocking thing that a woman should *address the congregation*" (1 Cor. 14:34-35). But even this salvo is hardly sufficient, for, as we have noted, the apostle allowed women to "prophesy" in church, and prophesying had a similar place in the worship of his day to "addressing the congregation" in ours by preaching a sermon.

In 1 Timothy 2:11-15 the reason for female silence in the church is spelled out in a way that defies hermeneutical ingenuity. Quiet submission to the man is required of the woman because, as the second created, it was she, not the man, who was deceived by the Tempter. Yet even in this text one should note, to the apostle's credit, that though he was steeped in rabbinic learning, he does not blame the woman for the Fall, as did many rabbis and Christian thinkers after him. It is not through *her* transgression but that of the one human being (δι' ἑνὸς ἀνθρώπου), the first Adam, that sin entered into the world and death by sin (Rom. 5:12, 19). Such restraint on the apostle's part is one further indication that he was not prepared to press the implications of Jewish patriarchalism.[30]

The Fathers and theologians of the church, unfortunately, have not shown the same restraint. For a thousand years they made the deception of Eve the basis of a demeaning theology of womanhood. Alone in the Garden without the man, the woman succumbed to the Tempter's wiles. Thus she occasioned the fall of the man and, through him, the perdition of the whole human race. Such a lamentable display of a lack of moral integrity and intellectual acumen is proof positive that the woman should learn, in submissive silence, from the man. Needless to say, there is no hint of all this in the biblical narrative of the Fall. One might just as well reason that the Tempter approached the woman because he knew her to be the key to the situation as the more astute. Indeed, some Roman Catholic theologians who pursue the mythical understanding of the feminine

29. So, traditionally, in some Plymouth Brethren Assemblies. One group of English Baptists proscribed *all* female singing, along with the use of instruments, as unscriptural. See Percy A. Scholes, *The Oxford Companion to Music* (London: Oxford, 1970), p. 83.

30. This is not to say that Paul blamed the man *instead* of the woman. In Rom. 5 he speaks in the singular because of the comparison and contrast with Christ, the one man who accomplished our salvation. Whether the text in 1 Timothy that notes the place of the woman in the Fall is from Paul's hand immediately is immaterial to the present discussion. We deem it Pauline in that it belongs, as the church has recognized, in the corpus of Paul's letters that are received as canonical.

principle as passivity and openness to God (the function of the Virgin) have argued in this way. The Tempter seduced not the "weaker vessel" but "the most powerful religious principle of creation," after which the man's ruin was easily achieved. So Willi Moll, *Die dreifache Antwort der Liebe* (Graz: Styna, 1964).

d. An Analysis of the Second Creation Narrative

Before considering other New Testament texts bearing on Paul's teaching about women, we must pause to look more closely at the second creation narrative (Gn. 2:18-23), which speaks of the woman's creation from, and for, the man. It is this narrative, never the first, that is reflected in what Paul has to say about the subordination of women. In these remarks, he assumes the traditional rabbinic understanding of the narrative, whereby the order of creation — first the man, then the woman — is made to yield the primacy of the man over the woman. Is this understanding correct? We do not think that it is. And why? Because the first creation narrative clearly teaches that men and women are equally in the divine image; and because, furthermore, the lifestyle of Jesus and the way he related to women implies their equality with men as persons.

How, then, should one understand this second account of creation, which speaks of the woman as created from the man in order that she might be a help to him in the ongoing tasks of life? We answer that the story of the woman's creation in Genesis 2:18-23 should be understood as a comment on the prior affirmation in 1:27 that we are made in God's image as male and female.[31] It tells us not only *that* God made us male and female, but how he did it and why he did it:

> "It is not good that the man should be alone; I will make him a helper fit for him." . . . So the LORD God caused a deep sleep to fall upon the man, and while he slept took one of his ribs and closed up its place with flesh; and the rib which the LORD God had taken from the man he made into a woman and brought her to the man. Then the man said: "This at last is bone of my bones and flesh of my flesh; she shall be called Woman, because she was taken out of Man."

In other words, "Eve was not taken from the feet of Adam to be his slave, nor from his head to be his lord, but from his side to be his partner."[32] This beautiful sentiment expressed by Peter Lombard, the "Master of

---

31. Prior, that is, in the order of the canonical documents.
32. Peter Lombard, *Sententiarum,* I. II. Dist. XVIII, as quoted by Schaff, *History,* 2.363, n. 1.

Sentences," reflects not only the imagery but also the meaning we shall give the biblical narrative of the woman's creation from and for the man.

As we turn to the exposition of the story of the creation of the man and woman, a word is in order about its literary genre. It has traditionally been understood as a literal piece of historical reporting. As such it has had an interesting secondary history. For centuries it was the basis of the doubtful anatomical theory that the male of the human species was minus a rib on one side. In fact, when Andreas Vesalius, a founder of the science of anatomy, dissected a cadaver and disputed the point, the church condemned him to exile (1564), not only for his temerity, but especially for his heresy. Somewhat later (1847) this same text, which was the undoing of Vesalius, proved the salvation of the eminent Scottish surgeon James Simpson. Beleaguered with controversy over his use of anesthesia to deaden the pain of childbirth — a circumvention of the divine will, as it was supposed — Simpson pacified his detractors by appealing to the "deep sleep" that the Lord God had caused to fall on the man as the first surgical operation. ("Probably the most absurd [argument] by which a great cause was ever won," observes Andrew Dickson White, *A History of the Warfare of Science with Theology in Christendom,* 2 vols. [New York: Appleton, 1896], 2.63.)

With the establishment of the empirical sciences of biology and anthropology, such a literal interpretation of the Genesis account no longer commends itself. This fact, however, in no way alters the significance of the narrative as a divine revelation. Indeed, the frequently alleged contradiction between this narrative, with its view of the *successive* creation of the male and the female, and the first narrative, which speaks of them as created *simultaneously* (Gn. 1:27), is of no account when the text is understood not as a literal piece of scientific reporting, but as a narrative that illumines the ultimate meaning of our existence in its polarity of maleness and femaleness.

The narrative in Gn. 2:18-23 is commonly classified by scholars as an "etiological myth," like Plato's account *(Symposium)* of the androgyne that Zeus split in two "like a sorb-apple halved for pickling" — each half a man or a woman — because of the insolence of original men in daring to scale heaven that they might lay hands on the gods. The difficulty with such a designation is that it conveys the misleading notion of a fictitious story written after the fact to explain the status quo. We prefer the term "narrative," therefore, in the sense of a story that clothes the truth it reveals to us about human origins in parabolic form. It is in this sense that we speak of Gn. 2 as the second "creation narrative."

One should note, as we turn to the text of Genesis 2, that in the biblical narrative the division of humankind (called אָדָם, *adam*) into a man and a woman (an אִישׁ, *ish,* and an אִשָּׁה, *ishshah,* respectively)[33] is not the result

---

33. אָדָם *(adam)* is the generic word in Hebrew for "humankind," while אִישׁ *(ish)* denotes the male of the species. As in English, the generic term אָדָם is sometimes used specifically of man in distinction from woman. Hebrew usage is further complicated by the fact that אָדָם is also used as the proper name of an individual, as in the phrase, "Adam knew Eve his wife" (Gn. 4:1).

of sin. It is rather a creative act of God. It is he who declares that the human creature is the creature who should not be alone. It is in the Garden of Eden, the biblical allegory of the bliss of the divine favor enjoyed before the Fall, that the mysterious division takes place, resulting in the creature who is man and woman. Our sexual polarity, then, is not a judgment, a rending asunder of that essential being that can be what it is intended to be only in unity. Our maleness and femaleness confronts us with an onto-logical polarity in the very being of humanity itself, a polarity wrought by a creative act of God. That the difference between man and woman is due to an act of God is seen, in the story, in the deep sleep that comes upon Adam while God works mysteriously to make the human creature (הָאָדָם, the Adam) into a man and a woman. Why a rib (הַצֵּלָע) should be mentioned, we cannot say. It has been suggested that the bodily member should be a bone, as a solid and substantial part; and what could be more appropriate than the bone that shelters the breast and heart, where the deepest and noblest affections reside?

More important than the precise significance of the "rib" — which probably has no precise significance — is that at this point in the narra-tive, the story is told in such a way that the sexual factor, in the narrower sense of the word, recedes into the background. The woman is not a man without a penis, as Freud crudely defined her; it is not the anatomical difference between the man and the woman but their essential relatedness that is emphasized. Woman is taken from the man in the sense that being distinct from him, she is yet like him, bone of his bone and flesh of his flesh.

In this description, to be sure, the language ("bone" and "flesh") is drawn from the physical realm. But this does not mean that the woman is like the man only or principally at the biological level, in contrast to the intellectual and spiritual level. She is described by God, her Maker, as a "helper fit for him" (עֵזֶר כְּנֶגְדּוֹ) — "corresponding to him," "equal and adequate to him." She is, to paraphrase in the words of Delitzsch, a "helping being in whom, as soon as he sees her, the man recognizes himself." Significantly, too, there is no suggestion that the woman is a helper in a particular way, as the bearer of children (Augustine) or the keeper of the home, to speak of the more common feminine stereotypes. Many women have borne children and kept the home in other generations, and many will continue to do so in the future. And this is, indeed, the will of God; but it is not the will of God for *every* woman by definition. To say childbearing is "what she was made for" is an arrogant male conclusion that the text does not warrant. The woman, then, is not the man's servant, his female valet, his little errand girl whom he needs for this or that. She is rather the help equal and adequate to him without whom he cannot be the man he is intended to be.

The word for "help" (עֵזֶר), used to describe the woman, is never used elsewhere to designate a subordinate. In fact, it is sometimes used of God himself, who is the help of his people in time of need (Ps. 146:5). Furthermore, as God takes counsel with himself before making humankind in general, and thus commends to us the dignity of our nature as human (Gn. 1:26), so he takes counsel with himself before making woman in particular, and thus commends to us the dignity of her nature as female (2:18). Further still, one should note that in making the woman, God is directly involved, even as he is in making the man. Whereas plants and animals are simply called into being by a divine word, it is not so with the man and the woman. Rather, God forms man by taking the dust up into his hands and stooping to breathe directly into his nostrils the breath of life (2:7). So also in making the woman; he takes the rib and fashions it into a woman and brings her to the man, and so humankind became man and woman (2:22).

By describing the woman's creation in this manner, the narrative underscores the point that she is not the creation of the man. As he does not owe his being to her, so she does not owe hers to him. When she is created, he is in an unknowing sleep. He contributes no more to her creation than to his own creation; the mystery of her being is the same mystery as his own being. Her being is as unmistakably her own as his being is his own; he cannot put her in his debt. Not that her being is alien to his, or competing with his, for she is bone of his bone and flesh of his flesh. But her being is hers even as his being is his; and both are given their specific being as man *or* woman, that as man *and* woman they may share life together as creatures of God uniquely endowed with the divine image. The narrative of Genesis 2 commits us to the integrity and freedom of the woman over against the man and of the man over against the woman, even as it commits us to their togetherness in an ineluctable relationship. This, in brief, is the theology of the second creation narrative. As D. S. Bailey observes:

> Such a theology will thus treat chiefly of what man and woman *are*, not what they *do* — though by applying the principles and insights so established, it will attempt to elucidate the many practical problems which constantly arise in connection with the . . . relationship of the sexes.[34]

We can only conclude, then, that when the narrative in Genesis 2 speaks of the woman as made from the man, the intent is to distinguish her from

34. Bailey, *Sexual Relation,* p. 276.

the animals, as essentially like the one from whom she is taken. Her superiority over the animals, not her inferiority to the man, is the fundamental thought in the immediate context. To reason that since the woman was taken *from* the man, therefore she is *subject to* the man is an obvious non sequitur; derivation does not entail subordination. (Would one reason that because the man is made "of dust from the ground" [מִן־הָאֲדָמָה, 2:7] he is *subordinate* to the ground?) Furthermore, even if one were to construe the narrative in Genesis 2 literally, so as to postulate a temporal priority in the creation of the male (Adam was *first* formed, *then* Eve, 1 Tm. 2:23), nothing in the thought of temporal priority implies superior worth or value. According to the first creation narrative, the animals were created first, then humankind; yet this does not imply their superior worth. Quite the contrary, the creature who is last is the crown of creation, with dominion over the other creatures. If one were to infer anything from the fact that the woman is created after the man, it should be, in the light of the first creation narrative, that she is superior to him.[35] We conclude, therefore, that so far as the traditional doctrine of sexual hierarchy is concerned, it must be read into the biblical account of the woman's creation; it is not required by the text as it stands.

5. THE MAN-WOMAN RELATIONSHIP VIEWED AS A PARTNERSHIP OF EQUALS

a. Introduction

The rejection of sexual hierarchy does not imply the rejection of all hierarchy as such. As a matter of fact, the Christian vision of reality is hierarchical in a fundamental way. What one may call the "hierarchy of grace," in Paul's thought, cannot be doubted from a Christian point of view. By the "hierarchy of grace" we refer to the Christian doctrine that God is the source of all

---

35. Milton, in fact, puts this argument on the lips of Adam:

> O fairest of creation, last and best
> Of all God's works, creature in whom excelled
> Whatever can to sight or thought be formed,
> Holy, divine, good, amiable, or sweet!

> *(Paradise Lost,* bk. 9, lines 896-99).

But, of course, this is Adam about to succumb to the charms of his consort turned temptress. Speaking of the woman's manifest excellence, one is reminded of the answer of a Sunday school pupil when asked by the teacher why God made Eve. "When he looked at Adam," she replied, "he decided to try again."

authority (Rom. 11:33-36; 1 Cor. 15:27); that the Son of God voluntarily humbled himself as the Messiah and Savior (1 Cor. 15:28), becoming obedient to his Father in all things even unto death (Phil. 2:6-8); that because of this obedience the Son has been highly exalted in his messianic office and made head over all things for the church (Eph. 1:22; Phil. 2:9-11); and that for this reason all Christians are subject to him who is the Head, freely confessing him as their Lord and Savior (Rom. 10:9). This hierarchy of God, Jesus the Christ, and the Christian believer, to which Paul appeals in 1 Corinthians 11:3, is at the very center of Christian revelation.

In this regard one might ask whether the "analogy of relationship" *(analogia relationis),* then, of which we spoke when comparing the I-thou relationship that is God's as a Trinity and the male-female relationship that is ours as the creature in his image, does not imply that the woman is subordinate to the man as the Son is subordinate to the Father. The answer is no, it does not, since the subordination of the Son to the Father is not an ontological subordination in the eternal Godhead, but a free and voluntary act of self-humiliation on the part of the Son in the economy of redemption. As the second person of the Godhead, the Son is equal with his Father; as the incarnate Messiah, he freely assumes a servant role in which he becomes subordinate to his Father in the fulfillment of his redemptive mission (Jn. 6:38). The "analogy of relationship" is a comparison based on the doctrine of the Trinity, not on the doctrine of the Incarnation. For a fuller discussion of this matter, see *God, Creation, and Revelation,* pp. 315-23, especially 322-23.

There is hierarchy not only in the realm of grace but also in the realm of nature. Were we to seek to live our lives as human by following a purely egalitarian model, the social structures essential to our common, communal life would disintegrate into anarchy. To conceive human life as an I-thou fellowship obviously does not imply an egalitarianism that knows no levels of authority and obedience, no supra- and subordination in society. In fact, in the concrete structures of life, women ought to be subordinate to men as the occasion demands. And, by the same token, men ought to be subordinate to women as the occasion demands. It is not the subordination of *some* women to *some* men, but the subordination of *all* women to all men, *because they are women,* that is the indefensible thesis, indeed, the unscriptural thesis.

Commenting on 1 Timothy 2:12, Calvin, one will recall, affirms that there is no absurdity in a man's obeying in one relationship and commanding in another. But this does not apply, he contends, to women, "who by nature are born to obey men." Here the argument is found wanting. Since men and women are equally in the image of God, what is true for one is true for the other. We should not, then, understand the hierarchical relations between the sexes ontologically. Neither men nor women are, by nature, born to command or to obey; both are to command in some circumstances and to obey in others. And because they are persons, the more personal the relationship between them, the less there is of either; the less personal the relationship, the more there is of both. For example, when one enters into marriage, the relationship is quite different from that which prevails when one joins the army. At no time can a true marriage be likened to an army. In the military enterprise, by reason of its impersonal character, hierarchy is essential; some must give the orders and others must obey.[36] In a marriage, by contrast, rarely will either party command or obey, and when such occasions do arise, one should not say that the husband must always give the orders ("make the basic decisions") because he is a man, while the wife must always obey because she is a woman. Husbands are not to wives what generals are to privates. So to conceive the husband-wife relationship is to threaten marriage with tyranny on the man's part and artifice on the woman's part.[37]

Sexual Complementarity and Wifely Submission

Since we will assume, when we develop our doctrine of marriage (see below, pp. 190-350), the complementarity and equality of husband and wife in the marriage relationship, a further word is in order at this juncture concerning Paul's admonition to wives (Eph. 5:24 NIV) to "submit to their husbands in everything" (ἐν παντί). This particular admonition stands, in the Ephesian epistle, at the beginning of what Luther called the house-table (*Haustafel*), a list of specific admonitions to wives, husbands, children, parents, slaves, and masters concerning their behavior as members of the Christian household. (See also Col. 3:18-19; Ti. 2:4-5; 1 Pt. 3:1-7.) The submission that Christians are to practice one toward another in Christ (Eph. 5:1) is determined by a certain order: wives are to be subject

36. See the eloquent apology for hierarchy delivered by Shakespeare's Ulysses before Agamemnon's tent in *Troilus and Cressida,* act 1, scene 3. In Molière's *École des Femmes* (act 3) Arnolphe reminds his bride-to-be that though the human race is divided into two halves, they are far from equal halves. One is the major half, the other, the minor, so that the obedience the

> Soldier displays to his appointed captain, . . .
> Is nothing at all to the docility,
> And the obedience, and the humility,
> And the profound respect that a wife should show
> to her husband, who is her master, chief, and king.

What the great dramatist meant as a comedy is taken with all seriousness by many husbands on the stage of real life.
37. The traditional Christian marriage ceremony has required of the woman the vow of obedience to her husband. If a woman chooses to take such a vow she is free, of course, to do so. But she should not be required to do so.

to their husbands, as is the church to Christ (5:22, 23); children are to be obedient to their parents, as the fifth commandment enjoins (6:1-3); and slaves are to obey their masters with sincerity of heart, as they would obey Christ (6:5-6). In antebellum America, slave owners in the South and divines in both North and South used this and similar passages to justify the subjection of slaves to their masters. In a similar way, this passage has been used to justify the submission of wives to their husbands. In fact, it was from the ranks of the women who took up the abolitionist cause that the first concerted plea came in America for the emancipation of women. As a result, American women have gained many rights; yet even today, when it comes to the home, it is often affirmed that the woman's place is "in the home," and that her duty as a wife is to submit to her husband. As the "head of the house," he has the final authority.

What may we say of this argument for wifely submission? For one thing, it is surely true that Roman society being what it was in the apostle's day, the quality of a Christian woman's life could be humanized by her chaste and reverential submission to her husband; especially in the light of the exhortation to husbands to love their wives as Christ loved the church (v. 25). Yet, in this regard, as in the case of slavery, one cannot but admit the limitations of the apostle's vision. Wives, he says, are "to submit to their husbands as to the Lord. For the husband is the head of the wife as Christ is the head of the church, his body, of which he is the Savior" (vv. 22-23 NIV). But husbands are not the lords and saviors of their wives, even in an analogical and symbolical way, any more than wives are the lords and saviors of their husbands. Such an argument rests on patriarchal assumptions about the man-woman relationship that we have already evaluated and found wanting.

It is sometimes alleged that if one questions the apostle's teaching about wifely submission, then one threatens to undermine his ensuing admonition to children that they should obey their parents (6:1). Thus the family, which is the basic unit in today's society, is threatened with anarchy. The screw that is loose in this reasoning is the failure to acknowledge the double meaning of the term "children." Obviously children ought to be subject to their parents until they grow up and become responsible persons in their own right. But when this happens, they are no longer subject to their parents as when they were literally children. Parents who are unwilling to acknowledge this fact often make their own and their children's lives miserable because they are unwilling to relinquish their parental rule over them. In a similar way, and perhaps more tragically, husbands make life miserable for their wives when they treat them as children in marriage. Ibsen's Nora complains to Torwald in their first (and last) conversation as equals:

> "You have always been so kind to me. But our home has been nothing but a playroom. I have been your doll-wife, just as at home I was papa's doll-child; and here the children have been my dolls. I thought it great fun when you played with me, just as they thought it great fun when I played with them. That is what our marriage has been, Torwald."

When her husband reminds her that before all else she is a wife and mother:

> "I don't believe that any longer," she replies. "I believe that before all else I am a reasonable human being, just as you are — or — at all events — that I must try and become one."

The right to be "a reasonable human being just as you are" is a right no woman should be asked to surrender in marriage. And we do not believe that Paul intended that she should, especially when we recall other things he had to say about the man-woman relationship in Christ concerning which we will speak presently.

*   *   *   *   *

The "chain of command" approach to marriage, advocated by many in our day who "focus on the family," prompts us to say just a word about domestic violence in the form of wife abuse. Happily, many men who assume a hierarchical view of marriage do not abuse their wives. And surely when husbands do batter their wives, many reasons — alcohol, drug addiction, unemployment, jealousy, insecurity — for such abuse have nothing to do with a hierarchical view of the husband-wife relationship. Yet research has shown that the behavior of many men who batter their wives is reinforced by a traditional view of male supremacy, a view that in contemporary American society has a distinctly "Christian" component. Televangelist Charles Stanley, a spokesman for the "pro-family" movement and a onetime board member of Moral Majority, Inc., de-claims: "There is a vicious, all-out Satanic attack on the American home — the whole concept of anti-submission and independence. . . . When two people in the family become absolutely, legally equal, there is no head; both become independent of each other and love is destroyed" (as quoted in the *Quarterly Report of People for the American Way,* Jan. 1982, p. 3). Lenore Walker has observed that those who are most overt in denying help to the woman who is victimized by an abusive husband "are the conservative fundamentalists and some orders of Catholicism" (*The Battered Woman* [New York: Harper & Row, 1979], p. 164).

b. The Magna Carta of Humanity: Galatians 3:28

Whatever historical limitations may be reflected in the apostle's comments on the behavior of women when he wrote to the Corinthian congregation, there can be no doubt that as a Christian apostle he had gained some remarkable insights into the man-woman relationship as a whole. It was he who first declared that in Christ there is no male and female. To contrast Paul with Jesus, then, is palpably unfair, for Jesus himself never said anything beyond what Paul said in writing to the Galatians. Indeed, he could not, for there is nothing more to be said; Paul's word in his epistle of Christian liberty is the last word. The time has come to look more closely at this groundbreaking affirmation.

Reminding the Galatians that they were all God's children through faith in Christ and that having been baptized into Christ they had put on Christ, Paul goes on to affirm: "There is no longer Jew or Greek, there is no longer slave or free; there is no longer male and female; for all of you are one in Christ Jesus" (Gal. 3:28 NRSV).[38] The thought of the apostle is that those divisions which threaten the fellowship in and for which we were created are done away in Christ. The areas that he mentions are race (Jew and Greek), class (slave and free), and sex (male and female).[39] These are bracketed together because they have been the source of some of the most bitter and intractable antagonisms that have divided the human family. This they have in common, and from this point of view they all stand, in the apostle's mind, over against the new oneness in Christ, in whom the fellowship of creation is restored.

These categories are obviously not alike in every respect. The distinction between slave and master is not a creation ordinance at all but an instance of man's inhumanity to man that perverts the purpose of creation. It is literally done away in Christ. The distinction between Jew and Greek, though hardly a creation ordinance, is consonant with the fellowship for which we were created so long as it is not used to foster religious arrogance and pride. It is done away in Christ only insofar as it has been the occasion for divisions that separate one from one's neighbor.[40] As a Christian, Paul still considered himself a Jew (albeit a fulfilled one) rather than a Greek. As for male and female, this distinction represents, indeed, an ordinance of creation. Humankind has always been male and female because of God's creative act. Sexuality, in a literal sense, is not abolished in Christ; it should not even be suppressed. It is not sexuality but the immemorial antagonism between the sexes, perhaps the deepest and most subtle of all enmities, that is done away in him. In Christ the man and the woman are redeemed from false stereotypes, stereotypes that inhibit their true relationship to each other. Thus redeemed, they are enabled to become what God intended them to be when he made humankind in his image — a fellowship of male and female.

Undoubtedly in all three of these pairs — Jew/Greek, bond/free, male/female — the apostle thinks preeminently *coram Deo,* that is, in terms of our relationship to God rather than our relationship to neighbor. His

38. While most versions translate, "neither male nor female," in order to retain the symmetry in the series, in the Greek original Paul shifts to "male *and* female," reflecting Gn. 1:27. One should also note that he uses ἄρσεν καὶ θῆλυ, the words found in the LXX rendering of Gn. 1:27. Here, then, he clearly has in mind the first creation narrative. This contrasts with his exclusive appeal to the second creation narrative when speaking of the woman's submission to the man.

39. "Race" is confessedly not adequate to describe the distinction between Jew and Greek. But, in our judgment, it serves as well as other terms that are sometimes used.

40. Unfortunately the church has responded to "Jewish" exclusiveness with "Christian" anti-Semitism, a denial in reverse of the apostle's thesis in Galatians.

emphasis is on personal, spiritual salvation in which fellowship with God, our Maker and Redeemer, is renewed. Yet it is important to note that the theological "breakthrough," if we might so speak, reflected in Galatians 3:28 had social implications even for the apostle. He saw those implications clearly enough in the case of Jews and Greeks. Accordingly, when Peter came under the influence of some scrupulous brothers from the Jerusalem church who would not accept dinner invitations from Gentile Christians in Antioch, Paul withstood him to his face (Gal. 2:11-12). He did not say, as those from James were trying to say, that Jews and Greeks are one as to their personal salvation and enjoy a "spiritual" fellowship in Christ, but in other respects, such as eating, things remain as they always have been — restaurants must be segregated since Jews cannot eat with Gentiles. Rather, he insisted on complete social integration.

In the second instance (slave/free) the apostle's social vision was not so clear. While he made it plain to Philemon that in Christ his relationship to Onesimus had radically changed — from slave to brother (v. 16) — he did not confront him on the slave issue as he had Peter on the issue of Jews and Gentiles eating together.

Admitting the apostle's limitation when it comes to slavery, what may one say to his admonition to slaves that they should obey their masters with singleness of heart, as to Christ? For the millions enslaved without the possibility of freedom in Paul's day, the exhortation that as Christians they should render an exemplary obedience to their earthly masters was undoubtedly a word from God that did much to ameliorate the evil of their bondage. In response to the call of Christ, slaves found their lives humanized by the inner strength and freedom gained as the Lord's freed people (1 Cor. 7:22). One should also note that for all the historical limitations reflected in his thinking, the position of the apostle was not without Christian insight when it came to slave-master relationships. Although he did not organize an "underground railway" (where would it have gone?), when he sent Onesimus back to his master, Philemon, he sent him back, as we have noted, "no longer as a slave but . . . as a beloved brother, . . . confident of your [Philemon's] obedience . . . knowing that you will do even more than I say" (Phlm. 16, 21). This last remark may be an oblique reference to manumission dictated by the stylistic proprieties of polite letter writing, of which the apostle here shows himself a master. When, therefore, one reads the apostolic admonitions to first-century slaves who were Christians in the light of his letter to Philemon, these admonitions take on a rather different meaning from that given them by early American slaveholders!

As for the third instance (male/female), here Paul was more cautious still when it came to the social implementation of his Christian insight. He even spoke of the woman as subordinate and unequal to the man (1 Cor. 11:7-10), admonishing her to learn from the man but not to presume to teach him. Yet the magnificent declaration that in Christ there is no male and female (Gal. 3:28) was for the apostle no mere theory, as can be seen from many incidental details of his ministry as reported in the New Testament. One can only conclude from these details that, in a most remarkable way for a former rabbi, he lived the truth that in Christ there is no male and female. In so doing, he began to implement his new understanding of the male-female relationship in his own life and in that of the church. For example, whereas in rabbinic usage a woman was designated only as a wife of a particular man, Paul greets women by name in the Roman congregation: Tryphaena, Tryphosa (Rom. 16:12), Julia (16:15), and Mary (16:6), commending the last for her diligent labors. Not only does he mention Priscilla (16:3) along with her husband Aquila, but he even names her before her husband.[41] In fact, the apostle, who has been maligned as a misogynist, greets by name no less than seven Christian women in Romans 16 — a cover letter carried by Phoebe, a woman whom he calls his sister and warmly commends as a servant of the church at Cenchreae (16:1-2). As a rabbi, Paul would hardly have deigned to address a group of women when no men were present; yet he did so in Philippi without a moment's hesitation (Acts 16:13). Even less would he have acquiesced in a woman's importunate invitation to abide in her house. Yet he accepted Lydia's invitation, it appears, without the slightest scruple (Acts 16:15).

In all this, one can hardly fail to see how far Paul had moved in his pilgrimage from Judaism to Christianity. In fact, the letter to the church at Philippi, a church that began with the conversion and baptism of a prominent woman and her household, and that met in her house (Acts 16:40), must be considered along with the letter to the church in Corinth if one is to have a balanced view of Paul's attitude toward women. If his correspondence with the Corinthian congregation reflects his Jewish background as one who had worshiped in the synagogue, his letter to the Philippians reflects a more liberalized view of the place of woman in the Christian church. Although the apostle addressed the Philippian church as constituted with bishops and deacons, all of whom were most likely males (Phil. 1:1), one can hardly reason that he simply used Lydia's conversion and hospitality as a means of establishing a bridgehead with men in the community. Women evidently played a prominent part in the

41. This same Priscilla, with her husband Aquila, instructed the eloquent Apollos, a Jew "well versed in the scriptures," in "the way of God more accurately" (Acts 18:24-26). While granting her the evident learning and ability implied by this incident, scholars have greeted with erudite indifference and condescension Harnack's suggestion that she was the author of Hebrews. They have preferred Luther's suggestion that the book was written by Apollos, her pupil!

church at Philippi, not only at its inception but also as it grew and developed. Two of them are mentioned by name, Euodia and Syntyche, whom Paul calls his "co-workers," who "struggled (συναθλέω) beside me in the work of the gospel" (Phil. 4:3 NRSV). These the apostle exhorts "to be of the same mind in the Lord" (4:2 NRSV). Although he does not disclose the nature of their misunderstanding, his appeal to them in a general letter to the church indicates that it was not simply a private affair. Rather, the difference between them threatened the unity and well-being of the whole church. Thus the apostle implies their prominence in the church and also their right to express themselves as leading members of the congregation.[42] To the same effect is the mention by Luke of "chief women," who were prominent among the apostle's converts in Thessalonica and Beroea (Acts 17:4, 12). There must have been something about Paul's gospel and the way he expounded it that made an impact on these sensitive and gifted women. And what could it have been but the profound worth, as *persons,* which they perceived themselves to have when they grasped the implications of his message?

We may conclude, then, that while Paul went all the way in living out the truth that in Christ there is neither Jew nor Greek, he by no means denied in his lifestyle the implications of the further truth that in Christ there is no male and female. Here he made only a beginning, to be sure, toward the social implementation of his insight. But it is high time that the church press on to the full implementation of the apostle's vision concerning the equality of the sexes in Christ. Thus and only thus will the church become a fellowship of men and women like that which is revealed to us in the life of our Lord himself while he lived among us — too briefly — in this sinful world.

c. Conclusion

Many, no doubt, will argue, as did our forebears in the days of the abolitionist movement, that the church should leave the social implications of the New Testament message to the civil government to implement. Let the church attend to its proper business, which is the salvation of souls, and not meddle in controversial social issues. If enough men are converted, then women will be treated justly and with love and concern. To raise up husbands who are more considerate in the home, husbands who are like the beneficent slave owners of a century ago, is what the church is com-

---

42. See the provocative article by the Reverend W. Derek Thomas, "The Place of Women in the Church at Philippi," *Expository Times* 83, no. 4 (Jan. 1972): 117-18.

missioned to do.[43] Some who argue thus do so in a deliberate effort to circumvent the truth. But many who do so are sincerely concerned to be biblical; and it is true beyond all doubt that the Bible is primarily concerned with the divine-human relationship. Those who deplore the "social gospel" have more than a grain of truth on their side; salvation with a vertical reference is the central theme of Scripture. Yet the social implications of this gospel of salvation are always implicit in Scripture, and sometimes explicit as well. What, then, may be said to those who have a sincere concern to be biblical when it comes to the place of women in society?

In response to this question we would suggest that it may be of help to distinguish between what the New Testament *teaches* about the new life in Christ and the actual degree of implementation of this vision in the first-century church. So far as woman's role in the partnership of life is concerned, it can hardly be the *degree of implementation* in the New Testament to which the church should look for authoritative guidance in our present moment in history. In its implementation, the New Testament church reflects, to a considerable extent, the prevailing attitudes and practices of the times. Because of this, we should look to the passages that point beyond these first-century attitudes toward women, to the ideal of the new humanity in Christ. Only thus can we harness the power of the gospel to make all history, not just first-century history, salvation history.

The example of slavery remains, perhaps, the best we have to illustrate this principle. If we believe that the abolition of slavery is the plain implication of the message of liberation in Christ, then we cannot regard the implementation of this ideal in the New Testament church as normative. Had the church through the centuries interpreted "neither slave nor free" in Galatians 3:28 in terms of its explicit implementation in the New Testament, the institution of slavery would never have been abolished. The same is true of woman's liberation. The church today should not strive to maintain the status quo of church life in the first century, as though it were normative for all time. Rather, the church should seek to implement fully the principle that in Christ women are truly free. Such an effort will contribute to the liberation of all, both men and women.

43. See the "Danvers Statement" of the Council on Biblical Mankind and Womankind, signed by evangelical advocates of male hierarchy, Rationale item 3, December 1987. "We have been moved in our purpose by the following contemporary developments which we observe with deep concern: . . . (3) the increasing promotion given to feminist-egalitarianism with accompanying distortions or neglect of the glad harmony portrayed in Scripture between the loving, humble leadership of redeemed husbands and the intelligent, willing support of that leadership by redeemed wives." Nothing is said about the "leadership" of the *un*-redeemed husbands mentioned in 1 Pt. 3:12.

Speaking to this end, D. S. Bailey makes the perceptive comment that achieving a right relationship between man and woman is a prime desideratum in all human affairs. God has laid upon us all, by making humankind male and female, the unconditional task of living in sexual partnership. And this obligation pertains not simply to marriage, but to all the manifold variety of associations in our communal existence as men and women. We have been created for each other and are bound together by a tie of mutual dependence. But in the past, this genuine partnership of mind and spirit between the man and the woman has been greatly hindered by theories of male superiority and domination. As a result, the woman has been excluded from many spheres of life, especially those where decisions are made. And her social and educational disabilities have deprived her of the means to refute the arguments by which the man has buttressed his position of privilege. The woman has had to compete with the man in a "man's world," on his terms, rather than relate to him as a partner who is equal to him in every way. In view of the many obstacles she has had to face in exercising her natural gifts as a female human being, her achievements are remarkable. Yet compared to the man's they are slight indeed. Little do we know what resources she has because she has been deprived of the spontaneity to express them through the stultifying effects of male supremacy.

In seeking a resolution to this problem, we must challenge the presumption that speaks of the "woman question." This very way of stating the matter presupposes that man's place in life has been determined and is beyond dispute. This is the first lie. If it is not good that man should be alone, if the Creator has given him a partner in life, then the "woman question" implies a "man question." The one cannot be discussed without the other. And the "man-woman question" is the question of their right relationship, a question that can never be resolved so long as one member presupposes that his role in the relationship is self-evident. Since God created humankind male and female, both must acknowledge the call of God to live creatively in a relationship of mutual trust and confidence, learning through experiment in relationship what God has ordained that they should learn in no other way. This calls for integrity on the part of the man to renounce the prerogatives, privileges, and powers that tradition has given him in the name of male headship. On the part of the woman it calls for courage to share the burdens and responsibilities of life with the man, that in love and humility they may together fulfill their common destiny as the creature in the image and likeness of God.[44]

44. See Bailey, *Sexual Relation,* pp. 282-84.

ADDENDUM: MISOGYNY IN PAGAN
AND CHRISTIAN THOUGHT

If the view we have espoused is true — that God has so created humankind that our very being is a being-in-fellowship; and if, at the human level, the fundamental form of that fellowship is the fellowship of man and woman, then any depreciation of the man by the woman or the woman by the man is a perversion of their common humanity. The female of the human species is by no means immune to this tragic propensity; but the male is undoubtedly the prime offender, the female more the hapless victim than the miserable sinner. In his selfish aggressiveness and pride, the man has made the woman's place in life a problem, not realizing that it is his attitude, not her existence, that is the fundamental problem.

After Achilles slew Hector outside the gates of Troy and celebrated the funeral of Patroclus, the Achaean warriors engaged in various contests for the prizes Achilles offered them. Whereupon mighty Ajax and crafty Ulysses wrestled valiantly till "their backbones cracked" for the prize of a "tripod ready for setting on the fire" — valued at twelve oxen. To the loser went the consolation prize, "a woman skilled in all manner of arts" — valued at four oxen.[45] This scene occurs in Homer's *Iliad,* the first work in the Great Books of the Western World, a series setting forth the fundamental ideas that have shaped Western civilization. Robert Hutchins has aptly called this series "The Great Conversation." Among the seventy-three authors who carry on this conversation, there is not one woman to speak on anything whatsoever. (The second edition of the series [1990] includes two women: novelists Jane Austen and George Eliot.) And when it comes to the subject of woman, it is some conversation! Indeed, it would be difficult to find a theme on which greater minds have expressed meaner thoughts.

Plato *(Timaeus),* having told us how God implanted immortal souls in material bodies, observes that he who lives an evil life will, upon reincarnation, become a woman. Aristotle, the father of biology, in his *Generation of Animals* (2.3.3), tells us that "the female is, as it were, a mutilated male," a piece of pseudoscience that Thomas Aquinas found not wholly incompatible with Christian theology. But it is not simply in classical paganism that such blatant misogyny is found. Some of the greatest minds of more modern times — Schopenhauer, Nietzsche, and others — have articulated similar vulgarities. But it remained for Sigmund Freud, in the name of the science of psychology, to explain in what sense Aristotle's "mutilated male," who is a "female," is really mutilated. She lacks a penis, and the

45. Homer, *Iliad,* 8.273, Great Books, 4.168.

envy that this anatomical deficiency has created in her is the key to the woman's psychosexual life. Her psychosexual life, in turn, is the key to understanding her life as woman. This crude bit of misogyny is set forth in Freud's *New Introductory Lectures on Psychoanalysis*. Lecture 33 is devoted to the "Psychology of Women," an analysis, Freud assures us, "containing nothing but observed facts, with hardly any speculative additions." He goes on to enlighten his audience with the observation that "throughout the ages the riddle of woman has puzzled people of every sort. . . . You too will have pondered over this question insofar as you are men; from the women among you that is not to be expected, for you yourselves are the riddle."[46]

In *The Feminine Mystique,* Betty Friedan offers a trenchant response to Freud. Noting the derision in which he held John Stuart Mill's views on women's emancipation, she goes on to observe, "The fact is that to Freud . . . women were a strange, inferior, less-than-human species. He saw them as child-like dolls, who existed in terms only of man's love, to love man and to serve his needs." Freud grew up, she observes, with this attitude built in by his culture — not only the culture of Victorian Europe, but that Jewish culture in which men said the daily prayer, "I thank thee, Lord, that thou has not created me a woman." In the same culture, women prayed in submission, "I thank thee, Lord, that thou hast created me according to thy will." Naturally, observes Friedan, a woman who secretly wished to have the freedom, status, and pleasure that men enjoy in life might wish she were a man and, in the shorthand of the dream, see herself with that one organ that made men unequivocally different. But you "cannot explain the woman's envy of the man, or her contempt for herself, as a mere refusal to accept her sexual deformity, unless you think that a woman, by nature, is inferior to man. Then, of course, her wish to be equal is neurotic."[47]

Instead of throwing Freud's book away, she complains, his popularizers threw it at their female patients. Thus they were driven back into the home, their proper "place," where they did not need an education and where, in lieu of their freedom and rights as human beings, they could have security and fulfillment as women. Awed by the authority of science, including the "science" of psychology, women were kept from questioning this "feminine mystique" elevated by Freudian theory into a pseudoscientific religion.[48]

46. Sigmund Freud, *New Introductory Lectures On Psycho-Analysis,* trans. W. J. H. Sprott (New York: Norton, 1933), pp. 154-55.
47. Betty Friedan, *The Feminine Mystique* (New York: Norton, 1963), p. 108.
48. Ibid., pp. 117-19, 125.

Not only Western thought in general but Christian thought in particular has been flawed by a disgraceful prejudice against women. Woman, declaims Chrysostom, is "a necessary evil, a natural temptation, a desirable calamity, a domestic peril, a painted ill."[49] Speaking of these and other contemptuous epithets with which the Fathers of the church loaded the name of woman, D. S. Bailey goes on to observe, "She is to be suspected and avoided as a subtle and dangerous temptress, always inclined to beguile man and to inflame him with evil passions."[50] In the traditional thought of the theologians, this sinister fascination of the female, by which she has beguiled mighty men like Samson and spilled the blood of holy men like John the Baptist, was grounded in the primal history of the race. Eve and all her daughters belong to that guilty sex whose sin led to the expulsion of the human race from the Paradise of God. "Do you not know," thunders Tertullian, "that each of you is also an Eve? . . . You are the devil's gateway, you are the unsealer of that forbidden tree."[51]

A millennium of Christian history hardly relieved this image of the woman as temptress. Novella O'Andrea, A.D. 1312-1366, one of the few learned women admitted to a chair in the venerable University of Bologna, lectured in philosophy and law behind a curtain lest her face should distract the students. But it is in the medieval theory of witchcraft, the alleged malevolent magic of women who had made a compact with the Devil, that this caricature of the woman as the ruin of the man reaches its apogee. The redemptive note, so prominent in our Lord's relation to women, is never heard in the fulminations of churchmen against the abominable practice of witchcraft. Rather, in their maledictions the traditional suspicion of the female character fuses with elements of folklore and superstition to betray the church into some of the most atrocious cruelties ever perpetrated by humans against their fellow humans. The bull *Summis desiderantes,* promulgated by Innocent VIII, December 7, 1484, assumed the evidence to be incontrovertible that humans, especially women, rendezvoused with demons in "witches' sabbaths," where they indulged every vice and were instructed in all sorts of fell arts. By these they made husbands sterile and wives barren, blighted vineyard and orchard, raised tempests, and rained down hailstorms. The response of the church to these straw women was vicious. Following instructions in the *Witches' Hammer,* a Dominican

---

49. As quoted by Kathleen Bliss, *The Service and Status of Women in the Churches* (London: SCM, 1952), p. 17, n. 1.

50. *Sexual Relation,* p. 63, with sources from Athenasius, Clement of Alexandria, et al.

51. *De cultu feminarum,* 1.1, as quoted by Bailey, *Sexual Relation,* p. 64. Although the ground of the misogynists' argument moves back and forth among bad biology, bad psychology, and bad theology, the result is always the same.

manual for detecting and prosecuting witches, the emissaries of the Holy Office interrogated thousands of women. Crazed by the agony of their torture, these hapless creatures confessed everything imagination could suggest. Even in the hour of death when, at last, they were delivered from physical torment, they were not buoyed by the sympathy and prayers of the church. Held in horror by those who had been nearest and sometimes dearest to them, subject to the indignity of having the hair shaved from their bodies, they were whipped, banished, and burned at the stake. Denied the glory of a martyr's crown and the prospect of a heavenly bliss, unpitied and unprayed for, they yielded to the cold scrutiny of the inquisitor and the consuming power of the flames.[52]

C. THE MYSTERY OF HUMAN SEXUALITY: A BRIEF COMMENT

The affirmation that our very existence as human is given us in the fellowship of male and female compels us to consider the question, What is the ultimate nature of this polarity on which such fellowship rests? Our sexuality permeates our being to its very depth; it conditions every facet of our lives as persons. As the self is always aware of itself as an "I," so this "I" is always aware of itself as "*her*self" or "*him*self." Our self-knowledge is indissolubly bound up not simply with our *human* being but with our *sexual* being. At the human level, there is no I and thou per se, but only the I who is male or female confronting the thou who is also male or female.

But what does it mean to say, I am a male; I am a female? What *is* a man? What *is* a woman? Recalling the deep sleep that fell upon Adam when Eve was created, D. S. Bailey observes that there is a divine secret here, a secret about our being that has never been disclosed. The intuitive awareness that one is a man or a woman does not convey an understanding of its meaning. "Thus sex remains a profound and baffling enigma of personal existence, the mystery of which can never be dispelled by excogitation — and certainly not by studying what is now both popularly and scientifically called 'sex.' "[53]

52. See Schaff, *History*, 6.514ff. The Protestant Reformers, lamentably, raised no word against the theory of witchcraft; and even Richard Baxter, the irenic peacemaker, applauded the worst cruelties in England, as did Cotton Mather in New England. As late as 1768, John Wesley opined that "giving up [belief in the reality of] witchcraft was, in effect, giving up the Bible."

53. *Sexual Relation*, pp. 280-81. Our inability to solve the ontological question of our sexuality, observes Bailey, is perhaps the most unpalatable of all truths to an age that thinks it "knows all about sex."

That there is something about human sexuality which is the Creator's secret, something concerning which the divine word has been sealed, as it were, is a truth theologians need to remember. Not that theology places a premium on ignorance, but it is always done best when it is done with a little humility. For example, Barth, who spends more time than most on our maleness and femaleness, admits that the difference-in-likeness between men and women is as mysterious as it is obvious.[54] Such reserve on the theologians' part is commended by the sheer complexity of the data available to modern science. This data makes one aware of mystery not only at the ultimate, but even at the penultimate, level of our understanding of human sexuality.

Beginning at the biological level, where it is easiest to say what a man is in distinction to a woman, matters are by no means simple. Scientists today distinguish at least five biological variables, ranging all the way from chromosomal factors in the cell nucleus to the external genitalia, all of which are ordinarily congruent in male and female human beings. (Incongruities at the biological level can create many problems of gender identity for the individual. Insofar as these problems have a moral component, we must leave their resolution to the ethicists.) Over and beyond our biological determination as male or female is the involved question of gender identity. The study of psychology, sociology, and cultural anthropology shows that our anatomy is not our destiny. Rather, we actualize the sexuality given us in our biological inheritance by interacting with our environment in a lifelong process of learning. Thus we who are born male and female become men and women as we internalize the cultural mores of the society into which we are born. In the study of this learning process, one sees how biological males and females acquire and maintain their respective masculine and feminine identities in society. Such a study cannot but impress one with the psychosexual malleability of the human subject in contrast to the animals.

It is this amazing plasticity, this "phenomenology" of human sexuality, as the philosophers and theologians call it, that discredits much of what has been said about the difference between men and women. Although it is still as true as ever that men and women are sexually different from birth, this difference is also a function of the roles assigned to the sexes in a given society and culture. When, therefore, theologians argue that man's nature is more "productive," woman's more "receptive"; man's more "outgoing," woman's more "introverted"; man's more "inquisitive," woman's more "conservative," etc., one suspects that such efforts have more to do with the traditional roles assigned men and women in Western culture than with the ordinance of creation.

---

54. In the first creation narrative "male and female" translates זָכָר וּנְקֵבָה (Gn. 1:27), two words of obscure origin that appear to derive from roots denoting, respectively, "the sharp one" (one with a penis) and "the perforated one" (one with a vagina). In the second narrative (Gn. 2:18-23), "man" and "woman" translate אִישׁ and אִשָּׁה, which some think come from roots denoting, respectively, "the strong one" and "the delicate one." Such terms, reflecting the primal data of experience, would seem to contribute little to an understanding of the ultimate meaning of our sexual polarity.

Not only have theologians been overly confident, in the light of empirical data, in their understanding of the difference between man and woman, but they have also erred in assuming that the woman is to be understood in terms of her sexuality in a way that the man is not. They have taken their text from Byron rather than the Bible:

> Man's love is of man's life a thing apart;
> 'Tis woman's whole existence.

To cite a case in point, Helmut Thielicke argues that a woman reveals more of her essential personhood through sexual encounters than does the man. This is supposedly because it is her vocation to be a lover, companion, and mother. Therefore, even in the career woman, who sublimates them, these fundamental characteristics remain discernible. By contrast, the man invests much less of himself in sexual relationships. In fact, in the sex act itself, the woman receives something to herself, whereas the man discharges something from himself — frees himself from it, as it were. In this freedom he gives himself to tasks and aims that carry him beyond his sexuality to confront what Schiller has called the hostile forces of life (*Theologische Ethik,* III, "Die Verwirklichung der Geschlechtsnatur" [Tübingen: Mohr (Siebeck), 1958], pp. 572-73; ET *The Ethics of Sex,* trans. J. W. Doberstein (Grand Rapids: Baker Book House, 1964), pp. 80-81). We see no ground whatever for drawing such a conclusion.

Even when Christian thinkers do not profess to understand the woman in terms of her sexuality, even when they admit to a mystery they cannot fathom, they tend to forget the duality of our humanity and focus on the mystery of the woman's nature in a derogatory way. For example, Kierkegaard looked on womanhood as something so complicated, strange, and confused that only a woman could live with the contradiction.[55] Simone de Beauvoir, animadverting on this female "mystery" so dear to the masculine heart, observes that it permits the man to find an easy explanation for all that appears so inexplicable in woman. Thus he can avoid admitting his ignorance. He can go on maintaining a negative relationship to the woman rather than relating to her authentically as a human being. The woman, hidden behind her veil, is for the man both angel and demon, one whose fundamental being is marked by ambiguity. In a truly perceptive paragraph, Beauvoir illumines the heart of the matter when she observes:

> Surely woman is, in a sense, mysterious, "mysterious as is all the world," according to Maeterlinck. Each is subject only for himself;

---

55. In attributing to Kierkegaard this view of woman, expressed, passim, in his *Stages on Life's Way,* we acknowledge that in the pseudonymous writings not all the opinions are Kierkegaard's. But this one surely seems to be.

each can grasp in immanence only himself, alone: from this point of view the *other* is always a mystery. However, to men's eyes the opacity of the self-knowing self, of the *pour-soi,* is denser in the *other feminine.* . . . The truth is that there is mystery on both sides: as the *other* who is of masculine sex, every man, also, has within him a presence, an inner self impenetrable to woman; she in turn is in ignorance of the male's erotic feeling. But in accordance with the universal rule I have stated, the categories in which men think of the world are established *from their point of view, as absolute: they misconceive reciprocity, here as everywhere.* A mystery for man, woman is considered to be mysterious in essence.[56]

To acknowledge that they have erred in that they have "misconceived reciprocity" is the first step male theologians must take when they address the mystery of human sexuality. Since we have our being as human in the sexual polarity of maleness and femaleness, we suspect that the ultimate meaning of our sexuality is to be found not in theory but in practice, not in reflection but in living; living, that is, in a relationship of equality and complementarity as men and women. Thus, and only thus, will we enjoy a mutually enriching life together as that life has been given us by the Creator.

EXCURSUS: THE ETERNAL FEMININE

The "Eternal Feminine," though a legitimate theological theme, is not exegetically grounded in Scripture in a specific way. It is rather an inference resting on the fundamental assumption — which we would not dispute — that the empirical world contains symbols whereby we see, as in a mirror, ultimate spiritual Reality. Specifically, it is argued, the woman's being uniquely mirrors this Reality; hence one may speak of the Eternal Feminine. In the phrase "the Eternal Feminine," the adjective "eternal" means that the woman is being understood, not in the light of biological, psychological, sociological, or historical considerations, but *sub specie aeternitatis.* That is, the woman, as the empirical bearer of the feminine principle, symbolizes the theological mystery of our true relationship to the Creator, a relationship in which the Creator's strength is made perfect in the creature's weakness (1 Cor. 12:9). In this relationship we find our summum bonum, the true meaning of our existence as those who live, move, and have their being in God.

56. Beauvoir, *Second Sex,* pp. 240-41. Italics added.

In Roman Catholic thought, the Eternal Feminine has been used to explain why the larger responsibility belongs to Eve in the biblical story of the Fall. Woman was tempted not as the weaker one but as the one to whom belonged the ascendency in the original creation. And the same ascendency also belongs to her in the redeemed creation. It is through the woman's "seed" (Gn. 3:15) that redemption comes to the human family. The metaphysical mystery of our humanity, therefore, becomes tangible, and hence intelligible, supremely in one woman; and this one woman is Mary, the mother of our Lord. Her virginity is the expression of the inviolable holiness and purity of life required of all who strive for the noblest achievement in the Christian pilgrimage. They who so strive are those who have "made themselves eunuchs for the sake of the kingdom of heaven" (Mt. 19:12). They are those who, having finished their earthly course, stand with the Lamb on Mount Zion because "these have not defiled themselves with women, for they are virgins" (παρθένοι, Rv. 14:4 NRSV).

Many modern translations obscure this last text (Rv. 14:4) by not translating παρθένοι as "virgins," which is its literal meaning. Rather than "they are virgins," we read, "they are chaste" (RSV); "they kept themselves pure" (NIV); "they are celibates" (NASB, also Phillips). Why do translators of this text not translate παρθένοι literally, as "virgins"? Perhaps because they wish to reflect contemporary usage, and in such usage men are not ordinarily called "virgins." But if this is the case, then why do they proceed to translate γυναικῶν literally as "women"? Could it be that male translators assume that when the author of Revelation says that the 144,000 "are those who have not defiled themselves with women" (οὗτοί εἰσιν οἳ μετὰ γυναικῶν οὐκ ἐμολύν-θησαν), he must be talking about literal women, since, obviously, men are defiled by — women? In any case, if one approaches this text from the perspective of the "Eternal Feminine," then the author is not talking about literal men, women, and virgins at all. Rather, he is referring to those (men and women alike) whose lives have not been defiled by the sinful world of the fallen creature. That is, he understands the triumph of the righteous over this defiling world and their beatitude in the world to come in terms of the feminine principle. Thus we can be sure that literal women are among the 144,000 who have the Lamb's name written on their foreheads, even as literal men were in the congregation at Corinth whom Paul presented to Christ as a "pure virgin" (παρθένον ἁγνήν, 2 Cor. 11:2 NIV).

In Roman Catholic thought, the feminine principle of virginity also enables us to see how male life intersects with female at the historical level in such well-known cases as that of the apostle Paul. Paul chose, as the better part, to refrain from marriage, that he might give his undivided devotion to the Lord (1 Cor. 7:32-38). But, of course, for the Roman Catholic, the feminine principle is most clearly exemplified in the life of Mary. This is not only because she remained a perpetual virgin, but also because she lived her life in a way that uniquely expresses the mystery of our humanity. To be truly human is not only to escape the defilement of the world, but to do so by surrendering our will to the will of the Almighty in all things. A unique instance of such surrender is Mary's response to the angelic annunciation of the birth of Jesus. In her words, "Behold, the handmaid of the Lord; be it unto me according to thy word" (Lk. 1:38 KJV), we have revealed the essence of our calling as creatures in the divine image, namely, openness to God's will and work through an act of total self-surrender. To symbolize such openness to God and so to one's neighbor is the ultimate meaning of the feminine mystery.

For believers in the Eternal Feminine, therefore, to disregard woman's symbolic significance is to fail to understand her insofar as her countenance is metaphysical. It is to disregard her *fiat mihi* ("be it unto me") and thereby to disregard the religious element in human life as a whole. Usually such a misunderstanding results from the self-assertive pride of the man, but it may also be the consequence of the woman's denial of her own symbol. Both are a repudiation of the Eternal Feminine. When this happens, the world becomes a "man's" world in the evil sense symbolized by the four horsemen of the Apocalypse (Rv. 6:1-8). This world without "Woman" is really a world without God, a world in which "Man" depends on human strength alone. Such a world is self-destructive, since "Man" can be truly human only in the spirit of the *fiat mihi* of the "Woman." Only when met by the power of a ready openness, the "be it unto me" of the Virgin, can the divine Power, breaking in from heaven, renew the earth to the glory of God.

The concept of the Eternal Feminine has never had the place in Protestant thought that it has had in Roman Catholic thought, where it is intertwined with Marian dogma. The Virgin of Catholic dogma is a *perpetual* virgin, *immaculately* conceived and *bodily* assumed into heaven. The Reformers' rejection of this Marian dogma — with which we concur — was so emphatic, however, that Protestant and evangelical theologians have given virtually no attention to Mary and the significant role belonging to her in salvation history. Should we not, as Protestants, in our gratitude to God for the gift of his Son, also show a little gratitude toward the mother of that Son? And should not this gratitude inspire positive theological reflection? "Through the annunciation," says the Angelic Doctor, "the consent of the Virgin, given in place of the whole human race, was awaited." Such a thought, in our judgment, is hardly heretical, whatever one may say of the subsequent development of Marian dogma in Roman Catholic theology.

In any case, the rejection of Marian dogma does not entail the rejection of the Eternal Feminine as such. The real problem, as we see it, with the Roman Catholic use of the concept is the inference that since the woman is the primary bearer of the Eternal Feminine, the man must be the primary bearer of the Eternal Masculine. Such an inference lies behind the thought that the *creaturely* submission to the Almighty, symbolized in the feminine principle, requires a *womanly* submission to the man, since the woman is the empirical bearer of that symbol. This is where the argument is skewed. The result is only too predictable. Mary's answer to the angel in the Annunciation symbolizes openness not only to the will of God on the part of the creature, but also to the will of the man on the part of the woman. Thus the man becomes the earthly counterpart of God. Now we grant that in the drama of the Incarnation, the Son has the *primary* role, the mother the *secondary* role; he *operates,* she *cooperates.* But the bearer of the Eternal Masculine in *this* case is the Son of God. We have no quarrel with the thought that the Son of God, who assumed our humanity as the son of Mary, symbolizes the Eternal Masculine, the divine Power breaking in from heaven to renew the earth. But when the male of the human species identifies himself as the symbol of this Power over against the female, we have one more instance of the man's proclivity to understand himself as being like the Creator, not along with the woman, but in distinction from the woman. Such an inflated self-understanding on the part of the male does not rest on an ordinance of creation; it echoes rather the thought of the Tempter, who was the first to talk of Godlikeness in this sense.

Probably the most able and comprehensive exposition of the Eternal Feminine is found in Gertrude von le Fort's *Das Ewige Frau.* This widely read work by a German baroness and convert to Roman Catholicism was published in 1934 and later translated into English as *The Eternal Woman* (Milwaukee: Bruce, 1962). Gertrude von le Fort embraces not only a full-blown Roman Catholic Mariology but also a very traditionalist view of the role of the woman, which she reinforces in her exposition of the Eternal Feminine. The woman is not endowed with the historically effective talents of the man; she is rather the silent carrier of those powers by which humankind shapes its destiny. (This is the theological statement of the Mother's Day sermon theme, "Behind the hand that wields the scepter is the hand that rocks the cradle.") When the man cannot meet the demands made on him, the woman does indeed come to the fore in history, as when a male seed fails and a daughter substitutes in the line of succession, even assuming royal authority. But such coming to the rescue is really an instance of the woman's *fiat mihi.* When she attains the height of achievement under these circumstances, a woman's charismatic vocation is evident (Joan of Arc, Catherine of Siena, et al.). It is this factor of charisma that has enabled the man, the bearer of the church's hierarchy, to recognize such specifically feminine achievement as authentic. This charisma does not imply power to produce in one's own strength but rather the obliteration of the self to the point of becoming simply the instrument of God in the moment. Hence the lives of the great women of history disclose the inner meaning of creaturely cooperation with the Creator as they follow the path that Mary took.

But this charismatic achievement within the boundaries of the feminine mystery is made to symbolize, in the Catholic view of the Eternal Feminine, not only the *creature's* cooperation with the *Creator* but also the *female* creature's cooperation with the *male* creature. As we have indicated, here the dislocation in the argument sets in. To be specific, the bride's lifelong cooperative response to her husband throws an eternal light on the "creative companionship" between the sexes generally. As friend and fellow worker, the woman is the spouse of the masculine spirit — the Victoria Colonna, as it were, of Michelangelo; the Frau von Stein of Goethe. Hence the woman's work merges into the creative work of the man in an attitude of self-giving and surrender. As the bride receives her name from the groom, as Beatrice is veiled when she approaches Dante, so the woman, as the bride of the masculine spirit, fulfills her role, inherent in the eternal order of creation, as the bearer of the feminine symbol.

To illustrate the dislocation in this Catholic use of the Eternal Feminine, one need only consider the priesthood. Like all the religious, in their vow of celibacy priests follow the example of the apostle Paul and make themselves eunuchs for the kingdom of heaven's sake. In this renunciation of marriage, we are told, they exemplify the feminine principle set forth in the life of the Virgin. But the woman, who is the primary bearer of this very principle, and who, in her role as mother, is most closely linked with the church in its feminine essence (the church is the "mother" of us all), has no right to the priesthood! In fact, were the church to entrust the priesthood to *her,* it would destroy, in symbol, the timeless significance of the woman as the bearer of the Eternal Feminine! We find this a powerfully *un*convincing argument.

Charlotte von Kirschbaum responded to le Fort in her *Die wirkliche Frau* (Zurich: Evangelischer Verlag, 1949; ET: *The Question of Woman,* trans. J. Shepherd, ed. E. Jackson [Grand Rapids: Eerdmans, 1996]). In her response, von Kirschbaum gives her attention largely to Mariology and its refutation. For us, her work in this area takes on special interest in view of her relationship to Barth as the woman without whom, by his own confession, he could never have written his *Dogmatics.* (See Renate Köbler, *In the Shadow of Karl Barth: Charlotte von Kirschbaum,* trans. K. Crim [Louisville: Westminster/John Knox, 1989].)

Something Fitting

*A Sermon Preached by Marguerite Shuster
at Knox Presbyterian Church, Pasadena, California,
Lord's Day, October 20, 1991*

*Then the Lord God said, "It is not good that the man should be alone; I
will make him a helper fit for him." So out of the ground the Lord God
formed every beast of the field and every bird of the air, and brought them
to the man to see what he would call them; and whatever the man called
every living creature, that was its name. The man gave names to all cattle,
and to the birds of the air, and to every beast of the field; but for the man
there was not found a helper fit for him. So the Lord God caused a deep
sleep to fall upon the man, and while he slept took one of his ribs and
closed up its place with flesh; and the rib which the Lord God had taken
from the man he made into a woman and brought her to the man. Then
the man said, "This at last is bone of my bones and flesh of my flesh; she
shall be called Woman, because she was taken out of Man." Therefore a
man leaves his father and his mother and cleaves to his wife, and they
become one flesh.*

Genesis 2:18-24

"Vive la différence!" goes the famous French saying, proclaimed, one
supposes, with the much vaunted French enthusiasm. "How like a man!"
remarks an observer, tolerantly excusing some mildly disapproved behavior. "Isn't that just like a woman!" someone exclaims, with the slightly
amused, deprecating tone that suggests that the person in question being a
woman explains everything. "Why ask why?" concludes the endlessly

184

repeated beer commercial, after playing out examples of the presumably typical behaviors of one sex that can be counted upon to irritate the other. In each case the speaker relies on what he assumes to be the most obvious thing in the world: men and women are just plain *different,* that's all. Anybody who doesn't know that is clearly beyond help.

But when it comes to specifying just *how* men and women are different, besides the grossest points of anatomy, things become quite a bit more complicated. The endless psychological research on sex differences comes up with a few seemingly assured results that appear not to rely on social and cultural factors: on the average (and one must always say, "on the average"), little boys show higher levels of activity and aggression than little girls and generally excel in spatial and mathematical tasks; little girls do better in verbal skills. In fact, early IQ tests that emphasized the verbal side of things showed women coming out on top so consistently that the construction of the tests was changed so that scores now show more parity of the sexes. The point is, though, that all this research has come up with a lot less by way of identifiable differences than one might have expected.

More recently, rather than seeking to torpedo old, false stereotypes, some groups of women and some groups of men have sought to retrieve and relabel what they think are positive aspects of the old stereotypes. Some women have done studies suggesting, for instance, that women differ from men in the way that they make ethical decisions, emphasizing interpersonal, relational values instead of relying on abstract principles (and they generally conclude that a world like ours can use a lot more emphasis on these interpersonal, relational values). Some men are seeking to develop a specifically male spirituality that, among other things, restores a place of honor to the heroic and even macho side of the traditional male identity, sometimes with the defensible argument that what society doesn't need is more passive, underresponsible men.

In the midst of all of this, one sometimes wonders what makes it so important to nail down *differences.* In a famous essay entitled "The Human-Not-Quite-Human," Dorothy Sayers begins:

> The first task, when undertaking the study of any phenomenon, is to observe its most obvious feature; and it is here that most students fail. . . . The first thing that strikes the careless observer is that women are unlike men. They are "the opposite sex" — (though why "opposite" I do not know; what is the "neighbouring sex"?). But the fundamental thing is that women are more like men than anything else in the world. They are human beings.[a]

a. *Unpopular Opinions* (London: Victor Gollancz, 1946), p. 116.

She concludes the essay with a brief analysis of how Jesus related to women and says,

> There is no act, no sermon, no parable in the whole Gospel that borrows its pungency from female perversity; nobody could possibly guess from the words and deeds of Jesus that there was anything "funny" about woman's nature.[b]

And that, of course, is a fundamental point of my text: the woman, unlike anything else in the whole creation, was created as a fitting counterpart for the man, more like him than anything else in all the world.

If some particular, key, and universally identifiable difference or differences between the nature and roles of the man and the woman were intended in the creation, it is strange indeed that we find no hint of it here. We certainly do not find it in the phrase that the woman was to be "a helper fit for" the man. Nowhere else in Scripture is the word "helper" used for a subordinate. Rather, we find it in such verses as, "My *help* comes from the LORD, who made heaven and earth" (Ps. 121:2); "Happy is he whose *help* is the God of Jacob" (Ps. 146:5); and so on. Over and over again, God himself, not a subordinate, is identified as our helper. "Fit for" means simply "corresponding to," "equal and adequate to," with the implication of both similarity and supplementation. The woman's fitness for the man is in no way prescribed or delimited, as if she were fitted merely for childbearing, or merely for certain kinds of work. Rather, the fitness includes that of body and spirit, entailing mutual help and understanding and joy and contentment in one another.[c]

Nor can we draw any confident conclusions from the fact that the man was made first: if priority in time were everything, the man should consider himself inferior to the trees. Nor will the woman's derivation from the man demonstrate her lesser worth: she was, indeed, made from his rib; but he himself was made from the dust of the earth. What we find instead of any suggestion of inferiority is a picture of God taking the same sort of initiative and care in the creation of the woman as he took in the creation of the man. He makes her himself, while the man is sound asleep. She does not owe her being to the man, any more than the man owes his to her. Certainly, she is not an *alien* creature, as her being made from his rib beautifully symbolizes; rather the man and woman belong to each other from the beginning, as being of fundamentally the same substance. But neither is

---

b. Ibid., p. 122.

c. Claus Westermann, *Genesis 1–11,* trans. J. J. Scullion, Continental Commentary (Minneapolis: Augsburg, 1984), p. 227.

she something made according to specifications the man made up. He wasn't even consulted.

One may wonder why the man wasn't consulted, since the matter was, after all, of some concern to him.[d] He had shown the good sense to recognize that the animals, however beautiful or useful or whatever they might be, were not quite what he needed. But to know what doesn't meet one's need is not the same thing as knowing what will, especially if one has never met it before. My guess is that if we were consulted about such a thing, we would choose for ourselves either a sort of carbon copy of ourselves who would in no way challenge or threaten us, or else some vastly inferior being with a few skills we lacked and therefore useful as a flunky. But then we would still, in the most basic sense, be alone. Try talking into a tape recorder, if you think having your own views echoed is all that matters. Or spend your whole life with those who are not your peers, if you think you will find satisfaction in simply ordering others around in accord with your own wishes. In either situation one remains alone, and a clear implication of my text is that to be alone is precisely to be help-less.[e] To be alone is to be helpless.

Human beings do not find the meaning of their life simply in the fact of their existence, but rather in human community; and fundamental to an understanding of what human community *is* is the relationship of man and woman — *not* their sexual relationship in itself, but their relationship as those creatures both of whom are created in the image of God.[f] Human community is not just more of the same. To say that it is not good that we should be alone is to imply that it is not good that we should define ourselves simply in terms of ourselves — our own sex and self-development and needs and preferred style of relating. We can fulfill our destiny only in mutual assistance.[g] And, let us grant it, we can assist each other only if we are in some sense different from one another and do not seek to abolish the differences, whatever they may be. So we are back at last to acknowledging differences, you say? And it's about time, you add? Well, yes; but let us hold the idea lightly as we push forward a little further.

Let us suppose that we do rightly fulfill our destiny in mutual assistance rather than in the single-minded pursuit of a self-centered agenda. That idea presupposes that we must then be content not only to help (the role,

d. Elie Wiesel, *Messengers of God,* trans. Marion Wiesel (New York: Pocket Books, 1977), p. 26.

e. Gerhard von Rad, *Genesis,* rev. ed., trans. John H. Marks, Old Testament Library (Philadelphia: Westminster, 1972), p. 82.

f. Westermann, *Genesis 1-11,* p. 227.

g. Delitzsch, cited in ibid.

you recall, assigned here to the woman and characteristic of God himself), but also to be helped (the role assigned in this text to the man). Do you get the feeling that described this way, things are beginning to be stood on their heads? That's because we have learned too well the false lesson that to need help is to be culpably weak. The true lesson is that simply to be human and finite, even apart from being the sinners we also are, is to need help. But we can receive help only when we don't feel threatened at the core by the one who offers it, only when help can be given and received in love.

To know that one needs help is to know that one has limits; and Bonhoeffer remarked that "where love towards the other is destroyed man can only hate his limit."[h] Any other person limits me by his or her very existence: I am no longer everything. Any other person who can do something I cannot do makes plain what some of my limits of ability or character are. If I do not love that other person, I will want to destroy or deny or at the very least possess and control him or her. The language is strong, but not too strong, I think, to describe the tragic acts of competitiveness and oppression between the sexes.

So let us acknowledge that there are differences between men and women, but let us be very careful in our suggestions of what they are and what they imply, lest we find ourselves caught in what will prove to be manifest absurdity. Take the case of Stanford University and women. The school was always coeducational, but an archivist reports on the popular view held around the turn of the century that exposing a woman to an education designed for men would deform both her character and her physical health, a view propounded in a book published in 1873. However discredited that theory might be and whatever other factors entered in, not until one hundred years later, in 1973, less than twenty years ago, was the ceiling on the enrollment of women at Stanford lifted.[i]

Today, with efforts being made for inclusiveness, a woman like me is from time to time asked to serve on some sort of academic panel in order that "a woman's point of view" might be represented. As if women simply as women have a unified and distinctive point of view! I may well participate if I am interested in the topic; but imagine seeking out "a man's point of view" on, say, some aspect of Presbyterian doctrine! Presumably one would, instead, seek responses from those with knowledge of the subject under discussion.

h. *Creation and Fall; Temptation,* trans. John C. Fletcher, et al. (New York: Macmillan, 1959), p. 61.

i. *The Stanford Observer,* May 1985, p. 3.

Subtle sexism can even sneak into mathematics, believe it or not. In 1986 (October 29), the *New York Times* reported on a classic math problem, posed in 1891, whose solution was apparently hampered by sexist assumptions. The Menage Problem asks you to suppose that you have a certain number of couples to dinner and wish to seat them at a round table, with couples separated and men and women alternating. How many seating arrangements are possible? The mathematicians who came up with the most elegant solution claimed: "It appears that it was only the tradition of seating the ladies first that made the Menage Problem seem in any way difficult." The answer, by the way, is that with three couples, there are twelve suitable seating arrangements, but with ten, there are 3,191,834,419,200; which, the article concludes, "may not come as a surprise to anyone who has tried to organize a successful dinner party."

Of course there are differences between men and women, else we would not be as suitable and adequate helps to one another as the Lord created us to be; but exactly what those differences are is more mysterious than has sometimes been supposed by those who wish to make lists of roles and qualities and attitudes. Traditional, rigid assumptions hurt everyone, personally and practically. Indeed, if we are honest, surely we will start by admitting that we are profoundly mysterious to ourselves as human beings and as men or women; and that any other human, same sex or other sex, is likewise mysterious in a way past our fathoming. How would we answer from our own point of view what it *is* to be a woman or a man? We never discover the secret of ourselves and our own sexual being, much less that of anyone else.

But surely, if my text conveys anything by its whole mood and design, what it conveys is *not* that this mystery of our difference in similarity and similarity in difference as male and female is given us as a problem we are supposed to solve. It is not given as a problem at all, but rather issues in instantaneous, joyful, forceful welcome: this, this one here, this — in the Hebrew text the man repeats himself three times — "this at last is bone of my bones and flesh of my flesh." Whatever else she might be, he knew with a flash of recognition that she was right, just right, for him. And sometimes it seems to me that the whole history of our struggle to define things more closely than that is a manifestation of our endless determination to refuse to abandon ourselves to amazement and delight: "This at last is bone of my bones and flesh of my flesh."

D. SEX, LOVE, AND MARRIAGE

1. INTRODUCTION

As creatures in the divine image, we have argued, we have our humanity as a shared humanity, an I-thou fellowship whose primary form is that of male and female. Such a fellowship has many and varied manifestations, of which marriage is the most obvious and intimate. As such, marriage is redolent of all that it means to have our being as a being-in-the-relationship-of-male-and-female. This is not to say that marriage is the final purpose of our sexuality, the key that unlocks the mystery of our existence as male and female. That mystery, we have argued, has ultimately to do with our being in the image of God, not with our fellowship as husband and wife. Many men and women live full and meaningful lives apart from marriage. In our exposition of the Christian faith, therefore, we have given marriage a secondary place in our understanding and interpretation of human sexuality. This ordering of the materials of dogmatics so that we reason from the relationship of men and women in general to that of husband and wife in particular means that what we are about to say concerning marriage presupposes what we have already said about the complementarity and equality belonging to the man-woman relationship in general.

Although we subsume marriage under the larger reality of our existence as male and female, the integral relation between the two cannot be doubted. All that is right for the encounter of man and woman is right for the encounter of husband and wife; and all that is wrong for the encounter of husband and wife is wrong for the encounter of man and woman. Obviously, then, while marriage may be denied center stage in stating one's views of sexuality, it can never be disassociated from those views. Indeed, marriage is that specific instance of the man-woman relationship in which our sexual polarity is paramount. If ever the truism that we cannot escape our sexuality is evident, it is when two people enter into that most intimate of all human relations in which a man and a woman look into each other's eyes and say, "I take you to be my lawful, wedded husband/wife."

What is self-evident, as a matter of fact, in the existential encounter of marriage is implied, in principle, in the juxtaposition of sex and marriage in the biblical narratives of creation. No sooner do we read in Genesis 1:27 that God created humankind male and female, than we read in the next verse (28) of the divine blessing on them and the command to be fruitful and multiply, a blessing and a command that belong to marriage. By the same token, in the second creation narrative, the story of the woman's creation to complement and complete that of the man is followed immediately by the statement, "*Therefore,* a man leaves his father and his mother and cleaves to his wife, and they become one flesh" (2:24).

With regard to Gn. 2:24, which is the first express statement about the ordinance of marriage in the Bible, it is surprising to note how it reads. The text does not say, "Therefore shall a *woman* leave her father and mother and cleave to her *husband,* and they become one flesh." This, of course, is what actually happened in the patriarchal society of ancient Israel; the woman left her family to become a member of her husband's family. Why this striking reversal in the text? Here the observation of Heinrich Baltensweiler is worthy of note. The author, he suggests, in speaking as he does, means to convey the thought of the woman's worth. The man "loves her so much; so much does the thought of her fill his mind, that he is ready to break the closest family ties which blood relationship can establish. He will cleave to his wife and they shall become one flesh" (*Die Ehe im Neuen Testament* [Zurich: Zwingli, 1967], p. 21). The verb דָּבַק conveys strong personal attachment, as when Ruth cleaves to Naomi (Ruth 1:14), the people to their king (2 Sam. 20:2), and, in eight occurrences, Israel to their God.

As we turn to our task of making a Christian statement about sex, love, and marriage, one should observe that we are not primarily concerned with the so-called judicial question of marriage as an institution. Our concern, rather, is theological. The theological perspective we assume is that of the Protestant Reformers. Like them, we understand marriage in terms of creation rather than redemption. That is, marriage is not a sacrament of grace but an ordinance of creation;[57] it pertains not to the church but to the whole human family as made in the image of God. The right to marry is a right belonging equally to all people.

Although marriage belongs to the human family as a whole, we make no effort to frame a doctrine of marriage on which all will agree — an impossible task, given our sinful alienation from God and one another. Rather, our effort to understand marriage is one that interprets the marriage relationship and the responsibilities it entails in the light of the confession that Jesus is Lord.[58] As we turn to our subject, we venture a definition that determines the order — sex, love, marriage — we shall impose on the

---

57. We call marriage an "ordinance of creation" in the sense that it is a relationship which rests on the order and structure of our being as created male and female.

58. This is not to say that we shall simply ignore the problems confronting a Christian view of marriage due to the "sex revolution" brought on by technology and social change. It does mean, however, that we shall not approach our subject in terms of the "crisis of marriage." There is a vast literature of the marriage-and-family-counseling genre dealing with marriage from this point of view. Our approach will be that of the creation ideal as Christians have been given to understand that ideal through faith in Christ.

materials, as well as anticipates the nature of the conclusions we shall reach. *Marriage is that particular form of the encounter between male and female in which (1) a man and a woman (2) freely choose out of love for each other (3) to enter into an ongoing, exclusive, and lasting relationship (4) based on a mutual promise of fidelity.*[59]

2. SEX AS EROTIC PASSION[60]

In our definition, marriage is an encounter between "a man and a woman." Since, in this encounter, the "I" and the "thou" are two individuals of the opposite sex, marriage is obviously an encounter having a uniquely sexual quality. For those who are acquainted with the Christian tradition, it is no secret that the church has always been ambivalent about sex in the sense of erotic passion. This was especially true of the ancient Fathers. The heirs of a Greek dualism that denigrated the body, they extolled the virginity of Jesus and his mother and tended to look on sex as an unmentionable mechanism for procreation. The orgasmic climax of intercourse was viewed as a paroxysm of passion in which the animal appetites of the flesh threaten the proper balance between body and spirit. While "men ought always to pray," in coitus they obviously cannot.[61] The technical term used in classic theology to describe this inordinate passion is "concupiscence" *(concupiscentia).* Concupiscence is any compulsive urge to satiate one's desires, especially those fleshly desires pertaining to the sex impulse. When we succumb to such fleshly desires, we are out of control; the higher powers of reason and will are upset and the good life of impassive contemplation, the *vita contemplativa,* prized by the Greeks, succumbs to sensual pleasure and the gratification of animal appetite.

When it comes to the question of sex and passion, the Fathers' view of the divine impassibility returns to vex the theological enterprise. What they said about the way the divine Son of God, even as incarnate, transcended all emotions and bodily appetites — see *God, Creation, and Revelation,* pp. 398-401 — makes it obvious that the Fathers

59. The marriage relationship, so defined, makes the man a "husband" and the woman a "wife." We shall therefore avoid the common expression "*man* and wife." In other words, we shall not understand the man in terms of his essential humanity and the woman simply in terms of her role as wife.

60. In distinction from the foregoing discussion of the man-woman relationship in general, we shall now speak of "sex" and "sexuality" in a specifically erotic sense.

61. "Men" is quite literally appropriate here. The patristic discussion of sex is androcentric through and through. One wonders if the Fathers even thought of the possibility that a woman could experience an orgasm.

never thought of Jesus as experiencing any struggle with sexual impulses. And if Jesus, who revealed our humanity in perfection, transcended such impulses, the same must surely have been true for our first parents before they fell. They must have experienced their moments of sexual intimacy with no more passion and perspiration than when they were drinking water from their gourd. The Fathers could not deny that human generation pertained to the original creation, for the Creator himself had bidden our first parents to "be fruitful and multiply." But such procreation was sans passion. Augustine was of the opinion that Adam and Eve were expelled from the Garden before they engaged in intercourse. But even if they had come together in Paradise, the sexual organs would have tranquilly acquiesced in the bidding of the mind in full subjection to the will. In this serene and cerebral experience of togetherness, our first parents would have known a "gravity of glowing pleasure," yet without any "beastly move-ment" of the sort that inevitably compromises the marriage bed now that we are fallen sinners (*De civitate Dei*, 14.22-24). Thomas embraces Augustine's view of unfallen sexuality in all the essentials (*Summa Theologica*, pt. 1, q. 98, art. 2, "Whether in the State of Innocence There Would Have Been Generation by Coition?").

Of course the Fathers, having rejected the radical dualism of the Gnos-tics, could not condemn human sexuality out of hand, as though the Demi-urge had created everything below the navel.[62] Yet they were reluctant to affirm the sexual impulse as the good gift of the Creator to be used in a responsible way and enjoyed with gratitude. Part of their problem was undoubtedly their own experience before conversion. The way in which men like Tertullian, Jerome, and Augustine reproach themselves for the sins of their youth reveals the significant personal component involved in their attitude toward sex generally. Of the many issues leading to Augustine's conversion, to cite the best-known case, the sexual question was always prominent. This can be seen not only in the prayer he used, "Give me chastity — but not yet,"[63] but also in the Scripture passage on which his eyes fell when he opened Paul's letter to the Romans in the garden in Milan: "Let us conduct ourselves becomingly as in the day, not in reveling and drunkenness, not in debauchery and licentiousness. . . . But put on the Lord Jesus Christ, and make no provision for the flesh, to gratify its desires [KJV 'lusts']" (Rom. 13:13-14).[64]

62. In practical piety, however, such an attitude prevailed widely. "The story is told of a priest of his [Gregory I] time who kept his wife at a distance. When he was on his death bed she came to say goodbye, but he forbade her with the words, 'Depart, woman, take away the straw, for there is yet fire here' " (Roland Bainton, *What Christianity Says About Sex, Love, and Marriage* [New York: Association Press, 1957], pp. 53-54). On the church's rejection of Gnostic dualism, see *God, Creation, and Revelation*, pp. 440-42.

63. *Confessions*, 8.7.17.

64. For a careful analysis of the experiential component in the patristic comment on sex, with sources, see Bailey, *Sexual Relation*, pp. 48-49.

However, it would be a mistake to dismiss this ancient and long-standing reservation about sex, which continues in the church even down to the present, as a mere psychological aberration. There is something deeply wrong with our sexual impulse; and in this day of sexual "liberation," when many soundly reject the Christian virtue of chastity, it would be irresponsible not to speak a clear word on the side of a continent and chaste lifestyle. Furthermore, it is anything but prudish to confess that the way we express our sexuality — especially as males of the species — plainly corroborates the doctrine of original sin.[65] As C. S. Lewis observes:

> You can get a large audience together for a strip-tease act — that is, to watch a girl undress on the stage. Now suppose you came to a country where you could fill a theatre by simply bringing a covered plate on to the stage and then slowly lifting the cover so as to let everyone see, just before the lights went out, that it contained a mutton chop or a bit of bacon, would you not think that in that country something had gone wrong with the appetite for food?[66]

It is, perhaps, helpful in this matter of determining what is right and what is wrong with our sexual impulse to distinguish between "passion" and "lust."[67] When the ancient and medieval theologians talked about prefallen sexuality as without passion, they were doing apathic anthropology, which is no more convincing than apathic theology. There is no such thing (and there never was) as impassive sexuality. In its depth and vehemence, the sexual impulse can shake and overwhelm a person. It may rightly, in its intensity, be called a *ruling* passion, that is, a passion in which a person becomes aware of being acted upon as well as acting. Even the apostle Paul, who personally had the gift of continence, advises the Corinthians that it is better to marry than to be "aflame with passion" (πυροῦσθαι, 1 Cor. 7:9). And he is not talking about a sinful condition of

---

65. Some of the fiercest passions and darkest crimes in contemporary American life are sexual in nature; they are crimes — incest, rape — committed by men against girls and women.

66. *Mere Christianity* (London and Glasgow: Fontana, 1952), p. 86. Since people respond with passion to food when they are hungry, some have argued that the response to a striptease manifests sexual starvation. Lewis replies that today, as a matter of fact, people gratify their sex impulses more freely than ever before, yet the appetite for sex has grown with indulgence. Sexually speaking, we are not like hungry people; we are like gluttons who are still obsessed with food even when they have eaten more than their fill.

67. Since the New Testament uses ἐπιθυμέω of both lawful and unlawful desire, the distinction we suggest must be determined by context. Compare, for example, Mt. 5:28 with Lk. 22:15.

which they should repent, but rather of a human condition, to which, in his judgment, they would find marriage to be a happy resolution.

The apostle touches on the same matter in 1 Cor. 7:36, a notably difficult passage. "If," says the apostle, "anyone thinks that he is not behaving properly toward his virgin [τὴν παρθένον αὐτοῦ, i.e., "his virgin daughter" (NASB), "the virgin he is engaged to" (NIV), "his betrothed" (RSV), "the woman he loves" (Phillips)]"; and if he, the male, or she, the female, is ὑπέρακμος, a word otherwise unknown in the Greek language, meaning, "if she should be of full age" (NASB), or, "if she is getting along in years" (NIV), or perhaps, "if his passions are strong" (RSV), or perhaps, again, if "the emotional strain [for both] is considerable" (Phillips), "let him do as he wishes: let them marry — it is no sin." Paul may be referring to a betrothed couple, as most of these translations suggest. Or he may be referring to an early form of sexual asceticism, a "spiritual marriage," in which a man and a woman share the same abode in strict continence, working with the dubious principle that one augments merit by sharpening temptation. (One is reminded of the custom of bundling courting couples in early New England.) In any case, it is evident that once again the apostle recognizes the sheer power of the sexual impulse. It is not something to be condemned, but neither is it something to be denied. Rather, because of its power, it calls for the resolution offered in the fellowship of marriage whenever this is possible. (For statistics bearing on the strength of the sexual urge, especially in the male, see James McCary, *Human Sexuality* [New York: Van Nostrand, 1973], pp. 260-61.)

To acknowledge the passionate character of sexual (erotic) love is not to reduce such love to an irresistible biological drive whose sole purpose is the preservation of the species. Love is not simply a "cold sweat in propinquity." While humans share with animals the sexual instinct as a biological given, at the same time they transcend its driving impulse. The erotic encounter of a man and a woman is not like that of a tiger who stalks a tigress in heat, impregnates her with a snarl, and leaves her until another year rolls around. To be human is to discover the other as a personal self, a "thou," even in the sexual act. Thus our "animal sexuality" is caught up into our essential humanity in a way that transforms the impulse into something else quite different from that of the animals.[68] To designate this something else that is quite different, we shall speak of "romantic love." Such love is "a many splendored thing," and of its splendors we shall speak presently. For now our point is simply that the sexual component in such love means that it is unabashedly passionate. To be sure, there is a sexual component in all human relationships, for all humans are males or females; but there is something unique about the sexuality of romantic love. In such love one is moved with a gripping desire for someone of the

---

68. The difference is reflected in the way we speak: animals "mate," people "marry," etc.

opposite sex, not simply to gratify a biological urge, but in the awareness that the fulfillment and completion of one's own life is found in union with another who is of the opposite sex, a union that excludes all others. Queen Victoria, it is said, wrote to Albert that she had decided to accept his proposal of marriage because "I cannot live without you" — a very good reason indeed. Such romantic love, in the Christian understanding of life, finds its truest and most rewarding expression in the "one flesh" of the marriage bond.

To speak of sexual or romantic love brings us back to our definition of marriage. Marriage, we have said, is not only an encounter between a man and a woman, but its form is that of a choice which the man and the woman "freely make out of love for each other." We must now speak to this subject of romantic love, which we acknowledge as a genuine component of theological anthropology. But before we do so, we pause to say a word about the sinful perversion of love's passion, a perversion that turns love into lust.

Something, we have confessed, has indeed gone wrong with our sexuality. This is seen in the sad fact that we cannot affirm the passion of love without at the same time lamenting the lust that compromises such passion. Jesus' word in the Sermon on the Mount that "whosoever looketh on a woman to lust after her hath committed adultery with her already in his heart" (Mt. 5:28 KJV) condemns us all. We have taken the position that the Fathers erred in understanding all sexual passion as concupiscence. The passionate quality of romantic love is not per se symptomatic of sin. At the same time we must acknowledge that sin vitiates this passion and turns it into lust from which none escapes altogether — including the most abstemious ascetic. (See Sessetta's "St. Anthony Tempted by the Devil in the Form of a Woman," *Metropolitan Seminars in Art,* Portfolio 2, plate 24. For remarks on the misogyny implicit in such an artistic representation, see above, pp. 173-76.) This dialectic of love and lust calls for a comment. Our inability as sinners wholly to free ourselves from lust in the experience and expression of our sexuality does not mean that love and lust are ultimately one and the same thing. Indeed, a great gulf is fixed between them. The failure of theologians to clarify this point explains, at least in part, why they have had so little to say about romantic love. While they have discoursed copiously on marriage, some even treating it as a sacrament, they have been singularly reluctant to talk about romantic love, without which marriage falls short of the Christian ideal. But more of this presently. For the moment, we must speak of the perversion of that ideal, a perversion that we call "lust."

Theologians have traditionally understood lust as any urge to gratify one's sexual desires that does not aim at procreation. Lust manifests itself not only in adultery, incest, rape, bestiality, etc., but even in intercourse with one's own spouse if it is indulged for pleasure alone. The only equivocation in the tradition has concerned prostitution. Prostitution has been viewed as necessary in that it preserves feminine virtue in society as a whole. Hence, though evil in itself, prostitution contributes to the well-being of the body politic. (See Bailey, *Sexual Relation,* pp. 158-59, with sources in Augustine and Thomas. Note also Simone de Beauvoir's acrid comment on the Fathers' assumption that one part of the female sex had to be sacrificed in order to save the other [*The Second Sex,* p. 523].) Such sordid reasoning reflects the unconscionable assumption of the double standard on the part of the male. One is reminded of Jeremy Taylor's telling remark on prostitution: "Men make necessities of their own and then find ways to satisfy them" (cited in Bailey, *Sexual Relation,* p. 210).

For ourselves, assuming that our sexuality is given us by our Creator in and for fellowship, we understand lust as any expression of sexual passion that destroys that fellowship by craving self-gratification; it is a passion that desires the other apart from any value or worth seen in the other. When Amnon "made himself ill because of his sister," the beautiful Tamar, and, being the stronger, forced her, his "love" showed its true face when it turned to hate and he thrust her out of his presence and bolted the door (2 Sam. 13:1-19). Such self-centered passion is fatal; it not only threatens the other with destruction but reduces the self to bondage. Lust drives the rapist in his grisly quest for conquest; it leads to the brothel and the prostitute's embrace; it ends in disillusionment and frustration. The souls of the lustful in Dante's hell are tossed on a howling wind that never relents.

One form of lust is evil beyond all others; it does not make us like the animals but like the demons. We refer to that lust which shows its countenance most clearly in the person of the seducer. (Dante, one may recall, placed the lustful in the second circle of hell, just below limbo; the seducers, in the eighth circle of nether hell.) The seducer is one who is not satisfied simply to satiate his own appetite. Like Don Juan, the legendary incarnation of perverse sexuality, the seducer takes pleasure in the arousal of passion in the other, in leading the victim from innocence to desire that finally ripens said victim for conquest. (Christian tradition has fostered the myth that the woman is *the* seducer; in real life most seducers are males.) By unlocking the hidden passion of his victim, the seducer seeks to rejuvenate himself with each new conquest and thus defy satiety. He exults in the conquering of many rather than seeking fulfillment in giving himself to one with whom he can share the joys of love.

In *The Seducer's Diary,* Kierkegaard prefaces the entries with a letter from Cordelia to Johannes. Having laid his plan of attack and having deprived his victim of her honor, he leaves her, "never wanting to see her again." In her letter she writes:

> Johannes,
>
> Never will I call you "my Johannes," for I certainly realize you never have been that, and I am punished harshly enough for having once been gladdened in my soul by this thought, and yet I do call you "mine": my seducer, my deceiver, my enemy, my murderer, the source of my unhappiness, the tomb of my joy. . . . I call you "mine" and call myself "yours," and as it once flattered your ear . . . so shall it now sound as a curse upon you, a curse for all eternity. . . . Love a hundred others, I am still yours. . . . You have had the audacity to deceive a person in such a way that you have become everything to me, so that I would rejoice gladly in being your slave. Yours I am, yours, yours, your curse.
>
> Your Cordelia
>
> (*Either/Or,* Part I, ed. and trans. Howard V. Hong and Edna H. Hong [Princeton: Princeton University Press, 1987], p. 312)

3. ROMANTIC LOVE

a. Some Historical and Theological Observations

The I-thou encounter of romantic love, we have argued, transcends the sexual instinct that we share with the animal world.[69] The unique aspect of such a romantic encounter is, indeed, the sexual attraction lovers have for each other. Each is aware, acutely aware, of the other's sexuality. While this experience differs from individual to individual, such an encounter, we have further argued, always involves feeling and passion. Though viewed with suspicion by the theologians, this passionate love (eros) has stirred the imagination of the poets; and they have celebrated its glories with all the powers of language at their disposal.

> Love is a smoke raised with the fume of sighs;
> Being purged, a fire sparkling in lover's eyes;
> Being vex'd, a sea nourish'd with lover's tears;
> What is it else? A madness most discreet,
> A choking gall and a preserving sweet.[70]

This passion, this "motion of the soul" in its attraction to the beloved, is self-authenticating, scorning all analysis.

> Where both deliberate, the love is slight;
> Whoever loved, that loved not at first sight?[71]

To speak of such love as "love at first sight" is not to make a literal statement about reality. It is an artistic conceit for the decisiveness of love that compacts all time into the moment of decision and action. Romeo not only loves Juliet "at first sight," but woos her, wins her, weds her, and dies with her all in the space of a few hours! "Love does not question; it gives an answer. Love does not think; it knows. Love does not hesitate; it acts. . . . Love puts behind it all the Ifs and Buts."[72] But what prompts such love? Whence does it come? Who can say? No one really knows why

69. In other words, such love is not (as someone has said) simply "an irresistible impulse that cybernetically flows through the molecular structures of deoxyribonucleic acid."

70. Shakespeare, *Romeo and Juliet*, act 1, scene 1, lines 195-200.

71. Christopher Marlowe, "Hero and Leander," in Untermeyer, ed., *Great Poems*, p. 323.

72. Barth, *KD*, III/4, p. 249 (cf. *CD*, III/4, p. 221). In his very first letter to Elizabeth Barrett, incarcerated in her own home by a possessive father, Robert Browning wrote, "I love your verses with all my heart, dear Miss Barrett." Then he adds, impulsively, "And I love you too." Here was love *before* first sight.

Helen's face was "the face that launched a thousand ships,"[73] and no lover ever asks the question. He simply knows that Rosalynde is "fair Rosalynde," and that

> Her lips are like two budded roses
> When ranks of lilies neighbor nigh,
> Within which bounds she balm encloses
> Apt to entice a deity.[74]

All search for the origin of such love, Kierkegaard reminds us, "ends in the inexplicable." "Its happy awakening is unacquainted with work, and there is no advance preparation. Even if love can give birth to pain, it is not brought forth in pain; lightly, jubilantly, it bursts forth in its enigmatic coming into existence. What a wonderful beginning!"[75]

Although love's beginning is beyond causal explanation, "miraculous," in Kierkegaard's word, its proximate cause, as philosophers tell us, is perceived worth in the beloved that enriches the lover. While women who are lovers perceive worth in the men whom they love, in literature we generally hear about the worth men perceive in women. (This is simply because men, in our patriarchal society, have written most of the great love poetry.) Milton, often dismissed as a dour Puritan, puts a speech about Eve on Adam's lips that says it all.

> when I approach
> Her loveliness, so absolute she seems
> And in herself complete, so well to know
> Her own, that what she wills to do or say,
> Seems wisest, virtuousest, discreetest, best;
> All higher knowledge in her presence falls
> Degraded: Wisdom in discourse with her
> Loses, discount'nanced, and like Folly shows:
> Authority and Reason on her wait,
> As one intended first, not after made
> Occasionally: and, to consummate all,
> Greatness of mind and nobleness their seat
> Build in her loveliest, and create an awe
> About her, as a guard angelic placed.

In his comments on the theology of romantic love, Charles Williams quotes this passage from *Paradise Lost,* bk. 8, lines 546-59, as a definition of romantic love (*He Came*

73. Marlowe, *Doctor Faustus.*
74. Thomas Lodge, "Rosalynde," in Untermeyer, ed., *Great Poems,* p. 231.
75. "On the Occasion of a Wedding, 'Love Conquers Everything,' " in *Three Discourses on Imagined Occasions,* vol. 10 of *Kierkegaard's Writings,* trans. H. V. Hong and E. H. Hong (Princeton: Princeton University Press, 1993), p. 47.

Down from Heaven [London: Faber and Faber, 1950], pp. 65-66). We would concur. When one is "in love," as the saying goes, this is the way one speaks.

*   *   *   *   *

Although love breaks forth "jubilantly" in the beloved's presence, it can, as Kierkegaard notes, "generate pain." Shakespeare reminds us that love is not only a "preserving sweet" but a "choking gall." This is most obviously the case when love is unrequited. To speak of unrequited love is to acknowledge that while love is essential to a true marriage, true love does not entail marriage, for marriage presupposes a mutual choice; love must respond to love for love to be fulfilled in marriage. Unrequited love, love that does not win a response in the beloved, is a theme that has inspired many a poet, from a Virgil, who tells us in the *Aeneid* of the "ill-starred Dido," the Phoenician queen left behind by Aeneas; to a Tennyson, who writes movingly *(Idylls of the King)* of the grief of "Elain, the lily maid of Astolate," who dies for the love of Lancelot, whose heart belonged to another. In real life, such suffering love does not ordinarily end in death, though disappointment in love can last throughout life. Like all suffering, love's suffering may have its redemptive moments. The woman with whom George Matheson was deeply in love broke off their engagement when she learned of his impending blindness. Alone, years later, on the day of his sister's marriage (June 6, 1882), he wrote the hymn, "O Love That Will Not Let Me Go." He states that he wrote down the lines in five minutes and never retouched them!

Love may also bring pain when the beloved belongs in marriage to another. As one follows the troubadours in their romantic adventures, one is made aware that the love of which they sing is a "dishonorable love." The women who are the objects of their amorous lines are "ladies" of noble estate for whom marriage is determined by birth and status rather than the heart's affection. The romantic liaisons of which the troubadours sing, therefore, are inspired by a love outside the bond of marriage. "I am yours, not Arthur's, as you know, save by the bond," confesses Queen Guinevere to Lancelot (Tennyson, *Idylls of the King*, "Lancelot and Elaine"). For this reason, courtly love is anything but lighthearted. Although it sometimes mocked the happy married couple, it is, at bottom, a love that is despairing and tragic. Even the adulterous love of which the troubadours sang, however, had a redeeming aspect in that it recognized the worth of the beloved and thus ennobled women. And when it was "domesticated," it contributed to a new understanding of marriage as a union of romantic love.

In the drama of real life one thinks of Francesca de Rimini and Paolo. Given for political reasons to the deformed Gianciotto, lord of Rimini, Francesca fell in love with his younger brother, Paolo, and became his mistress. Having surprised them one day together, her husband stabbed them both to death (A.D. 1285). Significantly, Dante places Gianciotto in "Cain's place," far below his victims (*Divine Comedy*, "Hell," canto 5, lines 103-5).

The celebration of romantic love on the part of the troubadours and their followers, down to the poets of the present day, has made it seem to the heirs of western European culture that such love is a natural and universal phenomenon. But this is not the case. Whatever Christianity may have contributed to the awareness of woman's worth and the sanctity of the body, such change did not deepen the understanding of romantic love. The conception of romantic love with which we in the Western world are familiar is something of a novelty, first clearly expressed toward the close of the eleventh century in the poetry of southern France and northern Italy.

> French poets, in the eleventh century, discovered or invented, or were the first to express, that romantic species of passion which English poets were still writing about in the nineteenth. They effected a change which has left no corner of our ethics, our imagination, or our daily life untouched, and they erected impassable barriers between us and the classical past or the Oriental present. Compared with this revolution the Renaissance is a mere ripple on the surface of literature.[76]

Lewis goes on to argue — convincingly to us — that it is in Spenser's *The Faerie Queen* that we have the final defeat of the adulterous liaisons celebrated in the poetry of courtly love by the romantic conception of marriage.[77] Here, at last, the romance of adultery is overcome by the romance of marriage. "In the history of sentiment, he [Spenser] is the greatest among the founders of that romantic conception of marriage which is the basis of all our love literature from Shakespeare to Meredith." This whole conception of romantic love, Lewis goes on to lament, "is now being attacked. Feminism in politics, reviving asceticism in religion, animalism in imaginative literature, and, above all, the discoveries of the psychoanalysts, have undermined that monogamic idealism about sex which served us for three centuries."[78]

At this juncture we are confronted with the question: If romantic love belongs to a Christian understanding of marriage, why is our catena of

---

76. C. S. Lewis, *The Allegory of Love* (London: Oxford, 1951), p. 4. "The new thing itself," says Lewis, "I do not pretend to explain. Real changes in human sentiment are very rare — there are perhaps three or four on record — but I believe that they occur, and that this is one of them" (ibid., p. 11). For all its newness, it seems plausible to us that the revolution of which Lewis speaks could not have prevailed had not the way been prepared by Christianity.

77. Ibid., pp. 298, 338-39. The publication of *The Faerie Queen* began in 1590. In 1594 Spenser married the wealthy Elizabeth Boyle. In the eighty-eight sonnets of the *Amoretti* he indites his love for her, assuring her that

> "Dark is the world where your light shined never;
> Well is he borne, that may behold you ever."

78. *Allegory of Love*, p. 360.

quotes celebrating love's glories drawn from the poets rather than the
theologians? How shall we explain the virtual silence of the latter on the
subject, even down to the present? Although they do more to extenuate
than to justify, there are some obvious reasons for this silence. Preeminent
among them is the simple fact that while the Bible has much to say about
marriage, it associates love with marriage only in a peripheral way.[79] In
the patriarchal society of the Old Testament, the decision of the parents,
especially the father, took precedence over the choice of love on the part
of those joined in marriage. Although Isaac is said to have loved Rebekah,
their marriage was brought about by Abraham's resolve to seek a wife for
his son of his own kindred (Gn. 24). Although Jacob is said to have loved
Rachel rather than Leah, he had to accept Leah as his wife because Laban,
her father, considered it his prerogative to give the older daughter first (Gn.
29:20-26). In the Old Testament, even when love ennobled a marriage, the
relationship itself was understood primarily in terms of procreation rather
than erotic fellowship. Elkanah loved Hannah, we are told; but when he
sought to console her with the thought that his love was better than ten
sons, she yet languished in her barrenness and would not be comforted
(1 Sam. 1:1-8).[80]

In the New Testament even less than in the Old is romantic love made
essential to the marriage relationship. Indeed, marriage itself no longer has
the place given it in the Old Testament, due to the eschatological orientation
of the church as the community of faith. There is no more a need to propagate
the seed of Abraham through marriage and procreation, since in Jesus the
promise of the seed is fulfilled (Gal. 3:16); the heir of David's throne, whose
kingdom knows no end, has come (Lk. 1:32-34). In this kingdom "they
neither marry nor are given in marriage" (20:34-36). The blessing is not upon
the womb that bears nor the breasts that give suck, but upon those who hear
and keep the word of God. Such are the true sisters, brothers, and mothers of
Jesus (3:35). Jesus is the heavenly bridegroom who will return as the glorified
Christ. His bride is the church and his nuptial feast the consummation of all

---

79. The Hebrew word denoting a man's love for a woman and a woman's for a man
is אָהֵב (Gn. 24:67; 1 Sam. 18:20). However, אָהֵב is also used of the love one has for a son
(Prv. 13:24), the love of a slave for a master (Ex. 21:5), the love of neighbor for neighbor
(Lv. 19:18), and the love of friend for friend (1 Sam. 18:1).

80. Judges 21 tells the story of the Benjaminites and how they obtained wives in a
pinch. Hiding in the vineyards when the daughters of Shiloh came out to dance in the yearly
feast of the Lord, each man seized a wife for himself. Since the whole purpose of this
whimsical artifice was to prevent their tribe from dying out for want of offspring, it graphically illustrates the primacy of procreation over the fellowship of love in Israel's understanding of marriage.

things (Rv. 19). It is this eschatological perspective that explains Paul's comments on marriage when writing to the Corinthians. With the passing away of this present world order, marriage will also pass away. In fact, now that the Spirit has been poured out on the church, the new age has already broken into this present age and will soon be consummated in the return of Christ. Hence the apostle suggests that the unmarried should remain unmarried, while those who have wives should live as though they had none (1 Cor. 7:25-35).[81] And so we see that not only in the Old Testament but in the New as well, romantic love has only a marginal place in the biblical understanding of marriage.

This circumstance surely bears on the way in which theologians have ignored the subject when framing a Christian doctrine of marriage. However, their lack of interest in romantic love is not due simply to the way the Bible speaks of marriage. Another consideration, unfortunately, comes into play at this juncture. We refer to the theologians' inheritance of the Fathers' suspicion of sex; a suspicion, as we have seen, that became deeply entrenched in the thought of Augustine and thereby in the thought of the church as a whole. We call this inheritance "unfortunate" because it reflects a dualistic approach more Hellenistic than biblical in its denigration of the body. Such dualism leads to an ascetic repudiation of all sexual passion as a kind of animal intoxication to be suppressed.[82] Even down into the Middle Ages sexual intercourse was burdened with a peculiar taint; there was something about it that was polluted, defiling, shameful, and obscene. Obviously sinful outside marriage, even within marriage it had the potential for sin. A too passionate desire for one's own wife, according to Peter Lombard and others, was really adultery; hence the conclusion that sexual indulgence was unworthy of one who aspires to the high ground of a truly holy life. While the church was always careful to extol marriage as good, since it had been blessed by the Creator in the beginning (Gn. 1:28) and sanctified by Christ's participation in a marriage feast (Jn. 2), yet virginity was better. It is little wonder, then, that the Scholastics, having followed the early Fathers in their disparagement of sex, had almost nothing to say about romantic love. After all, romantic love is distinguished precisely by its sexual component; it is a love that is sexual (erotic) in its very nature.

81. In their depreciation of marriage, the Fathers relied heavily on 1 Cor. 7. We shall have more to say about this passage presently. See below, pp. 218-22.
82. By "suppression" of the sex impulse, the Fathers meant resistance to, a determination not to indulge, said impulse. There is no warrant for accusing them of fostering "sexual repression" in the modern psychological sense of something being pushed into the unconscious. They rather advocated a constant vigilance against the gratification of sexual impulses that was anything but unconscious.

When we come to the Protestant Reformation, the picture is little changed, so far as romantic love is concerned. The Reformers, as we know, went out of their way to repudiate the Catholic view of celibacy by extolling wedlock as an honorable estate. They did not argue that coitus within marriage is evil when indulged for the sake of pleasure alone, though without sin when motivated by a desire for offspring. Yet they had precious little to say about marriage as a union of romantic love. Luther was married suddenly at age forty-one to Catherine von Bora, a poor, fugitive nun, after she refused a match he had arranged for her with someone else. He said at the time he took her as his wife that he did so to please his father, injure the Pope, and vex the devil. The marriage turned out to be a happy one; and he soon came to speak of his wife with affection as "gentle, obedient, compliant in all things beyond my hopes."[83] But the union did not begin romantically. For Luther, the ideal bride was Rebekah, who willingly left her father's house to marry Isaac sight unseen (Gn. 24:58). Love is important to marriage, but it is simply a heightened form of the love that we owe our neighbor as Christians. After all, our wife is our closest neighbor and therefore should be loved most. As for Isaac's dalliance with Rebekah when he was eighty and she seventy (26:8), the Holy Spirit records such a scene simply to refute the fanatics and show how beautiful conjugal harmony can be.[84]

Calvin's views were similar to Luther's. He asked his friend Farel to help him find a wife, reminding him that he was not one of "those insane lovers who, when once smitten with the fine figure of a woman, embrace also her faults. This only is the beauty which allures me, if she be chaste, obliging, not fastidious, economical, patient, and careful for my health."[85] Several prospects in his quest to find such a wife having failed to materialize, at thirty-one Calvin married a widow from his own congregation, Idelette de Bure, whom he called "the excellent companion of my life," "the ever faithful assistant to my ministry," and "a rare woman."[86] A lot has happened since the days of the Reformers. As a result, the place of romantic love in marriage has come to be generally acknowledged by the church, especially in the Western world. This significant change, however, is not due primarily to the teaching of Christian theologians; rather it reflects the impact of the poets of romantic love going back to the eleventh-century troubadours of southern France.

83. Schaff, *History,* 7.460.
84. See Bainton, *What Christianity Says About Sex,* pp. 80-81.
85. Schaff, *History,* 8.414.
86. The grief Calvin expresses in a letter to Farel on the occasion of his wife's death is touching (ibid., pp. 416-18).

Though we applaud the recognition of romantic love as belonging to the Christian doctrine of marriage, we must register a demur. A romanticized view of marriage, widely held today, constitutes a significant departure from Christian teaching. We refer to the widespread assumption that if two people "fall in love," they should get married. If, after getting married, they cease to be "in love," then they should dissolve the union and marry someone else. They are joined for "so long as they love," not "so long as they live." (Increasingly, such couples are simply living together without benefit of matrimony, which makes separation simpler because legally unencumbered.) Contemplating such a state of affairs, in which romantic love is not simply an important element in a true marriage but the *only* element, Emil Brunner has made some sharp comments.

> Where marriage is built on love everything is lost from the beginning. One who loves can guarantee neither that one's feeling of love will endure nor that it will be exclusive. . . . To ground marriage in love is to build one's house on the sand. It is this subjective individualism more than anything else that has caused the present marriage crisis. (*Das Gebot,* p. 329)

This observation by Brunner is an overstatement, in our judgment. Yet it is an overstatement that says something that needs to be said in today's society. Married love as romantic love may be passionate, but it is much more than the feeling of the moment; it is a love that commits itself to the other in a promise of fidelity, a subject on which we shall have more to say presently. (See below, pp. 255-59.)

b. Concerning the Song of Songs

When it comes to the romantic expression of our sexuality, the dogmaticians' understanding has been darkened, we have argued, by the lengthened shadows of gnostic dualism. Hence erotic love, being sexual in nature, has been given short shrift in theology, to the impoverishment of the Christian understanding of marriage. While Scripture as a whole has little to say on this subject, theologians, for the most part, have missed even what it does say. We have in mind, particularly, the Song of Songs which is Solomon's (also called Canticles), where the overt expression of romantic love has been muted with the help of an allegorical hermeneutic.

The allegorical interpretation of the Song begins with the Jewish rabbis. While they were not as deeply suspicious of sex as were the early Fathers of the church, they struggled with the question of how the erotic lyrics of the Song could be read and recited in the synagogue without embarrassment. One could tolerate the veiled references to conjugal love in the proverb, "Drink water from your own cistern, flowing water from your own well" (Prv. 5:15). But the Song is more explicit. Of course it too contains a great deal of symbolism and double entendre. For example, when the beloved summons the winds to blow on her garden and waft its fragrance abroad; when she invites her lover to come into her garden and taste its choice fruits (Song 4:16), the devout company gathered for worship need not blush when they hear these words.[87] At times, however, the text is not veiled in figures. "Let him kiss me with the kisses of his mouth" (1:2 NRSV) is hardly referring to the holy kiss of fraternal greeting. A book that talks about a lover who "lies between my breasts" (1:13); a book in which this lover, in his turn, is enraptured by the beauty of the beloved, describing not only her eyes, hair, teeth, lips, and temples, but also her breasts ("your two breasts are like two fawns," 4:5), is a book that is ripe for allegorizing.

> Taking their cue from the mystical East . . . , the zealous rabbis hid the simple and forthright design [of the Song] under a fantastic structure of elaborations. They drew out the rich lifeblood and substituted an injection of thinly sugared parable. Thus even the youngest child could be told that the lover was God and the beloved was Israel.[88]

It comes as no surprise, in the light of the foregoing discussion, that Christian theologians followed the example of the rabbis and allegorized the Song, simply substituting Christ and the church for God and Israel.

The substitution of "Christ and the church" for "God and Israel" is of no theological moment so far as our present discussion is concerned. The God revealed in Christ was understood by the theologians to be the God of Israel, and the church was spiritual Israel. The real problem, theologically, is the allegorizing hermeneutic used by both Jewish and Christian scholars in the interpretation of the book. Assuming such a hermeneutic, the great Schoolmen not only tolerated the book but reveled in it. They exercised their imagination as interpreters in a way that appeared on the surface to be entirely innocent. In reality, they were sublimating those yearnings of the heart that are too natural to be overcome and too deep to be denied.

Dismissing the literal meaning out of hand as unworthy of Holy Writ, Bernard preached eighty-six sermons to the monks of Clairvaux on the first two chapters of the book, metamorphosing the content into a mystical apostrophe to God's love for the soul and the soul's love for God. Protestant interpreters have traditionally done the same thing. Charles Spurgeon, in his enormously popular devotional *Morning and Evening: Daily Readings* (London: Marshall, Morgan & Scott, n.d.), took his text some thirty-five times from the Song of Songs. "Let him kiss me with the kisses of his mouth" refers to Christ's kiss of *reconciliation,* of *acceptance,* of daily *communion,* of

---

87. While the figure of a fruitful garden, used to describe the delights a lover finds in his beloved, is "suggestive" enough to the initiated, it is a figure nonetheless, not a piece out of D. H. Lawrence.

88. Untermeyer, ed., *Great Poems,* p. 2.

reception that removes the soul from earth, and of *consummation* that fills it with the joy of heaven (ibid., p. 334). Thus the real meaning of the text was subverted. As a result, as Marvin Pope observes, getting at the text has been like opening a lock to which the key is lost. Actually, the door has been open all the time, but people have not had the courage to enter and see what is inside. Pope likens the problem to that of the emperor and his new clothes. "The trouble has been that interpreters who dared acknowledge the plain sense of the Song were assailed as enemies of truth and decency. The allegorical charade thus persisted for centuries with only sporadic protests" (*Song of Songs,* Anchor Bible [Garden City, N.Y.: Doubleday, 1977], p. 17).

The King James Version, we note in passing, translates 5:4 of the Song, "My beloved put in his hand by the hole of the door, and my bowels were moved for him." Pope reproduces the title page of a book containing the sermons of a Dr. Sibs on Canticles, which reads:

Bowels
Opened
or
A Discovery of the Neere and Deer Love, Union and Communion betwixt
Christ and the Church.

Pope reports that he found a copy of this work, whose title page has been abused by time, in the medical library of Yale University, classified under "historical," on the apparent assumption that it concerned the relief of constipation. (See ibid., plate 6, p. 360.)

The fundamental problem with the allegorizing of the Song of Songs is that it assumes a faulty theology of sex and love. Such a theology understands sex basically in terms of human sin rather than divine creation. Hence it implicitly denies that sexual — that is, romantic — love is the gift of the Creator to be enjoyed by two lovers. Rejecting such a theology and assuming that the book of Canticles is a collection of amorous love poems, we make the following observations with a view to illumining the biblical basis for a theology of romantic love.

First of all, we see no need to allegorize the Song to make it fit the canon. The sexual love that it celebrates is implicit in the creation narratives with which the Bible begins. The first narrative speaks of God's giving us our humanity as male and female (Gn. 1:27); and the second tells us of the man's grateful response (2:23) when he first encounters the woman. Commenting on 2:23, Westermann notes that the man's reaction is one of jubilant welcome; in fact, it is an emotional cry of joy and surprise. "This one," he exclaims, or, "this one here" (זֹאת), "now at last!" (הַפַּעַם); the article carries a demonstrative force.[89] Here we have the exegetical basis

89. See Westermann, *Genesis 1–11,* p. 231.

of the rapturous apostrophe, cited above, that Milton placed on the lips of Adam as he contemplates the loveliness of Eve; Adam's love was the first instance of "love at first sight," to borrow Marlowe's phrase.

> In one sense, the Song is an extended commentary on the creation story — an expansion of the first recorded love-song in history. "Then the man said, 'This at last is bone of my bones and flesh of my flesh; she shall be called Woman because she was taken out of Man.' "[90]

Second, one should note that the Song includes all the elements of erotic love commonly found in love poetry. Much is said, for example, about the physical attractiveness of the beloved in her lover's eyes. "How beautiful you are, my darling! Oh, how beautiful"; to which the woman replies, "How handsome you are, my lover! Oh, how charming!" (1:15-16 NIV).[91] Furthermore, the lovers are always excited when they are with each other, and the presence of outsiders is something of a distraction (1:6). By contrast, separation is intolerable and leads to risk taking and even the suffering of abuse without thought of retaliation (5:6-8), so intent is the beloved on finding her lover.

Third, the Song includes that element of erotic love that has most troubled the theologians, namely, passion. The beloved seeks to be refreshed with raisins and apples, "for," she says, "I am faint with love" (כִּי־חוֹלַת, 2:5 NIV).[92] The lover, in his turn, confesses, "You have ravished my heart, my sister, my bride . . . how much better is your love than wine" (4:9-10). Such love is "strong as death," as "unyielding as the grave" (8:6 NIV); it burns like a vehement flame. "Many waters cannot quench [such] love" (8:7).

Fourth, while the Song reflects all the elements of romantic love found in the poetry of love, including passion, it differs from such poetry in the ancient Near East and the modern West in that it is concerned with two lovers whose love is mutually expressed, with no hint of the primacy of the man. Here, for once, we escape the androcentricity that dominates the

---

90. G. Lloyd Carr, *The Song of Solomon*, Tyndale Old Testament Commentary (Downers Grove: InterVarsity Press, 1984), p. 35.

91. Semitic metaphors of beauty are often different from those we are acquainted with. The beloved's teeth are not like pearls but "like a flock of shorn ewes" (4:2). Some of the Song's metaphors have mightily challenged the commentators. They have tried hard, for example, to determine in what sense a nose is attractive that is "like a tower of Lebanon, overlooking Damascus" (7:4).

92. Commenting on 2:5, Bernard observes, "When the soul contemplates the cross, it is itself pierced with the sword of love" (as quoted in Schaff, *History*, 5.641). Thus the text becomes a proof text for an Abelardian view of the atonement!

great love poetry of the Western world, in which the aggressive male, in quest of the female, does the seeking, talking, and conquering. In the Song, when the woman is asked how her beloved is better than others, she speaks of her lover with all the transport that male poets have shown in extolling the irresistible charms of the beloved. In fact, in the so-called lost-and-found section of the book (5:2–8:4), some 80 of the 111 lines are the words of the woman. As Carr observes, "this is really *her* book."[93]

Finally, one should note that the love celebrated in the Song of Songs is not love outside marriage — the adulterous love of which the troubadours sang. Yet neither is it a love that begins with courtship and ends in marriage. "My bride" on the lips of the lover does not imply marriage any more than "my sister" implies incest (4:9, 10, 12). This is simply the way lovers talk. Such terms of endearment denote the intimacy of the relationship. Yet they also denote its permanency. The Song knows nothing of love as a passing encounter, an infatuation of the moment. The relationship is one of total dedication in a lasting commitment. Each lover lives for the other alone and will be faithful even unto death.[94] In brief, here in the Bible itself is poetry about romantic love, not as something incidental to our humanity, much less something from which we long to be delivered that we may become more holy. Rather, it is poetry that celebrates such love for its own sake, a love that is the gift of the Creator.[95]

ADDENDUM: A CHEER FOR HELOISE

During the first half of the twelfth century, Peter Abelard became master of the Cathedral School of Paris. Having attained this supreme eminence as a teacher of philosophy and theology, he found himself literally surrounded with students. They came from far and near, attracted by the brilliance of his dialectic and the magnetism of his classroom presence. A handsome young man, gifted of intellect, proud and ambitious, his place

93. *Song of Solomon,* p. 130. For his helpful exposition of this entire section, 5:2–8:4, see ibid., pp. 130-68.

94. Such an affirmation does not depend on a demonstration of the unity of the book and the existence of one male lover. However, we are inclined to the position that there is one male lover, a shepherd.

95. Since the Song itself does not mention God, this last comment is obviously a theological inference drawn from the canonical context that belongs to the book as part of Scripture. The situation in this instance is analogous to that of the book of Esther. The text of Esther as it appears in the Protestant canon makes no mention of God (or prayer); yet, since the book is canonical, the church has rightly understood it in terms of the biblical doctrine of divine providence.

in the world of academia was as secure as destiny could make it — until he met Heloise.

At the time, he was about 40 and she 17, the niece of a certain Canon Fulbert. Already renowned throughout France for her learning, Heloise was in a class all by herself. Abelard, who evidently had lived a life of continence up to that time, now laid his plan of attack with all the calculated care of a seducer. Appealing to her uncle's vanity, he persuaded Fulbert to entrust the education of his niece to his personal tutelage. He even took up lodging in the canon's residence so that he could be available to his pupil day and night. Heloise was so overwhelmed, it would seem, by the name and fame of her teacher that, in her own words, she did whatever he wished. The scruples she felt, the resistance she at first offered, were soon overpowered by a passionate love that never left her. In the grief and suffering occasioned by her ill-starred romance, she remained true to Abelard till death drew the final curtain on the drama. Heloise was Juliet in real life long before Shakespeare ever dreamed of the maid from Verona. "In the order of human love," Gilson concedes, "she was without a peer."[96]

The story of how the guilty liaison between the two lovers became known, the birth of their son Astrolabius, their secret marriage to which Heloise vehemently protested, the sending of Heloise to a convent, the cruel revenge of Fulbert in mutilating Abelard, Abelard's establishing Heloise as the abbess of the Oratory of the Paraclete, and his own tribulations in the monastic life, are all told in the *Story of Misfortunes (Historia calamitatum),* written in his own hand to a friend. This lengthy letter happened to fall into Heloise's hands; and the reading of it inspired her first letter to Abelard, which began the celebrated correspondence between them. It would take us far afield even to summarize the content of these letters. We must content ourselves with brief excerpts from Heloise's first two letters (nos. 2 and 4 of the correspondence). These letters have never been surpassed in their expression of romantic love — love, that is, of a woman for a man; specifically, the love of the unhappy Heloise for the unworthy Abelard.

We have argued that while romantic love is not the only expression of our nature as male and female, it is a natural and legitimate expression of that nature, to be enjoyed as a gift of the Creator rather than impugned as a carnal indulgence of our animal appetites. For this reason we have rejected a theology that would allegorize such love out of the canon and affirmed that, for all its perversion in a fallen world, romantic love should be understood not in terms of our sin but in terms of our creation. Since the theologians have had so little to say about the love of a man for a woman

96. Étienne Gilson, *Heloise and Abelard,* trans. L. K. Shook (Ann Arbor: University of Michigan Press, 1960), p. 39.

and a woman for a man, we do well to listen to a woman whose knowledge of such love none can doubt, even though her credentials as a theologian some might dispute. What she has to say about love is as profound in its insight as it is poignant in its simplicity.

We note, in the first place, that *Heloise's love is a proud love* for which her heart did not condemn her. She reminds Abelard, "Though exceedingly guilty, I am as you know, exceedingly innocent." She could blame herself for marrying him but not for loving him. Hence the cold silence Abelard observed once she was secure as the abbess of the Oratory of the Paraclete was a bitter pill to swallow. It defrauded her of her right. When she chanced upon his long letter detailing his misfortunes to a friend, she broke the silence.

> Tell me only one thing, if you can, why after our conversion [to the religious life] which you alone decreed, I am fallen into such neglect and oblivion that I am neither refreshed by your speech and presence nor comforted by a letter in your absence. Tell me, if you can, or let me tell you what I feel, nay what all suspect. Concupiscence joined you to me rather than affection, the ardour of desire rather than of love. . . . When in time past you sought me out for temporal pleasures, you visited me with endless letters, and by frequent songs put your Heloise on the lips of all. . . . How much more should you now excite me to God whom you excited then to desire. Consider, I beseech you, what you owe me, pay heed to what I demand. My long letter I conclude with this brief ending: farewell, my all.

Remembering the theologians' penchant for apathic anthropology, which deplores passion as a threat to the higher faculties of reason and will, we note, second, that *Heloise's love is a passionate love*. Writing to Abelard from the nunnery, "So sweet," she confesses,

> were those delights of lovers which we enjoyed together that I cannot despise them nor even efface them from my memory without great difficulty. Wherever I turn, they bring themselves before my eyes with a desire for them. Even when I am asleep, they do not spare me their illusions. In the very solemnities of the Mass, when prayer ought to be most pure, the obscene phantoms of those delights so thoroughly captivate my wretched soul that I pay heed to their vileness rather than to my prayers. And when I ought to lament what I have done I rather sigh for what I have lost. Not only the things that we did, but the places also and the times in which we did them are so graven in my heart that in the same times and places I re-enact them all with you.

These and other ardent protestations led Gilson to suggest that Heloise herself would gladly have written at least four lines in Pope's "Eloisa and Abélard."

> Still on that breast enamour'd let me lie,
> Still drink delicious poison from thy eye,
> Pant on thy lips, and to thy heart be press'd;
> Give all thou cans't — and let me dream the rest.[97]

Third, we note that *Heloise's love is utterly self-sacrificing;* hers is a love that never counted the cost to herself.[98] "I call God to witness," she writes,

> if Augustus, ruling over the whole world, were to deem me worthy of the honor of marriage, and to confirm the whole world to me, to be ruled by me forever, dearer to me and of greater dignity would it seem to be called your mistress than his empress. For it is not by being richer and more powerful that a person becomes better; one is a matter of fortune, the other of virtue. Nor should she deem herself other than venial who weds a rich man rather than a poor, and desires in her husband things more than himself. Assuredly, whomever such concupiscence leads into marriage deserves payment rather than affection.

Grieved that Abelard had clothed her in the religious habit before taking up the monastic profession himself, as though, like Lot's wife, she might have looked back, she later exclaims, "God knows, I would without hesitation proceed or follow you unto the fires of hell according to your word. For not with me was my heart, but with you. . . . For without you it cannot anywhere exist."

Finally we must comment on Heloise's solemn avowal that in her relationship to Abelard she preferred free love to the bond of marriage.

> Nothing, God knows, have I ever sought of you, save yourself, desiring simply you, not what was yours. . . . And if the name of wife appears more sacred or more valid, sweeter to me is ever the word friend — or even — be not angry — concubine or harlot. For the

---

97. Ibid., preface, IX. In her third letter to him, Heloise reminds Abelard, "Nothing is less in our power than the heart, which we are forced rather to obey than able to command."

98. It is, we have argued, in its sacrificial character that eros rises to the level of agape. Thus the marriage relationship becomes an analogy of the relationship between Christ and the church. See *God, Creation, and Revelation,* pp. 235-36.

more I degraded myself for you, the more I hoped to gain your favor and so also to bring less damage to the fame of your renown.

These are not the words of a paramour or prostitute. They rather reveal the essence of true love, whose glory is its utter disinterestedness. Perceiving as much, we suspect, is what prompted Abelard to remark that God is not to be loved as Abelard loved Heloise but as Heloise loved Abelard. She expresses herself in the way that she does, not because she was a sinner but because there was no way that her love, which was all that love should be, could find fulfillment in marriage, given the erroneous theology of sex, love, and marriage that prevailed in the church of the twelfth century. It was because of the teaching of the church that she perceived marriage as compromising Abelard's ideals as a philosopher and demeaning the honor belonging to him as a cleric. She would willingly, therefore, have risked her own honor to preserve his. In so stating her case, Heloise is expressing the tragedy of her love as a student of Jerome, not its sinfulness as a daughter of Eve. God only knows how many Heloises and Abelards of a lesser breed have known the same tragedy in love due to the teaching that extols celibacy above marriage even down to the present day.[99]

For an elaboration and interpretation of the details of our drama, including efforts to resolve numerous problems of a historical nature, one may consult George Moore, *Heloise and Abelard* (New York: Liveright, 1923). In our excerpts from Heloise's letters, which are taken from the first two she wrote to Abelard, we have relied, for the more part, on the translation of C. K. Scott Moncreiff, *The Letters of Heloise and Abelard* (New York: Cooper Square, 1974), pp. 59, 61, 81, 109, 60; 57-58, 57. Also Gilson, *Heloise and Abelard,* pp. 76-77, 56. As for Gilson's learned work, while we have found it helpful, his theology of sex and love, as a Roman Catholic, make him more sympathetic with Abelard and less with Heloise than we are. When he talks about "the cruel blow that God had struck them" (p. 99), we cannot but suggest that maybe it was the church rather than God that struck the blow.

99. Hence we are dismayed that Gilson should find it necessary to write a whole chapter entitled, "The Mystery of Héloïse," and to conclude it with the thought: "For Héloïse to have wished to tell the whole world about her sorrow was a little less noble than to endure it in silence. That she may have found a sort of bitter pleasure in this is not impossible. That she may have taken pleasure in her misfortunes as her surest claim to glory and that this pleasure may have been mingled with bitterness is almost certain" (*Heloise and Abelard,* p. 104). We see no grounds in her letters for any of these speculations. Indeed, the evidence points the other way! See Enid McLeod, *Héloïse: A Biography* (London: Chatto & Windus, 1971).

4. THE COVENANT OF MARRIAGE

a. The Volitional Nature of the Marriage Bond
(Vinculum Matrimonii)

We have defined marriage as that particular form of the male-female relationship into which a man and a woman freely enter out of love for each other. The choice of marriage is a lover's choice. We grant that reality often mocks this Christian ideal. People often choose marriage for the wrong reasons — to please their parents; to gain wealth; to secure advantage, fame, or social status.[100] They may even choose to marry someone out of sympathy for them.[101] God in his grace may turn such utilitarian marriages into true marriages; but one should not presume upon the grace of God in such matters. As Heloise wrote to Abelard, when one follows a selfish path into marriage, one deserves payment rather than affection.

While marriage should be the choice of lovers, lovers may not always choose marriage. There are many reasons why lovers do not choose marriage, some admirable and some not. For example, fidelity to one's marriage vows is an admirable reason for not marrying someone else. By contrast, when love cannot free the will of racial prejudice, the choice not to marry is anything but admirable. Indeed, it is tragic. (See James Weldon Johnson's *Autobiography of an Ex-Colored Man,* in *Three Negro Classics* [New York: Avon, 1965], the story of a black man who passed for white — until he met *her,* a white woman; especially pp. 348-51, where the proposal of marriage to a white woman meets the moment of truth. In this case, the pair did later marry.)

In speaking of love as that which should motivate one's decision to enter the marriage relationship, we do not mean to imply that marriage is based on love. Marriage is not based on love but rather on an act of the will. It is a union that rests on a mutual decision and choice, not on the love that motivates the choice. In other words, we should not try to compensate for the theologians' neglect of love by making love the very foundation of marriage. Love is not "the ontological basis of the marriage union," as is sometimes argued

---

100. Our literature abounds with illustrations of the machinations people use to achieve some dubious end by means of matrimony. (One recalls the case of Becky Sharp in Thackeray's *Vanity Fair.*) It is to be lamented, even as it cannot be denied, that the church has solemnly blessed these unchristian, utilitarian unions, declaring them to have a holy, even sacramental character.

101. The marriage of C. S. Lewis to Joy Gresham in a civil ceremony was so motivated. Happily, the relationship came to be one of mutual love and was subsequently blessed by the church. See George Sayer, *Jack, C. S. Lewis and His Times* (San Francisco: Harper & Row, 1988), pp. 211ff.

(Bailey). The basis of the marriage union is rather the *choice,* the *decision,* which two lovers make to enter into that most intimate of all relationships. In making such a decision they recognize each other not simply as friends but as partners in a unique, ongoing sharing of life together. It is this decision, expressed in their mutual consent *(consensus mutuus)* to be joined to each other in the marriage covenant, that makes a man and a woman husband and wife. Whereas one is a male by the Creator's choice, one becomes a husband by his own choice; whereas one is a female by the Creator's choice, one becomes a wife by her own choice.

To be created in God's image, we have argued, is to be given our being in such a way that we ourselves determine who we are and who we shall be. (See above, pp. 72-77.) Surely such self-determination, which qualifies human relationships in general, should qualify the marriage relationship in particular. The statement that marriage rests on a mutual choice admittedly describes the Christian ideal. In the real world, by contrast, this choice has been and still is violated, especially in the case of women, who are sometimes treated as "the mute object of gift or barter" (Lewis). To cite a biblical example, Michal was given by her father, Saul, to David as a wife, "that she may be a snare for him" (1 Sam. 18:20-21). Unsuccessful in this stratagem, her father took her from David and gave her to Palti, son of Laish (25:44). When David later demanded that she be returned, the relationship was renewed with trauma (2 Sam. 3:13) and ended in mutual contempt (6:16-17). If one or both parties are pressured into marriage, it is no true marriage. Again, God, in his grace, can turn even a "shotgun marriage" into a true marriage, for he can make good come out of human folly. But for the most part, such forced marriages are doomed to failure because true marriage rests, by definition, on a free and responsible decision on the part of both parties to the marriage covenant. In the light of this ideal of mutuality, the assumption that the man should always take the initiative and "pop the question" to the coy maid is more cultural than commendable.

The tragedy of forced marriage is a theme provocatively explored in many a literary masterpiece. In Tolstoy's *War and Peace,* for example, Pierre is maneuvered by Prince Vasíli into marrying his daughter, the beautiful and depraved Hélène. Subsequently, when Pierre kills her lover in a duel, the marriage, so-called, ends in a last devastating encounter between husband and wife that forever terminates the relationship (see bk. 3, chaps. 1-2; and bk. 4, chaps. 4-6). In *Don Quixote* the forced marriage of "Quitena the Handsome" to "Camacho the Rich" ends on a much happier note, managed by the consummate skill of the great storyteller Miguel de Cervantes (see especially the Modern Library edition [New York: 1930], part 2, bk. 3, §§ 19-21).

In taking the position that the basis of marriage is the mutual consent of the covenanting parties *(consensus facit matrimonium),* we understand consent in the sense of a voluntary concurrence in a mutual commitment and promise. Marriage is based on a commitment which takes the form of a promise that one will be faithful to one's intended spouse. The basis, then, of the marriage bond is not sacramental and ontological in nature; rather, it is volitional. To affirm the volitional, consensual basis of the marriage bond is not to deny its sexual character. The marriage union, which rests on a mutual promise of fidelity, is described as a union of "one flesh" just because it is a union expressed in the act of sexual intercourse. This is not to say that every instance of intercourse is an expression of the true oneness *(henosis)* of marriage; but it is to say that the sex act, in the context of marriage, expresses the giving of the self to the other according to the mutual promise made by the covenanting parties when they entered into the marriage relationship. For this reason, sexual intercourse, though not always possible throughout a given marriage, is rightly called the "consummation" of marriage.

Our basing the marriage union on a mutual act of will and choice, on the one hand, and our acknowledgment that this choice is expressed in the physical act of love which is passionately sexual, on the other, call for comment. One should note, first of all, that when sexual passion overrides the will, the result can be tragic. Romantic love is turned into sentimentalism. The familiar adage that "love is blind" is simply a popular way of describing what happens when one succumbs to such pseudo-romanticism. This sentimental love, which is the counterfeit of true love, is idealized in trashy films and drugstore novels. It encourages the notion that "falling in love" is a kind of fate, a given — "like catching the measles" (Lewis). This fatalistic view assumes that lovers are thrown together, as it were, by the stars under which they were born. Such an approach

> is encouraged by the irresistible, sometimes almost demonic power of sexual attraction and emotion. Men and women feel that control has passed out of their hands, and that they act under the compulsion of an inexorable destiny against which they are powerless to assert their own wills and exercise the responsibility demanded by true love. (D. S. Bailey, *The Mystery of Love and Marriage* [London: SCM, 1952], p. 24)

Related to the thought that sexual passion is destiny is the view that marriages are "made in heaven," a view that easily lends itself to the mystical apotheosis of the erotic encounter of lovers. Barth is well taken in his acknowledging the truth in much of what Schleiermacher has to say, in his philosophical ethics, about romantic love. But he is also well taken when he distances himself from Schleiermacher's view that marriage is "itself an eternal work of a love which is eternal." Such divinization of the romantic encounter between a man and a woman — the embrace of the spouse is the embrace of God — construes the romantic encounter as a metaphysical absolute and thus confuses it with the *divine*-human encounter. As a result, the analogy between husband and wife, on the one hand, and Christ and the church, on the other, is threatened because the analogy is turned into an *identity*.

Barth cites some extreme statements from authors who have romanticized love and marriage in terms of Schleiermacher's feeling mysticism. For example, "Authentic sexual love is a *testimonium Spiritus Sancti*" (Walter Schubart). Again (Schubart), "It is possible for an eye that is pure to see the phallus and the cross, the holy symbols of creation and redemption, together without being shocked." (See *KD,* III/4, pp. 134-35 [cf. *CD,* III/4, pp. 125-27], with sources and further comment.) In the light of such reveries we can only commend Barth in his effort to demystify and demythologize the encounter of erotic love, for all its ecstasy, rapture, and transport. It is because of the problems we have with this mystical approach to eros that we have found Denis de Rougemont's *Love in the Western World,* trans. M. Belgion (New York: Pantheon, 1905), less than helpful.

One final word must be spoken about the mutual choice whereby a man and a woman enter into marriage: for the Christian, at least, such a choice is anything but an autonomous act of the will. It is a choice, rather, that one freely makes in the awareness of one's responsibility to God and with a desire to please him. Christians believe that God has given the ordinance of marriage to the human family to intimate the fellowship he himself enjoys with his people in the covenant of grace. Given this understanding of marriage, it is God's blessing and approval, resting upon one's choice to take another as husband or wife, that affords the Christian the confidence to enter into the marriage relationship, with all its promise and peril. We shall discuss these matters at more length presently.

Since love's choice of marriage is, for the Christian, a choice made in the light of God's will, one can understand why the question of "mixed marriages" — marriages, that is, between believers and unbelievers — became an issue in the church early on. Paul did not consider such marriages invalid. In fact, he told the Corinthians who raised the question that if the unbeliever consents to remain with the believer, then the believer should not seek to dissolve the marriage bond. "For the unbelieving husband is consecrated (ἡγίασται, 'sanctified,' 'made holy') through his wife, and the unbelieving wife is consecrated through her husband" (1 Cor. 7:14). In other words, the marriage covenant, which sets one apart for exclusive fellowship with one's conjugal partner, remains valid in God's sight after one is converted, even as it was before. Grace does not destroy nature; it may even redeem it. Hence believers can be assured that their Christian witness is not compromised by their cohabitation with an unbelieving spouse, so long as the latter accepts them and willingly lives with them. Since they obviously do not regard their children as unclean (ἀκάθαρτα), but rather holy (ἅγια), that is, legitimate, why should they suppose the marriage relationship of which the children were born to be defiling (v. 14)? (Unfortunately, 1 Cor. 7:14 has been conscripted in the cause of infant baptism, a subject quite alien to the larger context of the passage. The resultant exegetical confusion in understanding the verse is, in Barth's word, "hopeless." See our *Infant Baptism and the Covenant of Grace* [Grand Rapids: Eerdmans, 1978], pp. 122-23.)

In 1 Cor. 7:12-16, Paul is speaking to people who became Christian converts after they were married. His advice to Christians before they are married differs significantly. Should they choose to be married, a choice that they are quite free to make, they should marry "only in the Lord" (μόνον ἐν κυρίῳ, 7:39). He would presumably not consider a marriage to an unbeliever, under such circumstances, to be invalid, though he could not regard such a choice as a proper response to the grace of God on the part of believers. As those who now live their lives "in the Lord," they should choose a spouse who can share such a life with them. "For what do righteousness and wickedness have in common? Or what fellowship can light have with darkness?" (2 Cor. 6:14 NIV).

The grace of God may be manifested, of course, even to those who enter into such a mixed marriage. Here one thinks of John Bunyan. At the age of nineteen, he married a woman of whom we know only that she came from a godly home and spoke often to him about his spiritual needs. Her dowery was two Puritan books, *The Plain Man's Path to Heaven* and *The Practice of Piety* (Lewis Bayly). Gradually his wife induced him to read these books and to go with her to church. The rest of the story is history. As we noted before, however, one should not presume on the grace of God. To put the claims of love above the claims of Christ is to compromise deeply one's Christian confession, and it may even destroy it. Advising Wormwood on how he might frustrate the hopeful beginning his subject had made in the Christian life, Screwtape writes, "There must be several young women in your patient's neighborhood who would render the Christian life intensely difficult to him if only you could persuade him to marry one of them" (Lewis, *Screwtape Letters,* no. 19).

In conclusion, one should observe that while marriages between believers and unbelievers may go wrong for obvious reasons, it does not follow that marriages between two believers will go right simply because they are believers. As Brunner once remarked, "The love that supposedly 'comes of itself where true Christians marry' belongs to the realm of Christian legend" (*Das Gebot,* p. 345).

Excursus: The Celibate Life

If the basis of marriage is a choice freely made, on the part of two lovers, to enter into the marriage relationship, then it is only reasonable that one is free not to enter into such a relationship. This choice also can be made in responsibility to God. In the Christian understanding of things, not all have the same vocation; some are called to marriage and some to celibacy. In setting forth our views of the celibate life, we begin with a brief historical comment.

The ancient Fathers, as we have noted, bequeathed to the church a deep suspicion of sex as especially compromised by the taint of original sin. While marriage, for them, was not an unmitigated evil, as the extreme ascetics taught (1 Tm. 4:3), neither was it an uncontaminated good. It was not to be despised, yet it was inferior to the celibate life. Although marriage came eventually to enjoy sacramental status, the unmarried state was commended to the priesthood, since priests were supposed to embody the moral ideal in a special way. This priestly celibacy was voluntary in the ancient church; however, by the fifth century, rules began to appear that led eventually to mandatory celibacy. First came the rule forbidding more than one marriage to a member of the priestly class. Then came the proscription of marriage after ordination and the forbidding of intercourse to those married before ordination. Finally, the prohibition of all clerical marriage became the official position of the Western church. Though widely resisted, it was reinforced by appeal to the most learned authorities in the Nicene and post-Nicene church. Augustine refers routinely to the "weaker brethren who enjoy married life," whom he contrasted to "those who live at a higher level, who are not entangled in the mesh of married life."[102] In spite of ongoing disciplinary problems indicative of widespread failure, the institution of sacerdotal celibacy finally triumphed over all opposition and was firmly entrenched at the time of the Reformation.[103] Its rejection by the Reformers on the ground that forced celibacy was contrary to nature only increased the vigor with which the institution was defended by Rome in the Counter-Reformation.

In view of what we have already written, it is obvious that we are in fundamental agreement with the Reformers. We concur in their judgment that a vow of perpetual celibacy is contrary to nature. Not only so, but we also applaud their insistence that marriage, as blessed by the Creator, is consonant with the highest ideals of Christian piety. By removing the stigma from wedlock as inferior to the life of an ascetic, they rendered a lasting service to the church.[104]

But we must also acknowledge that the Reformers overreacted. In their zeal to celebrate the blessings of marriage as an ordinance of creation, they tacitly, if not explicitly, implied that the unmarried state falls short of the Christian ideal.[105] Such a position turns the redemptive clock back to the Old Testament, where marriage alone completed the man and delivered the woman from reproach. Now that Christ, the seed promised to Abraham and Sarah, has come, marriage has been relativized. There is no need in

102. *The City of God*, 1.9. "Cut down the wood of marriage," Jerome fulminated, "with the axe of virginity" (*Ep.* XXII, as quoted by Schaff, *History*, 2.413).

103. It was often alleged that Luther began the Reformation so that he could get married, an aspersion that even Erasmus did not dispute.

104. At the practical level the Reformers obviously served the church well in that they made it possible for the theologians, when they set out a doctrine of marriage, to experience something of what they are talking about!

105. Barth animadverts on the fact that even at this late date, Althaus can write (*Grundriss der Ethik* [1931], p. 91): "Marriage is the instrument by which new life is produced — no one has the right to evade the creative will of God, who in our human situation and natural impulses commands us to be fruitful" (*KD*, III/4, pp. 156-57 [cf. *CD*, III/4, p. 141]).

the New Israel to continue the literal generations that carried the covenant promise to fulfillment. Indeed, Jesus, in whom the promise is fulfilled, was neither joined to a wife nor had a family — save those who do the will of God (Mk. 3:34). This community of the redeemed is his spiritual bride, and he the heavenly bridegroom.[106] In this community are those who have "left home or wife or brothers or parents or children for the sake of the kingdom of God" (Lk. 18:29 NIV); those "who have made themselves eunuchs for the sake of the kingdom of heaven" (Mt. 19:12), that is, have forgone marriage for the sake of their calling and mission (1 Cor. 7:7). Protestants should not let their traditional polemic against clerical celibacy distort their perception at this point.

In other words, not only is the option of celibacy entailed in a theology that bases marriage on a mutual choice, but it is also authenticated as a genuine Christian calling by the very structure of biblical revelation. Not that celibacy is the ideal to which we strive in order to suppress our sexual impulses as sinful. But celibacy has become a truly Christian option because the eschatological form of the kingdom in which one "neither marries nor is given in marriage" has been made manifest in the person of Jesus Christ. In this kingdom, men are men and women are women, truly and completely. And so also shall they be in the final manifestation of the kingdom. But in this final kingdom of glory they shall be neither husbands nor wives. Jesus' celibate life not only anticipates such life in the age to come; it also reveals that even in this life the sexual congress of husband and wife is not essential to a Christian's calling. Christians who choose the celibate life, as the apostle Paul did, testify that "the present form of this world is passing away" (1 Cor. 7:31 NRSV) and, by the lives they live, anticipate the new age that has already broken into the present world.

*   *   *   *   *

In this community of the coming age are not only those "who have made themselves eunuchs for the sake of the kingdom of heaven," but also those "who have been made eunuchs by others" (Mt. 19:12 NRSV). Unlike the community of ancient Israel, which excluded "one whose testicles are crushed or whose penis is cut off" (Dt. 23:1 NRSV), this community is a community into which the Ethiopian eunuch is baptized and sent on his way rejoicing (Acts 8:26-39). Thus is fulfilled the Lord's promise, "let not the eunuch say, 'Behold, I am a dead tree.' For thus says the LORD: 'To

---

106. For an appraisal of a recent argument that Jesus was married in his preitinerating life, see our *Man as Male and Female,* pp. 105-11.

the eunuchs who keep my sabbaths, who choose the things that please me and hold fast my covenant, I will give . . . a monument and a name better than sons and daughters; I will give them an everlasting name which shall not be cut off' " (Is. 56:3-5).

*   *   *   *   *

Paul argues in 1 Corinthians 7 that the Corinthians would do best to accept the status quo as God's calling διὰ τὴν ἐνεστῶσαν ἀνάγκην (v. 26), that is, "on account of the impending distress" (RSV), or better, "the present distress" (KJV), referring to the hostile environment in which his readers were living at the time. If people are married, let them remain married; if unmarried, let them remain unmarried. This is his judgment, to which he adds, δοκῶ δὲ κἀγὼ πνεῦμα θεοῦ ἔχειν: "I think that I also have the Spirit of God" (v. 40). Of course there are exceptions to this general rule that one should remain in one's present state. To enter into marriage, he grants, is no sin; and any Christian is free to marry in the Lord at any time. Nonetheless, the apostle's tone is somewhat different from that of the Protestant Reformers when it comes to marriage, a point that Roman Catholic defenders of celibacy have been quick to note. This fact calls for comment.

We are not persuaded, to begin with, that Paul means to say that he is simply giving his private opinion about a matter concerning which he had no revelation and could make no claim to apostolic authority. Although we do not agree with the demeaning view of marriage taken by the Fathers, they were justified, we believe, in reading 1 Cor. 7:25-26 as inspired Scripture. We could wish, to be sure, that they had paid as much attention to what the apostle had to say about sin and grace in Romans and Galatians as they did to what he had to say about sex and marriage in 1 Corinthians. But be that as it may, surely the apostle is not deceived in supposing he had the Spirit when speaking candidly about sex and marriage to his own converts. He simply speaks with modesty, even with a touch of irony — "I think that I have the Spirit [you know I do]" (v. 40) — as he counsels his readers, who lived in the most sexually immoral city of the empire, concerning delicate and personal matters. He does distinguish between what the *Lord* requires of those who are married (v. 10) and what *he* has to say to them as an apostle (v. 12). But such a distinction reflects simply the difference between a situation concerning which, in the tradition Paul had received, Jesus had clearly spoken, and one in which he had not. In the latter, the apostle speaks to the subject directly, as one who has the Spirit of Jesus.

The Fathers, then, did not err in supposing that what Paul says in 1 Cor. 7, he says with apostolic authority. But they did err, in our opinion, in that they misconstrued his argument as one that not only extols celibacy but depreciates marriage. And they erred in this matter because they failed to recognize the eschatological perspective underlying his remarks. The apostle speaks as one who is profoundly convinced that this world in its present form is passing away. While the Parousia may not have been as immanent as he supposed when he wrote these words, they express what has always been the expectation of the church. This hope of a new world that informs the apostle's comments on marriage as indifferent is quite another matter from the Greek dualism that lies behind the Fathers' disparagement of sex and marriage. It is one thing to live a celibate life in anticipation of the coming kingdom, another to live such a life out of the conviction that one must avoid sex and women if one is to escape this sinful world. This latter view, though it is not really Pauline, has cast its lengthened shadow over the ongoing theological discussion, with the result that marriage has often been viewed as a divine concession to human weakness, a remedy for male passion, useful primarily as a means for generation. In our view, the correct understanding of 1 Corinthians is one that recognizes both marriage and celibacy as options to which God calls people as he leads them in the differing times and circumstances of life.

Speaking of the times and circumstances of life, obviously many Christians choose celibacy not in response to a divine call to live in anticipation of the coming kingdom, but simply because of the particular circumstances of their lives. Having embraced a Christian view of chastity and having met no one to whom they could make a loving, lifelong commitment, they choose the celibate life as single persons. (This is especially true for women, who outnumber men. See Brunner, *Divine Imperative,* pp. 365-66.) Christian theology can offer no quick fix for the disappointment and loneliness such a life often entails. But it does assure such people that their lifestyle is in every way acceptable to God. The subtle rejection of such persons as odd, even as failures, on the part of many church congregations that "focus on the family" is unconscionable.

b. Further Comment on the Marriage Relationship

1) The Personal Quality of the One-Flesh Union

While marriage belongs to the whole human family, we admittedly are making no effort to frame a doctrine of the marriage relationship that will command universal acceptance. Our approach is confessedly Christian; furthermore, it is Protestant rather than Catholic. We will, therefore, simply summarize the Roman Catholic view, with comment, by way of introduction to our own statement.

Excursus: Marriage Viewed as a Sacrament

A précis of the Roman Catholic (and Eastern Orthodox) view of marriage naturally begins with Eph. 5:22-32. In this passage Paul cites Gn. 2:24, which speaks of a man leaving father and mother and cleaving to his wife, with whom he becomes one flesh. He compares this one-flesh union of husband and wife to the union of Christ and the church. That the former should typify the latter, he says, is "a great mystery" (τὸ μυστήριον τοῦτο μέγα ἐστίν, Eph. 5:32). The Vulgate translates μυστήριον with *sacramentum,* "sacrament." While present-day Catholic scholarship would not use this translation, the dogma of the Catholic Church reflects it, in that the marriage union is numbered among the sacraments. As such, it is viewed as an efficacious sign *(signum efficax)* of grace, which means that it is the efficient cause of the grace it signifies. The mutual consent *(consensus mutuus)* of the two parties entering into the marriage covenant is, in and of itself, only a natural event. If the consenting parties are not baptized Christians, such an event may be recognized by the state as legitimate matrimony; but it is not a true marriage in the proper sense. If, however, the two consenting parties are baptized, then their consent increases the grace first given in their baptism in order that they may be, by this increase of grace, enabled to maintain conjugal fidelity and bring up their children in the fear of God. Thus their love is taken up into the divine love. (The Catholic doctrine of marriage seems not to be concerned with the difference between eros and agape.)

When this happens — and it happens retrospectively when a couple already legally married in the eyes of the state is baptized — marriage becomes an effectual sign of grace that is given by Christ himself. In that Christ has won by his merits that grace which shelters and strengthens husband and wife, and in that their relationship is an efficient sign of this grace and an image of the mystical marriage of Christ with the church, matrimony is raised to the dignity of a sacrament. Hence those who enter the state of matrimony by their own free consent, which consent is essential to the constitution of marriage, must yet remember that "the freedom of man has no power whatever over the nature of matrimony itself, and, therefore, when once a person has contracted marriage, he becomes subject to its essential laws and properties." "This sacrament . . . adds special gifts, good impulses and seeds of grace, amplifying and perfecting the power of nature and enabling the recipients, not only to understand with their minds, but also to relish immediately, grasp firmly, will effectively and fulfill in deed all that belongs to the state of wedlock and its purpose and duties" (Pius XI, encyclical letter, *Casti Connubii,* 1930).

Deploring contemporary "disfigurements" of the institution of marriage — divorce, free love — and the profanation of married love "by excessive self-love, the worship of pleasure; and illicit practices against human generation," Vatican II reaffirms the traditional Catholic doctrine of marriage and the family, though it does place a new emphasis on conjugal love and the uniquely personal relationship that it presupposes. In keeping with this emphasis, the Council seeks to avoid the traditional distinction between the primary and secondary ends of marriage, the former being procreation and the latter conjugal love. Nonetheless, the Pastoral Constitution *Gaudium et Spes* affirms, "Marriage and conjugal love are by nature ordained to the begetting and educating of children." The Constitution even cites as a proof text Genesis 2:18, "It is not good that the man should be alone," that is, without offspring! Paul VI, in the encyclical letter *Humanae Vitae,* makes the same point, insisting that the conjugal act has two meanings that are inviolably connected. These two meanings are the union of mutual love, on the one hand, and procreation, on the other.

It remains only to note that in Catholic doctrine the officiating priest is not the dispenser of the sacrament. He simply performs those ceremonies necessary to insure the proper treatment of marriage in its public solemnizing. His word, whereby a man and a woman are said to be joined in marriage, has only a declaratory character. The marriage partners themselves are the mutual dispensers of the sacrament. This dispensing to each other of sacramental grace does not occur in sexual intercourse but in the freely given mutual consent to enter into the marriage relationship. Intercourse is rather a privilege that the sacrament of marriage affords. In fact, intercourse can be entirely renounced and the marriage remain a true marriage — as was the case with the marriage of Mary and Joseph. (Catholic dogma, one must remember, affirms the perpetual virginity of Mary.) Hence a couple may have a so-called Joseph marriage, a marriage without intercourse.

Even in this brief summary of the Catholic view of marriage, one can sense a somewhat rigid, legalistic approach. The Catholic view is long on theological niceties and short on scriptural exegesis. And, in our judgment, it reflects a deep antinomy. On the one hand, marriage cannot escape the ancient shadow of dualism. The ideal relationship between spouses is that of Joseph and the Virgin, whose marriage was without sex. On the other hand, in an act of overcompensation, marriage is exalted to the level of a sacrament of grace. This latter argument is a theological tour de force if ever there was one. Such an effort to shift the ground from nature to grace, from creation to redemption, only makes the difference between marriage as an ordinance of creation and as a true sacrament of grace all the more obvious. This can be seen by recalling that the cleansing symbolized in baptism prepares us for life in the holy city, where nothing unclean shall enter (Rv. 21:2, 27). Likewise our participation (fellowship, κοινωνία) in the body and blood of the Lord (1 Cor. 10:16), symbolized in the Holy Supper, prepares us for life in the Father's kingdom. In this kingdom our Lord will drink of the fruit of the vine with us anew in a fellowship beyond the reach of death (Mt. 26:29). But how can we say that marriage prepares us for a life of holiness and fellowship in the world to come? That world is the kingdom in which "they neither marry nor are given in marriage" (Mk. 12:25). Heaven is, of course, likened to a marriage feast (Rv. 19:7-9). But it is also likened to a sabbath rest (Heb. 4:9); yet this latter analogy does not make the observance of the Lord's Day a sacrament. We can, then, make no progress in our effort to understand the nature of marriage by going down such a theological cul de sac. We shall seek, therefore, to understand the marriage relationship along quite different lines.

When a man leaves father and mother and cleaves to his wife, they become "one flesh" (וְהָיוּ לְבָשָׂר אֶחָד), we are told in Genesis 2:24. Asked about the Mosaic law of divorce, Jesus cites this text, with the added comment: "So they are no longer two but one flesh. What therefore God has joined together, let not man put asunder" (Mk. 10:2-9). In writing to the Ephesians, Paul also cites this Genesis text and then goes on to say, as we have noted, that while it is a great mystery, he is speaking of Christ and the church (Eph. 5:31-32). The word "mystery" (μυστήριον) refers, in the New Testament, to truths revealed to believers but concealed from unbelievers. Here the apostle's thought seems to be that the intimate marriage union, referred to in Genesis 2:24 as a union in one flesh, serves as a "type" or "symbol" of an intimate union of a very different sort, namely, the spiritual union between Christ and the church. Thus the unity of husband and wife in marriage illumines, for the Christian, the unity of Christ and the church in salvation.

There can be no doubt that when Scripture refers to the marriage union as a union of one flesh, the immediate reference is to sexual intercourse. It is in sexual intercourse *(copula carnalis)* that marriage is "consummated," to use traditional language.[107] This sexual intimacy at the physical level is what makes marriage a unique relationship. While all men and women are related sexually, for men are males and women females, in the Christian understanding of male-female relationships, the physical intimacy of coitus belongs to marriage. It is a privilege enjoyed by a particular man and a particular woman who are related as husband and wife. Christians have generally agreed on this matter. They have also agreed that to understand the one-flesh union of marriage exclusively or even primarily in terms of the physical is to understand it too narrowly. The unity of the marriage bond is not simply a matter of what one does with one's sex organs. The physical intimacy of intercourse gives tangible form and expression to the larger reality that marriage is a life fellowship of an all-encompassing nature. Understanding marriage in terms of fellowship, Protestants have viewed the marriage union as a personal, not a sacramental, one.

Since Vatican II, the Catholic Church has also emphasized the personal side of the marriage relationship. However, the sacramental character of the marriage bond remains the fundamental matter. Pius XI's insistence *(Casti Connubii)* that once a couple enters this relationship, their freedom has no power over the *nature* of matrimony and that they are subject to its *essential* laws and properties, is still the official position of the Catholic Church. Thus the Catholic Church seeks to have it both ways, maintaining the sacramental view of the marriage union, on the one hand, yet taking more than a furtive glance in the direction of the voluntaristic view, on the other.

To understand marriage in terms of personal union does not imply that when two people are married, the individual identity of the one is absorbed into that of the other. There is no mystical loss of the self in the self of the other; husbands and wives remain two people.[108] Yet they are no longer two as once they were. In the union of marriage, they have become one in the sense that both partners are more and more conformed to a common

---

107. Animadverting on the tendency in this oversexed age to reduce the oneness of the marriage union to physical sexuality, Boman suggests that to call the marriage bond a union of "one flesh" refers not only to the lasting fellowship of which intercourse is the physical expression, but also to the offspring of a marriage union. The child is one flesh from both parents in a literal sense *(Hebrew Thought,* p. 96). So also Gerhard von Rad, *Old Testament Theology,* 2 vols., trans. D. M. G. Stalker (New York and Evanston: Harper & Row, 1962-65), 1.170. This argument is more sentimental than substantive. Gn. 2:24 is not concerned with offspring but with the fellowship of marriage, which is so radical that it takes precedence over the blood ties of family.

108. In view of our rejection of sexual hierarchy, we obviously do not believe in the traditional view that the wife's identity should be merged with that of her husband. Even if she takes his surname, she retains her Christian name. And the same is true of the husband, if he takes his wife's surname. On the inviolability of the individual self, see above, pp. 23-25.

personality, as it were, of which each partakes and in which each shares by virtue of the ongoing marriage relationship.[109] Thus the relationship may be described as a "bond," a tie that binds, not in the sense of coercion but of a oneness *(henosis)* of heart and mind. It is a tie in which each gives the self to the other in an unreserved and ongoing commitment.[110] About to leave on a trip to Paris, the poet John Donne sought to cheer his tearful wife with lines that beautifully express this sentiment:

> Sweetest love, I do not go,
>   For weariness of thee,
> Nor in the hopes the world can show
>   A fitter love for me. . . .
> When *thou* sigh'st, thou sigh'st not wind,
>   But sigh'st *my* soul away;
> When *thou* weep'st, unkindly kind,
>   *My* life's blood doth decay.[111]

The "oneness of mind and heart" that describes the marriage bond is, in our judgment, entailed in the biblical expression "to know" as used of sexual intercourse. ("Adam knew [יָדַע] Eve his wife, and she conceived" [Gn. 4:1].) Such an expression is no mere euphemism. To know another person, that person must disclose him- or herself to the other. While it is true that husband and wife come to know each other through the fellowship of married life generally, the physical intimacy of coitus in the larger context of married love is an apt symbol of such disclosure. The verb "to know" describes what happens in intercourse with a depth of meaning that goes far beyond the physical act itself as a biological mechanism for procreation. Hence it is unfortunate that some modern versions, in an effort to make the text plain to the present-day reader, translate, "Adam lay with his wife Eve" — a doubtful effort to make scriptural revelation "relevant" by lowering it to the level of the reader rather than lifting the reader to the level of revelation.

The experience of marriage, to the degree that the ideal of oneness is achieved over the years, shapes both partners so that they complement each other and become ever more congruous to each other. As the Christian must say, "To me to live is Christ" (Phil. 1:21), acknowledging that her

---

109. While marriage is a "state" into which one enters, it is not a static condition — except in the eyes of the state, which construes marriage as a legal contract. Theologically, the operative word is not "state" but "relationship," a relationship whose dynamic quality we here seek to express by the adjective "ongoing."

110. In other words, while married couples retain their *individuality,* they give up their *independence.* To the extent there is failure in either direction, the ideal of marriage will be compromised.

111. "Sweetest Love, I Do Not Go," in Untermeyer, ed., *Great Poems,* p. 357. Italics added.

life would not be life apart from her oneness with the Lord, so it is with husband and wife. United in the bond of marriage, each partner feels the inadequacy of a life without the other. The self is complete only in the other, so that the life of each is fulfilled as life together. Such unique and intimate fellowship is what makes the relationship between husband and wife in the marriage covenant a parable of the relationship between Christ and the church.[112]

To summarize: we understand the oneness *(henosis)* of marriage as an instance of the I-thou encounter that rests on a unique, lifelong fellowship with one's sexual partner. The quality of this unique, ongoing fellowship should not be understood narrowly in terms of the physical, even though sex, in the physical sense, is the Creator's gift to be enjoyed in the bond of marriage. The time has come to fill out our understanding of this fellowship of sexual (romantic) love as it is perceived in the Christian ideal of marriage.

As we turn to the task before us, we pause to note that Paul, in contrast to the Fathers, obviously deemed sex, in the physical sense, to be an essential part of the fellowship of marriage. He calls it the "debt" (ὀφειλή, *debitum*) owed to one's partner. To withhold it is to defraud (ἀποστερέω) the partner, unless it is by mutual consent for a time, that one or both parties may give themselves to prayer (1 Cor. 7:1-6). In the ancient and medieval church this text, intended to limit the occasions for abstinence, was instead used to multiply such occasions. Some authorities required newlyweds to abstain even on their wedding night! Others counseled abstinence on the night before receiving the sacrament of Holy Communion, even though marriage itself was regarded as a sacrament. (Thus one sacrament hindered the receiving of another!) There were those, however, who condemned such views as "rigorism."

The frequency of intercourse cannot be legislated, though it is obvious that the apostle regarded it as an ongoing expression of the one-flesh relationship of marriage. Therefore it is not too much to say that he regarded marriage as a *remedium concupiscentiae*. It is also obvious, however, that the apostle thought of these matters in terms of mutuality. Each should render what is owed to the other. Not only does the wife's body belong to her husband, but likewise the husband's body belongs to the wife (1 Cor. 7:3-4). One can only deplore the loss of this mutuality as a result of male bias, which has traditionally looked upon the marriage *debitum* as the husband's "right" and the wife's "duty," an abuse that has been justified by the wife's promise, in the traditional wedding ceremony, "to obey"; and reinforced by the fiction that the male has greater need than the female, who is "passive" in coition. Thus it is not marriage that becomes the remedy for concupiscence, but the *woman* who becomes the remedy for the man's concupiscence. The abuses women have suffered because of such an attitude are unmentionable. (Of the many manuals offering counsel and advice bearing

112. When we come to the locus of ecclesiology, the concept of *koinonia* (fellowship) with one another in Christ will be central to our understanding of what the church is.

on the physical side of the marriage relationship — sexual technique, the wedding night, etc. — one may consult with profit Theodor Bovet, *A Handbook of Marriage* [Garden City, N.Y.: Doubleday, 1958], especially chap. 3, "The Fellowship of Love," pp. 47-80.)

2) *The Blessings of Marriage* (Bona Matrimonii)

As already noted, theologians have generally understood our creation as male and female in terms of the command to be fruitful and multiply. Hence, when speaking of the *bona matrimonii* ("blessings," "benefits," "ends," "goods," of marriage), the Christian tradition has always emphasized procreation and the family.

Having rejected this traditional approach to the Genesis narratives, we have sought to understand our male- and femaleness not in terms of marriage and procreation, but in terms of what it means to be in the image of God. The God who is in himself a fellowship of Father, Son, and Spirit has given us our humanity as a fellowship of male and female. As for marriage, it is a specific instance of this larger fellowship. It is the fellowship of romantic love enjoyed by a man and a woman who have become sexual partners. The first express reference to marriage in Scripture, one should note, speaks not of procreation but of fellowship; marriage is a fellowship of a uniquely intimate sort — the man cleaves to his wife and they become "one flesh" (Gn. 2:24). In keeping with this approach, we understand the blessings of marriage primarily in terms of the fellowship of love, implicit in the man's original response to the woman's presence — "this at last" (2:23).[113] The fellowship of marriage, being sexual in nature, may indeed produce children, and "happy is the man who has his quiver full of them" (Ps. 127:5). But the fellowship of love is in and of itself the essential blessing of marriage.[114]

Such an understanding of the marriage relationship is admittedly not emphasized in Scripture, for reasons we have already reviewed. Yet it is an understanding that is compatible with Scripture; and the same is true of the Christian tradition generally. While marriages of love are infrequent, they are by no means unheard-of throughout Christian history. For example, Christina of Pisa (1364-1429) speaks not only of the gentle kisses she

113. See above, pp. 205-9.
114. Unfortunately the masterpieces of literature and music are primarily concerned with love's premarital conquests. Once the heart is wooed and the hand is won, the ongoing love of marriage is regarded as dull and uninteresting. Among the many happy refutations of this artistic fiction, in real life, is the love of Edvard Grieg for Nina Hagerup, for whom he composed his expressive and tender "I Love You" ("Ich Liebe Dich"). The touch of melancholy in his "Last Spring" reflects the vintage love of a life spent with her as his wife and companion.

received on her wedding night, but sighs as she recalls her husband's troth reiterated throughout the years of their life together.

> That he is mine, all mine to be
> Until the grave shall quell
> The ardor of our amity —
> From such sweet anguish I could die!
> Truly he loves me well.[115]

Even Luther, at times, extols married love. Such love says:

> "I wish not yours, I wish neither gold nor silver, neither this nor that. I want only you. I want everything or nothing." All other loves seek something else than that which is loved, but this love alone desires the beloved completely. If Adam had not fallen, the love of the bridegroom and the bride would be the loveliest thing.[116]

Such encomiums to love, however, are admittedly the exception that proves the rule.

When we hold the primary blessing of marriage to be the ongoing personal fellowship of romantic love expressed in the sexual intimacy of husband and wife, we must acknowledge that the passionate character of this love subsides with time. But the subsiding of passion does not turn married love into a cerebral fellowship of kindred minds. Nor does the one-flesh bond of marriage become, through the years, a "spiritual" relationship. If they are Christians, married couples may sing in church, "Blest be the tie that binds our hearts in Christian love"; but they do not sing it to each other. No; married love is always erotic love. But as youthful passions subside, love becomes a mellowed eros. This mellowed eros is not a love that is dying but a love that is maturing, plumbing ever greater depths of meaning, expressing itself in ever new and manifold ways. It is a love that brings joy and accepts sacrifice.

---

115. Translated by S. L. M. Barlow, *Saturday Review of Literature* 44 (Feb. 2, 1952), as quoted in Bainton, *What Christianity Says About Sex,* pp. 67-68.

116. WA, 62.167, as quoted in Bainton, ibid., pp. 76-77. For the most part, Luther was a traditionalist little given to romanticizing married life. Marriage was a yoke — though much easier than monasticism — that called for the exercise of patience. "He marveled at the patriarchs who had been able to stick it out for six or seven hundred years. How often Eve must have said to Adam, 'You ate the apple,' and Adam retorted, 'You gave it to me' " (WA, 42.151 and 550, as quoted by Bainton, ibid., p. 82). Luther also stressed the *remedium concupiscentiae* view of marriage. In a letter to Reissenbusch he expressed the opinion that taking a wife was just as much a necessity as eating and drinking. See Bailey, *Sexual Relation,* p. 171.

Theologians have no special term to describe this maturing love, for the obvious reason that they have had little to say about romantic love in any form. Bailey quotes Jeremy Taylor's observation that the sexual union of husband and wife has as its purpose, among others, "to lighten and ease the cares and sadness of household affairs, and to endear each other," and goes on to observe that "this is probably the first express recognition in theological literature of what may be termed the relational purpose of coitus."[117] What Taylor is talking about may be called "tender affection." A husband and wife, in coitus and in the larger fellowship of love that it symbolizes, become increasingly affectionate toward each other. As love has many splendors, so the love relationship of marriage partners displays many qualities; one experiences such love as endearment, as companionship, as mutual enjoyment of each other, as shared pleasure in times of prosperity and shared suffering in times of adversity.

Traditionally theologians have found it difficult to use the word "pleasure" when speaking of the blessings of married love. For centuries it has been assumed that pleasure is at best an incidental aspect of sexual intercourse, whose true purpose is procreation. The only reason a sexual encounter could bring one pleasure is that one did not seek pleasure in it. To indulge in intercourse for pleasure itself rather than procreation, even with one's spouse, is to succumb to concupiscence. In this matter Calvin was more liberal than most in his day. He allowed that pleasure is, indeed, a proper use of the sexual fellowship of marriage. Yet he admonished husbands and wives to indulge such pleasure only in moderation and with all sobriety. He would never have written a book entitled *The Joys of Sex*.[118]

The thought that the pleasures of sex in the larger fellowship of married love are to be enjoyed as gifts of the Creator is by no means a baptized hedonism. The enjoyment of sexual love on the part of husband and wife is of a different order from the selfish gratification of desire and appetite one finds in the momentary encounter with a prostitute. In the latter instance, there is no love, no giving of the self to the other, no lasting commitment; in short, no true fellowship. The "I" does not relate to the other as a "thou" but as an object — a sex object. And the same is true of the notion, so popular in our day, that we have been delivered by the "sexual revolution" from the restraints of marriage and (with the help of contraceptives) from the fear of pregnancy. We have found out that sex is fun; we can enjoy its pleasures without suffering its penalties. Thus we are free to indulge our appetites, which are "normal," "natural,"

---

117. Bailey, *Sexual Relation,* p. 208, citing Taylor's *Holy Living: Works,* 3.63. Bailey's thought is that procreation and the remedy of sexual desire had all but eclipsed any thought of fellowship as a benefit of intercourse.

118. "Zinzendorf endeavored to spiritualize marriage as a type of the relationship of Christ to the soul. The marriage bed he declared is as pure as the sacrament of the altar. Yet there should be no more enjoyment of sex in marriage than of wine in the sacrament" (Bainton, *What Christianity Says About Sex,* p. 104).

and "healthy." This is the πρῶτον ψεῦδος. In sex as in everything else, to live without restraint is to destroy life, not to enjoy it. One is here reminded of Barth's remark, "Coitus without coexistence is demonic" (*KD,* III/4, p. 148 [cf. *CD,* III/4, p. 133]).

In treating the fellowship of erotic love as the fundamental blessing of marriage, we are consciously reversing the traditional order of the *bona,* viz., (a) procreation, (b) remedy of desire, (c) mutual society. We are making the last to be first. The primary blessing of marriage is the fellowship of erotic love that unites a man and a woman in a uniquely intimate, sexual relationship. According to Dt. 24:5, the newly wedded soldier was exempt from service for a year, not in order to start a family — though such might happen — nor to satiate his passion, but "to be happy with his wife" ("to bring happiness to his wife," וְשִׂמַּח אֶת־אִשְׁתּוֹ). Generally alluded to with a knowing smile as hopelessly idealistic, this is a passage in which one easily misses the word of the Lord.

3) Marriage and the Gift of New Life

a) Introduction

Although we understand the fellowship of erotic love to be the primary blessing of marriage, we would by no means exclude from its many other blessings the gift of children. In procreation, husband and wife are privileged to share with the Creator in the marvelous work of bringing new life into the world. If one is a Christian, one cannot doubt the honor nor deny the responsibility that such a privilege entails. By the gift of new life, God, who is likened in Scripture to a father and a mother, makes a husband a father and a wife a mother. Thus the blessing of offspring enlarges the one-flesh fellowship of marriage and provides opportunity to express that fellowship in challenging and rewarding ways. This larger fellowship is, in other words, an extension of the marriage fellowship itself.[119]

Speaking of the challenging and responsible ways in which parents express the enlarged fellowship of the family, we pause to remember Monica, the mother of Augustine. One must acknowledge that she was in many ways a child of her times. Perhaps the account of her life contained in the *Confessions* is colored by the pious sentiment of a devoted son. Yet one cannot doubt that her importunate prayers were the means heaven used to bring the young Augustine to embrace the Christian faith. Thus she put all Christians in her debt. Noting her dismay when he became a Manichaean, Augustine tells how she wept for him more than most mothers weep for the bodily deaths of their children. "For she, by that faith and spirit which she had from you, discerned the death wherein I lay, and you heard her, O Lord; you heard her and despised not her tears when,

---

119. While such a larger fellowship rests, ordinarily, on blood relationship, it is essentially spiritual in nature. Hence the possibility that a married couple may become father and mother by adoption. One will recall that Paul uses the figure of adoption to describe the believer's relation to God in Christ. Thus he seems to commend adoption in the literal sense as securing essentially the same blessing that is ordinarily given through biological procreation.

streaming down, they watered the ground under her eyes in every place where she prayed; yea, you heard her" (3.11.19). When Monica entreated a bishop to reason with her son, he reassured her with the words, "Go your way and God bless you, for it is not possible that the son of these tears should perish" (3.12.21).

Having left Africa, Monica was in Milan when her son was converted and baptized by Ambrose. Subsequently, on their way back to their native land, they were detained in the port of Ostia by civil war. While staying in the home of some affluent citizens (the Anicii family?), Monica was stricken ill and died (A.D. 387). Augustine speaks of their last days together, in which they were led to the very gate of heaven as they contemplated a blessed reunion in the life to come. One should read especially 9.10.23-26, which relates the conversation they had one day when they found themselves alone, leaning on a window that overlooked the garden of the house where they were staying.

Because our subject is marriage, we cannot, at this juncture, pursue the many questions that confront one who would frame a Christian doctrine of the family. We must limit ourselves, rather, to matters bearing directly on procreation. As for procreation, our understanding of this subject will reflect the view of marriage we have espoused, which gives primacy of place to the fellowship of erotic love. Such an understanding will, of course, lead to conclusions about procreation concerning which Catholics and Protestants do not agree. Indeed, we must acknowledge that even a Protestant consensus on these matters is beyond the reach of theologians, at least for the present. This is so, on the one hand, because modern medical technology and new social and environmental issues have thrust upon the church the need for an in-depth reexamination of some assumptions about marriage and procreation on which the traditional consensus has rested. On the other hand, the insight needed for such a task comes only with theological reflection, and such reflection takes time. While the pastoral needs of the church are pressing, and while theology comes out of the needs of the church, good theology is never a quick fix. Theology cannot deny that life as we know it today compels us to make tough ethical decisions in areas of procreation; but theology does remind us that when, under the pressure of circumstances, we make such decisions, we should be prepared to repent of them. On this tentative note we venture the following observations.

b) Induced Conception

Given the structure of biblical revelation, marriage and celibacy, as we have noted, are equal options for the Christian. And by parity of reasoning, the same is true when a married couple contemplates the privilege and responsibility of bringing offspring into the world. The promise of offspring given to Abraham and Sarah has been fulfilled in Christ (Gal. 3:16); hence

Christians do not stand on Old Testament ground. Parenthood is, indeed, a gift of God, but husbands and wives are free in their choice to embrace or not to embrace such a gift. A childless marriage is not a sub-Christian marriage.

But what if married partners, earnestly desiring the gift of children, cannot embrace the gift because of some biological impediment that cannot be overcome without the help of modern medical technology? Christians do not suppose that reproductive technology takes such matters out of God's hands any more than scientific agriculture takes the blessing of providing our daily bread out of God's hands. If we put our trust in scientific agriculture, if we abuse the soil to reap abundantly in the short term, we will in the long term lose the blessing of him who gives us our daily bread. By the same token, if we take the creation of new life into our own hands in a way that denies the dignity and denigrates the quality belonging to human life, the God who is the source of all life will call us to account for our temerity. Whatever remedies, therefore, Christians may use to overcome a childless marriage, they should be not only technically feasible but also consonant with God's will insofar as we are able to discern his will.

When it comes to the question of human procreation and the will of God, it does not appear to us, as it does to the Vatican, that the act of intercourse and the event of conception are linked by the Creator in such a way that their deliberate separation is necessarily contrary to the will of God. In arguing that intercourse and conception may be separated, we are not implying that conception should ever be apart from parenting. New life, if it is to be human, should always be brought into the world in a context in which responsibility for the nurturing of that new life is acknowledged and accepted. (For the Christian such a context, obviously, is marriage and the family.) But this canon of responsible Christian behavior is not, in our judgment, necessarily violated whenever conception takes place apart from the act of intercourse. When fertilization cannot be achieved in a normal way, the use of medical technology, so far from violating "natural and divine law," would seem to acknowledge it and work within it. While we agree that the conjugal act is "designed for the procreation of offspring," as the Catholic Church teaches, why may we not seek that good end by artificial means when a natural impediment frustrates the use of ordinary means? Such artificial means do not demean the act of love any more than the use of lens transplants to improve one's eyesight demeans the gift of vision.

The technology to which we refer takes several forms. For example, the wife may be artificially inseminated with her husband's sperm (AIH). Some moral theologians have opposed such a procedure, not only because conception is achieved apart from inter-course, but because the husband must perform the sex act independently (masturbation) to provide the semen. In the Christian tradition, masturbation has been all but uniformly condemned. In the medieval penitentials, it was lumped together with homosexuality, fornication, adultery, incest, and even bestiality. The scriptural basis for such a judgment is wanting, however. The one text cited (Gn. 38:9), where Onan spilled his semen on the ground *(coitus interruptus)* because he did not want to provide his brother's wife with offspring, according to the law of levirate marriage, has nothing to do with masturbation. (Hence to call masturbation "onanism" is misleading.)

As for masturbation (autosexuality) in general, we must grant that the ideal expe-rience of an orgasm is one enjoyed in partnership with a spouse; it is one of the pleasures of the love that unites husband and wife. But such ideal circumstances are by no means always present, even to married people, as in the event of war, imprisonment, prolonged illness, and the like. Furthermore, the many sexual fantasies — "unclean thoughts" — that are indulged, under some circumstances, in masturbation are not caused by mas-turbation and, some have argued, may even be relieved by it. In any case, since there is no express basis in Scripture for condemning the practice (though there is no basis in Scripture for commending it, either), it is unrealistic rigorism to condemn it un-equivocally, especially in the case of those who are unmarried due to circumstances that are not of their own making.

*   *   *   *   *

As for artificial insemination by an anonymous donor rather than one's husband (AID), such a choice on the part of a childless couple presupposes the ability of both husband and wife to acknowledge, as Christians, that parental ties are essentially spiritual in nature rather than biological. Here again one must remember that the Christian does not stand on Old Testament ground. In Ezra's day, all were excluded from the priesthood as unclean who were not enrolled in the genealogies, since they could not prove their pedigree (Ezra 2:59-63). Such Old Testament ceremonial considerations are irrelevant when it comes to accepting a new member into the family on the part of Christian parents. The choice that parents make under such circumstances is akin to that made in adoption. In the case of adoption there is no biological continuity between the parents and the child whom they embrace as God's gift; in the case of artificial insemination by an anonymous donor there is no biological continuity between one parent and the child. Of course, if either parent cannot bring him- or herself to accept as their own offspring one who is not biologically related to them, it would be folly for a childless couple to pursue such a course of action.

*   *   *   *   *

Surrogate motherhood, in our opinion, is not the same thing as anonymous (surrogate) fatherhood (AID). In terms of blood relationship it may be so, in the sense that in the former instance the child comes into a family biologically related to the father only, while in the latter it is biologically related to the mother only. But here the incidental similarity ends and the significant difference begins. Surrogate motherhood, unlike sperm donation, involves all the suffering and risks of any pregnancy. Furthermore, the bonding that begins to take place between mother and unborn child goes far beyond the merely biological. In other words, surrogate motherhood involves the dimension of the personal; a significant personal relationship exists between the biological mother and the child she carries and bears for someone else. The Christian faith teaches us that in personal relationships we should not impose risks and burdens on others for the sake of satisfying our own desires. When a husband wants a child that is biologically his and his wife is barren, it is not right to put his wife emotionally at risk and at the same time burden her surrogate to achieve his own ends. One cannot but wonder, were the situation reversed so that the risk and burden fell on males instead of females, whether surrogacy would be tolerated in today's society. Furthermore still, surrogacy often involves paying money to the surrogate for her "services." Such a procedure is, in our judgment, paltry; it cheapens rather than commends the whole endeavor. What may be called the first instance of surrogate motherhood in the Bible is recorded in Gn. 16:1-6. Here Sarai instructs Abram to "go in to my maid; it may be that I shall obtain children by her." For all the cultural differences between then and now, the sequel to this ill-advised maneuver on the part of Sarai and Abram should tell us something about the present practice of surrogacy.

*   *   *   *   *

Like artificial insemination, in vitro fertilization (IVF) is, in our judgment, neutral technology. It is not to be faulted for separating intercourse from conception. Nonetheless, when sperm and egg are united in a petri dish and the embryo that forms is implanted in the mother's body, a new factor is introduced if several fertilized eggs are produced, only one of which is used. The human embryos that are destroyed (or frozen for subsequent nontherapeutic experimentation) are potential human selves. Such treatment of embryonic materials that are biologically human raises the problems that are also associated with abortion. In such an instance we are using technology not simply to aid those who desire to bring new life into the world; we are, at the same time, destroying that life. True, such destruction also happens in the case of therapeutic abortion; but when embyronic human life is treated as a mere glob of protoplasm to be used in experiments and discarded, then technology is on a collision course with the Christian doctrine of the sanctity of human life. (The same difficulty may emerge with zygote interfallopian transfer [ZIFT], though not with gamete [sperm and egg] interfallopian transfer [GIFT].)

All techniques to induce conception and so overcome infertility confront one with larger questions concerning which each couple must be persuaded in their own minds. Such techniques involve stress and risks that one may or may not be justified in taking. They also place a demand on human resources at a time when the world very much needs to devote its resources to limiting births rather than increasing them, and to improving the quality of life available to infants born under difficult and sometimes tragic circumstances. Finally, all such techniques may fail. This reminds

Christians, as we have already noted, that our lives are in God's hands. The Lord may give the gift of offspring, as he did to Zechariah and Elizabeth (Lk. 1:5-24); but again he may not. The greater blessing in the Christian life is not to receive whatever we desire but to desire whatever we receive because we receive it as from the Lord's hand.

c) Birth Control

In today's world it is not the use of medical knowledge to increase the birth rate but rather the use of that knowledge to control it that presents the greater challenge to the church. The former concerns the few who desire an end (birth) that the church has always blessed; the latter, by contrast, concerns the many who desire an end (the prevention of birth) that the church has traditionally condemned. Throughout the centuries of Christian tradition, the condemnation of birth control has been all but universal; and such condemnation is found even today in the official teaching of the Roman Catholic Church. This consensus has rested on the assumption, Protestant as well as Catholic, that the chief end of marriage is procreation and that any effort to avoid procreation violates the ordinance of creation enshrined in the divine command to be "fruitful and multiply, and fill the earth" (Gn. 1:28).[120]

In our previous discussion of the blessings of marriage we have rejected this approach, arguing rather that marriage is basically a fellowship of romantic love. In this fellowship the blessing of children is to be received with gratitude. It is, however, a blessing incidental rather than essential to the relationship, a blessing not even mentioned in the initial reference to marriage in Scripture (Gn. 2:24). In the light of what we have said about the structure of biblical revelation and the eschatological nature of the kingdom Jesus came to establish, many might think that the view of marriage we have espoused is sufficiently evident to have commended itself to the church throughout Christian history. But this is by no means so. Rather, the view we have espoused reflects a significant departure from the traditional teaching of the church. This fact becomes evident when one reviews the controversy over birth control that continues even to the present day.

When Walter Lippmann published *A Preface to Morals* in 1929, he affirmed that the Christian churches were right in perceiving that birth

120. Having grown up in a conservative Baptist church, I recall from childhood days a tract of the sort read by adults in the congregation. It was a broadside against Margaret Sanger (1886-1966), an early proponent of birth control in America. The title of the tract, which reflected the pervasive attitude in the congregation, was something like, "Margaret Sanger and Pail of Filth."

control was "the most revolutionary practice in the history of sexual morals."[121] He then went on to summarize the impact of this revolution on society in general and the profound changes it brought about for all concerned.

Lippmann, of course, when speaking of birth control as a "modern revolution" in morals, had in mind the advocacy of birth control as public policy. Such advocacy began in the nineteenth century. The practice, however, is much older. The use of contraceptives antedates the Christian era and first evoked controversy in the church when Callistus was bishop of Rome (A.D. 217-222). At that time women of aristocratic rank outnumbered men of equal standing, especially in congregations in and around the city of Rome. (One will recall the "Greek women of high standing" among Paul's converts in Berea, Acts 17:12). Because the church counseled against marriage to pagans, and because marriage to slaves and others of inferior rank meant the loss of all status and privilege, these Christian women were allowed to enter into lifelong relationships with freedmen and slaves who shared their faith as Christians, even though these relationships were without legal recognition. As this custom increased, many of the women involved were reluctant to bear children who by law would inherit the father's status. For this reason they had recourse to various means of contraception. When this situation became known in the church generally, the most vociferous protests came from the rigorous disciplinarians; but the church as a whole also condemned the practice as abhorrent and inimical to the true purpose of marriage. (See Bainton, *What Christianity Says About Sex,* pp. 37-38.)

Having already committed ourselves to the view that the chief end of marriage is the enjoyment of conjugal love for its own sake, it is obvious that for us the revolution of which Lippmann speaks has had a salutary aspect. Birth control ought to be public policy, and it ought to be accepted by the church as consonant with the Christian doctrine of marriage. We no longer live in the world of the Scottish economist Adam Smith, whose *Wealth of Nations* (1776) assumes that the increase of population is essential to the prosperity of the body politic. In our day the economic enterprise does not need more people to supply cheap labor, nor does the political enterprise need more soldiers to fight the battles of state. Rather than the world of Adam Smith, we live in a world in which the warnings of Thomas Malthus, whose *Essay on Population* (1798) first made us mindful of the inexorable law that human population must be adjusted to the limited resources of the planet, take on ever-increasing urgency. We also live in a world where modern medicine has for the first time made such population control a genuine possibility. These two, the need that is urgent and a solution that is at hand, have led the majority of theologians to look anew

---

121. *Preface to Morals* (New York: Macmillan, 1929), p. 291.

at biblical revelation and to acknowledge the limitations of the traditional understanding of that revelation when it comes to marriage and procreation.

As for the need to control the birthrate, what was a cloud the size of a man's hand in Malthus's day has become a flood that threatens to whelm the entire human race. World population at the beginning of the Christian era was somewhere in the neighborhood of 250 million. By A.D. 1600 it had doubled, and by 1850 it was at the one billion mark. United Nations demographers tell us that the world's population was 5.2 billion in 1990 and will have reached, by the turn of the century, nearly 7 billion. The present rate is three people per second or about a quarter of a million new arrivals on planet Earth every day. The decade of the nineties will add the equivalent of another China to the world's population (Nafis Sadik, executive director of the U.N. Population Fund, in the *Los Angeles Times,* Feb. 22, 1990, pt. I, p. A10). At this rate, in 650 years each member of the human family will have about one square foot of land to stand on! Little wonder that many speak of a population "explosion," and some have even suggested darkly that the world is afflicted with cancer and the cancer cell is the human individual. Lurking behind the cold statistics, the grim specter of famine and the apparition of disease are already at work in our world, wreaking widespread catastrophe that beggars description in the human family. (For further discussion of this problem in the context of the environmental crisis, see below, pp. 402-6.)

The problem of overpopulation has reached such staggering proportions — many believe that it has now eclipsed nuclear war as a threat to the human race — that it has called forth numerous responses. We must, we are told, increase the supply of food; industrialized nations must share scientific knowledge and technical skills with less developed nations; we must give economic assistance on a humanitarian rather than political basis; we must aid in public health education worldwide; and so forth.

One of the less plausible solutions is to encourage migration from heavily populated to less populated areas. The trend worldwide is actually in the reverse direction — to the cities. (As of this writing, Mexico City has nearly 30,000,000 inhabitants, and the children fourteen and under who live there outnumber the total population of New York City.) With the dawn of the space age, some have dreamed of exporting people to other planets. Commenting on this chimera, the *Christian Century* editorialized a number of years ago: "A recent issue of the *Population Bulletin* disposes of this hope: Around 7,000 people, argues the *Bulletin,* would have to be shot off from Cape Canaveral each hour to keep the world's population from increasing. At $3 million per emigrant — the current cost of a space shot — this project would cost $500 billion a day, or approximately the equivalent of our economy's annual gross national product" (as quoted in *Christian Century* 80, no. 46 [Nov. 13, 1963]: 1393).

When all is said that can be said about the need for a multifaceted, integrated, overall program to balance world population and resources, nothing

— neither more food, nor more money, nor more education — will work without a deliberate effort to regulate conception and birth. This is the firm conclusion on which all population experts agree.[122]

We grant that any such program has ethical dimensions that cannot be resolved by simply quoting the statisticians and demographic experts. But it is unconscionable for theologians, in the name of Christian morality, to advocate some solution that is at best a temporary palliation because they want to skirt the issue of birth control. The church must say clearly that it cannot be pleasing to God that natural fecundity should run its unimpeded course with its wretched train of poverty, suffering, degradation, and death.[123]

At the Second Vatican Council, the Roman Catholic Church recognized the need for reconciling its teaching on marriage and procreation with the sociological problems of our time. The Council, however, refrained deliberately from making specific pronouncements that would commit the Catholic Church on birth control because this matter was being studied by a special papal commission. In the Pastoral Constitution, *Gaudium et Spes* (1965), all the Council affirmed was that "the sons of the Church are not allowed, in the matter of regulating procreation, to adopt methods which are reproved by the teaching authority of the Church interpreting the divine law." After some delay, evidently because his own commission had overwhelmingly favored liberalizing the Catholic Church's position, Pope Paul VI finally issued his encyclical *Humanae Vitae* (1968). In it he condemned "every action which . . . proposes, whether as an end or as a means, to render procreation impossible." Such action, even in spacing a family, is wrong because it violates the particular laws that God the Creator has established as intrinsic to the marriage act. Any act that interferes with procreation "is in contradiction with the innate design of marriage and with the will of the Author of life." This position was reaffirmed in 1995 by Pope John Paul II in his encyclical *Evangelium Vitae,* in which opposition to techniques of artificial reproduction, most embryo research, and most instances of capital punishment, as well as long-decried abortion and euthanasia, was also given the weight of an encyclical. See *Christian Century* 112, no. 12 [April 12, 1995]: 384-85). Happily, the majority of American and European Catholics have rejected this particular piece of natural theology. But in Latin America the effect has been deleterious in the extreme. When one reflects on official Catholic teaching about

---

122. The enormous demands those who live in wealthy nations make on the environment by their lifestyle also contributes to a world in which population and resources are thrown out of balance. We shall speak to this problem presently. See below, pp. 392-445.

123. In view of the vexed problem of abortion, which we are about to consider, the church should not only recognize contraception as consonant with God's will but approve further research in the interest of improving the present options. In the United States alone, 8,000 people a day, we are told, become pregnant "by mistake" (Thomas Parker, *In One Day* [Boston: Houghton Mifflin, 1984], p. 94). Current studies indicate that of the 1.5 million abortions performed annually in this country, half are related to pregnancies brought on by the failure of contraceptives.

marriage and procreation in the light of Scripture and the demographic data, one is reminded, somehow, of the conflict with Galileo. The day of reckoning must come. We can only hope that the Catholic Church will not take as long to accept population control as it did to accept a heliocentric solar system.

By way of conclusion, we note that those who oppose artificial contraception espouse a position that actually threatens rather than affirms the sacred character of human life. The overpopulation that results from uncontrolled fecundity confronts the human race with unmitigated disaster. In saying as much, we have in mind the brute fact that starvation is already overtaking the human family. Surely "the design and will of the Author of Life" is not that we should bring people into the world whose only option is death by starvation.

The control of conception and birth, then, is not a life-denying but a life-affirming act in today's world. And this affirmation of life goes beyond the thought that everyone has the right to eat and enjoy physical health in the most literal sense. It includes the thought that women have a right to enjoy a greater measure of both physical and psychological health than is possible when submission to their husband's embrace involves one pregnancy after another. It also includes the thought that parents have a right to the prospect of providing their children with those better things that give their lives a truly human quality. Thus the earth will be filled, as the Creator has commanded (Gn. 1:28), not simply with children who must struggle to survive, but with those who have at least the possibility not only of receiving but of enjoying the Creator's gift of life.

We are not unmindful of the fact that the Catholic Church approves the so-called rhythm method of birth control. But this method is relatively less reliable than other approaches (20% failure rate). Such a risk factor is too high to remove the anxiety and fear of pregnancy. Furthermore, it calls for limited yet constantly recurring abstinence, which curtails the freedom and spontaneity of love. Such abstinence can be stress-inducing to the marriage relationship. We grant that many situations in marriage are stressful, but surely the act of love should not be made one of them.

d) Abortion: A Question of Life and Death

(1) Introduction. As astronomy has changed our picture of the universe, so biology has changed our picture of how each of us as individual selves becomes part of the universe. It was once thought that at conception the germ cell contained a complete, fully formed organism that developed simply by increasing in size. Some who embraced this doctrine (preformationism) were ovists, who supposed that the complete little human was

in the egg when it was activated by the sperm. Others, the homunculists, supposed that the complete little human was in the sperm head. Only in the nineteenth century was it discovered that a new individual life begins as a single cell and develops gradually into a fully formed human by a continuous sequence of cell multiplication and differentiation (epigenesis). Modern science has filled in the details of this picture in a brilliant way.

According to this picture, in a single act of intercourse, approximately a quarter of a billion sperm cells are released into the vagina. Setting out on a journey through the womb and into the fallopian tubes, one of these countless sperm meets an egg (if the woman has ovulated) as the latter moves through the fallopian tubes and into the womb. In this encounter, as the sperm penetrates the egg, the genetic material (DNA) from each combines to form a remarkable new cell called a zygote (fertilized egg). This new cell contains an incredible store of "information" — half from the father, half from the mother — that shapes and determines, biologically speaking, the entire life of the new individual from birth till death.

As this cell, which is the biological basis of each human life, continues its journey down the fallopian tubes toward the womb, a trip of about six days, it begins to divide into two cells, then four, eight, sixteen, and so on. About a week after fertilization, this tiny group of cells (blastocyst) arrives in the womb. At this point the blastocyst must implant itself in the lining of the womb or it will not develop into an embryo. Approximately one in four fails in this critical effort and perishes in a natural way. The same result can be achieved by scraping the uterine lining before the blastocyst arrives (curettage). When this is done, no blastocyst can attach itself; it is simply carried off in menstruation. (The "pill" is another way of achieving the same result. It functions to keep the menstrual cycle activated so as to carry off any blastocyst that might otherwise permanently lodge itself in the womb.) The failure of the blastocyst to implant itself in the womb obviously means that no embryo will form, no fetus develop, and no pregnancy take place. (This is why the argument over the use of the pill is sometimes referred to as "the after conception, before implantation debate.") If the blastocyst does implant itself in the uterine lining, a hormonal signal will turn off the woman's menstrual cycle so that fetal development may proceed undisturbed.

When left thus undisturbed, in about two weeks the cells of the blastocyst begin to multiply rapidly, and it becomes an embryo. Now begins the complex differentiation that leads eventually to the development of organs like the liver, the heart, the brain, and so on. The interruption of menstruation, which makes this rapid development possible, is the first sign a woman has that she may be pregnant. In about six weeks the

242 WHO WE ARE: OUR DIGNITY AS HUMAN

embryonic development of all the internal organs of the human body will have begun in a rudimentary way. By the end of eight weeks, fingers and toes are recognizable, the skeleton begins to form, and the embryo becomes a fetus capable of simple reflex actions. By the end of twelve weeks fetal heartbeat can be detected, while nerves and muscles are sufficiently developed for the fetus to move arms and legs ("quickening"). Beyond this point, fetal development is primarily a matter of growth of what already exists in the womb, until the time of birth, when the fetus is called an infant or baby.

The twelfth week is significant, medically speaking, since it marks the last possibility of abortion by simple dilation and curettage. (At this time the fetus is about 3½ inches long.) The twenty-eighth week of pregnancy marks the time when the fetus can survive a spontaneous, premature birth. This is an important milestone, for it is the time when the fetus is said to have attained viability. This so-called time of viability is significant legally, since laws often define "legal abortion" as the termination of a pregnancy "before viability." (The difficulty with such legal definitions is that technology is constantly shortening this time by perfecting the care of the prematurely born.) After twenty-eight weeks, the primary outward change in the fetus is in its size. As it grows, the development of certain organs like the brain accelerates rapidly in anticipation of the last event in the drama, when the umbilical cord is cut, the first breath is taken, and a new individual person joins the company of the human race some forty weeks after conception.

As one reflects on this mind-boggling process, which moves from a single cell to an individual self, three considerations bearing on the question of abortion come immediately to mind. The first is that the potential for new human life is present from the moment of conception. This is why a woman may not say of fetal tissue, "this is mine," as she may of kidney tissue when she donates it to another.[124] The second consideration is that as this potential human life moves toward actuality, each stage of the

---

124. We grant that fetal tissue is uniquely related to the woman's body, and we shall pursue the implications of this fact presently. Intimacy of relationship, however, does not entail possession. The woman does not *have* a fetus, she *carries* a fetus. Only penultimately does fetal tissue "belong" to her. Ultimately — as becomes obvious if the pregnancy is carried to term — this tissue belongs to the developing fetus. For a counterstatement, see Rachel Conrade Wahlberg, "The Woman and the Fetus: 'One Flesh'?" *Christian Century* 88, no. 36 (Sept. 8, 1971): 1045-48. "Consider the decisions you can make about your own body. . . . You can have your body tatooed, your ears pierced, your nose reshaped. You can decide to have an operation. Your appendix is your own and you can have it removed. . . . You are free to control your body in these and a hundred more ways. But if you are a woman?" (ibid., p. 1045).

process merges with the next so that it is impossible to impose any sharp lines or fix any exact point at which something unique happens. The boundary between human fetal tissue that is alive in the biological sense and human individual life that possesses dignity and worth in the theological sense cannot be precisely drawn. The third consideration is that matters are greatly complicated by the fact that abortion directly involves not only the life of the fetus but the life of the woman in whose body fetal development takes place. And the dignity of her life as human, whatever one may say of the fetus, cannot be doubted. That the fetus is human is a decision we must make. That the woman is human is a decision that has already been made. Hers are all the rights and privileges that pertain to the creature made in God's image. When, therefore, we talk about abortion and the need to reverence human life, the life we are talking about must obviously include the life of the woman who carries the unborn in her womb. This is why even the most ardent opponents of abortion will (ordinarily) sacrifice the life of the fetus to save the life of the mother.

One will recall that at the beginning of our discussion of marriage and procreation, we acknowledged that in the area of procreation some difficult decisions have been forced on the church today, decisions calling for theological reflection that the church has not had time to pursue. When this happens, the theologian becomes painfully aware of her finitude and can put forth her opinions only with an informed tentativeness. Hoping that we are informed and acknowledging that we cannot resolve all the issues, we venture the following comments on the "terrible choice" posed by the abortion dilemma.[125]

(2) Concerning Slogans and Moral Simplicities. The discussion of abortion is not advanced by oversimplification, for the obvious reason that it is not a simple question. We therefore reject slogans and moral simplicities when used by either side to win the argument. Slogans polarize and simplicities betray when applied to difficult ethical decisions such as the one before us.[126] To abort or not to abort has about it something of the elemental and existential quality of Hamlet's "to be or not to be."

125. See the account of The First International Conference on Abortion, with foreword by Pearl S. Buck, under the title *The Terrible Choice* (New York: Bantam, 1968). "White shall not neutralize the black, nor good/Compensate bad in man, absolve him so:/Life's business being just the terrible choice" (Robert Browning, "The Ring and the Book").

126. Even more disturbing than moral simplicities are misrepresentations of fact. One thinks, for example, of the oft-repeated story of the professor who submitted the following case to his students: "Here is the family history — The father has syphilis. The mother has T.B. They already have had four children. The first is blind. The second has died. The third

Speaking of moral simplicities, we have in mind such things as the tendency of some to equate abortion with murder *simpliciter,* a view taken by Tertullian as early as A.D. 200. (Tertullian, as a traducianist, believed the soul derived from the parents through procreation and was therefore present from the moment of conception.) Although Tertullian's view of the propagation of the soul has not commended itself to the majority of theologians, his condemnation of abortion has. Knowing nothing of the complexities of epigenesis, theologians, Catholic and Protestant, through the centuries, have generally opposed abortion, regarding the life of the unborn as sacred without qualification. This all but universal opposition to abortion in the Christian tradition has remained the official position of the Roman Catholic Church down to the present day.

In the Protestant tradition, by contrast, this consensus has given way to a qualified acceptance of abortion, especially in the early stages of pregnancy. If one argues that such qualified acceptance is a betrayal of the Christian vision, one should remember that not too long ago those who opposed birth control argued in the same way. Some who oppose abortion, even in the early stages of pregnancy, have hinted darkly that to favor abortion is to identify with the slaveholders who did not believe black folk had souls. If we believe that the slaves were people, then we should believe that the unborn are people. "The Dred Scott decision [that Blacks are not fully human (1857)] discriminated by skin color; Roe vs. Wade [the Supreme Court ruling of 1973] discriminated by place of residence — the womb. Each is a civil rights outrage." "We simply cannot continue to solve her [the woman's] personal problems by allowing the ghastly violence of killing a tiny, innocent human" (John C. Willke, "The Fetus Is Life Itself," *Los Angeles Times,* March 3, 1990, p. B6. Willke is president of the National Right to Life Committee).

In the same vein is the oft-heard complaint that the *Roe vs. Wade* decision of the nation's highest court, giving a woman the right to choose abortion in the first three months of pregnancy, has brought on an "abortion holocaust" reminiscent of the attitude toward human life espoused in the Nazi era.

> I am convinced that there are unmistakable similarities between what they [the Nazis] did then and what we are doing now. They too asked and answered the question, Who shall live and who shall die? And, Who belongs to the community entitled to our protection? Then and now, the subject at hand is killing, and letting die, and helping to die and using the dead. Then and now the goal is to produce healthier human beings and, perhaps, a better quality of human being. (Richard John Neuhaus, "Bioethics and the Holocaust," *First Things* 1 [March 1990]: 33)

To us such an argument appears profound on the surface, but deep down it is shallow (to borrow a phrase from Peter DeVries).

---

is deaf. The fourth has T.B. The mother is pregnant. What do you think?" Most of the students favored abortion. "Congratulations," said the professor, "you have just murdered Beethoven!" The trouble with this story is that Beethoven's father was an alcoholic, not a syphilitic; Beethoven was the second, not the fifth, child; and the first, supposedly blind when Beethoven was born, actually lived only six days. Such facts are easily obtainable in any standard biography of the composer.

(3) The Biblical Data. The theologian's difficulty in reaching an informed opinion about abortion stems not only from the rapid advance of scientific knowledge but also from the paucity of scriptural comment bearing on the subject. As we know, the biblical story of human origins contemplates the man and the woman as full-fledged (Gn. 2). When our first parents come on the scene, the umbilical cord has been cut. It is "humankind come of age," if we might so speak, that Scripture presents to us — the archetypical man and woman made in God's image and likeness. Adam and Eve are representative figures in whose life and destiny we see the life and destiny of the whole human race. Infancy and childhood have been left far behind, not to mention the mysterious beginnings of individual life in the dark recesses of the womb.

Since the biblical narrative speaks of God's "breathing into man's nostrils the breath of life" (v. 7), it might seem plausible to argue that the soul informs the body when the first breath is drawn, that is, at birth. But obviously we cannot take such language, so metaphorical in nature and theological in content, and apply it with such scientific literalism. One might as well argue that the soul informs the body when the fetal skeleton is formed, since the narrative also speaks of the Lord God's making the woman from the rib of the man (v. 22).

The ancient law found in Exodus 21:22-25 is sometimes cited as implying that the unborn are only potentially, not actually, human. According to this law, if a man maliciously causes a woman to miscarry, he shall be fined; but if an injury is sustained, he shall give eye for eye, even life for life. The ambiguity in the text — is the injury an injury suffered by the child due to premature birth, an injury suffered by the mother, or both — cannot be fully resolved. However, the text obviously focuses attention on the woman and what happens to her when she is hit. Such a focus implies that in contrast to a mere fine if she miscarries, a more severe penalty is exacted for any permanent injury she may suffer. This traditional understanding of the verse, reflected in the King James translation, surely does imply a hierarchy of values in which a woman's life takes precedence over the life of the unborn in her womb.[127] But such a hierarchy of values does not imply that life in the womb is merely biological. That Israel regarded fetal life as more than biological can be seen from the way the psalmist speaks when he reflects on the mystery of his own being — "For it was you who formed my inward parts; you knit me together in my mother's

---

127. As we have observed, this hierarchy of values is tacitly acknowledged by almost everyone, even the most stringent antiabortionists. It is the basis of the general acceptance of therapeutic abortion.

womb. I praise you, for I am fearfully and wonderfully made" (Ps. 139:13-14 NRSV). The use of the personal pronoun — "You formed *my* inward parts," "you knit *me* together," "*I* am fearfully made" — implies that the psalmist thought of himself as a self, an "I," even before he was born.

However, the question that confronts us today as to when fetal life is human is a question the biblical writers had no occasion to ask. They were convinced, in the words of Jeremiah the prophet, that God knew them even before he formed them in the womb (Jer. 1:5); and they confessed with the apostle Paul that the God whom they worshiped was the God who separated them from their mother's womb (Gal. 1:15). And Christians still affirm these fundamental truths; but they do so whether they believe that the human spirit is present from the moment of conception, or only at some subsequent stage of fetal development. In other words, Scripture gives Christians every reason to assume that fetal life is human life even in the womb. We do not find in Scripture, however, an answer to the question, When precisely is such life present? This is a question that cannot be resolved by simply citing chapter and verse; it compels us to consider the larger issue of the nature of human life in the light of scriptural revelation as a whole.[128]

In the abortion debate, pro-life apologists have conscripted Ex. 21:22-25 in defense of their cause, affirming that this passage does not distinguish between the life of the fetus and that of the mother; both are of equal worth. Given such an assumption, they then argue, "This law found in Ex. 21:22-25 turns out to be perhaps the most decisive positive evidence in Scripture that the fetus is to be regarded as a living person." And since the fetus is a living person, just as is the mother, "to be criminally responsible for the destruction of the fetus is to forfeit one's life" (Meredith Kline, as quoted by John Ankerberg and John Weldon, *When Does Life Begin?* [Brentwood: Wolgemuth & Hyatt, 1989], p. 196). Elaborating on Kline's argument, Ankerberg and Weldon go on to note, "The sixth commandment, 'Thou shalt not kill' (Hebrew: murder), refers to every act of murder: child, wife, husband, stranger, self, etc. Since it is scientifically established that the fetus is a human being, the commandment applies to abortion as well. 'Thou shalt not kill' is equivalent to, 'Thou shalt not commit abortion' " (ibid.).

This is, indeed, the logical conclusion implied in the thesis that the fetus is fully human from the moment of conception. Such an interpretation means that the party whose fighting caused the pregnant woman to give birth should get off with nothing more than a fine if, and only if, there is no permanent harm done either to the mother

128. The use of Scripture in the literature circulated by Christians on both sides of the debate is often more curious than convincing. On the one hand, pro-life people observe: "In Deuteronomy 30:19 God instructs his people how to properly solve the matter of choice. 'I set before you this day death and life, choose life.' God declares himself. He is 'pro-life.' " On the other hand, pro-choice people urge us to read Jn. 6:53-63, where Jesus says, "He who eats my flesh and drinks my blood has life. . . . It is the spirit [note lowercase *s*] that gives life, the flesh is of no avail."

or to the newly born. Why a fine should be exacted under such circumstances is not made clear. By contrast, the traditional interpretation suggests that the fine is paid the husband for the loss of a prospective offspring due to his wife's suffering a miscarriage.

(4) Soul and Fetus: A Theological Comment. When we say that the question of abortion cannot be resolved by quoting Scripture, we do not mean to imply that it can be resolved by science. If science has the answer, why have lawyers, legislators, psychiatrists, sociologists, ethicists, and even philosophers been drawn into the debate? The answer is that left un-molested, human fetal tissue develops into a human being whose life is sacred. But such a judgment of value rests on considerations that are theological in nature rather than scientific.

In our exposition of the doctrine of the *imago Dei* we attempted to state what these theological considerations are from a Christian point of view.[129] We recognize, of course, that in a religiously pluralistic society there is no way to achieve a consensus on such matters. We can only state what Christians believe. In fact, when it comes to abortion, even Christians, who affirm that human life as the image of God is sacred, disagree because they embrace different views concerning the nature of fetal life. Is all fetal tissue, which is biologically human, theologically human? Is a fertilized egg in the image of God? If we affirm that it is, what basis do we have for making such a judgment? If we affirm that it is not, when is the transcendent factor, what we have called "human nature on its immaterial side" — soul/spirit — present?[130]

The question, When is the fetus human? evokes at present (1990) more depth of feeling on both sides than virtually any other theological issue. On the one hand, a king abdicates his throne (temporarily) rather than affix his signature to legislation allowing abortion in his kingdom for the first time. (We refer to King Baudouin of Belgium, a devout Catholic.) On the other hand, women's abortion rights activists have threatened Idaho with a potato boycott if restrictive abortion legislation is ever passed in that state. (Potatoes are Idaho's number one cash crop.) Meanwhile the National Conference of Catholic Bishops in America has hired a Madison Avenue public relations firm to help them win the battle against abortion. It is estimated that the campaign may cost as much as five million dollars.

            *   *   *   *   *

In the matter of determining the humanity of the unborn, we must again caution against the tendency of some to embrace moral simplicities. John C. Willke, in the article quoted

129. See above, pp. 53-99.
130. See above, pp. 35-53.

above ("The Fetus Is Life Itself"), declares that religion can never answer the question: Is the fertilized egg a human being? The answer to that question is to be found, rather, "in books on biology, embryology and fetology. In these sciences there is no disagreement on the fact of when human life begins." When the fertilized egg — a cell that "contains more information than could be contained in all of NASA's computers" — is present in the woman's body, at that moment, Willke assures us, another human being is present. "To deny that fully human life begins at fertilization is to deny the known facts of fetal development and biological science." We must confess that we are not persuaded by such a reductionist argument, which equates human life with biology. The question, When does human life begin? is a theological question with ethical implications. Such a question, therefore, cannot be answered by a simple appeal to the "facts" of science. Books on biology and fetology have their place, but for us, another book, the Bible, is a better place to look for help in answering the questions before us.

As Christians we should listen to what scientists have to say, for what they say does bear on the question of whether fetal life is human life. One can see this, for example, in the testimony of a group of scientists who recently gave information to the United States Supreme Court. In an amicus brief, twelve Nobel laureates and fifteen distinguished biologists and physicians stated that neurobiologists have determined that development of the neocortex in the fetus sufficient to support the functions of "personhood" found in newborn infants is not reached until after twenty-eight weeks of pregnancy. Willke, however, does not so much as mention this particular "known fact of fetal development and biological science." Obviously at this point fetology does not support his confident affirmation that human life is present from the moment of conception. Therefore, it would seem, he makes no mention of it. But more of this presently.

In our previous efforts to frame a theological anthropology, we have rejected the notion that humans are simply cerebrating animals. To be human, we have affirmed, is to transcend the world as personal subjects. That is, we are essentially spiritual beings, uniquely endowed by God our Creator, who has made us like himself. At the same time, we have acknowledged that we are given our humanity as a bodily existence. The body is the visible form of the self in its specific individuality. There is, then, an indefeasible relationship between soul (spirit) and body. Specifically, we have argued, this relationship is evidenced in the correlation between our self-awareness as transcendent subjects and the wonderful patterns of neural activity that occur in the cerebral cortex. In this obscure and marvelous place, the transcendent world of spirit mysteriously interpenetrates the immanent world of our bodily existence.[131]

The implications for our present discussion are patent. How so? We are seeking to reach a decision about abortion; and to reach such a decision, we must deal with the question: Is fetal life human? This is the crucial

131. See above, pp. 7-10.

question. May it not be that the answer to this crucial question will yield at least some of its inscrutable opacity to our knowledge of brain development in the unborn fetus? May it not be that as we have come to associate the end of human life in the body with "brain death," so we may associate the beginning of human life, that is, the life of the human spirit in the body, with "brain birth?" Believing that human life is a transcendent, spiritual reality uniquely related to brain activity in its bodily manifestation, it seems to us that abortion in the early stages of pregnancy does not necessarily violate the dignity of such life, since the biological basis of said life is not yet present.[132]

We pause at this point to summarize the present state of scientific research. The first brain cells appear in the human embryo about three weeks after conception. About six weeks after conception the brainstem begins to form, which may account for the first embryonic movement. More important for our discussion is the appearance of the neocortex, that portion of the brain which is the biological seat of self-consciousness and thought. While the initial neocortical cells appear about a month after conception, the neocortex is not fully formed until about the sixth month (twenty-fourth week) after conception. The really dramatic turning point in fetal brain development begins in the twenty-eighth week. Before this time, as one scientist has put it, "the phones are in place but there are no wires connecting them." In the twenty-eighth week there is a burst of cell multiplication establishing the essential communication system that "turns on the neocortex," and by thirty weeks fetal EEG recordings are like those of a newborn baby. Both this evidence of brain-wave activity in the fetus and the fetal behavior that accompanies it plainly indicate the presence of personal self-awareness well before birth, if the fetus is carried to full term. (This brief account of fetal brain development is drawn from Margie Patlak, "Starting Point," *Los Angeles Times,* March 29, 1990, p. B2.) The conclusion that in the more advanced stages of fetal development human life is present is reinforced by the development of the nascent science of fetology, which

---

132. Such a viewpoint, modern as it may sound, is clearly articulated by Dante:

> When the articulation of the brain
> Has been perfected in the embryo,

> Then the First Mover turns to it, full fain
> Of nature's triumph, and inbreathes a rare
> New spirit.

(Purgatory 25.68-72)

If one takes such a position, it does not follow that by parity of reasoning the life of the severely retarded may be taken with impunity. The retarded are not without functioning brains, as is the fetus in the initial stages of development. While their brain functions are defective, the retarded may, as we have seen, not only have self-awareness but occasionally express it in unexpected ways. (See above, pp. 67-69.) The argument that toleration of abortion, even in the early stages of fetal development, undermines the value a society places generally on human life seems not to be confirmed in fact. For example, present-day Japan has legalized abortion, while in Nazi Germany abortion was illegal.

provides the same medical care, both diagnostic and therapeutic, for the unborn fetus that pediatrics affords to the newborn baby.

In view of what we have said about the unique nature of human fetal tissue and its marvelous development, it appears to us that nothing will ever make the choice of abortion an easy one, at least for the Christian. Abortion is never an unmitigated blessing, as some have argued. But under some circumstances, if the choice is made in the early stages of fetal development, it is a choice that is morally justifiable. It may be (we personally believe it is) a *tragic* moral choice; but it is not necessarily an *immoral* choice, much less a criminal one. We grant that since fetal tissue is not the woman's own body tissue, her choosing to be rid of it is never a purely private and individual right. Yet the right to make such a decision is preeminently hers, as she counsels with her physician and those closest to her. In the more advanced stages of pregnancy, she could never justify making such a choice — unless her own life were endangered — since another human life is present in her womb. But in the early stages of pregnancy, the only rightful coercion of a woman's will, as she contemplates the possibility of abortion, is the coercion of her own conscience.

Anti-abortionists often observe that during the seventeen years that *Roe vs. Wade* went unchallenged, 25,000,000 abortions were performed in the United States. This is indeed a staggering number that a Christian can contemplate with nought but dismay. But one should remember that 91% were performed before twelve weeks, 99.2% before twenty weeks, and only .01% after twenty-four weeks, when the neocortex is fully formed.

*   *   *   *   *

At this juncture a comment is in order concerning fetal pain. The statement is frequently made that we must understand "that the unborn are people, people who can feel pain and who suffer when abused or killed."

> No symbol has so dramatically captured this specter of fetal pain as the real-time ultrasound, "The Silent Scream," released in 1984. This film pictures a twelve-week unborn baby undergoing death-by-dismemberment in a suction abortion. (*Common Ground*, Occasional Papers from Presbyterians Pro-Life, May, 1988, no. 3, p. 10)

Once again we must register a demur at what appears to us an oversimplification. The event recorded in "The Silent Scream" is unquestionably a piteous one, fraught with tragedy; but the thought that a twelve-week-old fetus, in which the neocortex is not even formed, much less functioning, is an "unborn baby" screaming in pain is simply unfair to the evidence. Under such circumstances an abortion undoubtedly inflicts human pain, but the pain that is suffered is the pain of the woman, who may already have suffered in a deeper sense through the circumstances in which she became pregnant. We must not, then, in our concern for fetal pain, forget the pain of the woman.

*   *   *   *   *

Further evidence that one should not speak of a twelve-week fetus as human in an unqualified way is the fact that we do not memorialize the death of such a fetus with a funeral; nor do we criminalize (as in days past) the act of abortion with trials and incarceration. Although some Catholics may still baptize a fetus, most Christians do not. No country includes the unborn in a census count or provides added child support for an indigent mother before her child is born.

*   *   *   *   *

Still another matter relating to the question of when, in the course of fetal development, a human subject is present concerns the so-called abortion pill or the "morning-after pill." The French drug RU486 is about 96% effective, with few undesirable side effects. Through hormonal modification the drug causes the blastocyst to slough off, as in menstruation. If the fertilized egg in the earliest stages of development is more than the biological potential for human life, if human life is actually present from the moment of conception, then using a drug like RU486 is ethically no different from the practice of infanticide. Infanticide is a willful taking of the life of the newly born; the use of RU486 is a willful taking of the life of the newly formed.

It seems to us, however, that there is a screw loose in this argument. We refer to the assumption that a human being is present from the moment of conception. It is indeed an awesome thought that I would never have been I, much less would I have written these words, had no blastocyst implanted itself in my mother's womb. It does not follow, however, that *I* entered her womb on the day the blastocyst entered her womb, in the way that *I* left her womb on the day the umbilical cord was cut and I took my first breath. It may well be, then, that the use of a drug like RU486 is not essentially different from contraception. In the latter instance (excepting the pill, as noted above), sperm and egg are not able to unite; in the former the blastocyst is not able to attach to the womb and hence no biological basis for human life can develop. Yet the mysteries of conception and birth are so intertwined that the Christian answer to the urgent need to control human reproduction must principally be found in the prevention of conception rather than the aborting of fetal tissue. A Christian can never regard abortion in any form as merely an alternate form of birth control.

*   *   *   *   *

Finally, it must be said that we ought not to be so concerned with the question of when human life begins that we forget that it does not end with birth. A conservative Christian magazine reports on its cover that today "4000 unborn babies" will die in America. Concomitantly, *Time* magazine reports that "40,000 [born] babies" die of starvation every day in the Third World. Any fair discussion of abortion will take into consideration both of these melancholy figures. Faced with the tragic prospect of children being born to die, both physically and spiritually, how can we avoid the question of whether, in such circumstances, an early abortion may not be the lesser of two evils? Furthermore, one must ask why many who are the most opposed to abortion support a public policy that curtails nutritional programs for pregnant mothers, aid to poor families with dependent children, and food stamps. Some would even criminalize abortion, while at the same time they would curtail public health initiatives.

Speaking for ourselves, we can only say that while there is much abuse and waste in such health initiatives, the conviction that human life is sacred, which moves people to oppose abortion, should also move them to show equal concern for those whose lives are in jeopardy from the moment of birth and even before. Between 1980 and 1990, a pro-life administration in Washington increased the military budget by 37% while reducing social services for the care of children and the elderly by 35%. The U.S. military budget in 1985 consumed $555,000 a minute. "One minute's worth of military spending would pay for the 14,000 monthly WIC food packages to feed pregnant women and infants that were cut from the budget in 1985" (*Black and White Children in America: Key Facts* [Washington: Children's Defense Fund, 1985]). "Aborted children," reads the bumper sticker, "will never have a nice day." Neither will millions of other children who have not been aborted. In fact, they will have many miserable days and nothing but miserable days. (For a shocking account of the deaths suffered by countless unwanted babies and children before the days of effective birth control, medically safe abortions, and programs of public assistance — even down to the present — see Henry F. Smith, "Notes on the History of Childhood," *Harvard Magazine,* July/August 1984, p. 64A.)

(5) Abortion and Women's Rights. I once participated in an evangelical symposium on the control of human reproduction sponsored by the Christian Medical Society and *Christianity Today.*[133] Participants came from all parts of the country: physicians, lawyers, psychiatrists, social workers, ethicists, and theologians. Papers were read and responses made; but the moment of truth came when a psychiatrist played back a portion of a taped conversation with a client, a deeply distraught woman who was pleading with him to grant her an abortion on psychiatric grounds. The reason this brief episode proved to be a *kairos* moment, for me at least, was not the emotional shock that her anguished entreaty delivered, but the realization that hers was the first and only female voice heard in three days of deliberation. Here we were, all experts in our fields and all *males,* talking about and trying to decide what to do about abortion, a question that can never involve a man in the way it involves a woman. The wives who were present either sat as silent observers in the rear or spent their time at the exclusive

133. The papers presented were published under the title, *Birth Control and the Christian* (Wheaton: Tyndale House, 1969).

shops in the environs. Out of the conviction of that moment, we make the following observations on abortion and the rights of women.

First, the life of a pregnant woman, as we have already observed, takes precedence over the life of a fetus. This is so because the humanity of fetal life, in the early stages of pregnancy, cannot be established, while the humanity of the woman's life cannot be doubted. This is the theological basis for the generally recognized right of women to therapeutic abortion.[134]

Second, the life of the woman has been wrought into the lives of others: she is a daughter; she may be a wife; and she may already be the mother of children. These I-thou relationships, which manifest the human character of her life, mean that others have claims on her life along with the claims of the fetus that she carries. Of course, as fetal life develops, an I-thou relationship also develops between that life and the woman who carries it. Hence the later the abortion, even to spare the woman's life, the more tragic the choice. But in the early stages of fetal development, the woman's relationship to her parents, her husband, her children, and others, as the case may be, should be given their due in evaluating the claims of the fetus. If, for example, her strength to be a mother to the children she already has, her ability to feed them and to care for them, would be taxed beyond reason by the birth of another child, the sacrifice of fetal life in its early development seems the lesser of two evils.

Third, God has given each woman her being as human in a way that implies the freedom of self-determination. She has the right to be who she chooses to be as a responsible subject. To be sure, she does not have the right to use her freedom in a way that violates the rights of others. But if we have reason to suppose — and we believe that we do — that only a potential, not an actual, human other is present in her womb in the early stages of pregnancy, then it is a violation of her God-given rights as a human being to compel her to carry a fetus to full term against her will. This is not to deny that a woman should be counseled about the options and helped to make a decision in favor of the unborn, even when this involves sacrifice on her part — postponing a career, giving the child up for adoption, and so on. But while her decision should be informed, it is

---

134. In the encyclical letter *Casti Connubii,* 1930, Pius XI denied even this right, declaring the life of the mother and the unborn equally sacred. By contrast, most anti-abortionists also allow abortion in the case of rape and incest; a woman should not be compelled to have the child of her ravisher. In other words, they allow abortion not only for life-*threatening* but also for life-*devastating* reasons, that is, for psychiatric as well as for ordinary medical reasons. However, they often advocate laws that require detailed evidence as proof and so add to the woman's trauma as the one violated, treating her as though she were guilty until proved innocent.

a decision that no one has a right to make for her. To coerce a woman under such circumstances is one more instance of that unrelenting and punitive hostility that compromises the man-woman relationship in a society dominated by men. Mute witnesses to this sad truth are the thousands of women who have lost their lives in illegal abortions, or inflicted on themselves permanent injury in a desperate effort to abort an unwanted pregnancy.[135]

The hostility of the male toward the female is seen not only in the effort of predominantly male legislatures to make virtually all abortions illegal, but also in the evil use of abortion for gender selection, an abhorrent practice by Christian standards. Such a use of abortion can, of course, threaten either sex. But in the real world, it is the female that is in jeopardy. "In the northeast city of Shenyang, a woman committed suicide by drinking seven bottles of DDT because her husband beat and cursed her for having a girl. 'Go and die,' he ordered her. 'I will go and find a woman to bear a son.' " "Many Chinese women, convinced that boys are better, are seeking unethical sex-tests for their unborn babies and rushing to abort healthy female fetuses. In sophisticated Shanghai, many women weep on learning they have borne a girl" (*Los Angeles Times*, Nov. 14, 1982, pt. IV, p. 2). Another source reports that of 8,000 abortions performed in a Bombay hospital, all but one involved a female fetus (*The Other Side* 25, no. 1 [January/February 1989]: 5, from Tranet). Unfortunately, the use of abortion for gender selection, after the sex of the fetus has been determined by amniocentesis, occurs in America. Along with sickle-cell anemia, Down's syndrome, and other genetic diseases, just being female can put a fetus at risk. (See John Lauerman, "The Time Machine," *Harvard Magazine*, January/February 1990, p. 46. We shall have more to say about human engineering in general when speaking of human dominion over the natural order.)

(6) Conclusion. We have acknowledged repeatedly that abortion can never be an unmixed blessing; to abort the unborn is sometimes sinful; and it always confronts us with the tragic in life. The tragedy is not simply the termination of a potential human life, which we mourn; nor is it simply the trauma suffered by the woman who submits to the experience; nor again is it simply the shame that the woman endures, beyond anything the man involved has to endure. The full measure of the tragedy confronts us only when we reflect on the fact that most abortions involve healthy conceptions by healthy women resulting from careless sex within marriage, promiscuous liaisons outside marriage, experiments in sex by teens, and an ever increasingly casual attitude toward intercourse, which flouts the Christian view that the sexual act is the symbol of the lasting commitment of married

---

135. The nightmares women have endured in seeking illegal abortions are unspeakable. More tragically still, these horror stories generally involve the young and the poor.

love. This larger context of abortion reveals the tragedy of our existence as sinners, manifest in our alienation from God and each other. And within this larger context, abortion, in its own way, reminds us that our sins will surely find us out.

But it is hopelessly simplistic, in our judgment, for Christians to suppose that they can resolve this tragic situation by making virtually all abortions illegal as a matter of public policy.[136] It is indeed our calling as Christians so to live by the teachings of Christ as to lead others to the responsible use of the Creator's gift of sex. It is likewise our calling to encourage, by precept and example, a change in the minds and hearts of people so as to promote responsible behavior toward others in the realm of the sexual. Finally, it is also our calling to strive to alter the structures of society so as to provide more help for pregnant women who are poor and for children born out of wedlock. But we must take heed in this area, as in all others, lest we compound the tragedy of our sinful existence by our fervor to do good; lest in our zeal to make the world better we actually make it worse; lest, as Christians, we become "good people in the worst sense of the word."

4) Fidelity Within the Marriage Bond

We have affirmed that the bond of marriage rests on the consent of the covenanting parties. This consent takes the form of a promise to be true to one's intended spouse "till death do us part." In the words of our definition, marriage is "a *lasting* relationship based on a mutual promise of fidelity." In our day such a view is often contemned. The demon Screwtape boasts to his nephew Wormwood that in recent times the idea has taken hold, thanks to poets and novelists, that the only respectable ground of marriage is the evanescent experience of "being in love." When a marriage no longer renders this excitement permanent, it is no longer binding; everything is over.[137] If one embraces such a parody of marriage, then this conclusion inevitably follows. The thrill of erotic love is sustained only by the uncertainty of adventure and the challenge of new conquests. The traditional view of matrimony appears by contrast to be a dull and uninteresting proposition. As the glow of romance fades, as the ecstasy of passion subsides, the only antidote to the tedium of married life is the adventuresomeness of the libertine.

---

136. For example, one may believe as a Christian that divorce is sinful, a putting asunder of what God has joined together (Mk. 10:9); yet at the same time recognize the legality of divorce as public policy. So also one may believe as a Christian that abortion is sinful and yet recognize, as public policy, the legal right of those who do not share this conviction to choose abortion.

137. C. S. Lewis, *Screwtape Letters,* XVIII.

In view of what we have already said, it is obvious that we do not accept this freewheeling approach to marriage. Such an approach bases marriage on a selfish love, a self-centered eroticism that stands in contrast to true love, which "alters not when it alteration finds" (Shakespeare). We have, indeed, affirmed that romantic love is passionate; but we have also affirmed that it transcends passion in that it motivates one's will to a lasting commitment; and it is this commitment that grounds the marriage union. No one can promise feelings, but one can promise faithfulness. Such a promise is essential when two people enter into the marriage relationship. And the reason is obvious: the promise of fidelity authenticates love. It may be true that for the one who loves, love is self-authenticating; but for the other, the one who is the object of love, love can be authenticated only by the promise of the lover to be faithful. Hence we shall conclude our exposition of the doctrine of marriage with a brief comment on the subject of fidelity, for fidelity is the cornerstone of the Christian understanding of the husband-wife relationship.

We begin by noting the self-evident truth that fidelity is essential to all human relationships. To be unfaithful to one's promise is to destroy that fellowship in and for which we were created; and when fellowship is destroyed, our very humanity is threatened. We must remember that we have been made in God's likeness, and the God who has made us in his likeness is a faithful God.[138] Therefore, our lives are so structured that we are constantly confronted with the need of making promises and the responsibility of keeping them. Nowhere is this more evident than in the marriage relationship. This is so, obviously, because of the intimacy of the relationship, the only relationship that can be spoken of as becoming "one flesh." But, for the Christian, the need for fidelity in marriage is essential also because the mutual promise on which the union rests is ultimately made to God. It is he who has ordained marriage and placed his benediction on it (Gn. 1:27-28). This element of transcendence in the Christian understanding of marriage is the reason that Christians commonly speak of the marriage promise as a "vow" and the marriage contract as a "covenant."

The word "vow" conveys the thought of a promise that has special solemnity as made to God. In Christian wedding ceremonies, the man and woman are often reminded that the vows they have made are taken "in the presence of God and before these witnesses." The word "covenant" is properly used of the relationship God has sovereignly established with his people. In this relationship he commits himself to his people with a promise of salvation; and his people, in turn, commit themselves to him with a promise of obedience. (See *God, Creation, and Revelation*, pp. 404-7.) When used derivatively

---

138. See *God, Creation, and Revelation*, pp. 438-512.

of the marriage relationship, "covenant" conveys the thought that the mutual commitment of the consenting parties is regarded as an act of obedience to the divine will. In this vein, Christians sometimes speak of marriage as a "vocation." That is, it is God who calls two people to covenant with each other to live their lives as one flesh.

In the eyes of the civil magistrate, marriage has no such transcendent aspect; it is simply a legal contract between two consenting parties. For the Christian, such a mundane understanding of marriage has its place. Since marriage is an ordinance of creation rather than a sacrament of grace, the state should seek the commonweal by laws that guarantee the right of all to marriage, and secure a measure of justice to those who enter into it. A Christian view of marriage does not (ordinarily) conflict with such a concept of "civil marriage," marriage, that is, as defined by the laws of the state. But at the same time the Christian faith postulates a deeper understanding of the marriage relationship. Since, in the last analysis, it is not the state or the church that joins husband and wife, but God the Creator (Mk. 10:9), the promise of mutual faithfulness on which the union rests is a promise made, as it were, to God himself. He is the One whose will for our lives we seek to fulfill by entering into the married state. To break faith in marriage is, in a real sense, to break faith with God.   .

Finally, we must note that fidelity to one's marriage vows requires resolution. Resolution in such an instance is not resignation, an enduring of an intolerable yoke, a living in holy deadlock. Rather, the resolve to be faithful gives love its proper context; it requires that love be responsible love, a love that is willing to sacrifice. Such sacrificial love is committed love. It is a love that says, "I want you — not this or that which is yours, but you." In making such an unconditional request, love recognizes that it must commit itself in return. A lover cannot ask for everything on the part of the one loved and at the same time hold back as a lover. A love that says, I take not yours but you, is a love that has no strings attached. It says, I take you in sickness as well as in health, in adversity as well as in prosperity, in the twilight of life as well as in its meridian prime.

Such unreserved commitment to one's partner in marriage not only grounds the union on which marriage rests but also gives that union its permanent character. One cannot plight one's troth to the other, pledge faith and fidelity to the other, "for the time being" only.[139] It is arguably the case that the permanent character of the marriage vow has proved to be

---

139. Viewing marriage simply as a civil contract, some have sought to legalize "trial marriage." In this way marriage is reduced to the same level as any other legal contract between two parties entered into for a specific time. Such an approach, it is argued, would curtail prostitution, the practice of "keeping a mistress," and the trauma of divorce.

the most widely rejected aspect of the Christian doctrine of marriage. It may also be argued, in this regard, that Christians should not try to enforce their view that marriage is a lifelong relationship on the whole of society by making divorce illegal or by seeking to ground the legal right to divorce on the teaching of Scripture as they understand the Scripture.[140] But in any case, for a Christian, the marriage relationship is a permanent union. Sustained by a promise of mutual fidelity, the union between husband and wife powerfully witnesses to a mysterious union of another kind, in which Christ and the church are one according to a promise that cannot be made void (Gal. 3:17).

The expression "free love" is sometimes used of liaisons entered into apart from legal recognition by the state or the blessing of the church. Such cohabitation "without benefit of matrimony" (which has added the word "palimony" to the English language) is often looked upon as the way couples discover whether they are compatible before they "tie the knot" with a mutual promise of fidelity. Sociologists, therefore, have expressed surprise to find that people who live together before they are married are actually more likely to get a divorce than those who do not. This is really not so surprising after all, though, since such people are apt to be those who look upon happiness as an inalienable right for *me* rather than for *us*. They are people who value intimate relationships in terms of individual satisfaction rather than mutual fulfillment. Hence they desire to confirm "compatibility" with a sexual partner before they commit themselves; and they tend to leave a relationship that calls for sacrifice, even though they have made a commitment.

As for the term "free love," it most aptly describes a departure from the Christian ideal of marriage that is much more radical than cohabitation before marriage. Free love, properly speaking, is a love that will not acknowledge any constraints, a love that will not commit itself. It is love without obligation to another, love without the responsibility of fidelity. Such an approach to love strikes at the very heart of the Christian view of marriage, in which the freedom to love is disciplined by faithfulness to the one loved. It has been argued that the refusal to make a promise (free love) is better than making a promise that one breaks (infidelity). But to press such distinctions is to indulge a paltry casuistry.

*   *   *   *   *

The promise of fidelity to one's spouse is, we grant, never perfectly kept; the sinful heart and the roving eye betray all who embrace the marriage covenant. Here, as in all human relationships, we all offend. But the tendency to speak, in this regard, of the female as the fickle one is a male caricature. Too often the husband's jealous suspicion of his wife's affections (Nm. 5:14) — a frequent theme in literature — is but an act of projection. (Here see Cervantes's *Don Quixote,* pt. 1, bks. 4, 6: "The Novel of the

---

140. We shall treat the question of divorce presently. See below, pp. 273-89.

Curious Impertinent," a fascinating and pathetic story of the pain Anselmo suffered in his desire to know whether his beautiful wife Camilia was as virtuous as she seemed.) One should remember that the life of Gomer, the faithless wife of Hosea, is a parable — in a patriarchal society — of Israel's faithlessness to Yahweh. It is not intended as a comment on women as lovers. Indeed, we would venture the opinion that, as a class, women are more faithful lovers than men. In a sixteenth-century lullaby of unknown authorship, "By-Low, My Babe," a deserted mother sings to her baby:

> I cannot choose, but ever will
> Be loving to thy father still;
> Where'er he stay, where'er he ride
> My love with him doth still abide.
> In weal or woe, where'er he go,
> My heart shall not forsake him; so
> By-low, lie low.

(Untermeyer, ed., *Great Poems*, p. 171)

First Addendum: Monogamy and Polygamy. We have defined marriage as a relationship between *a* man and *a* woman, a relationship that is not only lasting but *exclusive* in character. In keeping with this definition we have assumed throughout our discussion that marriage is monogamous. The time has now come to speak more directly to this subject. Why have theologians supposed that monogamy best expresses the Christian ideal of marriage, especially in light of the widespread practice of polygamy in the Old Testament? How should the church understand the Scriptures of the Old Covenant in this regard?

We must admit that Christian missionaries have been slow to perceive the implications of the Old Testament institution of polygamy for their own ministry among polygamous peoples. That God was pleased to make and keep covenant with Israel, whose culture was polygamous from the beginning, reminds us that divine revelation is historical; it redeems rather than denies the historico-cultural reality of those to whom the revelation is given. This being the case, the traditional refusal of the church to baptize converts in a polygamous culture who will not renounce all wives but the first seems to us to reflect a Donatistic rigorism that will not learn from past mistakes.

We are not suggesting that the church should put its approval on the distortion of the Creator's will reflected in the institution of polygamy. Were the church to bless such marriages, where then would be the cultural redemption that the gospel promises? Yet when the church insists that a hopeful convert must renounce all but one of his wives in order to receive baptism, where then, in the case of the wives forsaken, is the fidelity that is basic to the Christian view of the husband-wife relationship? How can the church make the validation of a man's confession of Christ to be his repudiation of those women and children whose very lives depend on his faithfulness as a husband and father? One may protest that to allow the younger churches on the mission field to compromise the Christian ideal of marriage is unworthy of those who profess to be disciples of Christ. Yet we must remember that divorce, which is increasingly allowed in the older, sending churches of Europe and America, is also a compromise of the Christian ideal. In the younger churches, some have even suggested, wryly, that divorce, Western style, is a kind of serial polygamy.

While it is true that Christian theology does not approve compromise of the ethical ideal, it is also true that it recognizes that such compromise is implicit in the sinful human situation this side of the eschaton. The precise form that such compromise may take, as the church confronts polygamy in the pursuit of its missionary mandate, depends on the circumstances in a given situation; it is, therefore, beyond the scope of a general theological statement. This is not to say that one's theology has no bearing on those specific compromises one may accept in order to resolve the difficulty of polygamous marriages in other cultures. Obviously it does. We have affirmed, for example, that marriage is an ordinance of creation rather than a sacrament of the church. Having embraced such a theology of marriage, we could never suppose, as have some who look upon marriage as a sacrament, that all polygamous marriages are to be declared null and void, freeing converts to enter into a new marriage fortified by the grace of the sacrament and blessed by the church. Becoming a new creature in Christ changes the quality of the marriage relationship; it does not change the parties to the relationship. While one's theology thus defines the parameters within which compromise is possible, however, it does not determine the specific form that a given compromise may take in an a priori way. This is what we mean when we say that the precise resolution of the problem of polygamy is beyond the scope of theology.

As for the Old Testament, obviously one cannot say that it condemns polygamy; yet neither can one say that it teaches polygamy simply because it reports the prevalence of the institution in Israel. While the institution was widely accepted in Israel, the second creation narrative, which speaks of the man's cleaving to his wife as a "one flesh" union (Gn. 2:24), constitutes a tacit rejection of polygamy in favor of monogamy.[141] According to the narrative in Genesis 2, the Creator did not relieve the lonely solitude of the primeval man with a harem but with one woman, whom he embraced in a transport of delight — "this at last" (2:23). The implication of monogamy found in the second creation narrative is reinforced by the Song of Songs. The love poems in this document obviously presuppose two, and only two, lovers. Indeed, when probing the question of why monogamy best expresses the Christian ideal of marriage, were we to draw

141. Indeed, given the monogamous context of Jesus' appeal to this one-flesh union as an act of the Creator (Mk. 10:9), the Lord, in our judgment, goes beyond a tacit to an explicit approval of monogamy. Brigham Young, one of the founding fathers of the Mormon Church, was of a contrary opinion. In one of his sermons he affirms that Jesus was a practicing polygamist. Mary and Martha were among his plural wives, as was Mary Magdalene. (See William E. Phipps, *Was Jesus Married?* [New York: Harper & Row, 1970], p. 10.)

out the implication of the creation ordinance found in Genesis 2, we would have to say that romantic love is in its very nature monogamously disposed.[142] As we have seen, such love is single-minded. It says, "I cannot live without you," and that "you" is in the singular. What Elizabeth Barrett said to Robert Browning in her *Sonnets from the Portuguese* can be said to one man and one only.[143]

Because we understand the blessings of marriage *(bona matrimonium)* primarily in terms of the fellowship of love rather than procreation, we do not give great weight to the traditional argument that monogamy is entailed in the fact that each human self is born of one man and one woman. We would certainly agree that a happy monogamous marriage is best for the rearing of children, but what is best for the proper care and nurture of children is a different question from that of the monogamous proclivity of erotic love.

When we affirm that erotic love is "disposed toward" monogamy, this is not intended to be an ontological statement. Erotic love is not essentially monogamous. While only one can be loved supremely, more than one can be loved truly. This is implied in our commendation of the suffering love that respects the beloved's marriage vows to another. That erotic love is not absolute is implied also in our rejection of that romantic mysticism which views monogamous marriages as eternal. (See above, pp. 214-18.) When one loses one's beloved in death, one may forbear to marry another because love lives on in the lover's heart. Such faithful lovers may say with Elizabeth Barrett, "and, if God choose, I shall but love thee better after death" (Sonnet 43). But however such love may be expressed in the life to come, it will not be in marriage, for in death we enter a kingdom where "they neither marry nor are given in marriage." This is why death frees the living partner to marry another (Rom. 7:2-3). (Whether such freedom

---

142. This is not to deny that economic considerations are perhaps the main reason for the advance of monogamy against polygamy in many cultures today. But such economic considerations are pragmatic in nature; they do not bear in any direct way on the theological defense of monogamy as the implication of the man's, "this at last!" (Gn. 2:23).

143. See especially Sonnet 43:

> I love thee to the depth and breadth and height
> My soul can reach, when feeling out of sight
> For the ends of Being and ideal Grace.

Countering the view that such exclusivity is contrary to the natural proclivities of the male of the species, we may take G. K. Chesterton's remarks: "Keeping to one woman is a small price for so much as seeing one woman. To complain that I could only be married once was like complaining that I had only been born once. It was incommensurate with the terrible excitement of which one was talking. It showed, not an exaggerated sensibility to sex, but a curious insensibility to it. A man is a fool who complains that he cannot enter Eden by five gates at once. Polygamy is a lack of the realization of sex; it is like a man plucking five pears in mere absence of mind" (*Orthodoxy* [1908; reprint, Garden City, N.Y.: Doubleday, 1959], pp. 57-58).

to marry again is proscribed in 1 Tm. 3:2 and Ti. 1:6 to one who aspires to be a bishop [ἐπίσκοπος, presbyter, overseer] is moot.) Although the church has always recognized that the death of one's partner frees the other to remarry, it has commended those whose sense of loss is evident and frowned on those who remarry with undue haste. See Hamlet's complaint against his mother,

> O, most wicked speed, to post
> With such dexterity to incestuous sheets!
> (Shakespeare, *Hamlet,* act 1, scene 2, lines 156-57)

Second Addendum: Sex and Sin. We have confessed that as sinners we never achieve a perfect conformity of heart to the Christian ideal of fidelity in marriage. It is also sadly true that many marriages, hopefully entered upon, are threatened by lapses in deed as well as in thought. What may be said of these sexual sins that beset us all? Are sexual sins exceeding sinful above all others? A comment would seem to be in order at this juncture.[144] For the ancient church fathers, as we have seen, the principle of sin was somehow — just how was never made clear — uniquely related to our sexuality. As a result, in the tradition of the church, the ideal of the Christian life has sometimes been defined more in terms of one's sexuality than in terms of one's love of God. For example, Martin of Tours likens a life of virginity to an ungrazed field, marriage to a field cropped by cattle, and fornication to a field uprooted by swine.[145]

Now one must admit that some sexual sins are heinous in the extreme. Indeed, some — rape, child abuse, and the like — are crimes of the most vile sort. But it is unfortunate, in our judgment, that the ancient tendency to look upon sexual sin as quintessential sin continues down to the present day. As a result, Christians tend to equate all immorality with sexual immorality. They speak as though the seventh commandment were the first, and they seem to think that the seven deadly sins can be reduced to one common denominator. Dorothy Sayers recalls how a young man once said to her, "I did not know there were seven deadly sins: please tell me the names of the other six." She goes on to animadvert, "A man may be greedy and selfish, cruel, jealous, and unjust, violent and brutal, grasping, unscrupulous, and a liar; stubborn and arrogant; stupid, morose, and dead to every noble instinct — and still we are ready to say of him that he is not an immoral man."[146] One thinks, in this regard, of how frequently adultery is the occasion of church discipline, especially against ministers. Such an

---

144. This question of sin and sex will concern us more at length when dealing with the doctrine of original sin in a later volume.

145. See Bailey, *Sexual Relation,* p. 44.

146. *Christian Letters,* p. 138.

offense surely does call for church discipline. But so do lots of other offenses that are often overlooked in the church, though they would land an offender in a much lower circle of Dante's hell.[147]

The business of rating sins is admittedly complicated by the fact that "some sins . . . by reason of several aggravations, are more heinous in the sight of God than others" (Westminster Shorter Catechism, q. 83). This is certainly true of sins involving sex. The affair of the Reverend Arthur Dimmesdale with Hester Prynne in Hawthorne's *The Scarlet Letter* is surely an offense far less heinous in the sight of God than many. David's affair with Bathsheba is reprehensible; but it is especially so because of aggravating circumstances, as Nathan's parable makes abundantly plain (2 Sam. 12:7-15). (In this regard, see Marie M. Fortune, *Is Nothing Sacred? When Sex Invades the Pastoral Relationship* [San Francisco: Harper & Row, 1989], a case study of the manner in which a pastor exploited the confidence women parishioners placed in him. In such a case, illicit sex is obviously involved; the basic issue is not sex, however, but the abuse of trust while in the pastoral office, and the male's use of power to seduce females by dominating and manipulating them when they are in a vulnerable position.)

We do not mean to suggest that in such circumstances the sexual aspect of the offense be taken lightly. Rather, what we are protesting in this addendum on sex and sin is the way in which, in some Christian circles, all manner of offenses are tolerated except those which are sexual. To give an example from the present day, it was sexual indiscretions that led to the downfall of some prominent televangelists. The greed, deception, and plain dishonesty by which they fleeced the flock, in one instance even to the point of criminal activity, were overlooked as long as they were not found in a compromising sexual liaison. To solicit favors from a secretary is much worse, it seems, than swindling thousands of people out of millions of dollars. Conversely, in the same circles, the praiseworthy accomplishments of people are sometimes discredited because of their sexual foibles and failures. In this regard it is well to recall Barth's warning that the tendency to limit the word "immorality" almost exclusively to the man-woman relationship, especially in its narrower sexual character, is based on an opinion that is nothing less than disastrous (*KD,* III/4, p. 130 [cf. *CD,* III/4, p. 118]).

Jesus was obviously not among those who looked on sexual sins as the worst of all transgressions. While he by no means approved the lifestyle of the woman at the well who had had five husbands, he commended her for her candor in not dissembling the fact (Jn. 4:16-18). And when another woman was taken in adultery, though he admonished her to go and sin no more, it was the judgmental attitude of her male accusers that he rebuked: "Let him who is without sin among you be the first to throw a stone" (Jn. 8:3-11). By contrast, Jesus reserved his severest condemnation for religious

---

147. One will recall that Dante puts the lustful in Circle II of Upper Hell, just below limbo and far above the flatterers, hypocrites, sowers of discord, falsifiers, and others who are in Nether Hell.

hypocrites. Against those who make a profession of religious belief and indulge in pious practices — giving alms and praying — in order to be seen and admired by others, he denounces the most solemn woes and calls them "children of hell" (Mt. 6). In his *Mere Christianity,* C. S. Lewis admits that he has had much to say about sexual morality. But his concluding comment is:

> I want to make it as clear as I possibly can that the center of Christian morality is not here. . . . The sins of the flesh are bad, but they are the least bad of all sins. All the worst pleasures are purely spiritual. . . . For there are two things inside of me, competing with the human self which I must try to become. They are the Animal self and the Diabolical self. The Diabolical self is the worse of the two. That is why a cold, self-righteous prig who goes regularly to church may be far nearer to hell than a prostitute. But of course it is better to be neither.[148]

When we turn to the epistles of Paul, there is, indeed, a marked emphasis on sexual sins and the need for Christians to flee from them. One passage in particular, 1 Corinthians 6:12-20, calls for special attention, for it seems to contravene our thesis by treating sexual sins as heinous above all others. In this notably difficult passage, the apostle begins by granting the principle of Christian liberty: "All things are lawful for me," though, he goes on to say, they may not be especially helpful (v. 12). This is certainly true of the food we eat. " 'Food is meant for the stomach and the stomach for food' — and God will destroy both" (v. 13). But, he quickly adds, it does not follow, as some had evidently argued, that the general principle of Christian liberty makes whatever one does to satisfy bodily appetites indifferent. How we satisfy our sexual desires is a matter that is quite different from how we satisfy our desire for food. While both our stomach and the food we put in it will pass away, the body, as the object of God's redemptive purpose, will never pass away. Hence the body is not meant for sexual immorality (πορνεία), but for the Lord, as is the Lord for the body (v. 13). That is, our bodies are destined to be transformed in the resurrection, for God, by his power, will raise us even as he raised the Lord from the dead (v. 14). Such a relationship to the Lord means that our bodies are members of Christ himself (v. 15). Indeed, our bodies are the temple of the Holy Spirit, who already indwells us in anticipation of the resurrection. Hence, as Christians, we must honor God with our bodies (vv. 19-20). Now all this is the context for a remarkable affirmation on the part of the apostle:

148. *Mere Christianity,* p. 91.

Shall I then take the members of Christ and unite them with a prostitute? Never! Do you not know that he who unites himself with a
prostitute is one with her in body? For it is said, "The two will become
one flesh." . . . Flee from sexual immorality. All other sins a man
commits are outside his body; but he who sins sexually sins against
his own body. (vv. 15b-16, 18 NIV)

What may be said of this unequivocal denunciation of sexual immorality? First, it does seem strange that the apostle should quote Genesis 2:24,
which describes the one-flesh union of husband and wife, when speaking
of the union of a man with a prostitute.[149] The one-flesh union to which
Genesis refers, as Jesus reminds us, is that lasting union God has established
between husband and wife, a union that no one is to violate by putting
asunder those whom God has joined together (Mk. 10:8-9). By contrast,
the union with a prostitute is for the moment only and has as its purpose
not the expression of love but the gratification of lust. (For Judah, Tamar
was simply "the harlot who was at Enaim by the wayside" [Gn. 38:21].)
Why, then, does the apostle associate the two as he does in this passage?
Possibly, in making such an association, Paul means to say that there is no
such thing as casual promiscuity. A sexual union is never indifferent, it is
never like "drinking a glass of water." The Creator's blessing on the true
union of one flesh in marriage condemns the false union of a man with a
prostitute as a parody and caricature of the worst sort. Such a union seeks
the pleasures of marriage in a hedonistic way by isolating sex from its
God-given context. Here one is reminded of Barth's repeated comment,
"Coitus without coexistence is demonic."[150]

Not only is Paul's likening the union with a prostitute to that of
marriage — as the negative to the positive — strange at first sight, but so
is his affirmation that every other sin that one commits is "outside (ἐκτός)
the body," whereas sexual sin is "against (εἰς) one's own body" (v. 18).
What about gluttony, one might ask, or drunkenness, or drug abuse? Are
they not sins against the body? Excessive drinking may damage the liver
and sexual immorality give one venereal disease. In this they are alike. But
over and above what one may do to the body by overeating and promiscuous sex, sexual immorality uses the body in a way that the sinner, who
exists in, with, and as the body, sins against himself not just as object but
as person, and more particularly as one whose personhood is defined by
his union with Christ.

149. The problem is not the use in v. 16 of both σῶμα and σάρξ. Obviously in this
instance the apostle, quoting the LXX, understands the two terms as synonymous.
150. *KD*, III/4, p. 148 (cf. *CD*, III/4, p. 133).

To understand why Paul speaks with such abhorrence of this "sin against one's own body," one must remember the context in which he speaks: this context is Christological in nature. His concern is with a sin that only a Christian can commit. A Christian is one who is united with the Lord so as to become one spirit with him (v. 17). This spiritual union whereby we are one with Christ is symbolically set forth in the union between husband and wife. As husband and wife are one body, so Christ and believers are one body, analogically speaking. As such, believers are "members of Christ himself." Given one's Christian status, acts of sexual immorality become for Paul a "taking away of the members of Christ and making them members of a prostitute" (v. 15). How could one do such a thing? How could one suppose — even in the licentious city of Corinth — that one who is joined in one Spirit with the Lord can also be joined in one body with a harlot? The encounter with a harlot is an encounter that denies the true I-thou encounter with Christ. As infidelity is bad because it breaks the marriage vow, so, for the Christian, prostitution is especially bad because it is infidelity to Christ, who is the true Bridegroom. In this context sexual sin symbolizes one's surrender to the world, which is the community of evil and the Evil One (1 Jn. 5:19). It is this Christological context, we would suggest, and not the nature of sexual sin per se, that explains why Paul, when writing to the Corinthians, speaks of such sin by a Christian as so exceedingly sinful.

5) Marriage as Institution: The Wedding

Alone with Friar Laurence in his cell, Juliet reminds him, "God joined my heart to Romeo's, thou our hands."[151] Throughout our discussion of the Christian view of marriage, we have been primarily concerned with the essential matter, the joining of hearts in love, and have left to the last the joining of hands in a wedding ceremony.[152] For us there is no theology of the wedding ceremony as such. Yet the theology of marriage we have espoused lifts such a ceremony above mere propriety and sentiment. More is involved than a sentimental recalling of the fact — which should not be forgotten — that our Lord once graced a wedding with his presence (Jn. 2:1-11). Hence this comment on the significance of ceremony in a Christian doctrine of marriage.

---

151. Shakespeare, *Romeo and Juliet,* act 4, scene 1, lines 55-56.
152. The popular tendency to identify a marriage with a wedding is unfortunate. While the two are related, it almost seems that the relationship is one of inversion. The more the wedding is grand with pomp and circumstance, the less the marriage is likely to succeed. See Hogarth's painting, *Marriage à la Mode.*

The consent on which a marriage union rests is, to be sure, a matter of individual freedom; and the sex act that consummates a marriage as a one-flesh union is a private affair. But for all the freedom and privacy that belong to the relationship, when two people enter into marriage they cannot simply say, "We are free to do as we please, and what happens between us is no one else's business." No. The marriage relationship constitutes the beginning of a new family, and the family (the household, the clan) is the basic unit of society. Hence marriage is not only a private but also a social event, and the ceremony that marks this event is more than mere homage to bourgeois respectability.[153] That is, marriage has an institutional aspect; it is a state into which two people enter publicly. When two individuals are married, they are henceforth related in a markedly different way not only to each other but also to those around them — family, friends, and society as a whole.[154]

In the ancient church no specifically Christian rites solemnized marriage. Christians simply followed the general customs of the Greco-Roman world, avoiding whatever was suggestive of pagan superstition. In lieu of sacrifices to the gods, for example, Christians would often substitute the Eucharist; and, of course, when Christians gathered to celebrate a marriage, there was a Christian blessing pronounced on the newlyweds. Inevitably, as time went on, distinctively Christian rites and wedding ceremonies were developed, which we need not detail here.

Once the Reformers rejected the notion that marriage is a sacrament, some of their followers went so far as to reject the idea of a *Christian* wedding ceremony altogether. This was especially true of the New England Puritans, who, to protest the claims of the Catholic Church, would allow a civil ceremony only. "As late as 1685 a Huguenot minister in New England was fined for solemnizing marriage. But the future was with him and in 1692 legal authorization was obtained for a religious ceremony" (Bainton, *What Christianity Says About Sex,* pp. 105-6). In the United States, presently, Christian ministers serve in a double capacity. Functioning as civil servants, they are authorized

---

153. The social aspect of marriage is reflected in the older usage of charging those present at a wedding to declare any impediment against the intended marriage or "forever hold their peace." To feel the drama latent in such a charge, see Charlotte Brontë, *Jane Eyre,* chap. 13.

154. There is, to be sure, "common law" marriage, that is, marriage without benefit of public ceremony, civil or ecclesiastical. Such a relationship does, indeed, fall within the parameters of a Christian view of marriage when marked by mutual commitment and fidelity. There comes to mind, for example, the practice of "secret marriage" *(matrimonium clandestinum)* by priests in the Middle Ages. These "marriages" were sometimes recognized as legitimate even by the church prior to the twenty-fourth session of the Council of Trent (Nov. 11, 1563). One also thinks of those faithful liaisons that defy laws of miscegenation. Only extenuating circumstances of this sort, however, could justify a Christian's entering into such a private union that is without social ceremony.

to pronounce a man and a woman husband and wife; functioning as ordained clergy, they speak for Christ when they invoke his blessing.

*   *   *   *   *

We have spoken intentionally of a "Christian" wedding rather than a "church" wedding. The outer form may be similar in both instances, but the inner reality is surely different. A Christian wedding is one in which two Christians say and do what they say and do because they believe that God wills that they should, not because they simply desire to cloak their marriage in traditional respectability. Indeed, there is reason to ask why those who do not make a profession of the Christian faith should even be granted the use of a church sanctuary for their wedding.

When Christians choose publicly to announce and declare their marriage with a Christian wedding, they will naturally use a ceremony that not only satisfies the requirements of the state but also contains elements of Christian worship — prayer in the name of Christ (especially a prayer of blessing), the reading of Scripture, song, and perhaps a brief meditation (homily) befitting the occasion. A Christian wedding ceremony will also contain specific acts and affirmations that symbolize and declare the essential nature of the marriage union as Christians understand it. Important among these are the announcement of intent, the joining of hands, the taking of vows, the giving of visible tokens, and the declaration of marriage. And, now that romantic love is recognized as an important element in the Christian understanding of marriage, the ancient custom of exchanging a kiss is at least appropriate, if not essential.[155]

Erotic love has had such a marginal place in the theology of marriage that its introduction into contemporary Christian wedding services often jars on one's liturgical sensitivities. I have heard complaints of the impropriety of erotic kissing by newlyweds while "still in the church." Such songs as "I Love You Truly," "Because You Came to Me with Naught Save Love," etc., seem not to fit exactly. But then, what else is there?

Speaking of those acts and affirmations that symbolize a Christian understanding of marriage, we find the traditional "giving of the woman to the man" in the marriage ceremony to be of more than doubtful merit. Some contemporary Christian marriage services retain this practice while giving it a new meaning, but these efforts are generally botched and inept. For example, in some ceremonies the giving of the woman is oddly

---

155. One should remember that this kiss is not the holy kiss with which Paul admonished the Roman Christians to greet one another (Rom. 16:16), but rather the kiss of Cant. 1:2: "Let him kiss me with the kisses of his mouth" (NRSV). Hence, it is unfortunate that even down to the present Christian wedding ceremonies seldom speak of the romantic love of the Song of Songs, but only of the agape love of 1 Cor. 13.

associated with the thought that marriage subordinates former family ties to the new bond of matrimony. Of course this is true; but in Scripture it is the *man,* not the woman, who breaks family ties that he may cleave to his wife and become one flesh with her (Gn. 2:24). Yet no one ever gives the man to the woman — which might not be a bad idea for a change. [I did once officiate at a ceremony where, at the young couple's request, the groom's parents "gave him away" even as the bride's parents gave her — an innovation obviously disconcerting to the largely conservative and traditional crowd. — Ed.] Others may construe "the giving of the woman" in the marriage ceremony as symbolizing the Creator's original act of bringing the woman to the man (Gn. 2:22). Again, it is true that God did not leave the woman to be discovered by the man (much less conquered by him); she was indeed brought to him as the divine gift that complements and completes his own being. This act of the Creator, however, is the presupposition of marriage, not the marriage itself. Gn. 2:22 is not the first wedding.

The real difficulty with "giving the woman in marriage" or "giving the bride away" is that it rests on the patriarchal view that invests the father with the right to choose a husband for his daughter. Given the view of marriage we have espoused, the father has no such right. No third party can give the woman to the man, any more than a third party can give the man to the woman. Both give themselves to each other. (In the sixteenth century, arguing for the custom of giving away the bride, Richard Hooker pontificates, "It putteth women in mind of a duty whereunto the very imbecility of their nature and sex doth bind them; namely, to be always directed, guided and ordered by others" [*Ecclesiastical Polity,* bk. 5, §73]. Indeed!)

*   *   *   *   *

Barth once remarked that the so-called marriage altar *(Traualtar)* is "a free invention of the flowery speech of modern religion" *(KD,* III/4, p. 255 [cf. *CD,* III/4, p. 228]). Such "altar" language leads us to say a word, in conclusion, about the increasingly popular custom in American evangelical circles of giving the elements of the Lord's Supper to the bride and groom as part of the wedding ceremony. One can understand, though not approve, the way in which the ancient church came to regard the Eucharist as a sacrifice on an altar rather than a fellowship meal around the Lord's table. And, given this unfortunate development, one can further understand why early ecclesiastical marriage rites substituted the eucharistic "sacrifice" for the religious sacrifices offered in pagan marriage rites. But surely the heirs of the Protestant Reformation, who have been delivered from the notion that marriage is a sacrament, should not look on a wedding as a Protestant equivalent of a nuptial Mass.

We have granted that a Christian wedding ceremony will include various elements of worship as essential. But it does not follow that the sacrament of the Lord's Supper is one of them. When a Christian congregation gathers, with friends and relatives of the bride and groom, to solemnize marriage in a wedding service, what is being solemnized is a relationship wherein a man and a woman are united in one flesh. We do not question the analogy that Paul draws between the intimate one-flesh union of husband and wife and the close spiritual union of Christ and the church (Eph. 5:31-32). The fact, however, that the two are analogous should not be so pressed as to obscure their real difference. The union of husband and wife is a union symbolized by the joining of hands and the repeating of vows; the union of sinners with Christ in his death is symbolized by the eating and drinking of bread and wine. The former union rests on the work of God the Creator; the latter, the work of God the Redeemer. Hence we are not carried by the many arguments that confound the difference between creation and redemption in order to justify the celebration of Communion at a Christian wedding.

An instance of such unconvincing argumentation is the following from D. S. Bailey:

> The significance of the Marriage Service is weakened by the habitual omis-
> sion of the Communion, and the restoration of its celebration is a much needed
> reform. As the couple kneel at the altar and partake of the Sacrament of Unity
> they declare their solidarity in Christ with their fellow-members of his mys-
> tical Body; and the Church, in her administration of that sacrament to them,
> recognizes their new status and their new relation to the whole company of
> the faithful. (*Mystery of Love and Marriage,* p. 69)

To the contrary, as we see it, the proper way for a couple to "declare their solidarity in Christ with their fellow-members of his mystical Body" is not to kneel at a wedding altar but to gather at the Communion table when the congregation as a whole celebrates the Lord's Supper. To merge these two events is to confuse nature and grace. Confusion is also reflected in the thought that the church, through the administration of Communion to the newly married couple, "recognizes their new status and relation to the company of the faithful." As a matter of fact, the new status and relation of people to the company of the faithful has always been recognized by the church, sacramentally speaking, by the administration of baptism, not Holy Communion. But no one would suppose that a marriage service is the appropriate time for baptism. We grant that sharing bread and wine may make the newly married couple "feel good," and no one would want them to "go away hurting"; but the proper celebration of the Lord's Supper cannot be determined by such sentimentalism.

Addendum: Arranged Marriages. In the foregoing effort to frame a Christian doctrine of marriage, we have placed considerable emphasis on freedom of choice and the love that motivates such a choice. Marriage, we have said, is a relationship into which a man and a woman "freely choose to enter out of love for each other." Such an understanding of marriage, however, is by no means common to all places and times. In fact, in most cultures in the past and in many even down to the present, marriages are arranged rather than chosen out of mutual love. Surely one cannot regard such marriages as null and void simply because they come short of the Christian ideal. But if the Christian view of marriage most clearly reflects the will of the Creator, what may we say of marriages that are not entered out of mutual love but arranged by parental choice?

We begin by noting that some arranged marriages are more, some less, a departure from the Christian understanding of marriage. From a Christian and theological point of view, that form of arranged marriage which imposes the union on one or both parties against their will is obviously the most objectionable. Although God's grace can make good come out of evil, we find it difficult to say anything good of such forced marriages. Having made self-determination under God essential to our humanity and having stressed in particular the volitional nature of the marriage bond, we can only deplore the suppression of choice in marriage as an egregious departure from the will of the Creator.[156]

At this point it would be tempting to dwell on some unspeakable horrors like "bride burning" in India to underscore the dire consequences of marriages that are not free. But here the Christian theologian needs to remember that they who live in glass houses should not throw stones. Examples of arranged marriages, in which the will of the parents, especially the father, overrides that of the child, are found in Western as well as Eastern cultures. Although in theory the church has always opposed forced marriages, it has in fact not only allowed but even solemnized them. Throughout the Middle Ages, marriages were arranged by the parents and blessed by the church without any consideration of the will of those being joined as husband and wife. Speaking of the importance of land as the basis of all life and institutions in feudal society, Bainton observes:

> In such a scheme marriage served not simply for propagation but even more for the unification of families and estates. . . . The daughter of Count Roger of Sicily was still a child when her hand was given to King Conrad in 1095. Adelheid was eight when in 1110 she was engaged to Henry V. . . . King Louis of France betrothed his daughter when yet in the cradle to the thirteen-year-old son of King Henry of England in 1158. The son of the Count of Brabant was only just born when he was affianced in 1207 to the daughter of Philip of Swabia. (Bainton, *What Christianity Says About Sex,* p. 48)

In some cases, the church did insist that espoused couples should not be forced into marriage; but given the social mores of the day, filial rebellion was infrequent and acquiescence the norm. This acquiescence, as Bainton notes, was secured not only by a sense of family loyalty but also by the early age at which marriages were consummated. For girls the average age ranged from thirteen to fifteen; and for boys, from fifteen to nineteen. If, when they were old enough to know their own minds, one or both parties sought to be free from such a marriage, the church declared the union indissoluble and used every means to enforce commitment to adolescent vows. By contrast, the church forced couples apart who were happily married if the marriage was found to be against the ecclesiastical canons defining consanguinity and spiritual relationships.

> Robert the Pious, for example, had been living happily for some years with his wife, Bertha, when it was discovered that he was related to her physically as fourth cousin and spiritually as godfather to her child by a previous

---

156. See above, pp. 214-18.

marriage. Protracted excommunication at length constrained them to separate.
(Bainton, ibid., pp. 50-51)

Little wonder that the love of which the troubadours sang was so often an adulterous love!

Marriages arranged in such a way as to violate individual freedom ("forced marriages") are not the only sort of arranged marriages that offend the Christian ideal. Those arranged out of utilitarian considerations, even when freely entered into, are likewise offensive. Such "marriages of convenience," as they are sometimes called, contracted for the supposed benefits arising from them rather than from the mutual attraction of those entering into them, mock the true purpose of marriage. Indeed, along with androcentricity in male-female relationships and hedonism in the gratification of the sex impulse, especially on the part of the male, utilitarianism is one of the vices that, in our judgment, must bedevil the marriage union.[157]

By no means, however, are all arranged marriages to be condemned out of hand, as though they were all forced or self-serving. While some may come short of the Christian ideal of love, this fact alone does not doom arranged marriages to a necessary failure. In fact, arranged marriages may prove more fulfilling than "marriages of love" when two people bring nothing else but love to the relationship. After all, romantic love has not had a prominent place even in the Christian understanding of marriage until relatively recent times. And, as everyone knows, along with romantic love many qualities of character make for compatibility in marriage. Here one recalls the marriages of the Reformers, into which they freely entered, though hardly out of romantic love. Catherine von Bora (having escaped from a convent) may be said to have "arranged" Luther's marriage — to herself; and Calvin, as we have seen, sought the help of others in arranging a marriage because of the demands that his work made on his time.[158]

In today's Western society, perhaps nearest to an "arranged" marriage

---

157. See Browning's "My Last Duchess," in his *Men and Women*.

158. In the present day, one might also mention the marriage of Benazir Bhutto, not only the first woman to rule in a Muslim country (Pakistan), but the first ever to become a mother while head of state. "Although," notes Peter Galbraith, "many of Benazir's Harvard friends expressed amazement at the willingness of one of our contemporaries to enter into an arranged marriage, I was not surprised. Benazir is an amalgam of East and West, and very much the product of a tradition in which such marriages are the norm. More practically, her prominence in a fundamentally conservative society made dating impossible; an arranged marriage provided the only feasible means for getting married at all" ("The Return of Benazir Bhutto," *Harvard Magazine,* July-August 1989, p. 24). Speaking of "East and West," there comes to mind the marriage arranged for Wang Lund to O-lan, engagingly described in the opening chapter of Pearl Buck's *The Good Earth*.

are those marriages negotiated (for a fee) by marriage brokers.[159] Brokered marriages, freely entered into, need not be utilitarian. After all, matchmaking by family and friends (without a fee) is a commonplace both in and out of Christian circles. What many so-called marriages of love need most is the wisdom that comes from advice and counsel given by a competent professional. Better to consult a marriage broker before marriage than go to a marriage counselor after marriage, when the relationship has fallen hopelessly apart.[160]

5. DIVORCE: THE DISSOLUTION OF THE MARRIAGE BOND

a. Introduction

Back in 1984, according to the all-knowing computer, 13,500 Americans were married on any given day — and 6,500 were divorced.[161] This latter figure can hardly be dismissed as a mere statistic, especially if one has a Christian understanding of marriage. Rather, it is a jarring reminder that the idea of marriage as blessed by the Creator — and set forth in the above discussion — is never found in reality as such but only, in our sinful and broken reality, as the ideal toward which we strive, God helping us. This being so, any theological statement about marriage must include a comment on failed marriages.

As we turn to the task of making such a statement, we shall simply assume that one's understanding of divorce comes out of one's understanding of marriage. We do not make such a statement because people have first to be married in order to get divorced, but rather because of the inner coherence of thought. The way in which one's view of marriage determines one's view of divorce is dramatically illustrated in Charles Williams's aphoristic comment, "Adultery is bad morals, but divorce is bad metaphysics."[162] Such an aphorism is true if one accepts the Roman Catholic view that the bond of marriage rests on natural law elevated to the sanctity of a sacramental sign. But if one affirms, as we have done, that the bond of marriage is ultimately volitional rather than sacramental in nature, then Williams's affirmation that divorce is bad metaphysics is itself bad theology.

159. Marriage brokers should not be confused with those who offer dating services. We are not talking about the hucksters who can provide a "girl" for every occasion.

160. Evangelical Christians whose pious sentimentalism would be shocked at the thought of consulting a professional in seeking a marriage partner too often pay a counselor large sums to salvage a marriage headed for disaster from the beginning.

161. Parker, *In One Day*, p. 94.

162. *The Forgiveness of Sins* (Grand Rapids: Eerdmans, 1942), p. 117.

In evaluating this Catholic and sacramental argument about divorce and metaphysics, we shall begin with a brief historical summary.[163] Our story goes back to the consensus among the ancient Fathers that in the teaching of Jesus, the marriage bond is inviolable. Obviously, then, it ought not to be broken. But it can be; and all the Fathers agreed that in the case of adultery, it was. Hence adultery constituted a possible ground for divorce.[164] But this did not mean that the "guilty" party could remarry. On the contrary, the Fathers all insisted that the offending party, whether husband or wife, could not contract a second marriage. In fact, the majority went further, denying even to the "innocent" the right to enter into a second marriage. This was because they believed that only the death of one's spouse could finally free one from the marriage bond.[165] Early in the history of the church, therefore, the marriage relationship was held to be, in some sense, indissoluble. As the theologians came on the scene, the doctrine of the indissolubility of marriage was more and more vigorously defined in the direction of absolute inviolability. This rigorous view prevailed in the West, and by the eleventh century it was the received teaching of the church. Divorce did not give anyone, not even the "innocent" party, the right to remarry. Even when marriage partners were irrevocably separated, the marriage bond, in some sense, was still to be reckoned with.

The Scholastic reasoning behind this doctrine that the marriage bond is, by its very nature, indissoluble is set forth in detail and defended by Thomas Aquinas in the *Summa Theologica*. In the very first article on the Sacrament of Matrimony, Thomas defines with care the sense in which matrimony is a matter of natural law. It is not a natural law in the sense that the upward movement of fire is natural, but rather in the sense that our God-given nature inclines us, through the intervention of free will, to the marriage union.[166] Thus Thomas prepares the ground for his denial, in the fifth article, that one ever has the right to remarry after one is divorced. In this article, he not only assumes that the marriage relationship rests on

163. Here one may be helped by reading Bailey, *Sexual Relation*, pp. 80ff.

164. In treating of the grounds of divorce, both the Fathers and the Schoolmen assume, for the most part, a double standard. An adulterous husband is dealt with more leniently than an adulterous wife. This chauvinistic attitude rests on the argument that adultery in the wife is the greater offense because it risks a confusion of progeny *(confusio prolis)*. It was deemed of cardinal importance that the husband should be sure of the paternity of his wife's children. The paternity of the illegitimate children he sired by another woman was of less concern — naturally.

165. Obviously, then, the Fathers used the term "divorce" to describe what we would call separation of bed and board *(a mensa et thoro)*. Failure to reckon with this usage sometimes confuses the discussion.

166. *Summa Theologica*, Suppl., q. 41, art. 1.

nature as structured by the Creator in the beginning but also cites Paul's admonition to the Corinthians (1 Cor. 7:10-11) that "the wife should not separate from her husband (but if she does, let her remain single)." He goes on to note that were one freed by adultery to contract a more agreeable marriage, this would be to gain advantage from one's sin. Since God cannot possibly bless a marriage under such circumstances, we must conclude, "Nothing supervenient to marriage can dissolve it: wherefore adultery does not make a marriage cease to be valid. For, according to Augustine (*De Nup. et Concup.* 1.10), *'as long as they live they are bound by the marriage tie, which neither divorce nor union with another can destroy.'* "[167]

This view that the marriage bond is, in its very nature, indissoluble, is reinforced in official Catholic teaching by the notion that marriage is a sacramental sign of the union between Christ and the church.[168] Spelling out the implications of this reasoning, the Council of Trent (Twenty-Fourth Session) affirmed that Christ by his passion merited for us that grace which perfects natural love, *confirms the indissoluble union of marriage,* and sanctifies the married couple.[169]

Though a bit more restrained in its pronouncements since Vatican II, the Roman Catholic Church continues to teach that the marriage union is indissoluble. Whereas the sacrament perfects the marriage bond in that it conveys the grace necessary to achieve fidelity, the bond itself rests on what God has done in creation. It is he who has so joined husband and wife together that they are, in the words of our Lord (Mt. 19:6), one flesh. Hence, while the freedom of the consenting parties is essential to the constitution of marriage, such freedom does not give the consenting couple, once they have entered into marriage, any power whatever over the nature of matrimony as such. Given such a view of the marriage union, as metaphysical in nature and sacramental in significance, the words of our Lord, "What therefore God has joined together, let not man put asunder" (Mt. 19:6), really means, "What God has joined together, no one *can* put asunder." In the words of John A. T. Robinson, "a physical or metaphysical union is created by wedlock which cannot be abrogated any more than two persons can cease to be brother and sister. Marriage is not merely indissoluble: it is indelible."[170]

---

167. Ibid., Suppl., q. 62, art. 5. Thomas recognizes, of course, that a divorce entails separation, so that a woman is not bound to her husband as regards the marriage debt; but she is bound as regards the marriage tie so long as her husband lives. See Rom. 7:2-3. Thomas does not comment on the fact that Jewish law proscribed the woman's right to initiate divorce, but not the man's right.

168. See above, pp. 222-24.

169. Italics added.

170. *Honest to God* (Philadelphia: Westminster, 1963), pp. 107-8.

This Catholic view of the indissolubility of the marriage bond is obviously behind Charles Williams's remark that divorce is bad metaphysics. It is also obvious that because we reject this Catholic view of marriage, we also reject Williams's view of divorce. While we would surely affirm that the marriage bond *ought* not to be broken, we believe it can be. Because the question of indissolubility is often burdened by disputes over "ought" and "can," we have avoided using the term in our own definition of marriage, choosing rather to speak of marriage simply as a "lasting relationship."

b. Marriage, Divorce, and the Divine Will

In contrast to the Catholic view, which looks on the marriage bond as ontological in nature when sacramentally constituted, we have argued that the basis of the marriage union is volitional in nature. Marriage is a personal relationship that rests on the mutual consent of the covenanting parties *(consensus facit matrimonium)*. This relationship, then, has no "nature in and of itself" with "essential laws and properties" that are distinct from the will of the marriage partners. Marriage is not a union that in its ultimate being is somehow mysteriously independent of the mutual choice and consent by which a man and a woman enter into said union and by which it is sustained as an ongoing reality day by day and year by year.

At the same time, we have insisted that the mutual choice whereby two people are joined as one flesh is by no means an autonomous act of the human will. At least, for the Christian it is not. The Christian, rather, understands matrimony as *holy* matrimony because it is an ongoing relationship that is according to the Creator's will and enjoys his blessing. For the Christian, then, marriage is a calling; and the vows of fidelity that unite two people in marriage terminate ultimately upon God. While such a position does not mean that the marriage relationship is ontological — two people are not, in God's eyes, husband and wife as they are male and female — it does mean that marriage has a transcendent reference. It is a covenantal relationship entered into and lived out according to the will of God. In this respect marriage symbolizes the union between Christ and the church. Since marriage has this transcendent reference, since it is to be entered into and lived out in the light of God's will, our rejection of the view that divorce is bad *metaphysics* does not imply that we think divorce is good — or even neutral — *morality*.

The loss of transcendence, the rejection of any "thou shalts" or "shalt nots" from Sinai (or anywhere else), the autonomy in which one tells oneself what is right and what is wrong — these lie behind the modern view that marriage and divorce are simply this-worldly correlatives. Since there is no thought of a God who is to be loved and feared, marriage is entered into without a desire to obey him and left without repentance for disobeying him. One chooses to enter, even as one chooses to leave, marriage for purely mundane reasons. Now it is surely the case that in a religiously pluralistic society, the state should grant its citizens the right to such a secular view of marriage. Christians ought not to impose their view of marriage on atheists and humanists by the coercion of civil law. From the standpoint of the state, therefore, marriage is rightly treated as a legal contract; and it may even be that justice for those who seek release from this contract is best served by "no fault" laws of divorce. But it is dismaying, to say the least, when those who claim to speak as Christians seek to baptize such a secular view of marriage by decking out a so-called divorce service in the trappings of a traditional wedding ceremony.

In "An Amicable Divorce," *Christian Century* 88, no. 18 (May 5, 1971): 553-55, Mary McDermott Shideler relates how two of her friends "solemnized the dissolution of their marriage with a religious ceremony." Observing the value of certain rites associated with marriage — announcements, wedding, reception — Shideler finds it unfortunate that "no such rites have yet been established for divorce, which is also the beginning of a new life." She then describes the service for the Dissolution of Marriage that she wrote for her friends, whom she calls "Matthew" and "Anne," in order that they might celebrate their divorce as they enter upon a new way of life. This service began with all saying, "Oh Lord, our God, how excellent is Thy name in all the earth." Then the officiant said:

> Dearly beloved, we have gathered here to solemnize the end of one time in Matthew's and Anne's lives, and the beginning of another. . . . Thirteen years ago the time was right for Matthew and Anne to be joined in holy matrimony. Then they needed for their growth in grace and truth the visible bond of marriage. Now the time has come when that bond is hampering both their growth as individual persons, and their common life. They have resolved, therefore, to sever the ties of their marriage, though not of their mutual love and honor, and have asked us, their friends, to witness that affirmation of their new lives, and to uphold them in their new undertakings.

Matthew then solemnly relinquished his status as Anne's husband, freed her from all claims and responsibilities except those she willingly gave to all other children of God, and Anne did likewise for Matthew. Each released the other with love, blessing, and gratitude. These vows of release were followed by a prayer: "Almighty and loving God, who has ordered that seasons shall change and that human lives shall proceed by change, we ask thy blessing upon thy children who now, in their commitment to thee, have severed their commitment to each other. Send them forth in the bond of peace, Amen." The service closed with a benediction of peace, and the blessing of God Almighty, the Father, the Son, and the Holy Spirit. The rite was followed by a period of "glorious affirmation." Awaiting them, we are told, "were homemade bread of that morning's baking, and wine that flashed red."

We find such a "service" of "holy" divorce a sacrilege. To ask the Almighty to bless those who "in their commitment to him have severed their commitment to each other" is pure doublespeak. So to sanctify divorce, without a word of repentance, reminds one of the bold speech found on the lips of Milton's Satan, "Evil be thou my good." We grant that the church, as the community of faith and love, should renounce the judgmental attitude that would deny all compassion to those whose marriages have failed. As such people struggle with their grief and guilt, as they endure the pain of divorce, members of a congregation should uphold them in prayer and so learn not only to rejoice with those who rejoice but also to weep with those who weep (Rom. 12:15). Under certain circumstances, members of a congregation may even wish to express their concern and support in some formal service. But at the very least such a service should be penitential in nature. (For an attempt at such a penitential service, see "Order for Recognition of the End of a Marriage," *Book of Worship*, United Church of Christ [New York: Office for Church Life and Leadership, 1986], pp. 289-95.) There is no way to celebrate the failure of the marriage relationship. To seek to do so is simply to defame marriage.

If, over and beyond the choice of the consenting parties, one grounds the marriage relationship in the will of God; if one says that marriage partners are they whom God has joined together, and therefore they ought not be put asunder; then, obviously, every divorce is in some sense contrary to the will of God. Divorce is something God allows, not something he enjoins. Hence the parties to a marriage covenant, if they are Christians, will leave marriage only when they must and, even then, not without seeking God's forgiveness for having made a wrong choice that now compels them to break the solemn vow with which they entered marriage.

But how does one know that the moment has come when one *must* leave a marriage? If to leave a marriage is an act that calls for one to repent of the wrong which he or she has done, what is the greater wrong that compels one to commit the lesser wrong of leaving a marriage? As we grapple with this difficult question of determining when divorce is the "lesser of two evils," we shall begin by looking at the way the Reformers approached the subject. As we know, they broke with the ontological/-sacramental view of the marriage union. This theological shift, in turn, made it possible for them to acknowledge that the marriage union is not indissoluble in an absolute sense; the covenant of marriage can be broken. Divorce *a vinculo*, that is, with the freedom to remarry and not simply as separation of bed and board *(a mensa et thoro)*, is allowed.

Obviously the Continental Reformers were more liberal in their approach to divorce than the Anglicans; and Luther was the most liberal of them all. While he extolled the bliss of marriage as better than all celibacy, he always added the caveat: when it turns out well. When it does not, it is the very devil (Bainton, *What Christianity Says About Sex*, p. 82). In the Church of England, by contrast, many of the bishops sought to hold the line against the right of remarriage, taking a position similar, for all practical purposes, to medieval canon law. The exceptions in which divorce and remarriage were allowed tended to favor the rich and powerful (Bailey, *Sexual Relation*, pp. 211-12).

The prototype of this abuse was Henry VIII, that "remorseless incarnation of Machiavelli's prince," who embraced and dispatched wives at his pleasure.

In keeping with the Reformers' emphasis on the authority of the Bible, it comes as no surprise that they sought to answer the question, When is divorce allowed? by appealing to Scripture. As a result, the Protestant ethical tradition has been marked by an ongoing effort to establish the so-called scriptural grounds for divorce. In evaluating this effort, we begin with a review of the biblical data with which theologians and ethicists have worked, giving attention especially to the teaching of Jesus.

In the ensuing discussion, one should remember that the phrase "grounds of divorce" describes those conditions allowing for, but not requiring, divorce. The conviction that marriage is permanent is such a fundamental element in the Christian view of things that few Christian ethicists have been inclined to follow the rigorists of the ancient church who required the husband to put away an adulterous wife. Against such rigorism one recalls the marriage of Hosea to Gomer, which symbolized Yahweh's faithfulness to his covenant people Israel in spite of their infidelity to him. In like manner, the permanence of the marriage union has made it, in Christian thought, the symbol of the lasting relationship between Christ and the church. Therefore, Christian writers, while allowing divorce, have generally applauded the effort of two people to stay together in a difficult marriage when they have the courage of conviction and the strength of faith to do so.

Christian history affords many examples of such courage and faith. One thinks of the marriage of John Wesley. Although he was among the most gifted and influential men in the history of the church, when it came to women, all Wesley's talents left him. As a young missioner in Georgia (1730s), he had a love affair with a Sophia Hopkey that ended in a tangled suit for slander. Later (1749), having been frustrated in his purpose to marry Grace Murray by the resistance of his friends, especially his brother Charles, he precipitously entered into a marriage (1751) with a London widow, Mrs. Vizelle. Determined to keep up his travels, of which she, understandably, grew tired, Wesley soon found himself in a marriage that became a textbook case of marital incompatibility. Plagued with a monomaniacal jealousy, his wife traveled many miles to spy out who rode with him in his carriage. She ransacked his desk, showed his private papers to his critics, interfered with his guests, and, in a huff, left him from time to time. When she finally deserted him for good, he observed in his *Journal,* laconically, "I did not forsake her, I did not dismiss her, I will not recall her." Yet throughout the years of married life, he never spoke of divorce; and his letters to her reveal the tender affection with which he treated her. (See Abel Stevens, *The History of the Religious Movement of the Eighteenth Century Called Methodism* [London: Wesleyan Conference Office, 1878], vol. 1, p. 290.)

The real unsung heroes in this whole matter of bearing the burdens of a difficult marriage are the many anonymous women whose heroic courage in the midst of marital trials and tribulations, unlike those of prominent men, have never been chronicled. While they cannot be named individually, the encomiums inspired by a suffering fidelity belong primarily to them.

Deuteronomy 24:1-4 proscribes the right of a man to take back a wife whom he has divorced, even if she is widowed. The ground for divorce in this passage is that the man has found in his wife עֶרְוַת דָּבָר, literally, a "nakedness of a thing," often translated as "some indecency." This Old Testament text has been of interest to Christians primarily because the Pharisees cited it when they asked Jesus what he thought about divorce (Mk. 10:2-12; Mt. 19:3-12; see also Mt. 5:32; Lk. 16:18). Jesus answers that Moses wrote this commandment, granting a man the right to divorce his wife, because of "the hardness of your hearts." He went on to say that inasmuch as God in the beginning created male and female and joined them together in the one-flesh union of marriage, there is really no place for divorce. This answer shows plainly that Jesus believed that sin is at work whenever a marriage is terminated.[171]

When one looks more closely at the answer our Lord gave to the divorce question, as that answer is reported and elaborated in the various strands of the synoptic tradition, it would appear that he taught that a man who divorces his wife and remarries commits adultery (Mk. 10:11; Lk. 16:18). Such an interpretation presupposes that the Greek verb ἀπολύω, literally, "to put away," has the equivalent meaning of divorce in the modern sense, though this is not certain.

Matthew 19:9 reports this saying with a qualifying clause: "whoever divorces [literally, 'puts away'] his wife, except for unchastity (μὴ ἐπὶ πορνείᾳ), and marries another, commits adultery." This qualifying clause in Matthew's report is generally looked upon as an addition to the original teaching of our Lord, reflecting the understanding of that teaching in Jewish-Christian circles. We are inclined to construe this "exception clause" as explanatory on the part of the evangelist; that is, he believed that such an exception was entailed in what Jesus taught. For a wife to be involved in an adulterous liaison with another man is, for all practical purposes, to dissolve the marriage bond by violating it. Hence a man has a right to recognize such a fact for what it is by legally ending the marriage through divorce.[172]

171. Whether, as is often supposed, the Pharisees queried Jesus to see if he sided with the liberal school of Hillel or the conservative school of Shammai in interpreting Moses is uncertain and, for our discussion, unimportant. In any case, Jesus' hearers would not have understood his answer to contradict Moses. To require more than the law is not to defy the law. "Moses did not *command* divorce, he permitted it; and to prohibit what he permitted is by no means the same as to permit what he prohibited" (E. P. Sanders, *Jesus and Judaism* [Philadelphia: Fortress, 1985], pp. 256-57).

172. Here one recalls that it is Matthew who reports the intent of Joseph to "put Mary away privately," that is, divorce her, when he learned that she was "with child" before their marriage had been consummated, Mt. 1:18-19.

Along with the interpretation of Matthew's "exception clause," other questions are raised by the way Jesus' sayings on divorce are reported. These questions have invited many ingenious efforts at explanation and harmony. Especially puzzling is the saying, reported in Matthew 5:32, that a man who puts away his wife, except for unchastity (πορνεία), causes her to commit adultery (μοιχευθῆναι); and anyone who marries such a divorcee commits adultery (μοιχᾶται). We need not review in detail the efforts to clarify this and other difficult passages; we simply note that none of these efforts seems wholly satisfactory.

In conclusion, we can only suggest that whatever questions concerning Jesus' teaching on divorce remain unresolved, surely he regarded the permanency of marriage, based on lifelong fidelity, to reflect the Creator's original intent. This conclusion is inescapable even if one affirms that he used the word "adultery" (πορνεία) as a synonym for marital unfaithfulness of every sort. Therefore, if he did not absolutely proscribe divorce, he certainly looked on the termination of marriage as a grave violation of moral obligation.

When we turn from the teaching of Jesus to that of Paul on the subject of divorce, the interpretation of the relevant texts is not so difficult; but the larger implications of what the apostle says have been much debated. Speaking first to the unmarried women in the Corinthian congregation (1 Cor. 7:8-9) and then to the married (7:10-11), the apostle instructs the latter not to depart from their husbands; but if they do, to remain unmarried or to be reconciled to them. Likewise, husbands are not to leave their wives. In giving these instructions, he speaks as one who is simply passing on what Jesus taught ("I give charge, not I but the Lord," v. 10). But then (vv. 12-15) he goes on to speak to a situation that our Lord never faced, namely, the disruption of the marriage relationship through the conversion of one of the parties. In such a situation he could not appeal to a tradition going back to Jesus. Hence he speaks on his own authority as an inspired apostle ("But to the rest I say, not the Lord," v. 12). Paul's counsel is that even under such circumstances, fidelity to the marriage covenant is the Christian's calling (vv. 12-13). The believer, therefore, must not initiate a separation. However, if — here we translate the text literally — "the unbeliever separates himself/herself," then "let him/her separate himself/herself" — εἰ δὲ ὁ ἄπιστος χωρίζεται, χωριζέσθω (v. 15).[173] When the unbeliever initiates the action and walks out of a marriage to a believer, "in such a case," the apostle concludes (v. 15), "a brother or sister is not bound" (οὐ δεδούλωται ὁ ἀδελφὸς ἢ ἡ ἀδελφὴ ἐν τοῖς τοιούτοις).

173. In passing, one should note that while Jewish law gave the privilege of divorce to the man only, in this passage Paul assumes a reciprocity of the sexes in such matters.

This last remark has caused so much discussion that it has acquired a technical designation: the "Pauline privilege" *(privilegium Paulinum)*. For all the discussion, however, the apostle's meaning is still not clear. He may mean that a believing spouse, when deserted, should simply consent to the separation and feel no responsibility to try to restore the relationship through cohabitation. The brother or sister, under such circumstances, is no longer bound vis-à-vis the marriage debt. However, the Protestant church has generally understood the apostle to mean that the believer, whose faith occasioned the separation on the unbeliever's part, is no longer bound by the marriage covenant, but free to enter into a new marriage. In fact, the majority in the Protestant tradition have gone even further and reasoned that not only separation for religious purposes but any irremediable separation, whatever the reason, gives the party that is forsaken the right to remarriage. Having noted that an innocent party in a case of adultery may sue for divorce and marry another, the Westminster Confession concludes the chapter on marriage by affirming that "nothing but adultery, or such willful desertion as can no way be remedied by the church or civil magistrate, is cause sufficient for dissolving the bond of marriage."[174]

Here we conclude our review of the biblical data with which Christian moralists and theologians have worked as they have sought to determine the "scriptural grounds of divorce." Cursory as this review has been, it is sufficient to highlight some of the difficulties that beset such an endeavor. Outstanding among them is the seeming asymmetry between the teaching of Jesus and that of Paul. While he does not say in so many words that the bond of marriage is indissoluble, Jesus does hold that all divorce violates the will of God as manifest in the original creation. Hence he opposed divorce and remarriage. Even if one construes the "exception clause" in Matthew 19:9 as an original word of our Lord, this conclusion is inescapable. In fact, his disciples, sensing the import of his response to the Pharisees, protested that if this is the way it is between husband and wife, then it is better not to marry in the first place (Mt. 19:10). If one construes what Jesus says in verse 11, "Not everyone can accept this word, but only those to whom it has been given" (NIV), as a response to their complaint, then it may be that our Lord is conceding that his teaching reflects an ideal that is beyond the reach of many.[175]

However one may understand the teaching of Jesus, it would appear that Paul, when confronted with a new situation that Jesus did not contem-

---

174. Chap. 24 of the edition of 1647.
175. If this is the correct understanding of v. 11, then what is said about eunuchs in the following verse (12) is simply a discrete saying whose original context has been lost.

plate, went beyond anything our Lord had allowed as grounds for divorce. At least this is the case if one construes the Pauline privilege as it has been widely understood in the Protestant tradition. Given the difficulties that confront the interpreter of the Gospel accounts of Jesus' teaching on marriage and divorce, and considering the way Paul approaches the same question when confronted with the Corinthian problem, one cannot apparently deduce from Scripture the grounds of divorce in a tidy and orderly way. The traditional lists — adultery, impotence, separation, and the like — have merit; but their merit does not rest on specific proof texts apart from larger considerations, to which we must now give our attention.

c. Conclusion

We have come to the place in our discussion where we must face the "existential" question, How does one who is a Christian know when her leaving a marriage is the lesser of two evils?[176] How does she know when she must "sin bravely," to use Luther's phrase? In seeking to frame an answer to this question, we begin with another look at the teaching of Jesus.

One cannot doubt that the ideal of marriage which Jesus upheld did not allow for divorce. This ideal is the standard of perfection toward which we strive as Christians. To the degree a marriage reflects this ideal, the one-flesh union brings an ongoing fulfillment and satisfaction to the marriage partners. But when we construe this ideal as a rule to which we must conform without exception, we put ourselves under law rather than grace in our effort to know God's will for our lives. Such a legalistic approach to the question of marriage and divorce can exact untold suffering; and it has done so, in that it compromises the meaning of grace, understood as God's compassion toward those who confess their sin and his readiness to forgive them. In its judgment and condemnation of all whose marriages fail, the law obscures the truth that the God whom Jesus revealed is a God who, in the midst of judgment, remembers mercy.

We would suggest, therefore, that when Jesus appealed to the creation ideal, in the light of which all divorce stands condemned, he should be understood as setting forth a basic principle, that is, a fundamental truth that exercises a guiding influence in our decision making. Such a fundamental truth has a general application; it is not meant to be an inflexible law that defines our course of action in every instance. Suggestions, at least, that Jesus' words should be understood in this manner are found in

176. In this section when we speak of "leaving a marriage," we have in mind divorce *a vinculo*, not simply separation *a mensa et thoro*.

Scripture itself. We have already alluded to the response he made to his disciples that not all are able to receive his word about divorce, but those only to whom it has been given (Mt. 19:11).[177] Furthermore, the apostle Paul, as we have seen, when faced with the desertion of a Christian by an unbelieving spouse, acknowledged that in such a situation the Christian was free from the marriage covenant (1 Cor. 7:15). It seems unlikely that he would have spoken as he did had he construed Jesus' teaching as a law denying the possibility of divorce for any cause whatever.

Furthermore still, while the creation ordinance to which our Lord appealed when he condemned divorce is the fundamental truth on which the whole Christian understanding of marriage is based, this fundamental truth must be held in tandem with a second truth, and that is that our present reality is a broken and sinful reality. As a result, the goodness of the original creation is deeply flawed in our present existence by our fallenness and alienation from the Creator. Hence there is always the possibility that they who have joined themselves together in matrimony, according to the laws of the state and even with the blessing of the church, may not have been joined together by God. This is not to say that the church is ever in a position to make such a negative judgment about a marriage union. (The church cannot bless a divorce as it would bless a marriage.) But it is to say that the community of faith should be prepared to accept those who are penitent, those who confess that they can no longer continue in a given marital relationship because they entered upon it "unadvisedly, lightly, or wantonly." Forgiveness is open to all who truly repent and are sorry for the mistakes they have made; the grace of God is not selective in granting forgiveness of sin.

The admission that sin has so deeply flawed our human existence that two people may be joined together in marriage without heaven's blessing calls for a word concerning what Barth refers to as the "inner genesis" *(inneren Zustandekommen)* of a marriage, namely, the *mutual* desire and volition out of which a marriage arises and by which it is sustained.[178] This mutuality of purpose and desire, which is the basis of marriage, is the context in which the marriage vow is taken. This means that the promise of fidelity on which a marriage rests is never unconditional and without qualification. When one promises fidelity to one's partner in marriage, it is with the tacit understanding that the other will likewise show fidelity to the one making the promise. Faithfulness, in such a context, is faithfulness-in-fellowship, faithfulness that assumes faithfulness in return. When,

177. That is, some may have resources of faith to sustain a marriage that for others is intolerable.

178. *KD*, III/4, pp. 239-40 (cf. *CD*, III/4, pp. 213-14).

therefore, unfaithfulness has destroyed the fellowship of marriage beyond the possibility of renewal, the church has no warrant, in our judgment, to insist that the external relationship must continue as a legal fiction. We grant that divorce is a breaking of the promise contained in the marriage vow, and promise breaking calls for repentance. But to say that under no circumstances may one be forgiven for such an act, and that only death can release one from the marriage vow, is, as we see it, an untenable position in view of the context of mutuality and reciprocity in which such a vow is taken.[179]

Finally, when we speak of the failure of a marriage in its "inner genesis," we are actually speaking, in a general way, of what, in a specific way, the Protestant church has already acknowledged by listing adultery as one of the grounds of divorce. Adultery is obviously a ground of divorce inasmuch as the adulterous life of a philanderer destroys the mutuality that inwardly sustains the marriage relationship. What we have protested, therefore, as legalism is not the listing of adultery along with other grounds of divorce, but an appeal to such lists as inflexible rules that know of no exceptions. We grant that if we believe divorce is a possibility in the light of scriptural revelation, then we ought to be able to say on what grounds such a possibility is admitted. But when we list possible grounds, such lists are simply pointers in the direction of responsible decision making; they are not to be treated as the law of the Medes and Persians.[180]

The need to recognize any list of scriptural grounds for divorce as pointing in the direction of responsible decision making rather than constituting an inviolable rule is evidenced by the fact that for all the effort to specify the grounds of divorce, the Protestant church has never been able to avoid the more general approach implied in the term "incompatibility." Divorce, it has been argued, should be allowed for "incompatibility."

Before commenting on the approach to divorce implied in the concept of incompatibility, we pause to say a word about the way the traditional list of specific grounds has

---

179. Speaking of divorce and the breaking of the marriage vow, we do not understand the phrase "for better or for worse," found in that vow, to include the utter failure of the marriage relationship as such. We understand it, rather, to refer to that mutual readiness on the part of marriage partners to share not only the blessings but also the burdens that come to a married couple as they live together in this "vale of tears."

180. In the case of adultery, to be specific, a legalistic approach does not take into account the possibility that one may, in a single instance of weakness, be guilty of an act of which one deeply repents; while another, who never succumbed to such weakness, may through physical abuse and mental cruelty gradually destroy the mutuality on which a marriage relationship rests. A legalistic approach simply goes by the rule; adultery is on the list, physical and emotional abuse is not. Ergo. . . .

been altered by the addition of a new item in relatively recent times. We have in mind the belated recognition, at least in some parts of the church, that domestic violence constitutes a possible ground of divorce.

Before the rise of the modern feminist movement, Christian ethicists and theologians rarely suggested that a battered wife had the right to divorce her husband, even if her life were in danger. It was more or less assumed that since the man was the head of the house, if a woman were physically abused, she must be doing something to provoke her husband. In fact, those who listen most to the stories told by battered women and talk most to the men who batter them, testify that even down to the present day a fundamental issue is the place of authority over the woman that society has assigned the man and taught him to exercise in the name of his masculinity. Given such a social context, many men who batter their wives do not feel they are doing anything especially wrong, though at times they may be visited with remorse. As a result, the home has become for many women anything but a shelter from the pervasive, institutionalized violence she suffers covertly in a patriarchal society. Indeed, for some, the home has become the maelstrom of that violence in such an overt way that it threatens to destroy them. The evidence of such abuse is often hidden from view by the embarrassment and fear of reprisal that the victims feel and by the sanctity of the home, which shrouds what happens behind its doors with a mantle of privacy. But when a woman's well-being, emotional and even physical, is threatened so that she is not safe in her own home, what is she to do? Where is she to go? These are not hysterical outbursts of some bleeding hearts, but sober questions that the church cannot ignore.

Some evangelicals who are "pro-family" seek to make a bagatelle of this issue, reminding women that they can attain Christian fulfillment only by submitting to their husbands in everything (Eph. 5:24); that the Scripture (Eph. 5:33) does not say that the wife should "reverence her husband only if he deserves to be reverenced"; and that by submitting to their husbands under oppressive circumstance, women learn what it means to "suffer for righteousness' sake." (See the "Special Report" of the *Quarterly Report of People for the American Way,* Jan. 1982, pp. 3-4; also Scanzoni and Wells, "Make Sure Your Counselor Is a Feminist," *Daughters of Sarah* 6, no. 3: 8-9.) Others, more commendably, have sought to help women by providing shelters (since the 1970s) for those who have no other place to go. Still others advocate therapy, which may prove to be helpful in cases where treatment at the hands of a skilled practitioner is maintained over a sufficient time.

But in many cases only release from the marriage bond will relieve the woman's trauma. (See Philip Brasfield, "Stranger to Our Town," *The Other Side* [Sept.-Oct. 1990]: 18-19. Brasfield recalls from his childhood days the first attack on his sister Julia, who had been married less than a year. "Suddenly there was screaming, and Julia was running across the rutted, muddy street. Her clothes were in tatters; her face a nearly unrecognizable mask of swollen, bloody terror.") In a recent document entitled "Heritage of Violence," issued by the Social Affairs Committee of the Quebec Assembly of Catholic Bishops, some who speak for the Catholic Church have, for the first time, come remarkably close to acknowledging the inevitability of the divorce option in such cases. The document (in a working draft) deplores the fact that the Catholic Church is "sacrificing people to maintain the marriage bond." It goes on to say that "the unlimited and often unconditional forgiveness and perpetual reconciliation" that women are urged to offer "in the name of a mystical state . . . is very difficult to attain. There are cases where the marriage bond no longer makes any sense." Upon reading this document, one Catholic sociologist expressed astonishment that the Catholic Church would admit even an indirect role in aiding and abetting wife battering. "I've been told that some priests would warn battered wives, threatening to leave their husbands, that they would . . . go to hell if they broke their marriage vows and ended their marriage" ("Events and People," *Christian Century* 107, no. 4 [Jan. 31, 1990]: 95-96).

As we seek to evaluate the case for granting divorce on the grounds of incompatibility, we pause to recall what we have already said about marriage as an *ongoing relationship*. The unity of marriage, we have argued, is not simply a matter of what one does with one's sex organs. It is rather a lifelong, personal fellowship of an all-encompassing nature. As the ideal of oneness is achieved over the years, each partner becomes more and more congruous with the other, so that the life of each is fulfilled as life together. Although youthful passion subsides and eros mellows, love does not die; rather it matures, probing ever greater depths of meaning, expressing itself in ever new and manifold ways. Thus the initial decision and choice on which marriage rests is confirmed and strengthened.

But in a world where sin is at work, the very malleability of the marriage relationship means that as it develops and changes, it can move not only in the direction of the creation ideal, but away from it until it is a very parody of that ideal; indeed, its utter antithesis. As a result, in due time people whose lives are joined in holy wedlock find themselves living in holy deadlock. To be sure, we should not add to Scripture, when confronted with such situations, and say that what God did not join together, the church should now put asunder. Yet we must acknowledge that there are times when we cannot doubt that those whom the church assumed God had joined together seem now to have put themselves asunder. Instead of feeling inadequate without each other, some married couples can no longer stand each other. Their life together is not mutually fulfilling but mutually destructive.[181] Adultery or desertion may not be in the picture; but there

---

181. The seventeenth-century Puritan Thomas Gouge had a quaint piece of advice to help married couples avoid such mutual destruction: "And, therefore, I would commend this rule to married persons: be aware of both being angry together, but rather let one be to the other like David's harp to Saul's fury" (quoted in Bainton, *What Christianity Says About Sex*, pp. 98-99). The trouble with this otherwise delightful analogy is that the last time David played his harp before Saul, the king nearly shafted him with his spear (1 Sam. 18:10-11; 19:9-10).

can be no doubt that the partners in marriage are, in the language of our discussion, utterly incompatible.

Incompatibility should not be confused with the inevitable tension that is built into any union of two free and autonomous selves. Marriage is an encounter between an I and a thou in which, for all its intimacy, the I remains I and the thou remains thou. Marriage, therefore, will surely involve a clash of two wills at some level. But the mutuality of love, which moves two people to plight their troth, produces an ever-increasing tranquility of spirit that is deeper than any disparity of wills that two people bring to the marriage union. When we speak of incompatibility, by contrast, we are talking about a situation where the distinction of wills becomes a proud and selfish autonomy of wills that makes fellowship impossible.

The first major apology for divorce on the grounds of incompatibility was Milton's tract, *The Doctrine and Discipline of Divorce.*[182] In this tract the author points out that the Creator's first word was, "It is not good for man to be alone." "In God's intention, a meet and happy conversation is the chiefest and noblest end of marriage." "The chief society [in marriage], therefore, is in the soul rather than in the body; and the greatest breach thereof is unfitness of mind rather than defect of body." "It is no blessing but a torment, nay a base and brutish condition, to be one flesh, unless where nature can in some measure fix and unite the disposition." "What a violent and cruel thing it is to force the continuing of those together whom God and nature in the gentlest end of marriage never joined." He who missed the true end of marriage "by chancing on a mute and spiritless mate remains more alone than before." "Suppose he erred. It is not the intent of God or man to hunt an error so to the death with a revenge beyond all measure and proportion."[183]

The concept of incompatibility can, indeed, be used frivolously. It has been so used from the time of Hillel, who, in the first century, allowed a man to divorce his wife for burning the food. But the traditional

182. London, 1643, much enlarged in the 2nd ed., 1644. In 1643 Milton had married Mary Powell. She was seventeen and he thirty-five. A more perfect mismatch could hardly be conceived. He was already a recognized man of letters; she, a country lass who left him for the convivial life of her former country home within the first year of marriage. Although she eventually returned, it was not before Milton had written his tract, which brought an angry response from the members of the Long Parliament and the Westminster Assembly of Divines.

183. The above quotations are drawn from a larger compendium in Bainton, *What Christianity Says About Sex,* pp. 100-102. The full text may be found in *The Works of John Milton,* vol. 3, part 2 (New York: Columbia University Press, 1931), pp. 369-511. For a comment on Milton's argument that one may be more alone after marriage than before, see Charlotte Mew, "The Farmer's Bride," in Untermeyer, ed., *Great Poems,* pp. 1063-64.

approach that allows only specific offenses — adultery, desertion, and so on — can be used legalistically. And it has been so used in a way that substitutes judgment for mercy and inflicts suffering without redemptive purpose.[184] The frivolous mind knows only choices and does not acknowledge that there are moral and immoral choices. The legalistic mind knows only moral and immoral choices, and does not acknowledge that there are *tragic* moral choices. But life confronts one with such choices, choices that are tragic just because they are moral and moral even though they are tragic. (One does not speak of a tragic *im*moral choice.) A failed marriage is a case in point, since it confronts one with such a tragic moral choice. To choose divorce is to acknowledge failure in the form of a wrong choice that cannot now be undone — but only repented of.[185] But then, repentance and forgiveness and the opportunity to begin life anew is what the gospel is all about.

We conclude our discussion of the failure of marriage and the dissolution of the marriage bond with a brief word concerning the distinction commonly made between the "innocent" and the "guilty" party. While we have not approached the divorce question in terms of this distinction, we do not mean thereby to suggest that it is without merit. Obviously the Pauline privilege (1 Cor. 7:15) supposes the relative innocence of the believing sister or brother abandoned by an unbelieving spouse. But it is all too easy, when it comes to divorce, to use the categories of innocence and guilt in a way that turns the gray ambiguities of life into black-and-white simplicities. No doubt in many failed marriages the primary blame can be easily fixed. And yet, while there may be villains in such marriages, there are few heroes. Milton's wife deserted him; he did not desert her. But surely there is fault on his side. His failure to anticipate the problems with his marriage is both egregious and culpable. We applaud Wesley for patient forbearance in the midst of his marital woes. But was he justified in his conviction that he should continue his travels without the slightest abridgment after his marriage, in spite of his wife's sentiments, even quoting Scripture to the effect that the emissaries of the Lord who have wives should live as though they had none (1 Cor. 7:29)? As it takes two people to make a marriage, so, more often than not, it takes two to break it. We have chosen, therefore, in our treatment of divorce to stress the need for repentance on the part of those who acknowledge they must leave a marriage, and compassion on the part of the church toward those who make such a decision.

184. One has only to recall the suffering, mentioned above, that battered women and abused children have been made to endure.

185. On divorce seen as a tragic moral choice, we would make the following comment. A tragedy is an event involving misfortune, suffering, and misery for those who are overtaken by it because they cannot escape from it. When one chooses to leave a marriage, we call it a *tragic* moral choice because it is a choice arising out of a former choice (to enter the marriage relationship) that has now become one's destiny.

6. CONCERNING HOMOSEXUALITY: AN EXTENDED ADDENDUM[186]

a. Introduction

In the foregoing discussion we have simply assumed that the bond of marriage is heterosexual in nature. The love that moves two people to enter into the marriage covenant involves "a gripping desire for someone of the opposite sex." Marriage is not simply an I-thou encounter, but an I-thou encounter in which the eyes of a man meet the eyes of a woman in a way that speaks the silent rhetoric of mutual love. This is the love, we have argued, celebrated in the Song of Songs, a love in which the beloved is enraptured with the beauty of *his* lover; and his lover — "faint with love" — likens *her* beloved to a "bundle of myrrh, resting between my breasts."

When two such lovers plight their troth and are thus united in the bonds of matrimony, such an act, we have further argued, rests on what God has done as Creator. In the beginning, he gave us our humanity in the polarity of maleness and femaleness. Indeed, one may construe the Song of Songs as an elaboration on an original theme of Scripture, namely, the jubilant delight with which the man first received the gift that the Creator gave him; a gift, not of another *man,* but of a *woman,* that they might share life together as male and female.[187] Hence, at the outset of our discussion, we defined marriage as a relationship between "a man and a woman who freely choose out of love for each other to enter into an ongoing, exclusive, and lasting relationship based on a mutual promise of fidelity."[188] Should we have placed an asterisk at the end of this definition? Should we have said in a footnote, at least, that in some cases "a man and a man" or "a woman and a woman" may freely make such a choice out of love for each other? If one answers yes, on what basis could one make such a statement, given the evangelical perspective we have brought to the theological enterprise, a perspective that views the Scripture as normative for faith and life? If one answers no, then what should one say about homosexual relationships? Do such relationships constitute a perversion of the Creator's intent in giving us our humanity in a sexual polarity? Is homosexuality a sin of the deepest dye because it is a sin against nature *(peccatum contra naturum),* as the church has traditionally taught? Or is there some middle

---

186. In the ensuing discussion we understand "homosexuality" to mean: a distinct psychosexual phenomenon that implies the same sort of strong and spontaneous capacity to be erotically aroused by members of one's own sex as heterosexuality implies in relation to members of the opposite sex. Taken from Ralph Blair, *Hope's Gays and Gay's Hopes* (New York: HCCC, 1983), p. 2, and based on the definition of Judd Marmor, past president, the American Psychiatric Association.

187. See above, pp. 205-9.

188. See above, pp. 190-92.

ground, some via media, consonant with Scripture, that neither blesses such relationships unreservedly nor condemns them implacably?

However we may be inclined to answer these questions, we need first to listen. We need to hear what has been traditionally said — the No! of the church. We also need to hear what is being presently said, the Yes! of many gay and lesbian people, some of whom are confessing Christians who accept their homosexual orientation as the gift of the Creator. As we embark on this task of listening, a word on methodology would seem to be in order.

In our prolegomenon we described our theological approach as "orthodox" in that it is rooted in the old catholic tradition and the Protestant Reformation, particularly the Genevan Reformation. Yet our effort to frame an orthodox theology is consciously done in the context of life and thought in the modern world. Such orthodoxy we have called "contextualized" orthodoxy because it is an orthodoxy that seeks to listen as well as to affirm (See *God, Creation, and Revelation,* p. 16). When it comes to the question of sexual orientation, it is safe to say that the traditional orthodoxy has been more prone to affirm than ready to listen. And this affirmation, so far as same-sex orientation is concerned, has been one of all but universal condemnation: homosexuality is a perversion of our humanity, and homosexual acts are acts "against nature."

Today this judgment is being challenged in a way that chastens traditional confidence and calls for listening on the part of the theologian. Such theological listening involves a theologian's methodology. When she listens, her way of doing theology determines what she hears; and what she hears determines the conclusions she reaches. This is especially true when it comes to difficult questions like the one before us. Hence this brief aside on our own theological method.

Assuming that the truths of science and of theology are ultimately the one truth of the one God, we have rejected the thought that science and theology are necessarily related in an adversarial way because of their differing methodologies. Yet we have acknowledged that theology is first of all (and last of all) concerned with what God says, not with what "science says." Our openness, therefore, to the conclusions some have drawn in the name of modern scientific thought about God, the world, and our place in the world is by no means unqualified. The history of dogmatics painfully illustrates how efforts to restate the Christian faith in the interest of making it "relevant to modern thought" can end up with the loss of that faith. Too often accommodation has turned out to be capitulation.

To avoid such a fatal mistake, we have suggested an approach that may be pictured in terms of concentric circles around the center of a target. (See *God, Creation, and Revelation,* pp. 21ff.) At the personal center are those truths of revelation — God's disclosure of himself as the personal God who is reconciled to the sinner in Jesus Christ — truths that Christians accept by faith. It is in the light of these truths that Christians understand who they are as personal selves and what they are called to be as the people of God. But as we move out from this personal center, the truths with which we are concerned are increasingly impersonal and objective, truths that we discover for ourselves. And the more impersonal and objective these truths are, the more competent is reason in evaluating them and the less necessary is the corrective of faith.

Faith is always essential to a Christian Weltanschauung; but, to give an example, when it comes to questions of astrophysics, what a believing astronomer sees when she looks through a telescope does not differ objectively from what a nonbeliever sees. (Knowing by intuition that this was so, some bishops execrated Galileo's telescope as an abominable instrument of the Devil and would not so much as look through it.) However, when it comes to the question, Is homosexuality consonant with the will of the Creator? it is evident that the situation differs. One could wish that the answer to such a question were as objective as is the answer to the question, Does the earth revolve around the sun? One might even wish for that measure of objectivity with which one answers the question, Did *Homo sapiens* evolve from a common ancestry with the apes? But to claim such objectivity would obviously be to embrace a chimera. All questions pertaining to our sexuality have to do with who we are and how we understand ourselves, not as objects but as subjects; how we understand ourselves, that is, at the very core of our being as persons. Such questions cannot be reduced, therefore, to physical, biological objectivity. In other words, the answer we seek to the question of homosexuality involves a maximum interpenetration of reason and faith.

The Christian, then, has no simple way to relate the data of revelation to what present-day psychologists and sociologists are saying about homosexuality. In fact, those who speak for the behavioral sciences do not always agree on the subject even among themselves. Hence the challenge to the church to reconsider its attitude toward homosexuality is one that confronts the theologian with many issues that are neither black nor white, but gray. And the several resolutions suggested are often wanting in clear definition and fraught with ambiguity.

Speaking of objectivity and subjectivity, when Sigmund Freud invited certain persons to his home to discuss his new ideas on neuroses (1902), the Vienna Psychoanalytic Society was born. Shortly, however, rivalries and quarrels broke out and splinter groups were formed. Excommunications took place, the first major apostate being Alfred Adler, who left the fold in 1911. In 1912 Carl Jung broke with Freud. (See Arno Karlen, *Sexuality and Homosexuality: A New View* [New York: Norton, 1971], pp. 284-85.) Such divisions of the house are inevitable, given the nature of the "soft" sciences; and they remain with us down to the present day. In 1973, for example, when the American Psychiatric Association voted to expunge homosexuality from its official list of mental illnesses, some 40 percent of its own members protested. The question, Who was right? is not what concerns us at the moment, but the fact that a vote was taken in the first place. Imagine the American Medical Association voting on whether cancer is an illness or debating the normalcy of paralysis.

b. The Traditional Case Against Homosexuality in the Teaching of the Church[189]

While homosexuality is not discussed extensively by the Fathers of the early church, whenever the subject is mentioned, it is condemned without

189. Since we are seeking to frame a theological anthropology from a Christian and evangelical point of view, we shall not be concerned with the findings of cultural anthropology bearing on acceptance or rejection of homosexuality in those societies untouched by Christian thought.

qualification. Especially abominable are "frenzies of lust" (Tertullian) between men and men or between men and boys. "Chrysostom, in one of his sermons, inveighs against the paederasts who come to church to look with lustful curiosity upon handsome youths."[190] And Basil warns youthful converts to the monastic life to exercise every precaution against kindling illicit desires. Likewise, Augustine reminds nuns who are dedicated by a holy vow to Christ that the love they bear toward one another "ought not to be carnal but spiritual."[191]

The fundamental reason for the condemnation of homosexuality on the part of the Fathers is their conviction that all such desires and acts are sins against nature. Indeed, in the words of Tertullian such unnatural sins "are not sins so much as monstrosities." In the traditional polemic against homosexuality, this note is struck again and again. Homosexuality is a sin that not only feeds on "vile affections" (Rom. 1:26) but threatens the very existence of the human race itself by foreclosing the natural function of human sexuality, which is procreation. It is a sin, therefore, that constitutes an unpardonable affront both to nature and to nature's God. Fornication and adultery are bad, but they are at least natural; whereas "sodomy," as homosexuality was commonly called, not only offends against one's neighbor but transgresses the basic law of nature whereby our sexual life is to be governed. That law is the mutual congress of the sexes with a view to the preservation and increase of the race through procreation.

This natural law argument is taken up and elaborated by theologians in the Middle Ages. According to Thomas, while all sexual acts that exclude procreation are sins against nature, the sin of sodomy is, next to bestiality, the most grievous offense of all; it is not only a vice but an "unnatural" vice.[192] The Protestant Reformers are of the same opinion,[193] as one can see in the comment of Calvin on Romans 1:26-27, where Paul refers to men and women who exchange natural relations for unnatural ones, being inflamed with lust for one another. Expanding on this text, Calvin speaks

190. D. S. Bailey, *Homosexuality and the Western Christian Tradition* (London: Longmans, Green and Co., 1955), p. 83. In this place Bailey cites numerous original sources and goes on to review ecclesiastical legislation by which the church came officially to condemn those who were deemed guilty, not only of homosexuality but of perverse sexual passions and practices of all sorts.

191. *Ep.* 211.14, as cited by Bailey, ibid., p. 85. Such express prohibitions of lesbianism are infrequent in the sources. Its condemnation, however, is entailed in that of male homosexuality.

192. *Summa Theologica*, pt. 2-2, q. 154, art. 11, 12.

193. We do not mean to suggest that the Reformers embraced anything like a full-blown natural theology; simply that they condemned homosexuality for essentially the same reason the Scholastics had condemned it.

darkly of "the dreadful crime of unnatural lust." It appears, he says, that those who are guilty of such an offense have "not only abandoned themselves to beastly lusts, but became degraded beyond the beasts, since they reversed the whole order of nature."[194] Theologians have reiterated this argument in one form or another down to the present day. For example, in the light of his concept of humanity as cohumanity, manifest in the sexual polarity of man and woman, Barth calls homosexuality a perversion, a kind of inhumanity that seeks masculinity in freedom from the woman and femininity in freedom from the man. Such an approach leads to "transgressions against nature" *(widernaturlichen Vergehungen)*, which are obviously contrary to God's holy commandment.[195] Expounding the Christian interpretation of sex, Otto Piper affirms that homosexuality

> contradicts the very meaning of sex. When one of the two persons in such a case undertakes or attempts to undertake the sex function of a person of the other sex, this does not lead to any understanding of what manhood and womanhood signify to each other; rather, the case is repugnant to sense in so far as they do something for which they do not possess the natural qualifications.[196]

Piper's observation that homosexuals "do something for which they do not possess the natural qualifications" sounds a note, as we have observed, that is frequently heard in the traditional polemic of the church. In the teaching of the church, intercourse has been so universally associated with procreation as means to end that coitus in the precise sense of penetrating the vagina with the penis has been regarded as the only "natural" use of the sex organs. In present-day manuals on marriage and sexual techniques, however, other forms of physical contact, such as oral-genital sex, are not only allowed but recommended as ways of making love. Unless one holds that sexual acts must always be open to the possibility of procreation — a view we have rejected — there would seem to be no ground for condemning such other forms of sexual intimacy. (For our comments on the personal quality of the marriage relationship and our defense of

194. *Commentary on Romans,* trans. and ed. John Owen (reprint, Grand Rapids: Eerdmans, 1961), pp. 78-79. See also his comment on the sinners that are mentioned by Paul in 1 Cor. 6:9, the ἀρσενοκοῖται ("abusers of themselves with mankind" [KJV]; "sodomites" [NRSV]; "homosexual offenders" [NIV]). This sin, he says, is "the most serious of all, viz. that unnatural and filthy thing which was far too common in Greece."

195. *KD,* III/4, pp. 184-85 (cf. *CD,* III/4, p. 166). Barth in this place also uses the word "sickness" *(Krankheit)* to describe homosexuality, which shows that his vocabulary, at least, has been affected by the contemporary discussion. There is surely some distance between "vile affections" (Thomas) and "sickness."

196. *The Christian Interpretation of Sex* (New York: Scribner's, 1953), p. 143. Piper's charge that homosexual acts are "repugnant to sense" echoes Thomas's argument, *Summa Theologica,* pt. 2-2, q. 154, art. 11, that such acts are a form of lust because they are "contrary to right reason."

birth control, see above, pp. 222-28, and pp. 236-40.) Sex, even in the physical sense, is more than phallic penetration. The brain, after all, is the basic sex organ; and erotic pleasure is a basic aspect of sexual intimacy.

In view of such considerations, some have argued that the expression of physical intimacy on the part of a homosexual couple need not differ from that of a heterosexual couple. The basic issue is the genuineness of the mutual love and commitment expressed through such acts, whether one's partner be of the same or of the opposite sex. While this argument has some plausibility about it so far as lesbian acts of love are concerned, it is less plausible when it comes to male relationships. Copulation *per anum,* which is widely practiced by males who are gay, is an act that many heterosexuals find revolting at the visceral level. The bodily incongruity involved in such an act fortifies this revulsion and reinforces the notion that such intercourse is unnatural. Of course many would find the masochism and sadism practiced by heterosexuals likewise revolting. But no one has ever argued that such acts of kinky sex are a proper use of the Creator's gifts. In any event, when practiced on a regular basis, anal intercourse leads to anorectal disorders — hemorrhoids, fissures, venereal warts — earlier in life than is usual for heterosexuals. (See Karlen, *Sexuality and Homosexuality,* p. 196. In this place Karlen reports that 50 percent of gay men say they do not enjoy the passive role in intercourse but submit as a favor to their partners.)

Whereas theologians have condemned homosexuality as contrary to the act of the Creator in making humankind male and female (Gn. 1:27; 2:18-24), the traditional popular Christian response to those who are erotically attracted to members of their own sex has been most dramatically shaped not by the inference theologians have drawn from the creation narratives, but by the graphic account of the wickedness and judgment of Sodom (Gn. 18:16–19:29). Here we have to do not with definitions and inferences but with a gripping narrative full of drama from beginning to end; here we have a piece of story theology that has made an enormous impression on the popular mind. Sodom is a city so wicked (13:13) that even the intercession of an Abraham cannot save it. Warned of its impending destruction, righteous Lot and his family barely escape the carnage as the Lord rains down fire and brimstone from heaven on the city of the damned. And the baneful glow of Sodom's destruction still burns in popular imagination; the smoking ruins that Abraham saw the next morning when he surveyed the cities of the Plain still smolder in the eyes of many as they seek to chart their moral course in today's world.[197]

The impact of the Sodom and Gomorrah story can be seen in the way it has indelibly marked our language. "Sodomy," from the Latin *sodomia,* used to describe unnatural

---

197. The ghastly story of the Levite and his concubine, as told in Jgs. 19, is in many ways parallel to that of Sodom and Gomorrah and has been interpreted accordingly in the tradition of the church.

intercourse, first appears in the *Oxford English Dictionary* in the 1300s. Loosely speaking, every expression of sexual behavior deemed contrary to nature has been reprobated as "sodomy." However, the word refers primarily to the practice of anal intercourse because (supposedly) this is what the men of Sodom had in mind when they demanded that they might "know" Lot's visitors. In this strict sense of anal intercourse, sodomy is practiced by prisoners, soldiers, and others. A "sodomite," therefore, may be heterosexual in orientation. Such persons are sometimes said to be "circumstantially homosexual." As for the term "homosexual," it was coined by a Hungarian physician (Karoly Benkert) in 1869, though it did not become common usage until some time later. It describes one who is erotically attracted to persons of the same sex.

Although it may have a considerable historical pedigree, the word "gay" has only recently been used to describe persons who are homosexual. Significantly, "gay" is the word that people who are conscious of their same-sex orientation have increasingly chosen to describe themselves, since it means "merry or happy in a lively fashion" in contrast to "maladjusted, miserable, and neurotic." While the term may be used of males and females, as in the phrase "the gay community," it is sometimes restricted to males, as in the phrase "gays and lesbians." "Lesbian," the word generally used to describe women who are conscious of their same-sex orientation, is taken from "Lesbos" (now Mytilene), the island that was home to Sappho, the most celebrated woman poet of Greek antiquity. Her homosexuality has been masked by the traditional editing of her more overtly erotic lines.

Aside from the story of Sodom and Gomorrah, the Old Testament as a whole has little to say about homosexuality. But what it does say is congruous with the traditional understanding of the Sodom and Gomorrah story. In Leviticus 18:22 we read, "You shall not lie with a male as with a woman; it is an abomination"; and in 20:13, "If a man lies with a male as with a woman, both of them have committed an abomination; they shall be put to death, their blood is upon them."

Along with these two passages from the Holiness Code, some others in the Old Testament are often mentioned, passages in which the question of homosexuality has become intertwined with the larger question of cult prostitution (Dt. 23:17; 1 Kgs. 14:22-24; 15:12, 13; 22:41, 43, 46; 2 Kgs. 23:6, 7; Hos. 4:12-14). It is in these passages that the words קָדֵשׁ ("male shrine prostitute") and קְדֵשָׁה ("female shrine prostitute") occur. The KJV translates the former "sodomite" and the latter "whore." These translations are misleading in that they have fostered the assumption that the male shrine prostitutes were homosexuals. But the fact that there were male as well as female cult prostitutes does not entail such a conclusion. What could be the purpose of homosexual acts in the practice of the *fertility* cults? Such acts have nothing to do with fertility. Most likely, one of the tasks of male shrine prostitutes was to serve women (for a fee) who were barren and who hoped to remove their reproach by resorting to intercourse with a "holy man." (See Bailey, *Homosexuality*, p. 52.) To be sure, those prophets, priests, and kings in Israel who were zealous worshipers of Yahweh detested and abominated these fertility cult rituals and sought to exterminate all shrine prostitutes from the land. This is understandable, for if prostitution is sinful, it becomes exceedingly sinful when joined with the worship of a Canaanite fertility goddess, like Asherah or Astarte, on the part of those whose covenant obligation was to worship the one true God. It is unfortunate, however, in the extreme, to include gays and lesbians in a common condemnation with these cult prostitutes who plied their trade "on every high hill and under every green tree" (Jer. 2:20) in ancient Israel.

Like the Old Testament, the New Testament has relatively little to say about homosexuality. But what is said has always been understood by the church as condemning both the disposition and the act as sinful. As we noted above, Paul's judgment (Rom. 1:26-27) against both men and women who exchange natural intercourse with those of the opposite sex for intercourse with those of the same sex has been taken as confirming the conclusion that homosexuality is revolting to nature itself, since it violates the divine intent in creating humankind as male and female. It is an expression of that "reprobate mind" to which God has abandoned those who reject him and give themselves to the worship of idols.[198] And the same conclusion has been drawn from the apostle's listing of male prostitutes (μαλακοί) and homosexual offenders (ἀρσενοκοῖται) among those who shall have no inheritance in the kingdom of God (1 Cor. 6:9).[199]

c. The Traditional Attitude Shown Toward Homosexuals in the Life of the Church (and in Society)

Having heard the No! to homosexuality on the part of the theologians and having reviewed the way in which they have confirmed this No! by their understanding of Scripture, one might expect that we should now listen to the Yes! with which increasing numbers in our day affirm their homosexuality as consistent with a Christian understanding of what it means to be human. For the present, however, such listening must defer to another task, namely, a reflection on the *attitude* that the teaching of the church has fostered and the behavior that this attitude has evoked toward homosexual persons on the part of the Christian community.

198. Rom. 1:26-27 must be read in the context of Paul's condemnation of idolatry. Charles Hodge stresses this point when commenting on 1:18-23 in his well-known *Commentary on the Epistle to the Romans* (reprint, Grand Rapids: Eerdmans, 1955), pp. 41-42. Due to the time in which he wrote (1886), Hodge does not use the term "homosexual," but he does speak of "shameful lusts" and sins that are "peculiarly degrading," which makes eminently clear his understanding of the apostle's thought.

199. We shall review the question of the meaning of μαλακοί and the rare word ἀρσενοκοῖται, found only here and in 1 Tm. 1:10, when we look at the biblical data more closely.

Early on, as we began the task of making a Christian theological statement, we committed ourselves to the proposition that the end of all theology is morality (*God, Creation, and Revelation,* p. 20). We have come to a place where we must pause to reflect on this sometimes subtle but always essential relationship between the quest for truth and the practice of goodness. To illustrate our point, let us take a case sufficiently removed from the present to give perspective and obvious enough to carry conviction. We have in mind the Crusades, a spectacle the like of which the world has never seen. When Urban II, at the Council of Clermont (1095), called for the deliverance of Jerusalem — "the navel of the world" — from the Saracens, his sermon proved to be the most effectual ever preached. The conscience of Christendom was smitten and the chivalry of Europe aroused to repossess

> those holy fields
> Over whose acres walked those blessed feet
> Which fourteen hundred years ago were nail'd
> For our advantage on the bitter cross.
> (Shakespeare, *Henry IV, Part I,* lines 24-27)

This supposedly noble enterprise turned out to be one of the most lamentable chapters in Christian history. Thousands who set out with pious zeal were cut to pieces in the forests of Bulgaria; thousands more were massacred by the Turks in Asia Minor, and "their bones were piled into a ghastly pyramid, the first monument of the Crusade" (Schaff, *History,* 5.233). Others, on their way to the "Holy City," proceeded to pillage and slaughter the Jews of the Rhine Valley. Over three hundred thousand lives were lost before Jerusalem was so much as seen on the distant horizon. And when the city was taken, the conquest was a scene of savage butchery and slaughter against which neither the tears of women nor the cries of children were of any avail. Under the sign of the cross, the crusaders

> "cut down with the sword," said William of Tyre, "every one whom they found in Jerusalem, and spared no one. The victors were covered with blood from head to foot." In the next breath, speaking of the devotion of the Crusaders, the archbishop adds, "it was a most affecting sight which filled the heart with holy joy to see the people tread the holy places in the fervor of an excellent devotion." (Schaff, ibid., pp. 240-41, quoting William of Tyre)

When one asks the question, How could so many people be so devoutly yet disastrously misguided, much of the answer is to be found in the medieval mind. It was a mind deeply religious yet unbelievably credulous; superstitious and given to warlike barbarity when it came to infidels, Jews, and heretics. But one ingredient in the whole debacle — which is the point on which our discussion turns — was a faulty theology of space and place. The entire enterprise presupposed an Old Testament concept of holy space, which not only stirred the imagination of the common people but convinced the best theological minds of the church. As a consequence, the soul of Christendom could not tolerate the thought that the "holy land" should be occupied by the followers of the prophet Muhammad. The manger where our Lord had been laid, the ground on which he had trod, the hill where he had been crucified, the sepulcher where his body had reposed in death and been glorified in the resurrection — these holy places had to be delivered from the defiling feet of the infidel. It was as though Jesus had never said, "The hour is coming when neither on this mountain nor in Jerusalem will you worship the Father" (Jn. 4:21). How different might things have been had Urban, and those who heard him, espoused Milton's theology — "God attributes to place no sanctity if none be thither brought by men who there frequent or therein dwell" (*Paradise Lost*, bk. 11, lines 836-38). Had they brought to their deliberations such a theology of place, they might not have "confused the terrestrial with the celestial Jerusalem" and sought the living Christ in the tomb from which he had risen.

*   *   *   *   *

A more recent illustration of the relation between theology and morality is the experience of the young Karl Barth. In the Oct. 4, 1914, edition of the prestigious *Frankfurter Zeitung,* he read an open letter publicly defending the war policies of Kaiser Wilhelm II and bearing the signatures of ninety-three German intellectuals, "among which, to my utter amazement," he observes, "I perceived the names of virtually all my hithertofore trusted, honored, theological teachers. I could not but remark that having erred in their practice, I could no longer follow their dogmatics, their exegesis of the Bible and their representations of history." This, Barth continues, was the *dies ater* when he realized that the theology of the nineteenth century no longer had a future. (For Barth's later reflection on this letter, see *Evangelische Theologie im 19. Jahrhundert,* Theologische Studien 49 [Zollikon-Zurich: Evangelischer Verlag, 1957], p. 6.)

If the end of theology is morality, if truth is unto goodness, then the way in which the Christian community has related to gay people should give the theologian pause. It is here, in the area of attitude and behavior, that the first shadow of doubt falls over the teaching of the church concerning homosexuality. In this respect, as one reads the literature, one cannot but be struck by the vehemence and depth of feeling with which homosexuality is condemned. It is "an outrage on decency," a "detestable crime against nature," a "most shameful lust," a "peculiarly degrading sin," an "unnatural filthiness."[200] Even armed robbers, rapists, and serial killers do not provoke such emotionally surcharged language. The judge who pronounced sentence on Oscar Wilde declared:

> Oscar Wilde and Alfred Taylor, the crime of which you have been convicted is so bad that one has to put stern restraint upon one's self to protect one's self from describing, in language which I would rather

---

200. Lv. 18:22 speaks of a homosexual act as a תּוֹעֵבָה (abomination), which often parallels שִׁקּוּץ and שֶׁקֶץ. All three words denote that which is detestable and abhorrent, including everything from unclean animals to idols and idolatrous practices. Thus they are not reserved for homosexual sins exclusively but are also applied to offenses committed by heterosexuals.

not use, the sentiments which rise to the breast of every man of honour who has heard the details of these two terrible trials. . . . It is no use for me to address you. People who can do these things must be dead to all sense of shame, and one cannot hope to produce any effect upon them.[201]

Such an attitude of loathing gay people is wholly without warrant in Scripture. In fact, it rests on a distortion of the scriptural doctrine of sin, namely, the assumption that sexual sin is the worst sin and homosexuality the worst form of sexual sin. Against such a view we cannot but protest.[202] The sex lives of homosexuals are, no doubt, sinful, but so are the sex lives of heterosexuals. Even if one were to argue the traditional view that, in contrast to heterosexuals, homosexuals live a sexual life that is sinful per se, it would not follow that the sin of such persons is the most heinous of all sins. In the three New Testament passages (Rom. 1:26-27; 1 Cor. 6:9-10; 1 Tm. 1:10) that mention homosexual offenses, they are simply listed along with other sins, all of which are alike condemned. Were one to attempt a hierarchy (lowerarchy) of the vices mentioned in these passages, then idolatry, according to Romans 1, would be the basic sin, the sin of all sins.[203]

The distortion involved in the thought that homosexuality is the nadir of human depravity is highlighted by the chauvinistic form the argument has assumed from antiquity. Chrysostom reminds the one who is the passive partner in homosexual intercourse that "not only are you made into a woman, but you also cease to be a man; yet neither are you changed into that nature, nor do you retain the one you had." Both Augustine and Lactantius express similar revulsion at the thought of a man allowing his body to be used "as that of a woman," since, in Augustine's words, "the body of

---

201. Frank Harris, *Oscar Wilde: His Life and Confessions,* 2 vols. (29 Waverley Place, New York: printed and published by the author, 1916), 1.317-18. See also *Regina v. Wilde,* May 25, 1895; and the discussion in Karlen, *Sexuality and Homosexuality,* p. 254.

202. For our rejection of the view that sexual sins somehow embrace and epitomize all seven deadly sins, see above, pp. 262-66. Speaking of this distortion of scriptural doctrine, one is reminded of G. K. Chesterton's warning as to the consequences of such distortion: "If some small mistake were made [by the church] in doctrine, huge blunders might be made in human happiness. . . . A slip in the definitions might stop all the dances; might wither all the Christmas trees or break all the Easter eggs" (*Orthodoxy,* p. 100).

203. The notion that a homosexual act is of all offenses the most sinful is behind the legal notion that such an act is a capital crime. In his authoritative *Commentaries on the Laws of England,* 4 vols. (London, 1826), W. B. Blackstone speaks of homosexuality as a crime against nature which "the voice of nature and reason, and the express law of God determine, to be capital." He appeals to the destruction of Sodom as prior to the Jewish dispensation and therefore exemplifying a universal, not a provincial, precept. See Bailey, *Homosexuality,* p. 153.

a man is as superior to that of a woman as the soul is to the body." (See John Boswell, *Christianity, Social Tolerance, and Homosexuality* [Chicago: University of Chicago Press, 1980], pp. 361-62 and 157, quoting Chrysostom's *Commentary on Romans,* Homily 4, and Augustine's *Contra mendacium,* 7.10.)

* * * * *

One distortion leads to another. It is commonly supposed that assuming cross-identity in the explicitly sexual aspect of gender roles means that homosexuals are effeminate. They can be recognized, therefore, by their mincing gait, languishing eyes, and honeyed voice, along with their proneness to foppery and dandyism. While such personality traits are found in some homosexuals, they are also found in some heterosexuals. Hence such stereotyping is palpably unfair. Nor can it be justified by an appeal to 1 Cor. 6:9, a passage in which the apostle excludes the μαλαχοί from the kingdom of God. Most likely Paul has in mind young men and boys (catamites) who function as male prostitutes by allowing themselves to be used for homosexual purposes. We are not suggesting for a moment that such a lifestyle is acceptable to God. We are simply protesting that it is no more just to suppose that all homosexuals are like these male prostitutes than it is to suppose that all heterosexuals are like the πόρνοι (fornicators) and μοιχοί (adulterers) who are also excluded from the kingdom in this very same verse.

* * * * *

Speaking of fornication and adultery, it is often assumed that the heterosexual character of such sins mitigates, if it does not atone for, their culpability. Such offenses are, after all, "natural." But are they? If to be human is to enjoy fellowship with God and neighbor, if this is the "nature" of the life the Creator has given us, then what shall we say of those broken marriages in which fellowship is destroyed by the infidelities of the adulterer? What of the unwanted children brought into the world by the fornicator and abandoned to the cruelties of a life without love? In the light of these blighting effects on human life, such heterosexual sins appear to us to be anything but "natural." Those who argue that homosexuals have also broken marriage covenants and left children must remember that often homosexuals entered into marriage for the wrong reason. They embraced the ill-advised notion that through marriage they might alter their sexual orientation and so gain acceptance in the Christian community and in society as a whole.

The attitude of loathing from which gay people have suffered as the foulest sinners is reflected in the many defaming epithets with which they have been loaded. They have been castigated as "queers," "fags," and "freaks"; they have been accused of a practice "so foul that it is unknown even among animals."[204] And this attitude of abhorrence has, unfortunately,

204. Those who have condemned homosexuality as "unnatural" have often affirmed that same-sex bonding is unknown in the animal kingdom. As a matter of fact, the evidence does not warrant this conclusion. Homosexual behavior and pair bonding have been observed among animals both in the wild and in captivity. A recent (1990) program in the "Nature"

led to the abuse of homosexuals in those societies influenced by the Christian church in a way that goes well beyond the denigration of name-calling.[205] While it would take us far afield even to summarize the story of their inhumane treatment, we must speak at least a brief word of protest against the abuse of gay and lesbian people and the denial of their civil rights even down to the present day. The most notable case is the blatant effort of the Nazis in World War II to exterminate homosexuals as degenerates who were a threat to the Aryan race. Homosexuals were made to wear pink triangles, just as Jews had to wear the yellow star of David. Heinrich Himmler gave the order (1936) that all homosexuals should be sent to level three camps, that is, death camps. It is estimated that as many as five hundred thousand may have perished, one of the largest groups after the Jews. But although homosexuals suffered a common fate with the Jews, there was a unique pathos in their suffering. We say this because in the extremity of the hunted Jews, at least a few righteous Gentiles hid them; but no one reached out a helping hand to the despised homosexual.[206] Even after the nightmare was over, the difference remained. Whereas the Jewish Holocaust evoked a universal cry of horror and shame, the brutal extermination of the gay community elicited no tears, no mea culpas, no efforts to compensate the survivors. Indeed, since the survivors were still regarded as criminals under German law, they could not protest for fear of further reprisals. Moreover, they not only suffered, but for want of family ties they suffered alone, as isolated individuals, without the help of sympathetic friends and relatives.[207]

Even down to the present day, the dark cloud of bigotry has not lifted altogether from the gay community. The National Gay and Lesbian Task Force notes that in 1989 more than seven thousand hate crimes against

---

series on public television, concerned with the nesting habits of sea gulls, showed a female pair of gulls maintaining their nest and sitting on the unfertilized eggs in the same manner as heterosexual pairs. See George and Molly Hunt, "Female-Female Pairing in Western Gulls *(Larus occidentalis)* in Southern California," *Science* 196 (1977): 81-83. Six years earlier (1971), Karlen affirmed, with apodictic finality, "There is no homosexual behaviour among birds. Males do not copulate" *(Sexuality and Homosexuality,* p. 391) — as though what the male does or does not do is what the species does or does not do.

205. What we speak of is commonly called "homophobia," meaning, etymologically, "fear of that which is the same or similar." Since our discussion centers not so much on the fear as on the abhorrence it produces, and since homosexuals are not the same as heterosexuals but different from them with respect to that which engenders the phobia, we have chosen not to employ this term.

206. See Boswell, *Christianity, Social Tolerance, and Homosexuality,* p. 16.

207. See John McNeill, *The Church and the Homosexual* (Kansas City, Kans.: Sheed Andrews and McMeel, 1976), p. 82. Also ibid., p. 204 n. 91, for sources in English and German on gay genocide. A committee of concerned citizens plans to build a monument in Amsterdam in honor of these forgotten victims of the Nazi terror.

homosexuals were reported in the United States, including sixty-two murders.[208] Such gay bashings, ranging from harassment to homicide, can hardly be trivialized as so many pranks. Even in prison, gays and lesbians are victimized. The city of Los Angeles segregates inmates, not to protect heterosexual prisoners from the "perverts" but to protect homosexual prisoners from neo-Nazi gang members, skinheads, satanists, and so-called homophobes.[209]

The traditional aversion toward homosexuals manifested in church and society bears on the double lives homosexuals have lived, lives of secrecy and fear in which their familiar faces mask rather than reveal their true selves.[210] Given the attitude that has been dominant in the church throughout most of its history, one could easily assume that such lives exemplify the truth of Jesus' words that sinners love darkness rather than light because their deeds are evil. Such people will not come to the light lest their evil deeds be made manifest (Jn. 3:19-21). Another view, which considers itself more contemporary and sophisticated, speaks not of sin but of sickness. Homosexuals are emotionally damaged people, neurotic, shallow, and irresponsible. Hence, because they are misfits in society, they lead clandestine, double lives. Howard Brown, having abandoned his Christian upbringing, tells of how he naively hoped to find healing on the psychiatrist's couch and how this hope was dashed:

> Psychiatry used different terminology from that of religion to condemn me, but the condemnation was just as devastating. I was no longer a sinner, but a psychopathic inferior and moral defective. In the later stages of therapy I was privileged to learn that, as a homosexual, I was narcissistic and incapable of love. If love was the ultimate human good, and one could never love, then one was doomed to a hell in this life. I certainly felt I was.[211]

Observing that such textbook deliveries on homosexual maladies are based on case histories of sick individuals, Brown (ibid., p. 220, citing "Homosexuality," in *The Same Sex: An Appraisal of Homosexuality,* ed. Ralph W. Weltge [Philadelphia and Boston: Pilgrim, 1969], p. 13) quotes a comment by psychiatrist Wardell Pomeroy: "If my concept of homosexuality were developed from my practice, I would probably concur

208. *Los Angeles Times,* June 8, 1990, p. A22. More crimes were committed than were reported; we can be sure of that.

209. *Los Angeles Times,* Dec. 27, 1990, p. B1.

210. See Howard Brown, *Familiar Faces, Hidden Lives* (New York: Harcourt Brace Jovanovich, 1976). Brown, a prominent physician, was the chief administrator of all health services in New York City under Mayor John Lindsay.

211. Ibid., p. 181.

in thinking of it as an illness. . . . On the other hand, if my concept of marriage . . . were based on my practice, I would have to conclude that marriages were all fraught with strife and conflict, and that heterosexuality is an illness."

Doubly condemned as sick and sinful, it is no wonder that many homosexuals have believed (and many still believe) the worst concerning themselves. Condemning themselves to a life of private and secret shame, they become invisible, and their invisibility has enabled society as a whole to distance itself from them.[212] Thus society has remained ignorant of the fact that gays and lesbians are not all effeminate wimps and brawny dames of the sort that spend their days in gay bars and their nights in wanton orgies.

As for gay bars, from a Christian point of view there is surely nothing to commend the lifestyle of those who patronize such establishments. But in 1969 a gay bar in New York City became the theater for playing out a drama that marked the beginning of a social revolution. And it is, in our judgment, a social revolution that the church cannot ignore with impunity. We refer to the well-known confrontation at the Stonewall Inn (June 28, 1969) between New York City police and some four hundred gays, an event that has been called the "Lexington of the homosexual rights movement" and compared to Rosa Parks's refusal, back in 1955, to relinquish her seat to a white passenger on a Montgomery, Alabama, bus.

One night the New York City police routinely raided a bar catering to homosexuals. A South American exchange student, fearful of deportation if he were discovered, sought escape by leaping from a second-story window. He died in the attempt when he impaled himself on an iron-spiked fence. A few nights later, while the memory of this student's death was still fresh in everyone's mind, the police conducted another routine gay harassment raid, this time on the Stonewall Inn in Greenwich Village. The unexpected happened: instead of slinking into the night, gays for the first time joined in fighting back. Regrouping at a nearby square, the crowd exploded in frenetic fury and threw everything they could get their hands on at the police, who symbolized for them the oppressor. The riot, which lasted for two nights, broke the spell. The conspiracy of silence was over.

While the majority of Christians have been more spectators than movers in the wake of the Stonewall riots, they have not been able to ignore the issues raised. In fact, they have been increasingly compelled to change

212. This invisible life of gays and lesbians has been referred to as "living in the closet," an apt figure when one recalls the many references in literature to people hiding in closets and behind curtains when they do not want their presence known. By the same token, when homosexuals go public they are said to "come out of the closet."

their attitude toward homosexuals and to recognize the social implications of the revolution that the riots precipitated. That is, they have been brought to acknowledge that homosexuals have suffered gross injustices, injustices that the gay civil rights movement has rightly challenged.

Meanwhile, the movement has gained momentum as gays and lesbians have come out of the shadows into the light of public awareness and pressed for social acceptance. The effect has been dramatic on both sides. Nongays (the "normal majority") have been amazed (and in some instances shocked and angered) to learn that gay and lesbian people are everywhere: they sit behind editorial desks, consult at hospital beds, stand before the bar, manage large companies, and join learned societies. Not only are they musicians and hairdressers but also bankers, mechanics, farmers, policemen, professional athletes, and even clergy persons. Nongays have found these people to be among their friends, neighbors, and coworkers, and, yes, even in their own families.[213]

The emotional stress and mental anguish created by the discovery and disclosure of homosexuality in the inner circle of the nuclear family has been often chronicled and variously commented on. (See Brown, *Familiar Faces, Hidden Lives,* chap. 5, "Parents," pp. 68-82.) When it comes to Christian counseling and pastoral care for such families, evangelicals are divided. Some offer hope to heterosexual spouses and parents through prayer, and healing to homosexual spouses and children through repentance and trust in Christ. (See, for example, *Healing for the Homosexual* [Oklahoma City: Presbyterian Charismatic Communion, 1978].) Others advocate acceptance of homosexuality as one would accept left-handedness. (So Ralph Blair, director of the Homosexual Community Counseling Center [HCCC, 30 E. 60th Street, New York, NY 10022] and founder/president of "Evangelicals Concerned," an evangelical gay rights advocacy group with chapters in various cities across the nation.)

213. The question, How many homosexuals are there? is often raised. It has traditionally been supposed that in America there were relatively few till the modern "sexual revolution" gave free rein to licentious perversion. More likely, the number has remained constant, the difference being in society's awareness of a homosexual presence. Using a scale of 0 (exclusively heterosexual) to 6 (exclusively homosexual) and working with the data of the Kinsey Report (Alfred C. Kinsey, Wardell Pomeroy, and Clyde Martin, *Sexual Behavior in the Human Male* [Philadelphia: W. B. Saunders, 1948], followed in 1953 by a companion volume on female behavior), it has been estimated that 4-5 percent of American males and 1-2 percent of American females are exclusively or predominantly homosexual. This would mean there are as many homosexuals as there are Jews in American society. A more recent survey by the Battelle Human Affairs Research Centers, however, found only 1 percent of males aged 20-39 to be exclusively homosexual; while recent surveys in Europe and Canada come up with figures in the 1-4 percent range (Priscilla Painton, "The Shrinking Ten Percent," *Time* 141, no. 17 [April 26, 1993], pp. 27-29). The confidence that gays and lesbians are less frequently to be found in evangelical circles, a confidence that I have heard expressed more than once, appears to be wishful thinking.

The gay rights movement has changed not only the perception that nongays have of gays and lesbians, but also the perception that gays and lesbians have of themselves. From a sense of their homosexuality as an overwhelming fate, a burden of private shame and remorse, many homosexuals have moved to a consciousness of themselves as an oppressed social group.[214] In what they consider a flash of insight, a kind of latter-day revelation, the conviction that something is deeply wrong with themselves has been turned into the conviction that something is deeply wrong with society. Moving from self-negation to a new-found courage, they have turned from passive endurance to assertive action and marched under the banner, "Gay is Good." By losing their privacy — and sometimes their jobs — they have begun to win their civil rights.

In "coming out," gays and lesbians have overcome the isolation that in the past has made them especially vulnerable to discrimination and persecution. By identifying themselves, they have been able to identify others and so have found strength in unity. This can be seen (to give an example) in the way those gays and lesbians who identify with the Christian church have pursued what might be called the implications of an I-thou theology. As a result support groups like "Evangelicals Concerned," mentioned above, have emerged. In most mainline denominations gays have caucused. Both the United Methodists and the United Church of Christ have gay caucuses; the name of the Roman Catholic caucus is "Dignity," and the Lutheran, "Integrity." Presbyterians have not only a gay caucus but several "More Light Churches," which welcome homosexuals into positions of ordained leadership. The name "More Light" comes from a remark of John Robinson made back in 1620. As pastor of the Lyden Pilgrims, who were seeking religious liberty, he reassured them that "God hath yet more light to break forth from his word" (or words to that effect; see *The Works of John Robinson* [London: J. Snow, 1851], pp. xliv-xlv). Gays in the Pentecostal tradition have even founded their own denomination. The Reverend Troy Perry, a former Pentecostal minister, founded (in 1968) the Metropolitan Community Church in Los Angeles, which has developed sister congregations in other cities.

The purpose of all these groups is not primarily to preserve denominational distinctives but to give to homosexuals the opportunity to gather as Christians of whatever tradition in an open and accepting community. The assumption behind the decision to form such support groups deeply disturbs many in the Christian tradition. That assumption is not that there are Christians who are homosexuals, but rather that Christian homosexuals need not repent of their homosexuality. A group of avowed (in theological parlance, unrepentant) Christian homosexuals appears to them to be a contradiction in terms; one might as well talk of a Christian Mafia that trains Christian enforcers to provide Christian extortion services. But more of this later.

214. The experience of an increasing number of gays illumines the anatomy of hiding. Having abandoned the agony of a clandestine life, they have found relief from the guilt of living a lie only by coming out and being who they really are.

d. *The Contemporary Case* for *Homosexuality*

1) *Concerning the Distinction Between Sexual Orientation and Sexual Behavior*

As we turn from the churches' No! to homosexuality to the Yes! of affirmation with which increasing numbers in the gay community are affirming their sexuality, we cannot appeal to a tradition of long standing; the case *for* homosexuality is barely in the making. For want, therefore, of a broad consensus that we can summarize and critique, we will simply comment, in a somewhat desultory manner, on some matters that we deem relevant to the discussion. We have in mind, to begin with, information stemming from the so-called sexual revolution, which began with the modern use of contraceptives.

The phrase "sexual revolution" is commonplace in our day. For many it conjures up thoughts of X-rated movies, pornographic computer games, teenage pregnancy, abortion on demand, and a general flaunting of one's freedom from all sexual inhibitions. The exposition of a Christian view of sex, love, and marriage that we have attempted (see above, pp. 190ff.) entails the utter rejection of these abuses so widespread in today's society. For us, the suffering, confusion, fear, and doubt (not to mention disease) resulting from the casting off of all sexual restraints in modern society only confirm the Christian view of sex and give the lie to the supercilious cant one so often hears about progress and deliverance from Victorian scruples.

But one may speak of a sexual revolution in another sense. We have in mind the present-day scientific study of human sexual behavior. Such study (sexology) also constitutes a revolution. In this latter sense, the church should welcome the sexual revolution and the insight it brings to human sexuality. We say this because our sexuality is essential to our humanity and touches all phases of our lives as humans. Such an affirmation needs to be made in view of the near hysteria shown by the religious community (along with others) when the Kinsey Research on human sexual behavior first appeared in the 1950s. (See C. A. Tripp, *The Homosexual Matrix* [New York: New American Library, 1975], pp. 218-19, for an account of the initial response to Kinsey's statistics and studies as so many "toilet wall inscriptions.")

In present-day studies of human sexuality, a distinction is often made between sexual behavior and sexual orientation. This distinction has made an impact on the contemporary discussion of homosexuality. As we enter into this discussion, we shall begin with a word on the etiology (cause) of sexual orientation as such. If one's sexual orientation somehow determines one's sexual behavior, what determines one's sexual orientation? What gives one the capacity to be erotically attracted to a member of the opposite sex, and what gives one the capacity to be erotically attracted to a member of the same sex?

It should come as no surprise that what has been written on this subject is primarily concerned with the latter question. Given the traditional view of the healing professions that a homosexual orientation is pathological, many have assumed that such an orientation needs explanation so that it can be "cured," in contrast to a heterosexual orientation, which is normal and therefore needs no explanation.[215]

As one reviews the literature on the etiology of homosexuality, it becomes apparent that much of it is erudite ignorance, and some of it is not even erudite. Everything from the stars under which one is born to fluoride in the drinking water, excessive masturbation, and teaching a boy to knit and cook has been cited as the cause of homosexuality and given the magisterial form of published statement. A bit more plausible are widely held theories of a psychological nature. Homosexuality is a neurosis; it reflects an arrested state of development (Freud) brought on by this or that. Fathers of homosexuals are "cold and rejecting," mothers are "dominant and controlling," and so forth.[216]

Since World War II, with the adoption of better research methodologies, many psychologists and psychiatrists have moved away from this illness approach, recognizing that there are not only disturbed but also healthy homosexuals, even as there are disturbed and healthy heterosexuals. Given this breakthrough, one might suppose that a scientific understanding of our sexual orientation would be easily achieved. This has not proved to be the case. Rather, the whole question has turned out to be exceedingly complex.

Our own thinking on the subject reflects our general view of what it means to be a human being. Believing that to be human is to be an embodied spirit, it seems to us that sexual orientation must be the result of both heredity and socialization.[217] In other words, it is both constitutional and acquired; it

215. The traditional theological view that homosexual orientation is sinful is congruous with the psychiatric view that it is a sickness. The relationship between sinfulness and sickness will concern us when dealing with the doctrine of sin in a succeeding volume.

216. Of course some parents are cold and controlling in relating to their children. But this is true whether the children are homosexual or heterosexual. It is also true that many parents *become* cold and rejecting toward their children when they discover they are gay, even telling them they are a "mistake" and thrusting them out of the home. And while we are speaking of parents, we should also note that the effort of modern psychology to probe the relationship between parents and homosexual children sometimes exacerbates rather than relieves the situation for parents. The theory that children have become homosexual because of the way their father or their mother related to them when they were growing up can traumatize good and faithful parents. What did I (we) do wrong? One might as well ask, What did the parents of Mozart do right?

217. As bodies, our being is given us in terms of the cause/effect nexus of biological law (heredity). As spirits, our being in its interaction with the environment (socialization) transcends the biological. See above, our discussion of human nature as existence in the body and as transcendence of the body, pp. 30-46.

reflects a delicate balance of genetic, neurological, hormonal, and environmental factors. And this balance is fixed at a very early age, being largely in place from the time we are born.[218] As a result, we are aware of our sexual orientation not as a conscious choice in the past when we stood before an ethical crossroad, but as an inclination that is coterminous with memory itself.

Heterosexuals have shown no reluctance in accepting such conclusions so long as they are thinking in terms of their own sexual orientation. The difficulty arises when homosexuals make the same claim for themselves. Our sexual orientation, they are saying — and this is a pivotal part of the contemporary case *for* homosexuality — has also been shown to be deeper than any conscious, individual choice. It is, like heterosexual orientation, coterminous with memory itself. In this respect, therefore, they say, we homosexuals are like you even in our differentness from you.[219] We, like you, accept the conclusion that the learning of which life is made up surely does significantly affect how, when, and where one gives expression to one's sexual inclinations. But such learning, we would maintain, while it shapes our behavior, has relatively little effect on our sexual orientation as such. The latter is a constant that remains unchanged from early childhood.[220]

218. See Lee Ellis and M. Ashley Ames, "Neurohormonal Functioning and Sexual Orientation: A Theory of Homosexuality-Heterosexuality," *Psychological Bulletin* 101, no. 2 (1987): 233-58. We are indebted to Ralph Blair, of Evangelicals Concerned, for calling our attention to this article, in *Review* 12, no. 3 (spring 1988). See also Letha Scanzoni and Virginia Mollenkott, *Is the Homosexual My Neighbor?* (San Francisco: Harper & Row, 1978), chap. 6, "What Does Science Say?" Recent studies have found differences between homosexual and heterosexual men in a tiny portion of the brain believed to govern sexual activity; and a significantly higher incidence of homosexuality (slightly more than 50 percent, but *not* 100 percent) in the identical twins of homosexual males as compared to their nontwin and adoptive brothers (all pairs of brothers studied were reared in the same households, thus controlling for the effects of environment). See *Los Angeles Times,* Aug. 30, 1991, p. A40; and Dec. 15, 1991, p. A43.

219. There is no contradiction in the claim of homosexuals that they cannot remember being anything but homosexual and their admission that they can well remember when they first became aware of their homosexuality. "I was eighteen when I first perceived myself to be homosexual. . . . Being sexually excited by the sight of another boy made me aware that I was different, that 'there was something wrong with me.' . . . Homos were mysterious, evil people, to be avoided at all costs. And I was one. Often, when I thought of this, I would break out in a cold sweat. I couldn't be. I shoved the idea aside" (Brown, *Familiar Faces, Hidden Lives,* p. 32).

220. The lives of many heterosexuals while they are in prison illustrate the way in which the circumstances of life affect sexual behavior without altering sexual orientation. When incarcerated, heterosexual prisoners will often indulge in homosexual behavior. A 1968 study of Philadelphia prisons branded them as "sodomy factories," and reformers sought to stamp out the perversion by instituting conjugal visits (Karlen, *Sexuality and Homosexuality,* p. xv). Such homosexual behavior is obviously perverse. There is no mutuality, no I-thou fellowship in such unions. Rather, they are acts that at best gratify sexual

The perception that one's sexual orientation is not learned in the ordinary way that one's sexual behavior is learned (through the experience of living and growing up in a given culture), and the claim of an increasing number of homosexuals that for this very reason their erotic attraction to members of the same sex is not essentially different from the erotic attraction of heterosexuals to members of the opposite sex, obviously constitute a revolutionary approach to the whole matter. This approach challenges the traditional teaching of the church concerning homosexuality, as well as the attitude shown toward homosexual persons both in the church and in society. Before we turn to consider the ways in which those who speak for the church have sought to meet this challenge, we pause to comment on related developments in American society generally, developments in which professionals, Christian and non-Christian, have been involved.

2) Concerning Civil Rights and Medical Opinions

Considered as sin by the church, homosexuality has traditionally been condemned as a crime in American law.[221] Persons accused of homosexual acts, if found guilty, could be fined and were often sentenced to serve a prison term. In 1955 the American Law Institute broke with this long-standing tradition when, after considerable debate, it recommended the removal of homosexual acts between consenting adults from the list of crimes against the peace and dignity of the state. The argument was that whereas such acts may be considered sinful, this moral judgment rests on religious considerations; and it is not the task of the state, through the use of civil sanctions, to control the moral behavior of citizens when there is no threat to the public peace.

The argument for decriminalizing homosexual practices is obviously but a specific instance of the generally accepted argument for the separation of church and state as set forth in the United States Constitution. The recommendation of the American Law Institute was given a fillip by the appointment in 1954 of the so-called Wolfenden Committee by the British Parliament, for the purpose of investigating and making recommendations concerning homosexual offenses and their treatment in the courts. In 1957 this committee stated in their report that it is not the function of the law to intervene

appetite on the part of those deprived of heterosexual contacts. More often (in the case of males, at least), they are acts of sheer aggression and violence, a rape intended to denigrate and conquer the victim. Our only point in mentioning such sordid behavior is to note that when these prisoners are released, they revert to heterosexual activity. Their behavior in prison did not change their orientation.

221. The relationship between sin and crime will concern us when dealing with the doctrine of sin in a succeeding volume.

in the private lives of citizens to enforce particular patterns of sexual behavior simply because they are regarded as sinful and immoral by many for reasons of conscience and religious conviction. Society should not equate crime with sin *simpliciter,* but rather recognize a realm of private morality and private immorality that is not the business of the law. Accordingly, the committee recommended that "homosexual behaviour between consenting adults in private should no longer be a criminal offense." (That is, "Criminal law should take cognizance only of acts involving assault or violence, the corruption of minors, and public indecency or nuisance" [Bailey, *Homosexuality,* p. 164]. In other words, homosexuals should receive parity of treatment before the law with heterosexuals.)

In 1973 the American Bar Association called on the state legislatures to repeal all laws that made any sort of private sexual conduct between consenting adults a criminal offense. As a result several states repealed their sodomy laws. Some municipalities have begun to go even further and to enact antidiscrimination ordinances to secure the civil rights of gay and lesbian persons.[222]

The injustice wrought by sodomy laws is underscored for any who will take the time to review the anecdotal literature. See, for instance, John Gerassi's *The Boys of Boise* (New York: Collier, 1968), the story of a homosexual-hunting crusade that tore apart the city of Boise, Idaho, in 1955. (See Karlen, *Sexuality and Homosexuality,* pp. 607ff.) One of the obvious benefits of gay rights legislation is that it curtails blackmail, one of the most lamentable abuses of gay persons imaginable. In March 1966 a blackmail ring was uncovered in New York City "consisting of some seventy men who had extorted at least a million dollars from perhaps a thousand victims — among them a congressman, a minister, a surgeon, two university deans, a wealthy midwestern teacher who had paid $120,000 over four years, and a nuclear physicist who had broken security to avoid exposure" (ibid., p. 611).

In evaluating the modern case *for* homosexuality, even more significant than the position taken by the American Bar Association is the decision (also in 1973) by the American Psychiatric Association (APA) to remove homosexuality from its official *Diagnostic and Statistical Manual of Mental Disorders.*[223] This act, as Howard Brown observes, "made millions of

---

222. Impetus for gay rights legislation antedates this call of the American Bar Association, going back to the Stonewall riots. In fact, in the wake of what happened at Stonewall, many lawyers and legislatures began to change their thinking in a way that made gay rights legislation possible. The setback suffered by gay rights advocates due to the AIDS epidemic has not reversed this general trend. For example, as of this writing, equal employment laws and domestic partnership ordinances are being enacted.

223. The American Psychological Association followed suit in 1975, urging health professionals to take the lead in removing the stigma of mental illness from homosexuality.

Americans who had been officially ill that morning [December 15, 1973] officially well that afternoon."[224]

Such a decision is obviously controversial. At the time, the APA statement assured all "dedicated psychiatrists and psychoanalysts" that they should continue to treat homosexuals who were "unhappy with their lot," that is, homosexuals who suffered from "sexual orientation disturbance." On the one hand, gay activists issued a statement declaring this assurance to be a maneuver to keep psychiatrists who make lucrative careers out of allegedly helping homosexuals to change "from being drummed out of their profession." On the other hand, even down to the present, especially in conservative religious circles, the charge is made that the militant gay community pressured the APA into making its decision, even though it is contrary to the evidence.

There can be little doubt that the decision of the APA concerning homosexuality was a stunning victory for homosexual activists and all homosexual persons. This victory can be appreciated when one recalls that homosexuality has not only been declared a sin by the church but also a crime by the state and a disease by the medical profession. One can hardly imagine a more formidable phalanx of opposition. But now two of the three ranks in the phalanx have begun to give way.[225] And increasingly there are those even in the church who applaud the trend toward decriminalizing acts of homosexuality and press for laws securing civil rights for gays and lesbians.

Shaking off the labels of "criminal" and "neurotic," gays and lesbians are not only leaving the invisibility of the closet but also being brought out of the oblivion of past history. And again the result is surprising. Even if one discounts (as we do) many of the claims made for former worthies who have contributed to our cultural heritage, one cannot doubt that there have been famous and gifted people in the past — Leonardo da Vinci, James I (who commissioned the KJV), Tchaikovsky, probably Whitman — who were homosexual. And some of these gifted people were Christians — Michelangelo, W. H. Auden, Gerard Manley Hopkins. (See Scanzoni and Mollenkott, *Is the Homosexual My Neighbor?* pp. 32-38, 52-53, for helpful comments, together with a discussion, p. 34, of the disputed case of Shakespeare, whom they believe to have been heterosexual. Observing that many believe that in his sonnets Shakespeare "entered

224. Brown, *Familiar Faces, Hidden Lives,* pp. 200-201. Though present at the occasion, Brown was obviously bitter that the decision had come so late in his own life, "thirty years after I learned that as a homosexual I was a constitutional psychopathic inferior." Of course the APA understands what it means to be a "healthy" homosexual in psychological, not theological (spiritual), terms. The thought is that according to the scientific evidence, homosexuality does not cause "impairment of one's judgment, stability, reliability, or general vocational capability."

225. One obvious consideration making the APA decision significant is that it prevents people from being made sick by being constantly told they are sick.

the confessional," Untermeyer, ed., *Great Poems,* p. 273, quotes Wordsworth: "with this key Shakespeare unlocked his heart." To which Browning protested, "Did Shakespeare? If so, the less Shakespeare he!") One reason so many people feel what has been called "cognitive dissonance" when they discover the truth about famous homosexuals in the past is that scholars have written history so as to suppress the evidence. To alter slightly William James's phrase, historians have shown a "will *not* to believe." (See, for example, the comparison between the Jowett translation of Plato's *Symposium* and *Lysis* and that of C. A. Tripp in the latter's *Homosexual Matrix,* pp. 217-18.)

e. The Church and the Contemporary Case for Homosexuality

We do not hesitate to applaud the decision of the state to grant homosexuals their civil rights and the decision of the medical establishment to give them a bill of health. In these matters, for us the evidence is in and the argument is over.[226] When it comes to the church and its teaching, we do not find matters quite so simple. Indeed, we must admit straight off that we are unable to offer a theological resolution to the issues that confront the church; we cannot trace the thread of Ariadne through the maze of the argument. Much as simplicity and synthesis appeal to those who love the discipline of dogmatics, our treatment of the issues might rather be an instance of Abelard's *Sic et Non.* While many have assayed to overcome the antinomies, we shall simply attempt to set forth their several arguments, together with some critical comments. Nearly forty years ago, when Otto Piper published *The Christian Interpretation of Sex,* he conceded, "we do not intend to dispute that the undeniable fact of innate homosexuality faces us with a very difficult and thus far insoluble problem."[227] What we are about to do is take a look at some of the efforts to solve Piper's insoluble problem.

Some of these "solutions" are so far to the right or to the left that we will mention them only in passing. For instance, according to a segment of the theological left, with respect to its views on homosexuality, as well as on many other matters, a rigidly unchanging church has simply failed to keep up with a changing God — failed, indeed, to understand that in some respects God *must* change in order to keep up with developing circumstances. To the question, Is there a methodology whereby the God of the biblical community can be understood as having modified his ethical stance on such an impor-

---

226. This is not to deny that in both these areas today's society remains far from unanimous in its agreement. For instance, various gay-rights initiatives in several states have been followed by a near doubling of murders of homosexuals nationwide — 151 such murders reported between 1992 and 1994 (Kim Murphy, "Death in a Safe Place," *Los Angeles Times,* Dec. 20, 1995, pp. E1f.).

227. P. 143. With this truism, he dropped the subject without a further word.

tant issue? they answer with a resounding Yes: process theology. They do not deny that the Scriptures condemn homosexuality. They rather argue that to maintain his change-less attribute of love, God alters judgments about specific behaviors as conditions and persons change. For instance, homosexuality may be wrong when human reproduction is of the essence to the survival of the community, but unobjectionable once the population has reached a certain size. (See Arvid Adell, "Process Thought and the Liberation of Homosexuals," *Christian Century* 96, no. 2 [Jan. 17, 1979]: 46-48.) We have already denied, however, that God's loving concern for us entails a sort of "becoming" on his part, with the ethical morass such fundamental changeability would produce (see *God, Creation, and Revelation,* pp. 281-83). The idea contravenes the essential reliability of God's will and purpose. Further, one wonders how comforted a homosexual of Paul's day would be to learn that God (and not just society) would have viewed him differently if only he had been fortunate enough to be born a bit later.

Another approach is to rewrite Scripture in terms of our contemporary life and understanding. The report of the special task force on human sexuality of the Presby-terian Church (U.S.A.) (*Keeping Body and Soul Together: Sexuality, Spirituality, and Social Justice,* 1991, p. 97) calls the idea that the Bible "consistently and totally condemns homosexuality" a "myth" perpetuated by those who refuse to examine the context and assumptions of the relevant texts. If one does rightly examine these, one will discern, for instance, that in 1 Corinthians 6 Paul condemns no more than "a lifestyle of licentiousness and lust, and castigates those who know no higher calling" (ibid., p. 102). Galatians 3:28 teaches us that "the freedom of the gospel makes possible a higher morality" and "frames a theology of sexuality that affirms sexual expression which genuinely deepens human love and promotes justice" (ibid., p. 98). Another writer (Rachel Wahlberg, quoted by Richard R. Mickley, *Christian Sexuality,* 2nd ed. [Los Angeles: Universal Fellowship Press, 1976], p. 47) takes this same text to mean: "The goal of Christians is to be neither Greek nor Jew, neither slave nor free, neither male nor female, (neither heterosexual nor homosexual), but full persons doing the work of Jesus Christ." Although we will suggest below that many of the biblical texts associated with homosexuality deserve another look, this sort of freewheeling exegesis and interpolation will hardly do. It suggests a paraphrase of the remark of the wife of an ethicist, who said, "The job of a moral theologian is to find reasons why it's all right to do what everyone knows is wrong": in the current context, we might suspect that the job of a modern exegete is to find a way to make the text say what everyone knows it does not mean!

A third tactic we might dub "semantic theology," referring to the word games theologians and would-be theologians play: the way "in" words and phrases are tossed about, terms redefined, and incommensurate ideas and events associated as if they illumined one another. We hear of "the continuing revelatory activity of God in the world" that "confirms for the church the great theme of the Bible: God is active love, creating, responding to need, and liberating"; and of "mutually informing and correct-ing doctrines of biblical authority and interpretation" (report [1978] of Presbyterian Task Force to Study Homosexuality, pp. D-98, D-140) — without any further indication of what criteria determine what is, in fact, God's *revelatory* activity, or what might rightly give one doctrine the power to "correct" another. We see sin defined as "an action or omission which is harmful, which hurts either one's self or others, which is against the dignity, duty and rights of one's self and of others" (J. N. Pallikkathayil, "Homosexuality — What?" *Monday Morning,* Sept. 5, 1977, p. 3) — with no reference to offense to God or disobedience to his law. We find Peter's experience of the Spirit's work in the Gentile Cornelius and his recognition of God's abrogation of ceremonial food laws (Acts 10:1–11:18) used to argue that since one may see evidence of the Spirit's work in many self-affirming, practicing homosexual persons, therefore, "we are led to believe that God has cleansed and proclaimed clean their devoted hearts," and, "Who are we that we can withstand God?" (1978 Presbyterian Task Force, p. 169; see also the critique by Bruce Metzger in *Monday Morning,* May 15, 1978, pp. 9-11) — without any distinction made in the nature of the evidence received and with no recognition that the revelation to Peter spelled out the strand of Old Testament revelation that looks on the covenant with Abraham and the election of Israel as having as its purpose a larger universalism.

Impossible as are these attempts made by the theological left, the efforts of the right are surely no better. We mentioned in passing above (p. 129) the Reconstructionist inclusion of homosexuality among those capital crimes for which swift execution is the suitable punishment. When President Jimmy Carter invited homosexual persons to visit the White House, evangelist George Otis responded with a letter confidently stating that the president's action "was deeply disappointing to me and to God" and that "the Dead Sea area . . . is the Lord's most permanent monument to His personal attitude concerning perversion" (*High Adventure* 11, no. 2 [1977]). A mother apparently hired cult deprogrammer Ted Patrick to "deprogram" her twenty-year-old daughter out of lesbianism. Patrick and others were brought to trial on charges of repeatedly raping the young woman (see Ralph Blair's *Record,* winter 1982, p. 2). Such approaches, examples of which could all too easily be multiplied, neither require nor deserve comment.

1) Sexual Orientation and Sexual Behavior Revisited

Since we are a unity of body and soul, we should not, as we have said, be surprised to find a physiological basis of sexual orientation, whether it proves to be highly complex or relatively simple. But at the same time, we should not be surprised to find that physiology is not everything. A person who has fallen in love is attracted to one other person, not indiscriminately to all men or women. Romeo did not love just anyone, but only one — Juliet. Love remains not only a mystery but a highly individual mystery, so that the mere observer may often be moved to remark, "I wonder what she sees in him?" The bond between a man and a woman may be as opaque to objective, outside analysis as the bond between two men or two women. And anyone who has ever been deeply in love must surely be able to find in her heart some sympathy, at least, for homosexual people who testify that they, too, have that experience, but with reference to a person of their own sex. Theology must seek to keep in mind the irreducible uniqueness in such human relationships, while science properly concerns itself with general principles.

Current scientific understanding suggests that even human sexual identity is not a simple thing but consists of three elements: (1) our awareness
of ourselves as male or female; (2) our conformity (or lack of conformity)
to behavior expected of and generally learned by our sex in our particular
culture; and (3) our attraction to a person of the same or the opposite sex
as a sexual partner.[228] Homosexuals, unlike transsexuals, who feel as if
they are trapped in the wrong body, do not have difficulty identifying
themselves as male or female.[229] They do not want the body, clothes, or
manner of the other sex; nor do they necessarily desire roles commonly
played by the other sex in their society. But their choice of sexual object
is homosexual. And as we have just said, something about sexual attraction
is fundamentally mysterious.

Thus we soon find that it becomes difficult indeed to make a tidy
separation between what one *is* and what one *does,* such that the one is
entirely innocent and the other culpable.[230] One man, a physician, married
and a father, was told by two psychiatrists that he could not be a homosexual
because he had not had any homosexual experience for years.[231] From the
strength of his desires, even before they drove him to overt action, he knew
differently. Where does "orientation" stop and "behavior" begin? Most
people mean by "behavior" explicit genital behavior; but that is a definition
more appropriate to the state, which must decide what acts it will prosecute,
than to the church, which must deal with Scripture's manifest concern for

228. Scanzoni and Mollenkott, *Is the Homosexual My Neighbor?* p. 93, citing Richard
Green.

229. The case of the transsexual is instructive, however, in demonstrating that the
apparent facts of bodily existence do not definitively answer even the seemingly obvious
question of gender identity. Since the Christian vision admits that the self is more than the
body — indeed, essentially more — a discrepancy between self and body in this regard can
at least be conceived. A few such people who have undergone surgery and hormonal treatment
"fade away into respectable anonymity in their new lives" (John Money in Karlen, *Sexuality
and Homosexuality,* p. 404). This is a different matter than the case of transvestites, usually
clearly and exclusively *heterosexual* men who in some sense and for widely varying reasons
live a masquerade (with or without an intent to deceive) and whose cross-dressing is
specifically condemned by Scripture (Dt. 22:5). (See Tripp, *Homosexual Matrix,* pp. 25-30.)

230. That is, we are about to suggest that relying theologically on "the fundamental
distinction between sexual *orientation* and sexual *behavior*" (Robert Nugent, S.D.S., "Homosexuality and the Vatican," *Christian Century* 101, no. 16 [May 9, 1984]: 487), as have many
Roman Catholic theologians and an increasing number of evangelicals, is fraught with
difficulties when we are talking about those whose basic orientation is homosexual. It may,
however, have usefulness when considering prisoners, soldiers, temple prostitutes, and others
who may under pressure of particular circumstances engage in homosexual behavior that
they would not otherwise have considered. We will take up this problem again from a slightly
different angle when discussing the "celibacy" solution, below, pp. 342-47.

231. Discussed in Brown, *Familiar Faces, Hidden Lives,* p. 111.

disposition as a sort of behavior in itself. Envy, for instance, need not issue in theft for it to be condemned. A passionate glance, a meeting of the eyes, a feeling for another, the writing of a letter, and so on, are all behavior.[232] There is no way one can experience erotic love for another that does not involve behavior of some sort. Further, our sexuality, as something that is an integral part of who we are, is broadly involved in what we do (though of course our sexuality is not the sum total of what we are nor wholly determinative of what we do).

Precisely when we have the most difficulty in separating orientation from behavior, then, we have to face the potentially radical implications of views of the etiology of the orientation. We have marked the movement in scientific study from seeing homosexuality as a sin and a crime (a perverse personal choice to be punished), to seeing it as a disease (a misfortune, an indication of damage or inferiority to be healed), to seeing it more as innate, like left-handedness (an anomaly, but not pathology).[233] Sinners *should not* sin, however much they feel inclined to do so. Left-handed people, however, should by all means write and throw and so on with their left hands; and the view of another generation that their parents should try to force them to become right-handed is now universally seen to be misguided. If homosexual orientation or the potential for it is, like left-handedness, simply another manifestation of a perfectly natural *difference,* among the vast array of differences in the created order, and not a consequence of the Fall (as are our predilection to sin and vulnerability to sickness, from a theological point of view), then logic and fairness would seem to require us to cease blaming either the orientation or its expression.

This, indeed, is the position taken by many who note that the church Fathers, and presumably the writers of Scripture as well, appear never to have considered the possibility of a natural homosexual orientation, but only the unnatural, perverted, lust-inspired actions of heterosexuals.[234] The ancient condemnation by the church of all homosexual activity is thus, they argue, based on tragic ignorance and misunderstanding. That treatment of homosexual persons has been worse than tragic we have freely acknowledged. The nature of our hesitation simply to link homosexual orientation with the creation must emerge in our revisiting of the biblical data and our theological reflection upon it.

---

232. Note further that in Rom. 1:26, not just acts but passions are seen as dishonoring.
233. See Karlen, *Sexuality and Homosexuality,* pp. 181-95.
234. See, for example, McNeill, *Church and the Homosexual,* p. 96.

2) The Biblical Witness with Respect to Homosexuality

The pressing question for the evangelical faced with a challenge to long-held views on an important matter of faith and practice is whether there is, indeed, more light to break forth from God's word on the subject in question. We believe that traditional views supporting slavery and the subordinate status of women have rightly been corrected by an appeal to Scripture. Can a similar correction be made with respect to homosexuality, or is the alleged new light in this case not from but against God's word? To respond to that question, we must look both at specific texts and at the witness of Scripture as a whole.

a) Genesis 19

It seems clear, upon careful examination, that some of what homosexuals have called the "killer passages" do not as transparently condemn homosexuality as has often been supposed. Indeed, the passage most prominent in the popular mind — the story of Sodom and Gomorrah in Genesis 19 — is most vulnerable to interpretation in quite different terms. Despite Sodom's wickedness being mentioned frequently in Scripture, nowhere is that wickedness clearly associated with homosexuality.[235] When Jesus refers to Sodom (Mt. 10:14-15; Lk. 10:10-12), he does so in the context of instructing his disciples on how to respond to inhospitality. Violations of the sacred duty of hospitality were a very serious matter in Hebrew culture. Seeking to rape visitors, not to mention angel visitors, and thereby to demean and humiliate them, showed the grossest disregard of cultural values.[236] Indeed, the men of Sodom appear to have intended a gang rape,

---

235. See Dt. 29:23; 32:32; Is. 3:9; 13:19; Jer. 23:14; 49:18; 50:40; Lam. 4:6; Ezk. 16:46-48; Am. 4:11; Zeph. 2:9; Mt. 10:15; Lk. 17:29; Rom. 9:29; 2 Pt. 2:6; Jude 7 (Boswell, *Christianity, Social Tolerance, and Homosexuality,* p. 94). 2 Peter and Jude do refer to licentiousness and sexual immorality in a general way; but the reference to "strange flesh" (KJV) in Jude probably refers to a Jewish tradition that the *women* of Sodom had intercourse with the angels (ibid., p. 97; cf. Victor Paul Furnish, *The Moral Teaching of Paul,* 2nd ed. [Nashville: Abingdon, 1985], p. 56).

236. McNeill (*Church and the Homosexual,* p. 59) notes that it was a common practice, particularly of the Egyptians, to sodomize defeated male enemies as a symbol of domination. Bailey's suggestion (*Homosexuality,* pp. 1-5, 155) that no homosexual activity of any kind is implied in the passage, but that the verb יָדַע, "to know," should be taken in the sense of "get acquainted with," founders on the plainly sexual meaning of יָדַע in v. 8, where Lot offers his two virgin daughters as a substitute for his angel guests. (Hospitality and the safety of men were obviously more important than the dignity or even the life of women, as the similar story in Jgs. 19, where the townsmen accept the offer of the Levite's concubine and abuse her to death, further demonstrates. Whether an attempt to "restore the divine order" by the offer of women was intended [so Don Williams, *The Bond that Breaks: Will Homosexuality Split the Church?* (Los Angeles: BIM, 1978), p. 36] is less clear but may be implied in Jgs. 19:23, 24.)

for every last man of the city came out to surround Lot's house (v. 4). But surely we ought not to call same-sex rape "homosexuality," any more than we call other-sex rape "heterosexuality." We cannot take an easy step from condemning what the men of Sodom did to condemning what homosexuals in general do. Or, going at it from another angle, can we possibly assume that the whole male population of Sodom was homosexual in orientation? Far more likely is that this passage refers primarily to the debased behavior of heterosexual men. And acts of sexual assault on men or women are widely recognized as crimes more of violence and power than of sexual desire.

b) Leviticus 18:22 and 20:13

No such problem of the plain meaning of the text attends Leviticus 18:22 and 20:13. Everyone agrees that homosexual acts (at least male homosexual acts) are unequivocally condemned and assigned the death penalty.[237] The problem comes with the placement of these verses in the "Holiness Code," which intersperses matters of the highest ethical concern with those related to ritual purity, including proscriptions of wearing clothing made of mixed fibers or sowing one's land with two kinds of seed (19:19). That all these regulations had importance to Israel in keeping it separate from the customs and idolatrous practices of surrounding nations may be granted; but which remain valid today? Jesus abrogated the food laws. We take it as somehow "obvious" that blended fabrics and mixed crops are unobjectionable. Few see anything morally wrong with coitus during menstruation, forbidden along with homosexuality in Leviticus 18 and 20 and treated, it seems, as a moral and not just a ceremonial matter in Ezekiel 22.[238] Where to draw the line between the moral and the ceremonial is by no means clear. Thus many evangelicals have felt some nervousness about relying in an unqualified way on these texts, even when what should be given weight and what should not *seems* self-evident. They have to acknowledge how strongly culture conditions these assumptions of self-evidence, manifested, for instance, in the tolerant views many have come to have of masturbation and

237. That female homosexual acts are not mentioned, even though adultery, bestiality, and assorted other offenses are condemned for men and women alike, is curious. Possibly female homosexual acts were not considered truly "sexual," since they do not involve physical union or the ejaculation of semen (semen being seen as incipient life, the one substance necessary for procreation); or perhaps male homosexuality was seen as violating the "maleness" of the passive partner and thus demeaning him, while a woman has no such dignity to lose. In any case, female homosexuality has seldom inspired the horror produced by male homosexuality.

238. See Scanzoni and Mollenkott, *Is the Homosexual My Neighbor?* pp. 114-15.

oral sex — unthinkable, not so long ago, that these should be seen as permissible and even be advocated by some affiliated with the conservative wing of the church.

c) Romans 1:26-27

When we turn to the New Testament and the key passage Romans 1:26-27, we find a similar clarity in the text of Scripture: few would dispute that this passage condemns both male and female homosexual behavior. (This is, in fact, the only biblical text that mentions and condemns lesbianism.) Discussion, therefore, has centered not on obscurities of the text itself, but rather on such matters as its cultural context; its meaning and place in Paul's larger theological argument; and how we should understand φύσις, "nature," and that which is παρὰ φύσιν, "against nature." The Greco-Roman world of Paul's day had some considerable history of debased and degrading sexual practices. Suetonius's biographies of the twelve Caesars, from Julius Caesar through Domitian, provide "a catalog of astounding psychosexual disease, from incest to transvestism"; and the poet Juvenal wrote satires on perverted sex as taking over and destroying Rome.[239] Among homosexual practices, pederasty — the love of an older man for a youthful one — was a particularly prevalent problem. Plato and others had lauded pederasty as the purest form of love (though Plato came to condemn it in his later years); but it lent itself readily to abuse and exploitation because of the differential in age and power.[240] Young male slaves were forced to serve as prostitutes; some free effeminate youths sold themselves, serving as "call boys"; a Jewish tradition warned against sending a young man to a Gentile to study or learn a trade, lest he be used for pederastic purposes. These practices were sufficiently common that Scroggs states confidently, "We now know that the male homosexuality Paul knew about and opposed had to have been one or more forms of pederasty."[241] Perhaps. Paul did not, however, speak of men relating to *boys,* but of men committing shameless acts with *men* (ἄρσενες ἐν ἄρσεσιν τὴν ἀσχημοσύνην κατερ-

---

239. Karlen, *Sexuality and Homosexuality,* pp. 49, 51.

240. The general assumption of an age differential may be modified by Boswell's argument (*Christianity, Social Tolerance, and Homosexuality,* pp. 29-30) that "Beautiful men were 'boys' to the Greeks just as beautiful women are 'girls' to modern Europeans and Americans"; and that most ancient writers did not distinguish objects of attraction by age. In any case, however, leaving aside the literary apologists for pederasty, one might also find in ancient Greece a widespread attitude of mockery and disgust at homosexual behavior — for instance, the satires of Aristophanes, which were aimed at the mass, theater-going population (Karlen, *Sexuality and Homosexuality,* pp. 35-36).

241. Robin Scroggs, *The New Testament and Homosexuality* (Philadelphia: Fortress, 1983), p. 67 and passim. See also Furnish, *Moral Teaching of Paul,* pp. 58-67.

γαζόμενοι). Furthermore, this argument fails to consider the case of women, whose behavior Paul equally condemns. Were girls used by women as boys were by men in the Greco-Roman world? Apart from evidence that they were, the case that Paul inveighs only against *exploitative* homosexual relationships founders. Even if some Gentile sexual excesses provided especially salient examples of the destruction and chaos that result from unbounded sexual expression, examples that may well have been fresh in his mind, Paul does not appear to be speaking only of one particular form of abuse.

This point may be heightened by the observation that this condemnation of homosexuality comes just before and nearly as part of what may be termed a conventional vice list, used as an illustration of the vast and varied moral perversion to which God abandons those who idolatrously serve the creation rather than him. As many have observed, Paul's theological argument has to do with idolatry. He is not making an independent statement about homosexuality (nor does he ever do so). On the one hand, this may give us a measure of freedom in our thinking, since the force of illustrations is not argued but assumed and rests on the basis of common cultural understanding.[242] When cultural symbols and practices change, as in the case of hairstyles (1 Cor. 11:14-15), so does our choice of illustrations. On the other hand, not only does Paul obviously assume himself the evil of those things he mentions, but also he does not appear simply to have taken over unreflectively some extant Greek or Hebrew catalog of vices. We rather find a mixture of several streams of moral thought, with the abhorrence of homosexual practice a component particularly Jewish in its character and suggesting Paul's continued adherence to this aspect of the Levitical law.[243] Furthermore, the fact that Paul saw homosexual passion and practice, like the list of sins in Romans 1:28-31, as a result of idolatry and something to which people are given up by God as a matter of judgment, might at least give us pause in a society in which sexual needs seem often to be given almost absolute authority.[244]

---

242. See, for example, the argument to this effect by Helmut Thielicke, *The Ethics of Sex*, trans. John W. Doberstein (New York: Harper & Row, 1964), pp. 280-81.

243. "That Paul simply takes it for granted that the Jewish abhorrence of Gentile sexual license is still the appropriate ethical response of the Gentile believer in Christ means that he recognizes at least one distinctive element of Israel's covenant righteousness which remains unchanged within the wider freedom of the new covenant" (James D. G. Dunn, *Romans 1–8*, Word Biblical Commentary 38A [Dallas: Word, 1988], p. 74).

244. "In Paul's theology change of existence always takes place as a change of lordship. . . . A person's reality is decided by what lord he has. . . . He who evades the Creator runs into his Judge" (Ernst Käsemann, *Commentary on Romans*, trans. and ed. G. W. Bromiley [Grand Rapids: Eerdmans, 1980], p. 43).

But could it be that Paul's use of homosexuality as a general example of vice depends on a fundamental misunderstanding? Could it be that, lacking our contemporary understanding of sexual orientation, he simply assumed that all homosexual passion and behavior come from persons whose *natural* orientation is heterosexual, and that he never addressed or intended to address those who are *naturally* homosexual? For, leaving aside instances of exploitation and abuse, we have earlier noted that the traditional and seemingly obvious argument against homosexuality practiced by consenting adults is that it is "unnatural," "against nature" (παρὰ φύσιν).

The problem of "nature" and "sins against nature" is a complex and vexed one, not least because of the rigidity and violence with which the idea of "natural law" has been applied in later Christian thought. The idea of "nature" has little currency in biblical thought and does not become for Paul a major theological concept. There is no Hebrew word corresponding to the Greek φύσις, and the term and its derivatives are used only eighteen times in the New Testament, by contrast to frequent uses in Hellenistic literature. It can be used for descent, the regular order of nature, or what we could consider mere custom (perhaps because what is dictated by something's fundamental constitution and what is culturally determined remains open to debate). The phrase "against nature," παρὰ φύσιν, however, did have general currency in both Greek and Jewish sources in reference to sexual deviations. (See Gunther Harder, "Nature," in C. Brown, ed., *New International Dictionary of New Testament Theology* [Grand Rapids: Zondervan, 1976], 2.656-61; and Helmut Köster, "φύσις, κτλ," *TDNT*, 9.251-77. For the complexity of current uses of the term, applied in a somewhat different context, see Gordon D. Kaufman, "A Problem for Theology: The Concept of Nature," *Harvard Theological Review* 65 [1972]: 337-66.) But it was also used in other ways: for instance, Aristotle condemned the taking of interest as against nature (παρὰ φύσιν), reflecting the notion that money, being a dead thing, ought not to breed (Alfred Plummer, *A Critical and Exegetical Commentary on the Gospel According to St. Luke,* 4th ed., International Critical Commentary [Edinburgh: T. & T. Clark, 1901], p. 442).

Only centuries after Paul did the concept of natural law become fully developed, though we have already noted that denunciation of homosexuality on the grounds that it is unnatural can be found as early as Tertullian (Bailey, *Homosexuality,* p. 82). Thomas, however, makes clear his view that not only is homosexuality unnatural, but, because unnatural, it is "the greatest sin among the species of lust" (*Summa Theologica,* pt. 2-2, q. 154, art. 12). He argues that it is more serious than rape, sacrilege, or incest, on the grounds that, "Just as the ordering of right reason proceeds from man, so the order of nature is from God Himself: wherefore in sins contrary to nature, whereby the very order of nature is violated, an injury is done to God, the Author of nature." This motif of homosexuality as the *worst* sin keeps recurring. Heterosexuality can be *perverse* — witness prostitution, child molestation, pornography — but homosexuality is *perverted* to start with. It is disordered not just in its expression but in its essence.

One reason for this conclusion in the context of the natural theology of Rome, of course, is the thought that the rightful purpose of intercourse is always procreation. Even if at present the Roman Catholic Church may be hedging on this a bit, it remains basic to its teaching. By contrast, we have framed a doctrine of marriage that does not make procreation a necessary part of the relationship (see above, pp. 228-31). Nonetheless, it remains true that Genesis brings the creation of humankind as male and female in closest conjunction with the command to be fruitful and multiply.

We cannot say that in speaking of "nature" Paul generally differentiates sharply and consistently between what is innate and what is dictated by social custom (as seen most clearly in 1 Cor. 11:14). However, Romans 1:26-27 comes in a context emphasizing the work of the Creator and certainly seems to imply a violation of the created order.[245] Paul speaks not of a personal violation involving exchanging one's own natural orientation, but rather of exchanging the natural *use*, χρῆσιν (applied regularly to sexual relations, though also having the more general meaning of "usage"), of man or woman — that is, intercourse between a man and a woman, which is taken, evidently, as a universal standard. True, he does not appear to conceive of the possibility of "natural" homosexuality; but that is an argument that can be made to cut both ways and that becomes especially problematic in the face of the broader witness of Scripture, as we shall suggest below. For when we live in a situation in which all of our impulses and customs suffer from the corrupting impact of sin, how shall we determine not just what is "natural" in our current state ("we were by nature children of wrath," Eph. 2:3), but what reflects God's purpose for us? We must further note that it would be inconsistent to suppose that Paul's condemnation of homosexuality rests on an assumption that it is freely chosen: the overall force of his treatment of sin generally is that it is a power that precisely robs us of our freedom.[246]

---

245. "Paul does not share the ideal underlying the Stoic slogans φυσικός and παρὰ φύσιν, because there is for him no nature either detached from God or identifiable with God. For him these words . . . demonstrate degeneration: People refuse to be bound by the order immanent in the world and humanity" (Käsemann, *Romans,* p. 48, with reference given to Koester, *TDNT,* 9.267).

246. See Richard B. Hays, "Relations Natural and Unnatural: A Response to John Boswell's Exegesis of Romans 1," *Journal of Religious Ethics* 14, no. 1 (spring 1980): 184-215. Similarly, though from an entirely different angle, genetic determination does not make something "natural" in the sense that means we should affirm it without question. Many diseases and many anomalies are genetically determined or have significant genetic components. Diseases we try to cure. Anomalies (like, for instance, the YYX male, who is generally very aggressive; or the hermaphrodite, who has characteristics of both sexes), we handle by trying to limit the negative social and personal impact of the anomaly. But even the secularist does not say that we should pass no judgment of any kind on anything a person

d) 1 Corinthians 6:9-10 and 1 Timothy 1:10

The two remaining passages in the New Testament that seem to refer explicitly to some sort of homosexual practice are 1 Corinthians 6:9-10 and 1 Timothy 1:10.[247] Both use the rare term ἀρσενοκοῖται, which has not been found in the literature before 1 Corinthians 6; and 1 Corinthians 6 also refers to μαλακοί, a more common word (meaning "soft" — sometimes morally soft — or "effeminate"), but one whose precise meaning is not transparent in this context.

The difficulty of determining the precise meaning of these words may be seen in the variety of ways different versions of the Bible have translated them. The RSV, NAB, and NEB do not distinguish μαλακοί and ἀρσενοκοῖται but lump them both together as "homosexuals," "sodomites," and "who are guilty of homosexual perversion," respectively. Other versions try "effeminate, abusers of themselves with mankind" (KJV); "effeminate, homosexuals" (NASB); "effeminate, pervert" (Phillips); "male prostitutes, homosexual offenders" (NIV); "male prostitutes, sodomites" (NRSV); or "catamites, sodomites" (JB and Moffatt).

Problems with μαλακοί include its wide use by writers contemporary with Paul to refer to the weak or dissolute behavior of heterosexuals. (The identification of morally inferior attributes with femininity, as in the negatively valued word *effeminate,* belongs properly to the study of misogyny.) Further, it is the prejudice of heterosexuals that assumes males will be attracted only by what the culture defines as feminine. Richard the Lion-Hearted, for instance, was noted both for his martial skill and for his homosexuality (see Boswell, *Christianity, Social Tolerance, and Homosexuality,* pp. 24-25, 106-7).

> The exploits of the English king won even the admiration of the Arabs, whose historian reports how he rode up and down in front of the Saracen army defying them, and not a man dared to touch him. . . . One who accompanied the Third Crusade ascribes to him the valor of Hector, the magnanimity of Achilles, the prudence of Odysseus, the eloquence of Nestor, and equality with Alexander. French writers of the thirteenth century tell how Saracen mothers, long after Richard had returned to England, used to frighten their children into obedience or silence by the spell of his name, so great was the dread he had inspired. (Schaff, *History,* 5.264-65)

---

cannot help or did not choose. That is, we neither do nor can determine the "ought" from the "is," even if a considerable portion of the population represents a particular "is." The idea of "nature" as a standard has an inescapable teleological component that the Christian relates to God's purpose in creation, even though she may acknowledge that she cannot fully grasp or delimit that purpose.

247. Jude 7 and 2 Pt. 2:6-10 are also frequently included because of their mention of Sodom and Gomorrah and their reference to sexual misbehavior. These texts, however, are consistent with our treatment of the sin of Sodom being more incidentally than essentially homosexual. That is, they emphasize lawlessness and depraved lust and the hankering after "strange" (probably angelic, given the context) flesh. While they may assume homosexual acts of some sort, they do not name them directly.

Another point is that well into the twentieth century, the tradition of the church identified the term not with homosexuality but with masturbation; and the shift in interpretation came at a time when masturbation was no longer seen as a sin that could preclude entrance to heaven (Boswell, *Christianity, Social Tolerance, and Homosexuality,* p. 107).

With respect to ἀρσενοκοῖται, questions are raised not just by its rarity (indeed, absence from discussions contemporary with Paul), but by the fact that the term does not appear to have been widely or consistently picked up by later writers in their discussions of homosexuality. Nor are these biblical texts where the term occurs used regularly in these discussions. Thus one can ask if the term was understood as referring exclusively or even primarily to homosexual behavior (ibid., pp. 345-53; note, however, that translations from the Greek as far back as one can go [the Vulgate in the late 400s] all understand the word to apply to some sort of homosexual activity; so John Oswaldt, writing for a Daughters of Sarah Forum).

If Paul did intend to refer to homosexual acts by using the term ἀρσενοκοῖται, why would he have apparently coined or picked up this word, rather than using one of the several terms for homosexual activity current in his day? The most likely answer is that as a Jew, he was familiar with the rabbinical discussion of homosexuality, in which מִשְׁכַּב זָכוּר, "lying of a male," and מִשְׁכָּב בְּזָכוּר, "lying with a male," taken up from the Levitical texts, became almost technical terms. Paul, however, was writing in Greek. A literal translation of the terms in question yields ἀρσενοκοῖται; and indeed, the Septuagint of Leviticus 18:22 and 20:13 closely juxtaposes the components of the word.[248] Thus understood, the word refers generically to male activity with males, as its literal meaning would suggest in any case.[249]

---

248. Scroggs, *New Testament and Homosexuality,* pp. 83, 107-8; see also David F. Wright, "Homosexuals or Prostitutes?" *Vigiliae Christianae* 38 (1984): 125-33. The Hebrew and LXX texts of Lv. 18:22 and 20:13 read, respectively,

וְאֶת־זָכָר ל תִשְׁכַּב מִשְׁכְּבֵי אִשָּׁה תּוֹעֵבָה הוּא

καὶ μετὰ ἄρσενος οὐ κοιμηθήσῃ κοίτην γυναικός· βδέλυγμα γάρ ἐστιν. (Lv. 18:22)

וְאִישׁ אֲשֶׁר יִשְׁכַּב אֶת־זָכָר מִשְׁכְּבֵי אִשָּׁה תּוֹעֵבָה עָשׂוּ שְׁנֵיהֶם מוֹת יוּמָתוּ דְּמֵיהֶם בָּם

καὶ ὃς ἂν κοιμηθῇ μετὰ ἄρσενος κοίτην γυναικός, βδέλυγμα ἐποίησαν ἀμφότεροι θανατούσθωσαν ἔνοχοι εἰσιν. (Lv. 20:13)

249. The word and comparable phrases are used in this sense by Philo, Josephus, and Ps.-Phocylides (Wright, "Homosexuals or Prostitutes," p. 146). William Peterson ("Can ΑΡΣΕΝΟΚΟΙΤΑΙ Be Translated by 'Homosexuals,'" *Vigiliae Christianae* 40 [1986]: 187-91) argues that since male sexuality was assumed in antiquity to be polyvalent, ἀρσενοκοῖται must refer not to a category of persons but to a category of acts (and he wishes to preserve the term *homosexual* for persons of homosexual orientation). However, if Paul understood the Greco-Roman cultural norm to be a polyvalent male sexuality, it is all the more striking that he seems to be attacking the norm — and homosexual acts — generally and does not limit himself to decrying specific abuses. Nowhere does he give positive instruction for homosexual activity, though he does so regarding many other sexual issues (e.g., in 1 Cor. 7).

Whether the specific referent of ἀρσενοκοῖται should be at all nar-
rowed by its New Testament context cannot be said with certainty, though
its use with μαλακοί in 1 Corinthians 6:9 may be suggestive. The fact that
μαλακοί occurs between two words which both refer to sexual misbehavior
makes it plausible that it, too, should be understood here in its sexual sense.
It never became a technical term; but in sexual contexts it always had a
negative connotation. Specifically, it occurs several times in discussions of
the "call boy," "the youth who consciously imitated feminine styles and
ways and who walked the thin line between passive homosexual activity
for pleasure and that for pay."[250] If such a person was what Paul had in
mind, then "catamites" may be the best translation, with the ἀρσενοκοῖται
or "sodomites" being those who took the active role in homosexual intercourse (though in themselves, the ideas of passivity and activity do not
necessarily imply the abuses associated with this particularly corrupt form
of pederasty).[251]

That 1 Corinthians 6:9-10 and 1 Timothy 1:10 should be read as condemning homosexual acts, then, seems relatively certain. Whether they had
in view an especially destructive form of homosexual activity is less certain
but not unlikely. In any case, though, these passages neither seek to differentiate between an unacceptable and some putative acceptable form of
homosexual behavior, nor do they underline homosexual behavior as somehow more reprehensible than the other vices — including greed and
drunkenness — mentioned in the same list.

e) The Attempt to Find a Positive
Biblical Word on Homosexuality

Our survey of those passages that refer directly to homosexuality and our
brief consideration of their biblical and cultural contexts may leave us
with the sense that they may not prove quite as much as has traditionally
been supposed about the peculiar wickedness of homosexuality. Aggravating conditions seem always or almost always to be associated with
condemnations of it. Nonetheless, the problem remains that those who
wish to argue for the acceptability of at least some kinds of homosexual
behavior (by those, for instance, of "naturally" homosexual orientation)
have no alternative but to try to explain away the various biblical refer-

250. Scroggs, *New Testament and Homosexuality*, p. 106.
251. Scroggs further suggests that the placement of ἀρσενοκοίταις between πόρνοις
and ἀνδραποδισταῖς in 1 Tm. 1:10 may point to the enslaving of boys or youths for sexual
purposes, particularly if πόρνοις is taken in its narrower sense of male prostitute. The verse
would then be condemning "male prostitutes, males who lie [with them], and slave-dealers
[who procure them]" (ibid., p. 120).

ences, which are all on one side of the issue.[252] Not that traditional understandings of these texts need no modification: we would argue that they do. Nonetheless, when we turn to the Scriptures seeking a positive word, we find ourselves thwarted and having to argue from silence.[253] Even the most superficially promising case, that of David and Jonathan, does not hold up well under inspection. True, David proclaims in his lament on Jonathan's death, "Very pleasant have you been to me; your love to me was wonderful, passing the love of women" (2 Sam. 1:26). However, the same root, אהב, is used of David's love for Saul (1 Sam. 16:21), and regularly for Yahweh's love for Israel.[254] It seldom indeed has primarily sexual overtones. And it would be hard to deny the strength of David's heterosexual attractions.

Similarly in the case of Ruth and Naomi: we have every indication that these women were heterosexual, none that they were not. While one could conceivably argue that the consuming interest of the story that Ruth should have a husband was a function of the precarious position in that society of single women, we are given not a single clue that apart from such practical considerations, Ruth and Naomi would have found one another fully adequate to meet their personal needs.[255] The relationship of Jesus and John, spoken of five times, all in John's Gospel, as "the disciple

252. It is here that the issue of homosexuality differs from those of slavery and the role of women.

253. Much has been made of the fact that Jesus is silent on the issue. But then, he was also silent on being baptized for the dead, a fact of which the Mormons have made much in defending the practice. This silence may be likened to the silence of the Book of Confessions of the Presbyterian Church (USA) (apart from a single reference in the Heidelberg Catechism that quotes 1 Cor. 6:9-10). Richard Lovelace (in an unpublished paper entitled "The Active Homosexual Lifestyle and the Church: An Historical-Theological Evaluation," p. 5) plausibly attributes it to the likelihood that neither the Reformers and their successors nor their opponents would even conceive of suggesting or tolerating sexual activity outside the bounds of heterosexual marriage, marriage or chastity being the options laid out more generally in the confessions.

254. Furthermore, the LXX regularly translates it by forms of ἀγαπάω because the meaning of the Hebrew root is not well expressed by ἐράω or φιλέω. See Gerhard Wallis, "אָהַב," *Theological Dictionary of the Old Testament*, ed. G. J. Botterweck and H. Ringgren, trans. John T. Willis, rev. ed. (Grand Rapids: Eerdmans, 1977), 1.102-12. Bailey (*Homosexuality*, pp. 56-57) remarks on the relatively low view of marriage that then obtained as another reason that the love of a comrade such as Jonathan might readily be seen as surpassing "the love of women." See also note 79, above.

255. Scanzoni and Mollenkott (*Is the Homosexual My Neighbor?* pp. 94-95) rightly understand the David and Jonathan and Ruth and Naomi relationships as being close, same-sex friendships and remark, "Persons who are basically heterosexual need to realize that affectionate feelings toward friends of the same sex do not necessarily entail *erotic* feelings. . . . It is certainly possible to feel and speak of love for someone else without the slightest desire to express that love through genital sexual relations."

Jesus loved,"[256] was probably of the same general sort as the relationship between Jesus and Mary, or Jesus and other women (commonly cited by some heterosexuals to bolster the argument that Jesus must have been heterosexually active). In either case, one must jump from expressions of affection and tenderness, apart from which we can hardly imagine how Jesus would fully have revealed to us the love of God, to imputations of an illicit sexual component in these expressions. That the argument can be made equally plausibly, or equally implausibly, in the homosexual or the heterosexual direction should counsel caution.

Since it is rather widely recognized that these possible examples of a positive biblical treatment of homosexual relationships cannot be made to stick, persons seeking biblical grounds for their arguments have often turned instead to more general biblical principles, such as the command that we love our neighbor and the manifest concern throughout Scripture for the poor and oppressed.[257] In one sense these references are both proper and relevant: homosexual people are certainly our neighbors; and homosexual people, as we have sought to demonstrate above, have certainly been brutally and unfairly treated. In another sense, though, they tell us less than we need to know: What, exactly, does love require with respect to homosexuality — universal acceptance? acceptance with the same sort of boundaries applied to heterosexual behavior? acceptance of persons combined with lack of acceptance of their presumed sin? cutting off of persons from the Christian community until they change their ways? or what? And what does justice require? Even those who defend full civil rights for homosexual people might differ as to whether same-sex "marriage" should be considered a civil right, particularly when "marriage" is understood as including the right to have children, whether by adoption or, on the part of lesbians, by artificial insemination. While the person whose foot is being stood upon and not the person standing on it should be given the privilege of determining whether the position hurts, that point still does not obviate the other point that both church and society do and must impose limits that some people will find painful. General appeals to Scripture's demand that we be loving do not answer specific questions about where lines should be drawn. (They should, however, serve as a caution to those in positions of power, who turn out all too often to have been on the wrong side.)

The broader and deeper difficulty in seeking in Scripture a positive basis for affirming homosexuality — even if a fully convincing reinterpretation of the problematic texts were found — is that its silence in that regard is by no

256. Jn. 13:23; 19:26; 21:7, 20 using ἀγαπάω; Jn. 20:2 using φιλέω.
257. Hence, for instance, the title of Scanzoni and Mollenkott's book, *Is the Homosexual My Neighbor?*

means echoed when it comes to heterosexuality. Both creation narratives, however different their dates and tone and exact sequence, make plain that God's design for creating humankind is fulfilled not in the making of a man or a woman alone, or of two men or two women, but of a man and a woman. We have argued, indeed, that we are human, and in the divine image, only as male or female, male and female; and this not in the abstract but in relation to one another.[258] That this relationship is to be interpreted as heterosexual seems clear, in that it is immediately attached in Genesis 1:28 to the command to be fruitful and multiply, and in Genesis 2:24 to heterosexual marriage (granting that 2:24 may be a somewhat later addition to the original narrative).[259]

The Song of Songs unabashedly celebrates committed, heterosexual, erotic love. Jesus, in treating of divorce (Mt. 19:3-9; Mk. 10:2-9), combines both creation narratives in making his affirmation of God's intention for the permanency of (heterosexual) marriage. When pressed about the difficulty of such a lifelong commitment, he gives as an alternative only the choice of those "who have made themselves eunuchs for the sake of the kingdom of heaven" (Mt. 19:12); though he indicates that this sort of continence is not possible for everyone.[260] Similarly, Paul writes of marriage as the remedy for sexual passion, the fully acceptable option for those whose urges would otherwise overwhelm them (1 Cor. 7).[261] Also similarly, he refers back to

258. See above, pp. 131-36.

259. A gay interpreter writes, however, that "when majority folks read the biblical phrase 'male and female,' they read 'heterosexual' without a second thought. But the words stop me cold as I ponder what it means to be male and/or female biblically. In this culture [?], I'm a man — but not a 'real man.' I live somewhere close to womanhood in the popular myth — but I am not a woman" (John Linscheid, "Our Story in God's Story," in *The Other Side: Christians and Homosexuality,* updated ed., published by *The Other Side,* 1990, p. 28). He continues that he has learned that to equate "male and female" in the image of God with heterosexuality is to exchange the truth about God for a lie (Rom. 1:25). Such a reading is surely a strange distortion. Even the majority report of the 1978 Presbyterian Task Force to Study Homosexuality, a report noted for its pro-gay stance, suggests that a key reason Leviticus proscribes homosexual behavior is the belief that "Such behavior violates the integrity of primary categories of creation — male and female" (p. D-42).

260. BAGD confirms the seemingly self-evident reading of Mt. 5:12, that the three classes of "eunuchs" in question are intended to encompass those persons who have been physically castrated, those congenitally incapable of begetting children, and those who voluntarily abstain from marriage without being impotent.

261. Note that while his argument in favor of remaining unmarried is in order that one might give full attention to serving the Lord and not be anxious about pleasing one's partner, he does not countenance for an instant the possibility of relieving one's sexual needs in the context of a nonpermanent relationship. If nonentanglement and the meeting of a physiological need were the only considerations, the one-night stand with no-matter-whom would be the simplest solution. But again, such a possibility obviously does not even occur to Paul, who considers no options except marriage and continence.

Genesis in his treatment of marriage (Eph. 5:28-33). Even the symbolical
language in Revelation referring to the return of Christ is cast in terms of the
wedding feast of the Lamb and his bride (e.g., Rv. 19:7), so that the joy of the
reunion of God and his people is likened to the intended joy of the union of
man and woman. Thus, from beginning to end (and especially at the beginning and the end, where it is not spoiled by sin), the relationship of man and
woman is proclaimed and celebrated. It is difficult indeed to deny that
Scripture as a whole presents this relationship as reflecting something both
fundamental and good in the created order, something explicitly designed by
God. We simply cannot, as evangelicals, rightly approach homosexuality as
if this unified biblical testimony did not exist,[262] however deep may be our
sympathy for those who, through no conscious choice of their own, testify
that they experience the joy of recognition — "this at last is bone of my bones
and flesh of my flesh" — only with regard to a person of the same sex. What,
then, shall the church say to such persons?

3) Attempted Solutions

Before even beginning to look at the "solutions" that have been proposed
to and by homosexual people as a means of dealing with their circumstances, we must reiterate our conviction that we do not see a satisfactory
approach, though some options are doubtless better than others. For the
purposes of the discussion, we will assume that the "solution" must meet
the case of the exclusively homosexual person, with a normally high level
of sexual drive, who is aware of having made no "choice" about sexual
orientation but became aware of sexual feelings in the same way (though
doubtless — given prevailing societal attitudes — with more confusion and
conflict) that heterosexuals become sexually aware.[263] We will further

262. We do not see, that is, how to get from the Statement of Faith of the homosexual
group Evangelicals Concerned, which undoubtedly seeks sincerely to maintain its evangelical
faith as it affirms "the inspiration and authority of the Bible," to the same group's bylaws,
which state: "We believe that homosexuality is part of God's created order." For the latter
statement, as we have seen, we can find no warrant in Scripture.

263. Insofar as sexual orientation is not strictly biologically determined but has many
determinants, the distinction between what one *can* become and what one *cannot help but*
become can be very difficult to make. Hence one can perhaps understand why a gay person
might say that he made "the decision that 'I can't change' " (remarks by Chris Glaser in the
transcript of some Presbyterian Task Force discussions, Dec. 3, 1976); whereas one might
usually suppose that the affirmation "I can't change" comes as a recognition rather than a
decision (which may, of course, be what Glaser actually intended). Nonetheless, from our
perspective, if and when homosexuality reflects an active choice rather than being a manifestation of the same sort of deep component of one's being that heterosexuality is, the argument
on its behalf is simply lost. It does not follow from this distinction, however, and the possible
leeway it may give in considering homosexuality, that only what is the object of choice can

assume that this homosexual person is at least as sincere about his or her evangelical Christianity as is the ordinary heterosexual evangelical (though, again, with a lot more conflict, given the rejection or self-hatred he or she has likely experienced).

a) Change of Orientation

Those who are most certain that there is but one acceptable pattern of reality in the sexual sphere, and that heterosexual, have proclaimed the desirability and possibility of change — change, that is, from homosexual to heterosexual orientation (though some have been satisfied with the more moderate goal of reduction in overt homosexual behavior). They have referred not just to the boundless power of God generally, whose hand is not shortened, that it cannot save (Is. 59:1); but more specifically to 1 Corinthians 6:11, which follows the vice list including catamites and sodomites with the phrase, "and such *were* some of you" (emphasis added). Surely, they say, the text of Scripture itself affirms the possibility of change for homosexual people. And if change is possible, surely only perversity would fail to desire it.[264]

Some, indeed, would take a step beyond assuming that change should be desired and promoted to advocating that treatment be forced, even against a person's will — an approach potentially even more invasive than applying legal sanctions against the practice of homosexuality. The AIDS crisis provides a new motive, beyond the traditional terror that homosexuality itself can somehow be "caught" by association with homosexual people; and epidemiology provides a model (though, as a matter of fact, AIDS worldwide affects more heterosexuals than homosexuals): to prevent smallpox, for example, everyone must be inoculated, long before they experience any distress. A key difference, however, is the highly uncertain outcome of proposed treatments for homosexuality, as well as the risks associated with some modes of treatment. Persons have been subjected to castration, hysterectomy, vasectomy, electrical and chemical shock, and even lobotomy; have been treated with drugs ranging from hormones to LSD; and have submitted to aversion therapies using electric shock or nausea-inducing drugs. As a case in point:

> Aversion therapy was conducted with a male homosexual who had a heart condition. The particular form of aversion therapy involved the creation of nausea, by means of an emetic, accompanied by talking about his homosex-

---

be the object of moral judgment. We have noted before that a key characteristic of sin is precisely that it deprives us of freedom.

264. It would seem to confirm both the social problems and the personal depth of a homosexual identity that 90 percent of homosexuals would reportedly not "recommend" homosexuality to others, but a similar percentage would not elect magically to change their own sexual orientation (Tripp, *Homosexual Matrix*, p. 255).

uality. The second part of the therapy involved recovery from the nausea and talking about pleasant ideas and heterosexual fantasies, which was sometimes aided by lysergic acid. In this case, the patient died as a result of a heart attack brought on by the use of the emetic. (Quoted by Katz, *Gay American History* [New York: Thomas Y. Crowell, 1976], pp. 133-34.)

John Money makes the point that aversive therapies most likely will make patients sexually inhibited, anxious, or sexually apathetic, rather than change their orientation. Were such measures applied to heterosexuals, they would not become homosexual, as if homosexuality rushed in to fill an erotic vacuum; and the converse is likewise true. He concludes, "Therapeutic zeal in the absence of effective therapeutic technique produces charlatanism" ("Strategy, Ethics, Behavior Modification, and Homosexuality," *Archives of Sexual Behavior* 2, no. 1 [1972]: 79-81. See also his "Bisexual, Homosexual, and Heterosexual: Society, Law, and Medicine," *Journal of Homosexuality* 2, no. 3 [spring 1977]: 231-32). One must surely consider it unethical to impose such treatment on those who consider themselves well, and doubly so given results ranging from the dubious to the dangerous or even deadly.

The difficulty comes with the poor evidence of lasting change of orientation achieved by exclusively homosexual people, *no matter how much they may desire it* (with there being no question at this point of enforcing change on the unwilling). Not only did Kinsey Research fail, in a six-year search, to find anyone whose sex life had changed as a result of therapy of any kind; but also a member of the group has maintained a standing offer to administer the Kinsey Research battery of tests to any person a therapist might send as an example of a "cure" of homosexuality. Even those who have written extensively on allegedly successful work with homosexuals have not provided a single client who might substantiate their claims.[265]

Those who might wish to contrast this negative result in the secular arena with the claims of the Christian ex-gay movement have had to become increasingly cautious in their statements as one after another of the ex-gay ministries slips all too silently from the scene.[266] Their newfound caution sometimes exceeds their candor, that is, in acknowledging how many of the founders of such ministries have become ex-ex-gay, or have even become sexually involved with those sent to them for help — another manifestation of the way the facts about homosexuality have been

---

265. Tripp, *Homosexual Matrix,* pp. 236-37.

266. Witness the shift of *Christianity Today* from a banner headline in 1981 declaring "Homosexuals CAN Change" (Feb. 6) to the remark of editor Kenneth Kantzer in 1983 that, "The evidence is clear that such a turn is often not very successful" (April 22, 1983, p. 9).

suppressed throughout history.[267] The issue here is not the propensity of leaders to fall into sin, which has been amply illustrated in the heterosexual community. Rather, the issue is that both the leaders and the followers in the ex-gay movement give little evidence of change in sexual orientation, even when they have carefully governed their behavior and no matter what their quite sincere claims may be of having become new people in Christ. A Christian should not object to examining such claims critically, just as she should not object to taking the wine of Cana to a laboratory for chemical analysis.[268]

Even those who speak in the most glowing terms of their new identity as ex-gay often do so, particularly when questioned, in ways that suggest that they could in no meaningful sense be called heterosexual in their orientation. One young man, writing in praise of God's gift of a wonderful wife, adds, "This does not mean there is never any temptation," and expresses gratitude for God's gift of strength in what had been an uncontrollable area of his life.[269] Another man wrote of leaving his denomination because a minister whom he told about his past suggested he should not fight his homosexuality. He continued, "I can live in celibacy as I heal and move into my new heterosexual identity. . . . Temptation is painful enough without receiving support, and worse, without receiving criticism, at your

267. Ralph Blair gives continuing coverage to the fate of ex-gay ministries — and the ignorant or dishonest use made of their claims — in his newsletter *Record*. He notes, for instance, that the *Christian Herald* magazine promotes Exodus and Homosexuals Anonymous without telling readers that the two founders of the former (Michael Bussee and Gary Cooper) are in a committed gay relationship with one another and testify that nobody changed to heterosexuality at Exodus, while the founder of the latter (Seventh-Day Adventist Colin Cook, who has since tried again with another group) was forced to resign in 1987 after it became known that he had had sex with at least fourteen young men who had come to his ministry (*Record*, winter 1991, p. 1; spring 1990, p. 1). Doug Houck of Metanoia Ministries resigned due to continued homosexual activity (*Record*, fall 1990, p. 1). Jeff Ford, formerly of Outpost, no longer claims to have been "healed" of homosexuality and denies that any of the over three hundred people with whom he worked were healed, either (*Record*, summer 1990, p. 1). Guy Charles of Liberation in Jesus Christ, widely touted by evangelicals, was much earlier discovered to have had sex with those who came to him. Founders of Disciples Only, Love in Action, and EXIT of Melodyland, among others, are no longer in the ex-gay movement due to their continued homosexuality (Ralph Blair, *Ex-Gay* [New York: HCCC, 1982], p. 5). And now-bankrupt publisher Dan Malachuk continued to publish Kent Philpott's *The Third Sex?* even after the alleged ex-gays who were its subjects informed him that they were still gay and that the accounts in the book were misleading (*Record*, winter 1982, p. 3).

268. Contrast the remark of Ron Highley of L.I.F.E. ministry to a *New York Times* reporter, referring to statistics on change in the ex-gay movement: "When it comes to matters of truth, numbers don't count" (quoted in *Record*, fall 1990, p. 1).

269. Jeff Painter, "Saved By God's Grace," reprinted from *Good News* in the *Presbyterian Layman*, 1983.

334 WHO WE ARE: OUR DIGNITY AS HUMAN

own local church."[270] A lesbian claimed that although her body sometimes felt as if it were on fire, no matter what she was feeling, she knew she was a new creature and had been delivered by Christ from her lesbianism.[271] Since-fallen leader Colin Cook had even earlier called changing homosexual desires to heterosexual ones a "wistful hope" and spoke simply of claiming Christ's heterosexuality as one's own.[272] These expressions seem typical; and to say that the change they seek to affirm has not extended to the actual sexual orientation of the people involved is in no way to discount the possibility that these people have had a genuine encounter with Christ, or that they are now living more responsible lives than they had in the past. To call them ex-gay in anything but genital behavior would seem, nonetheless, to be a misuse of words.

That is exactly what those who have been the ex-gay route and have departed from it insist. When one speaks with those who have tried not only prayer but also everything from exorcism to electric shock, including twenty years of heterosexual marriage and parenthood, and who continue to have homosexual feelings as strong as ever, one senses the cruelty — unintended, of course, but real — of evangelicals who write confidently:

> God is eager to help anyone who really wants to change. Hence, no homosexual needs to feel he or she is bound and cannot change. He or she can, with God's help, be completely freed of the desire for homosexual relations and any other problems that may be associated with it.[273]

Such a statement (reduplicated many times in the literature) is surely a classic example of "the will to believe," which flies in the face of the testimony of those who, *because of their evangelical beliefs,* have persistently tried every avenue of change they know. It is unfair to such persons to presume that "probably few homosexual believers have made any consistent effort to lay hold by faith of the power of Christ for the progressive transformation of their lives";[274] indeed, it bears some analogy to the claim that those who do not experience healing from physical illness must lack faith, since Christ is surely able to heal them. Further, one may note the

270. Anonymous letter in *Presbyterians Pro-Life News,* fall/winter 1990-91, p. 1.

271. Deborah LaGanza, *Delivered from Lesbianism,* noted in Ralph Blair, *Holier-Than-Thou Hocus-Pocus and Homosexuality* (New York: HCCC, 1977), p. 28.

272. *Record,* winter 1987.

273. Letter from the session and ministers of the Parkminster Presbyterian Church of Rochester, New York, reprinted in the Presbyterian Charismatic Communion Newsletter, May/June 1976, p. 11.

274. Lovelace, "Active Homosexual Lifestyle," p. 25.

frequency with which pastors and theologians advocate psychotherapy for homosexuals, while evangelical psychologists and psychiatrists suggest spiritual remedies. Such humility creates suspicions.

Heterosexual marriage neither produces nor evidences change in homosexual orientation, though it does provide a cover for those who believe they must keep their sexual
orientation secret or who are seeking to convince themselves that they are not homosexual. While gay men who can "perform" heterosexually (often by engaging in
homosexual fantasies) may technically be bisexual and may care deeply for their wives
and children, those who have always been strongly homosexual in their orientation
report that they never come to enjoy a woman's body and do not find that sexual
relations with a woman meet their emotional needs. The women who fall in love with
such men and believe their love can change them end up defeated and wounded —
their needs, too, unmet. Such marriages are a tragedy for all concerned. Of course many
heterosexual men and women manage in marriages that are sexually unsatisfying; but
that fact does nothing to support the idea that marriage can serve as a "cure" for
homosexuality. (See, for example, Brown, *Familiar Faces, Hidden Lives,* chap. 7.)

What shall we say, then, about the implied promise of change in 1 Corinthians 6:11? If it is true, as we have acknowledged probable, that Paul did not know of or seek to make a distinction between homosexual orientation and behavior, and hence did not differentiate between homosexual acts by those deeply homosexual in their orientation and those carried out by heterosexuals engaged in perverted and exploitative practices, then it could well be that the change he observed took place in persons in the latter category. No one doubts that this sort of change in behavior is both possible and important, but it does not constitute a change of basic sexual orientation. Given our view of God's design as revealed in Scripture and the utter moral unacceptability of multiple sexual relationships, we would also affirm that those bisexuals who are torn between homosexual and heterosexual attractions should come down firmly and exclusively on the heterosexual side, whatever wrenches of desire they may continue to feel.[275] Most people know what it is to be attracted to more than one person while being called to remain committed to one only. But what shall we say to the person who has never known heterosexual feelings? That is, what is the relationship between empirical evidence of what one can actually expect to happen and what one can responsibly advocate? Would we

275. We consider it to be plausible that those rare testimonies of change that at least
appear to be convincing come from basically bisexual people who have been involved in
compulsive, impersonal, and therefore unsatisfactory homosexual lifestyles. (See, for instance, the review of *Straight: A Heterosexual Talks About His Homosexual Past* by William
Aaron [a pseudonymn] in the *Christian Century* 89, no. 46 [Dec. 20, 1972]: 1305-6.)

consider it to be *wrong* to pray for an amputee's leg to grow back? foolish? cruel?[276] The question is not whether the Lord could, theoretically, accomplish the miracle, or even whether we consider it desirable that he should, but whether it is fair to offer the expectation that he will.

b) Committed Homosexual Relationships

Evangelical homosexuals who have come to believe that they cannot change and both need and have a human right to an outlet for their erotic and affectional energies increasingly advocate committed, monogamous homosexual relationships, on the pattern of heterosexual marriage. Further, they ask that these relationships be given legal status — a demand that some may score as a manifestation of mere economic self-interest when it comes to, say, tax laws; but which takes on a whole different level of human meaning if the question is "family" visiting privileges when one's partner is critically ill in the hospital or inheritance rights of treasured mementos. They are understandably incensed that society uses evidence of homosexual promiscuity to support views of the perverted nature of homosexuality in general, and at the same time refuses to sanction, either legally or attitudinally, structures that would support instead of punish long-term relationships. Consider the tale of "two brothers, one gay and one straight. Both went to Wheaton College. One had no problem finding a nice Christian mate. The other got kicked out for trying!"[277] If we condemn promiscuity, we should not behave so as to encourage it.

Evidence of massive inconsistency in this regard is easy to obtain. When basketball star Magic Johnson admitted to being HIV positive, people were so relieved to find he had contracted the virus by heterosexual contact that they seemed not to be too concerned about his admitted enormous promiscuity before his marriage. After all, "boys will be boys." Tennis star Martina Navratilova, an acknowledged lesbian, remarked that a similar announcement from her would have received a different response. She said in an interview, "They'd say I'm gay — I had it coming" (quoted by James Wall, "Moral Wisdom and Sexual Conduct," *Christian Century* 108, no. 35 [Dec. 4, 1991]: 1123).

Even so, and granting that there may be some bias in the data, it would appear from a number of studies that the level of promiscuity among male homosexuals (not among lesbians, perhaps because lesbian relationships are both less suspected and less

276. We use this example only because it suggests a situation that the observer might wish to see changed but about changing which she would not be sanguine. The question here is neither the extent to which homosexual orientation is physiologically determined, nor the extent to which it is morally culpable, but only whether we have reason to believe it can be fundamentally altered.

277. "We're Living Who We Are," *The Other Side* 14, no. 6 (June 1978): 29.

abhorred) is extremely high, involving, on the part of more than 90 percent of gay men, from dozens to five hundred or more partners over the course of their lives (Alan P. Bell and Martin S. Weinberg, *Homosexualities* [New York: Simon and Schuster, 1978], pp. 81-102). While long-term relationships on the part of gay men and lesbians do certainly exist, such relationships tend generally to be much less stable than their heterosexual counterparts, and perhaps less likely to be monogamous. (See Brown, *Familiar Faces, Hidden Lives,* pp. 132ff.; but cf. the affirmation of some in the Metropolitan Community Church that those whose relationship has been recognized in a "holy union" ceremony are more likely to maintain a lifetime commitment [K. Cherry and J. Mitulski, "Committed Couples in the Gay Community," *Christian Century* 107, no. 7 (Feb. 28, 1990): 218]. Also see Dell Richards, *Lesbian Lists* [Boston: Alyson, 1990], pp. 132-33, for nineteen lesbian couples who lived together for from twenty to seventy-five years.) To gather such data is not, of course, to establish the reason for the phenomena. While some attribute them to particular difficulties of same-sex relationships or, on the part of males, to the tendencies of the male sex drive when not moderated by the somewhat differing demands of the female, others attribute them quite directly to social pressures. If discovery that one is homosexual threatens one's career and family ties, one might find anonymous and fleeting sexual contacts to be safest. If same-sex partners are vilified for living together, these pressures may add more stress than the relationship can absorb (just as outside pressures can threaten heterosexual marriages). If a Catholic homosexual recognizes that he will be denied absolution if he lives in "a state of sin," he may choose the occasional promiscuity for which he can receive absolution (John McNeill, cited by Scanzoni and Mollenkott, *Is the Homosexual My Neighbor?* p. 63). Where the truth lies in these matters can hardly be discerned as long as current social structures and attitudes prevail.

What may particularly trouble the evangelical, though, or anyone who takes seriously the profound human impact of sexual encounters, is the extent to which many writers doubt the importance of the monogamous ideal, particularly when there is no danger of pregnancy and there are no children to protect. (See, for example, Brown, *Familiar Faces, Hidden Lives,* p. 133; Tripp, *Homosexual Matrix,* chap. 8.) This doubt pervades the heterosexual community as well. We know of one congregation where the minister was criticized not for advocating "holy union" ceremonies for homosexual people, but for insisting that gay and straight people alike should restrict sexual behavior to formalized, permanent relationships. But there is a certain tension between saying that one's sexuality is central to one's personhood and demands an outlet — critical to the homosexual's argument for freedom of sexual expression — and saying that particular sex acts are *not* so important to one's personhood that they may not be engaged in with more than one other person.

* * * * *

Homosexual "marriage" is hardly a new idea. Such marriage was officially outlawed in Rome in 342, showing that it was previously at least de facto legal (Boswell, *Christianity, Social Tolerance, and Homosexuality,* p. 123). Further evidence comes from discovery of a large number of old commitment ceremonies for same-sex couples. (Boswell published his analysis of these ceremonies in his *Same-Sex Unions in Pre-*

modern Europe [New York: Villard Books, 1994]; and even those who deny that the "brother-making" liturgies in any meaningful sense resemble marriage still grant that they are very interesting. See, for instance, Philip Lyndon Reynolds, "Same-sex Unions: What Boswell Didn't Find," *Christian Century* 112, no. 2 [Jan. 18, 1995]: 49-59.) In more recent times, a wedding mass for two homosexual men was celebrated in 1967 in Rotterdam, the Netherlands, where homosexual acts between consenting adults have been legal ever since the Napoleonic Code came in force; but Rotterdam's bishop later claimed the officiating priest "was tricked into performing what he thought was a confirmation of a life-long friendship" (Charles Sanders, "Homosexuals Become 'Man' and 'Wife' in Unusual Wedding," *Jet* 32, no. 24 [Sept. 21, 1967]: 24-27).

When it comes to recognition of homosexual couples by the civil authority, Denmark allows homosexuals to marry and gives them most of the rights of heterosexual families, except for adoption and recognition by the state Lutheran Church (*Los Angeles Times,* May 27, 1989, pt. 1, p. 4). Sweden is considering similar legislation; and San Francisco, California, has also enacted a domestic partners law. The current trend seems to be in this direction; but one should note that even where homosexuality has long been officially tolerated, as in the Netherlands, problems of discrimination continue just below the surface. Toleration and acceptance are not the same thing.

Among churches, as of this writing, only the homosexual-run Metropolitan Community Church and the Unitarian Universalist Association officially approve the performance of "holy union" ceremonies. Individual clergy of many denominations, however, will bless homosexual unions; and many denominational leaders look the other way. More conservative ministers and laypeople may then appeal to the formal policy statements of their denomination to seek to prevent such ceremonies and to discipline those performing them. (See, for example, the *Presbyterian Layman* 24, no. 6, [November/December 1991]: 3.)

Many homosexual people argue both that those who are gay "by nature" should *rightly* relate sexually to those of the same sex (anything else would be, for them, *un*natural), and that sexual relationships should be evaluated not by the gender of the parties involved but by the quality of love the relationship exemplifies (an argument that has also frequently been made in support of sanctioning sexual expression by single heterosexuals). They do not wish merely to have their love tolerated, but to be able to celebrate as a positive good what they experience as the most precious thing in their lives — a privilege heterosexuals take for granted.[278] A union between two people is validated not primarily by procreation but by the fellowship they enjoy.[279] When it is understood that way, two men

278. One recalls the argument of Joseph Fletcher for affirming the best choice available to one: "*The situationist holds that whatever is the most loving thing in the situation is the right and good thing.* It is not excusably evil, it is positively good" (*Situation Ethics* [Philadelphia: Westminster, 1966], p. 65).

279. Recall that we have left ourselves open to this point of view in our treatment of "The Blessings of Marriage," above, pp. 228-31.

or two women may experience the blessings of union no less than a man and a woman. As a matter of fact, as the relationship continues, homosexual couples find, as do heterosexual couples, that sex as such plays a less consuming and dominant role, while other forms of intimacy grow in their importance. That is, marriage or a holy union is certainly not just a sex license, but rather allows sex to take its proper place as one component of one's life.

To the argument that same-sex relationships violate the creation principle that we are given our humanity as a fellowship of male and female and that any other pattern does violence to that cohumanity, one may make three rejoinders. First, while we must indeed interpret our humanity as cohumanity, we should not reduce that cohumanity to a matter of mere gender difference, lest we lose its general ethical significance. Instead, it is advised, we should understand it in terms of having our humanity only together with an *other* who is different from us and whom we may not seek constantly to make conform to our desires.[280] Some have even suggested a divine teleology in homosexual relationships, insofar as they may model a nonhierarchical style by which those involved in traditional heterosexual marriages might well be instructed. The second rejoinder is that homosexual people, like heterosexual people, see themselves and relate as either male or female: they do not deny their gender. Further, even though they choose same-sex sexual partners, they have friends of the opposite sex. Therefore, some claim, sanctioning homosexual unions does not violate the cohumanity of creation even in terms of gender differentiation. Third, if only heterosexually married people rightly fulfill the creation design, what shall we say about those who spend their lives single and celibate? Shall we impugn their humanity? Scripture clearly does not. Hence heterosexual marriage cannot be made the only legitimate mode of existence.

These arguments have some considerable force, particularly given the difficulties of the "celibacy" solution, which we shall discuss below. If we cannot fully embrace them, and thus construe committed homosexual relationships as properly having the same status among Christians[281] as committed heterosexual relationships, the reason lies not in our attribution to homosexual people of particular moral depravity, but rather in our understanding of God's purposes in creation, as attested by Scripture. That

280. Theodore W. Jennings, "Homosexuality and the Christian Faith: A Theological Reflection," *Christian Century* 94, no. 5 (Feb. 16, 1977): 138.

281. We are speaking here only of our theological understanding, not of the question of basic civil rights for homosexual couples.

is, we have not seen our way clear to attributing homosexuality to the creation side of the ledger rather than to the effects of the Fall.[282] And while we certainly ought not to blame people for suffering the effects of the Fall (we do not blame women for experiencing pain in childbirth, for instance), neither ought we freely to affirm those effects as a positive good, even when we do or should affirm the good that may come of them — good like deep love between two homosexual people, or heroic character built from suffering pain.

As we have already remarked, appeals to love taken alone — the quality or strength of love between homosexuals or the love Christians are enjoined to evidence for all people — will not suffice as an ethical norm. Should we doubt that our personal drives or our desires to be tolerant can blind us in this matter, consider the 1989 document the Roman Catholic group Dignity prepared to give theological direction on gay and lesbian sexual expression. One of its conclusions was not only that *all* "diversity of sexual and genital behavior" could be seen to reflect God's presence, but also that "we must explore together and learn from one another about . . . pornography, prostitution, sex with minors, multiple partners, anonymous sex, bondage and discipline," and so on.[283] The writers reported that they consulted their individual experience, reflection, and values in forming their judgments, and they spoke freely of "what God is doing in our lives" when talking about their own behavior.[284] An example of this kind makes clear that it is not just the holder of a poorly differentiated domino theory who may have qualms about where a love ethic grounded in nothing but what we experience as loving leads.[285]

282. The well-attested fact of animal homosexuality is not an argument to the contrary: we understand the whole of the created order to be marked by the effects of the Fall. (This is not to suggest a *temporal* relationship between the Fall and disruptions of the natural order, as if there were no illness or death before Adam sinned; but rather to find the *reason* for such disruptions in the Fall: causes but not reasons must precede effects.) Incidentally (though in a very different context), Thielicke notes that it was from a tree that God himself had created that he told Adam and Eve not to eat; and Thielicke puts in the mouth of the serpent the argument that surely nothing God had made could be bad or forbidden (*How the World Began,* trans. John W. Doberstein [Philadelphia: Fortress, 1961], p. 128). Obviously, though — if one wished to argue from creation, which we do not — one should count the difference in human cost between not eating of a particular tree and not expressing that sort of human intimacy for which one most longs.

283. Quoted (disapprovingly) by Ralph Blair in his *Review* 14, no. 2 (winter 1990).

284. Ibid.

285. Reinhold Niebuhr once remarked that we are "never as dangerous as when we act in love," for then we are at our worst as judges of what we are actually doing (quoted by John W. Turnbull, "Homosexuality: Some Neglected Issues," *Church and Society* 67, no. 5 [May-June 1977]: 77). As a further caution, we may note that there is some indication

Because the church must seek to uphold biblical norms and not simply redefine as normal our experience after the Fall, there is some reason for hesitation about its performing services of union for same-sex couples that are called or closely resemble "marriage." Not only does marriage have a range of functions that cannot be duplicated in homosexual unions (as is recognized when the latter are called "holy unions" instead of marriages);[286] but also we continue to believe that a person's being was intended to be complemented not only in an I-thou relationship, but in one in which the "I" is male or female and the "thou" is female or male. That is, we do not think that humanity could just as well have been all male or all female, with procreation managed as it is among some of the lower animals. Nor, given our view of how deeply our personhood and our sexuality are tied, is it enough simply to acknowledge that it is good that there should be both men and women, while denying that the goodness was necessarily intended by the Creator to have anything specifically sexual about it.

To make this judgment is not necessarily to deny out of hand the legitimacy of committed, same-sex relationships in our actual fallen estate. For one thing, in its legal aspect marriage and any analogs to it belong to the state, not to the church; and state and church do not have to operate according to the same principles with respect to it. Further, we have alluded to the fact that even for Christians, the ceremony is not the essence of the marriage; and under special circumstances Christians intending a per-

---

that many or most sexual predilections, including pedophilia, are established very early and are not a matter of conscious choice, any more than is homosexuality. Pedophilia may be rejected out of hand (though Dignity did not!) on the grounds that it involves obvious exploitation in a way that homosexuality does not. Rejecting it, however, means that one does not give the fact of the existence of a predilection or drive the power to determine its ethical status, even if the drive is strong. (We consider it dismaying that the most recent APA *Diagnostic and Statistical Manual* [4th ed., 1994] does not count one a pedophile just because one has sex with children, but only if one is distressed about one's behavior or because it causes impairment in some important area of functioning — and similarly as regards sexual sadism and masochism, exhibitionism, and voyeurism. Recall our earlier insistence that it is not the sick conscience but the healthy one that gives a person distress over wrong behavior [p. 92 above].)

286. To whatever extent it may be true that "We see increasing numbers of lesbian or gay couples who have children through artificial insemination or adoption" (Cherry and Mitulski, "Committed Couples," p. 219), and however much a desire for children may be understandable, the problematic character of homosexuality surely shows up here as much as anywhere. By no plausible argument about "nature" can children result from the union of two people of the same sex. Marriages are valid without children, and many children do not live in a two-parent family, and some intact families are abusive; but none of those facts should be used to argue that something other than heterosexual marriage is a *desirable* arrangement for the rearing of children.

manent commitment may forgo a public ceremony.[287] It would seem to us
possible that the church might accept what it would be improper to its role
actively to bless or to celebrate.[288]

We must acknowledge, however, that we can hardly expect what we
might consider a necessary reticence to be met with anything but hearty
resentment from the homosexual community. Not only do homosexuals
want the same freedom to affirm themselves and their relationships that
heterosexuals enjoy; but also they have every reason to believe that the
judgment implied in any reticence will result in continuing discrimination
against them, as it always has. Moreover, human relationships do need the
help of supportive structures and people, including the church. In fact, they
need all the help they can get. We must admit that anything that lessens
the degree of social support adds additional pressures to circumstances that
are already difficult and may foster behaviors that the church deplores.
Further, saying that the church may accept what it may not bless leaves
the church open to the charge: "We have asked, absurdly, the culture to be
more gracious and free than we are willing to be ourselves."[289]

c) Celibacy

While advocates of change wish ideally to address sexual orientation and
advocates of committed homosexual relationships wish to redefine the
criteria for responsible sexual activity (usually on the basis of a love ethic
combined with an assertion of the naturalness of homosexual orientation
for a significant minority of the population), advocates of celibacy for
homosexuals limit themselves to talking about behavior. Their bottom line
(and the official position of most denominations) is that all sexual activity
sanctioned by the church must occur in the context of heterosexual
marriage. Period. Some who take this position cast no moral aspersions of
any kind on homosexual orientation, counting it morally neutral, as well

---

287. See above, pp. 266-70.

288. An analogy might be to divorce: there are surely occasions, as we have argued,
when continuing a marriage causes far more harm than dissolving it; but we have also argued
that *celebrating* the dissolution of a marriage can be nothing but a travesty (see above, pp.
276-83). Similarly, refusing to acknowledge committed relationships between homosexual
people may, given the power of sexual drives, lead to serious harm; but it does not follow
that the church should *bless* what it cannot affirm as at least pointing toward God's intention
for human life. This "acceptance without celebration" rubric is similar to a variety of "lesser
of two evils" arguments, like Thielicke's suggestion that the homosexual "has to realize his
optimal ethical potentialities *on the basis* of his irreversible situation" (*Ethics of Sex*, p. 285).

289. "An Affirmation of Conscience" (responding to the 1978 Presbyterian General
Assembly's refusal to ordain avowed, practicing homosexuals), *Church and Society* 58, no.
5 (May-June 1978): 27.

as beyond many people's choice or control. Others do not see the orientation as quite neutral, given their view that it is a manifestation of the consequences of the Fall; but they see it as no more — if no less — culpable than any other indication of our common human condition. And some continue to lump everything related to homosexuality into the emotion-laden category "abomination." In any case, those counseling celibacy generally believe we ought to concern ourselves not with what people cannot help but with what they can, namely, their actions.[290] And if homosexuals govern their actions, or at least are duly penitent when they stumble, they ought to suffer no disability in church or society.

This solution has an attractive and deceptive tidiness about it. It is attractive because it asks of homosexuals what we in some sense ask of all of us sinners — that we not act on all of what we are, that some of our impulses go unexpressed. It is deceptive in that it may far too easily treat what is central to a person's identity and experience of self as if it were peripheral and incidental. While the church has always recognized and affirmed the vocation of celibacy, it has construed it as a special calling, voluntarily embraced, not something to be imposed. Such a calling might involve some critical ratio of a gift of self-control and dedication on the one hand, to one's natural drive level on the other (the higher the drive level, the more specially gifted one would need to be). Simply to assume that all homosexual people are so gifted goes against both reason and experience, and seriously disadvantages those who are both exclusively homosexual in their attractions and high in their need for sexual expression.

The question of the ordination of homosexuals has revolved around the demand for celibacy: most denominations are quite ready to ordain *repentant* and *celibate* homosexuals, just as they have always been willing to ordain repentant philanderers and nonpracticing adulterers. If the church did not ordain sinners, it would have no clergy. That there should be no barrier to ordaining celibate homosexuals, then, should be and remain obvious; and maintaining the standard of celibacy for homosexual clergy may be the church's best option. (Even so, in what may be the backlash department, the United Methodist Western Pennsylvania Conference passed a resolution in June 1990, including anyone who is "emotionally, mentally, spiritually, or physically practicing" in the category of "practicing homosexual," thus effectively barring celibate homosexuals from ordination — which goes to show that ground assumed won can quickly be lost again. See the *Christian Century* 108, no. 2 [Jan. 16, 1991]: 40.) However, demanding lifelong celibacy for a whole class of clergy puts Protestants in a bind, since they

290. For example, take the statement of Al Krass: "All of us accept the fact of homosexual *orientation*. And we don't feel compelled to call it a 'sickness.' So the nub of the issue for us concerns responsible discipleship — *behavior*" ("We're Living Who We Are," p. 25).

have explicitly rejected the Roman Catholic position in this regard. The Protestant church does not assume that a calling to celibacy and a calling to the ministry always go together for heterosexuals, so conservative theologians could be charged with egregious inconsistency for thinking it obvious that they must always go together for homosexuals. (Judaism, with its strong family values, has traditionally [apart from its Reconstructionist branch] taken a still stronger stand and refused to ordain not only homosexuals but also those who believe themselves called to celibacy.) While proponents of this position could obviously argue that they are rejecting not sex but sin, that argument will not help the homosexual.

Still, the terminology used by those advocating the ordination of "self-avowed, practicing" homosexuals is scarcely reassuring. These words sound much like "sexually active" when applied to the heterosexual, implying sexual activity not restricted to a single, lifelong partner. We count such activity unacceptable for everyone. Granted that church and society have hardly made committed relationships between homosexuals easy; but surely the standard for homosexuals cannot be set lower than for heterosexuals without impugning their human dignity — as serious an offense as asking for superhuman heroics of self-control.

We must also grant that under current conditions, a committed, monogamous, homosexual couple might well, as a political statement, describe themselves as selfavowed and practicing. This latter case is tricky, as is even the case when, as a matter of simple honesty, a homosexual couple, one or both of whom desire ordination, acknowledges openly their relationship. Theologians sometimes piously remark that to be a "self-avowed" sinner of any stripe is tantamount to endorsing sin, which no minister of the gospel should be allowed to do. However, we ordain self-avowed, practicing liars all the time: liars who defend certain lies as the best option open to them under particular circumstances (or who would defend themselves in this way if challenged). Of course such persons seldom celebrate lying, and we hope that they seek to avoid it; but lie and defend lying they do, and so, at least on rare occasions, do most of the rest of us. If we differentiate between ordaining these persons and ordaining a homosexual in a committed relationship who argues that that alternative is the best one realistically open to her or him, presumably it would need to be on some such grounds as the ongoing nature of the homosexual relationship (which, inconsistently enough, is exactly what we demand of intimate relationships!) and its visibility (like the fine homes and expensive, polluting vehicles of the wealthy?), which suggest approbation of that to which the church cannot point as embodying the biblical norm and which therefore can lead to confusion of the part of the faithful. Understandably enough, homosexuals respond that it is stances of this kind that keep them trapped in dissimulation and deception on the one hand and promiscuity on the other.

As far as self-control is concerned, it is quite a different thing to say "later" than to say "never." In the not-so-distant past the society at large managed with some success to support the church's "later!" directed at highly sexed teenagers. But can one imagine either society or church thinking it workable to tell these teenagers that they must abstain not just through adolescence but throughout their entire lives, and that they must *never* seek to meet their needs for sexual intimacy? Who would be surprised if such a dictum led to complete flouting of restraint? More importantly, most people would readily consider the demand both cruel and damaging. Yet many readily make it of all homosexuals, laying heavy burdens, hard to bear, on the shoulders of others (Mt. 23:4). One thirty-five-year-old farmer, a leader in his community, closeted and celibate, wrote as follows:

> I do not recommend my way of life to anyone. I am a homosexual, quite happy and capable of contributing to my community, but I am doing it by nearly impossible means. I have avoided all sexual relations; and I don't believe that this is mentally, physically, or socially healthy for young men. . . . I don't contend that I have more will power or that I have been less tempted or that I have less sexual desire than other healthy young men, but circumstances and conditions have been such that I can, with difficulty, lead a life that might destroy others. I pay a high price for this. I have to keep my distance from everyone. In this respect at least, mine is an impossible life.[291]

That this sort of loneliness is not only painful but also can be physically damaging has been shown by numerous studies that demonstrate a dramatically higher incidence of disease and premature death among those who live alone. Sometimes such premature death even results from suicide on the part of homosexuals with conservative theological convictions who are driven to despair by their inability to remain celibate.[292]

An analogy is sometimes drawn between the situation of the homosexual and that of the single woman in a society in which women outnumber men and in which, therefore, a certain number of women will, whatever their wishes, remain unmarried. Some women are essentially in the position of those to whom the realities of life have said "never," no matter what their need may be for sexual expression. From this analogy, two opposite conclusions can be and have been drawn. The traditional one states that since such women can and should remain celibate, so can and should all homosexuals. The other assumes that crippling sexual frustrations should be imposed on no one and that some sort of love ethic should be used to evaluate the propriety of sexual expression by heterosexual single people as well as by homosexuals (the position taken by the

---

291. Quoted in Brown, *Familiar Faces, Hidden Lives,* pp. 98-99.

292. One can only marvel at the naïveté of the suggested solution that homosexuals might live together with a lifelong commitment but without sexual intercourse. Were such a pair not sexually attracted to one another, their sexual needs would not be met (though they might gain some benefits of human companionship). Were they sexually attracted, the arrangement could hardly be other than torment (or else a failure in the celibacy department). (See Ralph Blair's *Review* 13, no. 2 [winter 1989], commenting on Tony Campolo's *20 Hot Potatoes Christians Are Afraid to Touch;* and also his pamphlet *Ex-Gay,* pp. 46-47.)

controversial Presbyterian study, *Keeping Body and Soul Together*). Either way, the problem is not one faced *only* by homosexual people; though it is legitimate to differentiate between disabilities affecting a whole group of people by definition and those affecting only a certain proportion of individuals in a group.

Even apart from practical considerations of physical well-being, which surely compassion must somehow heed, we face a difficult theological problem created by the attempt to drive a wedge between orientation and behavior (which is, in any case, almost impossible to do, as we have argued earlier). How can we possibly say that it is perfectly all right to *be* homosexual (orientation), with all the concomitant feelings and desires, but not all right to act on that orientation? If the orientation is morally neutral, how can there be no morally acceptable expression of it? But if the expression is always wrong, must not the impulse also be wrong? We might as well say that there is nothing wrong with being a murderer or adulterer in one's heart provided that one does not actually commit murder or adultery. Jesus said exactly the opposite in the Sermon on the Mount (Mt. 5:21-22, 27-28). The point is not that we can avoid sinful feelings and desires, and certainly not that the consequences for others are not worse when they are expressed, but rather that we do not label them as in themselves acceptable as long as they are kept inside. Everyone will find herself utterly unable to meet Scripture's demand for purity, but we do not for that reason change the standard.

It may, however, be relevant that, in the interests of reducing guilt feelings and maintaining self-esteem, much of modern psychiatry and psychology has sought to change the standard with respect to most or all of our deep and primitive impulses. They would make, for instance, the feeling of anger normal or neutral while suggesting curbs on its expression — the same split some evangelicals propose regarding homosexuality; except that curbs on expression would doubtless not be advocated by the psychologists if uninhibited expression did not clearly lead to negative consequences (as the "let-it-all-hang-out" school of thought learned to its sorrow). Furthermore, the traditional church has been scored by these disciplines on the grounds that its unrealistic, unreachable standards respecting heart attitudes make people sick and miserable. With respect to homosexuality, though, the oppressiveness for which the church is castigated is often currently located not in its ideal standards but precisely in its demand for curbs on expression. Such differences show once again how (changing) value judgments inevitably enter into allegedly scientific discussions.

Nonetheless, sexuality as such is not quite like these other impulses. When those of us who are heterosexual examine our own sexuality and the sinful misdirection to which it tends, we sense not only that we want to distinguish between the sexuality (which we affirm) and its misdirection (which we deplore); but also that we cannot quite desire that it be simply gone, as we can, say, a tendency to envy or lust.[293] We know we would be both better and happier were we free of envy and lust; most of us cannot imagine ourselves better or happier were our sexual orientation itself changed or nullified. Our sexuality is not only mysterious and powerful, but pervasive; not a merely bodily urge in a struggle between body and soul, but involved in our being as persons.[294] Thus we can perhaps see why the homosexual cannot separate her or his sense of self from her or his homosexuality. It follows that if we show concern for the heart as well as for the act, as Scripture insists that we must, and if we cannot on biblical grounds affirm homosexuality (as we have said we cannot), we find ourselves trapped into a more rigorist position than that of those who simply demand celibacy (who, we have suggested, demand what would readily be seen to be cruel and unjust if applied to heterosexuals). We find ourselves rejecting what homosexual people cannot separate from their very selves. The unsatisfactoriness of this result will be felt keenly by those who have known and respected Christian homosexual people.

4) A "Conclusion" of Sorts

Shortly before his death, Oscar Wilde said:

> I never came across anyone in whom the moral sense was dominant who was not heartless, cruel, vindictive, log-stupid and entirely lacking in the smallest sense of humanity. Moral people, as they are termed, are simple beasts. I would sooner have fifty unnatural vices than one unnatural virtue.[295]

These words haunt the theologian, for change "moral people" to "religious people" and they characterize all too accurately how the church, in the name of virtue, has behaved toward homosexuals. Something has to be wrong with

293. Recall the well-known case of Origen, who took Mt. 19:12 literally and castrated himself to try to secure himself against any temptations stemming from his sexuality. He later regretted his action (Schaff, *History,* 2.788). Perhaps this intuited sense of our sexuality as so permeating our being is involved in the church's long-standing inclination (which we have criticized above) to condemn sexual sins more strongly than others. It would indeed be an ironic twist, even though one blessed by Dante, if they were now to be treated most leniently!

294. We commented above on the deep and pervasive mystery of human sexuality (pp. 176-79); but we did not at that point make plain, as we by now clearly must, that the gender of those to whom we are attracted must be considered part of that mystery.

295. Quoted by Karlen, *Sexuality and Homosexuality,* p. 255.

teaching that evokes absolute hatred, loathing, and disdain for homosexual people, so much so that while, as we have noted, we experienced a devastating mea culpa with respect to the fate of Jews in Nazi Germany, we acknowledged nothing similar with respect to gays, who were also victims but who got neither sympathy nor help in recuperating. We are left with the feeling that the church has overdone it, no matter how you cut it; and that homosexuals have certainly suffered more wrong than they have committed; and that there must be flaws in whatever theology of nature or hierarchy of sins has made homosexuality be viewed as the nadir of depravity (even as something was wrong with the theology of place that was used to justify the Crusades). This feeling increases when one becomes acquainted with responsible, Christian, homosexual people and seeks to listen to their stories and their suffering. If stereotypes and destructive attitudes are to change, there is no substitute for knowing those who are oppressed by them (and perhaps discovering that many people whom one already knows and respects are in fact homosexual).

Apart from a deeply repentant change in overall attitude easier to advocate than to produce, the precise form the church's repentance should take is painfully difficult to determine: we have not been able to resolve the *sic et non* with which we began. Sharpening the issues leaves us with an increased sense of the inadequacy of every option of which we are aware, and also of how much more ambivalence of this kind costs the homosexual minority than the heterosexual majority. At the very least, we can insist that it is clearly and manifestly unjust that we should put up with the gravest evils and perversions provided that they take heterosexual form, but explode at homosexual sins. Surely, as we have said repeatedly, the question of the propriety of granting full civil rights should be regarded as settled: that differentiation between disposition and act that is so problematic for theology is entirely appropriate to the state, which must concern itself only with acts. Further, the state should concern itself with acts that harm the society as a whole, not those practiced in private by freely consenting adults. Of course the state must continue to seek to protect children. Pedophilia rights for school teachers do not comprise a legitimate subset of gay rights. But that there are homosexual sex crimes, even as there are heterosexual sex crimes, does not make homosexuality as such criminal.[296] Many things that are sins are not crimes.

---

296. While this point is surely obvious, one must recall that society, for no statistically legitimate reason, fears seduction of youth by homosexual people far more than it fears their seduction by heterosexuals. The prevailing view is further inconsistent in that it fears that seduction of a girl by a heterosexual male may make the girl frigid and fearful of men, discouraging future heterosexual activity; while it fears that seduction of a boy by a homosexual male may *encourage* him to engage in future homosexual activity. See Ralph Blair, *Holier-Than-Thou Hocus-Pocus*, p. 18.

The role that the theologian should grant to scientific and empirical insights in thinking about the place of homosexuality is particularly beset with difficulties, for how does she decide when such insights should be considered determinative or when they are properly applied? That the church once confidently opposed Copernicus on biblical grounds should give the contemporary theologian pause. Nonetheless, even if it were demonstrated beyond any possible doubt that homosexuality is determined either entirely biologically or by some combination of biological and social factors outside an individual's control, that does not, ipso facto, remove it from the realm of moral judgment. While the "I can't help it" defense rightly excites our sympathy, it cannot substitute for moral evaluation, unless we wish to fall into a completely materialistic, deterministic view of human nature that would make moral evaluation of any human predispositions or behaviors inappropriate — a view that would make human beings no longer subjects, but only objects. All human decisions take place in the context of the powerful influence of personal and biological history. None is a free choice if by that phrase one means "a reasoned, deliberate, fully conscious and fully self-determined selection among roughly balanced alternatives. . . . If in order to qualify as a 'question of morality' a condition or even an act must be 'chosen' in that sense, then it may be wondered whether in the view of these interpreters there is any such thing as a moral act at all."[297] (Of course the effort to understand scientifically and thereby to explain and solve — or do away with — the problem of sin, as if what we needed to conquer it were more knowledge, recurs in endless variation.)[298] If we understand the created order to suffer the effects of the Fall and humankind to be marked by original sin, we cannot label as acceptable everything we cannot help — which is precisely why we need a Savior. We cannot simply assume that whatever we observe about the so-called natural world is "natural" in the sense of belonging to God's purpose in creation. Nor can we argue simply from some abstract idea of fairness:

297. Turnbull, "Homosexuality: Some Neglected Issues," p. 78.
298. Karlen shows some ambivalence about the final efficacy of knowledge even in the secular realm when he says: "The study of 'problem' sexuality has only begun, and if enough information and insight accumulates, we may be able to start answering some very important questions. Once we understand the backgrounds of problem-ridden people, can potential offenders be recognized and helped? Or does having a fundamentally rewarding sex life depend chiefly on having picked the right parents or on growing up in a less sexually repressive society? Social scientists, especially American ones, tend to hope that solutions to problems are inherent in knowledge about them. Intellectually, our naturalism and social utopianism are at stake. More concretely, the stakes are the lives of thousands or millions of people" (*Sexuality and Homosexuality,* p. 562).

gifts and liabilities of all sorts — physical, intellectual, psychological, social, cultural — are notoriously unequally distributed among people.

The evangelical theologian remains bound by Scripture. But even if she concludes that the overall witness of Scripture points away from homosexuality (including orientation implicitly and practice explicitly) as a Christian alternative equal, for a particular segment of the population, to heterosexuality on the part of another segment, she has no basis for the inordinate horror with which homosexuality has been regarded. The apostle Paul simply lists it as a sin among other sins. But if the theologian seeks a way to get from the creation ordinance to the full validity of homosexual relationships, she must confront the problem that she can find no way to do so from Genesis 1 and 2 (or from any other texts).

So the final question remains the beginning one: when we defined marriage as a unique relationship between a man and a woman, should we have added, "or, on occasion, between a man and a man, or between a woman and a woman"? Is there a real possibility here that we have somehow missed? Or must the celebration of love between people of the same sex perhaps wait for heaven, when "they neither marry nor are given in marriage" (Mt. 22:30); but when, we trust, all that is precious in the myriad forms of frustrated love will at last be fulfilled?

V. The Divine Image and the Dominion of Humankind

A. INTRODUCTION

Immediately associated with the creation of humankind in the divine image (Gn. 1:26-28) is the idea that they have been given dominion over the rest of the creation. Indeed, so close is this association that some have argued that exercising dominion in the nonhuman world constitutes the decisive similarity between human beings and God. Human beings are placed on earth as God's representatives, just as earthly kings erected images of themselves to signify their authority in provinces where they did not personally appear.[1] While we would affirm that people act as God's vicegerents, we would prefer to say not that this responsibility and privilege *constitutes* the image, but rather that it *rests upon* it. That is, the divine image is the gift; the dominion of humankind is the exercise of the powers with which they are vested by God when he created them in his own image. We can see the difference between the two concepts rather easily if we consider the case of infants. Infants are in the divine image, but they do not yet exercise dominion — at least not in the sense in which theologians mean it!

We must say at the outset that this Christian doctrine of the divine image, with the power of human self-transcendence over the natural order

---

1. See, for example, Gerhard von Rad, *Genesis,* trans. John H. Marks, rev. ed., Old Testament Library (Philadelphia: Westminster, 1972), p. 60. G. W. H. Lampe marvels that such a high view of humankind's role was envisioned in a day when human dominion was actually so feeble ("The New Testament Doctrine of *Ktisis," Scottish Journal of Theology* 17, no. 4 [December 1964]: 449-62).

we have affirmed, does mean that human beings not only inevitably will, but also have a right and duty to, distinguish themselves from nature. (That they are also part of nature, which has its own value even without them, we will take up in due course.) Not only are they the crown of creation, but Jesus says plainly that they are of more value than many sparrows (Mt. 10:31) and freely sacrifices a whole herd of pigs in the interests of a single man's sanity (Mt. 8:30-32). Adam found no creature fit for him among the animals (Gn. 2:20); nor are people to confuse themselves with animals by engaging in bestiality (Ex. 22:19; Dt. 27:21). People could neither discuss their relationship to nature nor love it if they were simply part of it. "Bighorn sheep don't pause to admire the Rockies."[2] The problem, of course, is that the Christian doctrine of humankind has two parts: while we celebrate our dignity as created, we must also confess our fall and alienation from God, our proud usurping of God's prerogatives in our exercise of dominion, as in other areas of our lives. To the extent that we fail to reckon with our creaturehood and our sinfulness, we are headed for destruction and death — headed there, penultimately, because of what we do to the rest of creation.

It is by emphasizing the two parts of the doctrine of humankind, and by thus seeking to make a distinction between a proper and an improper exercise of dominion, that we would answer those who lay the current ecological crisis firmly at the door of Christianity. These charges cannot be satisfactorily countered simply by appealing to what the Bible "really" teaches about how human beings should relate to the natural world or by seeking to discern whether, in actual fact, Christianity provided a primary impetus for scientific achievement; for anyone can see that Christians, as well as others, do act exploitatively toward the creation. (Much less can the charges be dealt with by embracing new semi-pantheistic or panentheistic models like Matthew Fox's creation spirituality, which repudiates emphasis on the Fall; or Sally McFague's effort to picture the world as God's body, as a way of encouraging us to take matter more seriously; or by Loren Eiseley's disparagement of humankind as "the planetary disease" [quoted by Ian McHarg, "The Place of Nature in the City of Man," in *Western Man and Environmental Ethics,* ed. Ian Barbour (Reading, Mass.: Addison-Wesley, 1973), p. 174]. These all fail to take sufficiently into account one side or the other of our condition.)

    Lynn White's claim (in his seminal article indicting Christianity for the state of our world, "The Historical Roots of Our Ecologic Crisis," *Science* 155 [March 10, 1967]: 1203-7) that Christianity is anthropocentric is true. His assertion that Christianity has taught that God planned all of creation for human benefit, and that none of it had any purpose but to serve human purposes, may not be entirely true — note that the whole creation was deemed "good" (Gn. 1) before the creation of humankind and

---

    2. Peter Heinegg, "Ecology and Fall," *Christian Century* 93, no. 17 (May 12, 1976): 465.

seems to be celebrated for its own sake in Psalm 104; and note Job 38:25-27, where the Lord satisfies with rain "the desert, which is empty of human life" (NRSV) — but it can certainly marshal the witness of Thomas (*Summa Theologica*, pt. 2-2, q. 66, art. 1) and Calvin (*Commentary* on Gn. 1:26; see also *Inst.*, 1.14.2). The Christian doctrine of creation does destroy the old, pagan animism that militated against the exploitation of nature by positing spirits in natural objects; and it does leave nature available for investigation and use: Toynbee mourns, "monotheism, as enunciated in the Book of Genesis, has removed the age-old restraint that was once placed on man's greed by his awe" ("The Religious Background of the Present Environmental Crisis," in David and Eileen Springer, eds., *Ecology and Religion in History* [New York: Harper & Row, 1974], p. 145); while Brunner affirms that Ps. 115:16, "the earth he [the Lord] has given to human beings" (NRSV), makes the world the legitimate sphere for the exercise of human reason, and Gn. 1:28 is "the Magna Carta of all secular knowledge as well as of all the achievements of technics and civilization" (*The Christian Doctrine of Creation and Redemption,* trans. Olive Wyon [London: Lutterworth, 1952], pp. 26, 30; see also Helmut Thielicke, *The Evangelical Faith,* trans. and ed. Geoffrey W. Bromiley [Grand Rapids: Eerdmans, 1974], 1.337, for the argument that the doctrine of creation out of nothing makes possible an objective approach to the world and "noetic control" over it). This Jewish-Christian dedivinizing of nature remains, even though neither the work of historians of science nor an analysis of Israel's technical culture as compared to its neighbors' nor attention to the impact of Christianity in, say, Russia — where it gave rise to a mystical, nontechnically motivated civilization — establishes the vital relationship White suggests between Jewish-Christian doctrines and scientific and technical achievement (James Barr, "Man and Nature: The Ecological Controversy in the Old Testament," in Springer and Springer, eds., *Ecology and Religion in History,* pp. 48-75; Jacques Ellul, *The Technological Society,* trans. John Wilkinson [New York: Vintage, 1964], p. 33).

In any case, none of these components of a traditional Christian view of humanity's place in nature needs entail a charter to rape Mother Earth. Nor does the actual language of Gn. 1 and 2. The language of 1:26, 28 does sound harsh: especially כָּבַשׁ (subdue, bring into bondage) but also רָדָה (have dominion, rule, dominate) can carry a sense of treading down (an image also suggested by Ps. 8:6) and relying on force (see Nm. 32:22 for כָּבַשׁ). Despite such language, we may also note several moderating factors, including the point that the overall emphasis in Gn. 1 is not on power or exploitative activities; and the implication that both humankind and animals were apparently initially vegetarian suggests that dominion did not extend to killing animals (Gn. 1:29-30). Since כָּבַשׁ applies to the earth and not to animals, it perhaps should be understood to refer to undertaking those activities relating to settlement and agriculture, particularly the tilling of the land. Further, we need not see the physical sense of רָדָה as primary here: it can be used of kings and of God, and can refer to peaceful rule, as in the case of Solomon (1 Kgs. 4:24; see also Ezk. 34:4 for improper rule and its opposite, solicitous care). If the picture of a good king was in the mind of the writer of Gn. 1, then the ideas of subduing and having dominion imply not abuse but rather benevolent control and even protection (see Walter Brueggemann, "King in the Kingdom of Things," *Christian Century* 86, no. 37 [Sept. 10, 1969]: 1165-66; also Barr, "Man and Nature").

The second (but earlier, in date of composition) creation narrative further encourages seeing a benign rather than rapacious form for the dominion intended for humankind. Not only does this narrative show a more intimate concern for human well-being and comfort than the first, but it suggests a similar concern for the creation. עָבַד (till) can mean serve or even be a slave to something; and שָׁמַר (keep) implies vigilance and preservation (the same word, שָׁמַר, is used in the Aaronic blessing, Nm. 6:24: "The LORD bless you and keep you"). Naming the animals (Gn. 2:19-20) — the first exercise of dominion, which takes place by means of humanity's particular gift of language — involves establishing a particular order in the world but not the exploitation of the animals or even, at this point, their use for human ends (Westermann, *Genesis 1–11*, p. 228). Only after the first pair's disobedience do we find a rift between them and the rest of the creation: enmity with part of the animal world, strain in work, and the ground cursed (3:14-19). Only after the Fall are the animals given for food and do they come to fear people (9:2-3).

This ambiguity of our position as created and as fallen is not only *reflected* in the beautiful earth cursed and in bondage (Rom. 8:20-22) for our sakes, but it is also *compounded* by the effects of the Fall upon creation as a whole. The creation now presents itself to us with a dual aspect. The natural world at whose beauty we marvel (e.g., Ps. 19:1-6; 104) can terrify us (e.g., Ps. 46:2, 3; Mk. 4:37-38). While even wild animals, like the great fish that swallowed Jonah (Jon. 2) and the ravens that fed Elijah (1 Kgs. 17:6), can be pictured as helping to preserve humans; they can also, like the lion and the bear (Prv. 28:15) or the eschatological beasts (Rv. 12–13), be figures for terrible threats.[3] God coming in judgment may be depicted as a roaring lion or a bear or a moth (Ps. 39:11; Lam. 3:10; Hos. 5:12; 13:7-8; Am. 1:2) or as using "natural" disasters to punish his people (Am. 4:7-10; Nah. 1:3-5). Both the Lord's blessing and his curse may be manifested in the natural order (Dt. 28; see also Is. 24:6; Mal. 4:6; Rv. 22:3), even though he is also said to make his rain fall on both the righteous and the unrighteous (Mt. 5:45). Precisely, then, because we no longer find our world and its creatures entirely hospitable, precisely insofar as we feel threatened by forces beyond our control, we may be motivated to subdue the creation by any means we can muster.[4] By taking a short step, we become nature's enemies.

At that point we need to remind ourselves that although we do have

3. See Paul Lamarch, "Animals" (trans. John J. Kilgallen), and Pierre Grelot, "Beasts & Beast" (trans. Patrick J. Boyle), in Léon-Dufour, ed., *Dictionary,* pp. 18-20 and 43-44, respectively.

4. Note Brunner's comment that "civilization always extends beyond the limits of the merely useful and necessary, and in civilization man never seeks solely to secure the necessities of life, but in his dominion over nature he seeks an inward release from bondage to it, an expression of his superiority over nature" (*The Divine Imperative,* trans. Olive Wyon [Philadelphia: Westminster, 1947], p. 384).

an exalted place in nature, we are nonetheless creatures, part of the world of nature and not outside it. Like all living creatures, we depend absolutely on our environment for sustenance, without which we shall die — a point obscured by our purchase of plastic-wrapped steaks and precut particle board, far removed from bellowing animals and chain saws gouging graceful trees (witness the shock of a modern child confronted for the first time by an actual carcass in a butcher shop). Moreover, in what we share with the other creatures, we are not superior but inferior to them: we cannot see like an eagle, run like a cheetah, or navigate like a bat. God not only cares for birds and lilies (Mt. 6:26-30), but seems to delight in the careful fashioning of wild creatures not immediately useful to people (Job 39–40). More striking yet, God makes his covenant extend not only to people but to "every living creature of all flesh that is upon the earth" (Gn. 9:16). The nature psalms (Ps. 8; 19:1-6; 29), and especially Psalm 104, depict a cosmos unified by its permeation by a single will and by the relationship with God that all creatures have in common.[5] God created and intended the whole, not just us.

Essential to a proper view of this cosmos of which humankind is a part is that its material character does not compromise its goodness.[6] The verdict "good!" rendered of the original creation is confirmed anew by the Incarnation and by the indwelling of the Holy Spirit: matter can be affirmed and even hallowed. Thus we may be taught to honor our own

---

5. Walther Eichrodt, *Theology of the Old Testament,* trans. J. A. Baker, 2 vols., Old Testament Library (Philadelphia: Westminster, 1961-67), 2.112-13. Something of this unity, untroubled by nature's terrors, is reflected in what verges on nature mysticism in someone like Thoreau:

There can be no very black melancholy to him who lives in the midst of Nature and has his senses still. . . . The gentle rain which waters my beans and keeps me in the house to-day is not dreary and melancholy, but good for me too. Though it prevents my hoeing them, it is of far more worth than my hoeing. If it should continue so long as to cause the seeds to rot in the ground and destroy the potatoes in the low lands, it would still be good for the grass on the uplands, and, being good for the grass, it would be good for me. . . . I was suddenly sensible of such sweet and beneficent society in Nature, in the very pattering of the drops, and in every sound and sight around my house, an infinite and unaccountable friendliness all at once like an atmosphere sustaining me, as made the fancied advantages of human neighborhood insignificant, and I have never thought of them since. Every little pine needle expanded and swelled with sympathy and befriended me. I was so distinctly made aware of the presence of something kindred to me, even in scenes which we are accustomed to call wild and dreary, . . . that I thought no place would ever be strange to me again. (*Walden,* ed. Sherman Paul [Cambridge: Riverside Press, 1960], pp. 90-91)

6. Eichrodt, *Theology,* 2.108.

bodies and not attempt simply to subdue and disown them. Indeed, alienation from our bodily existence may well be, as Moltmann suggests, "the inner aspect of the external ecological crisis of modern industrial society."[7] Insofar as we denigrate the material aspect of ourselves, we wrongly remove ourselves from the natural world and quickly come to see it, too, as something to be simply used (or abused) rather than identified with, valued, and preserved.

To say that we are part of nature, then, need not be to demean ourselves. We are a part of nature not only because of our dependence on it and embeddedness within it (we cannot, whatever our proud fantasies, affect it without being affected in return — a fact that seems continually to surprise us and that we continually resist acknowledging), but also and just as importantly because of our common creaturely relationship to God. Yet we alone among the creatures wrestle, as persons and as theologians, with our place. We want to know and explain more than we do or can know and explain. We are both intrigued and troubled by the mysteriousness of the world. We take "views" of nature that then govern our behavior toward it and toward one another.[8] We have a sense of task with regard to the world, even a sense that, as Genesis 1:28 suggests, it is somehow unfinished and that we are *supposed* to put our mark on it.[9] But we are sinners, and our pencil slips.

So, as we shall see, it has been from the earliest days. There has never been any such thing as a completely "natural" environment: people have always sought to adapt it to their needs and ends — not to mention manipulating it simply because of what Eiseley calls "the age-old primate addiction to taking things apart."[10] And what they have done has done harm. As early as the Pleistocene period over one hundred species of large animals disappeared on this continent, likely because of wasteful hunting methods.[11] Soil laterization presumably attributable to improper farming methods has been discovered at ancient archeological sites.[12] A complaint about river pollution was brought to King Edward I of England in 1307; and London has been

7. Jürgen Moltmann, *God in Creation,* trans. Margaret Kohl (San Francisco: Harper & Row, 1985), p. 48.

8. Ralph Waldo Emerson went so far as to say somewhere that the views of nature held by any people are foundational to all its institutions.

9. Colomban Lesquivit and Pierre Grelot, "World" (trans. Thomas M. Spittler), in Léon-Dufour, ed., *Dictionary,* pp. 676-80.

10. *Firmament of Time,* p. 159.

11. Heinegg, "Ecology and the Fall," p. 464.

12. The cities and temple of the ancient Khmer civilization were built of *laterite* and sandstone: the Khmer people's farming of unsuitable land was likely a major cause of their demise (Paul R. Ehrlich, *The Population Bomb* [New York: Ballantine, 1968], p. 98).

known for its foul atmosphere at least since 1635,[13] And so on. Negative human impact on the environment is not new. The *newly* troubling factor is that never before have humans had the power they have today, nor have they existed in such large numbers. Never before have they had the sheer physical power to destroy the ability of planet Earth to support life as we know it. We are, and yet are not, part of nature. Like that of all crowned sovereigns, our power to do evil mirrors our power to do good. And who could deny that the majesty of our means has far outrun that of our ends?

B. THE RISE OF CIVILIZATION AND TECHNOLOGY

1. INTRODUCTION

Just as the author of Genesis reflects no particular concern with the vast drafts of time involved in the creation of the world, but telescopes his account, as it were, into events depicted as occurring in seven days; so he telescopes his account of the foundations of human civilization into the story of the seven generations stretching from Adam to Lamech (Gn. 4:17-18). With Cain and Abel we have the domestication of plants and animals, respectively; the descendants of Cain soon begin to divide between the different ways of life of the city dwellers and the nomads and to take up both arts (music) and crafts (metallurgy). On the one hand, then, humankind appears to be shown as exercising a rather high level of dominion almost right from the start, and developments that we now know to have taken millennia are depicted as taking place almost on top of one another; but on the other, the very fact that the author places these developments as part of a schematized primeval history makes clear that he does see them as in themselves very ancient and as part of the common history of humankind (a point of view also reflected in Dt. 6:10-12). Human progress is not in itself viewed negatively — as further evidenced in Deuteronomy 8:9, where the goodness of the promised land includes not only its fruitfulness but also its potential for mining. But its ambiguity becomes quickly evident: not only does increased killing follow immediately upon the use of metals, but also the city that was a sign of a newly settled life (Gn. 4:17) soon becomes the city with a tower that symbolizes human ambition over-reaching itself (11:4).[14]

13. John N. Black, *The Dominion of Man* (Edinburgh: Edinburgh University Press, 1970), p. 10.

14. See Westermann, *Genesis 1–11,* especially pp. 324-25, 454-55.

The sense of speed and of mixed results tending toward a descending spiral of sin that we get from the biblical account is mirrored in the most striking fashion by the actual course of the contemporary world. We can hardly keep up with the pace of change. We would not quite want to go back; yet we wish we could pluck only the less bitter of the fruits of progress, as an anonymous piece entitled "If You Were Born Before 1945" implies:

> We were born before television, before penicillin, before polio shots, frozen foods, Xerox, plastic, contact lenses, Frisbees and the Pill. . . .
> We never heard of FM radio, tape decks, electric typewriters, artificial hearts, word processors, yogurt and guys wearing earrings. For us, time sharing meant togetherness — not computers or condominiums; a "chip" meant a piece of wood, hardware meant hardware, and software wasn't even a word! . . . You could buy a new Chevy Coupe for $600, but who could afford one. A pity, too, because gas was 11 cents a gallon! . . .
> "Grass" was mowed, "Coke" was a cold drink and "pot" was something you cooked in. "Rock music" was a Grandma's lullaby and "AIDS" were helpers in the principal's office.

Changes on our immediate horizon — as, for instance, those resulting from genetic engineering — are even more spectacularly promising and threatening.

When the theologian sets out to examine this development of human dominion, she is chastened in making her evaluation by the church's sadly blemished record of taking what most would now consider indefensible positions with regard to human enterprise. Too often the church has been simply self-interested, approving conquest in the crassest sense when it enhanced the church's prestige, resisting new knowledge when it undermined the church's view of the world. One has only to think of the unfortunate and protracted debate between the church on the one hand and the scientists on the other to have an illustration of this problem, a debate that has sometimes been described as warfare.[15] The church has resisted everything from telescopes to lightning rods; and we smile and at the same time shudder at clergy refusal to look through Galileo's telescope at the moon and see that it indeed had bumps on it, because they had a theory about

15. For example, White's two-volume *History of the Warfare of Science with Theology in Christendom*. Most especially when theological arguments have relied on a "God of the gaps" to fill in holes in the causal sequence, they have suffered embarrassment (for a few among many possible examples, see ibid., 2.169-79).

the spherical shape of heavenly bodies.[16] Such errors counsel due humility but do not relieve us of the responsibility of taking some view of our journey — an aspect of the theologian's proper exercise of dominion!

2. CAIN AND CIVILIZATION

A modern Christian treatise on ecology begins, "Civilization imperils the creation."[17] While that sentence could only have been written in recent years, after the devastating impact of human progress on the natural world has become obvious to increasing numbers of people, the foundation of its judgment can surely be found in the primeval history. Even if it is true that the primeval history shows little interest in technology compared to the stories of beginnings of other cultures,[18] it nonetheless manifests a profound insight into its character that we may not yet have rightly grasped. With the *sinful* line of humanity, with the line of Cain, civilization begins. The writer seems to be suggesting that the wicked who forget God are those who settle down in this world and make it their home. Here is where they put down their roots; here is where their interests lie. These interests are frequently selfish, competitive interests; intolerant, to the point of murder, of those inexplicable inequalities of gifts and circumstances that divide a person from his or her brothers and sisters (Gn. 4:4-9).[19] The more human culture grows, the more irreconcilability and fierce self-assertiveness grow too (4:23-24).[20] Moreover, those who build a city are explicitly those exiled from the ground (4:11-12), an idea suggesting their alienation from the

16. The church has by no means been uniquely guilty of self-interest and fear of change, of course. Charles T. Salmon notes, "A century ago American society was grappling with a social problem — the threat of a substance that the governor of Minnesota said had been created by 'the ingenuity of depraved human genius.' " In some states the manufacture, sale, or possession of the substance was punishable by fines and prison. The federal government levied a "sin" tax on it. Only in 1950, after federal and state legislation and congressional hearings, was the product finally freed from restrictive controls. "Was it cocaine? Marijuana? Alcohol? Tobacco? No. It was margarine." The culprit in this case was the National Dairy Union, which had been striving to have margarine regarded as dangerous and needing restriction. (Quoted by Martin Marty, *Context* 22, no. 16 [Sept. 15, 1990], p. 3.)

17. Wesley Granberg-Michaelson, *A Worldly Spirituality: The Call to Redeem Life on Earth* (San Francisco: Harper & Row, 1984), p. 3.

18. See Barr, "Man and Nature."

19. "Why must a certain man always have two sons? Why not only one? Why not only me?" (Walter Brueggemann, *Genesis,* Interpretation [Atlanta: John Knox, 1982], p. 62). Such inequalities are reflected only too obviously in the unequal social circumstances of those born poor instead of rich, those born in Bangladesh instead of in Sweden.

20. Von Rad, *Genesis,* p. 111.

earth and a mutual antipathy with it. Sin, however, does not abrogate humanity's intellectual capacity to exercise dominion. Rather, it makes that exercise perverse and irresponsible, and often enough driven by the dream that humankind can somehow make void the curse and regain paradise by their own efforts.[21]

How dim — if present at all — that dream must have been two and a half million years ago, at the time when what are believed to be early hominids crafted the earliest stone tools yet discovered; but, say archeologists, "once tools appear in the record, they become continually more abundant and more sophisticated."[22] Continually? As archeologists count time, perhaps. Not for almost another million years (1.6 million years ago) do we find evidence of the control of fire. The Paleolithic (Old Stone) Age, characterized by rough or chipped stone instruments, lasted until maybe 12,000 years ago: that constitutes 99.52 percent of the history generally considered human, even though "modern" humans appear to go back at least some 100,000 years.[23] That is, it took "modern" humans something like 90,000 years to get from crude stone tools to the domestication of the dog and the making of the bow and arrow and pottery that are taken to characterize the Mesolithic Age.[24] (Dating is imprecise, both because of the limits of archeological data and because development did not take place at the same rate everywhere; indeed, remnants of Stone Age culture remain in some remote parts of the world even today.) But then we can see the beginnings of the great acceleration of change. The Neolithic Age brought not only polished stone and horn, bone, and ivory tools, but, by maybe 10-11,000 years ago, domestication of animals other than the dog, soon followed by agriculture. Then the wheel and weaving and settled village life — enormous gains over what looks like the brief span of 5,000 years,

21. Said Bertrand Russell: "It may be that God made the world, but that is no reason why we should not make it over" (quoted by Douglas John Hall, *The Steward,* rev. ed. [Grand Rapids: Eerdmans; New York: Friendship, 1990], p. 193. Hall notes that despite this proud assertion, by the end of his life, Russell was pessimistic that we would see the end of this century).

22. Tools recovered at Hadar, Ethiopia, along with fragments of bones of animals that had apparently been eaten. These tools are half a million years older than recovered remains of *Homo habilis,* the first member of the genus that includes humankind as we know it (*Los Angeles Times,* Feb. 2, 1981, pt. 1, p. 5). See below, pp. 380-92.

23. John J. Putman, "The Search for Modern Humans," *National Geographic* 174, no. 4 (October 1988), pp. 438-77.

24. This is not to imply that even Stone Age technology was uniform, as if development had to follow a set pattern. To the contrary, local, cultural variations appeared — for instance, some peoples made tools from flakes off a parent lump or core; others shaped the core itself. See V. Gordon Childe, *What Happened in History,* rev. ed. (Baltimore: Penguin, 1954), pp. 38, 43.

before the beginning of the metallurgy and cities of the Bronze Age: brief, comparatively; yet, we must recall, a longer span than all of recorded history. Then a mere 2,500 years until the Iron Age (about 1000 B.C.), presupposed by the writer of Genesis 4:22. One hundred times as long to get from chipped stones to polished stones as to get from the Bronze Age to the Iron Age. And now, in our own day, less than a hundred years to get from the horseless carriage to satellites mapping Venus.

Even if we can agree on some markers of significant change and the dizzying increase in its present rate, such agreement should not be allowed to hide the mysteriousness of the rise of civilization — and its fall, in some places; and its failure to rise, in others. That is, development of civilization does not appear to be either inevitable or unidirectional, as if humanity's capacity for dominion is self-explanatory or must take a preset course. We may speculate that hunting, which required toolmaking and impulse control and social cooperation (as contrasted with the solitary activity of gathering), helped promote human culture.[25] But we do not know why people innovated as they did: why, for instance, they chose specific plants to cultivate, or how they came to refine metals. Chance alone cannot be the answer.[26] One must have a capacity to recognize previously unthought-of potential. And one must find a way to engage in technological education so that progress is not lost (a process most likely in the realm of women, on the hypothesis that the men were of necessity out hunting). We cannot emphasize too strongly that none of this is automatic. Neanderthal, an early *Homo sapiens* whose burial rituals bespeak her human self-transcendence (but who apparently became extinct and was probably not an ancestor of modern humans), differs from modern humans in just this area of innovation: Neanderthal tools stayed the same for at least 100,000 years, despite the fact that Neanderthals had *larger* brains than do we.[27] And, as we have

25. "Puzzling Out Man's Ascent," *Time,* Nov. 7, 1977, p. 77.

26. See Ellul, *Technological Society,* p. 23. Teilhard considers it peculiarly characteristic of the development of humankind that "we think first in order to survive, and then we live in order to think" (Pierre Teilhard de Chardin, *The Future of Man,* trans. Norman Denny [New York: Harper & Row, 1964], p. 283).

27. Putnam, "Modern Humans," p. 453. We must further emphasize that such differences do not necessarily distinguish those who are from those who are not human. Consider the differences between peoples present today: in a single issue of *National Geographic* (February 1991), one can see on p. 83 the picture of contemporary Surma stick fighters — residents of a remote area of Ethiopia whose humanity is surely not in question — who paint their naked bodies with a chalk and water mixture to intimidate their opponents; and then can turn the page and see a citizen of Hong Kong dressed in a full-length mink standing in front of a Rolls Royce (p. 103). The former make clear that they wish to maintain their own culture.

noted in passing, Stone Age cultures, isolated from neighboring, more advanced ones, have persisted into the twentieth century.

By contrast, some very advanced cultures have risen only to stagnate and decline, with descendants losing arts and sciences understood by their ancestors. We have only to think of the Incas, who developed over three thousand separate varieties of potato;[28] or of the grandeur of the architecture and written language of the early Mayan Indian civilization. Ancestors of some Amazonian Indians made excellent pottery, while their descendants today make none.[29] Such particular instances, which could be multiplied, cannot really be made to suggest that humankind as a whole started off with a very high form of civilization and culture, which they then lost because of the Fall and have only recently regained (as early attempted harmonizations by the church suggested). We must simply take these examples as another indication that human cultural development is by no means strictly linear and predictable.

Whatever the zigs and zags of the development of civilization, though, our positive view of it as a whole manifests itself in the sense of regret and loss we feel at tales of magnificent civilizations that have declined and the judgment (whether scornful or sympathetic) that those who have not made particular kinds of technological progress are "backward" and proper objects of help from the more advanced.

This point of view has had a powerful impact on the church's missionary effort — in one sense very properly, since concern for human souls apart from human bodies is rightly seen as contrary to the gospel. Missionaries with particular skills — doctors, agricultural experts, teachers — have served nobly, sacrificially, and with love. (Such skills are sufficiently desired by some countries that they will now admit only those Christians whose declared purpose is to share them.) Nonetheless, missionary efforts have too often been marred by a proud confusion of our way of life with the gospel and, worse, by subservience to plans for colonialistic exploitation of the natural resources of the lands where the church has been established. Joseph Conrad described such colonialism by saying, "The conquest of the earth, which mostly means the taking it away from those who have a different complexion or slightly flatter noses than ourselves, is not a pretty thing when you look into it too much" (*Heart of Darkness* [New York: Signet, 1950], p. 69). However, separating the actual demands of the gospel from cultural imperialism is not entirely easy. Take the case of Irian Jaya in west New Guinea, in 1989 still a Stone Age culture of peoples who speak 250 distinct languages, chop trees with sharpened stones, count in base 27, have never seen a wheel, and have a life expectancy of about forty years because of their habit of sleeping in houses where

28. Clergy and Laity Concerned letter, fall 1990, p. 1.
29. "Stone Age Past and Present in Brazil," *National Geographic* 165 (January 1979), p. 79.

they leave smoke fires burning all night to keep them warm and to repel mosquitoes. Missionaries are credited with stopping a variety of traditional practices including cannibalism, ritual killing of widows and newborn girls, and endemic tribal wars — practices whose horrors lessen one's sympathies with anthropologists who complain about destroying culture. Introduction to a cash economy, though, has made the villagers avid consumers, eager for items like radios and wristwatches, and (therefore?) highly vulnerable to exploitation. (See Charles P. Wallace, *Los Angeles Times*, Dec. 22, 1989, pp. E1, 7, 8. However, the fact that some primitive cultures are violent and sexist should not be taken to imply that all are or were. For striking instances of peaceful, egalitarian, primitive cultures, see Walter Wink, *Engaging the Powers* [Minneapolis: Fortress, 1992], pp. 34-37.)

But, even though some vulnerabilities to natural threats and practices like cannibalism may diminish as civilization progresses, civilization is, as Genesis 4 implies, inextricably entangled with the impulse and the power to kill. The impulse has not declined, and the power has increased inconceivably: nowhere has acceleration of the rate of change been more evident than in the development of weapons. It took hundreds upon hundreds of thousands of years to get from stones and sharpened sticks and spears to bows and arrows; less than twenty thousand to get from bows and arrows to gunpowder.[30] Repelled by the power of gunpowder, Jonathan Swift mocked the European attachment to it when he had Gulliver visit the king of Brobdingnag:

> The king was struck with horror at the description I had given of those terrible engines, and the proposal I had made. He was amazed how so impotent and grovelling an insect as I (these were his expressions) could entertain such inhuman ideas, and in so familiar a manner as to appear wholly unmoved at all by the scenes of blood and desolation, which I had painted as the common effects of those destructive machines; whereof he said, some evil genius, enemy to mankind, must have been the first contriver. As for himself, he protested, that although few things delighted him so much as new discoveries in art or in nature; yet he would rather lose half his kingdom, than be privy to such a secret; which he commanded me, as I valued my life, never to mention any more.
>
> A strange effect of *narrow principles* and *short views!* that a prince possessed of every quality which procures veneration, love and esteem . . . should from a *nice unnecessary scruple,* whereof in Europe we can have no conception, let slip an opportunity put into

30. The Chinese apparently used gunpowder as early as the sixth century, although it did not begin to have its full effect as a weapon of war until it came to Europe some seven centuries later. See H. G. Wells, *Outline of History*, rev. by Raymond Postgate, 2 vols. in one (Garden City, N.Y.: Doubleday, 1956), pp. 465, 608.

his hands, that would have made him absolute master of the lives, the liberties, and the fortunes of his people.[31]

Humans have shown no such reserve as that of the imaginary king, whatever they have supposed about their capacity for self-control. In 1914 the London *Times* made confident editorial comment that no civilized country would bomb cities from the air — a procedure simply taken for granted by all civilized nations today.[32] The Second World War, in particular, served as a tremendous stimulus to technological advance, and most fatefully, to the use of atomic energy. Not a Pentagon bureaucrat, not some militaristic general in the field, but James Conant, president of Harvard University, went secretly to President Franklin D. Roosevelt to persuade him of the viability of the Manhattan Project; and Conant was himself present when the first atomic device was exploded in the flats of New Mexico. The power of such devices? "Picture a freight train stretching from New York to Los Angeles, with every one of its box cars filled with TNT — 20 million tons of it. That's the equivalent of *one* 20-megaton bomb."[33] Civilization has pushed Lamech's song — a song culminating the story of the development of civilization — to its logical limit: we have celebrated the fact that we can kill not only those who kill, not only those who injure, not only those who even insult us, but everyone on earth; not only everyone on earth once, but everyone on earth many times over. We have created a culture in which, in Walter Wink's phrase, "our smart bombs are wiser than our diplomats."[34]

31. *Gulliver's Travels,* pt. 2, chap. 7. Later, after having Gulliver further remark: "Neither are any wars so furious and bloody, or of so long continuance, as those occasioned by difference in opinion, especially if it be in things indifferent," Swift gave the Houyhnhnm king's opinion: "When a creature pretending to reason, could be capable of such enormities, he dreaded lest the corruption of that faculty, might be worse than brutality itself. He seemed therefore confident, that instead of reason, we were only possessed of some quality fitted to increase our natural vices" (ibid., pt. 4, chap. 4). Edward Gibbon (*Decline and Fall of the Roman Empire,* chap. 65), speaks similarly of gunpowder: "If we contrast the rapid progress of this mischievous discovery with the slow and laborious advances of reason, science, and the arts of peace, a philosopher, according to his temper, will laugh or weep at the folly of mankind." Wholly apart from war, handguns killed 9,000 Americans in 1978 (before the major ravages of gang violence). In 1992 the figure was 13,000 for murders, 24,000 if one adds suicides and accidents; but Americans insist on their right to keep guns. (A cartoon contrasts this attitude toward guns with attitudes toward other hazards, noting that saccharin was banned for killing four white rats [*Handgun Control News* 3, no. 3 (Aug.-Oct. 1979); S. Froman, T. Campbell, and J. Shover, "Gun Control," *Stanford* 22, no. 1 (March 1994): 51].)
32. Eiseley, *Firmament of Time,* p. 132.
33. James S. Kunen in *New Times,* April 16, 1976, quoted in *The Other Side* 13, no. 2 (July 1977): 16.
34. *Engaging the Powers,* p. 29, referring specifically to the nonnuclear Persian Gulf War.

3. BABEL, SCIENCE, AND TECHNOLOGY

If the story of Cain and civilization is that of humankind settling down on earth and doing their ambiguity-fraught best to reestablish paradise by their own efforts, the story of Babel is that of humankind displaying before heaven their prowess in such attempts, as if to dare God himself to thwart them — and the story of the divinely ordained futility of their arrogant pretensions. Even the structure of the story suggests a sort of presumptuous separation of people from their Maker: in the first part (Gn. 11:2-4) persons speak and act quite independently of reference to God; while in the second part (11:5-8), God speaks and acts in judgment, without any dialogue with the people. In a sense, the people's motives are understandable enough, human enough, even ordinary enough: they, like us, want to use their energies and skills, and they want the security that comes from unity and fame. But these understandable desires are set in the context of the drives of ambition and self-reliant autonomy, and hence of sin. It is against these aspirations, these propensities to overstep the assigned limits, and not against the building as such that God acts by confusing the language of the people and scattering them.[35]

It is surely significant that the mighty city of Babylon (to be identified with Babel) — appearing only here in the primeval history and apparently known by rumor and report — is the scene of these events. Cosmopolitan and materialistic, it was the center of power in the ancient world, and many passages mention it as an embodiment of arrogance (e.g., Is. 14:13, 14; 47:7-10; Jer. 51). Babel becomes the great Babylon that "I [Nebuchadnezzar] have built," which is destroyed in the midst of mirth at the feast of Belshazzar (Dn. 4–5); and the theme is renewed in the vision of Babylon that "I [Superman] have built," destroyed in one day in the funeral of the world (Rv. 18) — a funeral with its secular mourners grieving the loss of the things that have been their life, heaven's mourning of a deeper sort, and the counterpoint of the praise of the saints.

The story also reveals the same sort of ambiguity respecting the city as an entity that we see with regard to the natural world: the natural world may be idyllic garden or howling wilderness; the city may be the heavenly city or, like Babel, the wicked

---

35. See Westermann, *Genesis 1–11*, pp. 531-47; also von Rad, *Genesis*, pp. 148-51; Brueggemann, *Genesis*, pp. 100-101. The traditional (but now generally understood as a secondary and later) interpretation of this narrative was that it gave an explanation of the origin of language differentiation — the assumption being that everyone originally spoke Hebrew. When scientific comparative philology began to develop, experts for a long time sought to reduce all other languages to Hebrew, using such extreme expedients as declaring that since Hebrew is written from right to left, one might read it either way to produce a satisfactory etymology (see White, *Warfare of Science with Theology*, 2.180; cf. all of chap. 17). Those who challenged such procedures were sometimes relieved of prominent university posts.

city. Nor has sinful humanity ever abandoned the project of building vast monuments. While Egypt's ancient pyramid of Cheops may win the prize for cubic mass at 88,500,000 cubic feet, the skyscrapers of American cities probably hold the record for sheer height.

Even so, presumption and an almost blithe disregard for limits have surely been a hallmark of the fallen human enterprise, as if the effects of the Fall could be undone by human ingenuity. Not that human endeavor has always been explicitly Promethean, in the sense of humankind seeking intentionally and wrongly to take for their own use what belongs to God.[36] The religious motivation to "think God's thoughts after him" that scientists gave for centuries as the reason and reward of their work[37] could conceivably be consistent with a humble awe at and gratitude for the creation. Its danger of slipping into both naïveté and hubris at every seeming success, though, can be seen in the remarks of Francis Bacon, who expressed what would now sound like undue confidence in humankind's ability to govern their new powers by "right reason and true religion": "Inventions are a blessing and a benefit without injuring or afflicting any. Inventions are also, as it were, new creations and imitations of divine works." "Man, by the fall, lost at once his state of innocence, and his empire over creation, both of which can be partially recovered even in this life, the first by

36. In Aeschylus's version of the Prometheus tale *(Prometheus Bound)*, Prometheus defends his theft of fire and gift of it to humankind by saying at the end of his detailing of fire's benefits, "All human arts are from Prometheus," thus making all human progress dependent on an initial rebellion against the gods. This perspective obviously differs significantly from the biblical view, in which God gives dominion to humankind. Not all knowledge, but only particular knowledge, was forbidden in the prohibition of eating the fruit of the tree of knowledge of good and evil (Gn. 2:16-17). As early as A.D. 830, a picture in the Utrecht *Psalter* conveys the idea that technological advance is God's will by depicting a small body of the righteous, led by King David, confronting a large host of the wicked. While the latter use an old-fashioned whetstone to sharpen swords, the former "are employing the first crank recorded outside China to rotate the first grindstone known anywhere" (Lynn White Jr., *Medieval Religion and Technology: Collected Essays* [Berkeley: University of California Press, 1978], p. 250).

37. White, "Historical Roots," p. 27. White notes that this attitude prevailed from the thirteenth century through Leibnitz and Newton. Not until the eighteenth century would there be a Laplace, who, asked by Napoleon about the role of God in his *System of the World,* made the famous remark, "Sire, I have no need of this hypothesis" (quoted by Alexandre Koyré, *From the Closed World to the Infinite Universe* [Baltimore: Johns Hopkins University Press, 1957], p. 276). The Communism of Marx and Lenin took a more aggressively dismissive view of God. I can remember as a small child seeing cartoons brought by a Russian Jew who had earlier escaped from Russia. They depicted a ladder, symbolizing human technology, ascending up to heaven, being climbed by Lenin with other Communist leaders following him. They had ahold of God — a doting old man sitting on a cloud — and were pulling him down out of his heaven by his beard.

religion and faith, the second by the arts and sciences."[38] If we observe in such remarks that it has indeed been possible in days gone by to dream quite explicitly that science and technology could counter even the effects of the Fall, our day's apparent operating assumption — that we can try pretty much anything we want because science and technology will produce ways to fix anything we do wrong — may seem less extreme than it does at first glance.

Not that the dream of that earlier day was antinomian. The dream, ever since the Enlightenment, was the dream of scientific *progress* in the service of the good of humanity, the dream not now just of climbing up to heaven but of bringing heaven down to earth.[39] The spirit of Bacon and the ebullient hopefulness and self-confidence brought by the Industrial Revolution permeate the words of a Brooklyn pastor at the turn of the twentieth century:

> He who once baptized tongues is now baptizing tools. . . . Machines are becoming allies, making man invincible. All things in the heavens above and the earth beneath begin to stand about as servants and waiting. . . . Machines are to make the deserted fields of Europe to be productive again for the starving peasants. And tools toiling under India's tropic skies are to redeem the millions from their starvation and drudgery. Tools are to save what is now wasted and make poor men rich. Tools are to redeem our men of poverty and want. Within the next century, it is believed, tools are to make the college and university as free for young men and maidens, as public schools are now for boys and girls. Machinery is to increase intelligence and refinement; to put comforts and conveniences, with instruments of beauty, with those now called the poor and the weak. Through machinery wealth that now like snow sometimes comes together in drifts, is to be diffused and scattered evenly over the land. Tools are to become the almoner of universal bounty toward the church, the school, the library, the gallery, the Christian home.[40]

So much had been accomplished that anything seemed possible — even inevitable — from the conquest of disease to the elimination of war because there would no longer be any reason to fight wars. Indeed, we may still today experience a visceral incomprehension that we can build a space telescope powerful enough to spot an object the size of a fly in Australia

38. *Novum Organum,* bk. 1, 1.229; bk. 2, 1.52.

39. See Carl L. Becker, *The Heavenly City of the Eighteenth-Century Philosophers* (New Haven: Yale University Press, 1932), passim.

40. Newell Dwight Hillis, *The Quest of Happiness* (New York: Macmillan, 1902), pp. 400, 401, 418-19.

from the distance of New York[41] and yet, despite such amazing and continuing technical progress, find ourselves thwarted by famine, insurrection, and the common cold. Surely victory over these must lie just around the corner.

But if science and technology have not (yet?) brought us all the triumphs we had anticipated, we have not been slow to value what they indubitably have provided: a vast array of material goods, which seem to fulfill for us the Tower of Babel role of symbolizing security and success (fame). (Perhaps it is in part because we have believed and hoped so much in science that we have embraced so eagerly whatever it provides, trusting that this new god would never give us a stone for bread.) And material goods have become the emblem of the good life, and even of a secular salvation, to many of the world's less privileged: the Cristo Redentor, a statue of Christ presiding over the harbor of Rio de Janeiro, was featured in a quarter-page ad in a Brazilian magazine with the superimposed message, "Come Unto Us, All Ye Who Desire a Chevrolet."[42]

Such a message may, ironically, be harder to combat for Christianity than for faiths that have explicitly rejected the material world. We *do* affirm the value of reducing human pain and struggle in this life. However, the leap is short from a proper valuing of our bodies and the rest of the material creation to a greedy, disproportionate attention to them and a blithe and half-unconscious substituting of our vision of how a "more competent" God would have designed them. A broadcasting historian suggests that the underlying message of the entire commercial world is that God's "work of Creation has been largely a disaster, functionally and aesthetically. Almost everything done in the making of man and his environment was a mistake; fortunately, man himself has invented products to correct the errors."[43] It is commonplace that modern materialism and commercialism turn trivialities and luxuries into necessities, try to persuade us that happiness can be found behind the wheel of an air-conditioned, high-powered sports car, and lead us to pursue with evangelistic zeal the goal of making the world safe for Coca Cola.

41. *Los Angeles Times,* April 10, 1990, p. A2.

42. Quoted by Jan Knippers Black, "Brazil: New Hopes and Old Fears," *Christian Century* 98, no. 2 (Jan. 21, 1981): 49. Commercialization of the Christian message is not limited to developing countries. Robert McAfee Brown calls attention to a Smith-Corona typewriter ad (in those days — not so long ago as they seem — before typewriters had been made virtually obsolete by word processors!) in which an obviously affluent man holds his new Christmas present, captioned with the words, "When I was a child, I spake as a child, I understood as a child, I thought as a child: But when I became a man, I put away childish things. *I Corinthians*" (*The Hereticus Papers* [Philadelphia: Westminster, 1979], pp. 19-20).

43. Quoted by Granberg-Michaelson, *Worldly Spirituality,* p. 179.

Not that the craving for luxury, and the inordinate indulging of the craving, are new. The children of Israel quickly became dissatisfied with manna in the wilderness, however sufficient it was for their needs, and longed for the savory foods of Egypt. The prophets had occasion to condemn excess (e.g., Am. 6:4-6; Hag. 1:4). The very name *Babylon,* a city flourishing tens of centuries before Christ, has come to symbolize luxury and gratification of the senses. Roman emperors at the time of Christ, using the enormous wealth they took from conquered nations, "collected for a single meal peacocks from Samos, pike from Pessinus, oysters from Tarentum, dates from Egypt, nuts from Spain, in short the rarest dishes from all parts of the world, and resorted to emetics to stimulate appetite and to lighten the stomach"; and would display their wealth by dissolving pearls in the wine they drank (Schaff, *History,* 2.314). Suetonius says that Nero never wore the same clothes twice and used for fishing a golden net strung with purple and scarlet thread *(The Twelve Caesars).* Gibbon *(Decline and Fall)* traces seemingly endless examples of wanton display and waste: refusal to eat seafood unless it was rare and one was far from the sea (Elagabalus; chap. 6); transplanting a forest into the midst of the circus and stocking it with imported wild game for people to amuse themselves by slaughtering (Carinus; chap. 12; similarly the Persian Chosroes; chap. 46); kings keeping a thousand royal barbers, each generously salaried and having a daily allowance for twenty servants and twenty horses (just prior to Julian; chap. 22); a caliph with 38,000 tapestries and 22,000 carpets in his palace, plus 100 lions with a keeper each, and a mechanized gold and silver tree with warbling gold and silver birds (Almamon; chap. 52). Such extravagances rested on the spoils of war, the labor of slaves, and the extortion of inordinate taxes from the common people.

The indulgences of today's wealthy are just as exotic, even if their cruelty is frequently less overt. When Houston, Texas, was swimming in oil in the 1950s, a Houston millionaire's wife always purchased two extra first-class airline tickets for her travels — for her matched poodles, with their jeweled collars and chinchilla sweaters; and a man spent $50,000 in an unsuccessful attempt to keep penguins alive in a refrigerated room in his home (Thomas Thompson, "Blood and Money," *Mainliner,* March 1977, pp. 17-18). In 1925 William Randolph Hearst purchased a twelfth-century Spanish monastery, had it disassembled stone by numbered stone, and shipped it to the United States — and then lost interest in it (*Life,* Aug. 26, 1957). In 1991 the sultan of Brunei went on a ninety-minute, $190,000 shopping spree in Beverly Hills, accompanied by two men who carried his cash in a suitcase filled with $100 bills (*Los Angeles Times,* Jan. 4, 1991, p. E4); and the palace of the emir of Kuwait was restored to the splendor of gold-plated French bathroom fixtures and silk brocade wall hangings, in the midst of a war-ravaged city without running water and suffocating under smoke rising from still-burning oil wells (*Los Angeles Times,* Mar. 18, 1991, p. A1).

Moralists have seldom expressed great ambivalence in condemning luxury and waste, both because excess takes from the necessities of the many to supply the superfluities of the few, and because of its almost overwhelming tendency to corrupt without satisfying. The vacuity of the lives of the richest of the rich is legendary. Even in so apparently self-evident a matter, however, things are seldom entirely simple. A certain (and sometimes rather large) amount of superfluous wealth seems necessary to the development of some aspects of culture. Robber barons, whose business policies few would defend, built hospitals and museums and libraries and universities, whose services to elite and average person alike few would deny. In what sounds like an early version of trickle-down economics, Gibbon notes that the skilled mechanic or artist may receive a share of the wealth of the land that she could get in no other way, and generally stimulate the economy, by using her skills to supply pleasures to the wealthy (*Decline and Fall,* chap. 2). Some have seriously argued that building expensive buildings to form a powerful base for a church is the best way to generate funds for world mission. Any of these propositions, and any particular application of them, can (and generally should) be argued. Nonetheless, Jesus himself did not take an unrelentingly utilitarian view of the use of resources. He praised the woman who anointed him with costly ointment, against the protests of those who condemned this waste and said the ointment should have been sold and the money given to the poor (Mk. 14:3-9). And even the creation itself has an extravagance about it, not only in its astounding variety but also in, say, the overwhelming proportion of insect eggs or larvae destroyed for every one producing an adult insect. (We may, of course, contrast the extravagance that stems from largeness of heart with that which stems from largeness of ego; but in a fallen world, even distinctions of this sort cannot be made to stick absolutely.)

Rather than marvel at or debate the extravagance and waste indulged by the tiny minority or on the exceptional occasion, we may do better to consider that which is inherent in the way we Americans live our daily lives. Consider: the junk mail Americans receive each day could produce enough energy to heat 250,000 homes and costs 100,000,000 trees per year (quoted by *ESA Advocate* from *50 Simple Things You Can Do to Save the Earth*). We throw away enough aluminum to rebuild our commercial air fleet every three months, enough glass bottles and jars to fill both 1,350-foot towers of New York's World Trade Center every two weeks, enough iron and steel each day to supply all the nation's automakers each day, and 2.5 million plastic bottles every hour (*Keeping in Touch,* November 1990). The power used by a single Las Vegas resort hotel could supply an ordinary city of 60,000 people. And in the midst of all this, we still aspire to more. Barbara Ward and René Dubos ask:

> Is there a kind of biological limit to man's desire for food, shelter, leisure, entertainment, talking by telephone, moving about in a motor car, flying in airplanes, visiting distant lands? Is there a threshold beyond which desire and curiosity cannot be pushed? We do not know. . . . Perhaps no modernized societies have reached a consensus on what a "good life" means in economic terms save in relation to reaching other people's higher levels. In all of them, any general state of benign satiety seems a long way off. (*Only One Earth* [New York: Norton, 1972], p. 122)

God's judgment on our modern, scientific-technological Babel, with its presumption of control and its myth of progress and its materialism, has been sometimes more and sometimes less evident; indeed, its quality as judgment may often be obscured by our uncomprehending assumption that more of what produced the judgment is what is required to combat it. The simplest example of this process is the drive to fill up the emptiness generated by materialism with more material goods. Something much subtler than judgment of greed and the lusts of the flesh is at stake in this drive, however. Materialism is only secondarily a moral fault. It is primarily a statement about what is *real* and, as such, a manifestation of reductionism, an ignoring of the specifically human dimensions of life. The products of such reductionism cannot, virtually by definition, fulfill specifically human longings.

The very fact that Christianity has regarded matter seriously but not as divine has, as we have noted, been congenial to the scientific enterprise, the striking successes of which have fostered an attitude that — even in those too-rare instances when it refrains from metaphysical judgments about final realities — considers the only reality worth talking about to be that which can be investigated by scientific methods and, preferably, described mathematically. But these methods have produced a picture not just of a mechanized world (mechanized and meaningless, its very determinisms generated by the laws of chance operating on very large numbers), but a world from which we ourselves, in our human self-consciousness, are absent; and finally, a world of tasteless, colorless, soundless, whirling atoms rather than of crepe myrtles and dachshunds and bologna sandwiches with hot mustard.[44] These are not small losses (and doubly so because the more we come to see the world in the former rather than the latter terms, the less we are motivated to protect it); yet we are loath to give up the gains that come with them.

Some ambivalence soon enters in, however. Backing up a step or two from the more abstract reaches of science, we may begin by rejoicing in some concrete conquests of nature. We may count it well worthwhile to ignore and destroy the loveliness of a forest in order that we may treat its lumber as material for houses: houses may seem both more real and more necessary than loveliness. We may even agree to an electrode implanted in our own brains to reduce intractable pain. But propose moving that electrode to a location calculated to produce "happiness," and something we call "I" rises up to protest being reduced to an object.

---

44. "It is precisely as if some sect had insisted only that its followers believe they were invisible and all else would follow. Such a faith would be confined, we assume, to a few eccentrics and inadequates. Yet science's demand is even more extreme, and we do not notice our own acquiescence, our own eccentricity. And we do not notice because, astonishingly, the demand produces results. It works" (Brian Appleyard, *Understanding the Present,* quoted in *Context* 24, no. 18 [Oct. 15, 1992], p. 6). Similarly, "We know that two apples plus two apples make four apples. We have always taken it for granted that the apples exist, but . . . the mathematician gets on just as well without the apples, better indeed, since the apples have other attributes besides number. When sufficiently hard pressed, therefore, the physicist solves his difficulties by turning mathematician. . . . There is really no occasion for despair: our world can be computed even if it doesn't exist" (Becker, *Heavenly City,* p. 27). See also above, pp. 35-53, 72-77.

A starkly scientific approach to ourselves and our world, however potent and however amazing in its intricacy, simply does not take into account the most important things in our personal identities, much less those things that we intuit (for what can mathematics tell us about either importance or intuition?). Perhaps it is not so surprising after all, then, that magic and the occult have shown a resurgence right in the midst of a technological age, insisting in however dangerous and misguided a way upon a fuller perception of reality than that of science. And some have suggested that our reliance on *number* bears witness not to how much but to how little we have really grasped of the reality in which we live.[45] But science and the technology it spawns continue, understandably enough, to use the tools they have and, less understandably, to promise that these tools will produce a better *human* life.

No doubt it is in part this utter inability of science and technology to address the specifically human dimensions of life — and thus, unintentionally, their covert destruction of them — that has led to such disillusionment over what an earlier generation would never have dreamed of calling the "myth" of progress. Take the computer, in 1992 rated higher than churches as a source of positive influence on the country.[46] For all the vast quantities of information it can give us about what we do each day, it can tell us nothing about the value of what we do — calling to mind T. S. Eliot's line about the only monument of this generation being "the asphalt road/And a thousand lost golf balls."[47] Surely our powers exceed the human meaning of our goals. Confusion and emptiness result.

Furthermore, our focus on technology — on control of the environment as *the* solution to our problems — has at one and the same time robbed us of the sense of wonder and of reverence and of gratitude with respect to

45. See Karl Heim, *Christian Faith and Natural Science* (Gloucester, Mass.: Peter Smith, 1971), esp. pp. 80-81; Huston Smith, *Forgotten Truth* (New York: Harper & Row, 1976), chap. 3; and Moltmann, *God in Creation,* p. 39. One recalls Dostoyevsky's Underground Man's fear of the fixity and lack of freedom inherent in mathematical certainties, and his consequent revolt against number: "Twice two makes four seems to me simply a piece of insolence. Twice two makes four is a pert coxcomb who stands with arms akimbo barring your path and spitting. I admit that twice two makes four is an excellent thing, but if we are to give everything its due, twice two makes five is sometimes a very charming thing, too" (*Notes from the Underground,* chap. 9).

46. According to a Times Mirror Survey, noted in *Christian Century* 109, no. 24 (Aug. 12-19, 1992): 737. [I recall the remark of a minister who, having visited the central placement office of her denomination, expressed dismay at finding a person instead of a computer seemingly in charge of the process. — Ed.]

47. Choruses from "The Rock," in *T. S. Eliot: Selected Poems* (New York: Harcourt, Brace & World, 1964), p. 116.

the natural world;[48] and turned us away from what was once our primary human task: learning wisdom and self-control in the face of the often-recalcitrant and difficult "givens" of life. That is, a problem of morals has been transformed into a problem of technique.[49] Peculiarly human rewards and peculiarly human "soul-making" duties have been obliterated with a single blow. From thence it is but a short step to the verdict that "progress" that fails to produce better men and women does not deserve the name — a verdict reinforced by vast evidence that we have neither the wisdom, the courage, nor the self-control to govern our use of the immense power we have gained. We must make increasingly complex decisions for which we are absolutely not equipped. Nor do we know how to equip ourselves (mistrusting even the traditional means, many of which modern psychology has scored as producing unhealthy inhibitions, and hence being left with next to no means at all).

This dilemma is further complicated by the fact that technique is evaluated solely by its own efficiency and will not tolerate moral judgments — a point made at length in the writings of Jacques Ellul and, more recently, by Neil Postman.[50] Technique develops according to what becomes possible, not in accord with ideas of what uses will be made of its achievements: "Techniques of peace and alongside them other and different techniques of war simply do not exist, despite what good folk think to the contrary. . . . If atomic research is encouraged, it is obligatory to pass through the stage of the atomic bomb; the bomb represents by far the simplest utilization of atomic energy."[51] We simply cannot produce the good without the bad; and we have not only shown no ability to refrain from using whatever power we have, but we have also shown no ability to act on the thesis that the cost of obtaining some kinds of power may be too high. Those suggesting limits to human aspiration are attacked with a fury as having no concern for human welfare. Thus it has become an axiom that whatever is possible is necessary.

But it is not just failure to nurture the distinctively human or the

---

48. See Douglas J. Elwood, "Primitivism or Technocracy: Must We Choose?" *Christian Century* 88, no. 48 (Dec. 1, 1971): 1417.

49. See C. E. M. Joad, *The Recovery of Belief* (London: Faber and Faber, 1952), p. 54.

50. See, in particular, Ellul's *Technological Society,* pp. 97ff. and passim; also Postman's *Technopoly: The Surrender of Culture to Technology* (New York: Knopf, 1992). For Ellul, "technique" is not "technology" *simpliciter,* but rather, "the *totality of methods rationally arrived at and having absolute efficiency* (for a given stage of development) in *every* field of human activity" (ibid., p. xxv). Its amorality is embodied in the remark attributed to Wernher von Braun, that if the rocket went up, that was all that mattered to him. Where it came down was in another department.

51. Ellul, *Technological Society,* pp. 98-99.

inevitable production of bad along with good potential by each increase in human power that threatens the idea of progress. It is further compromised by the problem of unintended, unforeseen side-effects that tend to be more complicated than the original problem. DDT reduces some insect populations, at least in the short run, but leaves both pesticide-resistant insects and pesticide residues that threaten both animals and humans. Vaccination reduces the death rate, which produces population growth, which produces increased deforestation, which produces erosion, which produces desertification, which produces famine. Reduction of physical toil by new machinery produces nervous tension and all sorts of physiological and psychological ailments requiring further technical intervention. New detergents and biocides that have never existed in nature simply accumulate because organisms do not exist that can break them down.[52] And so on. Hence the judgments: "Every advanced country is overtechnologized; past a certain point, the quality of life diminishes with new 'improvements.' "[53] " 'Progress' is no longer an expression of hope, as it was in the nineteenth-century; it is a fate to which people in the industrial countries feel themselves condemned."[54] Its symbol might be the supersonic Navy fighter plane so fast that it overtook its own test-fired shells and accidentally shot itself down.[55]

Precisely in our efforts to gain control, we have produced more and more that we cannot control and hardly know how even to approach, including a whole array of new choices and unprecedented moral dilemmas. Consider: Who should have custody of stored embryos, produced by in vitro fertilization, when the prospective parents determine to divorce?[56] What do desires to use fetal tissue for research, and prospects of using it to alleviate, for example, Parkinson's disease, imply for abortion policy?

52. Paul B. Sears, "The Injured Earth," in Michael P. Hamilton, ed., *This Little Planet* (New York: Scribner's, 1970), p. 20. We may note that designer bacteria are now being developed to eat oil slicks — but what will then happen to the designer bacteria, if they have no natural enemies?

53. Paul Goodman, "Can Technology Be Humane?" in Barbour, ed., *Western Man,* p. 231. "Instead of rejoicing, there is now widespread conviction that beautiful advances in genetics, surgery, computers, rocketry, or atomic energy will surely only increase human woe" (ibid., p. 228). Some would go so far as to put the golden age for human beings back in the Stone Age, arguing that while we sentence ourselves to life at hard labor, hunters and gatherers likely worked three to five hours a day at food production, leaving the rest for recreation and sleep. "*This* is the era of hunger unprecedented. Now, in the time of the greatest technical power, is starvation an institution. . . . The amount of hunger increases relatively and absolutely with the evolution of culture" (Marshall Sahlins, quoted by Smith, *Forgotten Truth,* p. 125, n. 6).

54. Moltmann, *God in Creation,* p. 28.

55. *Los Angeles Times* clipping, date unknown.

56. *Los Angeles Times,* Aug. 8, 1989, pt. 1, p. 12.

What does computers' capacity to store and access records mean for privacy rights; and what does their vulnerability to viruses (and dependence on intact power sources) mean to a country increasingly unable to operate without them? We are confused because we do not know how to go back to a time before we built our tower of knowledge and expertise, even if we wanted to. We are faced, says Eiseley, with the problem of escaping from our own ingenuity.[57]

Who would have guessed that the ancient judgment on the people of Babel would come home in such striking ways in the modern world? We have been separated from one another and made unable to communicate with one another in ways that earlier generations could not have imagined. We are so specialized that we do not know what we do, as if we were with the best will in the world making screws for the atomic bomb: limits on what the human mind can assimilate militate against depth of technical knowledge and breadth of understanding of its possible consequences in the same person (and those who seek to major in breadth are open to the criticism that they simply do not understand the details of what they are talking about). Specialists in even closely related fields cannot talk to each other. We begin to wonder if we will be left with only computers talking to computers, since no person can process all the information necessary to make significant decisions.[58] Furthermore, we depend increasingly on tools and machines that, while they are easy to operate, can be repaired only by experts,[59] so that we are actually more helpless if the machine fails than we would have been had we not depended on the machine at all (witness what happens when a computer crashes before one has printed out a hard copy of the report due this afternoon). Babel, indeed. The Lord has looked

57. *Firmament of Time,* p. 159. For further expansion on this theme, see below, pp. 438-45.

58. See Jacques Ellul, *The Technological Bluff,* trans. G. W. Bromiley (Grand Rapids: Eerdmans, 1990), p. 90 and passim. A radio news broadcast, Feb. 24, 1993, noted that a Japanese firm has developed the prototype of a 256-megabyte chip the size of a postage stamp — a single chip with enough storage capacity to contain the complete works of Shakespeare five times over. Ellul remarks elsewhere, "Men do not *need* to understand each other in order to carry out the most important endeavors of our times" (*Technological Society,* p. 132, emphasis added).

59. "Indeed, unrepairability except by experts has become a desideratum of industrial design" (Goodman, "Can Technology Be Humane?" p. 231). This whole complex of specialization and of more and more elaborate tools does not spare the intellectually and economically less advantaged; rather, it wreaks especial havoc on them. Those not suited to technical or technically mediated work find themselves increasingly out of the mainstream; and the poor person quite capable of repairing her Volkswagon Beetle is helpless before the computer chips in modern engines: transportation becomes *less* accessible to her than before the "improvements."

down from heaven and confounded us. Having refused all limits, we have been set in slippery places, at risk of disasters we cannot ward off (Ps. 73:18-19; Is. 47:10-11). But we might scarcely notice were it not for the looming ecological crisis, which we shall take up in the next main section.

Excursus: The Mystery of Life and Evolution

Implicit in the story of the development of human dominion has been the assumption of development of some sort in the creature we designate as human. This assumption raises the underlying question of evolution and, when pushed, leads back yet further to the mystery of the origin of life itself on this planet. The issues here arise not from the untold eons of time that must, on anyone's estimate, be supposed for the evolution of so much as a one-celled animal; for we have already suggested that the telescoping of the biblical accounts leaves room for vast drafts of time. They do not even come in an unnuanced way from the thought that living creatures may have evolved from a single ancestor: few now doubt that something which can be called evolution has occurred with respect to both animals and hominids (though many debate both the extent and the mechanism of possible change), and we can see no compelling reason why God may not have determined on such a means to populate his world. Problems arise rather when we consider our own relationship to the animal world (is there anything *fundamentally* different about us that justifies use of the term *imago Dei?*) and when we ask about the nature of life itself (can everything at last be reduced to mechanism and determinism? — a position we have already rejected above with respect to the human person: see pp. 7-10, also 76-77).

When Pasteur, using aseptic techniques, demonstrated that life as we know it comes from other life, he put to rest the debate over spontaneous generation — the venerable idea that life simply appears or is created from time to time out of the materials of nature (as might be shown, according to a medieval recipe, by putting some grain into an old shirt and stuffing the combination into a corner: in a few weeks, this mixture would reliably produce mice! See Charles H. Townes, "How and Why Did It All Begin?" *Journal of the American Scientific Affiliation* 24, no. 1 [March 1972]: 1).

We might note in passing that Christians who initially opposed the theory of spontaneous generation on the grounds that it conflicted with their theology of creation, later embraced it because of what seemed to be overwhelming evidence in its favor. They even adduced such texts as Ex. 8:16-17, which states that Aaron struck the dust of the earth with his rod and it became gnats, in its support (see Jan Lever, *Creation and Evolution,* trans. Peter G. Berkhout [Grand Rapids: Grand Rapids International Publications, 1958], chap. 2).

Pasteur's work did not, however, address the question of life's most primitive beginnings or resolve in any lasting way the debate between the vitalists, who think that "life" cannot be reduced to or ultimately derived from its material substrate, and those whom we might call mechanists, who believe that it can. Understandably enough, vitalism is widely discredited as question begging by those seeking chemical explanations of life (though Darwin himself, at least at the time of the writing of *On the Origin of Species,* assumed as a starting point "some one primordial form, into which life was first breathed by the Creator" [quoted from the *Origin* by Man-schreck, ed., *A History of Christianity,* p. 446]).

While modern scientists have not been quite as efficient as medieval ones in creating life from their recipes, they can present some fairly impressive data. By passing a current through a solution comprising constituents of a posited "primordial soup" — an analog to the primeval ocean being struck by lightning — they have generated not only organic molecules but even proteins (*Los Angeles Times,* Sept. 6, 1989, pt. 1, p. 1). They have found physical evidence of primitive bacterial or algal colonies in 3½ *billion*-year-old Australian and South African rocks (*Los Angeles Times,* May 17, 1980, pt. 1, p. 1). And they can argue, in favor of a gradual transition from the nonliving to the living, that the line between the two is hard to draw: viruses, in particular, show characteristics of both living and nonliving beings (though because viruses cannot replicate outside living cells, they would appear to be dependent on prior life, not its precursor).

No one denies baffling problems in all current origin-of-life scenarios, from the overwhelming statistical improbabilities associated with supposing that enough of the right kind of molecules could be generated at one time and in one place to "get together" in promising ways (dust derived from disintegrating comets, containing the building blocks of life, has been suggested as one source [*Los Angeles Times,* Nov. 12, 1990, p. B3]), to chemical problems related to the likelihood of promising molecules being quickly broken down or unable to replicate properly even if they appeared, to "chicken-and-egg" problems concerning the interdependence of proteins and RNA in living systems as we know them (their interdependence is awkward, since one *or* the other is assumed to be the precursor of life: "No one believes that even a rudimentary form of life containing all three components — DNA, RNA and proteins — could have sprung up as a result of random processes" [*Los Angeles Times,* Sept. 6, 1989, pt. 1, p. 15]). The simplest one-celled organism shows a high degree of organization of hundreds of different kinds of molecules impossible to imagine as characterizing a truly primitive form. Even under the most ideal conditions, any life-generating process we can posit remains fantastically complex. It is likely, furthermore, to be subject to unknown environmental requirements that may be illumined by a story told by Jacques Cousteau. It seems that a European aquarium ran short of sea water needed to house a recent shipment of marine invertebrates. The curators therefore decided to manufacture some sea water, since its formula is well known. The curators soon found, however, that their chemically correct water would not support life until they added some real sea water to it (from a solicitation letter of the Cousteau Society written in the mid-seventies).

Let us suppose for the sake of discussion, though, despite the magnitude of the difficulties, that the mystery of the process was solved and life was indisputably generated in the laboratory. Even in this unlikely event, the theologian is not forced to a mechanistic conclusion. The mystery of the process of its appearance does not exhaust the mystery of life: process accounts neither for its prior conditions nor, we would argue, for its character. An environment that can even support life, much less one that can provide components for its emergence, can hardly be supposed just to have "happened," unless we posit a modern variety of spontaneous generation. (For the unlikeliness of our life-supporting world, see our *God, Creation, and Revelation,* pp. 486-90; see also the old [first published in 1913] but still provocative treatment by biochemist Lawrence Henderson, *The Fitness of the Environment* [Boston: Beacon, 1958].) But the problem is not just one of necessary components, but also that of the presence of some organizing principle that makes life possible (Michael Polanyi, *Personal Knowledge,* pp. 383-84). Critics like Jacques Monod (*Chance and Necessity,* trans. Austryn Wainhouse [New York: Knopf, 1971]) immediately cry "vitalism"; but note that such an idea proposes not the actual presence of life but only its possibility, and sounds remarkably like Monod's own claim regarding some structures: "No preformed and complete structure pre-existed anywhere; but the architectural plan for it was present in its very constituents. . . . The epigenetic building of a structure is not a *creation;* it is a *revelation*" (p. 87; we find obscure the difference between an organizing principle and an architectural plan). That there should be a world where molecules are so constituted that they even *can* come together in increasingly complex ways — much less that they should actually do so as if conforming to an inner necessity — strikes one as being in itself hardly necessary. (In fact, Monod himself, p. 138, quotes François Mauriac to the effect, "What this professor says is far more incredible than what we poor Christians believe"!)

Theologian Karl Heim, pondering the tendency of all creation from atoms to humans to maintain its "wholeness," suggests that we wrongly make a sharp distinction between "dead stuff" and "organic life" (see especially *The Transformation of the Scientific World View* [New York: Harper and Brothers, 1953], chap. 6; also *The World: Its Creation and Consummation,* trans. Robert Smith [Edinburgh: Oliver & Boyd, 1962], passim). What in the animal world we see as a struggle to preserve life is echoed in the inorganic world when crystals behave much like bacteria, dividing and then growing (an example also given by Monod, p. 86), and even in the atomic world, when atoms "resist" being split or "die" by emitting radiation (Heim quotes Mme. Curie: "In what appears to be lifeless material, there are births, collapses, deaths and suicides. They conceal dramas which unfold with ineluctable necessity. They conceal life and death" [*Transformation,* p. 242].) Plants even manifest some sort of "awareness," trees being able, for instance, to send out a warning to neighboring trees when they are under attack by insects, so that the others trees then defend themselves by exuding unpalatable chemicals.

It is curious, and perhaps significant for our present discussion, that while the terms βίος and ζωή were used synonymously for "life" in Hellenistic Greek, in the New Testament the former scarcely appears, and the latter takes on the qualitative sense of fullness of life, or eternal life, given by Christ (see Nelson, *Human Life,* pp. 104-18). In John's prologue, Jn. 1:3-4, the creation of all things by Christ and the affirmation that "what has come into being in him was life (ζωή)" (NRSV; nuance depends on punctuation of the Greek text) are brought into suggestive immediate conjunction, presenting at least some grounds for speculation that ζωή, or incipient ζωή, pervades the created order; and that nothing is properly understood simply as βίος (biological life or the means of living). (The understanding of λόγος [word] that includes "ordering principle" may also be relevant — the ordering principle, when identified with Christ, clearly being personal, not mechanistic, in nature.) See also Ps. 36:9 [35:10 LXX]: "with thee is the fountain of life."

Surely life, however it may have emerged according to empirical description, continues to strike us as a marvel, mysterious in its essence. All life, we would suggest, is a form of transcendence — perhaps only incipiently in the earliest stages of order prevailing over disorder, but more and more plainly as consciousness emerges. We are thus right to have a deep sense of life's sacredness, a sense of wrong at destroying life, from the sawing down of a mighty tree to the killing of a dog to, most of all, the killing of a human being. (Even the exceptions in this feeling we tend to make with respect to pests may prove, ecologically as well as theologically speaking, to have their hazards.) Furthermore, despite the fact that humans are "over" and the animals "under," we are bound up with the animals in particular in a common creaturehood, a continuity or relationship indicated in the Bible itself by the use of the term נֶפֶשׁ חַיָּה (living soul) for all living creatures, from the teeming beasts of the sea to humankind (Gn. 1:20, 24; 2:7). We share with all living creatures a vital, living, psychic being.

*   *   *   *   *

We come, then, to the question of evolution, eventuating in the ape's query, "Am I my keeper's brother?" (We add the requisite acknowledgment that evolutionists themselves would answer with a loud No, wanting to say more precisely that apes and humans share a common but very remote ancestor.) We must first recognize that evolution as generally understood involves a modern view of process that is, strictly speaking, absent from the original creation narrative, which presents successive creative fiats. Although the order of appearance of the creatures in the creation narrative is strikingly similar to that posited by evolutionary theory, the different orders of creatures appear instantaneously and full-blown; whereas evolution involves billions of years of more or less gradual change, with simple forms at last developing into more complex or "higher" forms, culminating in humankind. And just as allowing a heliocentric view of the solar system to displace a geocentric one once seemed to the church to threaten the validity of the Incarnation and the uniqueness of the world as the theater for the drama of salvation, so the theory of evolution has seemed to many Christians to threaten human uniqueness as created in the divine image and to relate human beings to animals rather than to God.

In considering the case for evolution, we need to separate the data that the theory seeks to integrate from the explanations it puts forth for these data, the former being more compelling than the latter. It would be folly to ignore the data. The fossil record does show significant continuities and discontinuities in life forms, including an increase over time in the diversity and complexity of forms. We see homologous organs in creatures superficially very different from one another; and presumably matters like the two kidneys of mammals are not a case of overendowment difficult for evolutionists to explain, but rather a carryover of the bilateral development of primitive ancestors that are therefore just what one might expect. Surely we must be impressed to learn that the four molecules constituting the genetic code are the same for all living creatures, that chlorophyll and hemoglobin are strikingly similar chemically (and that the line between plants and animals is very difficult to draw: take, for instance, the tiny dinoflagellates, some of which have chlorophyll and some of which do not but eat still smaller organisms [N. J. Berrill, The Life of the Ocean (New York: McGraw-Hill, 1966), pp. 50-51]), that humans and chimpanzees have more genes in common than any measured pair of species within the same genus: their DNA is 99 percent identical (though we choose to classify humans and chimps in different genera; see Stephen Jay Gould, "The Evolutionary Biology of Constraint," Daedalus 109, no. 2 [spring 1980]:

45; also Kenneth F. Weaver, "The Search for Our Ancestors," *National Geographic* 171 [November 1985]: 585). Plant and animal breeders can produce striking changes in form: consider the difference between a Great Dane and a dachshund. Every time we note the preponderance of white rabbits in the Arctic or the resistance of a bacterium to an antibiotic or of a weed or an insect to a pesticide, we may see natural selection at work.

To integrate this whole complex of data, the scientific orthodoxy has posited what is generally called the neo-Darwinian synthesis as its theory of evolution — a modification of Darwin's theory of natural selection and the survival of the fittest by combining the insights of paleontology, population biology, and genetics. Variability in the gene pool, particularly that induced by genetic mutation, provides the differences upon which selective pressures work; different and less heavily populated environmental "niches" give advantages to creatures that can adapt to different circumstances better than their fellows can; and isolation of populations leads to the perpetuation and intensifying of particular characteristics. By gradual increments, the theory goes, algae become Amazons. (Speaking of biological relatives, a recent study suggests that fungi are more closely related to humans than to plants and speculates that that may be why fungal infections are difficult to control: drugs that attack fungi often hurt people as well! [*Time* 141, no. 17 (April 26, 1993), p. 17].)

The first thing to note about this synthesis is that it is more adequate to some parts of the data than to others. Virtually no one doubts what has been dubbed "micro" evolution: evolution *within* a species. We can observe the achievements of animal breeders and the rise of "superbugs." "Macro" evolution, however — evolution of one species into another — is a different story, if not in its general outline, at least in terms of identifying a plausible mechanism. (Anyone who agrees that there was once a universe without an earth, an earth without living forms, living forms without land animals, and land animals without humans, accepts evolution of a sort.) Darwin was well aware of the lack of the intermediate forms his theory would require in the fossil record and assumed that with more research, such forms would be found. His confidence has not been vindicated. Indeed, evidence of abrupt transitions and lack of intermediate forms is sufficiently striking as to lead Harvard biologist and geologist Stephen Jay Gould and others to scrap the idea of gradual development of species in favor of a theory of "punctuated equilibria" and "hopeful monsters" that would allow for long periods of stasis and rather sudden large changes (generated by developmentally highly significant mutations — genetically and morphologically small as affecting the embryo and hence not imperiling survival, but still enabling a "key adaptation" producing profound differences in adults [Stephen Jay Gould, "The Return of Hopeful Monsters," *Natural History* 86, no. 6 (June-July 1977): 20-30]). While this theory may seem a desperate expedient, it does have the advantage of taking developmental biology — left out of neo-Darwinism and seen by some as the most hopeful cutting edge of evolutionary hypotheses — fully seriously. It has in its favor at least the discovery that "the genome of a rat pup or a child is unexpectedly fluid. Genes interact with one another, affecting characters all across the field of development, more intensely and intricately than was ever surmised" (Horace Freeland Judson, "A History of the Science and Technology Behind Gene Mapping and Sequencing," in Daniel J. Kevles and Leroy Hood, eds., *The Code of Codes* [Cambridge, Mass.: Harvard University Press, 1992], p. 63). Whether intraspecies fluidity can paper the gap between species is, however, still the question.

Of course the older theory positing intermediate forms has formidable problems of its own. One cannot imagine reasonable sequences of such forms: the intermediate structures would not even work, much less provide a survival advantage. Even if, against all conceivable odds, a set of mutations occurred that produced an exemplar of a new and viable species, "With whom shall Minerva from Zeus's brow mate? All her relatives are members of another species" (Gould, "Monsters," p. 28). Even smaller changes are not easier but harder to imagine than one might first suppose, when one considers that they involve simultaneous and independent changes in several different systems like bones, nerves, and muscles; or when one notes that as a matter of fact, a silk worm needs 180 genes just to build its eggshell: *one* promising mutation will not do the trick. (See Huston Smith, "Evolution and Evolutionism," *Christian Century* 99, no. 23 [July 7-14, 1982]: 755-57; also *Los Angeles Times,* June 3, 1983, pt. 1, p. 20.) Darwin himself hated to think about the problem of the eye, an enormously complex organ whose parts are of no use whatever until all are present; and the eye apparently evolved independently at least forty times (Boyce Rensberger, "Evolution Since Darwin," *Science* 3, no. 3 [April 1982]: 41-45). Natural selection will obviously not serve as a mechanism in such a case. Nor will it serve to explain the development of the fantastically elaborate, innate, inherited instinctual behaviors essential, for instance, to the reproduction of many insects: each of a whole series of what would in a person be prescient acts must be carried out in order for the creature to survive, and a partial success gives no advantage over total failure. Even the silken web of the spider is a second-degree miracle. In the face of challenges to Darwin's posited mechanisms, one critic concludes, "It is beginning to look as though what he really discovered was nothing more than the Victorian propensity to believe in progress" (Tom

Bethell, "Darwin's Mistake," *Harpers* 252, no. 1509 [February 1976], p. 72).

There are other problems as well. Even if some signs of life have been traced back 3½ billion years, the remarkable paucity of fossils in pre-Cambrian rocks, and the sudden appearance of virtually all phyla in the Cambrian rocks, remains a mystery. We may also be moved to caution by the hypothetical character of the interpretation of fossil remains. If we are impressed to take more seriously the possible relationship between birds and dinosaurs by learning that there are both "lizard-hipped" and "bird-hipped" anatomical types among dinosaurs, our new-found credulity may be strained to the breaking point by the further intelligence that birds are supposed to have descended *not* from the bird-hipped but from the lizard-hipped reptile! (Michael D. Lemonick, "Rewriting the Book on Dinosaurs," *Time* 141, no. 17 [April 26, 1993], pp. 42-49). Biologists may appeal to the fact that many genetic potentials are present even though unexpressed (for instance, hens' teeth are not so rare as we might suppose: chickens, when a specific gene is "switched on," *will* produce teeth); and some alternatives appear to present a "binary choice" — as in either bird-hipped or lizard-hipped, but nothing in between — to the organism. However, such facts neither reassure one about the reliability of anatomical deductions nor suggest where such full-blown alternatives came from. Some argue, in fact, that certain odd specimens, including some alleged protohumans, may be not early transitional forms but later dead ends (e.g., Smith, *Forgotten Truth,* p. 141; see also the confused treatment of the bird *Mononychus* in Lemonick, "Rewriting the Book," p. 48).

The business of how to conceive the production of alternatives — especially alternatives of increasing complexity dependent on new operational principles (Polanyi, *Personal Knowledge,* p. 385) — between or among which natural selection, or "chance," could "choose" is difficult. Pollard criticizes Lecomte du Noüy's famous argument that production by chance of a world like ours is absolutely incredible at the level of statistical probabilities (a later, non-Christian mathematician calculates the chance of fixing the minimum number of enzyme sites necessary for life at $10^{40,000}$, a number far exceeding all the atoms in the whole visible universe [noted by Smith, "Evolution and Evolutionism," p. 757]) by saying that the argument buys into the wrong premises: chance is not itself a causative agent but requires valid alternatives; and if which alternative is realized can be attributed to some natural *cause,* then we wrongly speak in terms of probabilities or chance (William G. Pollard, "A Critique of Jacques Monod's *Chance and Necessity,*" *Soundings* 56, no. 4 [winter 1973]: 433-45). Insofar as combinations and changes can take place only according to certain laws by which, so to speak, the dice are loaded, we are not dealing with mere chance — but neither have we explained why the dice are loaded (see Ian G. Barbour, *Issues in Science and Religion* [Englewood Cliffs, N.J.: Prentice-Hall, 1966], p. 387). Even more problematic is the expedient of positing all sorts of unrealized potential in the simplest creatures: such a strategy threatens to make the "simple" creature more complex, at least in its potentiality, than the creature evolved from it — a particularly unhappy prospect for the brand of Darwinist whose theory cannot account for endowment of species beyond their immediate needs. (In a curious comment affirming both a sort of process and a divine source of hidden potentials — hardly what those wedded to chance want — Thomas cites Augustine to support the idea that "the plants were not actually produced on the third day, but in their seminal virtues; whereas, after the work of the six days, the plants, both of paradise and others, were actually produced" [*Summa Theologica*, pt. 1, q. 102, art. 1].) Or take the remarkable fact that some processes must be almost, but not quite, perfectly reliable to enable evolutionary change:

> If our kind of mind had been confronted with the problem of designing a similar replicating molecule [DNA], . . . we would have made one fatal mistake: our molecule would have been perfect. . . . It would never have occurred to us, thinking as we do, that the thing had to be able to make errors. The capacity to blunder slightly is the real marvel of DNA. (Lewis Thomas, *The Medusa and the Snail* [New York: Viking, 1979], p. 28)

All of this can lead one to feel all over again the pressure for some driving force behind and within what we observe. One senses the need not for a God of the gaps, however many gaps there may presently be: empirical gaps call for better empirical science (Barbour, *Issues,* p. 389); rather, the need is for a dimensional view of the created order in which God is working out his own purposes through the means he has established and continues to govern. (In such a view, evolution as a means is no more incompatible with — and no more the explanation of — the creation of God's world than paint and canvas are incompatible with — or the explanation of — an artist's masterpiece.)

In any case, everyone agrees that "survival of the fittest" is a tautology that explains nothing, since fitness can be determined only by survival. Survivors may be more or less complex, more or less "evolved," than their ancestors. Likewise, "mutations," says Pierre Grassé (holder of the chair of evolution at the Sorbonne for thirty years) "provide change, but not progress" (quoted in Arthur Koestler, *Janus* [New York: Random House, 1978], p. 182).

Both these problems with the neo-Darwinian synthesis and the impressive evidence for continuities among forms of life must be kept in mind when we consider humankind. Without any doubt, races of beings with capacities we call human preceded us on this planet. As we have noted above, Neanderthal buried her dead and seems to have included provisions for another life with the body: food and worked flint tools. Even earlier, the workmanship on some hand axes suggests a concern for beauty as well as usefulness (Childe, *What Happened in History,* pp. 39-42). But as one looks at the by-no-means-straight line apparently going back from anatomically modern humans like *Cro-Magnon* through archaic *Homo sapiens, Homo erectus,* and *Homo habilis,* to 3½-foot-tall "Lucy," to yet earlier and more primitive hominids dating as far back as 4.4 million years, it is not possible to say with our current state of knowledge, "Precisely here, at this juncture, we have the first truly human beings, whom we may designate as Adam and Eve." New discoveries keep changing scientific perceptions. "Lucy," 3½ million years old, definitively breaks the long-assumed immediate link between upright posture (which is considered to distinguish hominids from apes) and an enlarged brain and use of tools (the first *"Homo"* was a toolmaker), since small-brained, bipedal "Lucy" predates tools by fully a million years (Donald Johanson and Maitland Edey, *Lucy* [New York: Simon & Schuster, 1981], p. 310). Fossil remains now suggest that species assumed to be in a single line of descent actually overlapped; and there is widespread disagreement as to which species should be counted as human ancestors and which were evolutionary "dead ends." Genetic studies suggest that hominids diverged from apes not 20,000,000 years ago, as had been assumed, but more like 5,000,000 years ago, further substantiating a rather close human relationship with apes. Genetic and molecular biological data now also lead many to assume a common and surprisingly recent source of modern *Homo sapiens* (in Africa maybe 100,000 to 200,000 years ago), and seem to substantiate the con-siderable gap between archaic and modern forms shown by fossils — without there being much time for such large changes to occur (John Tierney, with Lynda Wright and Karen Springen, "The Search for Adam and Eve," *Newsweek,* Jan. 11, 1988, pp. 46-52; *Los Angeles Times,* Feb. 18, 1991, p. B3; Robert Lee Hotz, "Genetic Study Says All Men Have a Common Ancestor," *Los Angeles Times,* May 26, 1995, pp. A1, A39.). We are a long way from having the final word on the exact nature of our biological relationship with the animal world.

Earlier (see above, pp. 53-59) we affirmed that human beings leave the animals far behind; but we must be careful of exactly how we frame the difference. Because humans have tended to think of their distinctiveness from the animals as being largely a matter of greater intelligence, much debate rages as to the actual capacities of animals. Montaigne considered it his duty to exalt God's special grace to people by minimizing or denying *innate* human differences from animals: "When I play with my cat, who knows whether I do not make her more sport than she makes me?" (*Essays,* 2.12). A modern naturalist notes that the insect brain, though laid out differently from our own, has the same structures; and he claims with no small cynicism that "one of the main functions of the rational mind is to deceive itself," allowing humans to commit moral atrocities in the name of progress (*Los Angeles Times,* Feb. 26, 1991, p. E8, review of William Jordan, *Divorce Among the Gulls*). Whether because of self-deception or not, surely we have a long history of understanding animals wrongly, from the common seventeenth-century view that they are machines totally lacking in feeling that may be kicked or dissected alive without unkindness, to such unfair characterizations as that of the jackal as a devious scavenger, when it is actually a monogamous, courageous hunter (Patricia D. Maelhman, "Jackals of the Serengeti," *National Geographic* 166 [December 1980], p. 841).

We have already commented in passing on the remarkable nature of instinct in animals, "instinct" being understood as involving not rational but rather physiological controls. It is the inherited capacity to respond in specific and complex ways to the environment. For instance, the wasp's nest is a marvel of engineering, accomplished without reflective thought, that defies our sophisticated analysis. Bottom-dwelling ocean creatures can detect differences in bottom sediments slighter than detectable by our instruments, and choose their habitat accordingly (William H. Amos, *The Life of the Seashore* [New York: McGraw-Hill, 1966], p. 126). Marvelous as instinct is, though — and despite the fact that it can in some cases be modified in its expression by learning, and in other cases must be supplemented by learning — its weakness is in its relative inflexibility. It may be a small matter that the openings to fiddler-crab burrows are either perfectly round or surrounded by a slight lip, depending neither on the circumstances nor on the individuals but on the species (Amos, *Seashore*, p. 121); but it is more serious when a male sage grouse's instinct to return to the same breeding grounds is so great that it will perform its courtship dance in the middle of a road built across its former territory (Ann and Myron Sutton, *The Life of the Desert* [New York: McGraw-Hill, 1966], p. 182). My wife is a bird lover, and she once showed me a picture of a finch who had built a nest in which a cowbird, a poacher, had laid its eggs. The finch, therefore, sealed up the nest and built a new one, only to have the same thing happen again. In the picture, the finch was sitting on top of a layer of seven nests, one on top of another, in the last of which were two cowbird's eggs; and the finch was looking at the eggs. Obviously a human being, not locked into instinct, would not put up with this but would find a way to eliminate the cowbird or move to a new location or build some different kind of nest.

Whatever the limitations of instinct, we may find it impressive because by it, animals can do many things we cannot do. By contrast, animals' learning and reasoning ability seems by no stretch of the imagination to compare with our own. Still, even earthworms can learn to solve some simple problems (Polanyi, *Personal Knowledge,* p. 122). Animals of the most varied sorts can be trained to do tricks. Apes will spontaneously use simple tools like reeds to suck water or ants out of a hole. But we have tended to assume that animals cannot think abstractly, that they have no capacity for comprehending symbols such as those necessary for language. Such assumptions have, however, been called into question by recent experiments not only with apes and dolphins, but even with the much less intelligent parrot and sea lion.

While no one can get inside the head of another creature and be certain of its thought processes, carefully controlled experiments suggest that an ape can respond to novel commands at the level of a 2½-year-old child and can combine symbols to express desires — for example, indicate symbols for "Fire" and "TV" to communicate a wish to watch a favorite movie, *Quest for Fire*. This same ape, named Kanzi, watched a favorite treat being placed in a box that was then locked and the key deposited in another box, which was tied with a cord. Kanzi solved the problem by taking a piece of flint he had collected earlier and slamming it against the floor. With the sharp chips thus produced he cut the cord; then he retrieved the key and opened the box to get his treat. Here we have not only tool using but also toolmaking and an impressive bit of reasoning (Eugene Linden, "Can Animals Think?" *Time* 141, no. 12 [March 22, 1993], pp. 54-61). Dolphins, too, can respond the first time to known commands combined in novel ways and can understand concepts like "small" used as a relative term: asked to fetch the small ball, the dolphin will not only do so, but will, on a second trial in which the original small ball is taken away and replaced by a ball even larger than the original large ball, choose the smaller of the two balls (which moments ago was the larger one; *Los Angeles Times,* July 23, 1990, p. B2). Rote learning obviously will not cover such cases. Chimps (but not gorillas or baboons) appear even to have some rudimentary self-awareness, acting surprised at their mirror image when an experimenter smeared red dye on their foreheads; they have in the wild demonstrated organized, systematic aggression against neighboring colonies, in one case persisting for months until all the neighboring males had been killed; and they have repeatedly been caught in what appear to be clear attempts to deceive (as may also the gorilla Koko, who years ago inadvertently knocked over a sink and signaled in sign language, "Kate there bad," while pointing to the sink, seemingly trying to blame an assistant of the experimenter for the accident. See *Los Angeles Times,* Dec. 7, 1988, pp. 1, 30; also Linden, "Can Animals Think?").

Such evidence of reasoning powers and even of what we would in humans consider to be morally culpable behaviors makes the line much less sharp than once supposed between humans and animals, though the gap in intellectual ability obviously remains huge: humans, not animals, take the initiative. They design the experiments, write the articles, and manufacture the cameras with which they take the pictures. Still, the commonalities may give us new eyes to look at the Old Testament solidarity between people and animals. As we have said, people and animals alike are נֶפֶשׁ חַיָּה, living beings. Animals are placed under the same penal code as humans, oxen being subject to stoning for goring a person to death (Ex. 21:28) and the animals of Ninevah being clothed with penitential sackcloth (Jon. 3:7-8). Likewise, animals are included in the hope and vision of a perfected world (Is. 11:6-8). Although human beings are more noble than animals, they need animals; whereas the animals, created before humans, have no need of people (Heim, *Creation and Consummation,* pp. 71-72; Barth, *CD,* III/1, p. 177 [*KD,* III/I, p. 198]).

All of this should surely teach us some respect for our fellow creatures, including a resolution not to use them wantonly or treat them cruelly, as if they were mere mechanisms having neither value nor sentience nor some power of thought. Our slaughter of animals for our luxury rather than our necessity — like the decimating of herds of buffalo for sport in the American West, using only the tongue for food; or the trapping of animals for furs for the wealthy, sometimes causing the animals to suffer for weeks; surely these can find no justification (and modern slaughterhouses and fur ranches may be little better in terms of abuse of God's creatures). Christians have been amazingly oblivious in this regard: in fact, it was the Perfectionist Oneida Community that perfected and manufactured the particularly cruel steel leghold trap (J. George Butler, "The Jaws of Hell: Cruelties of the Leghold Trap," *Christian Century* 92, no. 24 [July 9-16, 1975]: 662-65). Tolstoy's description of a brutal moment in a wolf hunt as the happiest moment in one of his characters' life (*War and Peace,* bk. 7, chap. 5) finds its counterpart in the recreational preferences of many Christians who would be shocked to be castigated for brutality. Use of animals for medical research and the testing of products poses more complex problems, being commended by its presumably worthier goals but being compromised by questions of comparability of test results on animals and humans, the doubtful necessity of some of the experiments, and failures to take all possible care for animals' comfort. Spurgeon wrote eloquently against vivisection, remarking, "How it must excite the righteous indignation of the all-merciful Creator! . . . One would think that the least enlightened conscience would perceive the evil of such cruelty" (*Autobiography,* 4 vols. [London: Passmore and Alabaster, 1898-1900], 4.128); and it has often been remarked that callous disregard for animals carries over all too easily to similarly callous disregard for people — mute testimony to the links between us. In Scripture we do not find animals regarded unfeelingly, as mere instruments for human use, but rather see them granted a share in the Sabbath rest and of the produce of the field in the Sabbath year (Ex. 23:11; Lv. 25:7). The fallen domestic animal is to be lifted up (Dt. 22:4), and the ox is not to be muzzled while treading out the grain (Dt. 25:4). All creatures should be treated with kindly sympathy (Andrew Harper, *The Book of Deuteronomy,* Expositor's Bible [New York: Armstrong, 1903], pp. 430-31).

Nonetheless, the kindly sympathy many do feel for animals — their desire to have them around and their sense of kinship with them, to which the tens of millions of pets kept by Americans bear witness — can surely go to seed when pets stand in for humans in people's lives and are treated to luxuries that not only can have no meaning to them, but deprive humans of resources necessary to life. The heavy-duty cut crystal food bowl, personalized with the pet's name, that we have seen advertised will mean as little one way or the other to the living pet as will an elaborate funeral with a silk-lined casket to the dead one; but we suspect, were we a dog, that we would find an umbrella to attach to our collar, a bikini with matching nail polish, a spray breath sweetener, or an electric fur drier, a positive nuisance ("Hungry People and Pampered Pets," *Christian Century* 85, no. 26 [June 26, 1968]: 833). Were we a dog, our verdict might be pending on the orthopedic bed to ease our arthritis; but being human, something in us protests a loss of proportion, a failure to recognize the nature of the differences between animals and people and to respond appropriately.

*   *   *   *   *

Whatever we may eventually learn about our physical relationship to the lower orders of creation, evolution is no substitute for theology as an explanation of the appearance of human beings or life or anything else. Description of a process does not constitute an explanation of it, nor is a process of this sort its own explanation. The Christian who is glad to affirm scientists' work in studying various forms of biological change must nonetheless insist on the absolute incompatibility of Christian faith with evolutionism as a worldview that has no room for anything but random variation and chance as the source of ourselves and our world. Indeed, she must protest such refusal to receive our being as a gift of our Creator and such insistence on understanding ourselves in terms of ourselves: all such efforts at self-understanding lead to an unchristian anthropology. And the Christian must likewise continue to affirm that when we look at human origins, people are to be seen not as a little higher than the animals but rather as a little lower than the angels. Even if the difference between animals and humans should prove gradual on the time line, it is nonetheless qualitative in nature — as attested by the fact that the cynic who says the human being is a clever animal still does not want to be treated like one (Emil Brunner, *Man in Revolt,* trans. Olive Wyon [London: Lutterworth, 1939], p. 82).

As we have implied, the ideas of process and of continuities in physical forms do not in themselves need to trouble the theologian. She may note that the Scriptures do not hesitate to speak in one place (Gn. 2:7) of humankind as formed from the dust of the ground, and in another as having been created on the same day as the land animals (Gn. 1:24-27; note also Eccl. 3:18-21; and see our earlier remarks affirming continuous creation in tandem with creation ex nihilo, *God, Creation, and Revelation,* pp. 459-61.) She might further recall that she herself, not so long ago, began gradually to develop out of a cell in her mother's womb — a very complicated cell, it is true, but one that looks not at all like her today. If she can nonetheless say with the psalmist, "I am fearfully and wonderfully made. Wonderful are your works; that I know very well" (Ps. 139:14 NRSV), then there would seem to be no absolute, theoretical reason why she might not affirm a similar process and divine superintendence in the development of the human race. She does not thereby learn exactly when, scientifically speaking, a pair of "*Homo* something-or-others" became human. (This is almost the same problem we face with abortion, though in the case of the developing fetus, we have the data immediately available to us. We also see no abrupt break at the purely empirical level when a child becomes a responsible agent or when an unbeliever becomes a Christian. Jesus himself said that the kingdom of God is not coming with things that can be observed [Lk. 17:20].) The biblical narrative is meant to show the meaning of God's creative activity, not to pinpoint its biological details. Thus questions of origin must finally have a theological answer to which the biological answer is indifferent.

Furthermore, descent does not determine nature: John the Baptist preached to the Jews that they ought not to rely on their Abrahamic descent, since "God is able from these stones to raise up children to Abraham" (Lk. 3:8; see Heim, *Creation and Consummation,* p. 67). What God will make of a creature depends on God's own act. Perhaps it took millennia for a creature to develop an appropriately complex central nervous system and large enough brain to be fit to bear the divine image, to receive the divine inbreathing that made it possible to hear God's address and enjoy an I-thou fellowship with God and others; but the bestowal of the image and the divine address, not the highly evolved nervous system, made her human. Thus Brunner distinguishes *Homo sapiens* as a species in the natural world from *humanus,* only the latter being human: *humanus* is one who knows God's law and is able to hear God's call. Not the intellect as such but the spirit related to God is the key difference between human and animal, the difference that also gives human beings a sense of aspiration for that beyond themselves and a desire for beauty, truth, goodness, justice, the holy, the infinite, the perfect, the absolute (*Man in Revolt,* pp. 59, 286, 419). Whatever animals' capacity for some measure of abstract thought, it is a human who speaks with the intent of revealing herself. However much animals may deceive one another or show shame when behaving in ways their masters have punished, it is a human who pursues the ethics of deception or who rises above her own instinctual impulses to evaluate them. When she does wrong, she is not behaving like a beast but showing herself to be a sinner. In that sense we sympathize with the precocious monkey of the following verse (source unknown):

> Three monkeys sat in a coconut tree,
> Discussing things as they're to be.
> Said one to the others, "Now listen, you two:
> There's a certain rumor that couldn't be true,
> That man descended from our noble race.
> Why the very idea is a disgrace.
>
> No monkey ever deserted his wife,
> Starved her babies and ruined her life.
> . . . .
> Yes, man descended, the ornery cuss,
> But, brothers, he didn't descend from us!"

Not only does descent not determine nature, it also does not determine destiny. If human destiny depended on human progress, evolutionary or other, an age like ours that has ceased to have its old confidence in progress might well despair. If only the fittest humans had a future, the church would have no business reaching out to the unfit. But the Christian hope is that the truly human future will be given by the hand of God, and that in the coming kingdom precisely the poor and the weak have special place (Lk. 6:20-22).

It remains to us to comment briefly on the relationship of what appears to be a lengthy human history to the primal history in Genesis 1–11, particularly the question of the genealogies in Genesis 5 and 11 and the question of the unity of the race. (We have already reflected on what we understand to be the telescoping of the creation accounts and of the story of the rise of civilization.) Here again, we will see the primal history as a type of *Heilsgeschichte* relating to a time prior to written sources or physical artifacts, a history that deals with events that really took place, but that are related in a form different from what we might call literal history. The narrative is a theological interpretation guided by the Holy Spirit and is "primal" not only because it comes first on the time line but also because it is basic to the whole human story. Because of the unreflective form of the story, not controlled by the canons of critical thought, some questions like those arising, for instance, from the positing of a first human pair (e.g., where did Cain's wife come from?), cannot profitably be posed; hence we will not take up such questions (see Westermann, *Genesis 1–11*, p. 311).

The actual length of human history has no direct consequence for our doctrine of humankind, for Scripture and hence theology are concerned with the gospel — a matter of the unity in creation, sin, and grace of the present race. However, we take momentary note of the precise chronological data supplied in the genealogies of Genesis 5 and 11, by which they are distinguished from other biblical genealogies and from which the traditional 4004 B.C. date for the creation of Adam and Eve was derived. No plausible amount of stretching can get these genealogies to cover a time span measured in six digits. About all we can say with reasonable confidence is that it is highly significant that this early history, to which the New Testament ties the descent of Jesus, is structured as history and not as a flight beyond history to some metaphysical, eternal principle. Adam is created and falls in history. The genealogy in Genesis 5 also underscores the effects of this historical fall, the outworking of God's judgment on humankind, by closing each account with the relentless refrain, "and he died." We do not, however, know just what to think about the longevity of the antediluvians before death overtook them. Numerical schemes, like supposing lunar instead of solar years, work for some figures but not others. Perhaps the numbers had some symbolic meaning now lost to us, as does the 666 of Revelation (see Jean de Fraine and Pierre Grelot, "Numbers" [trans. Patrick H. McNamara], in Léon-Dufour, ed., *Dictionary,* p. 795); or perhaps the figures were heightened to provide the more striking evidence that no matter what one's vitality and strength, the grim reaper will at last prevail. These genealogies might have as their text Romans 6:23, "The wages of sin is death."

The matter of the unity of the race is much more significant theologically than its antiquity as such. No one doubts the fundamental unity of all humans currently on the planet, whatever superficial racial differences we perceive. Not only can all intermarry, but differences in cultural achievement go less deep than one might think. A colleague of mine told me of an Australian physical anthropologist who, as a young man studying Stone Age Australian Aborigines, fell in love with one and married her. She subsequently earned her doctorate in physical anthropology at Oxford or Cambridge and for years lectured with her husband in various parts of the world. My colleague met her as a seventy-year-old widow and described her as a very charming woman.

The problem comes as we think of races no longer inhabiting the world (about whose relationship to Adam and to us we can say little) and, more importantly, when we debate whether we must think in terms of monogenism (all humans having a single pair of ancestors) or polygenism (humans having more than one more or less independent origin). At the moment, at least a significant portion of the scientific community seems to be leaning in the direction of monogenism, based on genetic studies of mitochondrial DNA (inherited only from the mother) which suggest that all current humans can indeed trace their ancestry back to a "mitochondrial Eve," probably African and presumably part of a group all of whom would figure in human ancestry but whose mitochondrial DNA disappeared somewhere along the line for want of having daughters; and also on studies of the male Y chromosone, which provide independent data consistent with the "Eve" theory (see Tierney, Wright, and Springen, "Search for Adam and Eve"; Hotz, "Genetic Study"). Establishment of this thesis would fit nicely with Genesis and with Acts 17:26, that God made "of one [KJV blood, αἵματος, is a textually uncertain addition] all nations"; and it would give a literal and badly needed force to Adlai Stevenson's conclusion that "all wars are civil wars, all killing is fratricidal" (quoted by Margaret Frakes, "Guidelines to Peace," *Christian Century* 82, no. 10 [March 10, 1965]: 296). The larger theological issue, though, has to do with Romans 5:12 and the traditional doctrines of the Fall and original sin: "sin came into the world through one man and death through sin" (see also 1 Cor. 15:21-22). It is hard to conceive a genuinely historical origin of sin without a single real individual who sinned — who fell, as we have insisted, not *into* but *in* history, and by whose act original righteousness was lost for the whole race. (To suppose that humans developed in several places and sinned as an inevitable consequence of their humanity is surely to impugn the work of the Creator.) That is why we do not consider it simply an indifferent matter to affirm that there was a first human pair, a man and a woman — a first human "I" who, as a result of the act of the Creator, was aware of himself in his relationship to a human "thou." This relationship brought responsibilities toward each other and toward God; and the first pair fell by transgressing God's will. All humans since have needed the salvation to be found in the Second Adam, Jesus Christ.

Despite our strong theological preference for monogenism, however, we confess once again our conviction that the primal history, though genuine *Heilsgeschichte,* is not a piece of modern historiography that absolutely forbids seeing Adam as a pro- totypical human: indeed, the Hebrew word for Adam, הָאָדָם, is simply the word for "human being." Further, since our spiritual unity in Christ is attained by faith, not biology, perhaps it is not imperative to ground our sinful unity in Adam in biology: the mysterious nature of our implication in original sin is not made notably more under- standable by embracing the assumption that sin is somehow transmitted biologically. (The traditional Roman Catholic teaching denies polygenism, either as involving a multitude of first parents or as the existence of true human beings not descended from Adam, on the ground of the reality and biological transmission of original sin; see H. J. D. Denzinger, *The Sources of Catholic Dogma,* trans. Roy J. Deferrari [St. Louis, Mo.: Herder, 1957], no. 2328. In a careful and thorough initial exploration of the issue of monogenism, Karl Rahner did not absolutely rule out polygenism but considered monogenism the theologically preferable view; see his *Theological Investigations,* trans. Cornelius Ernst [London: Darton, Longman & Todd, 1961], 1.229-96. His later in- creased openness to polygenesis actually changed little theologically, since he continued to affirm a unique and unified original group of human beings [see George Vandervelde, *Original Sin* (Amsterdam: Rodopi, 1975), pp. 234-38].) It is absolutely imperative, however, that our view of the unity of human beings maintain that they have a single origin and destiny in terms of God's act and purpose; that they all share in the divine image, original sin, and the need of salvation; and that creation, fall, and redemption designate events that take place in history.

C. THE ECOLOGICAL CRISIS

1. INTRODUCTION

The cover of a recent periodical shows sand in the design of an as-yet-but- slightly shrunken earth in the top of an hourglass, falling slowly but relent- lessly into a disordered heap at the bottom.[60] What the sobering image cannot depict, though, is how the sand is falling at an ever-increasing speed. As early as 1864, George Perkins Marsh wrote, "The earth is fast becoming an unfit

---

60. *Christian Century* 109, no. 12 (April 8, 1992).

home for its noblest inhabitant," and predicted dire consequences, and even extinction of the human species, if "human crime and human improvidence" persisted.[61] The fact that his gravest predictions, like the predictions of impending disaster generated by the computer programs of the Club of Rome, have not yet come true, allows the skeptical to ignore warning signs and go recklessly on their way, like a driver who passes the last gasoline station with her gauge registering virtually empty; but since she senses no diminution in her car's power, she presses the pedal to the floor and speeds out into the desert night. But of course the earth's resources, like the gas tank's, are finite; and in the twentieth century population, energy and other resource consumption, and waste production have multiplied at an unprecedented and rapidly accelerating pace. The scale of human impact has so grown that it is no longer even plausible to assume that the earth is too vast to be seriously affected by it. Yet changes — increasing levels of smog in the developing world, decreasing numbers of species — take place gradually enough, and sometimes at enough distance from us, that we do not quite feel the full force of them. Will we really refuse to notice our peril until it is too late — until we, like the prodigal son, have wasted all our substance?

We must not half-consciously assume that those of us who live in an affluent nation will somehow escape. We discover our human unity in a new way when we perceive that national boundaries have no effect on acid rain or nuclear fallout; and even if our greed gains for us an unfair proportion of the world's metals and fuels, when they are gone, they are gone for us, too. We dare not suppose, whether on evolutionary or on biblical grounds, that only the human line really "counts":[62] our dependence on

61. Quoted from his seminal *Man and Nature* by Larry Anderson, "Nothing Small in Nature," *Wilderness Summer,* summer 1990, p. 64. *Man and Nature* is sometimes considered the "fountainhead of the conservation movement" (Lewis Mumford). "Ecology" is a comparably old idea, Haeckel having defined it in terms of the "economy of nature" in his *History of Creation;* but the study of ecology long tended to focus on animals and plants and to overlook the impact of humankind on the environment (Black, *Dominion of Man,* pp. 2-3). It took fully one hundred years, until the widespread demonstrations of Earth Day 1970, for the environmental movement to take hold in the public consciousness (*ESA Advocate,* April 1990, p. 11).

62. Lecomte du Noüy (*Human Destiny* [New York: Longmans, Green, 1947], chap. 7) appears to argue almost this way. Some have criticized the "spaceship earth" image for seeming to offer ecological sensitivity while maintaining an anthropocentric, purely self-interested view of things that fails rightly to value the creation for itself (Lynn White Jr., "Continuing the Conversation," in Barbour, ed., *Western Man,* pp. 63-64). It is sobering to read that a study by Stephen Kellert of Yale found a direct correlation between negative or dominating attitudes toward animals and frequency of attendance at religious services (Wesley Granberg-Michaelson, "Introduction: Identification or Mastery?" in Granberg-Michaelson, ed., *Tending the Garden* [Grand Rapids: Eerdmans, 1984], pp. 1-3).

the balance of the whole, not to mention God's stated pleasure in his creation, is far too great to commend any such view. Nor ought we to let our confidence in the Lord's future coming (or the temptation to become otherworldly in reaction to crisis) lead us to irresponsibility in the present, after the model of Ronald Reagan's infamously antienvironmental Secretary of the Interior James Watt, who defended his policies by remarking, "I do not know how many future generations we can count on before the Lord returns."[63] Rather, we would do well to read with care the signs of the present time (Lk. 12:54-56), for we are surely courting catastrophe.

2. PARTICULAR ECOLOGICAL PROBLEMS

a. Pollution

All the elements upon which we depend for our earthly life — air, water, and soil — suffer seriously from pollution. Of these, many scientists consider air pollution to pose the most serious long-term threat because it contributes to global warming (by producing the "greenhouse effect": "greenhouse gases" allow the sun's rays to penetrate to the earth's surface but absorb heat radiating from the earth and prevent it from escaping into space), which, with a rise in average temperature of only four or five degrees Fahrenheit, could in turn melt the polar ice caps, inundating coastal areas and islands; drastically change the range of plants and location of prime agricultural areas; and destroy species with already limited habitats.[64] Burning of fossil fuels (particularly petroleum in automobiles and coal to generate electricity), producing carbon dioxide, and emission of chloro-fluorocarbons (particularly from auto air conditioning systems and foam insulation), which also destroy the ozone layer, are the worst culprits; but deforestation also contributes importantly to the problem, since trees take in carbon dioxide and give off oxygen. The carbon dioxide content of the

---

63. Quoted in Granberg-Michaelson, *Worldly Spirituality,* p. 34. (Note Paul's critique of those whose expectation of the Lord's imminent return led them to idleness, 2 Thes. 3:6-13.) Thomas's view that "plants and animals will altogether cease after the renewal of the world" (*Summa Theologica,* Suppl., q. 91, art. 5) scarcely helps motivate us to protect them now.

64. In February 1990, 55 Nobel laureates and over 700 members of the National Academy of Sciences signed an "Appeal by American Scientists to Prevent Global Warming," calling global warming the most serious environmental threat of the twenty-first century. See also David Maddox and Larry E. Morse, "Plant Conservation and Global Climate Change," *Nature Conservancy Magazine,* July-August 1990, pp. 24-25.

atmosphere has increased 25 percent in the last century; and ice core samples in Tibet show that temperatures there have been warmer during the last fifty years than in any comparable period in the preceding ten thousand years.[65] Although manufacture of chlorofluorocarbons is prohibited in the United States after the end of 1995, old stockpiles can still legally be used; and were there *no* new emissions, it would still take a hundred years to restore the ozone layer to 1960 levels.[66]

Besides the threat of global warming, air pollution threatens us in many other ways. The documented, rapidly growing hole in and general thinning of the ozone layer robs us of the protection from the sun's ultraviolet rays that is believed to be necessary for life, and that at the very least reduces the incidence of skin cancer. Pollutants from the burning of gasoline and diesel fuel in the United States may cause as many as thirty thousand deaths per year.[67] And acid rain, created when sulfur dioxide and nitrous oxides

65. Rudy Abramson, "Glacier Ice Has an Old Tale to Tell," *Los Angeles Times,* July 28, 1990, pp. A1ff.

66. Larry B. Stammer, "Global Talks on Ozone Described as Successful," *Los Angeles Times,* March 8, 1989, pt. I, p. 6. The danger of CFCs was suggested in 1974, but the warning was not heeded; indeed, it was actively discounted by industry (Lanie Jones, "He Sounded Alarm, Paid Heavy Price," *Los Angeles Times,* July 14, 1988, pt. I, pp. 1-2). CFCs remain active for up to 100 years in the atmosphere, and a single chlorine atom can break up as many as 100,000 ozone molecules. Unfortunately, alternative chemicals contribute to acid rain that may harm wetlands (Marla Cone, "Alternatives to CFCs May Harm Wetlands," *Los Angeles Times,* July 27, 1995, p. A3).

67. According to estimates by researchers at the Institute of Transportation Studies at the University of California at Berkeley (U. C. Berkeley, *Wellness Letter* 7, no. 5 [February 1991], p. 5). In smoggy midcentury Los Angeles, Nelda Thompson wrote a bit of verse entitled "The Smog or Me," containing these lines:

> And some remained and gasped for breath
> And were real good sports as they choked to death.
> But shyly suggested the time was ripe
> To clean up this aerial sewer pipe.
> And the wiser heads with their eyes cast down
> (Now living discreetly out of town)
> Were dreadfully sorry and twice as late
> Said, "Give us time to investigate."

Such sentiments, however, have not competed successfully with the American love affair with the automobile, depicted in these lines from Karl Shapiro's poem "Buick" (also midcentury):

> As a sloop with a sweep of immaculate wing on her delicate spine
> And a keel as steel as a root that holds in the sea as she leans,
> Leaning and laughing, my warm-hearted beauty, you ride, you ride,
> You tack on the curves with parabola speed and a kiss of goodbye,
> Like a thoroughbred sloop, my new high-spirited spirit, my kiss.
>
> (In Untermeyer, ed., *Great Poems,* p. 1218)

from the burning of fossil fuels are washed out of the sky, falls on the just and the unjust (Mt. 5:45), poisoning lakes and seas, killing forests, reducing crop yields, and corroding ancient monuments that have survived for centuries. Yet, not only do Americans continue to add at least a ton of pollutants *each* to the atmosphere every year, but the United States government (unlike governments of other industrialized countries) has consistently refused to take strong measures to curb greenhouse gases because of fear of the economic effects of such action. We are surely living in a fool's paradise that not even a fool will forever find paradisiacal.

Turning to water pollution, we might note that our appetite for oil contributes more than acid rain to the degradation of our water supply: five million tons of oil from spills and leaks ends up in the ocean each year, killing thousands of sea creatures and fouling beaches. Add to this twenty billion tons of wastes of all kinds — biodegradable and nonbiodegradable, nontoxic and highly toxic — poured into the ocean, sometimes secretly; and one can hardly be surprised at increasing numbers of beach closures due to high pollution levels and, worse, spread of DDT and heavy-metal compounds throughout the marine food chain, all the way to the Arctic. The effects of this dumping are heaviest on the coastal waters, which are also where the largest concentration of marine life is to be found.[68]

The long-term impact on the vast oceans of our too-often indiscriminate treatment may be presaged by the state of freshwater streams and lakes. Available fresh water constitutes only 1 percent of the total volume of water on earth; and of what is withdrawn of this one percent, 73 percent goes for agriculture, 21 percent for industry, and only 6 percent for domestic consumption — with two billion people lacking adequate drinking water. Worldwide, 10 percent of all rivers are heavily polluted, and water-borne diseases lead to 25,000 deaths *per day* in the Third World. In the United States, 700 chemicals have been detected in drinking water, including 129 considered dangerous; and underground water reserves are contaminated with seepage from landfills and chemical storage tanks.[69] Water pollution affects people and their food supply not only directly but also indirectly, when bacteria use up the available oxygen supply in breaking down biodegradable wastes, or when runoff acts as a fertilizer that promotes bacterial or algal "blooms" that in turn consume oxygen, finally leaving the water

68. United Nations Environment Programme, *Only One Earth,* 1990.
69. Ibid. The General Accounting Office said in 1989 that federally owned facilities violate water regulations twice as often as private firms — a dismaying statistic for those who count on central controls to reduce pollution (William J. Eaton, "GAO Says Federal Facilities Are Major Water Polluters," *Los Angeles Times,* Jan. 15, 1989, pt. I, p. 4).

uninhabitable for living things. Thermal pollution (water used for cooling then returned, heated, to the water system) also seriously disrupts the environment, since it stimulates some creatures and destroys others.[70]

Land pollution in the form of the mountains of solid waste we produce led a wag to speculate that we would reach Mars by standing up to our knees in garbage on planet Earth.[71] But not only are we rapidly running out of landfill space (which generates both technical problems and serious questions of justice in determining where to locate new dumping sites); worse, the huge majority of this waste is not disposed of in accord with minimal standards of public health. One study by the Environmental Protection Agency found that in 86 percent of the industrial land disposal sites it investigated, hazardous materials had escaped into off-premises water supplies, and soil tests in residential neighborhoods may reveal high levels of toxic substances. The effects of these — including miscarriages, birth defects, organ damage, and neurological problems — came to national attention in the Love Canal scandal of 1978; but that was only the tip of the iceberg. There are tens of thousands of toxic waste dumps, many larger than the one at Love Canal, but no one knows where they are all located or what they contain.[72] We do know that one-quarter of the population of the United States lives within four miles of one of the 1,300 superfund sites — particularly large hazardous waste locations.[73] Still worse, many firms dump toxics illegally or ship them to Africa or the Middle East. Worse yet, not only is the number of chemicals entering into commercial use increasing at a rate of 1,000 per year, but of the 48,000 listed by the Environmental Protection Agency, virtually nothing is known of the toxic effects of almost 38,000.[74] Often, as in the case of asbestos, we discover serious health risks of materials only after years of use.

70. Ward and Dubos, *Only One Earth,* pp. 66-68.

71. Ibid., p. 81. Recall the statistics on wastefulness in the remarks on luxury, above, pp. 369-70.

72. Letter from Environmental Defense Fund, no date. See also James N. Brewster, "Love Canal: Redefining Disaster," *Christian Century* 99, no. 25 (Aug. 4-11, 1982): 829-30. Not until 1995 were legal claims against the polluters finally settled (James Gerstenzang, "Firm Agrees to Settle Love Canal Suit," *Los Angeles Times,* Dec. 22, 1995, p. A43). In 1987 Los Angeles county industries alone released or transported elsewhere 91.7 million pounds of hazardous chemicals, of which 12.8 million pounds of the toxics have been linked to cancer; 25 million pounds have been suspected of causing birth defects, sterility, or genetic mutations; and 53.6 million pounds have been linked to damage to internal organs and the nervous system (Maura Dolan, "L.A. County Firms Blamed for 40% of Toxic Emissions," *Los Angeles Times,* April 21, 1989, pt. II, p. 1). We will consider the special problems of radioactive waste below, pp. 419-25.

73. "Shutdown Threatens Cleanup of Toxic Waste Sites, EPA Warns,"*Los Angeles Times,* Dec. 30, 1995, p. A20.

74. United Nations Environment Programme, *Only One Earth.*

Apart from pollution by waste of all kinds, the land also suffers from modern mining and agriculture. Rock and mill tailings accumulate in huge mounds, acid seeps into ground water, and mine dumps catch fire and burn obstinately, while land above abandoned mines sinks. Heavy irrigation waterlogs agricultural land; heavy use of pesticides contaminates it; and heavy use of commercial fertilizers apart from the normal organic components compromises the texture and humus of the earth.[75]

The list could go on and on. We could include as a pollutant nonnative species, introduced deliberately or by accident, that lack natural enemies and hence run rampant, like the European gypsy moth that escaped its cage shortly after the Civil War and has been spreading destruction across the United States.[76] We could mention indoor pollution and the rash of symptoms generated by exposure to the mass of chemicals in the ordinary, well-insulated, and tightly closed office building. Or we could speak of noise pollution in the city. We must not forget the frequency and seriousness of industrial accidents, as in the 1984 gas leak from the pesticide plant in Bhopal, India, that killed 2,500 people and injured 150,000. In each case, too much of something or something in the wrong place threatens human beings and the environment.

Pollution is cause for serious concern not just because of its immediate effects but because of highly unpredictable long-range risks. Exposure to low levels of toxic materials may not produce obvious health effects in people for years or even decades. Already, most human breast milk contains levels of toxic substances that would make it considered unfit for human consumption if it were offered for sale. Excesses of some pollutants may destroy on a broad scale the very processes by which contaminants are normally degraded, as in the case of Lake Erie.[77] We simply do not know the long-term effects or interaction of many chemicals already released in large quantities, though interaction of pollutants occurs more often than not and creates new and unpredictable hazards. We do not know, either, when we might reach a critical point of no return — or even if we already have. But surely no sane person could see it as conceivable that we continue to assume an "out of sight, out of mind" attitude about the by-products of

75. Ward and Dubos, *Only One Earth*, chap. 8.

76. Richard C. Paddock, "Threat of Gypsy Moth in State Prompts Environmental Debate," *Los Angeles Times*, Oct. 24, 1983, pt. I, p. 3.

77. Jørgan Randers and Donella Meadows, "The Carrying Capacity of Our Global Environment: A Look at the Ethical Alternatives," in Barbour, ed., *Western Man*, pp. 253-76. That Lake Erie has shown signs of recovery from what looked like death, after the flow of phosphates into it was radically reduced, is obviously an argument for continuing rigorous environmental standards, not a sign that they are not really necessary.

our civilization. The old option of migration when the land can no longer sustain us (Gn. 13:6) is no longer available (except, of course, in fantasies of the colonization of other planets, though we have even managed to park a fair amount of debris in orbit).

b. Habitat Destruction and the Loss of Species

Of the world's 5-30 (or more) million species of plants and animals (we do not know exactly how many, only 1.4 million having been formally identified), at least 1 million are currently endangered; and estimates of the rate of extinction range from a low of one species per day to as many as one per hour. Half of the world's known species, including half of known crops, originated in the 6-7 percent of the earth's land area that comprises tropical forests; and those forests are being lost at the rate of a football field per second. Surely these statistics are an affront to the Creator, who willed that the planet should teem with life (Gn. 1:11-12, 20-25); told Noah to preserve both unclean beasts and clean ones, implying the way all life is tied together (7:2-3); and made his covenant with all living creatures (9:8-17). Even in time of war, Israelites were not to destroy the food-bearing trees of their enemies (Dt. 20:19).

Of course extinctions have long taken place, as displays of exotic fossil creatures show us; but — aside from exceptional periods like the mysterious time of the extinction of the dinosaurs and many other species — the rate has been slow, perhaps at most a single species per year, or even per thousand years. Humans have long contributed to extinctions, too, by hunting endangered species: exotic birds for their feathers, whales for their oil, elephants for their ivory tusks, rhinoceri for their supposedly medicinal or aphrodisiacal horns, or any other species from which they might be able to make a profit or exact pleasure from the pursuit. Illegal trade in rare animals or their parts now threatens increasing numbers of species; as do legal techniques like driftnet fishing, which kills edible and inedible fish, birds, and marine mammals indiscriminately and in vast numbers. All such threats are serious, but the main cause of extinctions is habitat destruction by an ever-expanding population in need of land for agriculture, fuel and lumber, grazing ground, and settlements (not to mention landfills: once, these tended to be located in the nearest swamp; but now we realize the danger of encroaching further on these diminishing habitats, having lost 95 percent of the hardwood swamps in the United States in the six years between 1983 and 1989). Loss of the rainforests is most serious of all because of their unbelievable diversity, their fragility, the contribution they make to the world's oxygen balance, and the frightening speed at which they are being destroyed for very short-term gains (the unprotected soil is thin and quickly becomes unproductive, so poor farmers must move on, burning more forest, every couple of years).

Commercial and political interests often try to set the interests of land and species preservation against human needs, arguing, of course, for the primacy of the latter.[78] But these are false alternatives. The choice is not between *Homo sapiens* and one or another other species. The choice is whether all survive or all go down together. We are increasingly finding how intricate is the relationship among living creatures and how wide-ranging the effects of a single action. While charming giant pandas and panther cubs may serve best to raise conservation funds, humble bugs and even so-called pests may serve our planet's survival in undreamed-of ways — a lesson we should have learned from Noah's preservation of the "unclean" beasts. In fact, the tiniest plants and animals are the foundation on which the whole ecological system rests; and the demise of any species of whatever size is likely to be a signal that the system of which it is a part is in trouble.

As an example of interdependence of species, consider the almost nine hundred kinds of figs growing in tropical forests. The vast majority of these can each be pollinated by only a single species of wasp. No wasp, no fig. No fig, and the whole food chain depending on it, including bats, spider monkeys, peccaries, toucans, and jaguars, collapses (G. Jon Roush, "The Disintegrating Web: The Causes and Consequences of Extinction," *Nature Conservancy Magazine* 39, no. 6 [November-December 1989]: 7-8).

Or consider what resulted from a well-intentioned attempt to reduce malaria in a village in the Borneo jungle by spraying straw huts with DDT. Yes, the mosquito population was reduced. However, lizards inhabiting the wall of the huts also died from the DDT, as did the village cats that ate the lizards. Death of the cats led to an infestation of rats; death of the lizards left straw-eating caterpillars free to multiply, and they proceeded to devour the roofs of the village huts (noted by Jeremy Rifkin, *The Emerging Order* [New York: Putnam, 1979], pp. 70-71). Such tales of last states worse than the

78. The problem is worldwide. A congressman from the American Pacific Northwest remarked, "We now have two threatened species, the [northern spotted] owl and the thousands of families that depend on our forests for the food on their tables. Congress must act this summer to ensure that survival of the owl goes hand in hand with the survival of our North Coast way of life" (Mark A. Stein, "Owl Designated 'Threatened'; Impact in Doubt," *Los Angeles Times,* June 23, 1990, pp. A1-2) — as if it were unfair and unnecessary to ask for changes in lifestyle to protect the environment. In the Northwest, it is the timber industry that wants to proceed unimpeded. In Brazil, ranchers who want to turn forests into grazing lands have gone so far as to murder conservationists (*Los Angeles Times,* Jan. 22, 1989, pt. I, pp. 1ff.). In the Philippines, young divers risk their lives pounding on fragile coral reefs to drive fish into nets to feed hungry coastal villagers — reefs now 70% destroyed by this pounding plus various explosives, threatening the whole ecology of the region (Bob Drogin, "Death and Disaster on the Reef," *Los Angeles Times,* Nov. 22, 1989, pt. I, p. 1). Fish catches have been shrinking in the region (*Amicus Journal* 10, no. 4 [fall 1988]: 9).

first following injudicious pesticide use can be multiplied indefinitely. Not only do the pesticides become more and more concentrated higher in the food chain, as we have noted above, leading to such problems as falcons laying eggs too thin-shelled to hatch; but also pests tend to be rapidly multiplying creatures that quickly develop a resistance to or even a positive affinity for what once were poisons lethal to them. The pests not only are not eliminated but become harder than ever to control, so that the percentage of crops lost to pests has *grown* since 1900 for almost all major crops except apples (noted by Wink, *Engaging the Powers,* p. 381, n. 32, from *Los Angeles Times,* April 5, 1987, pt. I, p. 2). In short, attacks aimed at pests have proved more hazardous to the long-term survival of other creatures than of the pests themselves.

Loss of predators can be a very serious matter even when considering effects on creatures we have not considered pests. For instance, if all the eggs of one female oyster and their descendants were to survive, in five generations they would occupy as adults a space 250 times the volume of the earth; but in a normal environment fewer than 1 percent of the young survive (William H. Amos, *Life of the Seashore* [New York: McGraw-Hill, 1966], p. 138). We have had to learn to harvest for ourselves the small crustacean called krill, however, and at no small expense: it used to be harvested by whales, at the rate of a couple of tons per blue whale per day; but now there may remain as few as two hundred of these blue whales, the earth's largest animal, and most other whales are seriously endangered as well — which leaves krill all too free to multiply (David W. Ehrenfeld, *The Arrogance of Humanism* [New York: Oxford University Press, 1978], pp. 118-19; N. J. Berrill, *Life of the Ocean* [New York: McGraw-Hill, 1966], p. 126; Jane Fritsch, "Grim Report Notes Severely Depleted Whale Populations," *Los Angeles Times,* June 13, 1989, pt. I, p. 3). Again, it is not enough to preserve just a few exotic specimens; the balance of the whole must be considered. Sometimes, in fact, isolated, protected "islands" of a particular environment are compromised precisely by being isolated islands, as when fragmentation of a rain forest allows more light to enter, changes the climate, and leaves edges open to increasing invasion by nonnative plants and animals, resulting eventually in changes in the composition of the forest (*Nature Conservancy Magazine,* July-August 1990, p. 41). We keep finding things more complicated, and the balance more delicate, than we had supposed.

Preservation of species is vital not only because of the delicacy of the balance in nature but also because of the need to maintain diversity in the gene pool and to avoid losing resources we have not yet even explored. Inbred plants and animals, selected for particular traits farmers and ranchers desire, can be devastated or entirely wiped out by a disease because they lack the normal genetic variability that would ordinarily make some members of the species pest-resistant. When one considers that only about fifteen species of cultivated plants stand between humankind and starvation, loss of genetic resiliency and hardiness in any of these plants, or loss of the wild relatives that could replenish domestic stocks, is a very serious matter indeed.[79] Furthermore, because we

79. Philip Shabecoff, "Civilization's Folly: Million Species in Danger," *New York Times,* Nov. 22, 1981.

have classified such a small proportion of the earth's species, we have no idea what we may be losing. Already we depend on plants for the active ingredients in at least 25 percent of prescription drugs, including many drugs with anticancer properties, as well as materials like rubber and adhesives; and scientists have examined only 1 percent of the plant species in tropical forests.[80]

Species cannot be preserved without proper habitat; without intact systems, we have no way of knowing what it takes to constitute a workable environment (recall that the supposedly correct scientific formula for sea water would not support life until the genuine article was added to it — above, p. 378). While filling swamps and slashing and burning forests obviously devastate habitats, so, even if more slowly and less visibly, does pollution. We are rapidly loosening the strings on our fine-tuned environment and cannot blithely assume its continuing fitness to sustain us.[81]

c. Population Growth and Hunger

It appears that we have taken scarcely any divine injunction more to heart than the command to fill the earth. But surely this "obedience" of ours has been without discernment: the command comes with a responsibility, an obligation, that might well suggest to us that we ought not to *overfill* the earth. Nor ought we to think solely in terms of biological statistics, however much we may be tempted as Westerners to do so. Rather, we need to think in terms of the demands we make on the environment, for overpopulation occurs when people's demands outstrip the environment's abil-

80. Many have used as an additional argument for preservation of species the widely accepted hypothesis that complex ecological systems are stable, while simple ones (those with few components) are more subject to violent fluctuation or complete destruction in the face of external threats. While intuitively attractive, this hypothesis has been challenged as confusing cause with effect: the greatest diversity of ecosystems appears where the environment has been most stable for a long period of time; and these mature ecosystems (coral reefs, rainforests, and so on) appear in fact to fall apart quickly when stressed. Hence they particularly need protection (David W. Ehrenfeld, *Arrogance of Humanism* [New York: Oxford University Press, 1978], pp. 194-96).

81. Considering the seriousness of the environmental threats facing us, the refusal of the United States, in the face of corporate pressures, to support the international wildlife and habitat treaty proposed at the Earth Summit in Brazil is dismayingly shortsighted, to say the least (Rudy Abramson, "U.S. Will Not Sign Wildlife, Habitat Treaty," *Los Angeles Times,* May 30, 1992, p. A1). The United States' own Endangered Species Act comes under continual pressure from developers (not to mention being subject to changes in political climate in Washington); and while it has saved a number of species, as of 1988 some eighty species became extinct while awaiting formal designation as "endangered" under the law ("An Endangered Law," *Los Angeles Times,* April 5, 1988, pt. II, p. 6).

ity to supply them. If we calculate that way, we must conclude the United States is the most overpopulated section of the globe. A baby born to an American will stress the world's resources and environment one hundred times more than a Kenyan or Bangladeshi baby, which will not grow up relying on automobiles or air conditioners or grain-fed beef.[82] The American puts pressure not just on her immediate surroundings but on lands and people far away, as forests are destroyed to provide packing materials and grazing land for animals that will end up as pet food, oil and minerals are mined, and land needed for subsistence farming is devoted instead to cash luxury crops like coffee for export. As we have already seen, the world cannot continue to sustain even one United States with its current habits; but a growing population worldwide understandably aspires to a similar standard of living. And history provides no example of a nation mired in poverty and illiteracy experiencing a significant decline in fertility, both because many hands are needed for work and because parents want to increase the likelihood of some survivors where infant mortality is high.[83] Pressure on the environment increases either way.

Earth did not reach a population of one billion until 1835. Now there are more than five and one-half billion, and the number is growing at the rate of over ninety million per year — a rate that continues to increase. This increase testifies to the successes of science in reducing infectious disease, decreasing the death rate, and generally improving health, which leads in the end to more babies. And more babies demand, first of all, more food, just as the amount of land available to grow it on is being reduced by this same expanding population. People naturally begin to use marginal land that is not suitable for farming and is soon lost altogether for productive use: jungle soils turn to laterite and must be abandoned; six million hectares in Africa, Asia, and the Americas turn to desert each year due to overcultivation, overgrazing, deforestation, and improper irrigation; and another 21 million hectares become infertile. Wood and even dung are burned for fuel and hence no longer protect and enrich the soil.[84] Topsoil worldwide is being lost to wind and water

82. Paul R. Ehrlich and Anne H. Ehrlich, "Population, Plenty, and Poverty," *National Geographic* 174, no. 6 (December 1988), p. 917.

83. J. Edward Carothers, et al., eds., *To Love or To Perish* (New York: Friendship Press, 1972), p. 59. After sixteen years' effort promoting family planning in India, the population growth rate had *increased* from 1.3 percent to 3 percent per year (Paul R. Ehrlich, *The Population Bomb*, p. 87). By contrast, China has increased its standard of living and life expectancy while reducing its previously exploding population to near-replacement levels — at the cost of an increase in female infanticide, since families limited to one child have shown the traditional preference for males (Ehrlich and Ehrlich, "Population," p. 922).

84. Tom Hampson, "Lifescape: The Land and Its People," Church World Service newsletter, 1985.

erosion at a dismaying rate — for example, two bushels of topsoil are lost for every bushel of grain produced in the United States' "corn belt."[85]

Hope that the "Green Revolution" — a combination of hybrid, high-yield food grains with liberal use of fertilizers and pesticides — would solve the food problem has had to be modified because of its high costs in terms of energy input and soil degradation, and the vulnerability of hybrid monocultures to pests. Modern methods currently require three calories of fossil fuel to produce a single calorie of grain, making such methods unrealistic for poor countries (fertilizers and pesticides, and not just cultivating machinery, require petroleum products).[86] Just as serious, these methods compromise the soil itself, driving off earthworms and other creatures and changing its microscopic composition. Between 1984 and 1989, world food production dropped 14 percent; and the world fish catch per person has been declining since the early 1970s.[87] By 1995, competition over dwindling fish stocks was leading to international conflict.[88] Forty thousand young children die of hunger and related diseases every day. Two billion people are malnourished. Hunger in the United States increased 50 percent between 1985 and 1992.[89] Repeated famines, exacerbated by wars and debt, stalk Africa.

One can argue with a measure of force that we have not so much a food production problem as a food distribution problem. We could feed our current population if we ate less animal protein and if nothing interfered with getting supplies to those in desperate need. Particularly devastating are the kinds of statistics that inform us that 65 percent of food served in U.S. restaurants and 25 percent of food served in U.S. homes is thrown away (Tom Sine, *The Mustard Seed Conspiracy* [Waco, Tex.: Word, 1981],

85. Calvin B. DeWitt, "Introduction: Seven Degradations of Creation," in Calvin B. DeWitt, ed., *The Environment and the Christian* (Grand Rapids: Baker, 1991), p. 16.

86. Gerald O. Barney, "The Future of the Creation: The Central Challenge for Theologians," *Word and World* 4, no. 4 (fall 1984): 423-29.

87. United Nations Environmental Programme, *Only One Earth,* using data from the World Watch Institute; Ehrlich and Ehrlich, "Population," p. 943. The latter statistic is especially significant, given that in an article published as late as 1969, Philip Edgcumbe Hughes could suggest that the food resources of the ocean had scarcely been tapped ("Theological Principles in the Control of Human Life," in Walter O. Spitzer and Carlyle L. Saylor, eds., *Birth Control and the Christian* [Wheaton, Ill.: Tyndale House, 1969], p. 103). In 1993 the same World Watch Institute that noted the 14 percent drop declared, as a result of a four-year study, that for the first time population is increasing faster than the food supply: equal distribution of all food resources in 1993 would mean that everyone would receive less than they would have received as a result of equal distribution four years earlier (radio news broadcast, July 18, 1993; the seeming inconsistency may be due to attributing the decline in food production in the late 1980s largely to the 1988 drought).

88. Craig Turner, "Canada-Europe Flap over Atlantic Fish Intensifies," *Los Angeles Times,* March 15, 1995, p. A4.

89. *Bread for the World Newsletter,* January-February 1993.

p. 47), or that 90 percent of the world protein deficit could be met by the grain and fishmeal fed to U.S. cattle (Ian G. Barbour, *Technology, Environment, and Human Values* [New York: Praeger, 1980], p. 248). To see how much energy is lost as one progresses up the food chain, consider that a diatom traps 0.3 percent of the sun energy it receives, while fish that eat the animal plankton that eat the diatoms get 0.003 percent of that solar energy. If a human being gained a pound by eating a bluefish, she would be consuming the equivalent of production from 10,000 pounds of diatoms (Amos, *Life of the Seashore*, p. 185). But people could hardly be persuaded to survive on diatoms even if their nutritional needs could be met that way.

Our heavy American dependence on meat for ourselves and our pets, however, compromises our own health and the earth's environment, as well as hungry people's access to grain. It requires a large percentage of all our agricultural land for grazing and feed crop production (and contributes heavily to topsoil loss and to deforestation for grazing lands in poor countries), an enormous amount of our limited fresh water, and surprising quantities of energy and minerals for processing. It also contributes heavily to organic and inorganic toxic waste pollution of water, since water is used to flush slaughterhouses and feed lots and runs off fields laden with manure and pesticides. Thus livestock producers become the nation's biggest water consumers and polluters (Robin Hur and David Fields, "America's Appetite for Meat Is Ruining Our Water," *Vegetarian Times*, January 1985, p. 16). Everything thus argues for far more modest use of meat in our diets.

Even if we were to solve our immediate food distribution problems and reduce the inequities of diet around the world so that no one was now undernourished, such a triumph could only be short-lived if population continues to increase.[90] Surely it is obvious that if we do not voluntarily curb our reproduction, population will be drastically reduced not just by famine in somewhat limited regions, but by exhaustion of the resources required to support human life worldwide. But it is equally obvious that the affluent are in a poor position to press this point while protecting their privileges and being responsible for the majority of environmental damage. And being well fed and comfortable has a peculiar way of making people feel deep down as if threats of impending disaster must be overdrawn.[91]

90. We applaud the efforts of organizations like Bread for the World and their emphasis on public policy issues. We find persuasive their arguments that governmental policy decisions incomparably outweigh individual contributions and lifestyle modifications (see Arthur Simon, *Bread for the World* [New York: Paulist; Grand Rapids: Eerdmans, 1975], passim). Nonetheless, the most enlightened and self-sacrificial policies cannot prevail over unlimited population growth, or over the demands of the current population with an increasing standard of living. See above, pp. 236-40.

91. "For all the computers and measuring instruments and news gatherers and evaluators and memory banks and libraries and expertise on this and that at their disposal, their deaf and blind bellies remained the final judges of how urgent this or that problem . . . might really be" (Kurt Vonnegut, *Galapagos*, quoted by Hall, *Steward*, p. 9).

The seemingly surprising refusal of the Earth Summit (Rio De Janeiro, 1992) to press for population control can be attributed both to the anger of developing countries at industrialized nations and their policies, and to pressure from the Vatican opposing contraceptives (William R. Long, "Summit Gives No Support to Birth Control," *Los Angeles Times,* June 10, 1992, p. A8). As Protestants, we lack sympathy with the Vatican's position; indeed, we consider it disastrous. In fairness, though, we might press the point that social and cultural factors play as large a role as religion in governing rates of reproduction: while Roman Catholic birth rates in Latin America are among the world's highest, in Europe they are among the lowest (Ivan Bennett Jr., "People and Food," in Hamilton, *This Little Planet,* p. 100).

Unfortunately, slowing the birth rate does not free us from problems. Our success in prolonging the lives of older people, if combined with a severely reduced birth rate, means that we will create an aging and likely conservative society in which the political and economic power lies with the elderly (Hughes, "Control of Human Life," p. 113). America is already feeling the impact of an aging population's need for medical resources and various supportive services. Furthermore, if we so control the population that many have no children, those without heirs may feel as if they have that much less reason to be concerned for the future. Even so, problems associated with a declining birthrate do not make the alternative viable.

d. Exhaustion of Resources

Even apart from the threats to our survival that come from pollution and from destruction of the balance of nature through extinction, habitat destruction, erosion, and general misuse of the natural world, we are rapidly simply using up the earth's store of resources, accumulated over billions of years. Some of these, such as the diminishing stores of groundwater being tapped with deeper and deeper wells, could conceivably be restored if our demands were drastically reduced. Some, like arable land, are subject to competing interests: the same piece of earth cannot be used for a highway, a high-rise apartment, a strip mine, and crops; yet all of these are in increasing demand. Some resources, however, are at risk of being depleted absolutely, like metals and fossil fuels. Predictions suggest that in the last thirty years of the twentieth century, we will consume three or four times more minerals than have been used in the whole prior history of civilization.[92]

The seriousness of this threat tends to be obscured in a number of ways, one of which is the mathematical curiosity that when consumption is increasing at exponential rates, reserves appear not to be too seriously depleted only a few years before demand exceeds supply.[93] But, says the

92. From a study made for Congress's Joint Economic Committee, cited by Rifkin, *Emerging Order,* p. 55.

93. Edward Goldsmith, et al., "A Blueprint for Survival," *The Ecologist* 2, no. 1 (January 1972): 6. Alvin Toffler can write as late as 1970, celebrating the "throw-away

skeptic, predictions of imminent doom keep failing. New deposits of minerals have been discovered with some regularity; lower-grade ores become profitable to use when scarcity drives up the value of metals; the sea contains metals and offshore oil deposits; recycling enables reclamation of some materials; and we increasingly use synthetics, particularly plastics, as a substitute for almost everything. The trouble with these fallback positions is not just that they are costly, thus increasing the troubles of developing countries; or that use of low-grade ores produces enormous amounts of waste; but also that they require huge amounts of energy and that synthetics are made from products — particularly petroleum products — that are themselves in short supply. Thus the energy question looms particularly large.

Estimates called conservative that oil prices would reach $80 a barrel by 1985[94] have not come true; in fact, oil prices in 1993 are actually lower than in 1980. This is not necessarily good news because no one doubts that oil supplies are limited, or that we are using them up at unprecedented rates, or that we need them for a whole variety of petrochemicals used for everything from drugs to fertilizer to plastics and not just for power. How long we can extend the supply, by tapping shale and so on, no one knows for sure. Something similar is true of natural gas — clean and convenient, but probably in shorter supply than petroleum. By contrast, coal is abundant — but dirty to burn (a major source of greenhouse gases and acid rain), dangerous to mine, and leaving a terrible scar on the countryside when stripped from the ground. None of these fossil fuels can sustain us in the long run; so the development of renewable sources of energy is obviously a pressing concern.[95] Without them, and without concerted efforts at conservation and sharing, civilization as we know it will simply collapse, but probably not before scarcities have provoked increasingly desperate international struggles for control of remaining resources.[96] Meanwhile, rich

---

society": "We have . . . not yet outgrown the psychological attitudes that accompany scarcity. Thus there are still many people today who feel a twinge of guilt at discarding even a spent ball-point pen" (*Future Shock* [New York: Bantam, 1970], p. 61). Such a statement demonstrates how very far removed from recognizing the reality of limits we can be.

94. Kenneth F. Weaver, "Our Energy Predicament," *National Geographic* special report, February 1981, p. 2.

95. We will consider the particular problems of nuclear power below, pp. 419-25.

96. During the first "energy crisis," Ford, Kissinger, Schlesinger, and various journalists dropped hints about making use of the Marines to keep down the price of oil (Robert K. Musil, "How Defensible Is the Defense Budget?" *The Other Side* 13, no. 2 [July 1977]: 11); and if such an act could be conceived under conditions of a relatively minor crisis, what must we expect when faced with real stringency? (The cover of the same issue of *The Other Side* bears the ironic inscription, "War is healthy for the economy and other growing things.")

nations, like the rich young ruler (Lk. 18:18-25), continue to reject the way
of life because they have great possessions that they cannot bear to think
of losing but can keep only by refusing to gaze honestly at either the future
or their neighbors.

3. ECONOMIC AND JUSTICE ISSUES

Ironically, although economics and ecology belong together in terms of
their human meaning as well as in terms of their etymology (both derive
from οἶκος, "house," and deal with the functioning of our global "household"), economic and ecological interests have functioned at cross-
purposes for both the rich and the poor. Both the expanding economy that
produces profits and the prevailing vision of the good life as involving
more and more consumer products, not to mention relief of the urgent
necessity of many of the world's people, rest upon continued exploitation
of natural resources. We must therefore strive to think about the natural
and the social environment together, for it is people's needs and desires,
channeled through economic and political systems with self-perpetuating
agendas of their own, that have created the ecological crisis.[97] No one
looking soberly at a finite planet could seriously believe that our current
level of exploitation can continue forever, as we have seen; but the greedy
and the needy, for different reasons, focus on the present — the needy
with more just cause, of course, since they can fairly argue that unless
the present improves, they will have no future at all.

The rich have thus far found it cheaper to pollute, and even to pay
fines for polluting, than to install or develop cleaner technologies.[98] They
have likewise found it to their economic advantage to encourage a throw-
away society, whether by planned obsolescence or by shoddy construction
of products or by promoting the convenience of disposables. By viewing
people as consumers with an apparently unlimited array of desires that can
be skillfully turned into felt needs, they can evaluate positively that nemesis
of environmentalists, an increase in population. When their own resources
become scarce, they buy raw materials from less developed countries. And
so on. All of this is profitable, and hence the market does not work as a

97. For remarks on this theme see Moltmann, *God in Creation,* pp. 23ff.
98. Illegal dumping of toxic wastes and the shipping of them to developing countries
for cheap disposal are also serious problems programmed for increase as local controls
increase and make violations more costly. Or companies move to places that have less
stringent regulations, fouling someone else's backyard.

control. Nor does a centralized, controlled economy do better: Eastern Europe suffers shocking pollution. In part of Poland, for instance, heavy burning of coal has so fouled the air that life expectancy is fifteen years less than in Western Europe.[99]

Capitalist nations have tended to see the disintegration of Communism in Eastern Europe and the manifest failures of Communism at the level of production of consumer goods as proof positive of what they have always known: capitalism is God's own favored economic system. Some economic and religious conservatives have the added conviction that the Bible provides a blueprint for economic success. Billionaire Nelson Bunker Hunt put the bottom line concisely: "The most important thing to have is a spiritual environment in this country that will mean we can keep the money we can make" (Russell Chandler, "God as Capitalist: Seminar Promotes Religion and Riches," *Los Angeles Times,* June 1, 1981, pt. I, p. 3). The strongest rejection of that contention does not change the fact that one *can* defend private property scripturally (e.g., Acts 5:4; but always remembering that one's rights are not rights over against God, Job 1:21; that the earth and its fullness are the Lord's, Ps. 24:1; and that a right to possess something does not confer a right to endanger the environment); one can demonstrate from widespread experience that people will work harder and more productively if they benefit personally from their efforts; and one can even argue persuasively that an accumulation of wealth beyond mere necessities is essential to the development of the science and technology upon which improved welfare for many depends (see, for instance, Brunner, *Divine Imperative,* pp. 436-37). Even if Max Weber's thesis was somewhat overdrawn, clear hints of how a "Protestant ethic" relates to "the spirit of capitalism" appear in the work of seventeenth-century Puritan Richard Baxter: "If God shows you a way in which you may lawfully get more than in another way (without wrong to your soul or to any other), if you refuse this and choose the less gainful way, you cross one of the ends of your calling, and you refuse to be God's steward" (*The Practical Works of Richard Baxter* [London: George Virtue, n.d.], 1.377b). Baxter, however, firmly rejected all luxury and insisted that the worker must be wholly devoted to serving God — ideals that have not prevailed, as Scripture apparently warns us they would not in saying we cannot serve God and mammon (Mt. 6:24).

Given that we are sinners, we should scarcely have supposed that a system built on competition (with the most profitable case being elimination of the competitor) and tending in fact if not in theory to value money supremely, would end up being other than exploitative of people and nature both (see Robert McAfee Brown, *Creative Dislocation,* pp. 82-85; also Niebuhr, *Nature and Destiny,* 1.21). When self-interest is held up as the motor that makes the economic machine run, we can hardly expect it to make concessions for the needy neighbor or the threatened future: to do so would be a contradiction of its fundamental thesis of how the good for all will be achieved. But Scripture does ask us to take direct concern for the needs of neighbors (Phil. 2:4); it associates rewards with self-sacrifice, not with attachment to this world's goods, much

---

99. C. Theodore Dyrness, "The Earth Is the Lord's: A Christian's Musings on the Impending Ecological Disaster," *Theology, News and Notes,* December 1992, p. 12.

less with unlimited consumption of them (Mt. 16:25; Mk. 8:34; Jn. 12:24-26); and it has a great deal to say about justice, particularly for the poor (e.g., Ps. 9:7-12; Prv. 29:4, 14; Mt. 23:23). The pursuit of wealth, and capitalism insofar as it embodies that pursuit without sharp restraint and the inclusion of values of moderation, contentment, and responsibility to God and neighbor, is obviously inimical to the biblical vision of justice and righteousness and mercy.

In thinking about capitalism, we might direct a particular word to the vexed question of the taking of interest, warned against by Aristotle (noted by C. S. Lewis, *Mere Christianity,* pp. 76-77), clearly forbidden by Scripture, at least within the family of faith (Ex. 22:25-27; Lv. 25:36; Dt. 23:19-20; though often cited, Lk. 6:34 does not necessarily entail interest but only return of what has been borrowed), and condemned unequivocally by the church as usury up until the time of the rise of capitalism. Walter Lippmann noted, "The Council of Vienna in 1312 declared that any ruler or magistrate who sanctioned usury and compelled debtors to observe usurious contracts would be excommunicated; all laws which sanctioned money-lending at interest were to be repealed within three months"; and he continued, in a discussion of economics as one of the important provinces lost to church control, "The churches do not speak in that tone of voice to-day" (*Preface to Morals,* p. 81). Indeed they do not, but they are more likely to understand, even if sometimes with regret, that development cannot take place without large accumulations of capital impossible without borrowing, which is in turn impossible on a sufficiently large scale without the giving and receiving of interest. If the rules did not relax, economic progress would be stifled. But when they did relax, the church was left with nothing definitive to say about business, which ran according to its own rules. That the question needs revisiting can be seen in the crushing effect of interest payments on poor people and poor nations, who by borrowing at interest from private speculators or international entities become more and more tightly locked into the cycle of poverty; and even in the overwhelming national debt of the United States, increasing by thousands of dollars per second, which at the very least mortgages the future and compromises programs to help the poor in the present. Perhaps a moral distinction, even if not an absolutely clear line, can be drawn between loaning at interest to those who want money for a productive enterprise and those who seek it to supply their pressing consumptive needs (a distinction made already by Luther: see Brunner, *Divine Imperative,* pp. 673-75, nn. 16, 17). Perhaps, too, Christians who profit from interest without the investment of their own labor (one of the moral hazards of interest) might consider using such profits to fund no-interest loans to the needy, such as those by which an organization like Habitat for Humanity enables poor people to own their own homes.

Because of the biblical emphasis on sharing and concern for those in need, socialist experiments (Acts 2:44-45; 4:32-37) always remain a legitimate Christian option (though not, of course, theories like hard-core Marxism that would unseat God and replace him with purely economic forces). Even capitalist countries have acknowledged the necessity of conceding some powers to the state, like provision of public education, some regulation of public utilities and transportation, appropriation of land for public use, and even conservation. Unfortunately, though, sin does not beset socialist less than capitalist schemes of government. If the capitalist readily falls prey to greed, the person who knows her needs will be taken care of with or without her own effort falls prey

easily to sloth. Bureaucracies of whatever stripe become bloated and inefficient, per-
petuating themselves and serving their own interests despite costs to the public welfare.
Motivation for production of goods and services may be reduced, both the least-visible
very poor and international interests may continue to be ignored, and there may be no
checks on government's abuses of people and the environment (see, for instance,
Amy L. Sherman, "Rethinking Development: A Market-Friendly Strategy for the
Poor," *Christian Century* 109, no. 36 [Dec. 9, 1992]: 1130-34).

No economic system will do away with sin, injustice, and inequality among people.
National interest provides a further complicating factor, no matter what system prevails.
The Christian evaluating any economic system, however, may do well to ask what that
system or proposed changes in it might accomplish better to meet the basic needs of the
poor nationally and internationally; whether it puts a priority on increasing the participation of the marginalized in the society's privileges and governance; whether it safeguards
individual freedom and encourages initiative, creativity, and responsibility; whether it
takes seriously the constraints imposed by finite resources and the importance of maintaining the integrity of the environment; and whether there are adequate checks on those
with economic power. These things it must strive to do without leaving undone the task
of maintaining an adequate base of economic production (see "Economic Justice Within
Environmental Limits: The Need for a New Economic Ethic," *Church and Society* 67, no.
1 [September-October 1976]; also the Roman Catholic bishops' pastoral letter, "Catholic
Social Teaching and the U.S. Economy," *Origins* 14, no. 22/23 [Nov. 15, 1984]).

But if the environmental costs of policies promoting an indiscriminately expanding economy, whether capitalist or socialist, are disastrous,
the human costs of the stable or contracting economy environmentalists
generally recommend are likewise devastating. In the developed countries,
not profits but jobs go first when production shrinks or when formerly
labor-intensive tasks are automated to cut costs. And human beings do not
function well without work, which is a creation ordinance — a fact that
has tended to be obscured by both the grinding, discouraging toil of the
world's peasants and the dehumanizing effect of modern factories where
people are asked to produce like machines.[100]

Not so long ago — only about thirty years — a diverse, highly credentialed committee
suggested to then-President Johnson that advances in cybernetics and huge increases

---

100. "Unemployment" is a modern phenomenon that entered into public discourse only
in the 1890s, as mechanization and capitalization began to displace farmworkers (Richard
Luecke, "Faith, Work, and Economic Structures," *Word and World* 4, no. 2 [spring 1984]:
141-50). In 1995, according to the International Labor Organization, joblessness or under-
employment had risen to one-third of the labor force (Robin Wright, "A Revolution at Work,"
Los Angeles Times, March 7, 1995, p. H1). Even in the minority of cases in which people
have enough funds to cover their needs, long-term unemployment demonstrably does psychological damage, compromising a person's sense of worth and dignity and often leading
to family problems and recourse to drugs or alcohol ("Catholic Social Teaching," p. 359).

in productivity generating embarrassing surpluses of goods were soon to change radically the relationship of income to productivity in the labor force. We would soon have
so much, they thought, with so little expenditure of effort, that we would need to find
ways to guarantee an adequate income to everyone whether or not she worked, and
find ways to adapt to a new, leisure morality ("Bread Without Sweat," *Christian
Century* 81, no. 15 [April 8, 1964]: 451-52). The age-old curse on labor would be
broken and everyone would have enough, with minimal expenditure of effort. No more
would we gaze with pity on the landless, hopeless worker in Markham's poem:

> Bowed by the weight of centuries he leans
> Upon his hoe and gazes on the ground,
> The emptiness of ages in his face,
> And on his back the burden of the world.
> Who made him dead to rapture and despair,
> A thing that grieves not and that never hopes,
> Stolid and stunned, a brother to the ox?
> Who loosened and let down this brutal jaw?
> Whose was the hand that slanted back this brow?
> Whose breath blew out the light within this brain?

> Is this the Thing the Lord God made and gave
> To have dominion over sea and land?
>
> (In Untermeyer, ed., *Great Poems,* p. 992)

Nor would we be called to sympathize with Spurgeon's nineteenth-century pleas in
favor of the Early Closing Movement, meant to alleviate the crushing fatigue of city
workers pressed so long and hard that they had energy of neither body nor soul to
attend to the gospel; for those pleas would surely find fulfillment beyond his wildest
dreams (C. H. Spurgeon, *Autobiography,* 2.337).

The dream turned quickly into a nightmare, for it failed to reckon with the
recalcitrance of greed, with a burgeoning population, or with looming scarcity stemming
from the limits of a finite world. Automation has increased, all right: it has decreased
employment opportunities (unemployment due to changes in production techniques
was a problem in the automobile industry as early as 1956; in 1977 11,000 agricultural
jobs in California alone gave way to a mechanical tomato harvester); driven small
farmers and small business people who cannot afford big machines out of business;
encouraged scientists to develop tougher, more rubbery produce that will not be damaged by machine harvesting (never mind lost palatability); generally decreased the
bargaining power of workers and generated an inhuman pace of life, since machines
work when wanted and do not strike; and cost society billions in lost revenues, forgone
wages, and services for displaced workers. Not only laborers are affected. On the
"brain-work" end of the labor spectrum, a modern computer can calculate in a single
second the tables of logarithms and trigonometric functions that would be more than a
lifetime's work for an eighteenth-century mathematician — the kind of change in speed
as well as in human labor reduction that makes us smile that a historian of an earlier
era perceived a significant increase in the pace of life when nineteenth-century English
quarterly magazines began to be displaced by monthlies, and then by weeklies (James D.

Meindl, et al., *Brief Lessons in High Technology* [Stanford, Calif.: Stanford Alumni Association, 1989], p. 7; David Churchill Somervell, *English Thought in the Nineteenth Century* [London: Methuen, 1929], p. 59).

Many who have not been simply replaced by machines have paid high physical and emotional costs to use them. Modern techniques and machinery have made often crippling cumulative trauma disorders, caused by repetitive motions, the most prevalent form of industrial injury in the country, suffered by workers employed in as diverse occupations as slaughterhouse labor and keyboard entry tasks (Henry Weinstein, "Injuries Lead to Record Fine on Meatpacker," *Los Angeles Times,* Oct. 29, 1988, pt. I, pp. 1-2). Even genuine savings in physical effort have been accompanied by other kinds of physiological and psychological costs, not least those associated with nervous tension, when technological demands dominate over human styles and rhythms of work; and those generated by a sense of personal "absence" and purposelessness in executing tasks that nonetheless require one's full attention. High-status as well as low-status workers are affected: for instance, astronauts can suffer (presumably remediable) loss of bone mass under conditions of even moderately prolonged weightlessness. Simone Weil concluded, "Speaking quite generally, in any sort of sphere, it is inevitable that evil should dominate wherever the technical side of things is either completely or almost completely sovereign" (*The Need for Roots,* trans. A. F. Wills [London: Routledge & Kegan Paul, 1952], p. 196; see also Ellul, *Technological Bluff,* p. 42; and *Technological Society,* pp. 320, 399). In the realm of work as elsewhere, technology has proved a demanding, unreliable god, requiring much but *not* consistently distributing its boons to those it displaces or injures.

But even if technology had better kept its promises of providing the majority with both security and leisure, human beings were created to need not just the economic benefits work produces but work itself. Pascal observed (*Pensées,* no. 131):

> Nothing is so insufferable to man as to be completely at rest, without passions, without business, without diversion, without study. He then feels his nothingness, his forlornness, his insufficiency, his dependence, his weakness, his emptiness. There will immediately arise from the depth of his heart weariness, gloom, sadness, fretfulness, vexation, despair.

The command to have dominion, the duty to till and keep the earth (Gn. 1:26, 28; 2:15), precede the curse on labor (3:17-19). Although the Decalogue's commandment of Sabbath rest (Ex. 20:8-11) makes clear that work is not an end in itself but meant to serve human life (Brunner, *Divine Imperative,* p. 389), it is predicated on an assumption of six days of labor as both duty and blessing (John Murray, *Principles of Conduct* [Grand Rapids: Eerdmans, 1957], p. 83). Should we not get the point, Scripture does not hesitate to commend the busy ant as an example to lazy humans (Prv. 6:6-8). And Paul makes plain that whatever one thinks the future may bring gives no excuse for idleness in the present (2 Thes. 3:6-13). As the hymn puts it,

> Give every flying minute
> Something to keep in store:
> Work, for the night is coming,
> When man works no more.

> (Lowell Mason)

What we need, of course, is work with a human meaning, adequately compensated, and so situated in the social and natural worlds that it can be seen to be positively, not destructively, related to both. Not all work will provide those opportunities for creative self-expression that we tend to associate with "meaningful work," though we ought certainly to seek to maximize opportunities for pride in workmanship. (Workers enraged by being made subject to machines are famous for using their creative energies to sabotage products.) But when work is of necessity routine or even unpleasant, it may still make an essential contribution to the society, constituting part of the "moral relationship among people" (Robert N. Bellah, et al., *Habits of the Heart* [Berkeley: University of California Press, 1985], p. 66) that gives it more than merely instrumental meaning. It may still be done before God:

> Thine is the loom, the forge, the mart,
> The wealth of land and sea;
> The worlds of science and of art,
> Revealed and ruled by Thee.

(John Ellerton)

Seeing work only as a way of making a living leads to exploitative relationships to others and to the environment, to seeing the world only as a resource and not as a home (Mary Evelyn Jegen, "The Church's Role in Healing the Earth," in Granberg-Michaelson, ed., *Tending the Garden*, p. 108; also Moltmann, *God in Creation*, pp. 44-46).

In the developing world, to suggest that the environment cannot sustain further development or — what looks like the same thing — an increase in these people's standard of living, can generate nothing but hopelessness, rage, or both; for relief from poverty, hunger, and disease, if not the very survival of many, depends on some kind of development; and it is worse than disingenuous for those clinging to luxuries to say that the earth cannot bear to provide necessities to the poor. The poor see it as likewise disingenuous for already industrialized countries to ask them to pay costs for pollution control and abatement that industrialized countries themselves did not have to shoulder during their developing years (and to a significant extent refuse to shoulder now). Besides, many values important to the well fed, like amenities and bird sanctuaries and animal rights and clean air, have very much lower priority for the hungry:[101] some have even welcomed

101. Richard John Neuhaus makes some important observations about an elitism that ignores basic human need: conservationists have been noted for disengagement from larger social issues, enjoyment of the wilderness has been a flight from ugly social realities, and wildlife protection was originally game protection for the sporting rich. He says, "The project of greening America is obscene so long as vast areas of the world are parched by war and famine"; and continues, "The literature of the [environmental] movement is marked by a moving reverence for 'the seamless web of life,' accompanied by a shocking indifference to the weaker and less convenient forms of human life and by an almost cavalier readiness to

smog as a symbol of progress, bringing hazy visions of the comfort that
has accompanied the smog in industrialized countries.[102] Land may appear
to those newly in possession of it not as a fragile resource but simply as
opportunity: African-American writer Toni Morrison has an ex-slave's farm
say:

> Stop picking around the edges of the world. Take advantage, and if
> you can't take advantage, take disadvantage. . . . Grab this land! Take
> it, hold it, my brothers, make it, my brothers; shake it, squeeze it, turn
> it, twist it, beat it, kick it, kiss it, whip it, stomp it, dig it, plow it,
> seed it, reap it, rent it, buy it, sell it, own it, build it, multiply it, and
> pass it on — can you hear me? Pass it on![103]

The bumper sticker reading "RATS HAVE RIGHTS" will look much different
to a ghetto mother whose sleeping child has just been bitten by a rat than
to a middle-class activist concerned about misuse of laboratory animals.
To deny empathy for such persons' aspirations for a better life is to deny
one's own humanity.

Making the problem even more complex is that the poor of any
society, and poor countries as a whole, already doubtless suffer most from
the ecological crisis, even though the rich do a grossly disproportionate
amount of the ecological damage. In fact, a 1987 study shows that in
America, "the single most accurate predictor of whether a community is
likely to have an environmental problem . . . is whether or not it is a
minority community, and whether or not it is a poor, disadvantaged
community."[104] The rich can move away from blighted landscapes. They
usually have the political clout to refuse location of a toxic waste dump
in their backyards. They can buy food despite drought or blights on crops;
they can buy machinery to purify water. They can hire people with no
other option but unemployment to do health-threatening work in pesticide-laden fields, hazardous mines, or dehumanizing factories. And rich
nations can continue to import food and raw materials even when their
discretionary uses of them encroach on the necessities of their less advantaged neighbors.

---

disrupt the carefully woven web of civility and human values" (*In Defense of People* [New
York: Macmillan, 1971], pp. 59, 188). It seems to us that such remarks rightly draw attention
to our moral failures but would be wrongly used to suggest that the environmental crisis is
not really important after all.

102. Simon, *Bread for the World*, p. 49.

103. *Song of Solomon* (New York: Signet, 1978), pp. 237-38.

104. Albert Gore, speaking of a United Church of Christ study of environmental
problems, quoted in *Christian Century* 109, no. 20 (June 17-24, 1992): 608.

Both the Bible and Greek culture warned against the hazards of wealth: Theogonis, who complained much against poverty, nonetheless noted that money and spiritual nobility seldom go together (Werner Wilhelm Jaeger, *Paideia: The Ideals of Greek Culture,* trans. G. Highet, 2nd ed., 2 vols. [New York: Oxford University Press, 1945], 1.202); and Sophocles put in the mouth of Creon in *Antigone* the words: "Nothing so evil as money ever grew to be current among men. This lays cities low, this drives men from their homes, this trains and works honest souls till they set themselves to works of shame" — words readily recalling biblical warnings of how difficult it is for the rich to enter the kingdom of heaven, and how the love of money is the root of all evil, amounting to idolatry (Lk. 18:25; 1 Tm. 6:10; Col. 3:5). From such observations we are not, however, justified in drawing the conclusion that we are doing the poor a favor by promoting their poverty. Even in beginning to speak of poverty, we must be careful to distinguish between that poverty which can be the occasion for development of virtues of thrift, humility, and generosity (exemplified, for instance, in Alcott's *Little Women*), and that poverty which kills, cripples, and dehumanizes. If we refuse to recognize the real nature of the latter sort, and fail in the face of it to recognize as sinful the shockingly unequal distribution of the world's wealth, we do so culpably. There is nothing whatever ennobling in the childhood malnutrition that leads to widespread mental retardation, nor in the homelessness that leads people to sniff glue or guzzle alcohol to deaden them to the cold. If people cannot live by bread alone, neither can they live without bread, without a certain minimum — else why should Scripture commend the giving of alms and provision of food (Acts 10:31; Mt. 25:35)? Some earthly necessities can be obtained only through money, so that Chaucer could address his empty purse,

> Now purse, who are to me my life's own light,
> My saviour, the way the world runs here,
> Out of this trouble help me with your might.
>
> (In Untermeyer, ed., *Great Poems,* p. 117)

And Ruskin defended the poor, whatever their faults, as being "yet . . . holier than we who have left them thus" (quoted in Wayland Maxfield Parrish, *Reading Aloud* [New York: Nelson, 1936], p. 80).

Recognizing a legitimate human need for development to alleviate crushing poverty makes observation of its unkept promises and exorbitant costs the more dismaying. The gap between the rich and the poor in this country and elsewhere is not shrinking but widening. "Economic growth as we have experienced it over the last century in *no* way has resulted in increased equality among the world's people."[105] Wealth has, as someone put it, "trickled down like frozen molasses."[106] In short, our dominion, however

105. Randers and Meadows, "Carrying Capacity," p. 274.
106. Theodore Roszak's phrase, in *Where the Wasteland Ends* (Garden City, N.Y.: Doubleday, 1972), p. 439. In the United States in particular, not only have disparities increased greatly since the early 1970s, but also the rich are richer and the poor are poorer than in most of the rest of the industrialized world (Gary Burtless and Timothy Smeeding, "America's Tide: Lifting the Yachts, Swamping the Rowboats," *Washington Post,* June 25, 1995).

impressive its apparent gains, has misfired in the economic arena as in so many others. Reasons for this fact can no doubt be multiplied far beyond our competency to probe them, and affect our own nation's poor as well as others'; but a few examples may illustrate the bind in which the Third World finds itself. The main problem is simply the initial poverty of these lands and the cost of technology. Countries incur large debts to purchase technology and its fruits and then find themselves crippled by interest payments that consume much of their Gross Domestic Product.[107] They must thus use their best land for export agriculture (degrading the land and forcing peasants off it) and export raw materials no matter what the ecological cost (and no matter how seriously they compromise the future), while being left with nothing to invest in basic services for the people or with which to purchase food when needed (more, of course, being needed than if land were used for essential domestic food production). Technology transfer has often proved ineffective, either because of inadequate know-how in operating and maintenance or rapid change in knowledge: India spent eighteen years trying to purchase American technology for making chemicals used in refrigeration, which it finally obtained in 1986 — just as environmental hazards of these chemicals began to be known. Only three years later, the international community moved to phase out these chemicals rapidly, leaving an angry India with its investment very nearly wasted.[108]

Even when technology "works," according to its own rules, it can prove self-defeatingly costly. Take the hybrid, high-yield seed that requires heavy use of expensive fertilizer and pesticides, which proceed to pollute the soil. Technology can provide the (expensive) solution to the second part of the problem: try the "designer gene" seed that will thrive only in soil polluted by herbicides; or how about the hybrid seed that will produce mature fruit only if sprayed with a chemical also produced by the seed manufacturer?[109] In each case, the cost of the technology itself and the cost of financing debt incurred to procure the technology or its products ends

107. According to a Food First Action Alert, the debt of semi-arid, low-income African countries rose by 1986 to 90 percent of their Gross Domestic Product (Kevin Danaher, "Myths of African Hunger," Institute for Food and Development Policy, 1987; cf. Bread for the World's research showing that many such countries devote 25 percent of their export earnings to making payments on that debt [Sharon Pauling, "Africa: Crisis to Opportunity," Bread for the World Background Paper no. 132, March 1995, p. 2]). One reads continually of countries with unsustainable levels of debt but may not always attend to the terrible human cost of that debt.

108. Maura Dolan, "Clearing the Way to Clean Air," *Los Angeles Times*, June 10, 1992, p. A1.

109. Richard Cartwright Austin, "Jubilee Now!" *Sojourners* 20, no. 5 (June 1991): 27; Wink, *Engaging the Powers*, p. 345, n. 28.

up working economic harm to the least privileged and environmental harm to all. Such problems have led some to reject the development model altogether. Not only do less developed countries lack the uncharted frontiers whose resources currently industrialized countries plundered to finance cheap development, hence making the cost of development altogether different for them than it is today; but dependence on industrialized countries erodes the inner life of a poor country, provides economic rewards only to a small percentage of the population, and leaves the country with its economic and even political decisions heavily determined by the demands of international finance.[110]

But what are the alternatives? Part of the reason we focus obstinately on the present is that we have no viable vision for the future, the one relying on prosperity through development and security through violence having failed.[111] Some assume that technology will come miraculously to the rescue, just in the nick of time.[112] Those less sanguine about that eventuality have further questions about whether present conditions of shocking injustice and inequality of privilege can be sustained, especially when modern media make so evident to the needy what others enjoy. Will there be widespread revolution, made all the more destructive by whatever modern weapons revolutionaries can obtain? For the Western Christian, the more pressing question may be, What if there isn't? What if, instead, as resources become scarcer, they continue to be distributed increasingly unequally, as they always have been under such circumstances, since all the market can do about scarcity is drive up prices? What if precisely we Western Christians continue to be the beneficiaries of this inequality — we, who say we serve a God who sees suffering (Dt. 26:7), who judges oppressors (Am. 4:1-3), who identifies with the poor and brings them in particular good news (Mt. 25:31-46; Lk. 7:22)?[113]

4. TECHNOLOGICAL POSSIBILITIES AND RISKS

At about this point in a dismal tale, the reader might wish to remind us that many pages ago, we remarked on how humankind relate to the future by use of creative imagination, thus developing technology and culture in

---

110. Robert McAfee Brown, *Gustavo Gutierrez* (Maryknoll, N.Y.: Orbis, 1990), pp. 61-62.

111. Barney, "Future of Creation," p. 422.

112. For our doubts in this department, see below, pp. 437-45.

113. For an impressive collection of biblical texts dealing with hunger and poverty and God's justice, running to some two hundred pages, see Ronald J. Sider, ed., *Cry Justice* (New York: Paulist, 1980).

service of their vision — a rather more hopeful way of putting things than our more recent remarks suggest.[114] Surely creative imagination has not suddenly fled from us, leaving us, at a time of pressing need, bereft of power to envision a human future and to develop tools to pursue it. Much to the contrary, whole new vistas have opened up as we have probed the innermost nature of matter and of life. The possibilities of finding ways to rescue ourselves are intriguing, and the need to be willing to take a few risks seems evident — but the risks remain sobering.

a. Nuclear Power

When, in a fantastic triumph of scientific and technological skill, we learned how to split the atom, we tapped into almost unimaginable power. A pound of enriched uranium contains almost three million times the energy of a pound of coal.[115] Breeder reactors produce more fuel than they use. The hope lives of producing more power yet by fusion. How, then, can we speak of an energy crisis? Do we not have the solution already at hand?

The answer to that question provides a paradigmatic case of solutions many people have come to see as more threatening than the problems they address. Yes, we can produce a large amount of power through nuclear reactors. But we have to contend with the use of this same power for weapons of war and terrorism; the unsolved problem of what to do with daily increasing amounts of deadly nuclear waste; and the long history of failure and error in the most fail-safe, error-proof systems for handling hazardous materials. And we dare not forget that not some enemy to whom we blithely attribute inferior morality but our own nation dropped the first atomic bomb, and then the second: not for no reason do many of us immediately associate a mushroom-shaped cloud with nuclear power.

Until the startling changes and sudden relaxing of the cold war brought about by the breakup of the Soviet state, the amassing of nuclear weapons by both the Soviet Union and the United States seemed to pose the most immediate of all threats to the continued survival of humankind. As the stockpiles grew, anxious scientists moved the hands of the "Doomsday Clock" closer and closer to the midnight that would signal the end of the world. Never before had humankind had the power to destroy itself wholesale and make the world essentially uninhabitable for good measure. Easing of the most acute fears should not, however, lead us to forget the

114. See above, p. 64.
115. "An Atlas of Energy Resources," *National Geographic* Special Report, February 1981, p. 67.

possible consequences of detonating thousands of megatons of the nuclear warheads still in the possession of many nations:

> blinding of insects, birds, and beasts all over the world; the extinction of many ocean species, among them some at the base of the food chain; the temporary or permanent alteration of the climate of the globe, with the outside chance of "dramatic" and "major" alterations in the structure of the atmosphere; the pollution of the whole eco-sphere with oxides of nitrogen; the incapacitation in ten minutes of unprotected people who go out into the sunlight; the blinding of people who go out into the sunlight; a significant decrease in photo-synthesis in plants around the world; the scalding and killing of many crops; the increase in rates of cancer and mutation around the world, but especially in the targeted zones, and the attendant risk of global epidemics; the possible poisoning of all vertebrates by sharply in-creased levels of Vitamin D in their skin as a result of increased ultraviolet light; and the outright slaughter on all targeted continents of most human beings and other living things by the initial nuclear radiation, the fireballs, the thermal pulses, the blast waves, the mass fires, and the fallout from the explosions; and, considering that these consequences will all interact with one another in unguessable ways and, furthermore, are in all likelihood an incomplete list, which will be added to as our knowledge of the earth increases, one must con-clude that a full-scale nuclear holocaust could lead to the extinction of mankind.[116]

Schell concludes:

> The choices don't include war any longer. They consist now of peace, on the one hand, and annihilation on the other. . . . When nuclear weapons were invented, it was as though a battlefield on which two armies had been fighting for as long as anyone could remember had suddenly been bisected in an earthquake by a huge chasm, so that if the armies tried to rush at one another in order to engage in battle they would plunge into this chasm instead, pulling their nations in with them.[117]

We must keep the chasm before us, lest the years we have had nuclear weapons without destroying ourselves lull us into thinking we could, after all, afford to use "just a little one" to achieve some tactical end — a

---

116. Jonathan Schell, *The Fate of the Earth* (New York: Knopf, 1982), p. 93.
117. Ibid., p. 193.

scenario made ominously near-to-hand with admissions that the Pentagon has contemplated "limited" nuclear war,[118] "preemptive" strikes, the first-use possibilities of Star Wars technology, and so on.

The unprecedented destructiveness of nuclear war has led the churches, by and large, not only to reject actual use of nuclear weapons but also to oppose stockpiling them. Many rank all theories of nuclear deterrence as morally unacceptable; for effective deterrence relies on the credibility of the idea that such weapons might be used and rest hopes of security on force alone, ignoring the role played by justice and concerns for economic and social security (not to mention Scripture's clear warning against placing our confidence in the engines of war, Is. 31:1-3).[119] An additional and not inconsiderable incentive for disarmament comes with the fallibility of warning devices and the incredibly brief span of time, measured in minutes or seconds, decision makers have to judge whether what appears on the computer screen signals a massive enemy attack or a glitch in the machine. Such glitches are not infrequent: in 1979-80 in the United States alone, early warning systems falsely signaled a Soviet attack not once or twice, which would be dangerous enough, but 147 times.[120] Surely the "launch on warning" systems that have been discussed as a means of dealing with the narrowing of the time frame during which any counteraction could be taken must be counted the height of folly. Furthermore, apart from the morality or even rationality of keeping at the ready weapons that could destroy the whole earth not just once but many times over, we must not forget that they kill, and are killing today, while lying quietly in storage, simply by their enormous cost. They use up nonrenewable resources and divert desperately needed funds away from the needy and from research that could help the sick: in 1980, the world spent over a million dollars per *minute* on arms, while the World Health Organization estimated that 83 million dollars could wipe out smallpox; the United States by itself spent more than two trillion dollars during the 1980s.[121] In the words of a

118. John C. Bennett, "Countering the Theory of Limited Nuclear War," *Christian Century* 98, no. 1 (Jan. 7-14, 1981): 10.

119. Alan Geyer, "The Pains of Peace at Vancouver," *Christian Century* 100, no. 25 (Aug. 31-Sept. 7, 1983): 765-67, reporting on the sixth assembly of the World Council of Churches; and later, by unanimous vote, the Council of Bishops of the United Methodist Church (John J. Goldman, "Methodists Reject Nuclear Deterrence," *Los Angeles Times*, April 30, 1986, pt. I, p. 11).

120. Mark O. Hatfield, "The Age of Anxiety: Emerging Nuclear Tensions in the 1980s," Hatfield Backgrounder, June 1981, p. 9.

121. "1980 World Arms Spending Put at $500 Billion," *Los Angeles Times*, June 5, 1981, pt. I, p. 18; Ralph Vartabedian and John Broder, "Legacy of Failure in Defense," *Los Angeles Times* (clipping, no date); "Choose Life," statement on disarmament by represen-

Manhattan Project physicist, "Future generations, if there are any, will regard [the arms race] as a virulent case of collective mental disease."[122] Or, in theological language, here is human dominion gone badly astray.

But suppose — what is not yet the case — that we dismantled all nuclear weapons (and put strict limits on conventional ones for good measure, in the service of economic justice and of reducing the temptation to keep "just a few" nuclear weapons in the service of national superiority): could nuclear energy then change categories from bane to blessing? To the contrary, we still need to recall that, "what we are doing, in basing a larger and larger part of our energy supplies upon atomic energy, is bringing down to earth the powers which would have never permitted any kind of organic life to develop on this planet, had not billennia been spent in building up protective mechanisms."[123] The Three-Mile Island nuclear reactor accident in the United States and the more recent Chernobyl disaster in the Ukraine demonstrate rather forcefully that nontrivial dangers accompany even peaceful uses of atomic energy. Radiation from a reactor meltdown is no less deadly than radiation from a bomb. The protective covering of the destroyed Chernobyl reactor was reported to be leaking only six years after being applied; radioactive pollution is spreading to water sources; and officials have planned to fence off some hot spots in perpetuity, truck off several inches of topsoil in others, and keep people on still others despite risks to their health — acknowledging that none of these approaches is exactly satisfactory.[124] After nine years, an estimated 125,000 people had died as a result of the accident; and the worst may be yet to come, since resultant cancers are expected to peak in the second decade after the disaster.[125] All this from the meltdown of the core of a single nuclear reactor

tatives of churches of the United States and the Soviet Union, March 27-29, 1979, published in *Missionscope* by the United Presbyterian Church (U.S.A.). Figures for 1992 put world military spending at over $600 billion — still well over a million dollars per minute, with nearly half of this sum accounted for by the United States (which contributes more to the military than to education). Developed countries sold three-fifths as much in arms as they provided in economic aid to poorer countries. And after all existing (1992) commitments to reduce nuclear weapons are met, the five acknowledged nuclear powers will still have stockpiled more than 900 times the total explosive power expended in World War II. See the 1993 edition of *World Military and Social Expenditures* (noted by the *Christian Century* 110, no. 33 [Nov. 17-24, 1993]: 1151-52).

122. Victor Weisskopf of M.I.T., quoted by Anthony Lewis, "Who Are the Realists?" reprinted from *The New York Times,* 1985.

123. Ward and Dubos, *Only One Earth,* p. 129.

124. John-Thor Dahlburg, "A Nuclear-Tainted Russia Hunts for Affordable Cure," *Los Angeles Times,* Sept. 4, 1992, pp. A1ff.

125. Carol J. Williams, "Nine Years Later, Chernobyl Disaster Looks Worse," *Los Angeles Times,* April 27, 1995, p. A4.

— and the three remaining reactors at Chernobyl are still operating. More than two hundred nuclear power plants are in operation, some with more than one reactor and some built near known earthquake fault lines.

Add another speculation: suppose we learned to build truly accident-proof reactors (forgetting for the moment that we do not succeed in producing accident-proof anything, not just because of technical problems but because of the human factor: investigation shows that Soviet nuclear submarine accidents were due 75 percent of the time to people doing things they were expressly forbidden to do).[126] Then the problem becomes what to do with nuclear waste. We have not yet figured out what to do with the stuff. Leave aside the *millions* of cubic feet of mine tailings (in which, in the case of uranium ore, 85 percent of the radioactivity remains after milling)[127] and other low-level waste like contaminated rags and glassware generated by every reactor. Take only the eight kilograms of plutonium, an amount the size of a large orange, produced every two weeks not by breeder reactors but just as a by-product of *one* reactor's normal fissioning of uranium (plutonium exists in nature only in minute quantities):

> Microgram quantities can induce lung cancer. In theory, eight kilograms (eight billion micrograms) would suffice to kill every person on our planet. . . . The radiological toxicity of plutonium . . . persists through all chemical alterations. If I die of plutonium-induced cancer and my body is cremated, I yield up my plutonium through the smokestack into the biosphere where it may kill again, and this toxicity persists for 250,000 years. . . . If plutonium had been stored in the Great Pyramid of Egypt, it would remain 90% as lethal today as on the day when Pharaoh Cheops proclaimed, "They'll never find it there." . . . When we are told that wastes are to be stored in geological formations that are stable and dry, we shall do well to realize that plutonium will remain lethal for 20 times the epoch since the last ice age. . . . Indeed, since plutonium is a genetic mutagen as well as a radiological poison, our sour grapes of plutonium may set our children's teeth on edge for as long as the human species endures.[128]

126. Ibid., p. A16.

127. United States General Accounting Office, "Major Unresolved Issues Preventing a Timely Resolution to Radioactive Waste Disposal," July 13, 1978, p. 2.

128. Albert L. Blackwell, "Plutonium as a Religious Issue," *Harvard Divinity Bulletin,* June-July 1980, p. 15. Russia now generates something like two and one-half tons of plutonium a year (Dahlburg, "Nuclear-Tainted Russia," p. A15). Let us not fool ourselves by resting our hopes in "safer" reactor technologies; these still produce plutonium. There

Here is the kind of sword that cannot be beaten into a plowshare (Is. 2:4; Mic. 4:3), the kind of weapon that cannot be turned into an instrument of peace. Let us repeat: we do not know how to store radioactive waste safely, despite more than forty years of effort. Surely, then, we can continue to generate it only by resolutely shutting our eyes to the facts — a tactic apparently turned into policy by the Department of Energy: an official of the department allegedly told an environmental physicist complaining of leaks in storage tanks that it was Energy Department "policy that there will be no more leaks."[129] No level of exposure to radiation is "safe"; indeed, even electromagnetic radiation from computers and electric blankets is coming under suspicion.[130] Furthermore, black-market trade in nuclear materials is increasing, partly because of the economic turmoil in the former Soviet Union, where there are large amounts of such materials and people who are desperate for money. Weapons-grade material may already have surfaced on the black market; and plutonium provides particular temptations, for it is about as valuable as gold, and as little as eight kilograms would be sufficient for a Nagasaki-sized nuclear weapon. Thus proliferation in the service of terrorism is a serious threat.[131]

---

are already hundreds of tons of plutonium around the world, and the United States' highest priority is finding ways of disposing of these materials that reduce the security risk they pose. Officials recognize that hoped-for improvements in that regard will not have much impact on the pollution problem ("Plutonium and International Security," statement for the record by the honorable John H. Gibbons, Assistant to the President for Science and Technology before the Committee on Energy and Natural Resources, United States Senate, May 26, 1994).

129. "Clue to Volume: What a Reactor Makes in a Year," *New York Times,* July 9, 1979. In 1975 the Union of Concerned Scientists charged that virtually every waste facility started by the U.S. government has leaked radioactivity, and that more than half of the low-level waste disposal sites supposed to be secure for hundreds of years had leaked dangerously within ten years. By 1989 the problem had been anything but cured: revelations came of persistent violations of health and ecological standards at the Rocky Flats Nuclear Weapons Plant in Colorado (overseen by the Department of Energy), including an average of 32 "contamination incidents" every month and serious underreporting of the amount of waste generated, with no word as to what became of the unreported materials (Tamara Jones and Dan Morain, "Rocky Flats: Boon Turns into Ecological Nightmare," *Los Angeles Times,* June 20, 1989, pt. I, pp. 1ff.).

130. "Perilous Legacy," *MD Magazine,* April 1979, pp. 53-54; "New Look at Risk from Low-Level Radiation," *Los Angeles Times,* Jan. 29, 1990, p. B3.

131. A brief notice states that 26 ounces of weapons-grade uranium from Azerbaijan was seized in Turkey ("Police Arrest Man Selling Uranium," *Los Angeles Times,* Oct. 21, 1994, p. A9). A later article doubts that weapons-grade material has yet been smuggled but fears that it will be, given that Russia has two million pounds of it and scant means of safeguarding it (Mary Mycio, "Ukraine Seizes Uranium Cache; Two Russians Held," *Los Angeles Times,* March 22, 1995, p. A1; see also J. S. Goldman and W. C. Rempel, "U.S. Seizes 7 Tons of Vital Reactor Metal," *Los Angeles Times,* June 9, 1995, pp. A1f.).

These consequences of the use of nuclear power are not hypothetical or even future but actual and present. To fail to label them as the intolerable threat they are and to continue unheedingly to generate more and more plutonium can only be called unimaginable folly dependent on inertia and feelings of helplessness combined with willful blindness and dogged refusal to take seriously our history of human and mechanical failures.[132] Even something that *would be* acceptably safe if and only if no errors are made cannot be considered *actually* to be acceptably safe (and no scenario in which plutonium could reasonably be judged "acceptably safe" has yet been imagined even by the most wildly optimistic). Only where human hubris once again gets the upper hand will such technologies be pursued.[133]

b. Genetic Engineering and Biotechnology

What if we could make new plants with enhanced food value, or ones that *liked* to grow in salty or pesticide-laden soil? What if we could breed microbes that would eat oil slicks or produce alcohol for fuel? What if we could alter mosquitoes so that they would not give their victims malaria? Fantasy? We can already do these things, at least on a small scale. What if we could generate virtually unlimited quantities of genuine human insulin for diabetics? We can.[134] What if we could tell ahead of time that an apparently healthy child (or fetus) will in later life be at risk for, or will certainly manifest, devastating illness? In some cases we can do that, too. What if we could, by genetic manipulation, cure genetically caused defects or diseases? We cannot do that — at least not on a large

132. Schell quotes Pascal to the effect, "it is easier to endure death without thinking about it than to endure the thought of death without dying"; and applies it to nuclear buildups: "we have found it much easier to dig our own grave than to think about the fact that we are doing so" (*Fate of the Earth*, p. 148). So-called conscience funds (investments selected in accordance with various social screens) do tend to exclude the nuclear power industry.

133. We have not discussed other uses of nuclear energy that are not likely to be discontinued before better alternatives are found — as, for instance, in radiation treatment of cancer — because the scale is much different from that of weapons or energy production (nor is plutonium generated). Even so, such uses do produce hazardous waste in sufficient quantities to occupy our talents for finding reasonably safe ways of dealing with it.

134. See, for example, Robert F. Weaver, "Changing Life's Genetic Blueprint," *National Geographic* 166, no. 6 (December 1984), pp. 818-47; a whole issue of *Scientific American* (vol. 245, no. 3 [September 1981]) dealing with industrial microbiology, including genetic programming of industrial microorganisms; microbiological production of food and drink, pharmaceuticals, and industrial chemicals; and agricultural microbiology; Rick Weiss, "A Swat to Mosquito-Borne Disease," *Los Angeles Times*, March 11, 1991, p. B3.

scale.[135] But the hope inspires many suffering people and their relatives. Many hope that the food and energy crises can be alleviated by genetic engineering, too, which may be able to produce a variety of hardier, pest-resistant, faster-growing, more nutritious crops, as well as energy both from garbage and from specially designed plants.

Genetic engineering and modern biotechnology (a certain amount of biotechnology is as old as brewing beer using the good offices of yeast) provide unprecedented means of using and altering living organisms to suit human needs or to counter changes human beings have wrought in the environment. Some see them mainly as simply more efficient ways of carrying on the selective breeding that people have practiced throughout much of human history. That argument has some force when we are speaking of procedures like superovulation techniques, frozen embryos, and embryo transplants used to produce, say, cows giving twice the usual amount of milk.[136] The claim is less plausible when we consider the insertion of human growth hormone genes into mouse embryos, thus producing a giant mouse.[137] The latter creature, obviously, would never occur without drastic human intervention. The possibility of doing with genes things that could not happen without human intervention provides both the promise and the threat of genetic engineering.

Two lines of work are proceeding at the same time. One involves analyzing the exact sequence and location of genes on the chromosomes — probably some one hundred thousand genes in a human being (no one knows for sure how many). The genes constitute part, but not all, of the DNA in the chromosomes: writing the sequence of that DNA as a whole (in terms of the four — and there are only four! — chemical subunits called "base pairs" that form it) for a single person — three billion base pairs —

---

135. Gene therapy has been used, apparently successfully, on three babies with Bubble Baby Syndrome (defective immune system; see Leslie Helm, "Genetic Backlash," *Los Angeles Times,* May 24, 1995, p. D6). Even knowing the source of a disorder can under some circumstances spare its victims a measure of grief: some historians believe that many of the women burned as witches in Massachusetts may have suffered from Huntington's Disease, an incurable, late-appearing genetic disorder causing wild, uncontrollable movements, dementia, and finally death (Paul Jacobs, "Gene Maps: A Guide to Body Defects," *Los Angeles Times,* June 3, 1983, p. 21).

136. "Perfectionist," *Harvard Magazine,* March-April 1988, p. 87.

137. Weaver, "Changing Life's Genetic Blueprint," p. 821. To say that organisms produced by genetic engineering techniques are *fundamentally* no different from those produced by conventional crossbreeding, as a special committee of the National Academy of Sciences reportedly averred, sounds to us like an abuse of language (Thomas H. Maugh II and Kevin Davis, "Genetically Engineered Organisms Not Dangerous, Science Panel Finds," *Los Angeles Times,* Sept. 21, 1989, pt. I, p. 38).

would require at least as many pages as in thirteen sets of the *Encyclopaedia Britannica.*[138] The function of much of this DNA is unknown, though some segments are thought to control the expression of the genes or regulate their functioning. Scientists hope to be able to see precisely how humans differ genetically from animals and how the human organism develops (why one cell becomes a liver cell and another with the same genetic material becomes a brain cell is a great mystery), with an additional prospect of identifying and one day treating genetic diseases.

Genetic modification of plants and animals for commercial and research purposes and various sorts of gene therapy have not waited for complete knowledge of the genome, human or nonhuman. The U.S. Supreme Court allowed patenting of a genetically altered plant in 1980. The first animal ("OncoMouse" — a mouse genetically altered to develop cancer) was patented in 1988. By the end of 1988, there were one thousand different strains of mice that carried genes from other species, and hundreds of biotechnology firms are continually developing new "products."[139] In 1989 foreign (bacteria) genes were first inserted into human cancer patients as part of a program to track the effectiveness of a new therapy. New gene therapies, in which specially modified viruses can insert their genes into the DNA of, say, tumor cells, are being developed rapidly and show prospects of providing effective, specific treatment for some cancers.[140] In mice, defective genes have actually been replaced by normal ones by direct injection of DNA into muscle tissue.[141]

All of this is fantastically exhilarating, but also scary enough in terms of possible consequences that about 3 percent of the budget of the Human Genome Project has been recommended to be directed toward ethical concerns; and back in 1974, when some recombinant DNA experiments were in their earliest stages, anxious scientists took the unprecedented step of calling for a moratorium until risks could be assessed and appropriate precautions taken. The moratorium, though instituted, was short-lived. Guidelines for research were developed and scientists convinced themselves and most of their peers that the risks could be reduced "to levels far lower than other hazards which the public currently accepts without

138. Victor A. McKusick, quoted in *Context* 22, no. 21 (Dec. 1, 1990), p. 2. The Human Genome Project, expected to cost some five billion dollars, is the first really "big science" project in biology. Its completion is expected to take fifteen years.

139. United Nations Environmental Programme, *Only One World.*

140. Thomas H. Maugh II, "Treatment Cures Brain Tumors in Rats," *Los Angeles Times,* June 12, 1992, p. A29.

141. C. Thomas Caskey, "DNA-Based Medicine: Prevention and Therapy," in Kevles and Hood, eds., *Code of Codes,* p. 128.

question"[142] — not an entirely reassuring criterion! True, these guidelines do not deal with the kind of "shotgun" experiments now popular, in which all the genes of an organism are manipulated more or less at random and fragments that are essentially unknown quantities inserted into bacteria. And true, modified forms of *E. coli* — a bacterium that is a normal inhabitant of the human intestine and a human pathogen — are still being used as recipients of choice for implanting foreign genes, despite such a choice being deemed "reckless" and recommended for rapid phaseout almost twenty years ago by scientists concerned about adequacy of guidelines.[143] But a chorus of scientific voices asserts that we may be persuaded by experience: we have thus far suffered no adverse effects, which, they say, shows this experimentation to be safer than many once feared.[144]

One can hardly help recalling early enthusiasms for everything from cocaine (hailed by Freud as a wonder drug) to Thalidomide to DDT, not to mention the laboratory mistake that produced killer bees (now on the loose) or the devastating effects on some environments even of nonnative but genetically normal plants and animals. But surely genetic engineering brings far greater dangers than these now-known hazards, for organisms carrying transplanted genes may be affected in subtle ways not measurable for years or decades; and no one knows what to look for.[145] The dangers are particularly great when new organisms are released directly into the environment, as in the case of genetically modified bacteria that can protect strawberries against frost (first released legally in 1987). The question is

142. Lord Ashby, et al., *Report of the Working Party on the Experimental Manipulation of the Genetic Composition of Micro-Organisms* (London: Her Majesty's Stationery Office, January 1975), p. 4. This same report acknowledged the possibility, however, that "new combinations might (although this is only speculation) extend the host-range of a disease from animals to man, or provoke malignant cell growths, or confer new patterns of resistance to antibiotics" (p. 13). The Boston Area Recombinant DNA Group adds the caution: "disappointing precedent comes from work involving entirely known biohazards. The number of reported acquired infections in laboratories with special containment facilities has been around 1650 in the last 30 years [prior to 1975]" (Report of the Boston Area Recombinant DNA Group to Dewitt Stetten Jr., of the National Institutes of Health, Nov. 24, 1975, p. 18).

143. Report of the Boston Area Recombinant DNA Group, p. 4.

144. Contrast this assertion with the authoritative (and generally positive) report of Caskey: "Current gene transfer and replacement technologies have . . . high rates (between one in ten thousand and one in a million) of illegitimate recombinations, in which the gene inserts itself into the wrong place, sometimes in the middle of another gene. Illegitimate insertion of transgene sequences has produced disease in mouse embryos" ("DNA-Based Medicine: Prevention and Therapy," p. 129).

145. William Bennett and Joel Gurin, "Science that Frightens Scientists," *Atlantic Monthly* 239, no. 2 (February 1977), pp. 43-62. "The ultimate question is not whether bacteria can be contained in a laboratory but whether scientists can be contained in an ordinary society" (ibid., p. 62).

not just the safety of the bacteria themselves, but what they might eventually destroy or combine with and what unknown qualities may come with frost resistance. One of the curious things about genes is that they are enormously complex and behave differently under different circumstances, so we may not know soon what *can,* given appropriate conditions, be expressed.[146] Even worse is the potential contamination occurring from disposal of "genetic junk": waste products of experiments, organisms changed in obviously undesirable ways. What happens if they manage to reproduce themselves or infect other organisms? This new kind of "pollution" can occur even with organisms presumably confined to a laboratory. The likelihood that over time, genetic exchange will occur between presumably "safe," disarmed strains of *E. coli* used for experiments (not to mention by the pharmaceutical industry) and the widely distributed, airborne, wild strains indigenous to humans is quite large — and has the usual unknown, unquantifiable, even unguessable repercussions.[147]

Robert Sinsheimer (an early advocate of genetic engineering and one of the architects of the Human Genome Project) believes that recombinant DNA technique may prove, like nuclear energy, to be a field that would better have remained forbidden territory. He fears not only the spread of new slow viruses, cancers, or pathogens; not only intentional misuse of the technique by terrorists or the military; but more, manipulations "which

146. "Algae Shed Light on Gene Switching," *Harvard Graduate Society Newsletter,* April 1978.

147. Report by Boston Area Recombinant DNA Group, p. 5. Again,

one actual experiment that was terminated after some initial success was the introduction into *E. coli* of genes for making the enzyme cellulase. Cellulase, absent in humans, is the enzyme that breaks down the plant fiber material cellulose. The experiments were ended when the scientist conducting them realized that in addition to providing us with a new, digestible food source, plant fiber, the unaccustomed digestion would release carbon dioxide gas in the gut, and might cause us to swell like balloons whenever we ate vegetables, fruits, or grain products. Suppose he had not happened to think of this? (Ehrenfeld, *Arrogance of Humanism,* p. 95)

The other side of release of unwanted qualities into the environment is the unintentional loss of perhaps still unidentified desirable qualities, such as some kinds of adaptability or disease-resistance or medicinal potential, by genetic modification aimed at accomplishing something else, like high yield. While particular traits best fit one era in history, emphasizing them alone could diminish survival powers when the situation changes (thus, ironically, what is most lucrative at the moment may prove least "fit" when long-term survival is at stake; see Jeremy Rifkin, *Algeny* [New York: Penguin, 1984], p. 133). Dangers here are analogous to those of sacrificing any form of species diversity: we do not know what we are losing (Robert E. Rhoades, "The World's Food Supply at Risk," *National Geographic* 179, no. 4 [April 1991], pp. 74-105).

evolution has been at pains to prohibit," involving crossovers of cells from lower and higher organisms that have unknown consequences not just for individual organisms but for the evolutionary process as a whole.[148] We do not and cannot know ahead of time exactly what we are doing, yet we are irreversibly manipulating the mechanism that controls how life itself is expressed.

We may be moved to reflect in this day of ordinary and genetically engineered hybrids on the way Scripture speaks of each creature being made "after its kind" (Gn. 1). Claus Westermann said, "As long as the earth remains, there can never be a single plant among the hundreds of thousands that exist that does not belong to its own species within this whole. Just because it belongs to its kind, each individual is directed to the ordered whole, God's Creation" (*Creation,* trans. J. J. Scullion [London: SPCK, 1974], pp. 45-46). Scientifically speaking, such a remark no longer quite holds, but what does that fact mean for "the ordered whole"? Granting that selective breeding was practiced among the Hebrews (Gn. 30:37-40); granting the existence of mules (2 Sam. 13:29; 18:9; 1 Kgs. 10:25); granting the likelihood that taboos and magical customs of forgotten origin as well as culturally conditioned purity regulations lie behind Lv. 19:19 (cf. Dt. 22:9-11); could it yet be that an inchoate sense of some boundaries that need to be maintained and of species whose integrity should be respected can also be seen in the regulation against hybridization? Our current technological adventures might bring us to reexamine texts that have long seemed to be simply curiosities.

What is complicated enough in the case of plants and animals raises specters of a more ominous kind in the case of human beings, where determining what is desirable is associated with the name "eugenics" and brings with it a sobering history of use of various forms of sterilization and even lobotomies to purge society of everything from the sexually deviant to the insane, epileptic, retarded, or alcoholic. The Human Genome Project sets the eugenics question in a whole new light because for the first time we are gaining hard data, available before birth, about specific characteristics of persons. The usability of this information, apart from genetic engineering, is obviously tied directly to the question of abortion — whether abortion is permissible (or could become mandatory?), and under what circumstances, and, of course, who decides. One fetus will have a 95 percent chance of developing Huntington's Disease and dying horribly in midlife. Another has a 100 percent certainty of developing sickle-cell disease, though of unknown severity. Another will be female (in a family that strongly desires a male child). *Must* any of these fetuses be aborted to spare them and their families suffering, or to

148. Nicholas Wade, "Recombinant DNA: A Critic Questions the Right to Free Inquiry," *Science* 194 (Oct. 15, 1976): 303-6.

spare society the cost of caring for them and of keeping their faulty gene in the pool? (The economic factor will figure large, as we will see below.) Does a parent have a right, on the one hand, to bear an "imperfect" child or, on the other hand, to abort any child that does not meet her private definition of perfection? As tests become more reliable and cheaper, may one continue to refuse to make use of them? Might couples be required to get a license to reproduce, granting of which would depend on certain criteria of genetic soundness?[149] Will we by genetic testing create a "genetic underclass" with boundaries less permeable than those of any existing social class? Who will have access to the information?[150] Persons with various handicaps and of different racial groups have been understandably nervous that their worth as human beings is at least potentially called into question; while others try to make the case that both environmental pollution and our very successes in keeping the "unfit" alive have allowed the proportion of defective genes in the gene pool to increase dangerously.[151] (The prospect for "selective breeding" of humans is further complicated by the observation that the traits most of interest to those who wish to "improve" humankind, like intelligence, foresight, stability, compassion, and altruism, are precisely those least understood in genetic terms: many children of geniuses, for instance, have not done well themselves.)[152]

But what if, instead of isolating, stigmatizing, or sterilizing "defectives," we could "fix" them by replacing or rectifying a troublesome gene

149. Such proposals, made seriously, can be found at the level of newspaper reporting in 1964, where H. Bentley Glass of Johns Hopkins was quoted as making this suggestion, along with expressing the opinion that the Negro population of the United States will disappear entirely due to intermarriage with whites — an opinion blacks might with reason hear as ominous, however "scientifically" it may have been intended (George Getz, "Special Permit to Have Children Seen as Future Population Control," *Los Angeles Times,* June 3, 1964).

150. "One of the agencies most interested in the genome project is the FBI, a technologically very capable organization" (Charles Cantor, "The Challenges to Technology and Informatics," in Kevles and Hood, eds., *Code of Codes,* p. 106). Police want a DNA register of sex offenders; the public may want proof that a politician's children are really his own; the keeper of a small hotel in Wales actually wrote suggesting a DNA register of bedwetters (James D. Watson, "A Personal View of the Project," in ibid., p. 173).

151. See Kelsey, *Racism and the Christian Understanding of Man,* pp. 162-66.

152. Robert L. Sinsheimer, "All Men Created Equal," a paper read June 20, 1975; Charles E. Curran, "Theology and Genetics: A Multi-Faceted Dialogue," *Journal of Ecumenical Studies* 7, no. 1 (winter 1970): 61-89. We are reminded of the famous exchange between George Bernard Shaw and a beautiful actress who approached him with the suggestion that they have a child, since a child with her looks and his intelligence would be a remarkable specimen. Shaw punctured the balloon by reminding her of another, less appealing, possibility: that the child would have his looks and her intelligence!

or adding a normal gene to supply a missing function?[153] What seems benign on the surface carries a whole new set of dilemmas with it. Not least of these problems is that genes have more than one function, and in eliminating a problem, we may be unintentionally eliminating other things we do not know about as well. For instance, the gene that carries sickle-cell anemia also confers malaria resistance on African blacks;[154] and many have suggested that manic-depressive illness and creativity may be associated. But apart from such essentially technical questions, we have social questions. What is to be counted as a defect that should be remedied by gene therapy? Defining something like homosexuality or hyperactivity or aggressiveness as a disease (if we should discover that these are genetically predisposed) has vast repercussions for the human individuality of those who manifest them and for the society that induces people, forcibly or by judiciously administered rewards and punishments, to change them through genetic manipulation. Take hyperactivity in children:

> If treated behaviors are seen as the result of a disease, one has little compunction about altering them. . . . Here is where an end-product analysis is absolutely essential, but it cannot be performed because its questions are beyond our abilities to answer. . . . What are "hyperactive" and "minimally brain damaged" children like when they are allowed to grow up without stigmatization or specific treatment — not just at age twenty, but until death? Do they share any distinctive personality traits, do they have the same sorts of failures and achievements, are they different from other people? What is their net effect, as adults, on society? For example, do they promote war or peace? What does treatment do to these children, beyond improving their grades immediately after treatment? Is their creativity affected in any way? Their ambition? Their capacity for love? Their self-reliance? Their happiness? Their ability to resist tyranny? What is their later impact on society?[155]

Such questions need to be asked about all such interventions, with due attention to our dismal record of persecution and our historically changing opinions about what is and what is not a disorder.

153. Work in these areas is slow but progressing (Laurel Joyce, "Good Genes, Bad Genes," *Stanford Medicine,* Fall 1989, pp. 18-23); and we need not doubt that we will eventually gain some such capability.

154. "Gene-Altering Opposed," *Christian Century* 100, no. 20 (June 22-29, 1983): 609.

155. Ehrenfeld, *Arrogance of Humanism,* pp. 73-74. Ehrenfeld is speaking here about treatment coming far short of genetic intervention; but his cautions surely apply a fortiori to the latter.

Take the argument further. Should we draw the line on genetic manipulation between repair of damage (which we might justify by considering it to be restoring rather than changing creation) and enhancement of qualities someone desires? If so, where does this line lie? What image of normalcy or of perfection governs it? For instance, is aging a disorder?[156] How about the loss in humans of the ability to synthesize vitamin C or resist particular diseases?[157] Should we alter "somatic" cells only (limiting genetic corrections to those which will not be transmitted to offspring) or take human evolution into our own hands by correcting serious defects in germ cells, with a view to eliminating and not just treating genetic diseases? There has already been discussion of the possibility of some day patenting human characteristics as we currently patent genetically altered vegetables and mice (who would ever have dreamed that constitutional provisions against slavery would be a line of defense against patenting a whole person!).[158] Thus we are not sanguine about confident protestations that tampering with human germ cells and hence permanently altering the human gene pool "is a line that will never be crossed." But we are convinced that it *should not* be crossed, being reminded in a new context and with greatly enlarged consequences that our bodies are not our own to possess (1 Cor. 6:19-20).

Not theology but economics, though, will tend to govern major decisions in biotechnology as in so many other arenas. The reason for patenting forms of life is not, after all, scientific but economic. Money can be made from patented plants and animals (and, eventually, human traits?) that have highly desirable qualities, and that fact has several bad side effects: the rural poor are once again at a disadvantage in obtaining what is necessary to their livelihood; ownership of major components of the world's food supply comes to be concentrated in a few multinational corporations; and genetic diversity is lost when plant or animal stock is neglected or eliminated because, being a product of nature, it cannot be patented and hence generate profits. Money can also be made from various bioengineered

---

156. The life spans of fruit flies and roundworms have in fact already been extended by manipulation of so-called Methuselah genes (Thomas H. Maugh II, "Scientists Draw Back Veil on the Mystery of Aging," *Los Angeles Times,* Feb. 8, 1992, pp. A1ff.); but we can only marvel at the underlying fantasy that we will somehow, someday, learn by our own ingenuity to thwart death itself.

157. Caskey, "DNA-Based Medicine," p. 129.

158. Cary Fowler, "Biotechnology: Who Will Pay the Costs?" *Bread and Justice,* no. 64 (March-April 1988), p. 7. All of this comes ominously close to Aldous Huxley's *Brave New World,* in which human embryos are cloned (though he lacked the word, he had the concept) and designed for particular functions in the society.

products. Insulin is one thing: we can get enough human insulin to supply diabetics only by bioengineering. Products like vanilla and gum arabic are another matter: if the bioengineered products displace developing world exports of the natural products, cost to those developing countries could be devastating. Once again, from the have-nots, even what they have is taken away.

The economic morass surrounding genetic testing is just as deep; and pressures will assuredly increase as population increases and resources available to each person become comparatively smaller. Here in particular we seem to be generating an incipient paralysis by our increasing knowledge, knowledge that threatens to break down our cultural means of coping. Suppose, for instance, a woman at risk for bearing a child with Duchenne muscular dystrophy either refuses to be tested or, having had a fetus test positive for the disease, declines to have an abortion. Should all subscribers to medical insurance have to pay the increased costs stemming from the care needed by this child, multiplied by thousands of such children? On the one hand, suppose insurance companies or employers demand genetic tests of apparently healthy people to predict whom it is economically wise to insure or employ, or suppose they offer incentives to people who volunteer such information? (Obviously, the genetically sturdy will volunteer it, while those at risk, by withholding it, will actually supply the needed hint; and large numbers of presently well people will be uninsurable or unemployable.) On the other hand, suppose only the tested individual has access to the test results and no one else may legally request them: insurance companies could be put out of business by those at high risk buying large amounts of insurance, while the genetically sturdy buy little. All of this will add enormously to the push for universal, national health insurance. But universal insurance would not end the motivation to compile, buy, and sell libraries of genetic information. Nor would it solve the problem of who, under what circumstances, or at what odds for having a disorder, would be pressed (for economic reasons doubtless justified by supposed reasons of kindness) to have an abortion or submit to genetic manipulation. But how could we ever calculate ahead of time, or at all, the cost of Dostoyevsky's epilepsy and psychic misery over against the contribution of his literature, which is not a thing separate from his suffering? Or, perhaps more important for the discussion as a whole, what about his mother or father, in whom we might have found a faulty gene and who themselves may not have contributed greatly to society — except by producing Dostoyevsky? And in any case, if utility and performance were the key measures of human worth, we would all (especially theologians!) fail on somebody's scale. Contrast Jesus' particular care for the maimed, lame, and blind (Lk. 14:13, 21).

The enhanced temptation to evaluate a human life in terms of its likely economic costs is but one component of biotechnology's tendency to desacralize the created order. It disrupts our sense of relationship with other creatures and counts as significant precisely what can be counted, ignoring mystery and leaving aside those qualities of self-transcendence so crucial to our understanding of human dignity and personhood (including human ability to become scientists). Let the scientists speak for themselves: "What makes us human beings instead of chimpanzees . . . is a mere 1 percent difference between the ape genome and our own."[159] "By tweaking our computer programs, we will finally identify the regions of DNA that differ between the primate and the human — and understand those genes that make us uniquely human."[160] "I have spent my career trying to get a chemical explanation for life. . . . If you can study life from the level of DNA, you have a *real* explanation for its processes."[161] Really? When scientists say that the genes contain the "information" that determines the human individual, what exactly do they mean? We say there is information in an encyclopedia, but on a purely naturalistic basis we would do better to say that there is white paper with black ink on it in an encyclopedia. What makes the black ink on white paper convey information and what makes DNA do the building job it does are ultimately beyond naturalism to say. But the ink and paper on the one hand or the DNA on the other provides the essential means for transmitting the information. Tampering with the substrate that affects not only our bodies but also our emotional and intellectual capacities constitutes a serious threat that may rob not only us but also those who come after us of important aspects of their individuality and rightful dominion.[162] C. S. Lewis's remarks seem particularly prescient in this regard:

> The last men, far from being the heirs of power, will be of all men most subject to the dead hand of the great planners and conditioners and will themselves exercise least power upon the future. . . . Each new power won *by* man is a power *over* man as well. Each advance leaves him weaker as well as stronger. In every victory, besides being the general who triumphs, he is also the prisoner who follows the

159. Daniel J. Kevles and Leroy Hood, "Preface," in Kevles and Hood, eds., *Code of Codes,* p. vii.

160. Walter Gilbert, "A Vision of the Grail," in ibid., p. 94.

161. Watson, "Personal View," in ibid., p. 164 (emphasis added).

162. See Brunner, *Man in Revolt,* p. 321, for discussion of various ways in which the will and thought of some determine the individuality of others. Genetic engineering, however, encroaches particularly dangerously because it can permanently change the gene pool.

triumphal car. *Human* nature will be the last part of Nature to surrender to Man. The battle will then be won. . . . But who, precisely, will have won it?[163]

Because of, and not apart from, our human self-transcendence, how we regard ourselves and the rest of the creation has vital consequences for what we do. (Recall that those who regarded dogs as mere machines had no compunctions about behaving what we would now call cruelly to them; those who regarded Jews negatively had no compunctions about experimenting on them and killing them.) How much human genetic material can we transfer to an animal before the meaning of being human is called into question? How much genetic material from animals or how many "biochips" can we incorporate into ourselves before the same thing happens, and we begin to regard ourselves as animals or mere mechanisms?[164] If we insist (and we do) on the hopelessness of the effort to solve moral problems by chemistry, as if the right gene or the right pill could eliminate sin, must we turn the argument around and agree that anything that can be significantly influenced by pills or genes does not belong in the realm of sin at all? Already findings of likely genetic links to homosexuality have generated newspaper headlines and leads like, "Rethinking the Origins of Sin," "Should you condemn someone for something they're predisposed to do?"[165] It would be a fallacy at the scientific level to suppose that complex human behaviors are simply determined by variations in a particular gene.[166] But we further hold, from a theological perspective, that the amount of freedom and responsibility we believe we have will influence how readily we succumb to specific impulses. Nonetheless, our very

163. *The Abolition of Man* (New York: Macmillan, 1947), pp. 71-72.
164. The theory (supported by heavy investments in both biotechnology and microelectronics by some firms) is: "In the future, biocomputers will be engineered directly into living systems, just as microcomputers are engineered into mechanical systems today. They will monitor activity, adjust performance, speed up and slow down metabolic activity, transform living material into products, and perform a host of other supervisory functions. Scientists even envision the day when computers made out of living material will automatically reproduce themselves, finally blurring the last remaining distinction between living and mechanical processes" (Rifkin, *Algeny,* p. 22). That we already have medicines chemically regulating metabolism and mood and pacemakers electronically regulating heartbeat makes the line easier to cross than one might at first suppose. And a mathematician has used DNA to calculate the answer to a mathematical problem that, at its most complex, is beyond the capacity of current electronic computers (Robert Lee Hotz,"Unconventional Wisdom," *Los Angeles Times,* June 22, 1995, p. B2).
165. Larry B. Stammer, *Los Angeles Times,* May 15, 1993, pp. A1ff. For our discussion of this issue specifically, see above, pp. 315-18, 349.
166. Lauerman, "The Time Machine," p. 45.

successes in helping people via chemistry and biotechnology to control impulses or behavior they wish to change will increasingly call into question the meaning of their wishing.

Even apart from these ultimate issues of human freedom and dignity, we must face what new powers over human bodies can do to human relationships. What happens to human relationships if procreation is systematically and generally separated from love?[167] What about the "usefulness" of human bodies? Already parents of a leukemia-stricken child have had another child to obtain bone marrow for a transplant to save the sibling's life. Increasing use of fetal tissue from induced abortions raises fears of pregnancies begun with abortion as the goal (use of tissue from spontaneous abortions is risky because it has too high a probability of carrying infection or chromosomal abnormalities). A hardly less problematic issue is use of "spare" embryos produced for in vitro fertilization: may one do research on them? raise them in order to "harvest" organs or tissues? What about producing clones for such purposes?[168] Parents planning prenatal testing to guard against inherited diseases often delay speaking about a pregnancy and try to inhibit emotional attachment to a fetus until they get the test results — a major change in the human experience of pregnancy.[169] Sometimes, testing produces the need for grotesque choices, as when one twin is normal and the other is not. Our new powers thus bring before us the kind of decisions that may encroach on our sense of what it means to be human, no matter which decision we make. Again, our capacities have outstripped our wisdom and moral judgment — as we have demonstrated repeatedly, at Auschwitz, and Hiroshima, and Love Canal.

c. Conclusion

We are like kids who gleefully take apart things that they do not know how to put back together again. When it comes to blowing apart (or fusing) the nuclei of atoms or modifying the human germ line — rearranging not the external manifestation but the basic constituents of the natural world and of

---

167. See Curran, "Theology and Genetics"; also, for a fictional treatment, Huxley, *Brave New World.* Many have already deplored the reduction in our humanity brought by the separation of sex from love, the tendency to focus on the body apart from the person.

168. In fact, as of October 1993, scientists at George Washington University Medical Center have cloned human embryos, using methods similar to those used to clone rabbits. It happens that the cloned embryos were abnormal and did not develop, but surely the technical problems can be overcome. And then what? What happens to human dignity, to our understanding of every person as created in the divine image? (See "Cloning of Embryos Stirs Ethical Concerns," *Christian Century* 110, no. 32 [Nov. 10, 1993]: 1117.)

169. Allan Parachini, "Shadow of a Doubt," *Los Angeles Times,* Feb. 7, 1989, pt. V, p. 1.

humankind — we can only conclude that human dominion, given that we might "keep" and not only "subdue" the creation, has overreached itself. As creatures, we have been given creaturely limits. We must not continue to presume, after the model of our first parents, that whatever can be known should be known.[170] We must somehow learn at last the lesson that we must eschew certain gains where errors are too costly; for if we insist on sowing the wind, we will assuredly, sooner or later, reap the whirlwind. Errors *always* occur, due to technical failures, human mistakes, and simple human malice and sin. Serious nuclear or genetic errors carry with them inconceivable, irretrievable costs for all future generations. The genie, once out, cannot be stuffed back into the bottle. And with nuclear and genetic errors, it will sometimes be a long time before we even know if something terrible has occurred — if radioactive waste has been making its way toward a major water source, or if repair of a defective gene has eliminated an important but subtle human capacity. This time factor makes it doubly risky to comfort ourselves with reassurances that since nothing absolutely catastrophic has incontrovertibly happened yet, we can safely proceed on our present course.

Side effects often prove to be main effects in the long run. Worst of all the effects of both of these technologies may be a dulling of responsiveness to life itself. Maintenance of reverence and awe for the creation is incompatible with developing means to destroy or radically alter it forever. One must either blind oneself to what one is doing (that refusal to know consequences that is so often combined with insistence on knowing certain particulars) or regard differently that to which one is doing it. It is as if the technology has become a sort of Frankenstein's monster, having a life of its own but no soul, and threatening increasingly to revenge itself on its maker.

5. THE RECALCITRANT AND INTERLOCKING NATURE OF THE PROBLEMS

However serious our reservations may be about what we might call the boundary cases of technological intervention, surely most of us would see the various aspects of the ecological crisis as prime examples of problems

---

170. We cannot follow the sentiment of Teilhard de Chardin, who, reflecting on the opinion of some that knowledge of how to split the atom should have been suppressed and destroyed, opined: "As though it were not every man's duty to pursue the creative forces of knowledge and action to their uttermost end! As though, in any event, there exists any force on earth capable of restraining human thought from following any course upon which it has embarked!" (*Future of Man*, p. 140). The trouble is that when we wish we could forget, we do not know how (merely limiting access to knowledge is no solution), just as we do not know how to restrain the most terrible abuses of knowledge.

crying out for use of all of our technological skill. To think otherwise could signal a defeatism leading to a disastrous passivity, a refusal of the responsibilities we have been given. Quite obviously *something* must be done. And as a matter of fact, when we decide to devote the necessary resources, we can and do resolve an extraordinary array of difficulties. For instance, having driven the California condor to the very brink of extinction, we have, by an unbelievably elaborate (and costly) captive breeding program, made sufficient progress that some of the birds can be released into the wild again. Having polluted the soil with long-lasting pesticides and having made hard-to-dispose-of chemical weapons, we can now produce large quantities of an enzyme that can break down these toxins.[171] Having seriously depleted the Caspian Sea and increased its salinity by building irrigation dams that drain off fresh water — thus threatening oil drilling, fishing, shipping, and tourism — the former Soviet Union reversed the flow of two rivers to help make up for the loss.[172] Such diverse successes can lead to an understandable sense of exhilarating power that makes it unbelievable that anything could be too hard for us to handle. They also lead to a tendency to define everything as a technological problem, with a corresponding tendency to treat science soteriologically and be baffled if it fails us.[173]

And it has failed us in important ways. Given our legitimate triumphs, we may be taken aback to learn than since concerns about the environment began to increase in the early 1970s, not even one major trend of environmental degradation has been reversed.[174] Nor have we succeeded in humanizing our neighborhoods and cities. Part of the reason has to do with continuing population growth and unwise, exploitative practices, as we have already seen. Part of the reason is the speed of change: new technologies are applied so quickly that we have no time to sort out their implications or adjust at the human level to the new world they create. But part of the reason is just that everything turns out to be more complicated than we might at first suppose. With more time, we might be able to figure out what we did wrong last time, but no amount of planning can tell us what

---

171. "Researchers isolated the gene that the bacterium [*Pseudomonas diminuta*] uses to produce the enzyme, modified it slightly and inserted it into a virus, which was then inserted into insect cells to produce the enzyme in large amounts" ("Pesticide-Eating Enzymes," *Los Angeles Times,* Aug. 7, 1989, pt. II, p. 3).

172. *Geo,* July 1982, p. 119.

173. Ellul, *Technological Bluff,* pp. 48, 182.

174. Delegates and observers of the World Council of Churches meeting at Baixada Fluminense, Brazil, "An Open Letter to the Church," Pentecost, 1992, excerpted in *Theology, News and Notes,* December 1992, p. 4.

we will do wrong next time.[175] Perhaps even more importantly, presumed "solutions" reliably generate problems even more complex than those they solve. It is hard to believe that back in 1895, the automobile was hailed as a solution to the then prevalent problem of pollution: horse manure on the city streets.[176] Today we are finding that our efforts to curb smoke pollution by removing some solids from it leave free the material that causes acid rain — a serious problem no one even thought of predicting.[177] Life-saving antibiotics have ended up producing a new strain of tuberculosis, resistant to all known forms of treatment and having a 90 percent fatality rate. Tuberculosis is up 10 percent in the United States.[178] Captive breeding programs for threatened species generate genetic pools with very little differentiation, which ultimately threatens the species they are meant to preserve.[179] The point is not whether we will manage to solve these particular problems, too; it is rather that any such solutions will themselves apparently bring yet more and yet harder problems, so that our temporary successes may be bringing us closer to final collapse — just as with the drug addict who needs more and more chemical to prevent withdrawal symptoms.[180] But what are the alternatives? Needing more and more technology to counter the effects of technology, we are in a predicament like that of the sorcerer's apprentice, who has his broom drawing water but does not know the word to speak to get it to stop drawing water.

A related but slightly different problem is that we deceive ourselves if we think we can fix things one at a time, since everything interacts with everything else and many goods compete with one another. As a particularly distressing example, we might note the competing demands of energy production and food production. At the simplest level, an acre's corn output

175. Ehrenfeld, *Arrogance of Humanism*, p. 63.

176. Gilbert M. Grosvenor, "Will We Mend Our Earth?" *National Geographic* 174, no. 6 (December 1989), p. 767.

177. Ellul, *Technological Bluff*, p. 59.

178. Radio announcement Feb. 24, 1993, citing an article in the *New England Journal of Medicine*. There is an increasing variety of drug-resistant bacteria, raising the specter of a looming public health catastrophe — the kind of catastrophe that was assumed to be gone forever (Jack Cheevers, "Drug-Resistant Bacteria Pose an Increasing Threat," *Los Angeles Times*, March 25, 1995, pp. A1ff.).

179. Kathryn Phillips, "DNA Fingerprints," *Los Angeles Times*, Nov. 14, 1988, pt. II, p. 3.

180. Ehrenfeld (*Arrogance of Humanism*, p. 107) quotes Eugene Schwartz's book *Overskill* on the self-defeating process of addressing problems within too restricted a context (and a context must be restricted if anything even resembling a solution is to be found). Schwartz argues that techno-social solutions always generate new problems arising from incompleteness, augmentation, and secondary effects; that these problems proliferate faster than solutions; and that each set of residual problems is more difficult to solve than the last, until technological solution will finally become impossible.

takes the energy equivalent in fertilizer and other oil products of eighty gallons of gasoline — an increasingly hard trade-off as oil becomes scarcer.[181] But suppose we turn more to the use of coal for energy. Then the trade-off is just as bad because the coal lies beneath prime agricultural land, and strip-mining kills everything in sight, leaves a huge pit, and leads to mineralization of the water supply.[182] Burning coal also contributes heavily to acid rain, which threatens plants. How about biomass for energy, hailed as safe and renewable? Pretty good as far as the energy situation goes, not so good for food, because whatever vegetation is consumed for energy does not go back into the soil to keep it fertile. Sometimes a cruel irony thwarts good intentions, as when increasing food production in a developing country by use of modern techniques actually leads to increased hunger: former peasants are forced into cities where the food does not follow them, but is instead used for export crops to pay interest on the country's international debt.[183] Or, consider the disastrous consequences of the seemingly obvious moral imperative to pay a "fair price" for such countries' export crops: making export crops more profitable will result in fewer subsistence crops being grown.[184]

Such examples could be multiplied at great length, but they all tend to generate a conviction that piecemeal solutions are doomed. But the problem of instituting proper controls is at least as recalcitrant as the ecological morass. On the face of it, centralized and international controls seem more essential than ever before. People will not reduce pollution by automobiles without the kinds of federal action that set mileage and emissions standards, tax gasoline more highly, and provide alternative public transportation. Management of radioactive pollution is made almost impossible because no single agency currently has enough jurisdiction over all aspects of nuclear waste operations to enable development of the comprehensive program obviously needed.[185] Everything from control of acid rain to managing the environmental implications of international loans requires international cooperation. Even finding and instituting the combinations of small-scale technology and labor-intensive forms of work that many environmentalists encourage, or decentralizing industry, requires a great deal of centralized planning and capital.[186]

181. Simon, *Bread for the World*, p. 20.

182. Harry M. Caudille, "Farming and Mining," *Atlantic Monthly* 232, no. 3 (September 1973), pp. 85-90.

183. Austin, "Jubilee Now!" p. 28.

184. Ellul, *Technological Bluff*, p. 195, n. 10.

185. General Accounting Office, "Major Unresolved Issues," p. 9.

186. See Ward and Dubos, *Only One Earth*, p. 180; Ellul, *Technological Society*, pp. 199, 236.

However, we have good reason to fear both the inefficiency and the moral turpitude of large, powerful entities. A lot of profit can be made by, say, an unholy alliance of polluters and pollution-control forces.[187] Recall the dismal pollution record both of United States government agencies and of the governments of Communist countries, as well as the self-interested, environmentally reckless positions the United States took at the Earth Summit. Besides, big bureaucracies, like those that would be necessary adequately to enforce morally admirable environmental legislation, tend to become monsters that eventually die of their own weight. Add to these problems the nationalistic fervor aroused in some developing countries when they are pressed to submit to international supervision in order to preserve resources like the rain forests, and one can only conclude that adequately large-scale controls are not feasible.[188] Were we not sinners, we would not require such controls; since we are sinners, they will not work.[189]

So what will work? The ethical issues are recalcitrant, too. Hard-nosed realists, confronting the reality that people acting in their individual and immediate self-interest will do irreparable harm to the environment, continue to espouse mutual coercion (whatever its problems) as imperative.[190] But they may add a defense of "lifeboat ethics." A lifeboat (the earth) can contain only so many people. Add more, and everyone goes down. Or, in the phrase of "the dolorous economist" Malthus, "At Nature's Great Table there is no place for some." The best intentions may bring the worst consequences: "To send food only to a country already populated beyond

187. Neuhaus, *In Defense of People,* pp. 83-90.

188. William R. Long, "Drive to Preserve Amazon Sparks Nationalistic Reaction in Brazil," *Los Angeles Times,* Feb. 17, 1989, pt. I, p. 13. Still another factor is that: "A complicated system works most efficiently if its parts readjust themselves decentrally, with a minimum of central intervention or control, except in case of breakdown. . . . [If] a subject is wired to suffer an annoying regular buzz, which can be delayed and finally eliminated if he makes a precise but unlikely gesture, say by twisting his ankle in a certain way; then it is found that he adjusts quicker if he is *not* told the method and it is left to his spontaneous twitching than if he is told and tries deliberately to help himself" (Goodman, "Can Technology Be Humane?" p. 234). Sometimes precisely our vaunted human self-transcendence fouls things up!

189. Furthermore, as Ehrenfeld put it, commenting on the complaint of some that no one is at the wheel, "Of course nobody is at the wheel, because there isn't any wheel, nor can there be" (*Arrogance of Humanism,* p. 240). Again, the system is far too complex for a single tweak of something or other to correct the course of the whole.

190. They will continue to do this harm even if they perceive the ultimately disastrous consequences of their actions, because restraint on their own part will work against their interests unless matched by the same restraint on the part of everyone else. Game theory labels such a situation a zero-sum game. In such situations people opt for a bad outcome because if they are mistaken in trusting the reliability of others (everyone acting trustworthily would produce the best outcome for all), the outcome for them personally will be still worse.

the carrying capacity of its land is to collaborate in the further destruction of the land and the further impoverishment of its people."[191] The kindest thing we can do in the long run, such thinkers insist, is the cruelest in the short run — refuse "help" that will eventuate in further increases in population in already overpopulated areas.

But however accurate the calculations of the net misery fostered by an ethic of compassion as contrasted with a "lifeboat" approach, one can hardly escape the perception that the wrong people are making those calculations. The conclusions look different to those sitting securely in the lifeboat and those fighting a losing battle to keep afloat in the sea.[192] (And speaking of unintended consequences, a general espousal of lifeboat ethics, even in the name of reducing human misery overall, could be seriously morally debilitating, drying up springs of responsiveness to human beings.)[193] The ethical issue is not only "too many" (their problem) but equally "too much" (our problem). How do we determine the best balance of quantity and quality? (And what besides sheer power gave us the right to make the determination?) Who pays what to spare the environment? What are the chances, that is, that we would give up car air conditioners so that more Chinese could have refrigerators without further environmental harm; or that we would provide to the developing world nonpolluting technologies, either free or as cheaply as polluting ones? Not good?[194] What place, then, does the future have in our calculations, seen in the light of the somber fact that the balance of Earth's systems is in many respects more delicate than we had supposed, and of our increasing suspicion that we have already traveled far down many roads that all lead to points of no return? But the judgments of posterity, so long as a posterity remains, largely preserve our personal anonymity;[195] and in any case we may not perceive ourselves as being present to suffer those judgments. Hence care for the future of the world

191. Garrett Hardin, "Carrying Capacity as an Ethical Concept," *Soundings* 59, no. 1 (spring 1976): 131. See also Hardin, "The Tragedy of the Commons," *Science* 162 (Dec. 13, 1968): 1243-48; Erlich, *Population Bomb*, pp. 158-73.

192. As Richard John Neuhaus puts it *(In Defense of People)*, the further one is from the center of power, the better one understands the abuses of power.

193. This point is acknowledged by Joseph Fletcher, a moderate supporter of lifeboat ethics, and (by Fletcher's report) Hardin himself (George R. Lucas Jr., "Famine and Global Policy," *Christian Century* 92, no. 28 [Sept. 3-10, 1975]: 753-58).

194. Consider as an example this sobering datum: "Without exception, corporate management and boards have opposed every resolution filed over the past 20 years that has addressed social-justice issues" (David E. Provost, "Corporate Responsibility," *Christian Century* 110, no. 11 [April 7, 1993]: 357).

195. Black, *Dominion of Man*, p. 115.

has not sufficed as a motive for substantial and personally costly present change.

In short, self-interest — sin — makes most of the substantive questions facing us unanswerable. The best plans do not change human wants, nor does more information or more education. When a technologist defends technology against its detractors by saying that the fault lies not in the technology but in us, whose ends are not worthy of our means, the technologist is surely at least half right — but that is exactly our present point.[196] Nothing in our history should give us confidence that we will use our powers worthily. What we are able to do does not tell us, and will sometimes interfere with our carrying out, what we ought to do. "There are no technical answers to ethical questions."[197]

Our very successes in our exercise of the dominion we have been given, as well as our equally spectacular failures and follies, have increased creation's groaning, in the bondage and futility to which it was subjected by God on our account. Its fate is not separate from our own but is tied by God to both our guilt and our hope (Rom. 8:19-22; Gn. 3:17). The prophets tell us, more presciently than they could then have known, that the land mourns and the animals perish when God's people act faithlessly and without knowledge of him (Hos. 4:3; Jer. 12:4). The sins of God's people deprive them of the good of rainfall (Jer. 5:24-25); misuse leaves good land desolate (Jer. 12:10-11). An all-embracing catastrophe is pending. When the Lord brings judgment on the earth and leaves it utterly despoiled because the people have broken his covenant and polluted the earth by their disobedience, all classes of people — maid and mistress, creditor and debtor — will be equally affected.[198] No one is exempt. Population will dwindle, and "the gladness of the earth is banished" (Is. 24:1-11;

---

196. Thomas G. Donnelly, "In Defense of Technology," *Christian Century* 90, no. 3 (Jan. 17, 1973): 65-69. As the vice-president of a technological institute ironically put it, "If people could somehow be eliminated from socio-economic problems, the solutions would be quite straightforward" (Vernon L. Grose, "Constraints on Application of Systems Methodology to Socio-Economic Needs," a paper presented at the First Western Space Congress, Santa Maria, California, Oct. 27-29, 1970, p. 13). Given our discussion above of the increasingly complex problems generated by technological "fixes," however, we would hold to our opinion that technology does bring problems apart from the human and moral failures of its users.

197. Roszak, *Where the Wasteland Ends,* p. 441.

198. While it is uncertain to which of the Old Testament covenants Isaiah refers, some have suggested the Noachic covenant because of its universality (see R. E. Clements, *Isaiah 1–39,* New Century Bible [reprint, Grand Rapids: Eerdmans, 1980], pp. 201-2). If so, God's act to preserve the created order even in the midst of the Flood provides a striking contrast with this prophecy of (eschatological?) destruction.

see also Ps. 107:33-34; Zeph. 2:9). In a kind of moral sympathy (now in our day become all too concrete through our increased powers), the material world on which humankind depends is infected and corrupted by human sin, leaving guilty humans staggering "hopelessly like some broken insect on the quaking ruins."[199]

> Generations have trod, have trod, have trod;
> And all is seared with trade; bleared, smeared with toil;
> And wears man's smudge and shares man's smell: the soil
> Is bare now, nor can foot feel, being shod.

Is the day now past when the poet can continue:

> And for all this, nature is never spent;
> There lives the dearest freshness deep down things;
> And though the last lights off the black West went
> Oh, morning, at the brown brink eastward, springs —
> Because the Holy Ghost over the bent
> World broods with warm breast and with ah! bright wings.[200]

D. A MODEST EXERCISE OF DOMINION

1. INTRODUCTION

The human family has come to a point of critical decision, like Israel of old on Mounts Ebal and Gerizim, where Moses set before the people the choice between life and death, blessing and curses (Dt. 27–30). In their exercise of their God-given dominion over the creation, they may continue on their own way, trusting in the gods of science and technology to save them while forgetting, as Jonathan Schell put it, that "our swollen power is not a power to create but only a power to destroy."[201] Or they may have one more chance to relate positively to the creation by loving God and seeking to obey what he has said about the right ordering of life on this

199. George Adam Smith, *The Book of Isaiah,* Expositor's Bible, 2 vols. in 1 (New York: Armstrong, 1903), 1.418.
200. Gerard Manley Hopkins, "God's Grandeur," in Untermeyer, ed., *Great Poems,* pp. 978-79.
201. *Fate of the Earth,* p. 178. He continues, "Even our power of destruction is hardly our own. As a fundamental property of matter, nuclear energy was nature's creation [*sic*], and was only discovered by us" (ibid.).

planet. The first choice can bring only disaster.[202] The second, which promises blessing, involves (as it always has) a radical reordering of priorities and a humble acknowledgment that we will never succeed in saving ourselves in the ecological department any more than in any other.

Some of the problems we face, as we have seen, have complex technical components, like finding ways to use alternative sources of energy and to contain the nuclear waste we have already generated. We are at no risk of running out of appropriate scope for the creative intelligence we have been given. But no amount of tinkering with the system will go bail for a measure of sacrifice and restraint — for a measure of ordinary goodness. Not only has the vision of infinite progress proved illusory, but it has proved no substitute for virtue and morality. That is, if we fail to face the deeper spiritual problems, creative intelligence will meet its comeuppance. To stick with the former examples, we must reduce our need for energy and not just use cleaner, more renewable sources of energy; for the cleanest energy releases heat, of which our environment can tolerate only so much, and it also powers all sorts of environmentally damaging activities; and we must refuse to produce nuclear waste, not just find safer ways of storing what we have, lest contamination burgeon beyond all containing. Principles like these are neither complex nor obscure but perfectly simple and obvious. To heed them, though, means limiting use of some of the knowledge we have; decreasing the value we place on comforts, luxuries, and unlimited mobility as the components of a good life; and curbing short-term self-interest in favor of the legitimate claims of our neighbors and of future generations. That secular values are insufficient to motivate changes of these kinds has become sufficiently obvious that environmentally conscious politicians and scientists have advocated a resacralization of the earth, hoping that a change in attitudes will produce a change in our exploitative behavior.[203]

---

202. "Nowhere in the Old Testament is there a hint that human sinfulness cannot destroy mankind" (Brevard S. Childs, *Old Testament Theology in a Canonical Context* [Philadelphia: Fortress, 1985], p. 233). If we are not utterly pessimistic about the outcome, it is because of our frequently stated conviction that human beings are not absolutely determined but have some potential to exercise their transcendence and control the technology they have created. But we are not so sanguinely optimistic as not to see failure as a real possibility. And Rv. 11:18 makes the eschatological judgment sure: "Your wrath has come, and the time for . . . destroying those who destroy the earth" (NRSV).

203. Russell Chandler, "Religions Join the Crusade to Save Earth from Pollution," *Los Angeles Times,* April 19, 1990, pp. A3ff. See also Harold K. Schilling, "The Whole Earth Is the Lord's," pp. 120-22; and Ian G. Barbour, "Attitudes Toward Nature and Technology," both in Barbour, ed., *Earth Might Be Fair* (Englewood Cliffs, N.J.: Prentice-Hall, 1972), for arguments that only fundamental changes of attitude and not piecemeal attack on a succession of symptoms can stop our devastation of nature.

A proper understanding of the Christian doctrine of human dignity and the dominion of humankind, though, involves not a diminishing of human significance in comparison with other creatures, nor a turning of nature back into a sort of divinity, but rather a reemphasis on the relational character of the divine image that human beings bear. Having talked about humankind's increase as subject, about humans' breaking through the environment's disguise and learning more and more of its secrets, we must now not only marvel or express dismay at the creature endowed to do these things, but face anew the responsibility these powers bring with them. Responsibility and accountability before God are of the essence of what it means to be human. By *addressing* us, God gives us both our individuality and freedom and our duty to respond obediently.[204] Thus right exercise of dominion can never be heedless or independent of what we are given to know of the Lord's own purposes for what he has created. We may, then, speak of a *modest* exercise of dominion, an exercise full of humility before God but also free for proper use and enjoyment of the world. We might think of its components as including a sense of stewardship; love of the neighbor; sensitivity to the value of beauty, gratitude, and contentment; and a view to God's future.

2. STEWARDSHIP

The first and most vital of reminders to the human creatures drunk with their powers or overwhelmed by the challenges before them is to insist once again that they, like the rest of the created order, are precisely creatures. The whole belongs absolutely to God (Ps. 24:1; 50:10-12; Rv. 4:11). That is why we may appropriately sing at the time of the offering in public worship:

> We give thee but thine own,
> What e'er the gift may be:
> All that we have is thine alone,
> A trust, O Lord, from Thee.
>
> (William W. How)

Furthermore, everything continues to be absolutely dependent on him (Neh. 9:6; Ps. 145:14-20; 1 Cor. 8:6; Col. 1:17; Heb. 1:3). We have our role not by a Promethean wresting of power from the gods, but given us as gift and

---

204. Barth, *CD*, III/4, pp. 328-29 (*KD*, III/4, pp. 371-73).

task by the one God. And, being ourselves embedded in the natural world, we threaten ourselves when we threaten it.

Again, we do not have the choice of being stewards or being "free." Paul gave no choice of abstract freedom but only a choice of masters: we may be slaves to sin or slaves to obedience to the Lord (Rom. 6:16). Jesus set serving God and serving mammon as alternatives (Mt. 6:24). As respects our dominion, we will serve either God or else our own impulses and desire for domination on the one hand and our technological and economic systems on the other, both of which prove more demanding and recalcitrant and destructive than we could ever have imagined.[205]

To fulfill our role properly — to be good stewards — we must not only acknowledge our final answerability to God for our stewardship but also be aware of the value of that which has been entrusted to us. The steward who confuses dust and diamonds will not prove a good one no matter how excellent her intentions.[206] So we must recall the Lord's affirmation of the intrinsic created goodness of his works, before humankind entered upon the scene at all (Gn. 1:2-25). He continues his creative and preserving work in a way that gives each component place and worth (Ps. 104), and also a sort of subjectivity and dimension of mystery that militates against our treating it as mere object for exploitation.[207] It follows that the human being acting on God's behalf should uphold God's intent for the creation. The earth is worth saving. Ruling over nature does not mean destroying what we are supposed to rule.[208] But neither does it mean leaving what has been entrusted to us absolutely alone (despite our conviction that *some* things most certainly should be left alone): we are expected to invest, to improve the stock, to distribute benefits rightly, to make responsible choices (Mt. 25:14-46; Lk. 12:41-48). What is required may change as conditions

205. "An unrestrained desire to dominate the world and to enjoy the good things of the world destroys the meaning of life, destroys human personality, social relations, and, above all, man's relation with God. Civilization becomes a curse instead of a blessing; instead of elevating human life, it enslaves and degrades it" (Brunner, *Divine Imperative*, p. 391).

206. Reflecting on our propensity to value our own creations and lose the natural world, Elizabeth Achtemeier quotes George Buttrick to the effect that, "We admire Sputnik and ignore the stars" ("How Do We Know?" Payton Lecture delivered at Fuller Theological Seminary, April 7, 1992, and later published in *Nature, God, and Pulpit* [Grand Rapids: Eerdmans, 1992], p. 2). C. S. Lewis says, "A dogmatic belief in objective value is necessary to the very idea of a rule which is not tyranny or an obedience which is not slavery" (*Abolition of Man*, pp. 84-85).

207. "The doctrine of creation pictures every finite being as not merely reflecting but embodying a divine intent" (Richard Norris, "Human Being," in G. Wainwright, ed., *Keeping the Faith* (Philadelphia: Fortress; Allison Park, Penn.: Pickwick, 1988), p. 91.

208. Calvin DeWitt, quoted by Steve Woodruff in a newsletter from the New Creation Institute, spring 1985; see also Moltmann, *Future of Creation*, p. 134.

change: we have already remarked that the command to fill the earth should not be pursued in the same way when the earth has already been overfilled. We do wrong if we allow our choices to be dictated by self-indulgence or ambition. Certainly we do not seize control and do whatever we please (Mt. 21:33-46 and parallels). We also do wrong if we act helpless and powerless and passive when with effort and action we could gain proper increase from the resources we have been given.

A good steward, though, would not expect her master to be pleased by a splendid bottom line obtained by using up all the master's capital. The general principles of not wasting (Ezk. 34:18), not exploiting (Prv. 12:10), and not destroying (Dt. 20:19; 22:6) must be honored. With respect to the world of living things, Noah's ark (Gn. 6:19ff.) provides a paradigm. Insofar as it lies with us, we should preserve, not rearrange or annihilate, the species. We should preserve them all, "unclean" (pests?) as well as "clean," for they all have their role. True, some distinctions may be made: the older version of the narrative commands that seven pairs of clean animals be preserved, in contrast with only two of the unclean. Presumably we are not required to preserve the largest possible complement of cockroaches or of tuberculosis bacilli.

Here is where we would differ from those, like Albert Schweitzer, who make life a supreme principle:

> Man is only truly ethical if he is obedient to the constraint to assist all life as he is able, and if he refrains from afflicting injury upon anything that lives. He does not ask in what way this or that form of life merits or does not merit sympathy as something valuable, nor does he enquire whether it is sensitive. Life as such is holy to him. He does not pluck a leaf from the tree, or pull a flower, or trample on an insect. (Schweitzer, quoted by Barth, *CD,* III/4, p. 349 [*KD,* III/4, p. 397])

Schweitzer's adherence to his beliefs in this regard was apparently so consistent that according to a newspaper report, a minister who visited his hospital in Lambarene found it "filthy beyond description," with insects and animals of all description allowed even in the operating room (*Los Angeles Times* clipping, no date).

We cannot go this far. For all the reverence we rightly have for life, it cannot become an absolute. Even at the level of human beings, Jesus himself made plain that seeking to save one's own life was a route to losing it (Mk. 8:35). After the Fall, animals were explicitly allowed for food and commanded for sacrifices. That these changes are consequences of sin suggests some reserve in our acting on them; but they are a reality in our current state.

Even so, the critical thing is that the unclean animals were also to be saved. As we survey our world, we doubtless see a lot of things we would not have made and think we would much rather do without. God, however, did make them. That we do not know what they are "good for" says more about our arrogance, our ignorance, our tendency to crassly utilitarian motives, and our failure to value what God values than it does about them. Therefore Noah's example of inclusive preservation is a good one to follow.[209] And the more we can live cooperatively with other creatures, the better. We might perhaps join the biblical image of the good shepherd with the image of the steward and the example of Noah; for now more than ever it should be evident to us that other creatures require protection (from us!) and benevolent care.

With regard to our use of inanimate nature, we have the model of the Sabbath and Jubilee years (even if the latter in particular were observed primarily in the breach), speaking to us of *limits* in our exploitation of the land and of cycles of work and rest for the whole creation (Ex. 23:10-11; Lv. 25). These, precisely because they refuse to wrest the largest possible return from the land at every moment, testify to dependence on God and not finally on our own labor. Only she who trusts can really rest; but it is powerful witness to God's superintendence of the order of creation that letting the land lie fallow serves to maintain its future productivity (Lv. 26:3-5, 32-35; see also 19:23-25 regarding letting trees mature before harvesting their fruit, and Is. 5:8 regarding joining fields together greedily: while the last comes in a context of lamenting injustice, the practical effect of eliminating hedgerows and creating large expanses of fields is environmental degradation). The need for refreshment, shared by people, domestic animals, and land, is built in to God's world. The good steward, then, will exercise her stewardship accordingly and not allow even urgent necessities to make her apply that relentless pressure that disobeys the Lord's command and inevitably mortgages the future for all (Ex. 34:21). She might also extend the sense of reserve inherent in the principle of not exploiting the land to reserve in use of other resources — not overharvesting the forests, not stripping the earth of its fossil fuels and minerals, and so on.

It speaks volumes about our refusal of the limits God has set and our inability to exercise moderation that it is so doubtful that Sabbath and especially Jubilee years were ever

---

209. Augustine says of those who devalue parts of the creation, like fire, frost, and wild beasts: "They do not consider how admirable these things are in their own places. . . . Even poisons, which are destructive when used injudiciously, become wholesome and medicinal when used in conformity with their qualities and design" (*City of God,* 11.22). "And therefore, where we are not so well able to perceive the wisdom of the Creator, we are very properly enjoined to believe it. . . . It is not with respect to our convenience or discomfort, but with respect to their own nature that the creatures are glorifying to their Artificer" (ibid., 12.4). Ruskin has a wonderful short description exalting the freedom, bravery, and irreverence of the common housefly (*The Cestus of Aglaia,* VI, quoted in Parrish, *Reading Aloud,* pp. 67-68).

fully observed. By analogy, today it seems that the only way to assure the land protection and rest is for conservation groups to buy it, often with the express purpose of letting it alone. (Although such groups are now usually interested not in agricultural land but in specialized habitats, the day may come when our agricultural land will survive only with such drastic measures.) Deforested or badly eroded land can sometimes be reclaimed with a measure of success, but only with a lot of time, effort, and money; and even then, results far from equal the virtues of the original land (A. Kent MacDougall, "Forest Reclamation: Last Resort After Conservation," *Los Angeles Times,* June 22, 1987, pt. I, pp. 1ff.). So again, the need for conservation and hence for respecting limits becomes clear — something that those churches that observe Rogation Days, when prayers for the blessing of the land and the harvest are offered, might well add to their focus in that season. Furthermore, some churches in the Midwest that have land holdings are being encouraged by the Church Land Project to model environmentally sound practices and to sell or lease only to those who commit to continuing such practices ("Land reform asked of churches," *Christian Century* 110, no. 12 [April 14, 1993]: 393).

Other kinds of reserve a good steward might exercise include refusing to use products that deplete rare species or resources or that threaten vulnerable ecosystems. Taking recycling seriously will not halt our rush to destruction, but it will slow it. Every ton of recycled paper saves seventeen trees, significantly reduces both pollution and energy and water use, and saves landfill space. Reasonable stewardship of one's own health will lead to informed choices of foodstuffs and household chemicals; and selective buying does exert pressure on producers. Choices to reduce driving and other energy use, to avoid aerosols with chlorofluorocarbons, and to shun polluting products do make a cumulative difference: even 1 percent of the car owners in the United States leaving their cars idle one day a week would save about 42 million gallons of gas per year. So, small as these steps may seem, at least they provide a start; and environmental groups can provide a great number of further constructive suggestions.

The stewardship component of a modest exercise of dominion, then, emphasizes responsibility before God: we will assuredly be called to account by God for what we have done with what he has given us, and no measure of short-term gain will enable us to evade the final accounting. Thus it also focuses on right use: not losing or exhausting the "capital," working for appropriate gains, joining energy to humility in carrying out its tasks. As representatives of the heavenly King, stewards seek to further his interests, not simply pursue their own. Integrity of dominion may be judged by whether it is employed for the *benefit* of what exists.[210]

210. Eberhard Jüngel, "Toward the Heart of the Matter," *Christian Century* 108, no. 7 (Feb. 27, 1991): 232. Having left the Communist East for the free West, Jüngel came to a new appreciation of the divine power in creation and therefore wants not to abandon the ideas of power and dominion but rather to seek their right application.

3. LOVE OF NEIGHBOR

The neighbor is not one *over* whom we rightly exercise dominion, but rather one in whose presence and to whose benefit or harm we exercise it. Part of the ambiguity of our technological achievements is that they both bind us together in so many ways, from the effects of communications systems to those of pollution, that no one is any longer so remote as *not* to be a neighbor; and also provide new ways and reasons to express hostility.

"Dispersion" — the spread of the race over the planet — is also ambiguous, resulting on the one hand from the divine command to fill the earth (Genesis 1:28; 9:1) and on the other from the curse of Genesis 11:7, whereby the confusion of tongues destroys human unity (René Motte, "Dispersion" [trans. John R. Crowley], in Léon-Dufour, ed., *Dictionary,* p. 126). While we have spoken above about the fundamental unity of humankind (pp. 390-92) — a unity reinforced by the universalism of the gospel (Mt. 28:19; 1 Cor. 10:17; Eph. 2:17-18) and one which we see as God's final as well as initial purpose — the emergence of nationalism and the desire to preserve racial and cultural distinctives, the fundamentalists' fear of one world and resistance to ecumenism, and distrust of the United Nations all show how firmly we cling to differences. These pressures for continued separations persist even as cultural interpenetration on a spherical planet (Teilhard) and intermarriage work more quietly in the opposite direction.

Nonetheless, we are all inevitably part of a single household (οἰκία) whose administration or economy (οἰκονομία) depends on understanding the relationships within the household, its ecology (a word that we have noted is also derived from οἶκος, as is "steward," οἰκονόμος, and "ecumenical," οἰκουμένη).[211]

This fundamental unity does not mean that there are not and will not continue to be inexplicable inequalities among members of the household. We see such inequalities already in the story of Cain and Abel, in which we are told only that God regards Abel's sacrifice and not Cain's — we are not told why. Indeed, the narrator seems at pains *not* to give a reason but to leave the mystery intact.[212] Some individuals continue to be born who are more generously endowed intellectually than their sisters and brothers; some nations have more natural resources than others. These inequalities have nothing to do, at the outset, with individual or national virtue; though we

211. Wesley Granberg-Michaelson, "Earth-Keeping," *ESA Update* 7, no. 4, p. 2; Otto Michel, "οἶκος, κτλ.," *TDNT,* 5.119-59.

212. Westermann, *Genesis 1–11,* p. 297. Of course, such mysteries hardly justify a Lockean defense of unequal and unlimited individual appropriation of assets, in which property rights are severed from social obligations (Black, *Dominion of Man,* pp. 70-71).

usually say that gifts bring additional responsibilities with them (Dt. 8:12-20). Inequalities do, however, predispose people to particular temptations. Cain's murderous envy we have recorded in Genesis 4; the equally or more murderous self-righteousness of the privileged whom we might suppose to be Abel's spiritual heirs is recorded in the contemporary media. In the latter case as well as the former, surely the blood of the murdered brother or sister cannot be hidden but cries out to God.[213] We are not solitary; we may not ignore or conceal our relationships to others. Even unintended victims who may be wholly anonymous to us are not anonymous to God.[214] And surely the duty to love our neighbor includes efforts on our part to penetrate the veil of anonymity and to look around the blinders we use to hide the effects of our actions from ourselves. If stewardship rightly seeks the good of the creation, love rightly seeks the good of the neighbor.

The good of the neighbor cannot now and never should have been thought of in terms of everyone attaining an upper-middle-class American standard of living. That the environment can sustain no such thing, we have seen; but more, nothing in Scripture suggests that a self-centered, consumption- and pleasure-driven style of life does anything for human dignity. Neither, however — and this is the point we who are comfortable must not forget — does grinding poverty.[215] (It could hardly be more obvious that rich and poor alike would, given a choice, pick the moral hazards faced by the rich over those faced by the poor, even if the former were more eternally threatening.) At the very minimum, we must ask what our anonymous neighbor needs to receive in order to maintain her human dignity, and what we need to be willing to give up to retrieve our own (1 Jn. 3:17).

It would be hard to argue that the Bible does not show particular concern for the poor and oppressed, that they might have the necessities

213. Note also that Gn. 9:6 prohibits killing on the grounds that humans are made in the divine image.

214. Garrison Keillor remarked that you can't get rich in a small town because everyone is always watching. If you take an expensive vacation, they wonder if you charged them too much for that car they bought from you (*American Radio Company,* Nov. 14, 1992). Contrast the effects of the *lack* of anonymity with the effects of the distance between the rich and the poor, not just in terms of knowledge but in terms of moral, social pressure from peers upon whom one depends. Recall also the way the anonymity and depersonalizing bigness of bureaucracies undo feelings of personal responsibility and hence reduce pressures favoring moral behavior.

215. For a description of the desperate struggle to maintain any dignity at all in the face of crushing want, see Dostoyevsky, *Brothers Karamazov,* pt. 2, bk. 4, chap. 7. And Gibbon wrote, "if we are more deeply affected by the ruin of a palace than by the conflagration of a cottage, our humanity must have formed a very erroneous estimate of the miseries of human life" (*Decline and Fall,* chap. 24).

of life (Dt. 10:18; Is. 58:6-12; Lk. 6:20-26, etc.). Those who gather up wealth in larger and larger barns (Lk. 12:13-18), ignore the poor (Lk. 16:19-31), or pretend more generosity than they actually exercise (Acts 5:1-11) meet bad ends. Nor is Scripture shy about speaking of some forms of redistribution of property (Lv. 25:8-55; 2 Cor. 9). In a world in which unlimited growth cannot continue, only redistribution of one kind or another will meet the basic needs of the poor. Surely our resistance to such ideas is as clear an indication as one could wish of our refusal to love our neighbors as ourselves (Lv. 19:18; Mt. 22:39; Mk. 12:31; Lk. 10:27; Rom. 13:9), even though some preliminary steps are virtually painless. Simply the reduction of waste by us all would supply the necessities of many (Mt. 14:20 and parallels); as could the modern analog of not reaping the edges of the fields, not taking all we can get, but deliberately and creatively leaving opportunities for others (Lv. 19:9). If Americans ate only 10 percent less meat, the grain saved annually could feed all the people on earth who now starve to death.[216] And it has been remarked that the wealth of affluent church members could restructure the global economy.[217] Furthermore, Scripture links justice for the poor and oppressed with promises of the earth's fruitfulness (Ps. 72). The enemy of God's giving is human covetousness.[218] While the promises are made on theological grounds, we might also see a practical link between giving up graspingness and greed with respect to our own possessions, and a changed, less exploitative attitude toward the earth, which allows its produce to flourish.

Particularly difficult is how to use fairly, share, and protect the so-called

216. Transmissions Project for the United Nations Environment Programme, "Personal Action Guide for the Earth" (n.d.), p. 3.

217. Granberg-Michaelson, *Worldly Spirituality*, p. 165. We spoke above of "redistribution of one kind or another," because some believe that the redistribution will be achieved by violence if in no other way (though others argue that the truly poor are too debilitated to do anything but fight among themselves). Whatever our doubts about the brands of liberation theology that justify violence as a last resort, we must acknowledge the truth of the remark that "Liberation theology is a theology for those who have fallen among thieves. But we are the thieves" (Hall, *Steward*, p. 98). Waste, and even withholding from those in need, was condemned as early as Gregory the Great (Black, *Dominion of Man*, pp. 63-64); and that old radical Thomas Aquinas wrote: "In cases of need all things are common property, so that there would seem to be no sin in taking another's property, for need has made it common. . . . If the need be so manifest and urgent, that it is evident that the present need must be remedied by whatever means be at hand (for instance when a person is in some imminent danger, and there is no other possible remedy), then it is lawful for a man to succor his own need by means of another's property, by taking it either openly or secretly: nor is this properly speaking theft or robbery" (*Summa Theologica*, pt. 2-2, q. 66, art. 7).

218. Gustaf Wingren, "The Doctrine of Creation: Not an Appendix but the First Article," *Word and World* 4, no. 4 (fall 1984): 363.

commons: those resources of air and water and land on which we all depend. Thus far we have used them as if we need consider nothing but immediate self-interest; and when pollution or depletion problems have surfaced, we have reacted with a surprised innocence that refuses blame or responsibility — that wants to act as if the problem does not exist.

Contrast response to the Love Canal disaster with that to natural disasters. The latter usually spark a rallying of community and sometimes even international support and help. But almost no one championed the cause of the victims of Love Canal. Nor were there those signs of hope, like sunshine after a flood, that promise relief. People were stuck with a problem not of their own direct making and one that others were loath to acknowledge at all. (Similarly with Chernobyl; immediate coverage and provision of help were considerable; but who wants to deal with the long-term effects? And affected residents have little recourse.) Some have suggested that only the church and church-related agencies may have the will and tenacity to tackle problems of this kind (James N. Brewster, "Love Canal: Redefining Disaster," *Christian Century* 99, no. 25 [Aug. 4-11, 1982]: 829-30).

Obviously, we need to find ways of managing community property that both appropriately assess costs for violating it and make it available to all. For instance, presumably love and justice alike declare that factories must not pollute rivers and that one country must not divert a river and deprive its neighbor of the water. Less clear is how to avoid making the poor continue to pay disproportionately for pollution control, whether as victims or through increased product costs or higher taxes assessed to cover cleanups. Likewise unclear is what should be included in the "commons" and *how* they should be protected (we have already spoken of the dilemma of centralized controls). Should we include the genetic endowments of plants and animals? Or can these be owned, bought, and sold? How about irreplaceable mineral resources? How about environments like rain forests, with their barely tapped riches? On what grounds does a person or country say an unqualified "Mine!" about such gifts to the whole human family? Perhaps we might take as a suggestive analogy the biblical attitude to the land, which was central to God's promise to Israel. Above all, it was the gift of God, to whom alone it finally belonged.[219] It was an inalienable

---

219. A somewhat similar attitude may be seen in the often-quoted letter of Chief Seattle of the Duwamish Tribe in Washington, written in 1855 to President Franklin Pierce: "The Great Chief in Washington sends word that he wishes to buy our land. How can you buy or sell the sky — the warmth of the land? The idea is strange to us. Yet we do not own the freshness of the air or the sparkle of the water. How can you buy them from us? Every part of this earth is sacred to my people. Every shiny pine needle, every sandy shore, every mist in the dark woods, every clearing and humming insect is holy in the memory and experience of my people."

inheritance of which even a king had no right to deprive a peasant (1 Kgs. 21), and at the same time available in measure for the common good of all (Dt. 23:24-25). It was not to be sold in perpetuity — an arrangement, insofar as it was followed, that would prevent the development of a large class of landless poor and another class of very rich (an increasingly important point today as land becomes proportionately scarcer and hence a source of ever greater power: observers of many developing countries consider land reform essential, but nearly impossible to achieve). Such an approach both allowed for and controlled private enterprise.[220] Support of laws and policies embodying such values and attitudes with respect to all the commons, mutatis mutandis, might be an appropriate task for prophetic voices today, with particular emphasis on handling all of God's gifts in such a way that none is forever lost to the human family or any part of it.

Love of the neighbor would also teach us to change our priorities in the development of our dominion, directing it toward making resources available to our fellow humans and not just toward national prestige and technological achievement for their own sake. We should promote not the most spectacular but the most appropriate technology: technology that spares the environment, employs people productively, and meets legitimate human needs. That is, not flashiness but contribution to the common good makes a suitable measuring rod.[221] And we should foster selective growth that benefits the poor without being resource-intensive. Here we lack not the capabilities so much as the will. The dollars spent on the Vietnam War could have revolutionized agriculture in the whole developing world. The space program has been terribly impressive as a tribute to our skill at the technical level, but our failure to make *any* inroads on poverty or the deterioration of the cities even in our own land at the same time (or instead!) should cause us dismay.[222] Viewing it all from a distance, a Nicaraguan poet wrote:

220. See Harper, *Deuteronomy,* chap. 20, pp. 357-59.
221. Consider, for example, the Swiss-educated West German zoologist Dagmar Werner, who is using her doctorate earned studying iguanas to help Costa Ricans learn to raise them, thus providing a source of food and (the larger goal) preserving the rain forest that would otherwise be cut down to provide space for crops and cattle (Richard Boudreaux, "It's Feed an Iguana, Save a Tree," *Los Angeles Times,* Jan. 31, 1989, pt. I, p. 1).
222. Ian G. Barbour, "On to Mars?" *Christian Century* 86, no. 47 (Nov. 19, 1969): 1478-80. "In fact, few scientists would claim that the scientific benefits derived from the moon flight and the space program as a whole justify their enormous cost" (ibid., p. 1497). One can only wonder if this sober judgment of more than twenty-five years ago will still be being fruitlessly repeated another twenty-five years hence. We recognize, of course, both that human beings are so constituted that they want to pursue knowledge and achievement for more than purely pragmatic reasons, and that practical consequences often spin off unexpectedly from "pure" research. We simply argue here for a greater sense of proportion between means and ends.

The apollo 2 cost more than the apollo 1
the apollo 1 cost enough.

. . . .

The apollo 8 cost a whole lot but you didn't feel it
because the astronauts were protestants
they read the bible from the moon,
bringing glad tidings to all christians
and Pope Paul VI blessed them when they returned.

. . . .

The parents of the people of Acahualinca were
    less hungry than the people who live there now.
The parents died of hunger.

. . . .

Blessed are the poor, for they shall inherit the moon.[223]

4. THE VALUE OF BEAUTY, GRATITUDE, AND CONTENTMENT

Because our duties are real and our mishandling of them has been serious, discussion of our dominion can take on a rather grim tone. However, just as important as emphasizing obligations is reaffirming and celebrating the goodness of creation and enjoying the powers that allow us to experience it. These can all be compromised by an exclusively activistic sense of responsibility as well as by the lust to control and possess and dominate.

Part of the reason we want to protect the natural world is simply that it is beautiful, and human beings respond to beauty.[224] טוֹב, "good" (Gn. 1), has overtones of "pleasant" or "beautiful"; and in Genesis 2:15 a kind of amenity provided and to be maintained comes even before mention of food. Matthew 26:28-29 celebrates the beauty of wildflowers. Luther believed that apart from the Fall, people would not have used the creatures to obtain food, clothing, or money; "they would have made use of the creatures only for the admiration of God and for a holy joy which is unknown to us in this corrupt state of nature."[225]

---

223. Leonel Rugama, a Nicaraguan activist killed by government forces in 1970. Source unknown.

224. For our general discussion of this capacity, see above, pp. 96-99.

225. *Lectures on Genesis: Chapters 1–5,* trans. George V. Schick, ed. Jaroslav Pelikan, Luther's Works (St. Louis, Mo.: Concordia, 1958), 1.71. Contrast this attitude with those who believe that the only way to preserve the rainforests is to make them economically productive ("Amazon," *Los Angeles Times,* Jan. 22, 1989, p. 16).

Now if I believe in God's Son and bear in mind that He became man, all creatures will appear a hundred times more beautiful to me than before. Then I will properly appreciate the sun, the moon, the stars, trees, apples, and pears, as I reflect that He is Lord over all and the Center of all things.[226]

Similarly, affirming the immanence of God in the world as well as his transcendence over it may help us to perceive the glory of the creation and of God: Calvin taught that we should ponder deeply God's wisdom, justice, goodness, and power in all creatures; and Milton wrote,

> In contemplation of created things
> By steps we may ascend to God.[227]

We have already noted that the aesthetic sense relates to the intellect as well as the eye: scientists see beauty in the way things fit together. Perhaps emphasizing this side of the scientific endeavor that has to do with understanding and delight, rather than the offshoots that rush to produce changes, best suits our current situation. In fact, Augustine identified dominion with understanding, not with the exercise of power.[228]

Many have observed that when commercialization, overcontrol, and exploitation prevail, amenity is the first thing to go:

> I think that I shall never see
> A billboard lovely as a tree.
> Indeed, unless the billboards fall
> I'll never see a tree at all![229]

Others have complained that concern about billboards hardly suffices if no one is dealing with the ugliness of bumper-to-bumper traffic and urban

226. *Sermons on the Gospel of St. John: Chapters 1–4*, trans. Martin H. Bertram, ed. Jaroslav Pelikan, Luther's Works (St. Louis, Mo.: Concordia, 1957), 22.496.

227. *Institutes*, 1.14.21; and note 1.5.6; *Paradise Lost*, 5.511-12. See also Moltmann, *God in Creation*, pp. 13-15.

228. "That he judgeth all things, this answers to his having dominion. . . . This he doth by the understanding of his mind" (*Confessions*, 13.23.33). In its focus on creation, wisdom literature avoids stressing power and control and imposition of order but emphasizes mutuality and trust and observing orderliness (Robert K. Johnston, "Wisdom Literature and Its Contribution to a Biblical Environmental Ethic," in Granberg-Michaelson, ed., *Tending the Garden*, pp. 66-82). Luther said that we would die of wonder if we truly understood the growth of a grain of wheat (Paul Santmire, *The Travail of Nature* [Philadelphia: Fortress, 1985], p. 130).

229. Ogden Nash, "Song of the Open Road," *The Selected Verse of Ogden Nash* (New York: Modern Library, 1945), p. 97.

squalor.[230] Surely both points demand attention. On the one hand, even affluent human beings seem to have a need to escape from the artificiality and noise of any city environment and to find the beauty of nature restorative. Insofar as their distance from the natural world has become so great that this is not the case — insofar as they *stop* seeing beauty in the natural world and instead see only a commodity or a puzzle, and insofar as they are physically so removed as not to observe the negative effects of their actions on the environment — they will assuredly act destructively. On the other hand, deteriorating inner cities are a human and environmental disaster that squelch life and imagination even before they do bodily harm to their inhabitants, who usually cannot escape them. Obviously, those worried about ecology must be concerned for human as well as animal habitats. But note that it is precisely the ugliness of these city environments that immediately and viscerally alerts us to the fact that something is terribly wrong. We cannot simply put resources into human needs *instead* of beauty, since beauty is a human need and its lack usually points to other problems as well.[231]

Those whose hearts are moved by the beauty of the creation may be further moved by thanksgiving to God for his gifts. Gratitude that our needs are supplied may be heightened by the recognition that the Lord has done so much more for our enjoyment than would have been necessary had he simply wanted some creatures who would somehow manage to survive. The abundant life of nature breaks forth in the chorus of praise in which all creatures join (Ps. 98:8; 148; Is. 42:10-11); but joyful gratitude particularly behooves human beings (Dt. 28:47; Ps. 95:2; 100:4; Rom. 1:21; Phil. 4:6; Col. 2:7; 3:15; 4:2, etc.). Expressing praise and thanksgiving not only affirms our creaturely relationship to God but also helps us to recognize the goodness around us and in a sense increases and completes our enjoyment.[232] We might also speak of humankind as made to be nature's priest, to be the mouthpiece for all creation. Although galaxies and hummingbirds glorify God, they do not know what they do. Human beings who do know should therefore articulate praise for all.[233]

Gratitude and praise conduce to contentment, a great and necessary virtue in a society that appears to have no concept of "enough" (1 Tm. 6:6-9;

---

230. Goodman, "Can Technology Be Humane?" p. 233.

231. The poor, too, may wish to preserve what they see as attractive: the *Los Angeles Times* juxtaposed pictures of Calcutta's spotless billion-dollar subway and its squalid city streets. It quoted a rider: "This is ours. We feel that we cannot hurt it or let others hurt it" (Jan. 18, 1987, pt. I, p. 1).

232. "The duty exists for the delight" (C. S. Lewis, *Reflections on the Psalms* [New York: Harcourt, Brace & World, 1958], p. 97; see all of chap. 9).

233. See Moltmann, *God in Creation,* pp. 70-71.

see also Lk. 3:14; Phil. 4:11; Heb. 13:5).[234] Without development of a deeply felt sense of enough, there is simply no hope for the environment. But of things taken alone, beyond the certain minimum necessary for a decent existence, there can never be enough, which is why mere moralizing against luxury does not work: "since man cannot help seeking the infinite, he now seeks the meaning of his life in an infinity of things."[235] The search destroys the very relationships that could moderate it, loosening the bonds of community with people and the created order.[236] And it seduces us into thinking that real solutions to our problems will come with technological "fixes" or a bit more recycling, when inner change is actually what is required.

Interestingly enough, the early ascetical tradition recognized that we must moderate our appetites even to maintain our power of enjoyment. Demand to possess something (including health and life itself) cannot coexist with delight in it.[237] It seems that only profound reappropriation of something like this wisdom will enable us to say a firm No to continuing temptations to increase our power or to use to its destructive utmost the power we have. We need an intellectual asceticism that simply refuses to do all we can do.[238] Such an asceticism requires sacrifices that may, at least

234. "The solution for the third world's problems is that the poorest of the poor have enough; the need of the first world is that we must learn what *is* enough" (an interview with Job Ebenezer, "A Third World Christian Responds to Worldwide Concerns," *Theology, News and Notes,* December 1992, p. 22). "It makes no sense to propose a minimum income unless you define a maximum one — nobody can ever get enough who does not know what is enough" (Ivan Illich, "Education: A Consumer Commodity and a Pseudo-Religion," *Christian Century* 88, no. 50 [December 15, 1971]: 1467). "As I see it, the Christian's main task is to define the economic concept of 'enough.' If there is no concept of 'enough,' all problems become insoluble" (E. F. Schumacher, "Small Is Beautiful: Toward a Theology of 'Enough,' " *Christian Century* 88, no. 30 [July 28, 1971]: 902).

235. Brunner, *Divine Imperative,* p. 392.

236. When we consider the centrality of human relationships to people's sense of well-being, we should also recall that choices of types of technology to employ are also choices of forms of social interaction (Barbour, *Technology, Environment, and Human Values,* p. 303): for everyone who feels more connected to like-minded colleagues by virtue of E-mail, there are probably dozens who feel depersonalized by voice mail. It is hard even to imagine how social reality is reshaped for those who do much of their socializing (often anonymously) in on-line "chat rooms": the freedom from stereotyping by gender or appearance that many laud comes at the cost of a curious disembodiment and a lack of the restraints imposed by having to take public responsibility for one's views.

237. Margaret R. Miles, *Fullness of Life* (Philadelphia: Westminster, 1981), p. 40.

238. Although refusals to do all one can are rare, they are not absolutely unprecedented: Sweden intends to decomission all its nuclear power plants by the year 2005; Germany has placed strict limits on genetic engineering; the United States declined to develop a supersonic commercial airplane. In the sixteenth century, Japan, which became a weapons exporter shortly after firearms were introduced there, phased out gun production because it began to undermine the social status of sword-wielding samurai. When Commodore Perry "opened"

in some respects, seem greater and more arbitrary than the older bodily asceticism, since it means refraining from development and use of some technologies that could save lives and suffering, on the grounds that employing them entails too large a threat of destroying all of life. Seeking at any cost to prevent death inevitably leads to death — not only spiritual (Mk. 8:35) but also physical and moral.

Technological steps toward conquering death produce the need to foster death if overpopulation and increasing poverty are not to prevail: consider the problems of euthanasia and abortion as well as lifeboat ethics. What humanizes and what dehumanizes thus march forward hand in hand. Success in "conquering" nature seems to demand, as a result of the success and not only as a means, a certain brutality. Take the particularly wrenching, technologically generated dilemma of what to do in response to medicine's success in doing what often results in prolonging dying — at enormous financial cost, costs in deflection of resources from primary care of the poor, and cost in suffering to the patient. Despite knowing these costs, most of us who have such choices available to us can hardly bear the thought of not doing everything that might possibly preserve the life of a loved one. Our power confounds not only our wisdom but also our love. On a larger scale, consider the likelihood that deaths resulting from *not* relying on nuclear power and genetic engineering may prove fewer and in many cases kinder than those resulting from their use.

The corollary we have so much difficulty appropriating is that turning from our desperate attempts to secure life and happiness enables us to receive them from God's hand. Tilling and *keeping* the garden (Gn. 2:15) is fully consonant with great delight, provided only that the God-given limits are observed (2:17).

> Shame on us, who about us Babel bear,
> And live in Paradise, as if God was not there![239]

5. A VIEW TO GOD'S FUTURE

The future we cannot secure on our own and scarcely dare hope for on secular terms is a future God has secured for us, and not only for us alone but also for the rest of creation. We read of the creation longing to be set

---

Japan in 1855, a U.S. Navy commodore ridiculed Japanese innocence of firearms as a sign of primitiveness, apparently not comprehending that a people could deliberately have given up so powerful a tool (Gabrielle Strobel, "VTSS grads explore relationship of science, society — and get paid," *Stanford Observer,* July-August 1993, p. 4).

239. From the poem for the day of St. Matthew the Apostle in John Keble, *The Christian Year* (Philadelphia: E. H. Butler, 1867), pp. 311-12.

free from its bondage to decay and to obtain the freedom of the glory of the children of God (Rom. 8:21); of God gathering up and reconciling all things in Christ (Eph. 1:9-10; Col. 1:20); of the restoration of all things (Acts 3:21). How these promises relate to those others speaking of destruction of the earth by God's judgment (e.g., Zeph. 1:2-3; Joel 2:3; 2 Pt. 3:10-12; but cf. 2 Pt. 3:13), and how we should conceive and "locate" heaven, belong properly to the treatment of eschatology. Here we are concerned only to affirm that the Lord's plans concern more than just us human beings. The point is important to our exercise of dominion because we relate differently to that which has a future than to that which will be done away *simpliciter*.

The shorter-term future with which we must be concerned is plainly earthly — the bodily future we anticipate for ourselves and our descendants. God's covenant gift of the land was to Abraham and his offspring "forever" (Gn. 13:15; cf. Rom. 4:13). But God's judgment also visits the sins of the parents on the children (Ex. 20:5; 34:7; Nu. 14:18; Dt. 5:9), a judgment for which environmental degradation is a stunningly effective vehicle. Our children will be the ones to know deeply the meaning of West German poet Erich Fried's lines:

> Whoever wants the world
> to stay as it is
> doesn't really want the world
> to stay.[240]

Their earthly future depends on our making changes now, not waiting until evidence of the unsustainability of our behavior becomes utterly undeniable by everyone — by which time it is almost certain to be too late. Ecologists generally advocate combining a long-range and global perspective with action at the local level: "The right scale in work gives power to affection. When one works beyond the reach of one's love for the place one is working in, and for the things and creatures one is working with and among, then

---

240. Quoted by Hall, *Steward*, p. 230. Chief Seattle said, "The whites too, shall pass — perhaps sooner than other tribes. Continue to contaminate your bed and you will one night suffocate in your own waste" (letter to President Pierce). But he could not have known how they would threaten everyone's survival. Speaking out of a humanistic context, Schell says, "Evil becomes radical whenever it goes beyond destroying individual victims (in whatever numbers) and, in addition, mutilates or destroys the *world* that can in some way respond to — and thus in some measure redeem — the deaths suffered. . . . When crimes are of a certain magnitude and character, they nullify our power to respond to them adequately because they smash the human context in which human losses normally acquire their meaning for us" (*Fate of the Earth*, p. 145).

destruction inevitably results."[241] The Christian has the added motive of seeking to love what the Lord loves, which can help affection for particular creatures and places to broaden our vision rather than narrow it:

> He prayeth best, who loveth best
> All things both great and small;
> For the dear God who loveth us,
> He made and loveth all.[242]

Love for something carries the implication of a desire that it reach its proper end (Rom. 8:20-21; cf. Ps. 107:33-34). Here the theologian might extend the rubric of salvation to apply it to the natural order, which has become cursed on our account (Col. 1:23), with the role of humankind being extended to include that of reconciler. After the Fall, that is, the human power of dominion has not only been corrupted but also confronts a changed natural world that needs redemption and healing. Thinking of dominion as if the Fall had not occurred is not appropriate.

Note how the element of incompleteness and hope contrasts with efforts to ensure a future of our own design, whether by construction of an enclosed "biosphere" presumably able to support life for two years at a time (Thomas H. Maugh II, "Biosphere II," *Los Angeles Times,* Aug. 7, 1989, pt. II, p. 3; only two years? and what if the generator fails? Obviously, the inhabitants count on an ability to leave in case of real disaster, an option inhabitants of biosphere I, Earth, do not have!) or by desperate attempts to protect the earth by legislating environmental rights, after the model of human rights. We agree that there is at least some analogy between the oppression of nature and the oppression of people, an analogy picked up long ago by both Thoreau and English evangelical antislavery reformer William Wilberforce, each of whom had concerns for animals as well as for people (J. Ronald Engle, "Teaching the Eco-Justice Ethic: The Parable of the Billerica Dam," *Christian Century* 104, no. 16 [May 13, 1987]: 466-69). We also affirm that environmental destruction can hardly be significantly reduced apart from legislative constraints, as Justice William O. Douglas recognized back in 1972 (Richard Cartwright Austin, "Three Axioms for Land Use," *Chris-*

241. Wendell Berry, "Out of Your Car, Off Your Horse," *Atlantic Monthly* 267, no. 2 (February 1991), p. 63. This seemingly simple advice is not so simple in practice, for as Berry also remarks, "Ecological good sense will be opposed by all the most powerful economic entities of our time, because ecological good sense requires the reduction or replacement of those entities" (ibid., p. 62). On the issue of living beyond our environmental means, we note the complaint of a marquis residing in a castle and bewailing the financial drain of trying to live by modern standards in such circumstances: "In fact, we are an oppressed minority living a nightmare" (*Los Angeles Times,* Dec. 31, 1980, pt. I, p. 1) — increasingly the situation of the whole developed world.

242. Samuel Taylor Coleridge, "The Rime of the Ancient Mariner," in Oscar Williams, ed., *The Mentor Book of Major British Poets* (New York: Mentor, 1963), p. 124.

tian Century 94, no. 32 [Oct. 12, 1977]: 910-15). Thus we are far more sympathetic to (indeed, supportive of) the idea of strong legal protection for the environment we have than we are to constructing artificial environments to save us from our folly. We argue only that even worthy goals of protection, however necessary, are stopgap measures that remain compromised both by the limits of our vision of the Lord's purposes and by the limits on our legislative power. That is, we need hope for a far surer future than these expedients can provide.

Given the curse and human enmity with nature, it is most remarkable that renewal for human beings does still come through the elements of nature, most particularly in the bread and wine of the Lord's Supper. The Supper also confirms to us our hope of the resurrection of our bodies, a hope that leads naturally to the further hope of the recreation of the natural order of which our bodies are a part.[243] And the Supper can remind us of the nature of the dominion exercised by him in whose memory we celebrate it and to whom the whole idea of the dominion of Psalm 8 is referred in Hebrews 2:5-9. That the New Testament applies the psalm to Jesus does not mean that ordinary mortals have no real dominion; it means only that we have it not through our own technical skill but through Jesus, in whom alone we can see it aright.[244] What we have done on our own has miscarried; we do not see all things in subjection to us; our dominion has never been fully achieved. In Christ, it shall be. In Christ we have the truly righteous and benevolent king in whose reign the earth can indeed rejoice (Ps. 97:1; 1 Cor. 15:27-28).[245]

Thus we come to our anticipation of the longer-term future of the creation, when Christ's reign is without obstacle and *all things* are made new (Is. 65:17; 66:22; 2 Pt. 3:13; Rv. 21:1, 5). That the biblical images are far from our present experience while yet reminding us of it should make us neither homesick for some lost golden age nor despairing of the present, but rather hopeful with a hope that gives us new eyes and hearts for what God made and that for which he still has plans. "The garden [of Gn. 1–3] has become the city [of Rv. 21–22], but the city is reminiscent of the garden."[246] The earth will pour forth its goodness (Is. 55:12-13; Joel 3:18;

243. Lampe, "New Testament Doctrine of *Ktisis,*" pp. 455-56.

244. See Brunner, *Man in Revolt,* p. 409, n. 1; Barth, *CD,* III/1, p. 206 (*KD,* III/1, pp. 232-33).

245. Recall our discussion above of the image and the benevolent king, pp. 351-57.

246. Ronald Manahan, "Christ as the Second Adam," in DeWitt, ed., *Environment and the Christian,* p. 46. In the light of Rv. 22:1-2, we prefer this perspective to that which would set city and garden against each other as alternative and mutually exclusive views, as in Cowper's line, "God made the country, and man made the town" (in his poem "The Task," bk. 1, l. 749, *The Poetical Works of William Cowper,* ed. H. S. Milford, 3rd ed. [London:

and note the symbolism of Jn. 2:1-11). We will have fellowship once again with the animal kingdom (Is. 11:6-8; 43:19-21; 65:17-25; Hos. 2:18; but cf. Lv. 26:6; Ezk. 34:25). We will know what St. Francis meant when he spoke of all creatures — sun and moon and stars, wind and air and cloud and all weather, water and earth and fruits and flowers — as his kindred, in a tone wholly different from that of mere mastery.[247] The marvel of a world where life is possible will have become the greater marvel of one that freely and without impediment manifests God's glory (Is. 35; Rv. 5:13), one in which we along with all other creatures play our parts in the freedom of the glory of the children of God (Rom. 8:21).

Oxford University Press, 1926]; see also bk. 1, ll. 681-92, for comment on vices bred in cities; and bk. 3, ll. 721-27, for wonderment at human lack of appreciation for nature). The picture of a city reminiscent of a garden may also, by force of contrast, help us to see part of what is wrong with many of our own cities.

247. See his famous "Canticle of the Sun," cited in Schaff, *History,* 5.407-8 — a strong antidote to our proud refusal to identify with nature.

A Wider Sympathy

A Sermon Preached by Marguerite Shuster
at La Verne Heights Presbyterian Church, La Verne, California,
Lord's Day, August 29, 1993.

I consider that the sufferings of this present time are not worth comparing with the glory about to be revealed to us. For the creation waits with eager longing for the revealing of the children of God; for the creation was subjected to futility, not of its own will but of the will of the one who subjected it, in hope that the creation itself will be set free from its bondage to decay and will obtain the freedom of the glory of the children of God. We know that the whole creation has been groaning in labor pains until now; and not only the creation, but we ourselves, who have the first fruits of the Spirit, groan inwardly while we wait for adoption, the redemption of our bodies. For in hope we were saved.

Romans 8:18-24a (NRSV)

"The question from agnosticism," says writer Annie Dillard, "is, Who turned on the lights? The question from faith is, Whatever for?"[a] Because when you look closely at the world of nature — which is what Dillard spends her time examining — what you see does not inspire unqualified confidence in the designer of it all, despite the beauties and marvels some of us may have recently extolled while reporting on our summer vacations. The waste! The violence! The tornadoes and earthquakes and floods! The

a. *Pilgrim at Tinker Creek* (New York: Harper & Row, 1974), p. 144.

fleas. The poison oak. It's enough to make a bitter cynic like Housman observe in famous and memorable lines:

> We for a certainty are not the first,
> Have sat in taverns while the tempest hurled
> Their hopeful plans to emptiness, and cursed
> Whatever brute and blackguard made the world.[b]

Or more than enough to make a Christian believer like Pascal say that he could see too much of God in nature to deny but too little to be sure, leaving him in a state of doubt and concern.[c]

Why would a God who is *not* a brute and blackguard turn on the lights to reveal a world of so much suffering? The long-term answer, says my text, has everything to do with a hope so glorious that "the sufferings of this present time are not worth comparing" with it; but the short-term answer has something to do with the creation suffering a bondage not of its own making. One of the wonderful things about this passage is the tremendous sympathy Paul expresses for the natural world. It is in pain, says Paul. It, like us, longs eagerly — as if stretching out its neck in anticipation — for freedom. But it must wait for us, who long ago were given dominion over it but have terribly misused our powers, to its ruin and our own.

Sympathy for the creation, the kind of sympathy Paul shows in this text, has hardly been our dominant response to it. Far from it. We have distanced ourselves from our world. The child today is seldom taught to contemplate the creation with an open heart but, as someone put it, "the mysteries of nature are drummed into his head as if they were paragraphs in the penal code."[d] Oh yes, there was a romantic era when some philosophers and literary lights thought that if we could just return to the pure state of nature, all the ills of civilization would vanish. Such fantasies are remarkably susceptible to cure by encounter with a few underfed mosquitoes. Fear makes more sense than romanticism: nature not the savior but the enemy, in the guise of rattlesnake, lion, hurricane. Shoot them down! The hurricane refuses to fall? Then maintain the illusion of control by killing every lion you can find. In moments of comparative calm, take nature the resource. Take it, indeed — take ivory until the elephants are gone; take oil until the wells run dry and the sky blackens; take mahogany until the rainforests and all their creatures have given way to desert. Or

b. Quoted by C. E. M. Joad, *God and Evil* (London: Faber & Faber, 1942), p. 62.
c. *Pensées*, no. 229.
d. Arthur Koestler, *The Act of Creation* (1964; reprint, London: Arkana, 1989), p. 295.

take apart nature the puzzle, all the way down to the atoms and genes near
the core of matter and life. Surely, if we can take things apart, we can put
them back together again? So thinks every kid who has just pried the back
off grandpa's watch to see exactly where the tick is located. But whatever
our doubts about some of these enterprises, or at least about results that
have proved more harmful than we ever guessed back when the world
seemed vaster and hardier than it does today, we still seem io have trouble
seeing the world as Paul does, as our suffering fellow creature.

No doubt we have more trouble yet seeing its disarray, its threats and
thorns and thistles, as fundamentally our own fault. Or, even if we do, we
don't seem to do very well at changing our behavior. We're rather like the
construction worker who, each noon, opened his lunch sack and inspected
his sandwich. If it was peanut butter, he threw it out. If it was anything
else, he ate it. After watching this ritual for months, one of his buddies
said, "Hey! You've been married for more than ten years. Doesn't your
wife know yet that you don't like peanut butter?" The fellow responded
indignantly, "You leave my wife out of it! I make these sandwiches myself!"

We've made the creation the mess it is. And we go right on making
messes. When Paul refers to it as "subjected to futility, not of its own will
but by the will of him who subjected it," he is recalling God's curse on
creation because of Adam and Eve's sin. Remember Genesis 3:17-18? "To
Adam [God] said, 'Because you have listened to the voice of your wife,
and have eaten of the tree about which I commanded you, "You shall not
eat of it," cursed is the ground because of you; in toil you shall eat of it
all the days of your life; thorns and thistles it shall bring forth for you'"
(NRSV). And the man and woman were forever driven out of the garden,
that one place where their dominion over nature had not meant enmity with
it and where their work had not been fretful toil.

It gets worse. Isaiah picks up the theme, as you may recall from our
Old Testament lesson: "The earth shall be utterly laid waste and utterly
despoiled; for the LORD has spoken this word. The earth dries up and
withers, the world languishes and withers; the heavens languish together
with the earth. The earth lies polluted under its inhabitants; for they have
transgressed laws, violated the statutes, broken the everlasting covenant.
Therefore a curse devours the earth" (Is. 24:3-6a NRSV). Human sin affects
— we might almost say infects — our material surroundings, as if there
were a sort of moral sympathy between us and our world.[e] By God's own
judgment, what we have corrupted refuses to support us.

e. See George Adam Smith, *Book of Isaiah*, 1.417-19.

How modern it all sounds. Isaiah could never have dreamed how literally we would pollute our world. He didn't have in mind acid rain that would kill lakes and forests, or DDT that would so accumulate that now its concentration in people (not to mention Antarctic penguins) means you couldn't legally sell most mother's milk. He knew nothing of smog or of nuclear waste like the plutonium that takes 250,000 years — more than twice as long as so-called modern human beings have walked this earth — to lose its power to kill. Yet the course people have taken has come closer and closer to making Isaiah's vision of desolation a reality. In the words of Loren Eiseley:

> It is with the coming of man that a vast hole seems to open in nature, a vast black whirlpool spinning faster and faster, consuming flesh, stones, soil, minerals, sucking down the lightning, wrenching power from the atom, until the ancient sounds of nature are drowned in the cacophony of something which is no longer nature, something instead which is loose and knocking at the world's heart, something demonic and no longer planned — escaped, it may be — spewed out of nature, contending in a final giant's game against its master.[f]

A giant's game. We humans warring against nature; nature wreaking revenge. Nature carrying God's judgment against us, in more theological language, a judgment we are less and less confident of being able by some new exercise of technological ingenuity to escape. Witness, for instance, how the draining of wetlands and building of levees to keep the Mississippi within bounds has appeared to result in increasing the violence of the great flood when it finally came. We are at cross-purposes with our world.

But look back to Paul. This natural world that seems so recalcitrant, that refuses simply to bend pliantly to human maneuvering without exacting high and often unexpected costs, was not made to be our enemy. Paul describes its current state as a state of futility. Futility? Inability to reach its proper end, that is; inability for it freely to show forth all its magnificent properties to the glory of God, but instead being made subject to human sin. Bound to decay, to death. Groaning. Suffering agony, says Paul. Creation, like us, was meant for something better.

What would happen if we extended our sympathy to nature's pain; if, instead of exercising that kind of arrogant dominion that sees nature only as an opponent or a resource, we sought to tailor our behavior to its struggle? It's a hard question to answer, because another's pain — even the pain of another human being — is an inaccessible mystery. We cannot

f. *Firmament of Time*, pp. 123-24.

feel what it is like so as to take it at its full weight. Worse, we cannot "fix" it, any more than we can in our present state simply "fix" our struggling earth. Yet we cannot just disregard it, either. Sometimes what is required in the face of real pain is a deeply respectful restraint, the kind of attentive presence that tacitly acknowledges that "doing something" — doing just about anything at all — will only make things worse. An antidote to our pride may be acknowledging our terrible impotence. It's like the story of the atomic physicist, a prime architect of the atomic bomb, who was walking one day in the woods with a friend. He came upon a small tortoise. Delighted at the thought of being able to take it home to surprise his children with it, he picked it up and began to walk off.

After a few steps he paused and surveyed the tortoise doubtfully.
"What's the matter?" asked his friend.
Without responding, the great scientist slowly retraced his steps as precisely as possible, and gently set the turtle down upon the exact spot from which he had taken him up.
Then he turned solemnly to his friend. "It just struck me," he said, "that perhaps for one man, I have tampered enough with the universe." He turned, and left the turtle to wander on its way.g

Perhaps our first act of sympathy with nature's groaning should be an act of humility; a question to ourselves as to whether we do well to tamper further; a willingness, even at apparent cost to ourselves, to let atoms and genes and some tortoises alone. The better we know God's claim on both us and the whole creation he made good, the more we will see, and care about, the whole creation's pain.

But Paul's wonderful sympathy with creation's pain is only half the secret of this text. The other half of the secret is that the contortions, whatever they might look like, are not death pangs but birth pangs. The Lord is preparing something wonderful. What, exactly, we don't know, but it is something Paul describes in terms of the liberty of the glory of the children of God, and what Scripture calls elsewhere a new heaven and a new earth — *all things* made new. The most extreme ruin of nature by our sin can no more thwart the Lord's purposes for it than our ruin of ourselves by our sin can thwart the God who has determined to save precisely the ungodly. So we are also called to sympathize with nature's hope.

It isn't a hope independent of us, as some nature lovers — those who speak as if everything would be fine if humans would just disappear —

g. Ibid., p. 148.

suppose. Scripture clearly gives human beings a primacy of place; but it is a primacy that makes human importance *inclusive,* not *exclusive.* Nature's claims and our own must not be set in opposition to one another, as if it were, for instance, a simple question of the spotted owl versus human needs. No; we abide or go down together. If nature's bondage has to do with our disobedience, its hope of glory is just as tightly linked to our redemption. Note: our redemption, not some new technological triumph. Creation's groaning is, literally, a "groaning together"; creation's suffering of birth pangs is a "suffering agony together"; words suggesting better than the most passionate ecologist the profound interrelatedness of the whole created order. In short, we're all in this together.

What would it mean, then, to sympathize with nature's hope as well as its suffering? Especially now, before the Lord's return, before we are finally revealed as God's children; while sin and death still plague us and seduce us into misusing this earth? The simplest answer probably has to do with recognizing that God loves this world and has given it a future. What someone we love loves makes a claim on us. Perhaps therein lies the truth of the old Jewish teaching that anyone who loves God while hating or despising his creation will in the end hate God.[h]

We cannot save the world or fully restore it, any more than we can save or restore ourselves. That's God's job. But in our own eager anticipation of what God is going to do, we can sympathize with nature's hope by turning our hearts not first to defend against it or exploit it, but first to love it. Dostoyevsky had Father Zosima in *The Brothers Karamazov* say it this way:

> Love all God's creation, the whole and every grain of sand in it. Love every leaf, every ray of God's light. Love the animals, love the plants, love everything. If you love everything, you will perceive the divine mystery in things. . . . Love the animals: God has given them rudiments of thought and joy untroubled. Do not trouble it, don't harass them, don't deprive them of their happiness, don't work against God's intent. Man, do not pride yourself on superiority to the animals; they are without sin, and you, with your greatness, defile the earth by your appearance on it, and leave traces of your foulness after you — alas, it is true of every one of us![i]

It is true. The earth is corrupt and spoiled because we ourselves are sinners and because, being sinners, we have used our powers over nature

h. Elie Wiesel, *Souls on Fire,* trans. Marion Wiesel (New York: Summit, 1972), p. 72.
i. Trans. Constance Garnett (New York: Modern Library, 1950), pp. 382-83.

so as increasingly to destroy it. But the final word is not apocalyptic judgment, whether the bang of a nuclear explosion or the multiplied whimpers of one species after another going down in extinction. The final word is that we who love Christ together with the whole creation shall come at last to a better end than we can possibly imagine, the liberty of the glory of the children of God. And that's why God turned on the lights.

Index of Subjects

Index of Names

Aaron, Henry (Hank), 117-18
Abelard, Peter, 209-13
Achtemeier, Elizabeth, 448n.206
Althaus, Paul, 219n.105
Apollinaris, 44
Aquinas, Thomas, 36, 41, 42, 57, 64,
   65, 97, 142-43, 143n.10, 173, 181,
   193, 197, 274-75, 275n.167, 293,
   294n.195, 294n.196, 322, 353, 384,
   394n.63, 454n.217
Aristotle, 41, 65, 142, 173, 322, 410
Athanasius, 56
Augustine, 6, 15, 63, 64, 79, 134, 160,
   193, 196, 203, 219, 231-32, 275,
   293, 300, 384, 450n.209, 458

Bacon, Francis, 366-67
Bailey, D. S., 161, 172, 175, 176,
   176n.53, 214-15, 216, 230n.117,
   270, 327n.254
Bainton, Roland H., 271
Baltensweiler, Heinrich, 191
Barth, Karl, 16, 41, 132, 134, 135-36,
   145-48, 177, 216-17, 231, 263, 265,
   269, 284, 294, 294n.195, 299
Basil, 293
Baudouin I, King of Belgium, 247
Baxter, Richard, 176n.52, 409
Beauvoir, Simone de, 23, 178-79, 197
Benkert, Karoly, 296
Berdyaev, Nicolas, 132
Berkouwer, G. C., 36, 82, 133n.2

Bernard, Saint, 206, 208n.92
Berry, James, 126
Berry, Wendell, 463n.241
Bhutto, Benazir, 272n.158
Blair, Ralph, 333n.267
Böhme, Jakob, 132
Bohr, Niels, 76
Boman, Thorleif, 225n.107
Bonhoeffer, Dietrich, 62n.45, 86, 188
Boswell, John, 320n.240, 337-38
Boyle, Sarah Patton, 119
Brown, Howard, 303-4, 303n.210,
   309n.219, 311-12, 312n.224
Brown, Robert McAfee, 99n.96, 368n.42
Brunner, Emil, 26n.1, 57, 62n.46, 82,
   131n.1, 133, 133n.3, 205, 218, 353,
   354n.4, 389, 435n.162, 448n.205
Buber, Martin, 22
Bunyan, John, 218

Cairns, David, 27, 59n.39
Calvin, John, 18, 40, 40n.18, 58-59,
   65, 74, 78, 101, 127, 143n.10, 144-
   45, 163, 204, 204n.86, 230, 272,
   293-94, 294n.194, 353, 458
Chaucer, Geoffrey, 416
Chesterton, G. K., 261n.143, 300n.202
Christina of Pisa, 228-29
Chrysostom, 175, 293, 300
Coleridge, Samuel, 51
Conant, James, 364
Cone, James, 114, 115, 115n.17, 116

Index of Scripture References

481